Travels in the Slavonic Provinces of Turkey-In-Europe

THE SECOND EDITION OF THIS WORK

IS

𝔇𝔢𝔡𝔦𝔠𝔞𝔱𝔢𝔡

TO

SOPHIA, LADY MUIR MACKENZIE,

OF DELVINE,

IN TOKEN OF LOVING ESTEEM;

AND IN MEMORY OF HER DAUGHTER,

WHOSE NAME STANDS ON THE TITLE PAGE;

WHO MARRIED, IN 1871, SIR CHARLES SEBRIGHT, BARON D'EVERTON,
AND WHO DIED IN CORFU, JANUARY, 1874.

The Illustrations are from Original Sketches by F. KANITZ, Author of "Serbien," "Bulgarien," &c. The greater portion of the Text of the First Edition was Contributed by G. MUIR MACKENZIE, and has been Revised for this Edition by A. P. IRBY, who has added the Three Chapters: "Bosnia in 1875," "Journey in Bosnia in August, 1875," "Bosnia in 1876-7."

PREFACE.

UNTIL our own day, it has never been possible for the people of one country to obtain trustworthy information respecting the contemporary condition of the people of another. The press, the telegraph, the railway, the large and costly development of diplomatic and consular establishments, and the usages of popular governments, have, in their several manners and degrees, contributed to place within our reach this description of knowledge, in other times substantially inaccessible. In the general absence of it is to be found the best excuse for the seemingly heartless manner in which the statesmen of a bygone generation have argued for the maintenance of the Ottoman Government with a view to the general convenience of Europe, while they have seemingly omitted from the case all consideration of the question, how far the Porte fulfilled or defeated the main purpose for which every government exists—namely, the welfare of those beneath its rule. With the possession, even the partial possession, of such knowledge, we have obtained a great advantage. But we have also come under a new and very grave responsibility. We cannot now escape from the consciousness that we are dealing with questions which greatly involve the happiness or misery of many millions of human beings, whose condition we had formerly omitted from our calculations. In the case of Greece, the recollected glories of the past and the scandal of the servitude of a race once illustrious, were associated with the arguments drawn from the disturbance of the Levant, and probably told more in the production of the result than any keen sense of the specific character of Turkish oppression.

But, although this important change has been effected, it still remains a matter of difficulty, as well as of desire, that this knowledge, in cases with which we have chosen to concern ourselves, should be trustworthy, should be complete, and should be effectual. So to be concerned, is indeed a matter of great inconvenience, and even mischief. Ill able to cope with the problems which appertain to our own affairs, we can yet worse afford to meet drafts upon our care and attention for settling the affairs of others. Happily or unhappily, we have taken upon ourselves a heavy charge of this kind in the case of Turkey. Some found themselves upon British interests, others upon general duty, others upon the specific obligations growing out of our anterior proceedings, and especially out of the Crimean war. But all, or very nearly all, are agreed, that the question of the Ottoman Empire is one from which we cannot wholly withdraw. Very nearly all, whether freely or reluctantly, now confess that in treating it we cannot refuse to look at the condition of the subject races. And if we are to include that element of the case in our view, it is most important that we should see it as clearly and fully as may be possible.

I do not mean to disparage the labours and services of others when I say that, in my opinion, no diplomatist, no consul, no traveller, among our countrymen, has made such a valuable contribution to our means of knowledge in this important matter, as was made by Miss Mackenzie and Miss Irby, when they published, in 1867, their travels in some of the Slavonian Provinces of European Turkey. I shall not now dwell upon the information they have given us with respect to Montenegro: for, although it is highly interesting and instructive, it is subsidiary to the main part of the volume, on which I now dwell. Here, much more than in any other work I have been able to discover, is exhibited to view without passion or prejudice, as well as without reserve, the normal state of life among the subject races, the standing relation both between them and their government, and likewise between them and those Mahommedans, mainly descended from renegades, who are at once their fellow-subjects and their masters. At the time when these ladies undertook a mission of the purest philanthropy with a view to the diffusion of education in the Provinces, the Eastern question did not, among ourselves, wear even in the slightest degree the aspect of a party question. There was nothing from this side to disturb a perfect rectitude of view. It was still more important, that there was then nothing occasional, nothing exceptional, in the condition of the Provinces themselves. They had been, for some time, what would be called in Turkey tranquil. The journey was indeed one which would never have been undertaken except by ladies endowed with a courage and resolution as remarkable as their discernment and their benevolence. But they were able at the time to draw, with steady hand, all the lineaments of a picture, which is the picture of Ottoman rule over a Christian majority at its best, and in the absence of all exasperating circumstances. Without studying pictures so taken, our knowledge of the Turkish question must be essentially defective, and more or less misleading. The condition exhibited in it is that which determines the true measure of happiness or misery, growth or retrogression, elevation or depression, in the ordinary human life of these provinces. It shows us also the point of departure, from which begin the terrible processes, not indeed without example in former times, but never so fully exhibited to the view of Christendom as in the Bulgarian massacres of 1876, now ineffaceable from the memory of civilized mankind.

We thus come to learn, that there are two distinct phases of existence for the subject races of Turkey: the ordinary, and the exceptional. The exceptional phase comes when the ruling race finds or thinks itself threatened in the key of its position. This is on the rare occasions, when oppression is felt to be absolutely intolerable, and the down-trodden rayahs, appealing to force, seek to obtain their rights by the same instrument which has been the source and the vehicle of all their wrongs. Other conquerors, such as the Greek or the Roman, have relied, along with force, upon intellectual superiority, and upon the communication of benefits to the conquered. The Ottoman Turk, with his satellites, has relied upon force alone. Whatever intellect he has at any time displayed, and it has not always been small, has been intellect addressed to the organisation and application of force. The rebellious rayah for once meets him on his own ground. He is in a manner compelled to develop and apply on these occasions the whole of his large inventory of the weapons of violence and torture, and other yet worse and baser means of inflicting agony upon his subjects. For, if these instruments fail, he has nothing in reserve. It is now, therefore, coming to be understood, that the indescribable proceedings of last year in Bulgaria were not due to passion, ignorance, or accident; but to method, policy, and principle: the ends sought were absolutely vital to Turkish power as it exists in these Provinces, and the instruments chosen were admirably adapted to the ends.

With reference to this, which I have called the exceptional phase of existence under the Ottoman Power, Miss Irby, in the new edition of her work, has supplied illustrations of very great interest and importance. Although a considerable portion of the Metropolitan daily press systematically suppresses the too copious evidence of continuing Turkish outrages in Bulgaria, this portion cannot control its remaining organs, and it has become generally known that the reign of terror is still prolonged in that unhappy Province, and that what was done last May to hundreds and thousands is still, and daily, done to units, or fives, or tens. If the tempest has passed by, the swell still continues. Ottoman security is felt to depend upon keeping alive in the mind of the subject races the memory of the great massacres; for on the mirror of the past is drawn the image of the future. The work of Miss Irby, with the chapters she has added, widens our perspective. I have myself stated, months back, to the public that, while we were venting indignation about Bulgaria, the Turk was doing the very same foul work, though not on the same imperial scale, in Bosnia. The *Manchester Guardian* has rendered important public service with respect to the same afflicted region, through its very valuable correspondence. But Miss Irby, after her long and self-sacrificing experience, speaks with a weight of dispassionate authority, to which neither I nor any correspondent of a public journal can pretend. She now discloses, and that down to the latest date, upon information which she knows to be trustworthy, a state of things which exhibits a greater aggregate of human misery flowing from Turkish rule, than even the Bulgaria of 1876 could show. In Bosnia and the Herzegovina more than a third of the population are exiled or homeless; the mass of these (as we now learn) reduced to an allowance of a penny a day, but rather preferring to travel, and that rapidly, the road to famine and to pestilence, than to descend, by returning, into the abyss of a suffering which is also shame; and with this, the constant and harrowing recurrence of the cruel outrages, which are more and more fastening themselves, as if inseparable adjuncts, upon the Turkish name.

"I nunc, et versus tecum meditare cancros."

Teach, you who will, the duty of dealing effectually with the insurrection, and setting up again that fabric of Turkish rule over a Serbian people, which, redemption, which we may think to be now probably at hand, when acute suffering has been substituted for dull chronic pain, and when a people, too long patient, seems to be at length determined, in vindicating its own rights, to vindicate the insulted laws of the Most High.

W. E. G.

April 10*th,* 1877.

amidst all this misery, we may hope is tottering to its final fall.

Such is the aid Miss Irby gives us towards the attainment not merely of a theoretical, but of a practical and living knowledge with reference to the condition of the Slāv Provinces of Turkey after an insurrection. I however attach not a less, perhaps even a greater, importance to the less exciting picture which is drawn in the older part of the work. By the simple, painstaking communication of the particulars supplied from daily experience, it presents to us in comparatively quiet landscape, rayah life, under Turkish mastery, in the best condition it could attain, after many long years of peace for the Empire abroad, and of reforms promised at home, with facilities for effecting them such as are not likely to return. And what was rayah life under these happier circumstances? It was a life never knowing real security or peace, except when the Government and its agents were happily out of view. A life which never had any of the benefits of law, save when the agents of the law were absent. A life in which no object, that was valued, could be exposed. A life which left to the Christian nothing, except what his Mahommedan master did not chance to want. A life in which wife and daughter, the appointed sources of the sweetest consolation, were the standing occasions of the sharpest anxiety. A life debased by cringing, poisoned by fear, destructive of manhood, shorn of the freedom which is the indispensable condition of all nobleness in man, and shorn too of every hope, except such as might lie in an escape from it to some foreign land; or in the dream of a future

CONTENTS OF VOL. I.

CHAPTER I.
BOSNIA IN 1875 1

CHAPTER II.
JOURNEY IN BOSNIA IN AUGUST, 1875 24

CHAPTER III.
BOSNIA IN 1876-7 35

CHAPTER IV.
SALONICA IN 1863 54

CHAPTER V.
BULGARIA VIEWED FROM SALONICA.—PART I. . . . 65

CHAPTER VI.
BULGARIA VIEWED FROM SALONICA.—PART II. . . . 83

CHAPTER VII.
FROM SALONICA TO MONASTIR 90

CHAPTER VIII.
THE ANCIENT BULGARIAN CAPITAL AND THE MODERN TURKISH TOWN 102

CONTENTS.

CHAPTER IX.
KING'S SON MARKO: HIS CASTLE AND HIS STORY . . . 115

CHAPTER X.
THE BULGARIAN TOWNS OF PRILIP AND VÉLESA . . . 128

CHAPTER XI.
VISIT TO THE MONASTERY OF RILO, IN AUGUST, 1862 . . . 145

CHAPTER XII.
THE CITY OF JUSTINIAN 158

CHAPTER XIII.
KATCHANIK 168

CHAPTER XIV.
THE BATTLE-FIELD OF KÓSSOVO 182

CHAPTER XV.
THE MONASTERY OF GRATCHANITZA, AND THE TOWN OF PRÍSHTINA 193

CHAPTER XVI.
STARA SERBIA 209

CHAPTER XVII.
FROM PRÍSHTINA TO VUCHITERN 228

CHAPTER XVIII.
VUCHITERN 234

CHAPTER XIX.
FROM ARNAOUTLUK INTO BOSNIA 252

CONTENTS.

CHAPTER XX.

NOVI BAZAAR 265

CHAPTER XXI.

THE BOSNIAN BORDERS—NOVI BAZAAR TO TUTIN . . . 285

CHAPTER XXII.

THE BOSNIAN BORDERS—TUTIN TO ROSHAÏ 298

LIST OF ILLUSTRATIONS.

VOL. I.

SERBIAN BORDER GUARD	*Frontispiece*
MAP OF THE SOUTH SLAVONIC PROVINCES	*facing* p. 1
SALONICA ON THE ÆGEAN	54
BULGARIAN PEASANTS, WITH BULGARIAN MERCHANT AND HIS SON	69
CATHEDRAL OF OCHRIDA	103
BULGARIAN MONASTERY OF RILO	151
MAP OF STARA (OLD) SERBIA	209
SPECIMEN OF SERBIAN ARCHITECTURE	212
MUSSULMAN BEYS AND CHRISTIAN PRIEST	255
INTERIOR OF SERBIAN CHURCH—MANASSIA	275
SERBIAN PEASANTS AND CITIZENS OF A COUNTRY TOWN	281
BOSNIAN RAYAH PAYING TRIBUTE	311

CHAPTER I.

BOSNIA IN 1875.

THE rearguard of Mahommedanism in Europe maintains its last stronghold in the Turkish vilayet of Bosnia. Here, as the religion of the ruling caste, Islam has had a trial of nearly four centuries. What fruits has it borne?

In geographical position the nearest to European civilisation, but in social condition the most barbarous of the provinces of Turkey in Europe, Bosnia, including Turkish Croatia and the Herzegovina, extends to a point west of the longitude of Vienna, and interposes a savage and Oriental aspect between the Dalmatian shores of the Adriatic and the advancing culture of Serbia, Hungary, and Croatia. Cross the frontier from these lands, and you may fancy yourself in the wilds of Asia.

The soil of Bosnia teems with various and valuable minerals, her hills abound in splendid forests, her well-watered plains are fertile and productive, her race, under culture, proves exceptionally gifted. Yet her commerce is contemptible; "*plums*," to quote the report of Mr. Consul Holmes for 1873, being "the most valuable article of trade in the province;" her population is uneducated, not one man in a hundred knowing how to read, and the chief town, Serajevo, which contains from forty to fifty thousand inhabitants, possessing not a single book shop.

One or two English speculators have been tempted to inquire into the mineral riches of the land, but have prudently retired, being unable, on the one hand, to come to satisfactory terms with the government, and, on the other, to find a company to work the mines in face of the vexatious hindrances which baffle all enterprise under the present régime. The immense mineral wealth remains untouched.

An Austrian company has obtained some sort of local concession to work all the mines of coal, lead, and copper, within thirty miles of the proposed line of railway. But this concession has not yet received the needful ratification at Constantinople, and it appears that the Turks have a peculiar disinclination to give their neighbours, the Austrians, any footing in Bosnia. The beautiful marble of the country, white, and white with red streaks, is put to but sorry use in the rough Turkish pavements. Stone for building purposes is plentiful: yet even in Serajevo, wood, rubble and shingles still prevail; only here and there brick and stone houses, roofed with tiles, are beginning to appear.

A road now leads from Brood on the Save to Serajevo, a distance of about one hundred and thirty-eight English miles, along which passes once a week each way the post cart of the Austrian consulate in Bosnia; three places on the hay in the springless vehicle may be hired by those who do not object to jolt on continuously for two days and a night, or more. If a private cart be taken from Brood, at least three nights must be spent on the way, sleeping at khans, the discomfort of which is not to be described. It is necessary to take bed and bedding, or at least a mattress, and moreover to command the immediate expulsion of the carpets, mats and cushions, which form the only furniture of the rooms. A road is in course of completion from Serajevo to the Dalmatian frontier by way of Mostar, the chief town of the Herzegovina. Two years ago the rough carts of the country might be driven to Livno, and thence across the Austrian frontier to Spalato on the Adriatic; but the Turkish portion of this road is now impassable. There is a road from Serajevo by Travnik and Banjaluka to Gradishka on the Save, and other cart-roads and fragments of roads exist, but they are constantly out of repair and the bridges in most uncertain condition.

It is possible to traverse this rude land in many directions, on foot or on horseback, rejoicing in the ever changing beauty of mountain, wood, and water, which is enlivened by the rich colouring and picturesque variety of national costume. But the traveller may journey on for days, and he will come upon no works of modern enterprise, no monuments of ancient mediæval art. He may, indeed, if he search diligently, and if he know where to look, discover beneath weeds and brushwood, or scanty tillage, traces of Roman roads, one of which led across the province from Scissia (Sisseg) on the Save to Salona on the Adriatic. Such tracks of ancient passage he may find for the searching, and what is likely to be more to his purpose, he may come upon the fragment of a modern railway, lying detached and unconnected on the Bosnian plains. Along this railway, without beginning and without end, a train used to run once a day each way, conveying a ludicrously small average of goods and passengers between the village of Novi and the more important town of Banjaluka. The ideal and fragmentary nature of the achievement was owing to the collapse of the contract between an Austrian company and the Turkish government; but the whole, of which it should form a part, may some day become our main highway to India. It is to be seen on the map of the "Continental Guide," where Bradshaw has traced in anticipation a railway (elsewhere, by-the-bye, prophetically designated a branch of the great Euphrates Valley Railway), which, trending eastward off the well-known Semmering line between Vienna and Trieste, and traversing a part of Croatia, may at some future time cross Bosnia, Old Serbia, and Bulgaria, to Salonica and Constantinople. Such means of passage through the land, viz., lost Roman roads, of which scarce a trace remains, and the projected Turkish railways, of which, save the fragment here noted, not a Bosnian sod has been turned, constitute the chief works —with the exception of the roads, telegraphs, and bridges of the last few years, I should rather say the only works, for which Bosnia is indebted to ancient Roman and modern Turkish enterprise.

But what traces do we find of the intermediate centuries which elapsed before a part of the Roman province of Mœsia became the Turkish pashalik of Bosnia? Ruined castles of the ancient feudal nobility, ruins of Serb and Latin churches and convents; and the three Franciscan convents of Foinica, Kreshevo, and Sudiska, which, endowed with special privileges, have been maintained from the fifteenth century to the present day. The Paterenes, or Bogomiles, the early Dissidents of Bosnia, were very numerous from the twelfth to the fifteenth centuries, but they were scattered or exterminated with cruel persecutions, and have left visible traces only in graveyards popularly assigned to them.

Before the Turkish conquest at the end of the fifteenth century, the frontiers of Bosnia were repeatedly changed, and its inhabitants were incessantly harassed by the passage and encounters of hostile troops. For Bosnia has ever been the borderland of contending rival states and rival churches. Its history, in the Middle Ages as in later periods, is a distressing and tangled record of petty warfare, revolting treachery, and terrible crimes. A gleam of legendary light falls on the times of Ban Kulin, who held the faith of the Paterenes, and whose name is still remembered among the people, marking the era of a distant Golden Age. Its race is identical with that of Free Serbia, Old Serbia, and Montenegro, and with the Serbs of Hungary and Dalmatia. The name of the country is derived from the Bosna, a tributary of the Save. As in other Serb countries, the early princes of Bosnia were called *zupans*. At one time nearly all these lands acknowledged the supremacy of Byzantium. At another period Bosnia was incorporated in the kingdom of Hungary. In the middle of the fourteenth century it formed a part of the empire of Stephan Dūshan, that great ruler of the house of Nemania, who assumed the title of "Christloving Czar of all Serbs and Greeks," imitated the style and institutions, and aspired to succeed to the sovereignty of Byzantium, but died of fever on the march to Constantinople (1355).

Before the Turkish conquest, Bosnia was again a separate state under native *bans* and kings, and had been partly conquered by and partly reconquered from the Magyars. The Serbs belonged to the Eastern, the Hungarians to the Western Church, and then as now the jealousies of rival hierarchies divided the Serbian race.

Whatever germs of free institutions may have existed in the barbarous communities which we trace throughout the Serbian countries, and in Bosnia among the rest, were here stifled beneath the growth of feudalism, and the contending claims of the Eastern and Western Churches. Finally, the accidents of geographical position exposed the Southern Slāvs to the full sweep of the Turkish deluge. The Osmanli conquered; the Byzantine Empire was overthrown; there suffered also a younger race, the younger children of the European family, the Southern Slāvs, who, after centuries of repression, are asserting their right to independent existence.

After the conquest of Bosnia by the Turks, those of the nobility who remained alive in the land became Mahommedan. The Bosnian Begs were the offspring of an alliance between feudalism and Islam.

The feudal system, which had been established in Bosnia in the Christian period, was continued after the Mussulman conquest, with this sole difference, that the feudal lords changed their faith and their suzerain. Their own position was confirmed by the change. We have seen that Bosnia was continually the object of attack from Hungary. Now the Turkish policy was acute and masterly; there was also much that was noble and magnanimous in the Osmanli character; tempting terms were offered to the Bosnian nobles. Perceiving that under the shelter of their mighty conquerors, they would be able to preserve their nationality, maintain their caste privileges, and bid defiance to Hungary and the Pope, many of the nobles threw in their cause with that of the Empire of Othman, and the Bosnian Slavonic Mussulman became, in the words of Turkish writers, "the lion that guarded Stamboul." Bosnia was the bulwark of Islam against Western Europe. As in later times the *vis inertiæ* of the Turkish Empire in Europe has been considerably weighted by the Mussulman element in Bosnia, so in the sixteenth and first half of the seventeenth centuries, the days of its aggressive vigour, the spahis or feudal chiefs of Bosnia, led powerful contingents to the Turkish armies, and the ranks of the Janissaries were largely recruited by her sons.

But the tyranny and pretensions of the Begs waxed too great. They assumed entire independence, they coerced or chased away the viziers sent from Constantinople to reside or rule in Bosnia. It became necessary to subdue it as a rebel province. This subjection was accomplished in our own days by Omer Pasha, who in 1850-1 put an end to the feudal system in Bosnia, equalising the Mussulman Bosnian Begs, or magnates, with all other Mussulmans in Turkey, abolishing the rank and office of spahis, or military feudal chiefs, and compelling the tithe hitherto received by them to be paid into the government treasury.

All Mussulmans being equalised before the law in 1850, and political and social equality among all creeds and classes having been proclaimed by the Hatt-i-Humayoun of 1856, let us inquire what was the actual condition of the subjects of the Porte in Bosnia in the spring of 1875, immediately before the outbreak of the revolt.

The population of Bosnia and the Herzegovina, forming part of one Slavonic race, is still commonly spoken of as three different "nations," so great is the division marked by difference of creed. I give the following statistics gathered from Turkish official reports of 1874. Their accuracy cannot be relied upon: the number of Mussulmans is enormously exaggerated; the proportion between Greek and Latin Christians is fairly stated.

Bosnian Mussulmans	442,050
Christians of the Orthodox Eastern Church	575,756
Roman Catholics	185,503
Jews	3,000
Gypsies	9,537
Total	1,216,846

In addition to this native population should be mentioned some 5,000 Austrian subjects, and some hundreds of Osmanli officials.

It is only in the mutesariflik of Serajevo that the Mahommedans are in the majority. In the other six subdivisions of the land the Christians, Eastern Church Slāvs and Roman Catholics being taken together, on the whole greatly outnumber the Mussulmans.

I. The Bosnian Mussulmans are the owners of the land, and they reside on their estates, or in houses in the towns. They are also small merchants, and follow trades. Some are *kmets*, or farmers of the lands for richer Mussulmans. The Bosnian Beg par excellence, the powerful feudal chief of sixty years ago, is a chained monster with drawn teeth and cut claws. He was too decidedly a megatherion for our age. The brute force of the savage is greatly broken, and he has acquired no other force. For, with some possible exceptions, the Bosnian Begs of to-day are ignorant and corrupt, indolent, and wholly incapable of organization or combined action. Some have learnt a little Turkish, Arabic, and Persian, but very few know how to read and write their own tongue. The spirit of feasting and merrymaking, banished by Mahomet and his followers, but ineradicable among the Slāvs, still lingers among the Bosnian Mussulmans. Instead of the annual festival of the *Krsno imé*, when the friends and relations of every Serbian house gather to celebrate with feasting the day of their patron saint, the Begs still in many places make a festivity of the time of boiling down plums for *bestilj*, or plum syrup. But even this lingering opportunity for social union is being relinquished, and scarcely anything else of the kind remains.

The Mussulmans of Serajevo still keep St. John the Baptist's day (24th of June, O. S.), when the sun is said to dance at dawn on the top of the hill Trebovich: on that day, and on St. Elias's and St. George's days, the Mussulman population turns out of doors, and the whole side of Trebovich, especially the neighbourhood of the Moslem saint's tomb, is bright with red turbans and jackets and groups of women in white veils. They sit in separate companies smoking and drinking coffee, and there is a striking absence of life and gaiety among them.

Many of the Bosnian Begs are not indisposed to embrace the Christianity professed by their forefathers. They call a priest to say prayers over them when they are ill, they keep the name of the patron saint of their family, and they preserve with care the patents of nobility of their Christian ancestors. But on the other hand many of them are fanatic Moslems, and nourish a blind and savage hatred against their Christian fellow countrymen. This hatred finds vent even in quiet times in many a hidden act of cruelty. At the present moment of licensed insult and revenge (autumn of 1875), we hear of Christians being impaled and flayed alive, and cruelties of the worst ages committed on helpless women and children. In a season of perfect quiet (1871-2) some fierce Mussulmans of Serajevo swore to cut the throats of the Christians if they dared to hang bells in the tower of their new church. The conspiracy was discovered, and the leading Mussulmans held responsible for the quiet of the town. The pasha confessed the weakness of his authority to maintain the law when he called the principal merchants and asked them to give up their legal rights to the bells, on the ground that if their sound were heard he would be unable to restrain the fury of the Mahommedans.

The state of political feeling among the Bosnian Mussulmans was described to me before the outbreak by those who knew them well, as by no means unanimous. At present they have no leader of preponderating influence who might render them strong and dangerous by uniting them in one purpose. Some were amicably disposed towards Serbia; others were fanatically jealous of the Christian principality. The name of the late Prince

Michael of Serbia was not unpopular among them, but his assassination by men who were his own subjects greatly injured the Serbian cause, and is regarded by the Begs of Bosnia, among whom lingers the spirit of their aristocratic caste, as a crime which condemns the nation. Dislike to the Osmanlis and to Stamboul is universal among them, and has been much increased by taxation and by the obligation to serve in the Turkish army.

The conscription was first enforced by Osman Pasha in 1864. The Bosnian Mussulmans are drawn by lot for the regular army, or *nizam*, for a term of four years' service; and likewise for the *redif*, or reserve, in which they must serve one month in the year for nine years. Exemption may be purchased from the nizam by the payment of a hundred ducats, about £50, or a substitute may be found; but service in the redif is compulsory on each man on whom the lot may fall. The Bosnians are not required to serve outside the province. They are all infantry; the cavalry and artillery stationed in Bosnia are natives of other provinces of Turkey. Since the outbreak, robber bands of Turkish volunteers have been raised in different parts of the country.* The redif (or reserve) in many places have refused to serve.

The sacerdotal-legal profession is greatly desired by the Bosnian Mussulmans. Many of their ulemas have studied at Stamboul. Pilgrimages to Mecca are frequent. It is a not uncommon sight to see crowds of the Mussulman population sally forth from Serajevo to meet some returning hadji, or to escort pilgrims setting out for the Holy Places. Wandering dervishes visit the country, exciting the fanaticism of the faithful. Although no spirit of proselytism exists in Bosnia, yet renegadism has been

---

* Their method of suppressing suspected insurrection has been amply illustrated in Bulgaria. The like method is to this hour being pursued in Bosnia. But there are no reporters.

more frequent of late among the Christians. In the course of 1874, in Serajevo alone, ten women and four men, Catholics and Pravoslavs, became Mahommedan, and it is uncertain how many in other parts of the province. The immediate cause is generally the great poverty of the Christians, which often compels them to place their girls in service in Turkish houses.

The difficulty presented by the Mussulman element in Bosnia has been greatly exaggerated, together with its strength and numbers. Any well-organized Christian government would be able to deal with it. But as long as the Mussulmans alone are permitted to bear arms the difficulty is insuperable. With regard to toleration it should be remembered that since Serbia expelled the Turks from her own territory she still maintains a mosque in Belgrade for Mahommedan visitors, the expenses being defrayed by the Serbian government.

II. The Pravoslav Christians of Bosnia are merchants, small tradesmen, and farmers.

Some few Christians have attained to the possession of landed property; but the Mussulmans cannot endure the innovation, and they do their utmost, usually with success, to prevent a ghiaour from acquiring land, or to dispossess him if he has accomplished the purchase. This can be done in various ways; whether by bringing in Mussulman evidence—always ready at the call of Mussulmans—to prove that the late owner had no proper title, and that the sale is therefore invalid; or by making use of the law which exists in Turkey (or at least in Bosnia), that no property can be sold without first giving all the neighbouring owners the right of refusal. It is very seldom that a Mussulman can induce his neighbours to consent that he should sell his land to a Christian, and thus introduce a ghiaour into their midst. Public opinion prevents the sale, even though no one of the neighbours be able to purchase instead.

The Bosnian cultivator or farmer (here called *kmet*), usually a Christian, pays to his landlord, usually a Bosnian Mussulman, one third of the produce, or one half, according to the agreement, and as the landlord or the tenant may supply oxen, seed, and implements. A tithe, which is now actually the eighth, is paid into the government treasury, and is collected by the tax-gatherer, who farms the taxes from the government. Great and bitter complaints are made of the injustice and exactions of the tax-gatherer. The cultivator dares not gather in his crops till the visit of the assessor; while he is waiting it repeatedly happens that the harvests perish. The tax on the arbitrarily calculated value is, of course, exacted all the same. In fact the peasants suffer much less from the Mussulman landlord than from the government official, for the landowner is interested in the prosperity of his tenant.

The tax in lieu of military service which is paid by all non-Mussulmans weighs very heavily on the poor, who have to pay equally with the rich twenty-eight piastres for every male. In the poorest and most miserable family this sum must be paid for the male infant who has first seen the light a few hours before the visit of the tax-gatherer. This tax on the young children of the rayah is the most oppressive and galling to him, collected often by house visitations, in which the sanctity of his hearth is most vilely outraged. Great suffering results from the forced labour exacted by the government. For instance, in the making of the new road to Mostar, Christians were driven by zaptiés from great distances, and compelled to work for days without pay.

Systematic and legalised extortion has succeeded to the intermittent violence of former times; the mass of the people are ground to the dust under the present régime. They were materially much better off in the days of Begluk (the reign of the Begs). The Christian rayah was often less miserable when more directly under the Beg, or resident landowner, than he is now under the temporary official—the present farmer of the revenue—whose sole advantage lies in pocketing all he can for himself. The position of the landowner and his dependents affords opportunity for the development of much kindly human feeling: the tax-gatherer is by nature a bird of prey. Not long ago the Christian retainers of the Begs used to come into the town to church on the great festivals, decked out in the old-fashioned silver ornaments of the country, but now these ornaments are seldom seen, for their owners have been obliged to sell them.

I will here give a translation of the words of a native Bosnian woman, describing the changes which had taken place in the daily life of the Christian women of Serajevo, within the memory of the present generation and since the residence of the European consuls in that city has restrained the grosser outrages still committed in other parts of the country.

"When the vizier resided at Travnik, thirty years ago, the common people were much better than off than they are now, for then there were no taxes but the *haratch* (in exemption from military service). They were rich, and had horses, oxen, swine, sheep, and poultry; they wore fine clothes with silver ornaments, they had beautiful arms. Although there was no liberty, yet the Begs and Agas, lords of the land, protected and defended their own kmets. The greatest violence was in the days of Mental Pasha and Fazli Pasha, who plundered, killed, raged, tortured, and tormented just as they chose; there was no inquiry made and no evidence taken. This lasted till the time of Omer Pasha. As regards liberty (personal safety), from that day to this, the difference here is as great as between heaven and earth; at that time the women in Serajevo did not dare to go to the charshia (market place) or along the streets, they did not dare to stand at the doors; when they went to church, or wherever they were obliged to go, they went without ornaments, and covered down to the feet in a white cloth; the Turkish women rarely went along the streets, even covered up so that you could not see their eyes. Now for some time past Christian women and maidens, wives and daughters of the Pravoslav Serajevo merchants, adorned with ducats and pearls, in their best dresses, go along our streets, and in our charshia, as in their own homes, by day or by night without any fear."

With the exception of a few merchants, the Pravoslav population is miserably poor. There has been no development of the immense material resources of the country, no means of employment and occupation which might enable the poor to meet the ever increasing taxation, the extortions of the officials, and the heavy exactions of their own clergy. But in spite of all hindrances, the Serb merchants of Bosnia have advanced steadily, though slowly, in wealth and position. It was jealousy of their progress which led to the oppression of the thriving merchants at Gradishka, opposite the Austrian frontier, in 1873. False accusations were made against the leading Christians of the place and some were seized and put in prison; they petitioned the Porte, and, as usual, a counter-statement was got up by the medjliss, which Christians were made to sign, not knowing the contents of the document to which they had put their names. Fourteen Christian merchants fled over into Austria, and went to Vienna, declaring they would never return unless placed under Austrian protection. Through the initiative of Austria, Mustapha Assim

Pasha, the then governor of Bosnia, too zealous a Turk for the age, and determined by repression of Christian progress to restore the waning Mussulman prestige, was recalled from the province. Had he remained, the inevitable revolt must have broken out sooner. The immediate cause of the insurrection of 1875 may be found in the iniquitous manner of raising the taxes and the additional screw which had of late been put on the "naked Bosnian rayah" to contribute to the payment of Turkish bondholders. But this is not all. Far deeper than any temporary accident of increased taxation, lies the innate strength of Serbian nationality and the immutable determination of the Christian Serb to throw off the foreign yoke of the Turk—a yoke as foreign now to the Serbs of Bosnia as it was when first imposed on them four centuries ago. And it is certain, from the vengeful temper of the Mussulmans, that should the present insurrection terminate in the pacification of Bosnia as a Turkish province, the condition of the Christians will be worse than before, notwithstanding any amount of promises and professions from Constantinople.*

The Bosnian Christians of the Eastern Orthodox Church have the same peculiar customs, the same national saints and heroes, the same historic traditions, as the Serbs of the principality, with whom they count themselves one nation, though politically separated. In the house of every Christian Orthodox merchant you will find pictures or photographs of the princes of Serbia, and ornaments bearing the Serbian arms. Marinovich, some time prime minister at Belgrade, is a native of Serajevo, and related to the richest houses there. I know a Serbian family living in Belgrade which has in Bosnia Mussulman, and in Croatia Roman Catholic, relations of the same name. In Bosnia and

* Written in 1875.

Serbia there are many families related to one another, and who interchange visits from time to time. They call themselves alike Serbs; their religion is the Pravoslav. And the Pravoslav Serb, whether he find himself under Austrian or Turkish rule, or whether he be a Montenegrin or a native of Free Serbia, is the citizen of one Serbian fatherland, and nourishes an ideal national unity.

Considerable confusion has arisen from the term *Greek* being applied indiscriminately to all Christians of the Orthodox or Eastern communion. It is sometimes taken for granted that all the Christians of Turkey in Europe are Greeks by race as well as by religion. This has arisen from the habit of French writers describing them as "les Grecs." It is really less reasonable to call the Orthodox Slāvs *Greeks* than it would be to call the Roman Catholic English and Germans *Latins*. For the different branches of the Eastern Church are all distinctly national in this sense, that they acknowledge no foreign authority whatever. The Serbs of the Serbian Principality and the Greeks of Free Greece have their own metropolitans, who reside in Belgrade and in Athens, and are independent of the Phanariote Patriarch of Constantinople. The Serb Christians of Turkey reckon it among their chief grievances, that they are forced under the jurisdiction of the Greek Patriarch of Constantinople, and have not their own metropolitan. Appointed in Constantinople, and Greeks by birth, the Phanariote bishops placed over Serb flocks are tools of the Turks and play into their hands. They are the wolves and not the shepherds of the flock. The name Pravoslav, the old Slavonic liturgies and Church services, the Serbs have in common with the Russians; herein lies their bond of union with Russia.

III. The Roman Catholic Christians, or "Latins," of

Bosnia and the Herzegovina, are more orderly and submissive, but less sturdy and enterprising than the Pravoslavs. They are on a much better understanding with the Turks. Roman Catholic priests are never heard of in the Turkish prisons, Serb priests frequently, and for the most part on accusation or suspicion of political offences. Among the Roman Catholics of Serajevo there is not one single merchant; some follow trades, but for the most part the community are miserably poor. In the villages they are *kmets*, and cultivate the land for the Begs. In Travnik, Livno, and other towns there are "Latin" merchants; here and there they have recently acquired land. Notwithstanding the superior education and intelligence of the priests and the privileges granted to the clergy from the time of Mahmoud the Conqueror, their flocks remain ignorant and benighted. The paucity of schools is astonishing—unparalleled I believe among any other Roman Catholic population in Europe, except the Albanian. There are only from thirty to thirty-four Roman Catholic boys' schools in the whole province. Within the last few years girls' schools have been established in four places by sisters of the society of St. Vincent de Paul, who have their mother house in Croatia. Some improvement may also be expected from the future priests, who are receiving a more national and liberal training in Bishop Strossmayer's seminary at Diakovar in Slavonia. Up to this time they had been educated in Italy or Hungary, and to a great degree had lost sympathy with the spirit of their nation, although their superior learning gave them much influence with the people. They have succeeded in entirely abolishing among the Roman Catholic Bosnians the festival of the *Krsno imé*, on the ground of the expense which it involved to the impoverished people. But whatever are the abuses and the reckless extravagance of these festivals, they have served to keep up the brotherhood, courage, and sense of national unity among the Pravoslavs, and made them stronger to resist the Mussulman influence. The Bosnian Roman Catholic is to a great degree denationalised. He does not call himself Serb, but Latin. So far as he has any political intelligence whatever, he has the same aspirations as the Catholic Slāvs of Austrian Croatia and Slavonia. But the unity which is gradually growing there among the educated Pravoslavs and Catholics has not yet penetrated Bosnia. Bishop Strossmayer, however, is hopeful that the Roman Catholic Bosnians would coalesce with the others under a fair and free system.

The Jewish community of Serajevo is very prosperous; some of its members have grown rich within the last ten years and have acquired property in land and houses. Their poor are exceedingly well cared for, and a Jewish beggar is never seen. No Jew is ever accused of murder, theft, or violence, or found in the Turkish prisons, except on account of debt. This is the bright side of the picture; there is a dark side : in some respects they are miserably degraded; their houses and persons are filthy, they are small of stature, and the women always undersized. Their language, I am told by Dr. Thompson of Constantinople, probably the only Englishman who has conversed with them in their own tongue, continues the same as that spoken in Spain at the time of their expulsion, and is very nearly that in which "Don Quixote" is written. They have a boys' school only. They have many holidays and feasts, and more merrymakings at home than any other "nation" in Serajevo.

The wretched condition of education in Bosnia is one of its greatest misfortunes. Before the insurrection the Pravoslavs had in the whole province only six girls' schools, and at the highest estimate forty-seven boys' schools. The first girls' school was established by the

Bosnian woman Staka, with help from Russia. She travelled to Serbia to find a teacher. The population is carefully kept in ignorance by the Turkish government, the stupidity of the people being a necessary condition for Turkish rule. In the whole province there is not a single book shop, excepting the depôt of the British and Foreign Bible Society in Serajevo, which has been established for about eight or ten years. But no other books are to be bought in the place, save a few elementary school books, the old Slavonic "Book of Hours," and an occasional almanack. A Bosnian merchant, who recently attempted to have a few Serbian books in stock for sale, was obliged to give them up to the Turkish authorities. In fact, Serbian books and newspapers are strictly prohibited at the frontier; whatever enters the country must be smuggled in. So great is the perfectly reasonable jealousy with which newspapers are withheld from the eyes of Bosnian readers, that not long ago a formal complaint was made by the Turkish authorities to the Austrian consulate that one of its officials had shown Slāv newspapers received there to Bosnian merchants. There is a government printing press in Serajevo, but it has sent forth nothing save a few very indifferent elementary school books, a song book, and two newspapers in Turkish and Slavonic, whose contents are of the most meagre description, relating chiefly to the movements and changes of Turkish officials, which, indeed, are so frequent that their record leaves little space for the scanty scraps of news which fill up the remainder of the sheets. It may be supposed that this newspaper has no circulation among the Serb population.

One of the first questions asked by those who have any knowledge of a Turkish province and any human interest in its inhabitants will always be this: "Is the evidence of Christians against Mussulmans received in

Bosnia?" The evidence of Christians cannot be accepted in the *mehkeme* or kadi's court, the ancient Turkish court of justice, whose decisions are based on the Koran alone. In the modern courts of justice, councils or *medjliss*, the evidence of Christians against Mussulmans is admitted by law; their right is now in principle acknowledged, and even in Bosnia the evidence of Christians against Turks has sometimes been actually taken; more especially when backed by a bribe, by means of which, be it remarked, justice or injustice may at any time equally be obtained. But it is certain that the evidence of twenty Christians would be outweighed by that of two Mussulmans. The Turks have naturally shown little zeal, except under European pressure, in carrying out the design, which, taking from the kadis the decision of all disputes between Christians and Mussulmans, and referring such cases to the medjliss, threatens to destroy the essentially Turkish institution of the mehkemes.

In each of the medjliss of Serajevo there are four or six Mussulmans; one, sometimes two, Pravoslavs, one Roman Catholic, and one or two Jews. A knowledge of Turkish is necessary, as the proceedings are wholly conducted in that language. The influence of the non-Mussulmans is very small, and the office is most unpopular among the Pravoslavs, on account of the contempt with which they are liable to be treated by the Mussulman majority. Such being the state of things, the position of the Christian towards the Mussulman remains intolerable. The hereditary insolence of the Mussulman Bosnian is met by the hereditary cringing of the rayah. It will take some generations of another system than the present to restore to the rayah the virtues of the free. As an instance of Turkish insolence, under the eyes of the European consuls in Serajevo, where the Turks are on their best behaviour, I will give the following anecdote. A dervish, named Hadji Loya, met in the road near the town of Serajevo, a Pravoslav priest on horseback. He ordered him to dismount, telling him, "Bosnia is still a Mahommedan country; do you not see that a Turk is passing? Dismount instantly!" Three different times he met the same priest, and obliged him to get off his horse. This dervish also forced a whole wedding party of Roman Catholics to pass him on foot. This happened in 1871, and that same year, in Serajevo itself, a Christian boy of eighteen was stabbed by a Mussulman, who escaped in the midst of the market-place, in the presence of numerous Turks and zaptiés.

I used to find it very difficult to obtain circumstantial accounts of Turkish cruelties which I heard of as perpetrated in the distant parts of the country which I had not visited. I know that so recently as the spring of 1875, in the immediate neighbourhood of Serajevo, a rayah was tied barefoot to an Aga's cart, and made to run behind it. This was told me by a terrified eye-witness under strict promises of secrecy. The wretched Christians were too terrified to speak, for Turkish vengeance would have too surely pursued the reporters. When I complained to one of the more intelligent among the fugitives of the difficulty which I had found in Bosnia in getting the Christians to speak openly to me, he answered: "Why, we dared not complain to one another; how, then, should we tell strangers what happened? I did not dare to tell my friend, lest he should quarrel with me and betray me, or get drunk and repeat what I had said. The Turks would have marked me as a dangerous man, and I should have been imprisoned on some excuse or other, or have been put out of the way." I said to him: "Well, at least you may tell me now you are on Austrian ground and the Turks cannot hear you." In the course of our conversation he spoke as follows: "The extortions of the tax-gatherers and the Begs (land-owners) and the irregular exactions of the zaptiés (police officers) have reached a point never known before. What with the eighth paid to the government, the third or half to the Beg, the tax in exemption of military service, the taxes for pigs, cattle, and everything we have and have not, there remains nothing for us villagers to live upon. I have seen men driven into pigsties and shut up there in cold and hunger until they paid, hung up from the rafters of their houses with their heads downwards in the smoke, until they disclosed where their little stores were hidden. I have known them hung up from trees, and water poured down them in the freezing cold; I have known them fastened barefoot to run behind the Beg's cart; I have known women and maidens at work in the fields suffer the extreme of brutal violence, or be forcibly carried off to Turkish houses. If we complained or reported, we were imprisoned or put to death."

Now, the same true and horrid tale I have heard repeated again and again of deeds recurring throughout the length and breadth of the land. These were causes enough, indeed, to account for the rising. Encouraged, no doubt, it was by promises of help from without; and by so-called Serbian emissaries and agitators, who, however, to my certain knowledge, were native Bosnians and Herzegovinians living in exile in Serbia and Austria. The inhabitants of the Serbian principality are of the same race and speech as the Bosnians, and the Serbs dwelling in Austria are all exiles, of a more or less recent date, from the countries conquered by the Turks. In the neighbourhood of Pakrac, in Slavonia, we found the whole Serb or Pravoslav population mindful of their Bosnian origin, and for the most part looking forward to the time when they shall leave the fever-stricken districts between the Save and the Drave, and return to their own beautiful land, to the "Bosna ponosna," the "lofty Bosnia," of their songs.

CHAPTER II.

JOURNEY IN BOSNIA IN AUGUST, 1875.

TOWARDS the end of July, 1875, we left England to return to our school established at Serajevo for the purpose of training female teachers. We intended to make a recruiting expedition through some parts of the country which we had not yet visited, our plan being to induce the Serb communities in different parts of the country to send one or more girls to be educated as schoolmistresses, each for her own native place.

At Vienna we saw General Zach, the adjutant of the Prince of Serbia, who apprised us that the revolt in the Herzegovina was likely to become serious, that it would probably extend into Bosnia northward along the Dalmatian frontier into Turkish Croatia, and would spread simultaneously along the Serbian frontier and throughout the mountainous districts. He added that it would be impossible for the princes of Serbia and Montenegro to restrain their subjects from rushing to the aid of their brethren in race and religion. He urged us not to venture into Bosnia at a time when the desperate rising of the crushed and abject Bosnian Christians would call forth a terrible vengeance from the armed and fanatical Mahommedan population.

On the Save steamer we conversed with a Hungarian doctor in the Turkish service, on his way to rejoin the cavalry regiment at Banjaluka. He was of opinion that the rising would become "schrecklich ernst." The causes were deep and widespread. He knew the country too well to repeat fables about foreign instigation; but he related with the freshness of an eye-witness the ever-recurring facts of the intolerable oppression exercised by the farmers of the taxes, of the bribery, corruption, and extortion, systematic among the Turkish officials.

We visited Turkish Gradishka under the guidance of Vaso Vidević, a native Bosnian merchant, and the leader of the deputation to Vienna in 1873 to entreat protection from the Emperor. We were paddled over the river in one of the long narrow Save canoes, hollowed out of the trunk of a tree, and found ourselves once more amid the Oriental barbarism, the dirt, squalor, and misery which everywhere mark the frontier line of the Asiatic encroachments into Europe. The houses are built almost entirely of wood, here and there varied with plaster, and their condition was ruinous. In the tcharsia, or bazaar, were sitting turbaned Turks, cross-legged, in their shops, before the usual paltry stores of water-melons, Manchester cottons, leather shoes, rice, sugar, clay pipes, and little coffee cups. At last we came to a shop of European aspect, with counters arranged within, and the name Bozo Ljubojevich, painted in bright colours without. This was the shop of the richest Christian merchant in the place, one of those who had been obliged to flee into Austria two years before. He owned the largest house in the village, a very respectable building surrounded by a garden. Here we sat talking with his wife and family, served with coffee and sweetmeats. In 1873 armed Turks surrounded the house, insisting that ammunition was concealed there, and they made a rude but fruitless search. This house has been now completely sacked and demolished; the whole family are in exile in Austria, and Ljubojevich is a ruined man. In the poor little church Vaso showed us with pride a bell, which the brave Christians of Gradishka had dared to hang up in accordance with their rights: the only bell in any Orthodox church in Bosnia which could be heard from the outside. The Mussulmans would not tolerate the sound. But Vaso boasted that their bell could be heard even across the Save. Close to the church was a school, and on a plot of ground belonging to the community they were going to build shops, the rent of which would help them with their girls' school. At that time the town contained 150 Orthodox, 50 Latin, and 500 Turkish houses.

The next day we drove to Banjaluka, four hours distant, across a level plain, surrounded by hills, along the best road I have ever seen in Bosnia. At a short distance from the town we crossed the tramway of that fragment of railway which had been completed between Banjaluka and Novi. It has now been wholly destroyed, the bridges thrown down and rails torn up.

We paid a visit to a Bosnian family to whom we had brought a letter. The father, then absent, was one of the principal merchants in the place. The mother was an Austrian Slāv, a native of New Gradishka; the daughters, who were beautiful girls, had been educated by governesses from Austria, and are now married to Serb merchants, living in Belgrade. It was evident, with all their courtesy and real pleasure at seeing friends, that they were no little troubled at our coming. They told us that any intercourse with strangers rendered them objects of suspicion to the Turks. The father of the family had been seized and imprisoned in 1873, solely because he was on intimate terms with the then Austrian vice-consul, who was known to be friendly to the Christians, and eager to inform himself about their condition. They said that to avoid persecution they had requested the new Austrian vice-consul not to come to the house; that a Mussulman who had been long in their service had warned them to be exceedingly on their guard, and that they felt their lives and property were not safe. How much worse was it with the poor peasant, fleeced by the Mahommedan landowner, by the tax-gatherer, and by the native priest and Greek bishop, till nothing remains to him but the bare life! His food is the coarsest black bread, boiled beans, and maize; meat he does not taste once a year. In reply to our inquiries, they told us they had known instances of girls being carried off by Mussulmans in the villages in the neighbourhood of Banjaluka, but the cases were not so frequent now; though much that happened in the distant villages no one heard of.

Immediately after we left a zaptié came to the house, to inquire who we were and what we had come for. On our way to the inn we were met by another zaptié, who ordered us immediately to appear before the Turkish authorities. I replied that we were English ladies, and should do no such thing; and, producing our passport, told him to take it to the governor immediately, and to say that we must be supplied with an escort to Travnik the next day. The man said "Peki" (very well), and went off. Just then appeared the Turkish doctor, our friend of the Save steamer, who immediately went to the konak, to secure us a suitable guard for the journey.

Further information, however, as to the detestable condition of the hilly road between Banjaluka and Travnik, reported movements of Turkish redif (landwehr) about the country, together with the intense heat of the weather, decided us to give up the new route, and return to Gradishka, to take the steamer to Brod; much as we regretted the loss of a visit to the lake scenery of Bosnia, and the old historic fortress and castle of Jaica.

The day after we left Banjaluka, Sunday, 15th August, commenced the rising in North Bosnia, at Kosarać, in the district of Priedor, and in the neighbourhood of Gradishka. We first heard of it on the Monday morning, when at an early hour the two girls of the family we had visited at Banjaluka appeared at the door of our room in the inn at Austrian Gradishka, telling us their mother had sent them away in the middle of the night with all the children and those of a neighbouring family to join their relations in Austria. They reported that "a Christian had killed a Turkish tax-gatherer," and that "Turks and Christians were now killing one another in the fields." Vaso Videvich had been with us the afternoon of the preceding day, and he knew nothing then of what was taking place. He had told me a few days previously that the rayahs in North Bosnia could do nothing, that they were too weak to join the Herzegovinian example, and that they had no arms and no Montenegro to help them. Now we saw him earnestly consulting with some Bosnians in the garden of the inn. He was going away by the steamer, and he would never return to Turkish Gradishka. We found some months afterwards that he was then taking his whole wealth to purchase guns for the Christians. He conveyed these guns to Gradishka in Save boats, but the landing was ill arranged, and as the boats had lain there two or more days, it being perfectly well known that arms were on board, the officials were obliged to seize them. They were confiscated, and are to this day lying in the Austrian fortress at Gradishka. The same thing happened again and again. We heard that quantities of ammunition were confiscated, notwithstanding the readiness of every Slāv official along the Austrian frontier to wink at the transmission of arms for the insurgents. On one occasion the poor fellows had contrived to store some powder on an island in the river. It got damp; they spread it out to dry, it caught fire, and several men were killed or badly hurt. Another time they had made a wooden cannon, which they crammed so full of powder that it burst, killing one man and wounding several. What could be expected from peasants who were wholly unaccustomed to the use of firearms, and absolutely illiterate and unskilled? It is only surprising that the armies of the Porte have not been able long ago to put down the revolt of unarmed and ignorant peasants, but the rising is now stronger than ever,[*] and the Bosnian rayahs, who are apt to learn and keen-witted, now know better how to handle their weapons.

But to return to our own narrative. On board the steamer we found the Croatian *avocat*, Dr. Berlić, returning home to Brod. He had come that morning from Sisseg, and he told us that at a short distance from Gradishka, on the Turkish bank of the Save, he had seen from the deck of the steamer women and children hiding in the bushes at the water's edge, and peasants running to and fro with hoes and spades in their hands. Certainly the rising had commenced. Vaso Vidević, pale as death, called us down into the cabin, and

---

[*] "The capital error in Europe was the not aiding and encouraging the Turkish provinces to rise entirely and simultaneously, and helping them even, if necessary, in their self-liberation, as she has helped the Turks, with arms and means, leaving the discipline of war and military organization to establish the bases of political organization. The process would have been costly, but would have been profitable in the end; for it would have made of these slaves, men, as it has, to a certain extent, done in Herzegovina and Bosnia—would have brought forward their natural chiefs and established a moral authority of the highest importance in the new state of things. War and death are not so dreadful as slavery and corruption; and *it remains to be seen if the solution to be adopted will not in the end cost more bloodshed than the natural solution by a general insurrection.*"—"*Herzegovina and the late Uprising.*" By W. J. STILLMAN. Longmans. 1877.

implored us, with tears, not to go to Serajevo; persisting that it was highly dangerous to attempt the journey, and that the Austrian post-cart would very likely be fired at in the night. We told him, encouragingly, it might prove a very good thing for their cause if two English ladies were killed. To which he replied, "Yes; but not you." He was quite right in expecting the disturbances would spread eastward towards Brod. Many women and children were killed a few days afterwards at Kobash, near which place three Christians were impaled* two months later. A fierce Beg, named Osman Aga, from Dervend, on the post-road to Serajevo, sallied forth and effectively checked for a time the rising in that neighbourhood by the massacre of many defenceless men, women, and children. Corpses were seen floating down the Save, and were cast on the sand of the island near Brod. The body of a man was brought on shore at Brod, and was found on examination by the town doctor to be terribly burnt across the chest. This poor victim had suffered one of the well-known Turkish tortures, which consists of heaping burning coals on the breast. These horrors took place a day or two after we reached Serajevo. We left Brod in the post-cart August 17th, travelled through the night and the following day in

---

* "In the month of October, 1875, after the Turks had been two or three times defeated by the insurgents at Srbać and in the hills of Motaica, returning enraged and infuriated, they cut in pieces four peaceful Christian inhabitants, in the villages of Vlamka and Brusnika, named Simo Vrsoika, Marco Guzoica, Stevan Vrovać, and Jovan Lepir; and three they impaled alive on stakes on the banks of the Save above Kobash, opposite the Austrian churchyard and church of Kloster, namely, Mihail Snegotinać and his brother Aleksa Snegotinac, and Luka Drajovic, all three from the village Kaoć, in Bosnia, above Kobash. To this testify Kuzman Skolnik and Bozo Davidovish, who beheld it with their own eyes, and there are many others who will not give their names.

"(Signed)   Vaso Vidević."

The impalement witnessed by Canon Liddon and Rev. M. McColl was no solitary instance on the banks of the Save.

safety, slept at Kiseljak in the khan (where I remember being awakened at midnight by angry Turkish women flinging charcoal in at our open window), and reached Serajevo August 19th.

Our arrival was unexpected, and never had the aspect of the house, and the garden, and the whole little establishment been so encouraging. The holidays were over, and we found pupils and teachers at work in the school-room, three new girls having been just brought from Nova Varosh, on the Serbian frontier.

Mr. Consul Holmes was absent, having accompanied his friend Dervish Pasha to Mostar, the Turkish head-quarters in the Herzegovina. The aspect of affairs was considered very grave by the acting-consul, Mr. Freeman. Our Austrian friends held civil war to be imminent, and the wife of the Austrian consul-general, on the excuse of the illness of her mother, was on the point of starting with her little boy. Scarcely any regular troops were left in the town, every available man having been sent off to the Herzegovina. The Mahommedans of Serajevo are three times as numerous as the Christians, and are many of them exceedingly fanatical. They had sworn that it should go hard with the Christians in the town unless the rising in Bosnia was soon quelled. The defence of the place was almost wholly entrusted to some companies of the redif, composed of native Bosnian Mussulmans. The redif were being called out all over the country, and companies of fierce and wild-looking recruits on their way to the barracks were constantly passing our windows shouting their war-songs. One of the most cruel Bosnian Begs of Serajevo, Cengić Aga,* who had large properties in the Herzegovina, had started to form a

* Happily for the Christians, this Cengić Aga was wounded early in the insurrection, and died of his wounds at Mostar.

troop of Mahommedan volunteers, that is, to collect a band of licensed and fanatical marauders.

The situation was anything but hopeful. We decided to turn these adverse circumstances to the furtherance of our educational plans and to carry off the most promising of the pupils to continue their training at Prague, in Bohemia. The consuls assured us it would be impossible at that moment to obtain for these girls, or for any Turkish subjects, the necessary teskeré, or passport; the authorities were refusing the numerous applications now made, and objected even to women and children leaving the country. Mr. Freeman did, however, obtain the requisite permission, in exchange for a written promise, signed and officially witnessed, that we would bring back these subjects of the Porte to the lands of the Sultan. At the same time we received from the representative of the pasha an earnest request to remain, for our going away would give a bad impression of the inability of the Turks to maintain order. We thought matters too serious to admit of our staying for the sake of keeping up appearances for the Turks, and we therefore effected our departure early on the morning of August 23rd.

We were a party of ten in all, occupying four of the springless carts of the country. Three of our drivers were Mussulmans, the other a most miserable Christian boy in their service, who was always blubbering, and seemed literally terrified out of his wits. On the way we were obliged to take on another cart for the luggage. This was driven by its owner, a Jewish khangee. One of our Mussulman drivers, a black man, who went by the name of "the Arab," got frightfully drunk, and behaved so ill that we appealed to the kaimakam at Shebsche to put him in prison. Notwithstanding the order of the kaimakam, at our next halt the Arab appeared again, but he had been frightened into behaving himself better, and we had no further trouble with him. Another of the Mussulman drivers, a Turkish boy of sixteen, the son of a Bosnian Aga, owner of the horses, proved entirely beyond control. He stopped wherever he chose to stop, or he tore recklessly along the road, flogging his miserable horses and firing off pistols in the air. This boy was after the worst type of Bosnian Mussulmans. He was lank and small, with colourless eyes; wisps of his sandy hair escaped from the red handkerchief which was tied round a dirty white linen cap; his weazened boy's face was old with an expression of mingled cruelty, rapacity, and cunning. The day before we reached Dervend, the zaptiés told us the Turks and Christians were fighting there, and that the Turks were cutting the Christians to pieces; but we need not fear, whatever happened, for they had orders to defend us. These rumours referred to the raid of Osman Aga of Dervend, which I have already mentioned, and which had accomplished its cruel work some days previously. When we passed the next day through the Turkish portion of Dervend, which is on the post-road, all was quiet as the grave. Several times the new zaptiés, who seemed to suspect our sympathy with the Christians, volunteered to tell us about the revolt of the rayah; "Nasha rayah" (our rayah) "had actually dared to rebel, but the Sultan would send a great army to Bosnia along the Save."

Before we reached Brod, still expecting some difficulty in getting the Bosnian girls across, we made them put on European costume, which we had prepared for the occasion before leaving Serajevo. It may have been owing to this disguise that their teskeré, or passport, was never asked for, and we were allowed to cross the river with our whole party into Austrian territory, after a few lazy questions as to the contents of our luggage. A peal of bells from the church in Austrian Brod sounded more cheerily than ever across the water, while we were waiting for the ferry-boat in a golden breadth of evening sunlight. The loveliness of the earth and sky had all along uttered a protest against the odious sights and sounds of human degradation which we witnessed on the way, and the cloudless starlit heavens had invited us to forget the dirt and the disgust of the Turkish shelters. We had spent the nights in a cart, guarded by the zaptiés, and knowing even then but little of the terrible scenes enacted in this beautiful land, to which Humanity is faithless.

CHAPTER III.

BOSNIA IN 1876-7.

ANARCHY, insurrection, terror, massacres, "infernal chaos." More than one-third of the whole Christian population fled over the frontier out of Bosnia into the neighbouring lands—Austria, Serbia, and Montenegro. The number of those who have perished by the sword, the famine, and the pestilence within the land is unreckoned and unknown.

A letter which I have just received from a native Bosnian merchant will best describe the present condition of his wretched country. I can vouch for his trustworthiness. He writes from Austria Slavonia, on the northern frontier of Bosnia:—

"GRADISHKA, $\frac{10}{22}$ March, 1877.

"When the Bosnian refugees in Austro-Hungary heard that Serbia had made peace with Turkey they were struck dumb, as if a thunderbolt had fallen from the sky. They ask incessantly, 'What will become of us now? Do the Powers want again to force us under the Turkish yoke? Better each one of us should perish than return on the faith of the Turk.' They ask, 'What Power could have the conscience to wish or dare to drive us back under the Turkish sword, to ignore and forget our two years' struggle, and again hand us over into slavery?' I told them, only to see what they would reply, that perhaps Austria would send her armies into Bosnia. They answered, 'Why should we go from one slavery into another? Better we should slay our wives and children, and all seek death among the bands of the *haïduks* (outlaws), than go from slavery to slavery.' I think you will have already heard this sentiment from the Bosnian Serbs. As for Bosnia, and the Serb (Pravoslav) population of Bosnia, this is the condition to-day, as described to me from genuine sources within the province, and also by some who have saved their lives by flight. There is a complete clearing out of the Serb people of Bosnia, for the Turkish authorities themselves hunt them down, and give full licence to the Bashibazouks and Gipsies, also to the Catholics and the Jews; and every one is free to kill or do any violence to a Bosnian Serb, or to take away his property, and no Serb dares to make a complaint. They are fleeing incessantly out of Bosnia, wherever they are able. Below Brod, near Vuchijak, a hundred families have crossed over. I spoke with them myself, and asked them, 'Why do you fly, brothers, when here you must perish of hunger?' Weeping and groaning, they replied they would rather jump into the river than suffer what they have to endure. They said there were a hundred families in Gornje, the half of which had fled into Austria, but afterwards returned at the bidding of the Turks and of the Austrian government, who had assured them of perfect safety. They had been left in peace for some months, but now their sufferings were greater than ever before. They were incessantly harassed by Mussulman bands, composed of the worst murderers and evildoers, who violated women, carried off maidens, and seized whatever property they found. The principal inhabitants of the place had been carried off to Dervend, to Teshan, and to Prnjavor, and had never returned.

"These tidings gave me bitter grief. I said what I could to comfort them and went on my way to Diakovar. On my return I visited Austrian Brod, in order to get further information; and there again I heard terrible news. It so happened that I met there a merchant who is still living at Dervend, the first town on the post road between Turkish Brod and Serajevo. I asked him what was going on at Dervend and in the neighbourhood. He looked very anxiously round to see if any one was within hearing, and when he was satisfied that we were alone he went on to tell me that in the course of the last two months forty-two men, the principal Bosnian Serbs in the neighbourhood, had been murdered at Dervend. These butcheries had been perpetrated at night, behind the Turkish barracks. When the relatives of these men came to visit them in the prison and to bring them bread (as is the custom), they were driven away, and told to go home until the time came to shut them up too. Then they were also accused, and were sent off to Banjaluka. I hear now that this is the way the Turks are proceeding throughout Bosnia. Only to-day I heard that thirty families from Gashitza and other villages tried to escape into Austria across the Save below Jassenovatz, but the Turks came up with them, and murdered those who had not yet got over; a certain Jovo from the village of Medjedj was cut to pieces, and his two children flung into the water. Behold those woes upon woes, and behold the selfishness and inhumanity of Europe, which keeps us for centuries in slavery, and is resolved still so to keep us! There remains nothing for us but to fight. Better die than live in shame and misery. You know very well what sort of people are gone from Bosnia to represent the country at Constantinople. Misery, indeed, for us! Faim Effendi, from Banjaluka; Petraki, from Serajevo; Ephzem and Marotić, from Travnik, are all men who, together with the pashas, suck out the life of the rayah. No pen can describe the evil of the Turkish government, but the Turcophiles will neither see nor hear.

"In Bosnia the assessment and collection of the taxes is carried on in the following manner. Turks on horseback, with alibashis, go by twenties about the villages, demanding lodging, food, and drink for nothing, committing every sort of violence on men and women. Cattle worth 300 piastres have to be sold for 150 piastres in caimés (paper notes), on which the loss is 40 per cent., and the tax is to be paid in silver. The villagers have thus become so impoverished that about one-third of them have no live stock remaining, and the prisons are full of those who cannot pay. The various dues to the Beys and to the government, and other oppressive levies, are multiplied from day to day. Without excuse the bimbashis send zaptiés into the villages to terrify the inhabitants, and in some way or other to collect a few hundred piastres. For all the misery and wrong which the Christians are suffering at the hands of the Turks there is no justice and there are no judges, for none of the courts will give them a hearing. As for murders, they are happening every day. The last day or two there are fresh cases. Mahmoud Muftic, in the middle of the town, cut off the right hand of Pejo Savanević. Osman Shabio killed Josef Ervachenin in his own house, and flung the body into the middle of the road in the wood. Achmet Asnada killed Jovo Uvković in the village of Timara, together with another whose name I do not know. Also Sefto Jakupović, whom Faim Effendi let go that he might kill and rob the Christians, killed a housefather in his house in the village of Timar. In the quarters of the Turkish redif at Gradishka, he killed a peaceful villager from Kobatovća. Ifish Mlicharević killed the son of the Knez Ristic in his own house in the village of Miljević. Numerous like atrocities there are everywhere and in every place, and for all these misdeeds no one is answerable to anybody, for the government makes no inquiry, and will not even hear. Faim Effendi, the most renowned bloodsucker of the Christians, and the present representative of Bosnia and the Herzegovina at Constantinople, has spread a secret proclamation to be read by night to the Bosnian Mussulmans, in which it is declared that the Mahommedans will on no account accept any reforms, but that on the contrary they will everywhere oppose them with all their might, and that the utmost violence is to be carried out upon the rayah. The Turkish government has during the last few days distributed fresh arms to the Bosnian Mussulmans from 12 to 80 years of age. Three considerable encounters have taken place in the neighbourhood of Banjaluka, in the village of Verbać, three-quarters of an hour distant; in Klashonica, three hours distant; and the third at Mortanza in Zupa, eight hours from Banjaluka. Also in the Sandjak of Travnik in the villages of Pechko and Metko, between Livno and Travnik. We hear of encounters daily. Numbers are escaping to the mountains and to the camp of Despotović. Some of the richer villagers had fled from the country into the towns to be under the protection of the authorities. Turkish violence is now driving them all out of the towns, out of Travnik and Banjaluka, and other towns. They dare not go into the villages, for the Turks have taken to disguise themselves as insurgents. The Christians from the towns also are now escaping into Austria."

The rising was joined at the beginning by Roman Catholics. They were restrained by their priests, who received orders from Rome to stand aloof. Dread of the success of Serbia has also been a powerful withholding motive. As a rule, the Roman Catholics have aided the Turkish power in the insurrection; they have played into the hands of the Turks; they have acted as spies; they have gone on patrol with the Turkish soldiers. The rule, however, is not without exception, and at this moment Fra Buonoventura, a Roman Catholic priest, is one of the insurgent leaders in South Bosnia, and other priests, besides the well-known Herzegovinian Mussics, have led their flocks against the Turks.

I have just received the following account from Peter Uzelatz, a trustworthy resident on the Austrian frontier, of what is now passing in South Bosnia. He writes under date March 29 :—

"In Ochijevo the Turks have massacred the brothers Vaso and Jefto Karanović, have outraged women and girls, plundered 300 head of cattle, and burnt many houses. In the Klechovaca Mountains the Turks have fallen upon a quiet village, have killed three brothers named Kecman, stolen cattle, and exercised all kinds of brutalities. In the neighbourhood of Glamosh the Turks are attacking quiet Christian villages, and are massacring, plundering, and robbing in every direction. Near Glamosh four brothers Govzdonovic were murdered; their heads were cut off and carried to Glamosh.

"Turkish licence is driving numbers of the Christian population to Austria for safety. The help given by the Austrian government was reduced on March 20 from ten to five kreutzers (1*d*.) per day. From April 1 it will be given only to women and children and sick persons. Ablebodied men will receive nothing. Help is more necessary than ever at this very time, for it is a moment of the greatest poverty."

The diminution of assistance by the Austrian government is intended to check the immigration, and to drive back the fugitives into their own land. But these poor people, who have seen from the experience of their own lives and the lives of their forefathers what Turkish promises are worth, dare not return, knowing their certain fate to be massacre and outrage. The result of the Conference at Constantinople was announced to the Bosnians in the following manner by Kulinevic Beg at Vakup, in South-western Bosnia. The proclamation of the Constitution* being read in Turkish was then explained in Slāv, in the style of the Bosnian Mussulmans: "It is all quite right and very good; the Turk rules as before, and the rayah remains rayah. The Sultan, the Brother of the Sun, the Cousin of the Moon, Bond-brother of the Stars, the Friend of Allah, the Kinsman of Mahomet, the Son of

* The correspondent of the *Manchester Guardian*, writing from Ragusa under date February 9th, gives the following anecdote of the election of a Christian deputy for the Turkish Parliament:—"At Mostar, where consular supervision has also to be taken into account, these enlightened employés of the Turkish government have seized on and forcibly elected a Christian merchant as deputy for the capital of Herzegovina. The unfortunate Bilich, who was anything but ambitious of this unexpected honour, was so far intimidated that he dared not refuse it at Mostar, and was accordingly packed off to Stamboul by way of Ragusa. The instant, however, he set foot on Christian soil he despatched a letter to Mostar resigning his seat, and, fearing to return, is at present a refugee at Ragusa. Truly, it remained for the Turks to discover this new form of electoral intimidation." He goes on to say:—"Meanwhile the Mahommedan population of Herzegovina are becoming more and more dissatisfied with the first-fruits of the new régime. Among the merchants of the towns ruin has been sown broadcast by an enormous influx of paper money; Trebinje alone has been flooded with a new paper currency to the amount of 100,000 piastres. In the district of Trebinje, indeed, nothing but the neighbourhood of Turkish nizam has prevented Mahommedan discontent from bursting into open revolt. According to the law the heads of families are exempted from military service, but the kaimakam of Trebinje has been attempting to extort large sums of money, in some cases as much as 1,000 florins, from the heads of the richest Mahommedan families, in lieu of military service. Upon their appeal the tyrant tried to seize and imprison them, but has not been able to set hands on more than a dozen. The rest, to the number of over a hundred, and among them several Begs and influential landowners, have fled, and during the last few days no less than seventy Mahommedan refugees have arrived at Ragusa. Even as I write, I hear of fresh arrivals."

Osman, Emperor of Emperors, King of Kings, Prince of Princes, Lord of the Earth under the Sky, has commanded of those kings who came to him at Stamboul that they shall drive back for us our rayah into our lands again, and has decreed that whoever is not obedient on his return shall be put to death." Before the conclusion of the Conference, Bosnian Mussulmans had begun to spread the report that the Sultan would decree the massacre of every Christian in the land, in order that Bosnia might be preserved intact for the Faithful.

I have related in the last chapter the story of the beginning of the Bosnian rising in August, 1875, in North Bosnia. The following account of the spread of the insurrection was sent me by Herr Fric, in August, 1876:—

"The Bosnian insurgents, who are extremely numerous, and in some instances well armed, are for the most part distributed among the following troops and bands:

"1. The bands in the Rissovać and Grmeć mountains in West Bosnia. 2. In the Vucjak in East Bosnia. 3. In the Pastirevo and Kozara mountains in North Bosnia.

"The insurgents in the Rissovać and Grmeć mountains are under the leadership of the well-known Golub Babić, Marinković, Simo Davidović, Pope Karan, and Trifko Amelić. Latterly the Serb Colonel Despótovič has assumed the chief command, and has formed eight battalions out of the scattered bands. In Pastirevo and in Kozara are the bands of Marko Gjenadija, Ostoja, Spasojević, Marko Bajalica, Igumen Hadzić, and Pope Stevo. The new camp of Brezovać, not far from Novi, is held by Ostoja Vojnovic. The former camp of Peter Karageorgevic in Chorkovać is held by Ilija Sevic.

"The joint object of these bands at the present

moment is so fully to occupy the Turks as to prevent any greater concentration of Mussulman troops or irregulars on the Drina, on the western frontier of Serbia. As there is no possibility of systematically organizing an insurrection in Bosnia, the mode of warfare peculiar to the land is pursued. . . . . that is, by perpetual harassing to drive back the whole Mussulman population into their towns and strong places. Another object of the insurgent bands is the safe conduct, under cover of their protection, up to the frontier of Austria or Serbia, of the Christians who have escaped from the cruelties of the Turks into the forest mountains of Bosnia. Sometimes these poor exiles—unarmed men, women, and children —have been for months hiding in the woods, until the armed bands could open a way for them through the country into neighbouring Christian lands. They were driven from their homes by savage Mussulman soldiery, who suddenly appeared in their peaceful villages, murdering and plundering, and then setting fire to their houses. It is hard to realise the misery of these flights; the father loses the son, the mother the daughter; the young and the feeble perish on the way; weeks or months go by before the scattered members of a family find one another, and the fate of many is never known. No property, hardly the bare life, can be saved.

"It is especially to be observed that these Turkish onslaughts on Christian villages are not made exclusively by the Mussulman rabble of the land on their own account. These murderous raids are frequently ordered and authorised by the Turkish officials, and the regular troops take part in them.

"On my last journey from Kostainitza to the 'dry frontier,' near Novi, Bosnian fugitives who had just crossed over at Kuljani (between Kostainitza and

Podove), from Svinja on the Save, assured me that large Mussulman bands led by the recently appointed kaimakan of Bihac, Vessel Bey, had fallen on the village of Svinja and burnt it to the ground. The next day this account was confirmed to me in the presence of the Austrian authorities at Dvor by many other fugitives, who had fled before a similar incursion conducted by the Turkish Miralay. Driven by the kaimakam Vessel Bey, and this Miralay overrunning the land, 3,000 to 4,000 fugitives have passed over into Austrian territory, according to official report.

"With a heavy heart I call to mind the passage of the fugitives over the Unna at Kuljani, protected by a very large body of insurgents against an expected onslaught of the Turks. The miserable exiles this time reached the Austrian shore in safety in the little canoes of the river. What a scene of wretchedness! Hundreds and hundreds dragging themselves along the dusty road —men, women, and children. In the heavy despairing countenances of the tall strong men may be plainly read the hereditary misery of centuries. Weary women and little children can scarcely crawl along; some of the sick (for the most part smallpox cases) fall down by the way. I go up to a group which is gathering round some object on the road-side; a woman has been overtaken by the pains of labour, and, surrounded by her children, is giving birth to an infant. A few steps further on is another group; here lies in the last agony a woman who has been wounded; seven wounds on her body . . . . Here lie some others slightly wounded, who from pain and fatigue can crawl no further. Many sink down on the dusty hard roadside to seek on Christian soil the sleep to which for nights they had not dared to yield. By degrees the greater number reach the Gemeinde Haus in Divari. The whole group sit or lie about on the large grassy space in front of the building. Some begin to eat the ears of Indian corn which they have brought with them out of Turkey; for in the fields on the Turkish side is still lying Indian corn of last year's harvest, which neither Turks nor Christians, out of mutual fear, have dared to gather. Fathers of families go to seek bread in the village. Some have brought away a few coins, and can pay for it. Now, a father returns with some bread, which he divides among his family; the children watch every mouthful with longing eyes. Another father returns empty-handed; a cry of distress bursts forth. Alas! there are hundreds upon hundreds of such scenes; for fresh bands of fugitives are crossing daily at one or another point on the frontier into Austrian territory."

I spent the greater part of 1876 on the Croatian and Slavonian frontiers of Bosnia, engaged, together with Miss Johnston, in applying for the benefit of the exiles, the "Bosnian and Herzegovinian Fugitives and Orphan Relief Fund."*

Near Kostajnica, on the Croatian military frontier, Pope Mandic, of Meminiski, told us that he had in his parish over 2,700 fugitives, the number of inhabitants being 2,400. Thus the fugitives exceeded by 300 the number of inhabitants. The parish is extremely poor, and the house - room insufficient in ordinary times. In winter, not only one family, but several families, composing the *zadruga* or house communion, which prevails in this country, all sleep in one room round a fire made in the middle, the smoke of

---

* Some account of this work will be found at the end of the second volume. Donations are received by Messrs. Daldy, Isbister & Co., 56, Ludgate Hill; at Messrs. Twinings' Bank, 215, Strand; by the Clydesdale Bank; the London and Westminster Bank; by Lady Muir Mackenzie, 8, Eaton Place West; by Mrs. De Noe Walker, 10, Ovington Gardens, S.W.; and by the Hon. Treasurer, Andrew Johnston, Esq., 158, Leadenhall Street. The profits of these volumes will be given to the fund.

which escapes through the rafters of the unceiled dwelling. In common winters there may be found in such houses from twenty to thirty persons sleeping on the ground, round the fire, in this manner; when the poor fugitives were taken in there were sometimes upwards of forty. Was it surprising that first smallpox and then typhus had broken out, and that this priest had sometimes ten burial services a day to perform? Then there were newborn babies for whom their parents had no clothing, and for whom, when born on the flight, their fathers had cut up their stockings to make some sort of little covering for them.

The Bosnians' love of their own country is very great; they remain as close to the frontier as they can, within sight of their own hills. One poor man came from a distant village to Kostajnica, and crossed the bridge on to the narrow strip of land by the Austrian fortress on the other side to breathe his native air. "The air of Bosnia," he said, " smells like a rose." We heard from one and all the fugitives the same story—their houses are burnt, they escaped for their lives from the Turks, and they will never go back so long as the Turk rules there. The Bosnian villages, at a distance from the frontier, which had never risen, were frightfully plundered and maltreated by Turkish soldiers, regular and irregular, and by the native Mussulmans. We were told, on thoroughly trustworthy authority, that the former practice of the Turks was again resorted to of hanging up the rayah to a tree with his head downwards and pouring water over him, in the freezing weather, till he reveals the place where his little hoard of coin is hidden. At the present moment no Christian's life or property is safe in Bosnia, except under the eyes of the European consuls in Serajevo. The land is a desert. We hear from numerous Bosnians that three sowing seasons have passed, and nothing has been sown except in the gardens belonging to the towns. The fields are bare; the Turkish villages have been destroyed by the insurgents; the Christian villages by the Turks. Large tracts of country are absolutely depopulated. An enormous number of Mussulman widows and children are left, for the Christian Bosnian insurgents do not harm women and children, but let them go safe "in the name of Christ and St. John." On the other hand, the treatment of the Christian women by the Turks is now well known. The "Bulgarian atrocities" have been repeated again and again in Bosnia, from time to time, on a small scale, in different parts of the country ever since the beginning of the uprising.

In January, 1877, we went to the Dalmatian frontier of Bosnia, where the greatest distress prevails, and where there have been many deaths from sheer starvation. At this moment over one third of the whole Christian population of Bosnia and Herzegovina are in most miserable exile; the number of fugitives all round the frontier very considerably exceeds 200,000. The magnitude of the misery has been impressed upon us, eye-witnesses, by the constant repetition of the same scenes all through these many months, and along the extent of so many hundred miles. We found in the neighbourhood of Knin in Dalmatia the same misery, in a still greater degree, which we had left in the distant Slavonian district; we heard the same changes on the same sad story over and over again: "Our homes have been burned by the Turks, our crops destroyed; we fled for the bare life; we could save nothing, or we have spent all we were able to save. Our children are dying of hunger and sickness, but we will all rather perish here than return to encounter the armed and angry Turks." From whatever quarter you may approach the Bosnian and Herzegovinian boundaries, be it from Serbia or Montenegro, from Slavonia, Croatia or Dalmatia, you will find the same throng of ragged starving fugitives. They are in a worse condition than last winter, and the mortality among them is very great.

Mr. Arthur Evans thus describes a scene on the frontier:—

"We approached the Bosnian frontier by way of the village of Strmica, about which as many as 6,000 refugees are crowded. I had never come in contact with so much human misery before. They crowded round us, these pinched haggard faces, these lean bony frames, scarred by disease and bowed down with hunger; they followed till it seemed a dreadful Dance of Death. There was one lad of twelve, as pale as a spectre, who could not live many hours; and by him another younger child, whose only clothing was a few rags tied together and eked out by the long tresses of a woman's hair. Some English help has already reached Strmica, but in many cases it had come too late, and in this village alone over 500 have died in the last few months. A little further on the mountain side we came upon a new graveyard already well tenanted. We now crossed the Bosnian frontier, and followed a path along a precipitous mountain steep, passing the débris of a stupendous landslip, and beneath some extraordinary rock pinnacles, called "the Hare Stones" by the Bosnians. Near here we saw the first signs of Turkish ravages—the village of Zaseok burnt by the Turks at the first outbreak of the insurrection; and presently found an old Bosnian, who guides us by more difficult mountain paths to a lonely glen, where a torrent divides the Austrian from the Bosnian territory, and where, on the Christian side, we descried a series of caves in the rocky mountain side, to which we now made our way. Then indeed broke upon my sight such a depth of human misery as it has perhaps fallen to the lot of few living men to witness. We crossed a small frozen cataract, and passed the mouths of two lesser caverns, toothed with icicles three feet long and over, and then we came to the mouth of a larger cave, a great black opening in the rock, from which, as we climbed up to it, crawled forth a squalid and half-naked swarm of women, children, and old men, with faces literally eaten away with hunger and disease. A little way off was another small hole, outside which leant what had once been a beautiful girl, and inside, amidst filth and squalor which I cannot describe, dimly seen through smoke and darkness, lay a woman dying of typhus. Others crowded out of black holes and nooks, and I found that there were about thirty in this den. In another small hole, going almost straight down into the rock, I saw a shapeless bundle of rags and part of the pale half-hidden face of another woman stricken down by the disease of hunger; another den with about a dozen, and then another more horrible than any. A black hole, sloping downwards at so steep an angle as made climbing up or down a task of some difficulty, descended thus abruptly about thirty feet, and then seemed to disappear into the bowels of the earth. The usual haggard crowd swarmed out of the dark and fœtid recesses below and climbed up to seek for alms. A woman seated on a ledge of rock half way up burst into hysterical sobs; it was at the sight of old Lazar. The good old fellow had already discovered these dens of destitution, and had brought them some food from the English ladies all the way from Knin. They had tasted nothing then for three days, and would have all died that day, she said, if he had not come. Then, slowly tottering and crawling from an underground lurking place at the bottom of the pit, there stumbled into the light an old man, so lean, so wasted, with such hollow sunken eyes, that he seemed nothing but a walking skeleton; it was the realisation of some ghastly mediæval picture of the Resurrection of the Dead! He seemed to have lost his reason, but from below he stretched out his bony hands towards us as if to grasp our alms, and made a convulsive effort to climb the rocky wall of his den. He raised himself with difficulty a few feet, and then fell back exhausted and was caught by a girl in her arms. Poor old man! It was not hard to see that he would never leave that loathsome den alive; nay, I dare not say that those horrible recesses were not catacombs as well. Not far off we passed another cave, where the bodies of some women and children had been found."

Insurgent bands are again making sign from mountain and forest throughout the land. The rising has acquired compact strength in a district of South Bosnia, which is cleared of the Turks and held by Bosnian bands, who are at present under the command of Despotović, between the Austrian frontier and the Turkish fortresses of Kulin Vakup, Kljuc, and Glamosh. This district was visited, in February last, by Mr. Arthur Evans, who has fully confirmed, by the evidence of his own eyes, the accounts I have heard from many native Bosnians. He says the bulwark of this insurgent territory, to the east, is the great mountain range of Cerna Gora, or the Black Mountains, so that there literally exists at this moment a Bosnian Montenegro. "The fields and fertile lands of the peasants are circled, like a fortified town, by mountain walls, and often approachable only by difficult mountain portals. When this fact is appreciated, you will understand the great capabilities of defence possessed by a country whose mountain strongholds contain fertile fields, where corn may be sown and harvests gathered in. Against the Turkish towns the insurgents may show themselves weak; but, with ordinary leaders, they could defy the invader for generations in their mountain fastnesses. They are themselves beginning to appreciate their defensive strength, and the importance of dividing their energies between agriculture and defence; but during the period when the insurrection was confined to a few villages on the Dalmatian frontier, the Turks had penetrated into their secluded uplands, and several villages had been burnt." . . . .

" The district of Podić runs apparently in an undefined manner into that of Vidovoselo, to the north-west of this *polje*, and the whole of this district has been ravaged by the Turks in a most atrocious manner. As I have no wish to indulge in loose and unsubstantiated charges, I may say that I have taken down the accounts of three sets of witnesses. First, of the peasants, a man and a woman at the hut at Podić; secondly, of two peasants of Vidovoselo, by name Stojan Vasović and Gavran Tadić, whom I saw at Unnatz, and who actually witnessed what occurred from a wood above the village where they had hidden themselves; and lastly, from Boian Sterbać, who was horribly cut in the neck by a blow from a yataghan and his left hand nearly severed, and who lies at present in the insurgent hospital at Knin, where I saw him, and whose deposition and extraordinary signature I have before me. All these accounts agree in the minutest particular, and I do not think that even the Turks themselves would call them in question. On the 12th July of last year, about two in the afternoon, the peasants of this district were peacefully engaged in their fields, when a large band of Bashi-bazouks from Glamosh, under the leadership of Ahmed Beg Philipović, of that place, broke into the *polje*. They hunted down and killed—some on the plain and some in the houses—twenty-three unarmed peasants, nine of the village of Podić and fourteen of Vidovoselo. I have the names and families of all the victims before me. Among them were two children, one of five years old and the other about ten. The village pope, Damian Sterbać, was hacked to pieces; his wife, Stana Sterbać, was cut with yataghans about the breast; and his daughter Militća was wounded in the arm. The villages were first plundered and then burnt, and the Turks made off to Glamosh, carrying with them the heads of most of their victims. The hut we were in was saved from burning by the timely appearance of an insurgent band on the height above. A party of Bashibazouks were engaged in plundering the cottage when they caught sight of the enemy, and as unarmed peasants and women were their game, and not armed men, they decamped in a hurry."

I have a list of the names of these victims, and the signatures of some of the eye-witnesses whom I saw at Knin, among others of Boian Sterbać, whose scars are a frightful confirmation of his almost incredible story of escape, after being left for dead on the ground.*

* I give a translation of this statement: "On the 12th of July, 1876, Turks from Glamosh found peaceful villagers at work in the fields. They killed them all with the exception of the undersigned, whom they wounded terribly with a jatagan about the neck and hands. He lay on the ground, the Turks counting him for dead; when they were at a distance hunting other villagers along the fields, his wife and neighbours came, and carried him off, that he might tell it to the world, and relate the names of his murdered companions. The undersigned is the witness of this deed, and he writes with his own wounded and maimed body; other witnesses also sign who beheld the deed with their own eyes. *Murdered*—Pope Damjan Sterbać, Aleksa, Golub, Gliso Ilija, Vid, Nikola, Lazo Sterbać, Tode, Mijat and Stanko Vostica, Vaso and Ilija Knezevic, Sava Srećić Sava Tomic, Luka Mandic, Mijo, Pane, David, Jovan Radanovic, Peter Radun, Gavro Jovic, Vid Radun. *Left Wounded*—Stana Sterbać, wife of the pope, Milica, his daughter, Gliso Srećić, Kuzman Sterbać.

".(Witnesses) ○ Bojan Sterbac.
+ Vasilj Knezevic.
✕ Jovan Tomic.
✕ Ivan Vjestica.

"For the other wounded, above-named who cannot write, signs
"Unatz, 13th February, 1877. T. Sudievich."

No correct estimate can be formed of the numerical and military strength of the Bosnian insurgents. It is said that Despotović can summon 5,000 armed Bosnians, not counting other bands in Kraina, Kosarać, and elsewhere, who are not under his command. It is certain that the whole Pravoslav population would to a man join the insurgent ranks if they had arms. "We cannot fight the Turks with our pipes," said tall strong men whom we saw hanging listlessly and moodily about the frontiers, among the old men, women, and children, who are living on the scanty pittance doled out by the charity of the Austrian government. One of our hardest tasks lay in the absolute necessity we were under to refuse to assist them in any way with arms and ammunition. To have done so would have been to compromise our whole special work of education and relief. But it was impossible to resist the conviction that if the Christians had had arms last spring they would soon have learned to use them and have settled their own affairs for themselves.

In any proposal of Turkish disarmament it should be remembered that the Mussulman Bosnians have been recently supplied by the Porte with fresh arms for the defence of Islam after the approved method, and that it will be practically impossible to disarm them except in the presence of a superior force. The Mussulman population is armed to the teeth, and is even now carrying out the extermination of the Pravoslav inhabitants—that is, of the industrious, enterprising, and independent majority of the population of Bosnia.

CHAPTER. IV.

SALONICA IN 1863.

"The admirable situation of Thessalonica, and the fertility of the surrounding country, watered by several noble rivers, still enables it to nourish a population of upwards of sixty thousand souls. Nature has made it the capital and seaport of a rich and extensive district, and under a good government it could not fail to become one of the largest and most flourishing cities on the shores of the Mediterranean."—FINLAY's *History of the Byzantine Empire*, p. 317.

THE reader is now requested to go back into the quiet times of Turkey in Europe, and to start on a journey through Southern Bulgaria, Old Serbia, Northern Albania and Montenegro.

We first reached Salonica at the end of May, 1863, and had our best view of it from the deck of the steamer. But though cities that rise in amphitheatre round a bay are always most favourably seen from the sea, a Turkish city has a charm of its own whatever its situation, and looked at from what point you please. True to the pastoral instinct of his ancestors, the Turk ever seeks to absorb the prosaic town into the poetry of nature; he multiplies spires to atone for roofs, and wherever he builds a house he plants a tree. For the ground indeed he cares not, provided his horse be good, so in roughness his street outdoes a quarry, and in filth exceeds the wallowing-ground of swine. But potent is the magic of outward beauty. After a time one consents that nose and feet should suffer offence; if only, when the labours of the day are over, one may recline on the cool, flat house-roof, and feast one's eyes on masses of white and green, pierced by taper cypresses and glistening minarets.

Salonica has several points that repay a ride; among others the Fortress of the Seven Towers, which stands on the site of the ancient Acropolis, and commands a glorious view, bounded by Mount Olympus. But the citadel itself is in a very tumble-down condition, and the dwelling houses within its walls are mostly deserted.

The Chaoush Monastery stands also on a height above the town and offers healthy quarters for a traveller. Its monks live in somewhat ignoble comfort, for their convent was left standing and endowed with privileges as reward for one of its former inhabitants having betrayed the neighbouring castle to the Turks. The present caloyers are Greeks of that servile type which sets many an Englishman against the whole race; nothing could be more honeyed than their flatteries of England, because it was then popularly expected that she would transfer her patronage from Turkey to Greece.

As the precious things in the convent were almost all presents from Russia, it was necessary to explain this away; the monks did so by saying that the Czar had given them in exchange for relics of inestimable worth. For instance, a service of communion plate and a costly book were said to have been received in exchange for a gourd out of which our Saviour drank at the Last Supper, or, as others say, at the Well of Samaria. "Look!" said the Greek, "they gave us miserable gold for a treasure that kingdoms could not buy; they received from us a skin of oil and in return have sent us a single olive." Finally, it was declared that "if England will only protect us, she may count on our eternal devotion."

On the way down the hill we passed through the burying-place of the city. The Franks have secured themselves graves between those of the Turks and the walls. On the other side of the Turks lie the Jews, "that they may be obliged to carry their dead furthest from the town." The whole ground is unenclosed, and desecrated by asses and dogs. Some time ago a violent thunder shower washed the earth from an ancient sarcophagus which was found by the French consul and sent off to Paris.

The antiquities of Salonica occupied two days' sightseeing, and no kinder nor more persevering cicerone can be wished than the Scottish missionary. Almost every street, every fountain, shows fragments of coloured marbles and sculptured stones; and on the Vardar Gate and Arch of Constantine* may still be seen the processions of Roman triumphs. Among the principal objects of interest we may enumerate the churches of the Twelve Apostles, St. Sophia, and St. Demetrius; the pulpit wherein St. Paul is supposed to have preached; the so-called Rotunda; the remnants of a sculptured *bema* outside the Rotunda; and the five figures (called by the Jews *incantadas*) which formed the propylæum of the hippodrome. Except the two latter relics, which, though ruined, are not transformed, all that is of the pagan period has been byzantinized, and all that was Byzantine has been mahommedanized; so that while much may be traced to interest the antiquary, there is scarce beauty enough left to delight the unprofes-

---

* "The Egnatian way, which for many centuries served as the high road for the communications between Rome and Constantinople, formed a great street passing in a straight line through the centre of the city from its western to its eastern wall. This relic of Roman greatness, with its triumphal arches, still forms a marked feature in the Turkish city; but the moles of the ancient fort have fallen to ruin, and the space between the sea-wall and the water is disfigured by a collection of filthy huts."—FINLAY's *Byzantine Empire*, p. 317.

sional traveller. Perhaps the Christian who spoilt a classic temple in the attempt to render it cruciform, may be deemed as barbarous as the Mussulman who turned the cathedral of St. Demetrius into a mosque; but the latter achievement has had results so grotesque that we cannot forbear enumerating them.

The nave is supported by columns of precious marble; but these the Turk has painted green, and their capitals strawberry and cream colour. Icons and candles he has banished, and in their stead strings up ostrich eggs to ward off the evil eye; also garlands of little lamps, which look fairy-like by night, but wherein by day the oil floats cold and brown. The altar has been hurled from its site, but thereabouts stands the pulpit of the imaum, with its narrow stair and extinguisher canopy. A little side chapel is purged of its idolatries, and instead crammed with old mats, rubbish, and tools. As for the name and superscription of St. Demetrius, these must be sought on one of the doorsteps, but the tiny cell containing his tomb is respected and ostentatiously shown. This distinction it owes to its miraculous exudations, which attract hosts of Christian pilgrims, and bring to its Mussulman guardian a regular income of bakshish.*

But the real curiosity of Salonica is its population, that strange medley of antipathetic races. The Therma of ancient history and the Thessalonica of St. Paul's Epistles yields at present the curious instance of a city historically Greek, politically Turkish, geographically Bulgarian, and ethnographically Jewish.† Out of about 60,000 inhabitants some 40,000 are Hebrews;

* The Sahatli mosque is now notorious as the scene of the massacre, May 6, 1876, of the French and German consuls by a Mussulman mob.

† The number of Jews at Salonica is estimated (1863) at 40,000, but with their usual astuteness they contrive to avoid being taxed individually, and the community bribes the Turkish officials to let them pass without scrutiny for no more than 11,500.

and these, the most numerous citizens, are also the most wealthy and considered. They came, like most of the Jews in Turkey, from Spain, whence they were expelled by the Inquisition, and the comparative tolerance showed them by the Sultan renders them his good subjects. The Hebrews settled in Salonica are handsome, many of them auburn-haired, and their women often delicate, and even fair. In beauty the latter exceed the Hellene, which now-a-days is not saying so much, for, at least in Europe, the modern Greek woman falls short alike of the softness and fire of the Oriental and the refinement and loftiness of the Western lady.

Like most other numerous communities, the Salonican Jews are divided into three ranks—the tip-top, the middle, and the low. Of these the foremost, by their wealth and luxury, absolutely extinguish their Christian neighbours. The French consul, Marquis de ——, told us that for him and his wife society was out of the question. All the richest people are Jews. If they give a dinner, friends and relatives lend each other plate and other trappings, so that the pomp is overpowering, and in return one cannot receive them in any way that would not appear *mesquin*. Then, if one gives parties, the Jewish ladies come so apparelled that the Europeans feel *gênées* in meeting them: " on finirait par n'avoir que des Juives chez soi." The opinion of the French consul was shared by one of our English acquaintances. She would willingly have shown us some of these Hebrew dames, whom she described as accomplished and beautiful; "but the fact is," said she, "that my new summer gown has not yet come from London; and though in you, as a traveller, they might excuse a plain dress, I should not dare to go among them otherwise than spick and span."

The middle class of Jews are also rich, but less exacting in matters of toilette, so no obstacle existed to our visiting them. The first family we saw was that of a rabbi, and more interesting than others, as retaining some remnants of traditional habits and costume. The daughters had muslin dresses made in the European style, but their long hair hung loose down their backs. On marriage the hair is cut off, and the matrons wear a small turban fastened with a black handkerchief, which is passed under the chin and tied on the top of the head. The rabbi himself appeared in a sort of long loose coat bordered and lined with fur.

In Salonica, doctors disagree as to the advisability of adopting Frankish fashions, so we sought to learn the ideas of this good man, who is reputed liberal in his views. We alluded to the Jews of Cracow, to their peculiar dress, and to their unwillingness to change it. "Yes," quoth the rabbi, "but in Poland the Jews dress differently from us, and are of very different character. We came here from Spain, and at first all wore black, like Spaniards; what we now wear is Turkish, and some of us are beginning to imitate the Franks." "In that case," said we, "you do not connect any religious feeling with your costume?" He answered evasively, "Every dress has a religious value in the eyes of the people to whom it belongs." He then asked if we had remarked the curious out-door pelisses of the women. These are of scarlet cloth, lined with fur and bordered with gold. Over the head is worn a long scarf of the white stuff used for Turkish towels.

The rabbi whom we visited is a merchant, and carried on the conversation in Italian; he is also a rich man. We learned that here most of the rabbis are merchants and also rich; for wealth is one of the most needful qualications to obtain their office and sustain its influence.

Much of their commercial success is owing to their power of association, and their willingness to help one another. Herein they and their brethren excel the local Christians, who seldom seem able to trust each other or work as one.

Another distinction of our rabbi is that he keeps a printing-press. This privilege is not granted to the Greeks, and was lately denied to a Bulgarian bookseller. The request of the latter was supported by the English consul, who regarded it as most desirable that the Slavonic population in the neighbourhood should obtain books in its own language. Of course the excuse was put forward that the press would be used to circulate Russian proclamations; as if the lack of a printing-press in their own country were not precisely what hitherto has forced the Bulgarians to take their books from Russia.

The next house we visited was that of a rising coal merchant; a handsome dwelling, cleanly and cool. We came rather too near the middle of the day, so the lady and her daughters were enjoying a siesta, but they sent us a message so earnestly begging us to stay that we sat down patiently to wait. For this we were rewarded by seeing the maid carry three gowns and three "cages" upstairs, through the saloon, and past us into her mistresses' chamber. After the interval necessary for donning them, out came three ladies, elegant and smiling.

While waiting, our attention was directed to the extraordinary precautions adopted to secure the house against fire. The cause of this is that the Jews here will not touch fire on their Sabbath. Not only do they keep their candles ready lighted from the evening before, and a Gentile servant to do the necessary work; but should a conflagration break out among their dwellings, they must let it burn on, rather than meddle with it.

Jewish servant girls, whose clothes have happened to catch fire on the Sabbath, have been known to run burning to the nearest Christian house before they could obtain assistance. When a Salonican Jew sets up to be "liberal" one of his first symptoms is to smoke a cigar on the Sabbath. Sometimes the rabbis make an effort to reclaim him, *e.g.*, they bribe the pasha to put him in prison.

Another Jewish observance consists in saying prayers for the departed, a certain amount being sufficient for a good spirit and a longer time for a wicked one. Hence, while it would be considered undutiful for a son to omit having prayers said for his father's soul, he must take care not to have them said too long, lest he cast a slur on his father's character.

We were told that many of the poorer Jews are disposed to think that Sir Moses Montefiore will shortly prove to be their Messiah. The richer are said to be in no such hurry, "inasmuch as the coming of the Messiah would involve their own migration to the Promised Land, and being an exclusively commercial people they have little fancy to become landholders in Judea."

We cannot attempt to describe the Turkish residents in Salonica, as it happened that we saw nothing of them; but next in interest to the Hebrew comes the Greek community. Although it cannot vie in number or wealth with the Jews it counts some rich merchants, who were building fine houses while we were there. Besides these there are certain families which, from intermarriage for generations, are to all intents Greek, yet claim Western descent, and enjoy the protection of foreign powers. This, by sheltering them from Turkish interference, gives them great advantage in trade. In some cases the right to such protection is rather doubtful, and should a

European agent not prove himself above bakshish great abuses are certain to ensue.

It was with consternation that we heard of so-called British subjects stooping to farm taxation for the Turk. For "a man cannot carry fire in his bosom and his clothes not be burned;" and a tale was told us of the working of this system, in the particulars of which we would fain hope that there may be some exaggeration. Certain Frankish merchants undertook to farm the pig-tax, and hearing that the Christian peasants of a village were suspected of concealing pigs, they called on the Pasha to put five of their principal men into prison, where at the time typhus fever was raging. Out of the five, four took the fever and died.

Among the Greeks of Salonica, as elsewhere in Turkey, prevails the heinous custom of taking up dead bodies after a year spent in the grave, to look whether they be consumed or no. The scene on these occasions was described to us by a native who had often attended—the horrid curiosity, the superstitious terror, the fearful sight, and still more fearful smell, of which many women sicken on the spot. Should the body be preserved, it is taken as a bad sign and prayers must be said, for which of course the priest is paid. Then the corpse is reinterred for another year, and unless decay ensue the ceremonial may be repeated three times. So tyrannical is conventionality in this particular, that wealthy educated mothers—living in intercourse with Europeans—feel obliged to have their children disinterred. We heard of one instance where there was the additional agony of finding the little body in a state which relations and neighbours considered as indicating that the soul was in hell.

From these grim revelations, we turn to a quaint anecdote of the late sultan, Abdul Medjid. He came to

Salonica, and was invited to visit the garden of the rich Mr. John ——. Having walked about for some time, he asked to see "the merchant Jack." The merchant came, and with a profound bow gave utterance to the following Oriental compliment: "When I beautified this garden and planted these flowers I dared to hope that they might one day be honoured with a visit from your Majesty." The Sultan replied, with grave sincerity, "This day then God hath answered thy prayer."

Sight-seeing and visiting being accomplished, we had only to look if there was anything pretty in the shops, and then make preparations for the inland route. The Bazaar of Salonica is the finest in European Turkey next to that of Constantinople, and is far before the best in the interior, viz., those of Adrianople and Serajevo.

We had seen in Athens a dress made of the silk gauze of Salonica, a material stronger, and less like French *gaze de soie* than the gauze of Broussa. It was for this that we sought first, and then for silver bands to trim it; but we had to consume no end of time in collecting enough bits of a few yards each to make up the quantity required for a gown. The reason is, that the silk is made in private houses in pieces, each sufficient for a shirt.

We saw tailors working at splendid embroidery, and in many shops hung long trusses of what looked like golden straw—used to mingle with the locks of a bride.

One article we had made at Salonica, viz., the cover of a box. Our dragoman assigned the task to Jews, and we, soon after coming into the corridor, were startled to behold two venerable patriarchs, looking as if they had walked bodily out of an old picture Bible. These patriarchs seated themselves on the floor with the large chest between them; their bare feet extended on each side of it, their hands holding the ends of a long piece of sacking whereof they purposed to make the cover, and which they wound round and round the box by way of taking the measure.

CHAPTER V.

BULGARIA VIEWED FROM SALONICA.—PART I.

"The entrance of Russia into the political system of the European nations was marked by an attempt to take Constantinople,—a project which it has often revived, and which the progress of Christian civilisation seems to indicate must now be realised at no very distant date, unless the revival of the Bulgarian kingdom to the south of the Danube create a new Slavonian power in the east of Europe capable of arresting its progress."—FINLAY's *History of the Byzantine Empire*, p. 223.

"As for the Bulgarians, whether they remain yet awhile under Turkish rule or free themselves from it in our own time, as they must ultimately do sooner or later, it is in them alone that one can see any really hopeful prospect, on taking a broad general view of the probable future of these countries. This is afforded by their numerical preponderance; their utter primitiveness, which has learned nothing, and has nothing to unlearn; their industry and thrift; their obstinacy; and their sobriety of character."—LORD STRANGFORD.

WE have said that Salonica is geographically Bulgarian; in other words, it is one of the ports of that country with a Slavonic-speaking population which stretches from the Ægean to the Danube. Indeed, Salonica itself forms a point on the ethnographical boundary which, in this part of Turkey in Europe, divides the Slavonic population from the Greek. To a certain extent this frontier coincides with the line of the old Roman road between Salonica and the Lake of Ochrida; nevertheless some miles of country, inhabited by Bulgarians, stretch south of the Via Egnatia, Greek colonies lie to the north of it, and in the towns the population is mixed, in part consisting of Osmanli Turks. The other boundary cities are Monastir, Vodena, and Yenidjé; in all of which dwell few or no Greeks, whereas in Salonica itself there are only about 500 families of Slâvs.

On its south-eastern frontier, it is worthy of notice, the mass of the Slavonic population stops everywhere short of the sea, and leaves (or perforates only with stragglers) a coast-strip including part of Thrace, the Chalcidian peninsula, the cities of Constantinople and Salonica. This district is so variously peopled, so important for commercial and strategical purposes,— and it would so ill-suit any one that it should fall into the grip of any one else—that those who look forward to a readjustment of the Slāvo-Greek peninsula take it under their especial care. Among other plans, they suggest that it be erected into a neutral territory, and attached to the two great sea-ports, in the same manner as domains are attached to the Free Cities of Germany. These modifiers would give Greece her due in Thessaly and Epirus, and accord native and Christian self-government, as now exercised by the Principality of Serbia, to all the Slavonic provinces of Turkey.

Without venturing an opinion on this or other political projects, we may remark that any arrangement which would disincumber the thrifty and well-disposed Bulgarian of the yoke of his present barbarous master, would certainly prove a gain to civilisation, and in one respect especially to ourselves. Its immediate result would be the development of the resources of the country, and, among others, of its resources in cotton. The vast desert plain of Salonica is stated to be peculiarly adapted for the growth of Sea Island cotton; and a neighbouring district, not far from the town of Seres, is so favourable to the culture, that a man who planted the third of an acre with cotton realized a profit of £60. This cultivation is in the hands of Bulgarians; the Turkish landlord cares only to clutch half the produce, and the farmer of the Turkish revenue is the arch-foe of industry.

The labouring, *i.e.*, the Christian Slavonic, population of the country behind Salonica holds land on the following tenure: after a tenth has been paid to the Sultan, seed is put aside for the coming year, and of what produce remains the landlord gets half.

As for the taxation: in Turkey, grievances commence at the point where in other countries they are supposed to culminate; so we say nothing of the injustice to a population of millions that it should have no voice in the disposal of its money. Granted that the Bulgarians be ready to give all the government calls for, and, moreover, to pay for exemption from the army, that is, for being disarmed and held down by Mussulmans,* still the greatest grievance remains, viz., the waste and iniquity wherewith the revenue is raised.

Hitherto the taxes have been paid in kind, a method which always gives the gatherer much power to extort bribes, since he can refuse to value the peasant's standing corn until half of it be spoiled. But Turkish tax-farmers do not confine themselves to such by-paths of cheating. The following is an instance of what constantly recurs:—

Two men agree to keep a flock between them, the one in summer on the mountains, the other in winter on the plain. The tax-gatherer compels the first to pay for the whole, promising that he will ask nothing of the other; he then goes to the second, and with a similar promise forces him likewise to pay for all. In like manner, the Christian can be compelled to pay twice over for exemption from the army if the tax-gatherer declare his first

---

* "Exemption from the army" is the name now given to the tribute paid by Christians as such, which formerly was called *harateh*. The people still use the old word, for to them the tax remains the same, and so does its practical signification, *i.e.*, the Christian continues the disarmed tributary of the Mussulman.

receipt forged. The other day a Bulgarian brought his receipt to the British consul, who threatened the official to have it sent up for investigation. Immediately the charge was withdrawn.

A change of system is being introduced which will supersede payment in kind by payment in money. But it is hard to see how this is to prove beneficial without such means of transport and security of communication as would enable the peasant to bring his produce to market. At present, while he must sell it in the neighbourhood wherein it abounds, he is taxed for it at market value. The people declare that the oppression is now worse than before, and that this is one of the many *soi-disant* reforms which tell well on paper, while unless followed up by other reforms they prove actually mischievous. We ourselves saw the tax-gatherer swooping down on the villages, accompanied by harpy-flocks of Albanians armed to the teeth.

On occasion of the late cotton famine, the British Government instigated the Porte to encourage the growth of cotton, to give the seed for experiments, and, what is more important, to suspend, in favour of cotton, some of the modes of taxation which chiefly harass agricultural industry. The Christian Bulgarians have responded to this encouragement in a manner that gives fair promise of their energies should they ever be entirely free from vexatious interference.

By Bulgaria we understand, not that insignificant portion of the same termed "the Turkish Province of Bulgaria," but the whole tract of country peopled by Bulgarians. The population, usually given as four millions, is estimated by the people themselves as from five to six millions—forming the eastern division of the South Slavonic race. The Bulgarians are distinguished in all essentials from their neighbours—the

BULGARIAN PEASANTS, WITH BULGARIAN MERCHANT AND HIS SON, WHO HAS SPENT SOME YEARS OUT OF TURKEY.

Greek, the Rouman, and the Turk; they differ in a few points of character from their own western kindred, the Croato-Serbs. The chief of these latter points is a deficiency in what is called *esprit politique*, and a corresponding superiority in the notion of material comfort. Unlike the Serb, the Bulgarian does not keep his self-respect alive with memories of national glory, nor even with aspirations of glory to come; on the other hand, no amount of oppression can render him indifferent to his field, his horse, his flower-garden, nor to the scrupulous neatness of his dwelling.

How strongly difference of race can tell under identical conditions of climate, religion, and government, is exemplified in towns where Greeks have been dwelling side by side with Bulgarians for centuries. The one is commercial, ingenious, and eloquent, but fraudulent, dirty, and immoral; the other is agricultural, stubborn, and slow-tongued; but honest, cleanly, and chaste. The latter quality has from early times attracted respect towards the South Slavonic peoples. Their ancient laws visit social immorality with death, and at present their opinion, inexorable towards women, does not, like our own, show clemency to men. A lady told us that in the society of Greeks she could not be three weeks without becoming the confidante of a *chronique scandaleuse;* among Bulgarians she had lived for months, and never heard a single "story."*

In Bulgarian towns the Mussulmans are Osmanli colonists, who form, as it were, the garrison of the province. The Slavonians who have become Mahommedan mostly live in the country and continue to speak Slavonic.

* "The Greek cannot overcome the Bulgarian, nor lead him, nor incorporate him. He is of a less numerous and not of a superior race; his mind is more keen but less solid; roughly speaking, he is to the Bulgarian as the clever Calcutta baboo to the raw material of the English non-commissioned officer."—LORD STRANGFORD in *Eastern Shores of the Adriatic.*

In their bravery and warlike disposition the renegade Bulgarians evince the character of the nation before it was betrayed and disarmed, and they themselves adopted Mahommedanism only to avoid falling into the position of rayahs. In some parts they are known by the name Pomak (from *pomegam*, "I help"), and are supposed to be descended from those Bulgarian troops who served in the Sultan's army as "allies," until the Turks grew strong enough to force on them the alternative of surrendering their arms or their creed. Among our guards once happened to be a Bulgarian Mussulman, who allowed us to be told in his presence that he was still at heart a Christian; and in the neighbourhood of Salonica we heard of Mahommedan Bulgarians who excuse their apostasy by the following story. Being hard pressed they fixed a certain term during which they would fast and call on Christ, at the end whereof, if no help appeared, they would submit themselves to Mahommed. Help arrived not, and so Mahommedans they became. Since then, the old hatred of race has caused them to take part against the Greeks in more than one insurrection; but they equally detest the Turk, and thus sympathize with their own Christian countrymen in their national antipathies as well as in tenacity of their native tongue.

The rural population of Bulgaria is Christian, and hereabouts the rayah has a down-look and a dogged stolidity, which give one the impression that heart and mind have been bullied out of him. Of late years, however, he has presented an unflagging resistance to the Porte's imposition of foreign bishops; and those who have instructed him, both in his own country and out of it, assured us that he is of excellent understanding and zealous and apt to learn. The Christian Bulgarian is reproached as timid, but at least his is the timidity of shrinking, not of servility; he hides from those he fears, he does not fawn on them. His country, lying as it does on the road of Turkish armies to the Danube, has been subject to unceasing spoliation, and nothing is more melancholy than the tale told by its desolate highways, and by the carefulness with which villages are withdrawn from the notice of the passers-by. Cross the border into Free Serbia, and the cottage of the peasant reappears.

To give a sketch of Bulgarian history, one must go back to the end of the fifth and beginning of the sixth century, when a Slavonic population south of the Danube is spoken of by Byzantine authors.

Under the old East Roman Empire the people of Bulgaria appear both as subjects and as rulers. Justinian's birthplace was, as it still is, a Slavonic village, in the neighbourhood of Skopia, and his Latin name is the translation of his Slavonic one, Upravda. The great Belisarius is said to have been the Slavonic Velisar; Basil, the Macedonian, or, as Finlay calls him, the Slavonian groom, was the father of the longest line that ever maintained itself upon the throne of Byzance.

It would appear that the first colonists established themselves to the south of the Danube gradually, and recognised the imperial rule; but in the seventh century they were joined by tribes of a more warlike character, under whose leadership they rose against Byzance, and overran the greater part of the peninsula. These newcomers, who were of the same race with the Finns, adopted Christianity, and amalgamated with the Slāvs. From them dates the name of Bulgaria, and the first dynasty of her sovereigns. Though often at war with the Byzantine Empire, the Bulgarians profited by its neighbourhood so far as to imbibe a certain amount of civilisation. In the ninth century they fought covered with steel armour; their discipline astonished the veterans of the Empire, and they possessed all the military engines then known. Their kings and czars encouraged literature, and were sometimes themselves authors. As almost all accounts of them come from Byzantine sources there can be little doubt that this portrait is not flattered. Under their more powerful rulers the Bulgarians threatened Constantinople; under the weaker they acknowledged the Byzantine Emperor as suzerain, and more than once Byzantine armies effected a temporary subjection of their land; but their monarchy was not finally overthrown till the end of the fourteenth century, when they were conquered by the Turks. Coins of Bulgaria are to be seen in the museum of Belgrade, and a curious chronicle of Czar Asen has lately been published in modern Bulgarian.

At the Turkish conquest, 1390, Shishman, the last king of Bulgaria, surrendered himself and his capital to the conqueror's mercy; but the people submitted only by degrees, and always on the condition that if they paid tribute to the Sultan they should be free to govern themselves. Their soldiers were commanded by their own voivodes,* their taxes were collected, and towns and villages ruled by officers of their own choosing. The Bulgarian Church had native Bishops and a Patriarch, residing first at Tirnova then at Ochrida. All this is proved by firmans and berats accorded to them by numerous Sultans.

Those who take the scraps of liberty now-a-days octroyed to the rayah as evidences of a radical change in the maxims of Turkish rule, should bear in mind that far better terms were accorded by Turks to Christians five centuries ago. Those who put faith in Turkish

---

* In modern parlance, generals,—signification cognate with the German *Herzog* and Latin *dux*—hence also used for duke.

promises, should inquire how the liberties guaranteed to such Christians as submitted to the first Sultans came to be trampled under foot so soon as the Turks could call themselves masters of the land.

Of the Bulgarian voivodes the most resolute were cut off and the rest left to choose between emigration and apostasy. In 1776 the autonomy of the Church was destroyed, and in place of native bishops of one interest with the people, Greeks were sent from Constantinople, who plundered the peasants, denounced the chief men to Turkish suspicion, set an example of social corruption, and burnt all Slavonic books and MSS. whereon they could lay their hands. The last schools and printing-presses found shelter in the Danubian Principalities; when those lands came under Phanariote* government nothing was left to the Bulgarians save some old convents in the recesses of their hills.

Few points are more remarkable in the history of Ottoman rule than the mode in which Turks and Greeks have played into each other's hands. The Sultan could never have crushed the heart out of his Christian subjects without the aid of a Christian middle-man, and the Greek has used the brute force of his Mahommedan employer to complement his own cleverness and guile. Under the later emperors Greek dominion was unknown in Slavonic and Rouman lands; whereas under Ottoman sultans, we find Greek prelates and Phanariote princes ruling the Rouman, the Bulgarian, and the Serb. That nationality must be of tough material which gave not way under this double pressure.

The first break in the prison wall was made by the revolution at the beginning of this century. " Free

---

* Phanariote: so called from the Phanar, a quarter of Constantinople where the Greek Patriarch resides. The derivation of ".Phanar" is variously assigned.

Greece, autonomous Serbia: may not Bulgaria have her turn?" Gradually the wealthier Bulgarians sent their sons for education no longer to Constantinople, but to Russia, Bohemia, France. In the country itself were founded native schools; and even in districts already half Hellenized the national spirit began to revive. Persons who used to write their own language in the Greek character learned late in life the Slavonic alphabet, and we have ourselves seen parents who spoke Bulgarian imperfectly anxiously providing that their children should know it well. It was the obstacle presented by a foreign hierarchy to these efforts at national development that brought the people to the resolution of freeing their Church from the control of the Phanar.

This temper was taken advantage of by the Roman Propagandists, and emissaries were sent all over Bulgaria, promising self-government and services in Slavonic, with no other condition than that a nominal recognition of the Patriarch should be exchanged for that of the Pope.* This condition cannot be called hard, and at its first start the Romanist Propaganda was a success. The number of converts has been hugely exaggerated, yet it doubtless included some persons of influence. But the principal bait to the adoption of Catholicism was the promise of sharing the protection of France; and when it became evident that this protection could not be unlimited, nor exempt its *protégés* from payment of taxes, the new-made Romanists recanted in troops.

* The contest between Constantinople and Rome for the ecclesiastical supremacy of Bulgaria dates as early as the ninth century, on the plea that the Danubian Provinces were anciently subject to the Archbishopric of Thessalonica, in the times when that archbishopric was immediately dependent on the Papal See. The Bulgarian czars seem to have deferred their choice between the Greek and Latin Churches until they obtained from Constantinople the recognition of a Patriarch of their own.

Then, too, their leaders became convinced that the movement could have no other effect than to extend to Bulgaria what had already broken the strength of Bosnia and Albania, *i.e.*, a Latin sect, separated from the other Christians, cowering under foreign protection, selling its assistance to the Turks. With these views (we give their own version of the story), and not from any religious sentiment or scruple, many to whom the Propaganda owed its first encouragement withdrew their aid and opposed it with all their might.

But the indifference wherewith the common people had talked of transferring ecclesiastical allegiance proved to the thinkers in Bulgaria that the dangers of division might at any moment recur. For the second time in their church history it was recognised that the South Slavonians would remain in the Eastern Church only on condition of ecclesiastical self-government. If they are to have foreign bishops or a foreign head, it is all one to them whether their Pope resides at Constantinople or Rome.

At this juncture deputies from Bulgaria made their appearance in Constantinople. They came to demand that in virtue of the Hatt-i-Humayoun, their national patriarchate, formerly recognised by the Porte, should be restored, or at least that their Church should be declared autonomous, with native archbishop, bishops, and synod, and an ecclesiastical seminary at Tirnova. In short, they desired such a system of church government as succeeds admirably in the Principality of Serbia. It is years since the Bulgarians put in their claim, but the Turk is in no hurry to remove a cause of quarrel between his Christian subjects. With great subtlety he has tried to improve the occasion by hinting to the Bulgarians that they had better secede from the Eastern Church.

They have been told that by the treaty of Adrianople the Greek Patriarch is declared head of all the Orthodox communities in Turkey. "Be Catholic," says the Mahommedan judge, "or Protestants, or set up a sect of your own, and we will recognise you with pleasure; so long as you call yourselves 'Orthodox' we must know you only as Greeks."

But the Bulgarians avoided the snare. They replied that their demand affected no religious question, that they had no desire to separate themselves from the Orthodox communion. They were perfectly ready to yield the Greek Patriarch recognition as head of the Eastern Church; to be its *only* Patriarch he had never aspired. His predecessors had acknowledged a Patriarch of Bulgaria till within the last ninety years; he himself at the present moment recognised Patriarchs of Jerusalem and Antioch. Besides, the practical settlement of the business depends, not on the Patriarch, but on the Padishah. When the Bulgarian patriarchate was abolished it was by authority of the Sultan; to this day no prelate throughout the Ottoman Empire can exercise his functions without an imperial firman; and for such a firman a Bulgarian primate, already chosen by the people, was waiting in order to appoint his bishops, convoke his synod, and regulate internal affairs. Give him this, and the Greek Patriarch might defer his recognition so long as it suits his own convenience, while without a firman the recognition of the Greek Patriarch would be of no practical effect.

This statement places the Ottoman government in an attitude somewhat different from that which has been claimed for it; for it has been usually represented as striving vainly to reconcile Christians in a religious dispute, wherein it may mediate but not interfere.

No doubt, however, the Greek Patriarch might have done much to avoid an appeal to Mahommedan authority, and would have best consulted the interests of his own community by agreeing to accept the proffered recognition together with a fixed tribute.* But it must ever be remembered that in a post so important as that of the Constantinopolitan chair none but a pliant agent is tolerated by the Turk. Certain it is, that the Patriarch then in office behaved equally unworthily and unwisely. Three bishops (Hilarion, Accentios, and Paissios,) had declared themselves ready to resign their sees in Bulgaria unless confirmed therein by the choice of the people. They might have been used as mediators; on the contrary, they were seized and sent into exile. All such Bulgarians as did not accept the Patriarch's terms were anathematized and declared heretics.

By such measures the formidable wrath of a slow stubborn people has been thoroughly roused. The Patriarch who excommunicated them they have renounced; rather than receive his bishops, communities declare they will remain without any; should a Greek venture to impose himself upon them they resist him by every means in their power.

A series of scandals took place throughout the Provinces. Churches were closed, in order that the Greek liturgy might not be read therein. When the Greek

* Though some progress has lately been made towards a formal understanding between the Patriarch of Constantinople and the Bulgarian Church, recent confusions have prevented any real settlement. The Patriarch has declared his willingness to recognise the virtual independence of the Bulgarian Church, his own primacy, which has never been questioned, of course being retained. But he has limited the area to the territory north of the Balkan Mountains, which will be governed by an Exarch or Patriarch residing at Sophia. The Bulgarians contend that the independence should regard race, not territory; in which case a large portion of country between the southern slope of the Balkan Mountains and the Ægean Sea would be included within the rule of the Exarch of Bulgaria. Greek susceptibilities have as yet prevented this arrangement from being accepted at the Patriarchate.

bishops returned from their revenue-gathering progresses they found their palaces locked and were conducted beyond the city walls. If they entered a church to officiate, no Bulgarian priest would take part in the service; when they departed the floor was ostentatiously swept, as if to remove traces of impurity. In Sophia, when a new bishop was expected, men, women, and children filled the palace and blocked it up, till, unarmed as they were, they had to be expelled by Turkish soldiers. The bishop then dwelt in isolation, until, on occasion of a burial, he got hold of a Bulgarian priest and demanded why he did not come to see him. The priest answered that he must stand by his flock; that as it would not acknowledge the bishop neither could he. Thereupon the priest's beard was shorn, the fez of the dead man stuck on his head, and he was turned out into the streets as a warning and a sign. Again the unarmed citizens rose; shops were shut, houses evacuated, thousands of people prepared to leave Sophia. Their elders waited on the pasha and said, "Either the Greek bishop must go or *we*." The pasha advised the prelate to withdraw, and as the authorities in Constantinople would not permit the people to elect a new one Sophia resolved to do without a bishop at all.*

At Nish, a town on the Serbian frontier, the bishops anticipated an inimical demonstration by accusing the elders of the Bulgarian community of a plot to join the Serbs. The elders were called before the pasha, and without a hearing, without being allowed to say farewell to their families or to send home for extra clothing, they were hurried into carriages and sent off into banishment. This occurred in the depth of winter, and when in the ensuing August we were hospitably received by

* For some further details see "Donan-Bulgarian und der Balkan." Kanitz, Leipzig, 1875.

the family of one of the exiles, they besought us to apply to some English consul to learn if their relatives were yet alive.

Meanwhile a variety of evils pressed on Bulgaria —outbreaks of haiduks, some political outlaws, some highwaymen—influx of Mahommedan Tartars from the Crimea, for whom the Bulgarians were forced to build houses and provide food—emigration of Bulgarians to Russia, succeeded by their destitute return—attempt of other Bulgarians to get off to Serbia, frustrated by the Turkish authorities—finally, a shoal of Bashi-bazouks turned loose among the villagers, on pretext of guarding the frontier from the Serbs.* In the summer of 1862 we were witnesses to this state of things. Another means resorted to for holding down the Bulgarian is the introduction of Mahommedan colonists, who replenish the declining Mussulman population, and are kept well supplied with arms, of which the Christian is deprived. Since the Tartars, Circassians have been introduced, and the idea has been adopted of planting them along the frontier of Serbia, so as to bar off the Bulgarians. The Tartars were only idle, whereas these new immigrants come thirsting to avenge their own sufferings on all who bear the Christian name. It is said, however, that the Circassian mountaineers do not thrive on the Bulgarian plains and are rapidly decreasing in number.

In Constantinople we heard a good deal of the Bulgarian question—the Greek side of it from the Patriarch and his secretary, the Slavonic side from the Bulgarian deputies. Each party supported its arguments in pamphlets swarming with protestations of loyalty to the Sultan, and taunting its antagonists as emissaries of

* The Bulgarian horrors of 1875 are the intense aggravation of a chronic condition. They could astonish no one personally acquainted with the interior of the country.

Russia. Russia in Turkey plays the part of "cat" in a careless household; being charged with the doing of all mischief by those who wish to exonerate themselves.

As to probably impartial judges, we appealed to the opinion of foreign residents; these, especially French, British, and American, gave their verdict for the Bulgarians. British consuls assured us they were astonished to find a population in Turkey so industrious, thrifty, moral, and clean. As for the Americans, in a quiet way they are the best friends the Bulgarians have. Their eminent scholar, Dr. Riggs, has rendered the Old Testament from ancient into modern Slavonic, and numerous school-books have been translated from the English; American schools are in the Bulgarian principal towns, and their books are sold by native colporteurs in several parts of the country.

During our own travels we saw proofs enough that the people are trying to improve, and we were especially struck with their eagerness for education. The mountain chains of the Balkan and the Rhodope divide Bulgaria into three sections—northern, central, and southern. Of the northern district, between the Balkan and the Danube, we cannot speak from eye-witness, as the Turks declared it too disturbed for travellers; but we say, on the authority of persons who have lived there, that those Bulgarians who grow up with the great waterway of commerce on one side of them and their natural mountain fortresses on the other are more independent and enterprising than their brethren on the inland plains. Here, too, the people maintain numerous schools, of which the best are at Tirnova and Shumla. Tirnova, the ancient capital, is the site proposed for an ecclesiastical seminary, and if possible for a printing press, both of which the jealousy of the Porte as yet denies.

Central Bulgaria is that which lies between the ranges of the Balkan and the Rhodope. Here we visited the schools of Adrianople, Philippopolis, Samakoff, Sophia, Nish,—all supported and managed by the Christian communities without pecuniary aid from the government or bishops. The school-houses, mostly of good size and airy, are, like everything in Bulgaria, clean. The school-books, gathered from various sources, are eked out with those of the American Board of Missions. To conciliate the Turks, Turkish is frequently taught to a scholar or two, and phrases complimentary to the Sultan have been framed into a sort of school hymn. True, the same tune has another set of words in honour of him who shall deliver the country from Turkish rule. One or other version is sung before the visitor, according as he is judged to be Christian or Turcophile. We had opportunities of hearing both.

At Philippopolis, Samakoff, and Sophia, there are girls' schools. That at Sophia was founded by a patriotic citizen.* In his own words: "When my wife died and left me but one son I resolved not to marry again, but to give all my money and attention to this school." He has brought a female teacher all the way from the Austrian border, for Slavonic trained schoolmistresses are hard to find in Turkey.

Southern Bulgaria lies, as we have already indicated, between the Rhodope and the frontiers of ancient Greece. Such schools as we there visited were smaller and poorer than elsewhere, but we did not see those of

* In 1877 we found a young relative of this patriotic merchant among the Bulgarian students at Agram in Croatia. Ten lads and four girls had been sent to the excellent schools in this town before the recent disasters in Bulgaria, and are still continuing their studies, in spite of the privations consequent on the cutting off of remittances from home. We were glad to be able to render them some timely help from a sum entrusted to us especially for Bulgarians. The young girl from Sophia told me that the schoolhouse built by Hadji Traiko had been seized by the Turks and turned into a barrack for soldiers.

Istib and other towns lying on the more northerly route between Salonica and Skopia. Those on the line of our journey we will notice as we proceed.

Throughout the places we have hitherto mentioned, the Greek Bishop contents himself with ignoring the Bulgarian school, or from time to time expelling an energetic teacher; but nearer the Græco-Slāv boundary we found Slavonic education positively impeded. In Vodena and Yenidjé a Greek school is founded, and the community must needs support it; in case poverty should not be sufficient to deter them from supporting also one of their own, every possible hindrance is thrown in the way.

One result of this anti-national policy is, that the Bulgarians, elsewhere so eager to learn, are in these districts listless and dull; another result is, that being alienated from their own clergy, they lend an ear to overtures from Rome. Some of them calculate on using Latin aid to get rid of the Patriarch, and then finding means to get rid of the Pope; others still fear that the yoke they know not may prove heavier than the yoke they know. In Monastir the Unionists [*] had a school, and at Yenidjé they were building a church.

Meanwhile, in the neighbourhood of Salonica, awakes a party which bethinks itself that Protestants acknowledge neither Pope nor Patriarch, and that the protection of England would do as well as that of France. The question is asked whether, supposing they became Protestants, England would take them under her wing. For answer they get an emphatic "No." Still they turn to the Protestant clergyman at Salonica, and beg that he will procure for them books and teachers in their own tongue, duly offering to pay for both.

[*] The name Unionist is given to communities which retain the Oriental rite while they acknowledge the supremacy of Rome.

CHAPTER VI.

BULGARIA VIEWED FROM SALONICA.—PART II.

"The fame Methodios acquired among his contemporaries, as well as from those in after-times who saw his paintings, may be accepted as a proof that they possessed some touches of nature and truth."—FINLAY's *Byzantine Empire*, vol. i., p. 266.

WE have now worked round to our starting-point, the various-peopled city of Salonica. At no time were the Bulgarians its masters, yet its name is identified with the one incident in their obscure history which has left a mark in the annals of civilisation. We allude to the christianization first of Bulgaria and then of the whole Slavonic race, through the medium of a translation of the Scriptures in the dialect still called "Church" Slavonic. That dialect is generally considered to have been the ancient written language of Bulgaria, and the translators were natives of Salonica.

In the ninth century Salonica formed part of the Byzantine Empire, and its citizens are, without distinction, termed Greeks; but many Slāvs had settled there, their language was spoken in its streets, and long afterwards a Slavonic hero, named Doitschin, is celebrated in the national songs as having delivered the city from the exactions of a robber chief.*

* Even in Constantinople, and as early as the eighth century, the Slāvic element was sufficiently predominant for the Slavonian Niketas to fill the Patriarchal Chair, and the Greeks tell an anecdote showing that he was by no means

At this period their lived in Salonica the brothers Cyril and Methodios. Cyril, the elder, was learned and studious; the younger, Methodios, enterprising and energetic. Both were inspired to make known the Gospel to the Slavonic population outside the walls, and while at home Cyril prepared himself by study and cultivation of the language, Methodios went forth as a missionary. The latter presented himself at the court of Boris, king of the Bulgarians, and, as the legend goes, caught the humour of the monarch by offering to paint the walls of a favourite hunting lodge. Boris came to examine the work, expecting to see wolves, bears, and regal huntsmen; instead, he beheld the picture of a Great Day of Judgment, like those still common among peoples where justice is dispensed by the monarch in person. On the throne sat a King, not like Boris, frowning in wild pomp; but majestic and mild. His courtiers stood around him, but they did not flaunt Bulgarian horsetails, nor flourish bloody weapons; they had soft waving hair, and gold circlets, and white wings dipped in rainbow hues. The approved servants were being received on the right hand, above them opened a golden gate; the condemned were dragged off on the left, and beneath them yawned a pit of fire. But the strangest part was, that among the honoured and accepted were to be seen many frail and shrinking forms, the weak, the defenceless, the sick, the blind, and even figures in vile raiment, while among the reprobated were more than one fierce warrior, not altogether unlike to Boris and his lords. The king called the artist to give him the interpretation of this

completely Hellenized. One day reading the Gospel of St. Matthew, he pronounced the name Ματθάϊον, instead of Ματθαῖον. One of his people whispered to him that the vowels of the diphthong were not to be separated. The prelate turned angrily round, and exclaimed, "My soul abhors diphthongs and triphthongs!" This story is remarked on by Mr. Finlay.

picture, and Methodios expounded it thus: "The great King is the God of the Christians. He made the earth, and for a while dwelt on it in the likeness of man; but as He took on Him a humble form, and was holy and truthful, wicked men hated Him, and He suffered of them all that the evil still inflict on the truthful and the good. At the Last Day He shall come again in His glorious majesty, and shall judge both the living and the dead. He knows the sufferings of the oppressed, who Himself was once suffering and poor; He knows the cruel and violent deeds of great men: such men ill-treated Him and crucified Him on a tree." Boris considered the judgment throne, the winged messengers, the golden light that played over the throne; he felt himself in the presence of power and glory, higher, other than his own. Then he considered the dress and countenances of the guilty and the grisly monsters that were carrying them away, and his conscience gave him an uneasy twinge as to his own mode of treating the weak and defenceless. He turned to Methodios and said, "Canst thou teach me how I and my subjects may escape being sentenced to the pit of fire?" Methodios answered, "Send to Constantinople, and pray the emperor that he give thee wise men who can instruct thee and show thee how to tame thy wild people." One year from this time King Boris and his nobles bowed their proud heads in Christian baptism, and to this day the Bulgarians attribute their conversion to the picture-sermon of Methodios. Therefore he is represented in their schools and churches with his painting in his hand.

Some time after the mission to Bulgaria there appeared in Constantinople a deputation of strange men speaking the Slavonic tongue. They came from the western Slävic peoples, who were then welding themselves into that great kingdom of Moravia which, but for the jealousy of the neighbouring Germans, might have saved eastern Europe from disunion and barbarism.* The words of this deputation are given by old Nestor, the monk of Kieff: "The Moravian princes, Rastislav, Sviatopolk, and Kotzel, sent to the Emperor Michael and said, 'Our land is baptized, but we have no teachers who can instruct us or translate for us the sacred books. We do not understand either the Greek or the Latin language; some teach us one thing, some another; therefore we do not understand the words of the Scriptures, neither their import. Send us teachers who may explain to us the Scriptures.' When the Emperor Michael heard this, he called together his philosophers, and told them the message of the Slavonic princes; and the philosophers said, 'There is at Thessalonica a man named Leon; he has two sons who both know the Slavonic language and are clever philosophers.' On hearing this, the Emperor sent to Thessalonica, to Leon, saying, 'Send to us thy sons Methodios and Constantine,' which hearing, Leon straightway sent them; and when they came to the Emperor he said to them, 'The Slavonic lands have sent unto me requesting teachers who may translate for them the Holy Scriptures.' And being persuaded by the Emperor, they went into the Slavonic land, to Rastislav, to Sviatopolk, and to Kotzel. Having arrived they began to compose a Slavonic alphabet, and translated the Gospels and the Acts of the Apostles, whereat the Slavonians rejoiced greatly, hearing the greatness of God in their own language. After which they translated the Psalter and other books." (Nestor's "Annals," original text edition of St. Petersburg, 1767, pp. 20-23.†) Well says the monk Chrabr, writing in

* For history of the great Moravian State see Palatzky's "History of Bohemia," German translation. And for a sketch of the same, and of part of its territories, see "Across the Carpathians." London: Macmillan & Co.

† For an account of the mission of Cyril and Methodios among the Western

the eleventh century, "Dost thou ask any of the Slavonic authors who invented your characters and who translated the Books into your tongue? They all know, and will answer, 'The holy philosopher Constantine, called Cyril; he and his brother Methodios invented our characters and translated the Books into our language.' But dost thou ask at what time this took place? that also do they know and will tell thee: 'In the days of Michael the Greek Emperor, of Boris, the prince of the Bulgarians, of Rastislav, prince of the Blatens,* in the year of the creation of the world 6363'" (= 855 A.D.)

The strong presumption that the Salonican Apostles were not by race Hellene, but Slavonic citizens of a Byzantine city, rests less even on their perfect acquaintance with a tongue which the Greeks contemned as barbarous, than on their carefulness to make their mission a means of establishing the *Slavonic* language, not, as Greeks would have made it, a means of extending *Greek*.

The work of Cyril and Methodios bears date 855, and earlier than this it cannot be certain that the Slavonic was a written tongue. But that it was so is presumed, on the following grounds :—1st. Because unless the language had attained a certain degree of development, Cyril could scarcely have made what he did—a literal translation of part of the Scriptures—without borrowing largely from the Greek; nor could he have rendered almost all the terms and epithets of the

---

Slāvs, see Count Krasinski's admirable work on the "Religious History of the Sclavonic Nations." Shafarik gives his decision for the opinion urged by common sense, that the greater part of this translation was prepared before Cyril and his brother left Salonica. The dialects of the Slāvs north and south of the Danube must at that time have been sufficiently alike for one written language to be intelligible to both. The son and successor of Boris was himself the writer of several books.

* "Slāvs on the Balaton, Blaten, or Platten-see," in the south-west of Hungary.

original by Slavonic equivalents.* 2nd. Because the alphabet in which the earliest Slavonic MSS. are written bears trace of an existence prior to the introduction of Christianity, and would seem to have been first cut on sticks in the Runic fashion. This alphabet is called Glagolitic, from a letter named Glagol, which signifies "word."

The so-called Cyrillic alphabet is supposed to have been introduced as easier than the original character, both for copyist to write and for foreigner to acquire. Some of its signs are modified from the Glagolitic, but those which Greek and Slavonic have in common are simply taken from the Greek. Tradition calls its inventor St. Cyril, and history proves that it was brought into general use by his pupil Clement, first bishop of Bulgaria. It is adopted by all the Slavonic peoples belonging to the Eastern Church, and thus again their version of the Scriptures points back to its Bulgarian source.†

The Greek Christians of Salonica have always been left the use of certain churches and monasteries. Hence we looked for some testimonial to the memory of those missionaries whom their communion has to thank that at the present day it is represented in the councils of Europe by the Slavonic power of Russia. But no chapel, no monument, not even a house or a shrine, is pointed out as connected with Cyril and Methodios; and the monks whom we questioned on the subject would not

* Unlike the translations of the Scriptures in German, French, English, &c., wherein theological terms are borrowed wholesale from Greek and Latin, in the Slavonic they are mostly rendered by equivalents. Thus the word "theology" is translated *bogoslovie;* orthodox, *provoslav,* &c.

† There was long debate between Slāvic scholars as to the relative antiquity of the Glagolitic and Cyrillic alphabets, and it has been but lately decided that the former is the oldest. To recommend it to the court of Rome, it was said to have been invented by St. Jerome; and now, to recommend it to the Slāvs of the Oriental communion, the fact is insisted on that its origin dates from a period before the split between the Eastern and Western Churches.

know or hear anything about them. In fact, that Pope who in 1016 interdicted the Slavonic alphabet, and branded as a heretic the very missionary whom his wiser predecessor had consecrated archbishop,* did not bear more emphatic testimony to the national character of the ministry of Methodios than do these Greeks of the nineteenth century to the national character of the translation of Cyril.

It is to the possession of a liturgy and Scriptures in their own tongue that the Slavonic churches owe it, that they never have been utterly denationalised by foreign influence, whether proceeding from Constantinople or Rome. Nay, the common possession of these Scriptures and liturgy has proved a link between Slavonic peoples, even when long divided as adherents of Latin or Greek. In 1862 occurred the thousandth anniversary of the Salonican Apostles; it was celebrated by more than eighty millions of Slavonic Christians, without distinction of sect or denomination, from Prague to the Pacific, from the Baltic to Salonica.

* To obtain the Pope's permission for the establishment of a Slavonic ritual Methodios made two journeys to Rome, and was there consecrated Archbishop of Pannonia and Moravia, with full powers to carry out his plans. Even during his lifetime, however, this authority was qualified, and after his death the Council of Salona (1016) went so far as to brand the Slavonic missionaries as heretics and the Slavonic alphabet as an invention of the devil. It is no small proof of national tenacity that from that day to this the native liturgy should have maintained its ground in a part of Roman Catholic Dalmatia, and, so far from being likely to relinquish it now, the Croatians are taking measures to substitute it for Latin throughout their churches. In Bohemia the Slavonic Bible has held its ground, through struggles that form a long and important chapter in religious history.

CHAPTER VII.

FROM SALONICA TO MONASTIR.

OUR visit to Salonica happened in June, when silk merchants were scouring the country, taking up all decent horses, and over-paying the Turkish guards. The pasha, with so many buyourdís (passports) on his hands, neglected to send ours till late on the evening before we started; moreover he gave our escort no instructions to behave properly, and took no pains to secure us good steeds. Consequently the guards showed themselves generally disaffected, and refused obedience to various directions; the horses brought were so miserable that we had to send them away, and at the last moment sit down to wait for others. We did not get off till long after sunrise; and let no one attempt to ride over the plain of Salonica in the sun.

The first stage was Yenidjé, a town near the site of ancient Pella, about nine hours from Salonica and as many from Vodena. The whole way thither passes over the plain, which is for the most part desert, and here and there marked with hitherto unexplained tumuli. Through it runs the new road "Imperial," a rascally performance in the fullest sense of the term. In the first place it is badly made, and full of ruts; in summer it is as hard as stone, and in winter a Slough of Despond; furthermore, it was made by fraud. The pasha raised an extra tax from the country people, on plea that all their work on the road would be paid for, but having once got the money he put it in his own pocket, and made the road by forced labour. Families upon families were ruined by the double process.

The road Imperial crosses the Vardar, and to this end a bridge is in process of erection. Considering when it was begun, one might have expected it to have been finished long ago ; but this did not suit the private views of the workmen. They began at each end, and worked till near the middle ; then, where the stream runs deepest, they stopped, and bridged over the chasm by planks removable at pleasure. When a traveller appeared these planks were taken up until he paid what the workmen required, and then they were put down for him to pass over. At length the pasha made an end of this system of black-mail; nevertheless, when we traversed the bridge it was in a very imperfect state.

On the other side of the river stands a large new khan with several separate cells. Here we took shelter for our mid-day meal, and the great heat kept us within doors till well on in the afternoon. Even then we could not help envying the buffaloes that lay cooling in the shallow river—their heads and humps alone visible above water, and their muzzles just sufficiently approached to enhance felicity by companionship. These huge beasts are the only creatures on the plain of the Vardar that do not show signs of ill-treatment; slow and stubborn in disposition, they are too strong to be bullied and too useful to be neglected. The eye, turning from their repose, falls on the trains of patient horses carrying iron from Cardiff and cotton from Manchester to the markets of inland towns.

It was sunset when we reached the slightly elevated field which marks the site of ancient Pella. A large cistern lies between the rising ground and the road, on the other side of which is a khan with trees. The sight of carved stones in the walls of this khan attracted the British consul at Salonica, and he obtained permission to dig for further remains. His workmen had just begun, and we found the hole excavated by them at the foot of a rude fragment of Turkish wall. Leaving our horses, we descended into it, and carried off a sherd of ancient pottery.

From the site of Pella it is scarcely two hours to Yenidjé, for which place we had been provided with a letter to a principal Bulgarian. We sent it on by one of the zaptiés, and desired him to meet us outside the town, and conduct us to our quarters for the night. No one showing, we were obliged to follow the other zaptié to the khan, whence his fellow issued and deliberately stated that he had left the letter with the Bulgarian and had desired him to meet us; then, lazily giving some insufficient directions as to the whereabouts of the house, he returned to his rest. His comrade, gruffly murmuring, led us about and around Yenidjé, now stumbling over ill-paved alleys, now stooping under the boughs of enormous planes. The night had fallen, and after nine hours' ride in the heat the chills struck us through and through.

At last we gained the door of a court which proved to be our hoped-for *konak*.* Here the master of the house received us, and explained in consternation that he had been to meet us, but that we had missed him by entering by another gate. This he spoke in Greek, but the mistress welcomed us with the Slavonic "Dobro doshlé."† The room to which we were conducted was

---

* A Turkish word used hereabouts to express either the residence of a governor or one's night-quarters. It is one of those that has passed into use among the Slāvs: even in Croatia, *konatchiti* signifies "to pass the night."

† "Dobro doshlé" (f. pl.), lit. "You are welcome." To which greeting the response is "Bolié vas nashli," "Better we have found you."

upstairs, large and well-carpeted—one side all windows, mostly unglazed. We seated ourselves on the divan, waiting for our luggage, and here happened the greatest breach of respect we ever met with in Turkey. Our principal guard entered the room, threw himself down on the opposite end of the divan, and roared out "Voda" (water). We instantly rose and left the chamber, and on being followed to see what was amiss we pointed without a word to the zaptié on the divan. He dared not remain, and the master of the house was diffidently following him out of the room, when we called the latter back, requested him to be seated, and bade the woman shut the door, leaving the Turk in the dark outside.

The luggage had missed the road; it seemed ages before it came, and again ages till our beds were put up, our tea made, and chicken and rice ready. Overtired, our sleep was not refreshing. But the worst part was yet to come. Next morning the horses did not appear, and we saw with dismay the cool hours shortening while messenger after messenger went to summon them.

Then came one of the zaptiés to inform us that, before proceeding, the kiradgees wished to be paid for their last day's work. Perceiving that the zaptié himself supported their requirement, we immediately exclaimed, "Surely these kiradgees are Turks!" It proved but too true, and now we knew what we had to expect. The message being interpreted, meant that the kiradgees wanted to turn back. We answered, "If they turn back here, we do not give them a single piastre. The zaptiés must go instantly with the dragoman, show our buyourdí to the mudir of Yenidjé, and demand horses in place of these." When the kiradgees heard this they asked only for half their pay. We required obedience, and would listen to no terms. Next it was alleged that one of the horses was ill. "Then begone all of you, with your horses; as we have said, we will get fresh ones." More than once the dragoman actually left the court to go to the mudir, and was each time called back by promises of obedience. At length, all excuses being exhausted, they began to bungle over and misload the luggage. We saw that our poor dragoman, unsupported by the zaptiés, could do nothing, while his not wearing the European dress further detracted from his influence.

The sun always getting higher and higher—yet we would not go without a word with the master of the house; so when luggage and Turks were at last packed off we called in the Bulgarian for a talk. He gave us not much fresh intelligence, but confirmation of what we had heard from the most trustworthy sources at Salonica.

Yenidjé numbered about 6000 houses, half Bulgarian, half Turks; the Mussulmans being all Osmanlis. The Christians here, as in the country around, are Slavonic, the only Greeks being the bishop and the schoolmaster. The principal men speak Greek, for commercial purposes, but none of the women know it. As for the Papal movement, at that time two Bulgarian United priests celebrated a Slavonic service in a room—but a new church was being built. Converts once numbered fifty to sixty families, then not more than thirty-five; their number having declined because they were deceived as to exemption from paying the taxes. They would, however, increase again should the new church turn out exactly like those to which they are accustomed, for "they would then be persuaded that the Pope *does not want to latinise them*—only to supersede the Patriarch." Aware of this, the Greek bishop was doing his utmost to prevent the completion of the building; and should this be impossible, he hoped to obtain a mandate forbidding the Roman Catholics to imitate the Orthodox style, decoration, and service. Some Bulgarians regard the Unionists as deceivers, but our informant was evidently not quite decided as to his opinion of them. For himself, he felt an objection to do anything that would be considered a desertion of his father's faith, but at the same time entertained reasonable doubt that any real blame could attach to a person for substituting in his prayers the name of the Pope, whom he did not know, for that of the Patriarch, whom he could not bear. "What we want," said he, "is, protection, and some help to start with. We are not rich enough to build a second school, and since the bishop forces us to keep up the Greek one all we now ask is that his teacher should also know Bulgarian. But if we had the protection of some foreign power we could get on, and if a school with a Bulgarian teacher were once founded it is to it that we would send our children. Should we agree to go over to the Romanists, they promise us both church services and school teaching in our own tongue; and though we would rather get these benefits in some other manner, it is better to get them thus than not at all."

From Yenidjé we had but six hours to Vodena, but starting late, the first part of the ride was, as yesterday, in the burning sun. We halted at the khan of the little village of St. Georgio, inhabited by Bulgarians, but having a Greek school. This khan has no separate room, but the heat was too great to remain out of doors, so we had to dine in the stable, on a sort of platform raised round the poles that support the roof.

By the time we again started a cloud had come over the sun, and the last three hours of this day's ride proved delicious. We reached the Karasmak (the ancient Lydias), its banks dotted with grazing herds; and this boundary passed over, every step brought us nearer to the glen of Vodena, where the weary level of the treeless plain melts into mountain shadow, bowery verdure, and overflowing streams. It was evening when we entered the glen; in the mulberry gardens that fringe the road the nightingales were singing their serenade, while a light breeze shook the scarlet bells of pomegranate bushes in full bloom.

Presently we came on a meeting of waters overshaded by mighty planes, and there halted to take in the scene. We found ourselves at the foot of a precipice wherewith the upper glen suddenly breaks off from the mountains on either side. Over this precipice breaks the river, not in one sheet, but in five large cascades, while countless little watercourses flash out from the green on the height, and run races in the valley below—a glorious confusion of verdure and foam. Above, on the rock, at the head of the cascades—its glittering minarets seeming to rise besprayed out of the river—stands Vodena, the Bulgarian "city of waters," once the Macedonian Edessa.

In Vodena we were most fortunate in being accommodated in the house of a Swiss silk merchant. The family was absent, but, unlike our hosts of Salonica, had left its furniture behind. The manager of the factory, a Bulgarian, educated in Vienna, had been indicated to us as a person of intelligence; and besides the introduction from his master, we brought him a letter from a Bulgarian friend; hence he received us with great cordiality. We were soon at supper in a large airy room, comfortably furnished, and having but one fault, *i.e.*, two of its sides were glass windows, and this, during the sunny hours, made it like a hot-house.

At Vodena, fearing fresh carelessness in the orders given for our journey, we sent to desire the mudir would come to see us, and he duly appeared—the fattest, most stolid, most uncouth Turk we ever beheld. With him we tried to arrange our route to Castoria, but this turned out to be beset with obstacles. The authority of the mudir of Vodena, as subordinate of the pasha of Salonica, went no farther than Ostrovo, *i.e.*, about three hours distance, and at that station there were no officials and no horses. Then the mudir insisted that between Ostrovo and Castoria the way was infested by robbers, and that he did not know, and no one could tell him, whether we should find anything like a road between Castoria and Naum on the lake of Ochrida. Altogether we were obliged to come back to the plan we ought to have adopted from the first, and decide to go straight to Monastir. On this, after another endless series of conferences, a bargain was struck with some Bulgarian kiradgees. With Turkish carriers we would have no more to do.

So much time had been taken up by these affairs that we stayed a second day at Vodena in order to see something of the place. When the heat was past, our obliging and intelligent host came to take us a walk round the town. The character of Vodena is most peculiar, the river running alongside of the street; it might be called a miniature Venice, but for the difference between still canal water and rushing mountain streams. Straight out of the water rise the handsome houses of the wealthier citizens. Among them many are merchants, a few Swiss, and some Bulgarians. The lower story in these houses is stone, the upper, wood, and the great fashion here is to paint the walls white, picked out with blue. The lounge of the town is a grove on the river, over which plane trees throw their shade. Here we saw a group of Mussulmans seated in circle, holding grave and earnest converse. Our host told us that many councils are held there, and that at present the Turks are alarmed in prospect of a regular income-tax, for hitherto they have succeeded (as the consul at Salonica told us) in paying one piastre where the rayah paid twelve. Besides being engaged in a little row with the mudir, which it requires some organisation to prolong, they are busy consulting together on means to neutralise the effect of the new system; and as the valuation of property will be performed by Mahommedan agents, what through national partialities, what through bribes, they have every prospect of getting off as before.

We were next taken to see the place on the rock where materials were hauled up to build the school. Such is the steepness of the bank whereon the city stands that it cost less to wind up the stones with a windlass to the site of the building, than to bring them thither by road. From this spot the view is lovely, and as we exclaimed at the beauty of the landscape a Bulgarian muttered, "Aye, a good land; and it is *Turkish*. The pig always gets into the best garden." We were now invited to the garden of a neighbouring house, where we could sit down and enjoy the view at our ease. A carpet was spread on the brink of the cliff, and thence, with the scarlet pomegranate blossoms for our foreground, we looked down on a scene of beauty which has few equals. On each side of Vodena the mountains widen, and through gradual descents of glen and valley subside into the Vardar plain. The plain in its purple distance melts into the glittering sea, and on the rising ground on the farther side of the gulf the light falls on the white walls of Salonica. Such is the view right before us; but turn to the left and behold another picture: from the cascades and mulberry groves of Vodena rises a low range of wooded hills; above this a higher range and a higher, till all culminate in the Mount Olympus, whose broad snowy brow now shines golden in the setting sun. On scenes like these one must gaze and gaze till they are painted on the memory—every hue and line and shade—so that, in after times, among dull street walls and duller walls of drawing-rooms, one may have but to shut one's eyes and call back the living picture. For the sake of thus bearing away the views from Vodena we would have thought no price too dear save that which we paid for it. Sitting in the garden after sunset we both caught the fever.

Had we known what was the matter with us next morning, when we felt so aching and so heavy, we certainly should not have started, even after all the bother of getting the kiradgees to come. As it was, of course they came late, and were of more than Bulgarian stolidity, so that again, for the third time, we had to ride in the sun.

For some distance from Vodena the scenery is of the same enchanting character. You follow the river up a green luxuriant glen, from the head of which it falls in a cascade. Look back, the view is exquisite. On this road we came to a species of toll-bar, and saw foot passengers stopped by Albanians. To our surprise no demand was made on ourselves, our guides calling out that we travelled with buyourdí, and explaining that the toll was only meant for the "poor." Afterwards, for three hours, you descend abruptly on the Lake of Ostrovo. If not so bleak, this little lake would be pretty; its waters are picturesquely broken by a small island, with a mosque. The story is, that this mosque once stood in the centre of the village, and that the waters have submerged all round. But since last year they have taken the turn, and disgorged a strip of bare beach in place of all they swept away. The village of Ostrovo is miserable in the extreme, the dwelling-houses ruinous, and all of wood; the khan, where we halted for mid-day, is scarcely in a better condition.

Because of the steepness of both sides of the lake the zaptiés on this station are not mounted. Those who accompanied us changed every half-hour at the little "bothies" which serve them for stations. It is only on seeing these rural guard-houses that one recognises the mode in which this road is guarded or infested by its Albanian police.

After mounting to some height on the other side of the lake, we came to the khan of Gornischevo, where we were to spend the night. Great was our consternation to find it so very bad, that, but for the cutting cold of the high land whereon it stands, we should have preferred sleeping in our tent. This was, however, not to be dared, so we had to instal ourselves upstairs in a tiny room, with mud walls and floor, no glass in windows, and some difficulty in fastening the door. It may be imagined that, if it had been possible, we would have left this place of penance by next morning at daybreak; but, alas! it was not possible, and we found our only course was to lie still and tide over the fever fit.

At first the kiradgees were impatient, the guards unruly, and the villagers, as usual when one comes with Turks, declared they had nothing to sell. Our obstinacy conquered theirs, for we were too ill to be driven away. The guards we let go; the kiradgees were satisfied by promises to pay their expenses while we remained. The villagers, seeing the Turks depart and being spoken to in their own language, brought forth milk, fowls, and food for the horses, and finally negotiated for a Bulgarian spelling-book. But at the end of the first day we were no better. Then the objection to say "die" yielded to the fear of dying in reality, and dying in this detestable khan; we despatched a note to the consul at Monastir, to whom we had already forwarded our letters of introduction, and asked him to be so kind as, if possible, to send some sort of a carriage to fetch us. There is not, in Turkey, one out of a hundred places where such a request could be complied with ; nor, perhaps, one other place in the world where such a reception would await sick travellers as we met with in Mr. and Mrs. Charles Calvert's house at Monastir.

CHAPTER VIII.

THE ANCIENT BULGARIAN CAPITAL AND THE MODERN TURKISH TOWN.

"Samuel, King of Bulgaria, at the end of the tenth century, established the central administration of his dominions at Achrida. The site was well adapted for rapid communication with his Sclavonian subjects in Macedonia, who furnished his armies with their best recruits. To Achrida, therefore, he transferred the seat of the Bulgarian patriarchate. As a military position, also, Achrida had many advantages; it commanded an important point in the Via Egnatia, the great commercial road connecting the Adriatic with Bulgaria, as well as with Thessalonica and Constantinople, and afforded many facilities for enabling Samuel to choose his points of attack on the Byzantine towns of Macedonia, Hellas, Dyrrachium, and Nicopolis. Here, therefore, Samuel established the capital of the Bulgaro-Sclavonian kingdom he founded."—FINLAY's *History of the Byzantine and Greek Empires*, vol. i., p. 438.

"To talk with Turks, no men seem better to understand everything, or more fit to rule; to witness their real practice, no men so inapt for authority; all that is debased and debasing, ruinous and disloyal. . . . Those who have chatted with the elegant Turkish agent over a bottle of claret at the hotel, or held agreeable discourse with him in a carpeted kiosk on the shores of the Bosphorus, may find it hard to bring themselves to imagine how the burning houses and violated women of Damascus, the desolated villages and butchered peasants of Syria and Anseyreeyah, can be anyhow the work of a government headed by men so intelligent, so amicable, and, above all, so polite."—PALGRAVE's *Central and Eastern Arabia*, vol. i. p. 299.

DURING the fortnight we spent at Monastir our strength was not sufficiently re-established to allow of any lengthened expedition, and a ride or two to the neighbouring convents, with a visit to the schools in the town, were all that we could manage in the cool hours of the day. So far as our own pleasure was concerned, the loss of an excursion to the Albanian lake country proved a disappointment; for we had looked forward to enjoyment from the beauty of the scenery. On the other hand, our principal aim being to see those parts of Turkey least familiar to Europeans, we were consoled for missing the Albanian lakes by the knowledge that they had been well described in the travels of Mr. Lear. We heard too that another description was in progress from the pen and pencil of an accomplished lady.*

But even these considerations availed little to make up for foregoing Ochrida, not only a scene of unusual beauty, but to us a spot of unusual interest, as the "hundred-bridged city" of ancient Bulgaria. Here, towards the end of the tenth century, Samuel, czar of the Bulgarians, established the capital of a really formidable monarchy, in defiance of the then Byzantine emperor, himself the representative of a Slavonian line. We will not go into the story of those campaigns which at length won for Basil II. the grim title of "slayer of the Bulgarians," but we cannot refrain from telling a quaint love-tale, of which the heroine is Samuel's daughter, and the hero one of the early Serbian kings. We dwell on this legend the rather because it turns on an incident when Bulgaria, in one of its moments of strength, meets the slowly-growing power of its western sister-state, Serbia, with whose history we shall soon have to do. The subject of dispute between them, viz., the cities on the Adriatic, illustrates a point to which we must afterwards refer—that the first kinglets of southern Serbia were also rulers of the northern Albanians, and that the same state which comprehended Montenegro stretched to Alessio and Elbassan.†

* See "Through Macedonia to the Albanian Lakes," by Mrs. Walker.

† The early rulers of Serbia are properly called *zupan*, but the "chronicler of Dioclea" speaks of them in this chronicle as "kings," *reges*. Almost to the present day the hereditary pasha of Scutari, in Albania, was descended from a renegade branch of the old Serbian princes of Zeta.

Czar Samuel had resolved to extend his realm to the sea, so he began by taking Durazzo from its Byzantine garrison; but not content herewith he pushed forward to Dulcigno, a town belonging to the young Serbian king Vladimir. In the war that ensued Vladimir was driven to the mountains, where his warriors suffered greatly, and he then resolved to purchase peace for his people by resigning his own person to the enemy. "The Good Shepherd giveth his life for the sheep;" thus spake the King, according to the old chronicle, and for this among other reasons he is revered as a saint. Samuel led his captive to Prespa, a town not far from Ochrida, where he had a strong castle and kept his treasures; it was also at that time the residence of his family, among others of his daughter Kosara, a damsel fair, pitiful, and devout.

The pious Vladimir, praying in his dungeon, was comforted by the vision of an angel promising him speedy deliverance; the pious Kosara, praying in the palace, was bidden by an angel to visit the prison, and humble herself by washing the captives' feet. "In the process of this her good work, she came on Vladimir, and was struck with his noble looks, his dignity, his calmness; she spoke to him, and was equally astonished with his wisdom and piety; then hearing that he was of royal rank, and filled with pity for his misfortunes, she felt her heart move towards him, and bade him farewell, bowing herself before him. Resolved to free the noble captive, she hastened to the Czar her father, threw herself at his feet, and besought him, saying, 'My lord and father, I know that thou art thinking to provide me with a husband, as is the custom at my years; therefore I beseech thee of thy goodness give me thy captive the Serbian Vladimir, or know that, rather than wed any other than he, I will die.' The Czar, who deeply loved his daughter, and knew that Vladimir was a king, her equal, rejoiced at her saying and resolved to fulfil her petition. He sent for Vladimir, and after he had been bathed and dressed in royal apparel, he was brought before the Czar, who looked on him favourably, and before all his great men received him with a kiss and gave him to his daughter. After the marriage had been celebrated right royally, Samuel restored Vladimir to his kingdom, and gave him, besides his patrimonial lands, Durazzo and the district thereof. Further, the Czar sent messengers to tell Dragomir, the uncle of Vladimir, that he need no longer remain hidden in the mountain, but might return to his territory of Trebigne, call his people together again, and inhabit the land. Which all took place."

With this glance at the old Bulgarian days we will now return to the present Turkish days, wherein Ochrida has become a place of far less importance than the military station, Monastir. This town is beautifully situated at the extremity of a great plain, flanked by a majestic range of mountains, amid which the snow-clad crest of Peristeri attains a height of 7,500 feet. Besides its Greek name, Monastir has a Slāvic one, *i.e.*, Bitolia (from an older form, Butel), while the Turks uniting both, call the town Toli Monastir.

This variety of appellation is answered to by a variety of population almost as great as that of Salonica, though of somewhat different ingredients. The Jews are numerous, but do not outweigh the other races; the Mahommedans are Osmanli; the Slāvs, of whom but few live in the town, people its environs and all the country around; the Greeks, who people neither town nor country, contrive to have their interests and language represented by the wealthy and crafty Tzintzars. The story of this race, so called by their Slavonic neighbours, is very curious. It forms part of that which calls itself Rouman, and inhabits Wallachia, Moldavia, with a portion of Transylvania: without doubt, too, it once was numerous in Thessaly and Macedonia. At present it is represented south of the Danube by mercantile communities in Turkish towns, villagers in eastern Serbia, and shepherds on the Pindus and the Balkan. To this day the greater part of these speak their own language, which some call a barbarian dialect Latinized, others a Latin dialect barbarized. Of late years, however, Greek schools have been introduced among them, and the Hellenes have been clever enough to persuade them that they were originally Macedonian Greeks, romanized during the Empire; hence they identify themselves with Greek ambitions and antipathies, and make common cause with the Phanariote bishop in his determination to keep down the Slavonic element. The sly, grinding, and servile character of the Tzintzars in Turkey detracts from the respect one would otherwise feel for their industry and shrewdness; while the kindliness and honesty of the oppressed Bulgarian conciliates sympathy, even when, as here, his intelligence is at the lowest ebb. At that time the only Bulgarian school belonged to Unionists, and was superintended by a priest from Brittany, assisted by a native schoolmaster.

The Mahommedans of Monastir and in the country about it and Ochrida are said to be more numerous than the Christians. Wherever this is the case the state of the disarmed and disfranchised rayah is most pitiable, and open murder occurs frequently and unpunished. We will relate two instances which we had at first hand.

A lady with her husband and friend were spending Sunday at a village near Ochrida. Looking on the lovely and peaceful scene they said to each other, "Surely here at least violence has not entered in." But at that very moment, in the grove below, among the group of Christians who had been enjoying its shade, one lay dead, another maimed. The murderer was one of the Mahommedan zaptiés or rural police. This man had a grudge at the Christian elder, who had caused him to be reprimanded for a gross offence. He had been sentenced to a short imprisonment for burglary, but at the end of forty days was not only liberated, but received back into his former office, and thus let loose on the community he had offended—excited by revenge and armed. Forthwith repairing to a spot where the aged Christian was at dinner with his friends, he discharged his pistol at him, and hit, not the intended victim, but a young man sitting by his side. Three other zaptiés were present, yet none of them moved to stop the assassin. A young unarmed Bulgarian, a friend of the murdered man, raised his hand to arrest the murderer, and he was at once struck down by a blow which severed an artery and left him a cripple for life. The cowardly assassin afterwards made off to the woods, but except for the accidental presence of an European consul in the town, he need not have troubled himself even thus far. The mudir was dead drunk, and when forced to appear was scarcely able to give the order that the other zaptiés should pursue their colleague. They went just far enough to fancy they were not watched, but were seen to hold a parley with the murderer, who afterwards disappeared in the woods, the zaptiés returning to say that further search was useless.

Another case of the same kind happened shortly afterwards. A Bulgarian, one of the most prosperous men in Ochrida, had a sum of money borrowed from him by a Turk who did not repay it, so at length he made interest with the mudir to get his debtor put into prison. At the end of a few days, however, he let him out, only fixing a future time for payment; but this indulgence was vain; for the son of the Turk resolved that his father's imprisonment by a rayah should be bloodily avenged. He watched a moment when the merchant was taking his siesta under a tree, and then crept up to him and discharged a gun into his body. A few weeks later the merchant died of the wound; yet the murderer remained at large.*

In this manner murders are committed every day, and so long as the victims are rayahs the authorities take no notice; but even if they did the conviction of the assassin is hopeless, for a Christian cannot give evidence in criminal cases. It may be asked, why do the Christians not resist? In the first place, they are not, like the Mahommedans, armed; secondly, the injury of a Mahommedan by a Christian, even in self-defence or the defence of another, is rigorously punished in Mussulman courts.

A terrible instance of this deserves record. A late grand vizier, travelling through the provinces by way of doing justice and reforming abuses, stopped in his progress at Monastir. He found before the tribunal the case of two boys, a Christian and a Mussulman, who had been fighting, and were both hurt. The Christian remained long and severely ill, the Mussulman died; thereupon the grand vizier ordered the execution of the Christian boy. Now, it may not be known that in

---

* Since writing the above, we have found these and other stories related at length in "Through Macedonia to the Albanian Lakes," by Mrs. Walker, sister of the Rev. Charles Curtis, British chaplain at Constantinople. She also says:—"The Christians of Ochrida complain bitterly of the murders of their co-religionists which have taken place in that neighbourhood within the last three years. No less than thirty lives have been thus sacrificed, but in no single instance have the assassins been brought to justice" (p. 211). An American missionary told us (1863) that near Eski Sagra, in Bulgaria, where he was stationed, from seventy to one hundred Christians were killed annually by Mussulmans without inquiry being made.

Turkey capital sentences are rare. A criminal will be ordered to receive a number of lashes, under the half of which he dies, or he is assigned a term of imprisonment in a loathsome den, wherein he is certain to perish; but he is not *sentenced* to die. Hence the sentence of death pronounced on this Christian caused great and painful sensation. He had only struck in self-defence, while defending a friend from the molestation of Mussulmans; moreover, he had been himself wounded. It was felt that if in the face of all these extenuating circumstances the Christian lad were to suffer capital punishment, and that too on the sentence of the highest functionary of the central government, it was equivalent to a declaration that any Christian who might defend himself against the blows of a Mussulman should be punishable with the utmost rigour of the law. For this reason a petition for pardon was thrown into the vizier's carriage, and the consuls endeavoured to procure a revision of the sentence. But the very inference deprecated by the Christians was that which the vizier intended them to draw. Accordingly the consular remonstrance was disregarded, the petitioning citizens were punished and exiled, and the vizier himself (a europeanized Turk, who speaks French to perfection), although on the point of departure from Monastir, delayed his journey to witness the execution, and kept his carriage waiting at the door until he saw the Christian die.

No wonder the Bulgarian feels that, so long as the Turk rules the country, resistance to abuse of power is vain; the Christians of the Serbian principality, however, who have enjoyed at least one generation of freedom, already meet injustice very differently, and an instance illustrating their higher spirit occurred while we were at Monastir.

A Serb merchant, trading in wine, had the ill-luck to fall in love and marry out of his own country, and his wife, a Turkish subject, could not bear to be separated from her family. Hence he passed much of his time near Monastir. The man was supposed to be rich, and a scheme was entered into—and that among the highest personages—to get a sum of money out of him. Accordingly they trumped up an accusation, and got some creature to swear that six months before, on the bombardment of Belgrade, he and the Serb had agreed to seize booty together and to divide it. A share in the plunder was what he claimed. The falsehood of the charge was transparent, but it served as an excuse to put the merchant in prison, and so soon as he was there he received the message, "Only pay so much, and you shall be let out." He answered, "I owe nothing, and will pay nothing." The affair came to the ears of the consuls and some representations were made. Fearing he should escape, the authorities sent to the man, offering him liberation for half the sum originally proposed. He refused as steadily as before. Again representations were made, and at this juncture the Commissioner Subi Bey arrived. This commissioner must visit the prisons, and ask every prisoner the cause of his detention. The case of the Serb having attracted consular notice could not be shelved, and his mouth would not easily be stopped. Yet once more an attempt was made on him, and he was offered his liberty on the payment of only 100 piastres. It was then that the Turks found out they had to do with a man who was accustomed to take no less than justice. The answer was the same: "Do your worst. I will not pay a single para." Under the circumstances there was nothing for it but to try the merchant as fast as possible and to release him on bail. If he took the advice of his friends, he made the best of his way back to Serbia before the commissioner left Monastir.

In this last story we have alluded to a "commissioner," and will therefore explain his visit and functions. From time to time, and frequently at the instance of some European ambassador, the Turkish government despatches a so-called "commissioner" to perambulate the provinces, and root out and punish local abuse. If any further testimony were needful as to the corruption of Turkish officials, the results of one such commissioner's investigations would furnish all the evidence required. When we were at Monastir scarcely a day passed without some maladministrations coming to light, and so far as we heard, Subi Bey lacked neither energy to punish nor shrewdness to detect. But there is little use in ruining wretched subordinates while pashas and their secretaries escape; so a most unpleasant impression was made on those who heard that another commissioner in the western provinces, having presumed to arrest a high official, had forthwith been recalled. It was much feared that this example would not strengthen the hands nor sharpen the sight of Subi Bey.

One day a mudir entered the consulate. He was an honest, jovial-looking personage, and his face beamed with satisfaction in relating how triumphantly his examination had been passed. In a tone of decent regret he added, however, that of all those examined at the same time none had come out with clean hands but he. Nor did even this unique mudir pretend to have been acquitted of more than dishonesty and injustice; his mudirlik was in sad disorder, the local Mussulmans despising the law, Albanian brigands infesting the road. But these things were no fault of his, and encouraged by the commissioner's approbation, he had even ventured to tell him so, declaring himself powerless to effect improvement unless his authority were supported by better agents than the local zaptiés. The commissioner had of course promised him that all should be done as he wished; a body of regular troops should execute his orders, and he himself be raised to the rank of kaimakam. "If God will," ended the mudir.

Unfortunately his case is no solitary one. Supposing a new Turkish governor to come to his post, rapacious and cruel, all those who await him there will be ready to abet his plunder on condition of sharing his spoils. But let him be an honest man, with a desire to do justly and restore order, and he finds that all the traditions of his predecessors, all his own myrmidons, are against him; while the central government rarely puts him in a position to be independent of the local Mussulmans, who will only support him on condition of being suffered to prolong their corrupt régime. Nor, alas, is it only Mussulmans who thrive on abuses and strengthen wicked hands. We have already alluded to the miserable circumstance that in Roumelia Greek bishops are amongst the most decried hangers-on of the most decried governors; and hatred of race or greed of gain is ever sure to keep numerous rayah agents at a powerful Mussulman's beck and call. Such Christians, being the worst specimens of their own community, are of course still more reckless and base than their Mahommedan fellow-workers; consequently those travellers whose experience lies mainly in official circles are apt to affirm, and that with truth, that they found the Christians worse than the Turks. But these parasite Christians in Turkey are regarded by their honester brethren with horror as great as we can feel for them; and bitterly do the better sort complain that the material oppression of the Turkish

CATHEDRAL OF OCHRIDA.

system is a lesser evil than its demoralising action. Only those among the rayahs who are servile and unscrupulous can make their way to power; lawful demands are disregarded, outspokenness and independence of spirit crushed out; while prizes are held out to cupidity and treachery, and the scum of society is raised to the top.

At Monastir we strove to collect information as to ways and means of travelling between Macedonia and the southern frontier of the Serbian Principality. The lamentable plight wherein we had appeared before our kind hosts made us ashamed to tell them that we had purposed, after leaving Monastir, to visit all the places of interest in so wild a district as Old Serbia; on the other hand, we could not make up our minds quite to surrender this cherished plan. By way of compromise, we resolved on going straight from Monastir to Belgrade, seeing the battle-field of Kóssovo, and such other famous spots as could be taken en route. This, at the time, really seemed the utmost our scarcely restored strength could attempt, and even for this it was deemed necessary to ascertain that the road could be traversed in a carriage. Our furthest point on Turkish ground was to be the town of Novi Bazaar, and the way between Bitolia and this station is one of the regular tracks of inland commerce, therefore we had counted on being able to hear all about it at Monastir. But herein we were disappointed; for after asking all sorts of people, nothing but contradictory statements could be obtained, and we had to fall back on the strangers in the land. The consul and his wife could answer for having made their way *tant bien que mal* with a carriage as far as Vélesa. Then Hahn's book testified that he had taken a carriage between Vélesa and the town of Prístina on the field of Kóssovo. But beyond Prístina to the Serbian frontier went no man's ken, and one might have supposed that Novi Bazaar lay at the other end of the empire, instead of within a distance of about seventy hours. At last a Polish officer in the Turkish service, happening to pass through Monastir, declared that he had ridden over the whole road and knew that it was traversed by *cannon*, and thereupon some one remembered that talikas conveying the officials' harems must sometimes pass that way. On this collected evidence our bargain was made for a sort of covered waggon drawn by two stout horses, which, when necessary, were to be assisted by oxen. Some Tzintzar kiradgees undertook the luggage, and the consul allowed an intelligent young Albanian trained in his service to accompany us as cavass.

CHAPTER IX.

KING'S SON MARKO: HIS CASTLE AND HIS STORY.

"*King.*—Son Marko, may God slay thee! Thou shalt have neither monument nor posterity; and ere thy spirit leaves thy body the Turkish Sultan thou shalt serve.

"*Czar.*—Friend Marko, may God help thee! Bright be thy face in the Senate: sharp thy sword in the battle. Never shall hero surpass thee. And thy name shall be remembered so long as sun and moon endure.

"Thus they spake, and thus 'tis come to pass."—*Old Serbian Ballad: "Marko's Judgment."*

NOTWITHSTANDING all the comfort and kindness experienced during our stay at Monastir, it was no unwelcome change from a modern Turkish town to that atmosphere of poetry and romance which surrounds the mediæval sites of Serbian power. The site in question is the Castle of Marko Kralïevitch, *i.e.*, of the king's son Marko; it overlooks the town of Prilip, and is one of the rare feudal remains of any size to be found in this part of Turkey.

Even as Scādār, or Scodra, is common ground to Serbians and Albanians, so is Prilip, or Perlepé, common ground to Bulgarians and Serbs. The population of the town and district of Prilip is Bulgarian, but the presence of Marko Kralïevitch's castle connects the whole place and neighbourhood with Old Serbian memories and myths. Who Marko was, and how his name is interwoven with the web of historical legend, forms a story of no common interest; but one so long that, if we begin with it here, we shall afterwards be in no humour to climb a hill and see his tower. Therefore, with our reader's permission, we will do the castle first, our point of departure being that small monastery which stands at the foot of a three-horned rock, some hundred yards distant from Prilip.

Perhaps the monks might have been pleased to show us the ruin and tell us all manner of legends; at least so they usually did when we approached them through a Slavonic medium; but we had left the dragoman at home, and one of the party addressed the caloyers most affably in *Turkish*. Then all was over; the Bulgarians stiffened into wooden stupidity, and left us to make our way to the castle with no better cicerone than the guard. One attempt to mollify them we did make, but unsuccessfully, not being strong in Bulgarian, so began, "We would see Marko——," but then stopped short to recollect the next word. The monk shrugged his shoulders, with a smile, as if to say, "All your wilfulness cannot achieve *that*," and then answered, "God forgive us! Marko has been dead these 400 years." So he has; and yet, if all tales be true, this is no reason why we should not see him, if only we could wait until the anniversary of his festival or "slava," and hide ourselves in a certain little chapel where some of his family lie entombed. At midnight the doors burst open and in rides Marko, fully armed, and mounted on his favourite charger—that famous steed Sharatz.*

Left to make our own way to the ruin, we climbed thither straight up from the monastery, but soon found that in this, as in other cases, the longest way round is the shortest way there. An easier road, apparently the ancient approach, leads round the lower part of the hill, and had we followed it we should have avoided clambering over blank slabs of rock, whereon the gentle-

---

* Sharatz—literally "the variegated;" probably "piebald."

men's boots slid as on ice. At length we gained an open space, said to have been the old *place d'armes,* whence the horns of the rock branch upward right and left. The best view of the highest of these eminences is to be obtained from one of the lower, which we therefore ascended, and thereon found a group of enormous stones poised against each other, and in appearance not unlike rocking-stones; however, they would not rock.

Near the top of the hill is a ruined tower, but the path thither was barred by a lean grey form which stopped the narrowest part of the way, and seemed jealously to watch our meditated ascent. So steadily did it stand, that we had time to draw nearer and see what it was—a mountain goat, last sentinel in the feudal hold.

And now, reaching the higher brow of rock, we found it covered with walls, but without a single roofed chamber; so that though one enclosure is commonly called "the powder magazine," and another "the lady's weaving-room," they might as well pass for sheep-pens. On the highest crag poises another of the giant stones, so surrounded below by masonry that under it there runs a little corridor. On the top of this block stand the remnants of a cell, called by the country people "Marko's Kiosk," wherein Bulgarian legends describe him as seated, and viewing from afar all who approach his castle, either as guests or foes. On the kiosk walls are still to be found the traces of rude frescoes, horses and dogs—not that we saw them, but we had heard of them beforehand—and a zaptié who clambered up the big stone, which we could not, exclaimed at the wondrous drawings he found. Immediately below this perch one finds the enclosure of a lower chamber, to which the approach is over a slab of rock, so steep and smooth as to explain the necessity of the foot-rests therein hewn; some of these are in form like a horse's shoe; and it would be deemed hypercritical to question that they were made by Sharatz. From this point, looking over the fortified hill, the town below and the plain beyond, the landscape is picturesque, and might be pretty but from the scarcity of trees. Though less curious, it has some likeness to the view from Castle Blagaï in the Herzegovina.

Returning to Prilip by the proper road, we saw several graves cut in the rock, and passed by the walls of a small church. It seems that at the back of the hill there is a ruined chapel, containing some paintings and tombs, and on a high-peaked separate eminence stands a monastery, from whence the view is said to be fine. Dilapidated as Marko's Castle is, it has evidently been a place of larger dimensions than any mere watch-tower or Albanian kula. It recalls, not the hold of a robber chief, but the residence of a feudal potentate, and as such belongs to the date when careers like those of the King's Son and his compeers were possible in Turkey. Hence the sight of it gives local colour to that story of Kralïevitch Marko, whereon we will now enter without further delay.

With some writers it is as inevitable to draw parallels as with some speakers to make puns; but surely a bad parallel is even more vexatious than a bad pun. We begin with this remark, in order somewhat to excuse the irritation wherewith one cannot but reflect on those writers on the character of the King's Son Marko, who have called him the Serbian "Roi Arthur." No doubt Marko resembles Arthur in so far that he is the hero of a wide cycle of legend; but in no one of them does he occupy the position of a Roi; and the character of Arthur as chief of a circle of paladins, as champion of a falling cause, as perfect knight and Christian king, is realised, not in Marko, but in Lāzar, the last of the Serbian czars. Indeed, with one exception, the ballads about Marko belong to a phase later in date, lower and feebler in tone, than the highest strains of Serbian minstrelsy; and these lower-pitched songs group themselves around the Kralïevitch, just because he in his own person is typical of a lower period, because his class of achievements began when that of the heroes of the czardom was closed.

These legends convey to us the only extant picture of manners in Serbia during that dark period after the Mussulman had succeeded in overthrowing Christian rule, yet had not thoroughly substituted his own. At this time the policy of the Sultans exhibited, what some persons are pleased to term, an unprecedented regard for the feelings and rights of the vanquished; in other words, these rights and feelings were regarded until the conquerer had established himself in the country and could tread the vanquished down. Until in one way or another every noted Christian could be got rid of, it was necessary to begin by soothing and flattering such prominent aristocrats as would agree to do the Sultan homage; and during this interval the said aristocrats found themselves following the Grand Turk in his Asiatic campaigns and serving him against the Latin abroad, while yet at home they attempted to protect their countrymen from the lawlessness of Moslem spoilers.

Of these Slavonic nobles, in their eminently false and eventually untenable position, Marko Kralïevitch furnishes us the type. It is because of this his typical character that there is interest in examining into the functions and qualities attributed to the King's Son by popular song, for thus we may form some idea how the Serbian people looked on the leaders left to them during the first three centuries that followed the Moslem invasion. Over this whole transition period Marko's life is supposed to extend. He lives 300 years, and during this long career his character undergoes all the phases of a gradual degradation, such as undoubtedly showed themselves in the class he personifies, as it passed from its prime to its fall.

Marko begins life as one among the chosen circle of youths educated by the Serbian Czar Dushan to be the future ruling class in that empire which he hoped to leave more extended and more civilised. In spite of his high birth and warlike tastes, the Kralïevitch is studious and turns his studies to account. An archpriest instructs him in writing, and in reading books both clerical and lay; during the Czar's last campaign young Marko appears as his secretary and as the depositary of his testament.

Such Marko's spring-time; but the premature death of his master leaves his half-tame spirit to run wild in the mazes of the troubled times. He is well-intentioned, kindly, and dauntless, but devoid of settled purpose; he lacks the moral strength that can steadily sacrifice small aims to great ones, and subordinate egotism to an ideal: he is too haughty to yield place to an equal, and ends by falling under his inferiors. Marko becomes a Turkish vassal.

This is the first step downward; but for some time its pernicious consequences appear not in their full extent. Marko is still a champion to whom the Christian looks for protection, and whom the Mussulman flatters and fears: songs tell of his exploits in camp, castle, and court. A change for the worse comes on slowly, but surely. The King's Son is insulted by the Turks, and though he takes signal vengeance on the individual, his equal comradeship with them is at an end. He retires more and more from political scenes; his achievements become those of a slayer of monsters, or mere feats of strength, such as excite the wonder of the hunter and the hind. They grow, too, ever more mythical in character, till at length, merging into the lingering myths of heathenism, local legends of Marko can hardly be distinguished from those properly belonging to the ancient wood-gods.

Deeper and deeper Marko sinks into the forest, till his bond-sister, the Vila, or mountain-nymph, tells him he must die. The last we see of him—once knight in a Christian court, and long the pride of the Padishah's armies—is lying outstretched on his mantle, close to a mountain spring, his cap drawn over his eyes, dying like a worn-out haïduk—robber-outlaw. Yes, a haïduk; 300 years after Serbia's warrior nobles consented to do homage to the Mussulman the last trace of independent Serbians seemed to die out in the mountain forests as haïduks.

Marko leaves neither monument nor successor. The class to which he belonged sank into unknown, unhonoured graves; the Turk they had helped to establish in Europe suffered no Christian to continue in the position held by Serbian nobles; the Slavonic race in the empire of the Sultan came to be represented only by rayahs or by renegades.

Such is the story of Marko; nor less significant than the incidents of his career are the virtues and vices assigned to him by the popular song. This Serbian King's Son is never represented as an oppressor of the lower classes; on the contrary, we find in him the people's champion, defending them against outrages perpetrated by the Turk. Again, we find Marko sung by the peasants as manfully drubbing every Turk with whom he comes into antagonism; nor dares the Grand Seignor himself contradict him, even when he slays a vizier. "Of any Turk," so says the Sultan, "I could make another vizier; but where could I find another Marko?" Moreover, at least in his earlier days, Marko "fears naught save God and the truth," and judges righteously even to his own hindrance. Dutiful he shows himself to both parents—to a worthless father and to a mother noble as a Roman or Spartan, or, better said, as a *Christian* matron. Finally, Marko is hospitable and bountiful; he is the friend of the unfortunate, of little children, of dumb animals; and he is true to his creed; for, although a vassal of the Sultan, he never forsakes the Orthodox faith.*

Doubtless the picture has its shady shade. Marko is rough in manners, and a hard drinker; nay, he bursts into passion so sudden and violent as almost to equal the Scandinavian Berserk.† Though a true friend, he is relentless to those who affront him, even to women; and his outrageous treatment of one lady who mingled the refusal of his hand with a jibe, must be set off

* In Bosnia a blind minstrel was one day heard reciting a poem about Marko to a street audience of Orthodox, Latins, and Mussulmans, all equally interested in the Slavonic champion. The minstrel being himself a Latin, chose to represent his hero as belonging to the Western Church, when instantly one of the Mahommedans present interrupted him with a blow, exclaiming, "How darest thou make out Marko a Latin, when during 400 years we have never been able to make him out a Mussulman?"

† In one song a Serbian noble is represented as cautioning his attendants not to press too obsequiously to welcome Marko, not to kiss his mantle, or try to relieve him of his sabre, lest Marko, being in an ill-humour or excited with wine, should push his horse past them and ride them down. This instance has been cited to prove how mercilessly Serbian nobles must have treated their attendants. Surely it rather indicates the reverse. The noble in question would scarcely have thought it necessary to warn his servants against incurring treatment to which they were accustomed from his own hands or those of most of his guests. No doubt the times were rough enough; but Marko's violence is always instanced as exceptional. The very word for "oppression" used in the Serbian songs is a Turkish word.

against his disinterested championship of numerous damsels in need.

Other peculiarities of temperament are curiously characteristic of the still primitive race to which he belonged. For instance, although he asks more than one lady in marriage, and saves more than one lady from offence, the rough Serbian hero is never represented as performing his exploits under the influence of *la belle passion*. On the other hand, of all those questionable gallantries, deemed so excusable by Romance minstrels, Marko is guiltless by look, act, or word.

Another strongly marked trait is his rooted antipathy to the Osmanli, an antipathy perpetuated to this day among those renegade Serbian nobles — the Bosniac Mussulmans. Bitterly hating the Asiatic, Marko absolutely loathes the African. Taken captive by a Moorish king, he represents as worse than all the weariness of his prison the love-making of the Moorish princess. When at last the promise of freedom bribes him to flee with her, he only bears with her till she attempts to embrace him with her black arms, and then in a frenzy of disgust draws his sabre and strikes off her head. The graceless deed is humbly repented of; churches and monasteries are raised to atone for it; but still, when Marko confesses it to his mother, he half excuses himself by describing his sensations: "Oh, mother! when I saw her close to me, all black, and her white teeth shining!"

More excusable and more dignified is the last evidence of hatred to the Mussulmans given when Marko's deathhour is come. He shivers his lance that the Turk may not use it; he slays his horse that the Turk may not force it to carry wood and water in its old age; he breaks his sword into four pieces that it may not be used by the Mahommedan, and Christendom curse him as one who has put a weapon into the enemy's hand; he even desires that his grave may be concealed, lest the Turk should rejoice over his fall. Nay, the Serbian peasant believes that Marko's thorough detestation of the Mussulman, whom he himself detests so thoroughly, will yet find a more practical expression. "When the times shall be fulfilled the Kralïevitch will arise out of the cave where he is sleeping, and valorously lead the Serbians to drive the intruder from their fatherland."

So much for Marko's typical character; and long it was commonly supposed that he had no existence in any other. But some years ago a diligent numismatic collector brought to the Museum of Belgrade some coins found in Northern Macedonia, with the superscription "Marko Krāl." To no other person in Serbian history could this name possibly belong, so inquiries were set on foot, old records consulted, and the discovery made that Marko Kralïevitch actually reigned at Prilip, and had had an historical career.

He was found to be really, as tradition had reported, the son of the historic Kral Vukashine, one of the governors appointed by Czar Dūshan. Vukashine's territory extended from Macedonia to the Adriatic, and thus had for its two principal fortresses, on the west Scādār, on the east Prilip. At the sudden death of Dūshan, the regency of the empire and the care of his young son passed to the Kral, as to the second person in the realm; and he, to retain the power in his own hands, treacherously murdered his ward.

Marko took no part in this crime, nor did he even share the fruit of it, separating himself from his father and continuing faithful to the old royal line. But when both the young prince and the wicked Kral were dead, and the Serbian people met to choose a new czar, Marko considered himself a candidate whose claims ought to distance every other, and he could not forgive the election in his stead of Lāzar Greblíanovitch, Count of Sirmium. It would seem that in his disappointment he gave way to a burst of menace; for Lāzar, usually so mild, called on the assembled nobles to support him in reducing Marko, and finally deprived him of his fief. Landless and exasperate, Marko sought the camp of the Turks and offered his sword to the Sultan,—apparently for those campaigns in Asia wherein, Mahommedan warring against Mahommedan, adventurers from Christendom cared not on which side they fought, so that they earned booty and renown.

It is said that the Sultan at one time gave Marko the nominal investiture of " Castoria and the Argolide " (?) but afterwards, when Amurath marched on Serbia, the heir of Vukashine resumed possession of his own Castle of Prilip. Hence, whereas the Serbians know Marko only as Kralïevitch, or King's Son, the Bulgarians of Prilip call him " Marko Krāl."

That Marko fought for the Turkish Sultan in many a campaign is doubtless, but that he ever marched against his native country remains at least wholly uncertain. Indeed it appears impossible that he should have been in the habit of serving against any people of his own communion, when we read of his consternation at being summoned to fight the Orthodox Prince of the Roumans. Loyal to his suzerain, Marko Kralïevitch came into the field; but when he saw men of his own faith arrayed in battle against Mahommedans, and himself on the Infidels' side, horror took possession of his soul. "Oh, God!" cried he, "do thou this day destroy all those who fight against Christendom, and foremost Marko." Then, throwing himself upon the spears of the Christians, or, as some say, plunging into a morass, he met the doom he felt he had deserved.

Of this repentant death, the feeling, if not the facts, has been truthfully preserved in popular poetry. Taken in conjunction with Marko's life-long antipathy to the Turks, his proud bearing towards them, and his championship of the oppressed among his own countrymen —all these extenuating circumstances have contributed, in the eyes of the Serbian peasantry, to throw a veil over the one stain on the shield of their favourite hero, namely, that he served the Sultan. They cannot deny it, they would not palliate it, but they regard it less as a crime than as a calamity; indeed they set it down to the effect of a curse hurled against the Kralïevitch by his own father, when by one of his righteous judgments he prevented him from becoming Czar.

Unfortunately modern literati, emulous of the *naseweis* school of modern Germany, have showed themselves determined not to let the errors of the "peasants' hero" lie thus reverently enveloped in mist. On the stage of the little theatre of Belgrade, an author ventured to exhibit Marko Kralïevitch, not in his traditional character—rescuing the oppressed, and performing marvellous exploits—but in a situation wherein tradition and history have alike forborne to exhibit him: arrayed on the side of the Turks in a battle between them and the Serbs.

The announcement of an historical piece had, as usual, drawn to the little playhouse numerous spectators of the poorer class, and the entrance of each traditional hero was welcomed with delight. But when Marko, the well-beloved Marko, presented himself in so odious a character, a sudden chill fell on the audience: to enthusiasm succeeded (not even the expected hoots and hisses, but) a gloomy, restless silence; the silence of those who are at once puzzled and pained.

It appeared however as if, to the end of the scene,

the people hoped that Marko would do something to atone for his false position; but at last he quitted the stage without a redeeming act or word. Then one simple heart could bear it no longer; and bursting out, almost with a sob, a peasant's voice cried, "Marko is *not* a traitor."

CHAPTER X.

THE BULGARIAN TOWNS OF PRILIP AND VÉLESA.

THE distance from Monastir to Prilip is estimated at about six hours, and six very long hours it took us to jog over the rough and dusty plain that separates the two towns.

On the outskirts of Monastir we passed a church lately built by the Bulgarians for themselves, but in which, as we have since heard, the bishop insists on performing service in Greek. However, half-way between Monastir and Prilip one crosses the stream of the Tzerna Rïeka (Black River), and at every step on the other side the Greco-Tzintzar element becomes weaker, and the Bulgarians have got more and more the upper hand, both in church and school.

The spurs of the Babuna range, surmounted by the ruin of Marko Krāl's Castle, become visible some distance from Prilip, and a prospect of getting to hills and a river makes one quite impatient to arrive at the journey's end.

Prilip is a town of from 6,000 to 7,000 inhabitants, and forms the seat of a large yearly fair: hence it is one of the most prosperous places in southern Bulgaria, and boasts a very tolerable bazaar. On occasion of this fair the peasantry from the neighbourhood crowd hither, and are said to be well worth seeing. In one district the women are remarkably tall and stout, strong, thrifty, and industrious. It seems they are not allowed to marry until the age of thirty years, and that for two reasons: first, in order that their parents, who had the labour of bringing them up, may be rewarded for their services; and secondly, that they themselves may not be encumbered early in life with large families. A similar practice prevails in some of the country districts in Serbia, men marrying young, and choosing housewives in the full *force de l'âge*. This arrangement struck us as somewhat queer, and as unlikely to be agreeable to the woman, being conceived on the principle of getting the greatest possible amount of work out of her; but the men justify it by its results, and say that domestic comfort, social morality, and fine physical development prevail in the districts where it is followed. In the towns, both of Serbia and Bulgaria, the women follow the Oriental fashion of marrying and fading extremely young.

A letter from the British consul at Monastir procured us hospitable entertainment at the house of a rich Bulgarian merchant, where two rooms were given up to our use. The inner chamber was large, well stocked with cushions and carpets, and so cleanly that, although we prepared our beds on the divan instead of on our iron bedsteads, no disturbance of rest ensued. The merchant and his family trade in tobacco, which grows in abundance on the Prilip plain, and one of the brothers conducts the business of the house with Vienna. Unluckily he was from home, but his Viennese proclivities were represented by a musical clock, which strikes up tunes every quarter of an hour. We had been warned that we should find this article in our bedrooms, and that its performances would be fatal to sleep; but it seems our good-natured hosts had found out that it disturbed their former visitors, for just as we were vainly composing ourselves to rest, a daughter of the house demanded entrance, clambered up on the divan, and stopped the clock.

The civilised importer of the musical timepiece, and the grave and portly master of the house, are both members of a family of five brothers, who with their wives and children eat at one table and live in houses opening on one court, within the protection of one high wall. These family associations, or zadroogas, are general throughout Bulgaria, and have certainly tended to sustain the Christians under the lawless régime of the Turk. Besides securing to every household the presence of a number of men to protect the women from intruders, they ensure widows and orphans a maintenance and security in the bosom of their own kindred. Where land is to be cultivated, they enable a family to do its own work without hiring strangers, and they provide a sphere for younger sons without sending them out to service. Thus, too, family intercourse is kept free from the dread of spies; old ties, old memories and customs can be fostered, and foreign innovations can be withstood. Above all, natural affections find their due satisfaction; young women are preserved from temptation and young men are certain of a comfortable and well-regulated home. The Bulgarians may thank their united family life if they have preserved at once their nationality and their purity of manners while living under the yoke of strangers, and often side by side with people the most depraved.

Of course, however, the use of these family societies being mainly to defend and conserve, they become unnecessary when danger is past; neither can they co-exist with the movable relations and individual enterprise of modern society.

There are three Christian schools in Prilip, one for

the Tzintzar merchants who choose their children to learn Greek, the other two for the Bulgarians, who bring together 400 scholars, and manage them their own way. The Bulgarian books come from various places—Philippopolis, Pesth, Vienna, Belgrade; some are translated from the Serb reading-books, some from those of the Americans. The principal schoolmaster was a Serbian, and told us the children could read his language as well as their own. They showed us very fair writing, and seemed to know their way on the map. We asked if they could sing, and were at first told "No;" but presently a big boy was produced who was being trained as a priest, and he began to intone a psalm. We soon regretted having provoked his performance, for it proved at once dismal and monotonous, and was strongly sounded through the nose.

Not observing the usual picture of Cyril and Methodios we asked after it, and in the course of some incidental explanation we found that the children were well acquainted with the history of the national apostles. Nor did they omit to apply its teaching, for they coupled with the memory of the translators of the Slavonic Bible the name of a patriotic citizen of Prilip, who had been principally active in founding their own school.

Prilip was one of the places where some years ago the Greek clergy held their burning of Slavonic works; believing therefore that a present of books would be acceptable, we gave some to our hosts, to the schoolmaster, and to the best scholars. There was great anxiety for histories of Serbia, and scarcely were we returned to our quarters when a Bulgarian pope called on us, and requested that we should give a book also to him. We begged his acceptance of a New Testament, and seeing that it was in the common language of the people, he forthwith began reading it aloud. Another student in a humble line of literature was found in the little nephew of our host, who opened one of our spelling-books and began to read from thence an edifying description of the "Domestic Cat." The little girls collected eagerly to hear him, so we took the book and gave it to one of them, telling the boy that he would obtain access to it by offering to read it to his sisters. When the mother heard this she called to the other women, and they all blessed us heartily for letting the men know that women too should learn from books. The housefathers, thus challenged, declared that they did wish for a female school, and had room and money for it, but how to obtain a teacher they could not tell.

Conversation over the books induced a certain degree of cordiality; but as our letter of recommendation to our entertainers was not from one of their own people, they showed us little confidence, and eluded questions as to the state of the country. Having heard all we wanted from other sources, this was of less importance; but unluckily we found them equally unwilling to tell us any stories of Marko Kralïevitch, though Prilip, being his own patrimony, is said to produce a plentiful crop. Afterwards we obtained a book of popular poems, and therein found some Bulgarian tales respecting the famous Krāl, but they proved very inferior to the Serbian legends—long-winded, trivial, and full of Turkish words. As a grotesque specimen of a quasi-religious story, we will here give a Bulgarian song, which so far as we know has not hitherto been translated. It is called—

The Grudging Old Woman.

When St. Peter received his summons to enter into the Paradise of God, his old mother followed at his heels —a wicked mother, a sinful soul. And she called after him, "Stop, my son; wait for me, that I may enter with thee; for I also would see Paradise." Then St. Peter turned him about, and answered: "Begone, thou sinful mother; it is not so easy to enter Paradise; the gates of Paradise are closed, but open stand the gates of Hell. Hast thou forgotten thy conduct while we both were yet in the world? Thou wert rich; yes, my mother, a rich woman, with much substance, and flocks and herds more than enough [*lit.* over thy head]. But the mighty devil had power over thee, and kept thee from giving anything for God's sake to the poor. One day two beggars came to thee; they came to thee, and played before thee—from morning till evening did they play before thee; and yet, mother, thy heart did not melt to them, thou didst not take pity upon them. Thou didst bring forth a crust of bread, grown stale by three weeks' keeping; thou didst bring forth a flaxen girdle, and this thou gavest them as alms; and even as thou gavest it thou didst turn away, and cry out crossly, 'Ah, God! golden God! hast thou given me flocks and herds that my substance be eaten by strangers and foreigners, by the German and the dumb Turk?* What is left for my own children?' Alas, mother! sinful soul! those beggars were not beggars; they were two of God's angels: one of them was St. Elias and the other St. Nicholas.

"Of another sin I will convince thee. Thou didst accept the office of godmother—of godmother to little children—and thou frequentedst the christening feasts; but thou wentest to the christening for the eating and the drinking: to the children thou gavest no gift; not

---

* "Dumb" is an epithet applied by Slavonic peoples to all who do not speak their language; more particularly to the German, whom they call by no other name than *nemac*, the dumb. The word *Slav* is probably derived from *slovo*, word, and signifies those who can understand each other's speech.

a shirt, nor baby-linen, nor stockings, nor a little cap. Naked, barefooted, these children are standing to accuse thee before the Lord. How wilt thou answer to the Lord?

"Yet again I will convince thee. Thou, mother, wert a landlady, and thou didst pour out the glowing wine. Travellers came to thee, poor travellers, and asked of thee, 'How dost thou sell?' And, mother, thou didst swear to them, 'May God or the devil receive my soul, as I give full measure for full payment.' Then what didst thou pour out to them but one hundred drachms of wine mixed with three hundred of pure water? Oh mother! sinful soul! full payment thou tookest, short measure thou gavest. Wait, mother, while I condemn thee. The mighty devil had power over thee, and from thy poor neighbour thou didst borrow flour; pure flour didst thou borrow, and didst render again half flour, half ash-dust."

And now St. Peter and his mother came nigh to the Paradise of God; St. Peter walking first, after him the sinful soul. They had to pass the Bridge of Thread,* and over it the saint passed safely; but when the sinful soul would follow him, and had got to the middle of the bridge, in the midst it broke under her, and she sank down to the lowest Hell.

St. Peter became chief of the archangels, and prayed constantly to the Lord. Three years he begged and prayed—three years and three days: "Alas, Lord! golden God! grant me a pardon for my mother, for my mother's sinful soul!"

But he was answered: "Don't ask for that, St. Peter; thou mayst not beg pardon for thy mother; thy mother has many sins on her soul."

---

* Evidently an idea borrowed from the Mahommedans; as we have said, the legend is full of Turkish words.

Still St. Peter prayed on for three years and three days; and at the end of three years and three days the Lord said to him: "Cease now, St. Peter, for thou hast obtained pardon for thy mother's soul. Get thee to the sea-shore, and twist thee a slender rope, and lower it to the bottom of Hell. There may thy mother catch it, and be hauled up to the light of day. But, besides thy mother, there are seventy other souls; let them take hold of her skirts and her sleeves, that they too may be drawn out of Hell."

Off went St. Peter—off went he hastily to the sea-shore; and he tore off half his skirt, and he tore off his flaxen girdle, and of these he twisted a long slender rope, and lowered it to the pit of Hell. Alas! the little rope proved too short! But St. Peter wore a red feather; this too he tore off, and added it to the length of the rope.

And now St. Peter cried aloud: "Catch hold, sinful old mother! I have obtained a pardon for thy soul. And you seventy other souls, do you hear? You are to lay hold of my mother's skirt—of her skirt and of her sleeves—and you too shall be drawn up into the light of day."

But behold the old woman was *grudging*, even as she had been while yet in the white world. She called out to the seventy other souls: "Begone, you dogs! begone, you swine! what right have you to be saved with St. Peter's mother? I myself suckled St. Peter: I sang the lullaby of St. Peter: ye did not suckle him; ye did not sing his lullaby."

The Lord heard the old woman's words; suddenly the rope brake, and down she fell to the lowest pit. Alas, mother! sinful soul! thy place in Hell has been fully earned.

* * * * * *

From Prilip to Vélesa is a journey of eleven to twelve hours, too far for one day without travelling through the heat; we therefore started from the former place after dinner, and resolved to sleep in the Vezir khan, at the foot of the Babūna Pass.

The entrance to this pass begins about two hours from Prilip, but we had been led to believe the distance shorter; and had been warned that after entering the hills we must not attempt to sit in the carriage. We therefore concluded that it was not worth while to get into the carriage at all, and started on horseback at once; but we found, to our cost, that this was a mistake. Crossing the plain the heat was perfectly sickening; and when succeeded by the chill of the ravine produced sensations which caused us to anticipate a revival of all the horrors of Gornischevo. We were yet to continue for a few days the disagreeable part of our journey, so called in contradistinction to the agreeable part which followed. Certainly it is a difficult thing to know at what time of year to travel in Bulgaria. In winter the cold in the plains is terrible, in summer the heat; in spring, roads are all but impassable, while the mountain regions are exposed to the swelling of streams; finally, autumn is the unhealthy season, when most places become almost uninhabitable from fever.

Leaving Prilip by the road to Vélesa, one has on the left the Prilipska Rïeka, Marko Krāl's castle, and the range of Babūna hills. Here and there we perceived some small ruins, but heard that they are not old, only kulas, which, till lately, were tenanted by the haïduks. Instead of the haïduks, their next of kin, the zaptiés now hold a kula on the highest point of the pass; here one pauses to rest after scrambling up the vile Turkish road on one side of the ravine, and before scrambling down the vile Turkish road on the other.

The descent is certainly all but dangerous. Our poor beasts slipped most distressingly, and crossed and re-crossed in search of footing, that is to say in search of some spot of earth which the Turks have not attempted to pave. The attention necessary to get safely to the bottom was the more grudgingly bestowed on our part, because, after the bare ugliness of the Macedonian side of the Babūna, we wanted thoroughly to enjoy the wooded valley on which we had come among these recesses of the hills. Truly picturesque are the peaked summits of its steep green sides, whereon the little village of Czenitza lies in the midst of a patch of golden field.

Our mid-day halt on the morrow was at the Khan of Vranofzé, where we obtained access to a cool dark corner set apart for the drying of curd. There we found a victim to Bulgarian notions of hospitality, *i.e.*, a relative of the family in whose house we were to lodge at Vélesa, who had ridden out thus far in the scorching heat to meet us. It was cooler when we resumed our road, but a particularly rough bit of ground occurring shortly before we arrived at Vélesa the carriage lurched violently, and one of the horses sprained its foot. Nevertheless, when we begged to be set down at our quarters by the back door, which was easy of access, our remonstrances were disregarded, and we were mercilessly dragged up a steep street to the front. Thus ended for the second time (the first happened in the course of a journey between Constantinople and Belgrade) our attempt to traverse the interior of Turkey in a coach. The luckless harems, that cannot help themselves, may possibly be transported part of the way in talikas; and Consul Hahn, being resolved to make the experiment in the interest of his projected railway, succeeded in taking a light vehicle with good horses the whole distance from Belgrade to Salonica.

Vélesa lies on the banks of the Vardar, which at this distance from its mouth forms already a powerful stream, and is made use of by wood-merchants to float rafts down to the Ægean. The banks of the river are steep and high; and the town, climbing them on both sides, seems to contain a fair number of good houses. Indeed its situation affords such facilities for trade as made it even in early times a place of importance and comparative civilisation.

Vélesa is a thoroughly Bulgarian town; out of 4,000 houses only 1,000 were divided between Turks and Tzintzars, while the other 3,000 were Christian Slāvs. Under such circumstances the Bulgarians of Vélesa were able, till long after the Turkish conquest, to continue as the guardians of a certain amount of national learning. A store of valuable MSS. was said to be hidden in one of their monasteries; and for a short time it would appear that their city possessed a Bulgarian printing-press. All this adds evidence to the fact, which a nearer acquaintance with the Christians in Turkey in Europe is ever revealing to the traveller, namely, that the earliest times of Turkish oppression were not in all respects the worst, and that for the Bulgarians the cruellest trial of patience occurred within the last ninety years. Till the end of the last century the Slavonic patriarchates were not abolished; and while they remained, the conditions on which the Slavonic Christians parted with their national liberty did not appear to be altogether ignored.

The books stored at Vélesa escaped destruction during more than 400 years of subjection to the Ottoman; it was his Christian middleman, the Greek bishop, who ordered the bonfire that consumed them on the market-place; and it is said that this took place only thirty years ago. Hence, so long as the Porte continues to refuse to Bulgarian communities their native pastors, and to force on them a foreign clergy, its Slavonic subjects cannot but believe that it is even more disposed to trample on their liberties than it was in the first era of its rule.

Five or six years ago the Bulgarian movement gained strength sufficient in Vélesa to menace serious disturbances; at last, in the words of the people themselves, "The authorities saw that Bulgarians never could be made into Greeks and never would agree with Greeks, so we got some of the consuls to take our part in order to keep the country quiet. Since then we have been suffered to hold service in our own language and to set up our own schools."

The Bulgarians at Vélesa are certainly of a sturdy stock, as is shown by the following incident which has lately been communicated to us by letter. The deputy of the Greek bishop being on a tour to collect revenue, came to Vélesa, held service in the church, and began to read in Greek. The people instantly interrupted him, ordering him to read Slavonic. He replied that he did not understand it. "Then," said they, "we have some one who does;" and thereupon the service was performed in Slavonic as they desired. But besides being stubborn in the assertion of their rights, these people are really anxious for the spread of education, and to our knowledge have sent forth at least one active disciple of progress, Hadji Traïko, to whom we have already alluded as patron of the girl's school at Sophia.

Of course, such Bulgarians at Vélesa as have traffic with the south speak Greek, just as those who trade north of the Danube acquire German. The merchant in whose house we lodged spoke Greek fluently, but his wife and family did not know a word. European travellers who do not know Slavonic, or even know about it, are often deceived as to the extent to which Turkish and Greek are spoken in the interior of Turkey in Europe; inasmuch as in a Slavonic city they are frequently quartered with one of the very few citizens acquainted with either of these tongues.

The house in which we lodged at Vélesa was that of a rich merchant. It was furnished in the European style, and its master wore a phase of Frankish dress very common in Turkish towns, viz., loose white trousers, a black coat, and small red fez. He had had just converse enough with the world to rub the crust off that solid and shrewd intelligence which characterizes the Bulgarian mind, and which needs only the prospect that honest pains will be compensated to develop into as sturdy and practical a national character as any south of the cliffs of Dover. So long, however, as the Bulgarians live under an Oriental despotism they will scarcely get rid of their present defects, a sulky timidity and want of openness.

The master of the school at Vélesa is a priest, reputed among his own people for learning. We had a private letter for him, so he came to see us, and told us a good deal about the Bulgarian movement. Both he and our host declared that the state of the country was much the same as that which we have already alluded to in the neighbourhood of Prilip, Monastir, and Salonica. Christians are frequently murdered by Mahommedans, who thus pay off debts and get rid of any one whom they think in their way; highway robberies are constant. None of these vexations can be put an end to until the Turkish governors take to punishing Mussulmans with rigid and summary justice; this, however, they will not do, inasmuch as their rule depends for support on the interest which the Mussulman element has in perpetuating it.

The raising of the taxes in the new method was also bitterly complained of. When they were raised in kind, things seemed so bad that they could not be imagined worse; but now that the peasant is compelled to pay in money, while he remains without means of bringing his produce to market, the oppression is intolerably greater. As the government of the Porte must have money, taxes are now taken from Mussulmans as well as Christians, although not in the same proportion. But the Mussulmans being lazy are thus completely ruined, and those who were landed proprietors in the neighbourhood are trying to sell their tchifliks, but trying in vain. No one is willing to buy them, partly because few are rich enough, and partly because Christians, if they improved the land, would run a risk of having it taken back from them. These grievances relating to the sale of land are almost identical with those we heard of in Bosnia.

In all the principal rooms of the house at Vélesa the side that looked on the river was entirely given up to windows, and windows without shutters, while in these countries Venetian blinds are yet unknown. The glare was terrible, the heat that of a forcing-house; all day long we felt ourselves, as it were, melting in the sun. By the time of evening coolness the schools were closed, so we did not see them, and had to take the word of our informants that the Tzintzar school contains thirty to forty pupils, and the two Bulgarian schools 500 between them. There is also a curious little Bulgarian monastery, which is said to be worth seeing.

But what we could not do ourselves in ascertaining the state of education at Vélesa, was to some extent supplied by our dragoman, who opened the store of books he had received from the Missionary at Salonica, and announced that he was prepared to sell. Immediately purchasers flocked to claim them, and especially pounced upon the Old Testaments—of which the few books already translated into modern Bulgarian were bound together in volumes, costing half-a-crown a-piece. All our store was sold at Vélesa, and the priest was quite cross with us because we had not brought a larger supply. Some of the elder men slowly counted up the number of the prophetic books, and asked, somewhat suspiciously, why the *whole* Testament was not there. Our explanation appeared necessary to satisfy them that there was no intention of suppressing certain writers.

At Prilip—where the historical associations of Marco Krāl's Castle connect the town with the history of Serbia—the schoolmaster came from Serbia, and much interest was shown to possess Serbian histories. In Vélesa, where the historical associations are entirely Bulgarian, and only those of a seat of learning, the Serbian works of history and popular poetry were not asked for, and Bulgarian religious books were the thing desired. Apropos of this we may remark, that the Bulgarian's mode of cultivating his language necessarily differs from that of the Serbian. The written language now cultivated in Serbia is taken from the mouth of the shepherd and mountaineer, its root vocabulary is that of the national songs, and its pronunciation is borrowed from the minstrel warriors of Herzegovina and Montenegro. With the Bulgarians, on the contrary, the language of the common people has degenerated into a corrupt and frightful patois, full of foreign words, Greek, Turkish, and mongrel, with hurried enunciation and snarling accent. In short, if anything can excuse the Greeks for their inability to comprehend that the Bulgarian objects to part with his mother-tongue, it is the excuse suggested by one's ears on hearing Bulgarian spoken after Greek. On the other hand, the Bulgarians regard the Slavonic of Cyril and Methodios as their own ancient language, and are inclined to make use of it (as the Greeks of Athens make use of ancient Greek) for a model whereon to reform their modern tongue. Should they ever succeed in resuscitating this glorious old language, with its organ tones and rich depth of expression, they will do an unparalleled service to the whole Slavonic world, and their national life will find its expression in one of the noblest channels of human speech.

The editor of a Bulgarian newspaper aspired to make it equally readable by Serbians, Croats, and Bulgarians. Practically he succeeded, and he told us that the old Slavonic furnished him with words and forms intelligible to all southern Slāvs.

In the meantime, next to the patois of the Bulgarians, the Serbian spoken by the mongrel population of Belgrade may perhaps take rank as the least musical and dignified of all Iugo-Slāvic dialects; while the pure Serbian, wherein Montenegrīne pleaders advocate their own cases before the judgment-seat of Cetigne, is the most pleasing to the ear for its distinctness and harmony. A master in the gymnasium of Belgrade told us that among the scholars were a few from the mountains on the southern frontier, and that when they and the other boys were repeating the same lesson their intonation and style were as different as the declamation of orators and the chattering of apes.

Among the books we disposed of at Vélesa the translation of the Bulgarian Old Testament is due to the exertions of the American, Dr. Riggs; while the translation of the Bulgarian New Testament was undertaken for a Protestant society by John Neophytos, the present abbot of Rilo, a monastery in the Rhodope, about four days' journey north-east of Vélesa.* As we did not visit the convent of Vélesa itself, and we did visit the convent of Rilo, we will go back a summer and pass over a chain of mountains to describe the largest of the Bulgarian monasteries, and that wherein the national element has most successfully held its ground.

* Through Istib, Karatova, and Kustendil.

CHAPTER XI.

VISIT TO THE MONASTERY OF RILO, IN AUGUST, 1862.

THE traveller on the high road between Stamboul and Belgrade journeys for many a weary day along the sultry and feverish Thracian plain, nor until he approaches the town of Philippopolis does he espy in the west the boundary of the Rhodope, on the north the distant range of the Balkan. A day later he has gained the hills, and supposing him still to keep to the post-road he will cross the Balkan by its most westerly and most famous pass, the Kapu Derbend, or Gate of Trajan.

But we, though on the way to Belgrade, did not at this point keep to the straight line, for we wanted to visit an old Bulgarian monastery, said to lie in a gorge of the Rhodope, at the foot of its highest mountain, Rilo; so we struck into the hills, crossed the pass called Kis Derbend, between the Rhodope and the Balkan, made our first stage at the mineral waters of Bania, and our second at the little town of Samakoff.

The upland plain wherein Samakoff lies is crossed by the bridle roads from Bulgaria, Macedonia, Albania, and Thrace. Hence it forms a point of meeting, not, as might be expected, for commercial travellers, but for highwaymen escaping from one pashalik to another; for which purpose the Turkish authorities take care to allow an interval between each crime and the pursuit.

We came to Samakoff provided with a letter to one

of its wealthiest Christian inhabitants, who received us
hospitably, and conducted us to a chamber surrounded
by a broad divan. In arranging the cushions to form
our beds we lighted on a pair of loaded pistols. Of
course we covered them up again and said nothing,
but their concealment testified to what we had been told
already, *i.e.*, that although to pacify a revolt it was
nominally conceded that every Bulgarian may have the
means of defending his women from Mussulman intruders, yet while Mussulmans swagger about in belts full
of pistols, the Christian, if he have arms, must take care
that they be not seen.

Samakoff was the first place west of Constantinople
where we found Greek not even understood, but this
did not constitute the people barbarians. On the
contrary, they had two nice schools—one for boys, one
for girls; large airy edifices, built of wood, and gaily
painted, after the fashion of the country. Over the
doors was an inscription to the effect that they had
been erected by the elders of the community without a
farthing of help from any one; the emphasis being a
reflection on the late Greek bishop and existing Turkish
government. We visited these schools—examined the
work, the maps and the copy-books, heard the children
sing hymns and read, and rewarded the best scholar in
each with a copy of the Bulgarian New Testament.

Another object of interest at Samakoff is the convent
of Bulgarian nuns, which we came to visit under the
following auspices. We were scarcely settled in our
chamber before it was entered by a sweet-looking
young woman, dressed in a black mantle and a quaint
coif. To our amazement she accosted us in German.
She told us that she was an Austrian Slāv, and had
come from Vienna with her mother, who was servant to
a German physician; on her mother's death the old

doctor advised her to seek protection as a nun. She said the community at Samakoff was of the order of St. John of Rilo, and acknowledged as spiritual superior the abbot of the monastery of that name. It was formed by a number of elderly women, each of whom took a young woman to live with her, wait on her, and after death become her heir. The nuns supported themselves by their own spinning and weaving, and of their earnings have built them a church: they do not attempt outward benevolence, but on the other hand pride themselves on receiving help from none. To beg a livelihood they hold as degrading as we do ourselves. The works of merit constituting sainthood seem in their estimation to be five: diligence, obedience, abstinence from meat, wearing black garments, and making a pilgrimage to Jerusalem. This journey to Jerusalem is the event of each still life, and lends it its redeeming spice of expectation, retrospect, adventure, poetry. The nuns have not their goods in common; some are comparatively rich, others poor; some are assisted by their relatives towards defraying the expense of the expedition, others have to pay all from their savings. When the money is in hand two set out, and walk till they fall-in with one of those parties of pilgrims constantly passing to Jerusalem from Bulgaria. They cross the sea to Joppa, journey thence to the Holy City, and are received into a monastery, where they may remain a whole year, to join in all the feasts and festivals. On their return home they bring away with them a holy picture, a marvellous concoction of scarlet and gold, depicting all the Holy Places, all the holy persons, and the devil, distinguished by horns and a tail—as is not unnecessary among so many grim forms.

Primed with this information, we set out to visit the nunnery, and having hopped from one to another of the big stones which act as bridges to the muddy river-street, we entered a gate and found ourselves in a clean and dry inclosure in front of a neat little church. Behind it lay the gardens of the nuns with their little dwellings, containing two rooms—a tiny kitchen and divan-encircled parlour. Here we paid a succession of visits, first to the principal mother of the community, then to a very old and saintly mother possessed of a famous picture of Jerusalem, and beloved among the younger nuns for her endless stories of adventures by the way; finally, to the special mother of our guide, who caused her dear child to show us various little treasures and to bring out her best Sunday mantle. Then came evening service, which we attended, and in the dusk of the church the young nun whispered to us with sparkling eyes how the sisters prayed for the success of the brave Montenegrines, and that God would give all Christians a good courage and a united heart. "The great Christian Powers," said she —" is it true that they are leaving that little band to fight alone? Of the people here I say nothing, they deserve what they suffer, for they have not the hearts of men. But the Montenegrines are the soldiers of the Cross. No nation in all Christendom has battled with the Infidels as they."

We wished to have taken the nun with us next day to the monastery as an interpreter, but it was thought more discreet for her to stay at home, so we gave her at parting a Bulgarian Testament and she gave us each a rosary of plaited silk, marked here and there with large mother-of-pearl beads—a gift involving the sacrifice of some thirty piastres from the fund she was storing for her journey to the Holy Grave.

This day there had been rain, so the glorious sun of the morrow rose on an earth refreshed and green; men and horses had enjoyed a rest, and now set forth with glad spirits and bounding tread. Our shining-armed cavalcade was clattering and gay: eight well-mounted Mahommedan zaptiés—two of whom were cavasses of the pasha of Philippopolis—our dragoman, and an Ionian, deputed by the British consul to give us the benefit of one Christian sword in case we should be attacked in the mountains by the first cousins of our Mussulman guards. The Bulgarian driver of the waggon wherein we had come over the hot plain could not leave his horses even for a pilgrimage, but the boy was allowed to go, and on his nimble feet soon had the advantage of us all.

But all our enjoyment would have been marred had we ourselves been left to ride the sorry steeds furnished us by the mudir at Samakoff. Luckily a bakshish induced our guards to change with us, and we could not but laugh at the superstition current respecting horses "accustomed to carry a lady" when we felt these high-mettled animals treading proudly and gently under the unwonted side-saddle, the flowing skirt, and fluttering veil. A well-trained Turkish horse is delightful for a journey, being used to walk both for travel and parade. Hour after hour he bears you evenly, lightly, over the rough track, and when you enter the town he rears his head and marches with a procession step, representative of your dignity and his own.

But something more than fine walking became necessary when we left the plain for the pathless glen, and began to dispute with the torrents their rocky passage down the mountain side. When at length we reached the head of the pass we came to a bit of rough highland, where a halt was called, and the guard showed us the graves of a party of robbers here run to earth and killed. "Until quite lately," said he, "this was the worst glen in all the hills, but the new pasha of Sophia has lately put some robbers to death and caused their heads to be stuck on poles: that will stop it for this summer." Soon after they called our attention to the hollow sound of the earth beneath the horses' feet, and explained that it was caused "by prodigious wild boars, which lived underground and undermined all that part of the hill."

And now came a descent almost impracticable for horses, and yet so cutting to the human foot that we remained mounted far longer than was safe. The stiff stair led down to a basin, receptacle of waters from all the neighbouring mountain streams. One of the zaptiés pointed out to us a clear pebbly spot where the water escaped by an underground passage. This little tarn of the Balkan,* with its grey stones and solemn fir-trees, is one of those scenes which would repay an artist for the journey from England, only to carry it home in his portfolio. We sat down on its beach, and could have sat there till now, but the sun was sinking, and the road, ostensibly six hours, was very certain to take ten. The first sight on remounting was a view over beech forests opening on a grassy vale, at the extremity of which rose an outline of grey walls. "Here," quoth the guards, "is the boundary of the domain conceded by old sultans to the great monastery of Rilo." Scarcely had we crossed the frontier when we were met by the convent guard, dressed in white linen tunics and scarlet girdles, and commanded by a man in the garb of an Albanian, who, however, styled himself a Serb, meaning, doubtless, that he belonged to the Serbian creed. The array of armed men on horse and foot lent sound and colour to the long dark wood that followed, and once below, the passage through the narrow valley became every moment more beautiful. Exceptionally beautiful

* The Turkish name Balkan, though usually limited to the northern chain, or Hæmus, is in this part of Turkey given to all mountain ranges.

BULGARIAN MONASTERY OF RILO.

indeed, for the mountain scenery between the north of Albania and the Danube is usually rather wild than picturesque. Amphitheatres of hills, covered with wood, to which the blending of beech and oak with fir gives in the distance a bluish green; few sudden elevations, few rocky precipices—such is its character, answering exactly to its Slavonic name, "Plánina," that is to say, "forest mountain." Doubtless single scenes show extraordinary loveliness, and the gorge of Rilo is of this number. The hills terminate in horned crags of the most picturesque abruptness, of the most fantastic form. From these the wood sweeps down in masses, which break into groups and tufts on the park-like meadows which fringe the valley stream. On one side a large building lies to the right, which we took for the monastery, but which proved to be a house set apart for pilgrims, who crowd hither on certain days. To arrive at the convent itself the whole length of the valley must be traversed. The mountains draw nearer and nearer—they seem once more about to close—when, serried in their angle, rise the rugged towers and swelling domes. Outside the gate, in stately row, stand long-gowned, long-veiled, long-bearded caloyers, who gravely salute and sign to us to enter. As we pass through the portal out ring the bells—Christian bells. Who knows what it is to hear their voices in a Mussulman land? not in the city, nor in the villages of the plain, where they are forbidden, and where at any rate they would jar with a thousand conflicting sounds, but in the wild hiding of the Balkan, breaking on the stillness of convent air.

We were so thoroughly tired out by our long day's scramble, that we scarcely received more than a general sense of peace and beauty as we passed through the court and into the galleries of the monastery. They led us to a chamber painted in bright colours, and furnished with low well-carpeted divans. Here we remained, and had our supper served—as much chicken, fruit, and sweetmeat as the hungriest could wish, besides rice and clotted cream and a huge glass jar of excellent wine. We found also a little cupboard in the wall wherein a bottle of wine and sweetmeats were placed in store for private refection. But that night we wanted nothing but sleep.

Next morning we were invited to an interview with the abbot in his chamber of audience, and found him with two or three venerable monks, one of whom, with a long white beard, we had the night before mistaken for the superior. The real superior is not more than middle-aged, small and spare, with a refined intellectual countenance unusual among Bulgarians, who are generally large and ponderous men, with a wise expression rather than a clever one. But John Neophytos is no common person. His name stands on the title-page of the modern Bulgarian New Testament, and his knowledge of his own language, both ancient and modern, together with his zeal to educate and benefit his people, caused him to accept the offer of a Protestant society to undertake the translation. He has a store of the sacred books in his convent, and finding we had several with us he exhorted us to turn our journey to account by dispersing them abroad among the people. He told us that the American missionaries in Constantinople, who are translating the Scriptures, keep up a correspondence with him, and that two of them had that year been to visit him. Then were shown us the curious old documents which mark the early history of the convent. An inscription on the tower in the court states it to have existed under the mighty Czar Stephan Dūshan, who united Serbia and Bulgaria in his realm. But the earliest chrysobul is of the end of the fourteenth century, and from a personage who styles himself John Shishman, Faithful Czar and

Autocrat of all the Bulgarians and Greeks, *i.e.*, of the Greeks in Bulgaria.

The next documents are Turkish firmans, such as many of the richer monasteries were able to buy from the first Sultans. The monastery of Rilo, in virtue of its privileges, stands (like our Abbey of Westminster) under no bishop, and hence has been able to maintain its exclusively Bulgarian character. It consists of 150 monks, each of whom has a pupil, who becomes his heir. In all, the personnel of the convent amounts to 400 souls. Women are excluded, and it is even said that no one of them may dwell on convent land. This does not, however, extend to visitors, nor to the female relatives of pilgrims. The revenues of the convent depend partly on its mountain pasturage, partly on the gifts of pilgrims. Within the last century it has been benefited by the liberality of its northern co-religionists, and the monks have been allowed to gather funds for their new church by begging journeys through Russia, Serbia, Austria, &c.

The acquaintance which the superior showed with the history of his country and with the present needs of his countrymen, his services in the matter of the translation, —all struck us as strangely contradictory of a report we had heard at Constantinople, that the Greek Patriarch did not appoint native bishops to Bulgarian eparchies because there were no natives sufficiently educated. We afterwards heard that John Neophytos had been pointed out and demanded as bishop by his countrymen, but that the only effect of thus recognising his talents was for the jealous Phanariotes to banish him to this secluded abbey of the Balkan. As it is, he has a lithographic apparatus in the convent, and spoke of setting up a printing-press. Though, under the eye of jealous prelates, the light must be carefully hid under a bushel, there can be little doubt that the influence of such an abbot on the young students in the monastery of Rilo, will send them forth on their begging journeys able to sow as well as glean.

One remark of the abbot's struck us especially. We told him that the first Slavonic monastery we had ever seen was that of Cetigne in Montenegro. His brow grew dark, and after a moment's hesitation he said, "It is reported that that monastery is now given up to the Mussulmans and burnt." We asked him where he had read it? "In a transcript from the *Journal de Constantinople*." "Is that all?" cried we. "Then do not distress yourself; that journal has burnt Cetigne and killed the whole population of Montenegro already two or three times over."

"But," asked the abbot, "do you believe the great powers of Europe will sit still and allow that monastery to be burnt?" "We trust and believe not. France will do her best to save it." "France," said he, "perhaps; but England!" Feeling heartily ashamed of ourselves, we answered that the want of interest displayed by England in the Slavonic Christians arose in great part from her ignorance respecting them—that one really never heard their name.

"I have understood so," he replied. "The Americans have told me as much. It is, however, a pity that so great a country, whose children are free to travel where they please, and publish what they please, should remain in such profound ignorance of the *Christians* in a country where she is on such intimate terms with the *Turks*. For the rest," he added, changing his tone, "what have I to do with these matters? I live here as a mouse in a hole, and our Bulgarian people are quiet. Do you please to go over the monastery?"

The monastery is well worth going over, but first let us pause in its open gallery, and feast our eyes on the rich mass of wood that rises precipitately behind the towers in the court. The hill serves the convent at once for wall and screen.

The church standing in the court is new, the former one having been burnt to its foundations. The restoration took place in 1839, with money in great part gathered from alms. The building is in the form of a Greek cross, with domes, and has cloisters painted both within and without. The interior is supported on columns, and has a beautiful iconastasis of gilded wood, achieved by the Tzintzar carvers who do all that sort of work in Turkey. A Christ's head was pointed out to us as painted by a native of Samakoff who had studied at Moscow. It showed the softened Byzantine type of the modern Russian school.

Strange worshippers were in the temple—shepherds from the Balkan, talking a barbarous dialect of Latin and calling themselves "Romans," while they live as savages. These people herd flocks, and when the men are absent the women defend the huts, and like the female Albanians, are noted for their accurate shooting. Their wild mode of life was illustrated by their remarks on ourselves; for, seeing that we were foreigners and accompanied by a Turkish guard, they took it for granted that we had not come hither of our own free will, and pointing at us asked, " From what country have they been *robbed ?* "

But for such monasteries as that of Rilo these shepherds would be shut out from any form of worship, but here they assemble at certain times to confess and take the sacrament. How far these people are edified by services in a language which they understand not is perhaps an open question, but we were witnesses of the instruction which in such instances may be conveyed by sacred pictures. A fresco of the birth of Christ is painted on the wall of the church. The older of such frescoes are grisly icons, respecting which it may at least be said that those who bow down to them are *not* worshipping " the likeness of anything in heaven or earth;" but the modern pictures are more life-like, and this one was a genuine Oriental scene. One of the shepherd-pilgrims caught sight of it, and shouted out in rapture, " See, there is the birth of the Christ." The women crowded round him, and he pointed out to them the Babe, the mother, the star, the shepherds, the ox, the ass—explaining as he went on.

We afterwards attended evening service, at one part of which the monks took of their caps, and remained for some time bare-headed, their long locks flowing down their backs. The singing was good as to voices, but monotonous and nasal-intoned. It seemed to us to differ somewhat from what we had heard in Greek churches; but not to have improved as far as the Serbian psalmody, in which Western influence has counteracted the idea, apparently prevalent in the East as in Scotland, that there is something saintly in music through the nose.

The most interesting part of the Rilo monastery is the old tower containing the original church. The times wherein the latter was built reveal themselves by its position high up in the wall, which has no window or lower opening, except one overhanging the doorway through which to pour stones or boiling oil on the assailants of the gate. This is not the chapel of St. John of Rilo, who lived and died a hermit, worshipping in caves and hollow trees; it is not even the place of his interment, which lies at some distance on the hill. It is said to have been built at a very early date to defend the monastery from robbers, and was doubtless afterwards useful during the worst days of Mussulman fanaticism, when the life of a monk must have demanded a brave man. At the foot of the tower is a cell, wherein insane persons are confined, and whence they are brought into the church during service by way of being exorcised. The monk asked us if such persons were found in our country. We answered "Yes; but instead of cells we lodge them in large and airy dwellings, and instead of the priest they are brought to the doctor." "And do they recover?" "They do sometimes, but alas! not always." "Strange!" cried he; "that is just the way with ours."

The last place to be visited is the mortuary chapel, wherein we perceived numerous skulls on the altar. We were told that to have a skull placed there is a compliment to the departed, for which the relatives are willing to pay. Also that here, as in the Greek parts of Turkey, the dead are disinterred in order to judge by the state of their bodies whether their souls are in heaven or hell.

In recompense for our liberal entertainment at the convent we could get permission to leave nothing next morning save a donation, ostensibly for the church. On the other hand, we carried away some curiously carved wooden spoons, the portrait of old King Shishman, taken from a contemporary document, and a brand new history of St. John of Rilo, depicting his eccentricities, miracles, and burial.

CHAPTER XII.

THE CITY OF JUSTINIAN.

HAVING got to Vélesa, the thing was to get away again. The horse which had sprained its foot was not seriously injured, but could not be used again for some time, and the driver wanted us to wait at Vélesa while he rode back to Monastir to get another. But this was not to be thought of; so we paid him his bakshish, and gave him a letter of explanation to the consul at Monastir, while another letter of the same tenor was sent by the Turkish post.

Being rid of the coach, how were we to proceed? On horseback? But the road to Skopia passed over a broiling plain; besides, we felt too weak and ill to ride throughout a whole day. In a talika drawn by buffaloes, after the fashion of the country? But buffaloes walk three times as slow as the slowest horses, and can only journey during the few hours of cool. In this dilemma, our dragoman came to us with a suggestion from the master of the house, which, as he expounded it, sounded strange enough. "Listen," said he, "that I may explain to you how the Turks convey their women from place to place, and themselves travel when they are sick, for hereabouts no one goes in coaches. There is a little chamber, with a door and windows, made of wood, and fastened on poles; horses go between these poles, before and behind, to carry the chamber, and men walk, two on each side, to steady it. The Turks call this a taktaravān."* In other words, there was nothing for it but to travel in a litter, and, as it proved, a very rude one. Its sides were not padded, it contained no seats, and yet was not long enough to lie flat in. It was, moreover, too narrow for us to sit comfortably side by side, and in any other position one or other ran the risk of bursting open the door. The supporting poles were fastened to each side of the wooden saddles of the horses, but in the rudest fashion, with ill-tied knots which constantly slipped, so that now the equilibrium of the "piccola camera" was overthrown on one side and now on the other. The few men who attended on the litter paid very little attention to its balance; and but for our cavass, whose love of fault-finding and ordering about him stood us on this occasion in good stead, we should have been upset many times. The heat of the sun, beating on a low, dark lid, we avoided by nailing some sheets over the roof so as to form a white drapery. Of course it is vain to attempt to see country traversed in such a fashion, so the landscape through which we passed between Vélesa and Skopia may remain undescribed.

Our mid-day halt was in the Kaplan khan, and while there we became sensible that the weather was undergoing a change: the kiradgees predicted that on the morrow there would be a thunderstorm. We started again in the taktaravān, but ordered our horses to be saddled and led by its side. Soon, the heat abating and the day drawing near to its close, we began to fear being late in Skopia, and lost all patience with the slow motion of the litter. We got out, and found ourselves on a desert-looking plain bounded by low hills; over-

* We spell this as the pronunciation—possibly the mispronunciation—struck our ears.

head a grey sky lit up with a lurid sunset; the castle of Skopia in the distance. A sense of unwonted coolness was scarcely more refreshing than that of freedom to our cramped limbs. Usually we were very sparing of our horses, fearful of knocking them up by fast travelling, but the neighbourhood of their night's quarters and the comparatively easy ground now gave us an excuse for the gallop wherein we longed to indulge; so off we set, and arrived at the end of that day's journey in better spirits and far less wearied than we had felt or fancied ourselves when starting from Vélesa.

From the little window of the taktaravān we had looked out for the village of Taor, identified by Hahn with Tauresium, birthplace of the Emperor Justinian. After we arrived at Skopia, and were comfortably ensconced in the clean house of a Tzintzar merchant, we got out our books, and read up all such lore as we could find regarding the emperor and his cradle. The Goths, who from beginning to end have stood godfathers to so many Slavonic achievements and personages, were long set down as the country folk of Justinian, and his native name was derived from a Gothic word. Luckily, philology has lent its aid to the refutation of this error. "Upravda" is no longer forced into "aufrichtig," but allowed to be the genuine Slavonic equivalent of Justinian. Even the name of the emperor's father, Istok, is now assigned to its real origin. It is a curious coincidence that the famous Byzantine emperor of Slavonic extraction should also be the emperor famous for compiling a code of laws, for in the early history of every Slavonic people the kingly lawgiver is a person of higher repute even than the war-leader or conqueror. Whether it be the Bohemian Krok, Queen Libussa, the Polish Cracus, the Slovakian Svatoplūk, the Serbian Dūshan, or, nearer our own day, Peter the Great of

Russia, and St. Peter the bishop-chief of Montenegro; the warlike character is the subordinate, while that of the remodeller, the legislator, is the aspect under which the Slavonic hero is most admired.*

Justinian showed his regard for his native village by causing it to be defended by a square wall and four towers—a style of fortification termed a "tetrapyrgon;" he also built or restored towns and villages throughout the district, and especially the chief city Skopia. To it, when rebuilt and beautified, he gave the name Justinianea Prima, and made it the seat of the archbishop of Illyria. So it remained until Samuel, king of Bulgaria, established his residence at Ochrida, and removed the archiepiscopal seat thither, when it would appear that the name of Justinianea Prima, being identified with the see, was transferred from Skopia to the new capital. Procopius says that it would be hard to describe the churches, the magnificent houses, the pillared halls, the market-places, and fountains, wherewith Skopia was adorned in its Justinianea Prima days; it was also well supplied with water by an aqueduct; and altogether its prosperity was so firmly established that it long continued one of the finest and most opulent cities in that part of the world. Under the Serbian czardom it flourished, under the name of Skoplïe, as a free city with a great yearly fair, and specimens of its coins may be seen in the museum of Belgrade. In 1347 Skoplïe became the scene of that great Serbian *sabor*, or parliament, wherein Stephan Dūshan was proclaimed by the title of Czar, and promulgated the code that bears his name.

---

* As regards the present prince of Montenegro, Mr. Stillman gives the following testimony: "I have myself heard Turkish functionaries in Albania praise his justice and trustworthiness in terms which recalled Haroun-al-Raschid, while in any dispute in which Turk and Christian are engaged near the frontier, and in which the Turk believes he is in the right, the disputants go to a Montenegrin judge in preference to a Turkish one."—*Herzegovina*. W. J. STILLMAN. Longmans. 1877.

Here, too, the metropolitan of Serbia was raised to the rank of independent patriarch.

As the last czar of Serbia made his stand against the Turks on the field of Kóssovo, north of Skopia, this town was one of the first prizes of the conquerors'; nay, some traditions say that it became peaceably subject to them as part of the inheritance of Marko Kralïevitch. In the very year of the battle of Kóssovo certain it is that Sultan Bajazet sent Turkish colonists to Skopia, so that it must have fallen directly under Turkish rule long before other parts of the Serbian realm. The withering influence told on it surely, but at first slowly; the early colonists built handsome mosques; in 1686 a traveller describes it as still a flourishing city; and even in the last century Ragusan and Venetian merchants frequented it, and have left their names written on the pillars of the principal khan. But now Ragusa is no longer free, and Skopia is a decaying and wretched place, its inhabitants sickening under the unhealthy exhalations of undrained marshes. A still more melancholy fate has overtaken Novo Berdo, a town two days' journey north of Skopia, whose coins we also saw in Belgrade. In Serbian days, Novo Berdo was celebrated for its rich silver mines, and was called the Mother of Cities; Major Zach, who visited it in 1858, found only sixteen houses, of which one was Christian, and fifteen Mahommedan. The Mussulmans, who are descended from Asiatic colonists, say that the city used to contain 6,000 houses; this, however, is only half the number insisted on by the Christians. One source of decay is to be traced in the neighbourhood of a certain castle, now a ruin, but till lately the residence of an hereditary governor. Such governors were lawless Albanian chieftains, who, during the disorders of Turkish rule, exchanged their hills for the pillage of flourishing Serbian cities, and finally themselves perished in revolts against the Sultan's government.

At Skopia we found our quarters prepared for us in the house of a Tzintzar merchant, who lived in the most agreeable part of the town, *i.e.*, on the banks of the river Vardar. Our host was a grumbling old man, who astonished our servants by the extreme parsimony which, in spite of considerable riches, he practised in his own diet. The day we left, a younger man and a pretty-looking young woman in rich costume entered the garden, and we heard that it was a family festival. They seemed ready enough to enter into conversation, but the presence of the cross housefather tied our tongues.

The proverbial unhealthiness of Skopia led us to fear taking the fever while we remained there; but this time the change of weather saved us, though our cavass was unwell, and wore a livid hue during the whole time of our stay. To run no risk, we had intended remaining only one day, and then to journey through the pass of Katchanik to the monastery of Gratchanitza and the town of Príshtina, on the plain of Kóssovo. But the kaimakam of Skopia sent to urge our remaining two days, since by that time he could provide us with a carriage wherein we could travel the whole way to Gratchanitza. To this arrangement we agreed, and resolved to devote our second evening to a visit to the castle.

The citadel of Skopia stands on a low platform of rocks, which must have been fortified from a remote period. We were told that, properly speaking, we ought not to have been suffered to pass within the castle gate on horseback, but that we had been permitted to do so, lest, not understanding the custom, we might be offended by a request to dismount. Within the fort we found a few poor-looking Turkish artillerymen, and the whole place looked deserted and melancholy. The kaimakam used to reside in it, but his seraï (palace) was lately burnt down, so at present he lives in the town, while the blackened walls of his deserted dwelling by no means add to the trimness of the citadel.

Mounting by means of a stair in the wall to one part of the crenulated battlements, we enjoyed a singular though not a pretty view over the treeless level and low-topped hills.

On the north-east the plain of Skopia is bounded by a low chain of mountains, called by the Turks Kara Dagh, or Black Mountain, and by the Slavonians "Bulgarian Tzerna Gora." The zaptiés said that these hills were inhabited partly by Albanians and partly by Bulgarians. Northward lie the collateral ranges of the Shaar Plánina (ancient Scardus). In these are the sources of the River Vardar, which flows through the plain of Skopia. Part of the plain is planted with rice-fields, and the eastern half is occupied by a marshy lake, whose surface Hahn estimates at "an hour" in length, the same in breadth. It could easily be drained, but not being so, leaves Skopia a prey to pestilential fevers. From our position on the citadel we could trace the two highways, or rather high tracks, which traverse Skopia. That by which we were travelling leads from Macedonia to old Serbia and Bosnia; another, running from east to west, crosses a pass in the Shaar Plánina to Prizren, and unites Thrace and Northern Bulgaria with Albania and the Adriatic.

The only building of any beauty that struck our eye was a mosque with a particularly handsome minaret. The guide said it was "four hundred years old"—meaning that it was as old as a mosque hereabouts could be, for four hundred years is the term roughly assigned to Mahommedan occupation of the Slavonic lands. To say that any building is "four hundred years old," implies that it was built by the first conquerors; to say that it is "*more* than four hundred years old" is a significant mode of referring it to Christian times. "Now-a-days," added the zaptié, "they build no fine mosques, nothing but wretched little whitewashed things."

Next day our visit was to the Slavonic school, our host assuring us that the Greeks had none. In this direction, then, we had traced the Græco-Tzintzar influence to its vanishing point. Whereas at Monastir the Tzintzars have schools, and contrive to withhold them from the Bulgarians, at Prilip they have but one school, while the Bulgarians have two; at Vélesa, their one school is much smaller than those of the Slāvs, but at Skopia they have no school at all. Skopia is, indeed, the point where the Bulgarian element meets the Serbian, and in Serbian districts neither Rouman nor Greek can ever assert himself to the exclusion of the Slāv. It would appear that the historical pride and expectation of one day resuming empire, which gives the Greek so positive a power of self-assertion in face of the Bulgarian, meets its match in the historical pride and definite ambition of the Serb. The Tzintzar merchants at Skopia are its most wealthy citizens, but the Christian schoolmaster was a Serb, and in his sanctum we found pictures of the ancient Serbian kings and of the heroes who had flourished in those days when Skopia was the seat of a Serbian sabor.

There were three Slavonic schools in Skopia: two contained 60 scholars between them, and another, which was larger, held 100. The Christians had built a large church, apparently unmolested, for which liberty they were possibly indebted to the circumstance that Skopia was at one time a consular station. In districts between this and Nish there are places where the Christians, having received the Sultan's firman permitting them to build a church, have seen it twice thrown down by the neighbouring Mussulmans, and only succeeded in keeping it after the expense and labour necessary to rear it a third time. If any such story were connected with the church of Skopia we should probably have heard it; but we did not even hear complaints of the Greek bishop. At the time of our visit he was absent, and probably his substitute read the service in whatever language the people pleased.

While we were in the school at Skopia, there arrived a merchant who was anxious to see us, because, as he said, he had heard of us the year before in Bosna Seraï. He traded with that city, and told us that he had been taking thither cotton from Seres and tobacco from Prilip. He further related that his father was a Montenegrīne, banished from the mountains for breaking the laws; that he himself had made money as a travelling merchant, and settled in Skopia. Appealing to his experience of different parts of the country, we asked him whether he considered that Bosnian or Albanian Mussulmans behaved the better to the rayah. He said that the most cruel, rapacious, and lawless Mussulmans in Turkey were the Albanians at Ipek, Diakova, Prisren, Prishtina, and the Mahommedans near Prilip. The Bosnian Mussulmans are very oppressive, but after all it is "only because they are Mussulmans; they speak the same language as ourselves," whereas Albanians and Osmanlis, "not speaking our language," would be enemies, whether Mussulmans or no. We asked him if he had found the Albanians faithful to their engagements when they promised protection and peace. That he admitted. "If the fiercest Arnaout give his word of 'Bessa'—peace—to the poorest rayah, he will keep it; the Bosnians have no such talisman, and scarce think a promise to the Christian sacred."

CHAPTER XIII.

KATCHANIK.

ON the evening before we left Skopia, sounds of rumbling and crashing, as of a cart upset at the door, announced the carriage promised by the kaïmakam. We went down for an inspection, and found the horses tolerable, the driver an Arab. The vehicle was, we were assured, the best in the country, and had conveyed the harem of a rich official between Skopia and Salonica. Hence it deserves to be described. A little cart on four wheels, without springs or seats; four poles support its canopy, and from the canopy depend curtains: the curtains are cut in strips, and devoid of buttons or strings, so that they keep out neither sun nor rain, but when the wind blows they stream outward like banners or flap the faces of the inside passengers.

For the use of this family coach for two days we had been told that the due price would be at most 200 piastres; the proprietor, who accompanied it, demanded 700. We left the arrangement to be discussed, but were surprised when, after long debate, the figure did not come down. It was the old story: the proprietor was a Mahommedan, and the zaptiés had a finger in the pie. We had to send our cavass to the governor with this message: "Two days ago the kaïmakam induced us to wait here on promise of a coach. The coach has come, but the owner requires a price which every one assures us is exorbitant. We are willing to pay the usual price, *i.e.*, 200 piastres; he asks 700. What is to done?"

It was now late, so the chances were that the kaïmakam would be retired in his harem, and the subordinates refuse to attend to business. The cavass requested that he might take with him, by way of credentials, the buyourdí. But the buyourdí was with the kaïmakam already, and we had nothing left but the firman. The eyes of the cavass sparkled when we told him what it was; he seized it eagerly from our hands and made off. In about half an hour he returned in great excitement. The kaïmakam was gone home for the night, and the subordinates were enjoying *kef;* but at the sight of the firman the uzbashi had waked up at once, turned on the proprietor of the carriage like a tiger, and told him we were only too good to allow him anything for its use. He then sent us the message to give what we chose; "200 piastres was more than the tariff, but even if we did not choose to pay at all it would be made up out of the government money." It was not a little to the surprise of the driver, and, we fear, a good deal to the disappointment of our attendants, that we abode by our former bargain. Now that it was known we had a firman, the difficulty was to get along quietly or pay honestly for what we used.

Next morning we left Skopia; late, of course, but yesterday's thunder-shower had broken up the weather, so that the sun was no longer to be feared. The riding-horses were fresh, and we rode briskly forward, our coach following with streamers flying like a mediæval *carroccio*. Its intended use was to give us shelter in case of showers, but it creaked so frightfully that we fled out of hearing, and were generally too far off to get back before the rain.

A short distance outside the town we passed the ruins of Justinian's Aqueduct, and left the road for a nearer view. This aqueduct used to conduct water from a distance of about two and a half hours, supplying Skopia from a stream in the Kara Dagh: near the town there occurs a depression in the ground, which had to be traversed by the building whereof the ruins remain. There is still standing a double row of about 120 arches, all in the round style; between these larger arches come small ones, of which some are round and others pointed.

From one arch now pours a stream of water. Under the shade of another we descried a tiny garden of melons and pumpkins, and therein, seated and smoking, a white-turbaned Turk. Strange! to find thus in juxtaposition the witnesses of two conquering races: the Roman who builded, the Ottoman who destroys.

Pursuing our way, we in due time reached those hills which bound the feverish plain of Skopia. To get from thence to the green upland field of Kóssovo one must traverse the Pass of Katchanik, a long, narrow defile, through which flows the river Lepenać.

To render this pass traversable for cannon, a road has been made by the Turkish government, but not without considerable difficulty. In one place the passage is bored through a rock; in others, lack of earth on the side of the bank renders it necessary to support the path by a sort of wooden scaffolding or shelf. The sight of such a piece of workmanship in the backwoods of Turkey in Europe not a little edified the travellers Zach and Hahn, and they gave it a bountiful meed of praise; however, on nearer inspection one of them perceived that part of the wood used in construction was green. Not long after, this traveller met with the engineer under whom the road was made, and told us that he had remarked to him on the detected blemish, adding, "Your road is very well now, but in a year or two it will be thoroughly unsafe." The engineer, a European renegade in the Turkish service, shrugged his shoulders, and answered, "I know that as well as you." Five years after this conversation took place we passed over the road to Katchanik, and it *had* become thoroughly unsafe; the bridges were full of holes, the scaffolding over the ravines was nearly worn through.

The Pass of Katchanik is peopled by Albanians. Now the Albanians are great favourites of Austria, for in case of her ever getting hold of these regions she must, like the Porte, make use of these cut-throats to keep down the Bulgarians and Serbs. Accordingly, it appears that the observant and far-sighted Austrian consul Hahn gladly came to the conclusion—if indeed he was not actually told—that the work of the road of Katchanik, having been done by the inhabitants of neighbouring villages, must have been done by Arnaouts. This, if certain, would be a notable fact. Call the Albanians ruffians, robbers, what you will, see, with a little drilling, how useful they can be. But the consul's fellow-traveller was of opinion that the matter admitted of a different explanation. He said to us—

"Although Arnaouts hold the Pass of Katchanik, it is not likely that the Turkish governor, having a road to make, would seek the labourers in their glens; the adjacent plain of Skopia and other neighbouring districts are inhabited by industrious Christian Bulgarians; and here—let who will state to the contrary—it is most probable, and according to all precedent, that the workmen would chiefly be sought and found." Of course it is not for us to decide which of these opinions was correct, and possibly the truth rests between them; but in support of the latter we may quote the testimony of the Albanians themselves, of whom two, in the capacity of zaptiés, accompanied us through the defile. Indeed they seemed highly entertained at the idea of the Sultan asking Mussulmans to work when rayahs were to be had close by.

In the course of the ride these zaptiés told us some traits of their local countrymen, which, if less promising in a utilitarian point of view, were more in accordance with the nature of the Skipetār. For instance, at one point we stopped to look at the view, and our cavass told the zaptié that we thought the place beautiful. With a hard laugh he cried, "Beautiful? yes, indeed, a beautiful place for robbers!" He then explained that hereabouts a band of forty thieves had a fierce battle with a former kaïmakam of Skopia, who had been obliged to march against them in full force, and in reward for defeating them was made a pasha. Only two days ago six robbers had been captured on the very spot where we stood. At another point the zaptié bade the cavass attract our attention to a house perched near the top of a wooded hill. In front of it a space was cleared for an Indian-corn field and some haycocks, and from its position the inhabitants could survey the approaches on every side. "There," said the zaptié, "is a specimen of the houses hereabouts. They stand alone, and in strong positions, like so many kulas."* In these glens there are no villages, and more than three Albanian houses seldom stand together. We were not near enough to observe how this place was built; such Albanian kulas as we afterwards saw served for the residence of several brothers with their families, and were defensible, by shooting through loopholes, against any attack but a surprise. Presently we passed two women. "Look at them," cried the zaptié; "they are women

* *Kula*, or tower, is a Turkish name applied in those countries to all small forts or fortified houses, and even to the stations of the rural police.

worth looking at, for well do they know how to handle a gun." We asked, "Are they Mahommedans?" "Assuredly." "But they do not wear the yashmak?" "Not they, indeed; they have never worn it; and wherefore should they? they are fiercer and more unapproachable than the men." After these descriptions of the tenants of the Pass of Katchanik we no longer wondered that it is given in the Serbian songs as the scene of Marko's famous encounter with Mūssa, the bandit Arnaout.

We have already noticed that Sultan Amurath, or, as he is called hereabouts, the "Turkish Czar Murad," when leading his army to Kóssovo, is believed to have halted at Skopia, and hence an opinion has generally prevailed that he must have traversed the Pass of Katchanik. On this hypothesis, and not being personally acquainted with the ground, some Serbs of the Principality have wasted much good indignation on their own Czar Lāzar, for not having fallen on the Moslem host while entangled in the defile; others have even accused Marko Kralïevitch of traitorously holding the passage for the foe. But according to Turkish sources the Sultan went from Kustendil to Karatova, where he lay for some time encamped. From thence the army passed through the Moravitza valley, and near the village of Dolnia Chukarka a mound is shown as marking the spot where Sultan Murad's tent was pitched when he encamped on the way to Kóssovo. The only natural obstacle to the advance of the Turks by this route would be the necessity of crossing the river Morava, which they did cross, if their own records may be believed. It would have been almost impossible to transport a large army through the long and narrow Pass of Katchanik, even if uninterrupted by the Serbians, who had the Albanians on their side.*

* The famous Albanian hero, George Kastrioti, called by the Turks Scander-

We once held an interesting conversation on this subject with a Serbian officer, comparing our respective notes on the country with passages from "Hahn's Travels" and Hammer's "History of the Ottoman Empire." He was of opinion that if the Turks really followed this route, and debouched on the plain at Grachanitza, and not at Katchanik, the position wherein they were awaited by the Serbians, behind the rivers Lab and Sitnitza, admitted of explanation, and would in all probability be justified by future investigators of the question and of the ground.

A fight did take place at Katchanik, and our zaptié failed not to mention it. It occurred three centuries later than the great battle of Kóssovo, and in it the Turks drove back an outpost of the Austrian army, which at that time was encamped on the neighbouring plains. This was preparatory to the retreat of the Imperial army, which abandoned to the vengeance of the enemy those Christian inhabitants of the country whom Imperial promises had induced to join the campaign.

The scenery of Katchanik is hardly grand enough to require a particular description, but, like wooded river defiles in general, it is wild and picturesque. Near its mouth the way is closed by a singular bar of rock, reaching from the top of the bank to the brink of the stream. Hard by, the ruins of a bridge show that at one time this obstacle was avoided by crossing the river; now the road passes right through it by means of a tunnel, which an inscription at its entrance ascribes to a pasha of Skopia, 1794. On the other side of this tunnel

---

beg, was present at the battle of Kóssovo. (*See* Hahn.) He is said to have dissuaded Czar Lāzar from surprising the Turks at night, remarking, with characteristic Albanian boastfulness, that daylight was wanted in order that they might be utterly destroyed; in the darkness too many would escape. He himself survived the battle, to conduct the heroic defence of his own country.

one arrives at the best place for taking a last look at the pass, and at this point the view is striking.

As you proceed the precipitous banks abate, and the river Neredimka flowing towards you joins its stream to that of the Lepenitz. Low in the angle of their junction stands the ruined castle of Katchanik; the so-called town occupies the left bank of the Neredimka, and lies to your right as you issue from the ravine.

Outside the walls of Katchanik we found the chief citizens drawn up in a line to meet us—Albanians all, but showing by their dress that they lived on the borders of a Serb district; for the fustanella was exchanged for a simple short white tunic, and no dangling sleeves descended from the vest of crimson embroidered with gold. The chief man came into the middle of the road to welcome us, and then led the way through the town; say, rather, he sprang from point to point of the rubbish heaped where a town may have been.

On one hand lay the ruins of a large building; they said it was once a seraï (palace); the houses looked as if they could not stand a day longer, the streets were deserted, the shop-boards all but bare of goods, and tenanted instead by solitary and often sleeping forms. Much as we had seen of Turkish villages, still Katchanik was something startling; here, too, appeared that worst of all signs, namely, that the place was not only in a bad state, but in a state that grows worse every day. Some explanation was wanted, but it was not wanting long; in reply to our first question as to the population, we heard that the town consisted of seventy Mahòmmedan houses, "not one rayah among them all!"

Having traversed the street, we halted before a gate, and the Albanian shouted his order that it should be set open; then, taking our horses by the bridle, he pulled them into a large court, with dwellings at the further end, and stopped before a very low house. Here we dismounted, and were conducted through the kitchen into a room where we took our places on the divan and were served with coffee. The Arnaout, standing before us, and speaking in Albanian, desired our cavass to tell us that this was his house, and this the room where, in passing through Katchanik, all pashas, Begs, and consuls, invariably spent the night. Further, we were to be informed that he himself was a great Beg, and that under his roof we need fear no ill.

As we knew it had been debated at Skopia whether the Mussulmans at Katchanik could be induced to receive us at all, we acknowledged his hospitality in a phrase as elaborate as our knowledge of Greek would afford, and by the length of the cavass's translation into Albanian it seemed not to have lost anything in its passage. The Beg looked pleased, and again assured us that we need "fear nothing;" but as $μὴ\ φοβῆσθε$ was repeated again and again, we could not help interrupting to ask why it occurred to him that we were likely to be afraid. A longer experience of Arnaoutluk accustomed us to be told "not to fear," and moreover taught us not to take it for granted that we were sure to be safe.

So long as the master of the house was present, politeness deterred us from an examination of our apartment, but when he was gone we began to congratulate ourselves on its being so much better than the dilapidated outside led us to expect. Though extremely low, it was not small, and its windows had panes, of which some were filled with glass. The rest were covered with paper, and the excessive stuffiness of the atmosphere, added to the discovery that the windows would not open, at last reduced us to make an incision in one of these paper panes. All rooms in Turkey have a certain family resemblance, which renders a description unnecessary to those who have seen any of them; but, as the coldness of the climate in the northern provinces occasions some divergence from the best known models, we will herewith describe our Arnaout room at Katchanik, even at the risk of telling some people what they already know. The ceiling was carved, and both it and the plaster walls were painted in the gayest hues. In this instance the execution was rough and tasteless, but in richer houses it is often artistic. Unfortunately, the beautiful woodwork harbours insects, so that chambers literally "ceiled with cedar, and painted with vermilion," are often infested by innumerable plagues. In many rooms, we have already mentioned that two sides are entirely taken up by windows; but in mountain regions like Katchanik, where the climate is chilly and society unsettled, the apertures of dwelling-houses are small and few and overhung by the roof. Immediately within the windows is the divan, covered with cushions, and in front of the divan comes a raised part of the floor, usually of wood and carpeted, where it is ill-mannered to tread in shoes. Between the raised floor and the door intervenes a lower gradation, uncarpeted, and often of bare ground; this is subdivided into a standing-place for servants, a cupboard, and a stove. The cupboards are very convenient, even the space between their doors being provided with little cells; the stove, which in form is like a beehive and usually painted green and white, is on the outside pressed full of round holes, wherein we more than once baked apples for supper. There is also a fence of rails round the stove, on which garments can be hung to dry. Pegs abound in various parts of the room, and under the ceiling runs a high shelf, on which china dishes or other treasures may be displayed.

Such is the usual dwelling-room of a Mussulman house in this part of Turkey in Europe. As for the *kiosk*, it is the very poetry of a chamber, giving you at once a large open fireplace and large open windows, a comfortable sofa and the full enjoyment of the air. Unluckily, in rooms as well as in garments, the poor Turks are surrendering, for imitations of Europe, the few characteristics which they would do well to retain. On the other hand, they retain, even in good houses, certain blemishes in domestic arrangement, which cannot be sufficiently stigmatised. First, the plan of sleeping in rooms where they also sit and eat, and by day hiding away their bedclothes in cupboards; secondly, the harbourage of unnamable insects, which infest alike furniture, carpets, and clothes; thirdly, the toleration of accumulated filth under windows, under divans, in short, everywhere. This latter grievance is connected with a total absence of ways and means for removing impurities to a distance from dwellings. Certainly much of our own experience would go to prove that in their habits the Turks are dirty, and respecting the degree of cleanliness which results from ceremonial washings we confess ourselves unable to give a report. On this head, too, the accounts we received from others were absolutely contradictory. For instance, one resident would assure us that no adoption of Frankish fashion can make the Turk disregard his religious cleansing, while another had Turkish acquaintances who, being just europeanised enough to wear boots instead of slippers, limited their nether ablutions to besprinkling their *chaussure*. Again, we have been told by persons who professed to speak from experience, that Turks wash their hands and faces but very rarely change their linen; and in direct contradiction to this statement, we have been told that they change their linen every day. So far as our own observation is concerned, we must say that the Ottoman soldiers and officials, the Greeks, men, women, and children, and the Albanians of all clans and creeds, seemed to us heinously unclean.

Of their Slavonic neighbours, the least cleanly are the Montenegrines, who, however, are ashamed of it, excusing themselves from the fact that during a great part of the year their villages are ill supplied with water. On the other hand the Bulgarians are more cleanly than any people between them and the Dutch, and orderly and careful to boot. The Danubian Serbians are less dirty than Germans; they love fresh air, and let it well through their houses; though not as yet tidy, they are particularly anxious to become so, inasmuch as they regard "shiftlessness" as one of the attributes of the Turk. Their brethren of race, the Mussulman gentlemen of Bosnia, cultivate snowy linen and beautifully clean houses, and so do the Bosniac Christians as far as their poverty will permit. Indeed an appreciation of cleanliness is one of those points in which the Slavonic Christians differ in character from their southern co-religionists the Greeks, with whom they are so often confused.

Soon after we were settled in our room at Katchanik there came a message from the women of the Bey's family. They wished to visit us, and to this end, requested that we would send our men servants out of the house. Of course we agreed; and thereupon the Bey, having first seen our attendants to a safe distance, liberated his female relatives and himself withdrew. In a moment our room was full of Arnaout women, and we were reciprocally scanning one another—on our side with disappointment and disgust. For in Turkey, as elsewhere, it is usual for ladies, when paying a call, to be arrayed in their best, and we had expected to see some fine specimens of Albanian costume; instead of which these dames showed themselves in all the shabbiness of

Albanian *deshabille*. One of the maids spoke a few words of Slavonic, so we asked her whether her mistress had not anything better to put on; and thereupon it appeared that the poor creatures had not dared to sport their best clothes for fear of exciting our cupidity. The maid, anxious for her lady's honour, began to describe her *parure* of ducats, when her mistress snubbed her, fiercely snapping out, "Who talks of ducats? Hold your tongue." Failing the subject of dress (on which in such interviews we frequently relied), and the Slavonic words between us being few, we sought to amuse them with the pictures in a Bulgarian spelling-book. At this juncture the party was joined by a boy about twelve years old. To our surprise and the immense admiration of the rest of the audience, he knew all the Slavonic letters and read the alphabet aloud; he seemed, indeed, a quick enough child; but like every lad we saw in a harem, his manner to his female associates was not unlike that of a young turkey-cock among his silly troop of hens.

While all were thus intent suddenly a cry was raised, and the whole party bundled out, throwing their dirty wraps over their dirty and ugly faces, tumbling over one another, and in their haste leaving their slippers behind. The cause was explained next moment when our cavass entered bringing in the soup; but after all this fuss we happened to leave our room unexpectedly, and found two or three women in the kitchen while the dragoman was cooking. "Ah, ha!" said he; "they are not so particular as they would have you believe. When they want the kitchen they don't mind me."

Next morning before starting we made the discovery that the "great Bey" of Katchanik, like more than one Bey in Bosnia, was the proprietor of a khan, and only as such consented to offer distinguished guests the superior accommodation of his own house. He sent in his demand for so many piastres with no greater scruple than the most ordinary khangee.

Quitting Katchanik, *en route* for the monastery of Gratchanitza, we had to cross the river Neredimka; for this purpose, and in order to get safe out of the street, we mounted our horses and rode on during the next two hours. The way skirting the bank of the Lepenic traverses steep and broken ground, and it was to our surprise that the carriage rejoined us uninjured.

The hills that form the western wall of the Pass of Katchanik here meet the eastern extremity of the Shaar Plánina, and their point of junction is the pyramidal mountain, Liubatern, which rises to 6,400 feet. The zaptié who rode before us pointed to the cloud-veiled summit, and called out, "Look up there! Near the peak of that great mountain lies a lake whose shores are of snow; from that lake comes this river, but truly, it makes many twinings and twirlings on the hill-side before it gets down here."

We have never been so fortunate as to hear this assertion either confirmed or contradicted on competent authority, nor did we ever meet any one who had ascended the peak of Liubatern.

And now the unwinding of the mountain ranges showed us the great upland plain of Kóssovo, stretching to Mitrovic at the northern extremity, a distance of fourteen hours as the rider goes. It lies on an average 1,700 feet above the level of the sea, and forms the watershed of the Ægean and the Danube.*

* The whole surface was doubtless once a lake, and part of it still remains a marsh, while of the four rivers that drain it, two—the Lepenic and the Neredimka—fall into the Vardar (Axius); and two—the Lab and the Sitnitza—are carried through the Ibar and Morava into the Danube. The country people say that the Neredimka sends water both to the Black Sea and the White, meaning by the latter the Mediterranean. What they imply is, that while its principal stream falls into the Lepenic, a portion of its water contributes to feed a mill-brook which loses itself in the bog of Sasli, the source of the river Sitnitza.

CHAPTER XIV.

THE BATTLE-FIELD OF KÓSSOVO.*

"Cursed be Vuk Brançovic, for he betrayed the Czar on Kóssovo. But the name of Milosh shall be remembered by the Serbian people as long as the world and Kóssovo endure."—*Serbian Ballad.*

"Never let me hear that brave blood has been shed in vain; it sends a roaring voice down through all time."—*Saying of Sir Walter Scott.*

THE morning on which we entered Kóssovo was chequered by those alternations of cloud and gleam which usually herald a showery day. The wind blew fresh from the snow-wreaths on Liubatern, and swung aloft the boughs of the oak-copse, showing bright little lawns and dewy pastures, to which the grazing horses and cattle pushed their way through brushwood and fern: we felt that we had exchanged the yellow plains of the East for the green mountains and watered valleys of Europe. Unhappily, the verdure and the breeze are all that now testify of Europe on the field of Kóssovo. Old chronicles tell that at the time when a Turkish army first appeared on it the country was well cultivated and peopled with villages; roads and bridges were the especial care of the ruler; the Serbian parliament generally held its meetings in the neighbourhood; and the adjacent

* The name *Kóssovo Polié* has always been rendered by the Germans *Amselfeld*, *i.e.*, field of the blackbirds. Serbian etymologists now incline to derive the word not from *kos*, merula, but from *kositi*, to mow. Of the battle there are differing accounts; we have followed those most generally accepted both by Mahommedans and Christians, and which form the text of the principal national songs. Later ballads ascribe almost every engagement between Turks and Serbians to the battle of Kóssovo, and thus abound in contradictory details.

cities of Skopia, Novo Berdo, and Prizren, had great yearly marts, which formed the rendezvous of foreign merchants. Yes, in those days Kóssovo belonged to Europe—to a society, though rude, of activity and progress; but it was conquered to be a pasture-ground for Turkish horses, on just such a showery morning as this, some five hundred years ago.

The large plain of Kóssovo, situated in a mountainous region, and lying as it were before the doors of Danubian Serbia, Bosnia, and Albania, has in all ages been marked by its position as a battle-field, and it is still pointed out as the spot where combat may once more decide the fate of the surrounding lands. The earliest battle of Kóssovo of which there is a record, was fought between old Stephen Némania and the Byzantine governor of the adjacent castle of Svétchani, and it delivered the Serbs of this district from the last claims of Byzantine suzerainty. Again, it was on Kóssovo that the Turks first appeared as invaders of Serbia, and were on that occasion beaten and driven away; while in 1448 there was a celebrated combat, wherein the Hungarian general, John Hunyady, fought the Turks for three days running, in vain hope of recovering the land. But the great battle of Kóssovo was that wherein the last Czar of Serbia met the Moslem invaders of his country; and so fresh remains its memory that to this day it is scarcely possible for a traveller to converse for more than a few minutes with a genuine Serbian without hearing the name of Kóssovo. After five centuries, the lessons taught by the defeat are constantly applied; the loss of the country is an ever-rankling thorn. We have ourselves been present when Serbians quarrelling were quieted by the remonstrance, "What, will ye strive among yourselves like your fathers before the battle of Kóssovo?" and we have heard a Serbian peasant answer, when praised for bringing in a large load of wood, " Ay, but it is time we Serbians should gather in our wood from the field of Kóssovo." As for any one who has been much in Serbia, and has studied the national traditions and songs, he will at last come to feel almost as if he had been at the battle of Kóssovo himself, so minutely is every detail enumerated, so vividly are the motives and actions realised, so deep the lines, so strong the colours, in which the principal characters are drawn.

It was on "fair St. Vitus's day," June 15, 1389, that the Turkish and vassal hosts, led by the Ottoman Sultan Amurath, engaged the combined forces of the Serbs, Bosniacs, and Albanians, which were drawn up on the field of Kóssovo to repel further invasion of their land. The relative numbers of the combatants are very variously stated, each party raising that of its adversary to not less than 300,000, and declaring that itself was outnumbered as one to three.

The pride of the Serbs was their heavy-armed cavalry; and Turkish histories relate that on the evening before the battle it was debated among the Ottoman leaders whether it would not be advisable to try and frighten the enemy's horses by placing a row of camels before the Turkish line. Bajazet, eldest son of Amurath, objected to employ stratagem, inasmuch as it showed distrust of God. The grand vizier deemed it unnecessary, because, when he last opened the Koran, he had lighted on a promise of victory. Beglerbeg Timour Tash settled the question by declaring that the camels were more likely to run away from the Serb cavalry than the Serb cavalry from the camels. Another difficulty perplexed the Turks. All night long the wind blew strong from the Christian camp and towards theirs; the leaders were uneasy, lest, during the combat, it should blow the dust into their men's eyes. Sultan Amurath spent the night in gloomy foreboding that this battle was his last; he had recourse to prayer, and just before sunrise a light rain fell, laying the dust and wind. When the shower ceased and the sun shone out it was the signal for the armies to engage.

Meanwhile, in the camp of the Serbs counsel was darkened by domestic quarrels. Czar Lāzar had two sons-in-law; the one, Vūk Brankovic, was the greatest and best-born vlasteline in Serbia, the other, Milosh Obilic, was her bravest and most chivalrous warrior. The Czar loved Milosh, and trusted him as his own soul. Vūk was moved to jealousy at the sight of a man who owed his position to his sword preferred before himself; accidentally the jealousy of the brothers-in-law was brought to a point by a dispute between their wives. The quarrel had to be settled by a duel, in which Milosh unhorsed his antagonist, but forbore to follow up his advantage, and generously offered to make friends. But Vūk was envious, and envy does not forgive. It is said the Turkish Sultan had already been trying to weaken the resistance of Serbia by tampering with some of Lāzar's nobles, and had offered the crown to any one who would assist him to overthrow the Czar; it is said that Vūk Brankovic accepted the offer, and engaged to desert during the impending battle. Certain it is, that towards the end of the engagement he did lead his men from the field, and afterwards he applied to Amurath for the crown; hence to this day the popular voice of Serbia curses him as a traitor. But the Turkish chroniclers know nothing of Vūk's treachery, and in default of evidence, modern historians of Serbia are fain to suppose that he was no more than a mean sluggish character, who left the field because he deemed the battle lost. It is possible that he and Milosh mutually suspected each other of having listened to propositions from Amurath, and Vūk was too glad to undermine the credit of his rival by accusing him to the Czar. But Lāzar, true to his noble nature, was slow to believe evil; he would tolerate no private malignity, act on no private suspicion. If a doubt rested on the fidelity of Milosh he should be given the opportunity of justifying himself publicly; the accusation should be accompanied with a recognition of his former services and with a token of the gratitude of his prince.

On the evening before the battle the Czar sat at table with his vlastela. At his right hand was placed old Iūg Bogdan, vicegerent of Macedonia, and after him his nine sons—the brave brethren of the Czarine Militza. On the Czar's left was Vūk Brankovic, and after him all the other vlastela. Opposite the Czar sat Milosh Obilic, and on either side of him his bond-brothers, Ivan Kosanchic and Milan of Toplitz. Every Serb between the Danube and the Adriatic is as familiar with the names of all here mentioned as with those of his own brothers.

After supper, began the usual ceremony of proposing toasts; wine was poured, and the Czar, taking from his cupbearer a costly golden goblet, thus addressed the assembled voivodes:—

"To whom of you all, my lords, shall I drink this cup to-night? If the claim be age, I must drink to the aged Iūg Bogdan; if rank, to Vūk Brankovic; if affection, to my brothers-in-law, my nine brothers, the Iugovics; if beauty, I drink to Ivan Kosanchic; if height, to Milan of Toplitz; but if valour, then to Milosh. And to none will I drink to-night save unto thee, Milosh Obilic. Health to thee true! health to thee, traitor! Once thou wert true: traitor at last. To-morrow on Kóssovo thou wilt betray me—wilt desert me for the Turkish Sultan. Yet here's to thy health! And now do thou drink: drink out my wine, keep the cup as my gift."

To his light feet springs Milosh Obilic, and bows him before the Czar to the earth:—

"Thanks to thee!" cries he, "glorious Prince Lāzar! thanks to thee for thy toast—for thy toast and for thy gift—but no thanks to thee for thy words. Traitor I am not, was not, will never be. Rather, on the field of Kóssovo will I perish in defence of my faith. Traitor is he who sits at thy knee, under thy skirt—sipping the cool wine. The false, the accursed Vūk Brankovic. Enough. To-morrow is fair St. Vitus's day, and on the battle-field we shall see who is true and who is traitor. As for me, so help me God! my hand shall slay the Turkish Sultan, my foot shall stand upon his neck."

We next see Milosh in consultation with his bond-brother, Ivan Kosanchic. In the words of the song, he says to him:—

> "Oh, my brother, Ivan Kosanchic,
> Hast thou spied out the Turkish host?
> Have the Moslems many warriors?
> Are we strong enough to fight them?
> Are we strong enough to beat them?"
>
> And thus answers Ivan Kosanchic:
> "Oh, my brother, Milosh Obilic!
> I have spied out the Turkish army,
> And truly it is a mighty host.
> If we all were turned to salt
> We could not salt one Turkish meal.
> Full fifteen days I go around them
> And find no limit nor end of numbers.
> For wide-spread is the host, yet dense;
> Horse pressed on horse, hero on hero,
> Lances a forest, banners as clouds,
> And tents whitening the earth like snow.
> Should a storm-shower rain from heaven
> Not a drop could reach the earth,
> All would fall on steeds and warriors."
> * * * * * *
> The Sultan camps on Mazgit plain,
> And holds the rivers Lab and Sitnitza.

> Yet again asks Milosh Obilic,
> "Oh, Ivan, tell me truly
> Where stands the tent of Sultan Murad?
> For to our Prince I have vowed a vow
> That I will slay the Turkish Sultan
> And set my foot upon his neck."
>
> "Milosh, my brother, art thou mad?
> Dost thou ask where Murad's tent stands?
> In the centre of the camp,
> Hemmed in by the thickest squadrons.
> If thou hadst a falcon's plumes
> And couldst swoop on it from heaven,
> Verily thy wings would not
> Avail to bring thee out alive."
>
> Then doth Milosh thus adjure him:
> "Swear to me, bond-brother Ivan
> (Thou who, not my brother born,
> Hast to me a brother been),
> That what thou hast told to me,
> Thou wilt not tell to our Prince,
> Lest it weigh down his heart with care,
> And spread a panic through the host."

Next morning, the morning of the battle, Milosh had disappeared from the Serbian camp. Was he gone to fulfil his wild vow? or, as suspicion again hinted, had he indeed deserted to the enemy? Vūk Brankovic pressed the latter interpretation; Czar Lāzar was sore at heart; for, on what errand soever, Milosh was *gone*.

His arm, his word, his example, all were needed, and all were absent; the division of the army which he was to have commanded missed its leader and murmured. At this juncture in came spies, bringing such accounts of the mighty force of the Turks, that even now, at the eleventh hour, many of the Serb lords counselled negotiations. But this Czar Lāzar could not brook; in a few noble words he spoke courage to his troops and arrayed them for battle. But first the whole army confessed and took the sacrament. The Serbian Czar, in that priestly character still upheld by the Czar of

Russia, solemnly absolved them from their sins, and declared, that in fulfilling their allegiance to the Cross and to him they died as martyrs for their faith and fatherland.

Before the host the banner of the Cross was carried by the Czarine's eldest brother, brave Bosko Iugovic. Says the old song: "His chestnut steed is trapped with glittering gold, but o'er himself the great Cross banner flings its flowing folds, hiding him to the saddle. Above the banner shines the golden globe, out of the globe the golden crosses rise; down from the crosses golden tassels hang, and strike on Bosko's shoulder as he rides." True is the poetic instinct which thus represents the Christian standard-bearer: covered with the flag, his personality is lost in his office, and not he, but the Cross-banner alone, fills the eye.

We now return to the account of the Turkish historian. The battle raged and the left wing of the Ottomans had begun to give way, when Bajazet, surnamed "the Lightning," flew to its aid, crushing before him the heads of the foes with his iron mace. "Already streams of blood had dyed the diamond sword-blades to hyacinth, and the mirror-bright steel of the spear to ruby; already, by the multitude of heads struck off and of turbans rolling hither and thither, the battlefield was made to resemble a bed of many-coloured tulips; when, as a bird of prey rising from carcases, there raised himself from the heaps of slain a noble Serb." Milosh Obilic—for it was he—forced aside the crowd of myrmidons that surrounded the Sultan, shouting out that he had a secret to tell; Amurath signed that he should be allowed to approach. The Serb fell down before him, as if to kiss his feet, seized his foot, dragged him to the ground, and plunged a dagger into his body. The Sultan was mortally wounded: a thousand swords were drawn on the assassin; but he, strong of arm and light of foot, shook them off, struck them aside, and three times, by prodigious leaps, rid himself of the pursuing crowd. Almost he had reached the river's brink, almost he had regained his trusty steed, when a fourth time the multitude closed on him, overbore him, cut him down.

Some versions of the story say that he was killed at once, but most assert that he was brought back wounded and fainting to the Sultan's tent, and there kept till the end of the battle, when he was executed with other prisoners to glut the eyes of the dying Turk.

The hand of Milosh, who slew an Ottoman Sultan, was long preserved at the tomb of Amurath, near Broussa; and from his daring act dated the practice that strangers admitted to the presence of the Padishah must give their weapons in charge to his attendants, and even allow their hands to be held.

The deed of Milosh being thus related by his enemies, one fears not to give the version of his countrymen. Indeed this differs only so far as to make him appear before the Sultan with twelve companions, gain access to his tent in guise of a deserter, and take his life before the battle began. On both sides the deed is noticed as one of heroism; and even in our own day it deserves honour as an instance of self-devotion. Milosh, rendered desperate by calumny, resolved to show his patriotism by a desperate service; he beheld in Amurath an Infidel, a barbarian, and the invader of his country; but he used craft only to the point necessary to gain access to his victim, and he paid the price of blood with his own.

Meanwhile the combat raged on. Amurath, though dying, was still able to give orders, and Bajazet inspired his hosts with new fury by calling on them to avenge their Sultan. The tide of battle turned against the Serbs; and at this juncture Vūk Brankovic, who commanded the reserve, marched off the field without striking a blow. His brave men, 12,000 in number, believed they were only shifting their position, but their involuntary desertion decided the fate of the day. They were among the best troops of the army—the trusted, vaunted cuirassiers.

Still, however, the Bosniacs fought well, and the centre led by the gallant Czar bore all before it. But at length the Czar's horse broke down and he had to exchange it for another. For the moment he vanished from the view of his men, and the sight of his well-known dappled charger led from the front spread the report that he had fallen. The Christian ranks broke; and when Lāzar, remounted, strove with voice and example to rally them, he was borne along by the panic-stricken crowd; his horse stumbled and fell in a trench, he was surrounded and taken.

The Turkish Sultan lay in his death struggle when the Serbian Czar was brought before him, and over the couch of the dying Amurath the eyes of Lāzar met those of Milosh. Then all was told, and the prince solemnly rendered thanks to God that he had been spared to find Murad fallen and Milosh true.

Furiously, Bajazet asked of him how he had dared to cause the death of his father. Undaunted, the Czar replied, "And thy father, how dared he invade my realm?" "Gospodar," interrupted an attendant, "are then thy neck and shoulders of willow wood, that thy head, if cut off, can grow again?" But not heeding him, Lāzar spoke on: "And thou Bajazet, son of Amurath, thinkest thou if I had at my side a certain thing which I have not, that I would now delay to send thee after thy sire?"

Bajazet commanded the executioner to strike. The faithful squire entreated that he might share the blow; and then, kneeling down before his master, held outspread the royal mantle to receive the royal head.

Such was the end of the last Christian Czar of Serbia; her first Turkish Czar began to rule by causing his brother Jakub to be slain over the scarce cold body of their father; and justified himself by a maxim from the Koran, to the effect that, rather than let a man cause dissension, it is better to put him to death.*

Thus was Kóssovo severed from Europe, and thus it became a pasture for Turkish cavalry.

* Hammer. "History of the Ottoman Empire," vol. i., book 6. Among his exonerating motives is also stated the following:—"He considered that it became him to imitate the example of God, who is alone and without rival. Wherefore God's shadow on earth, the Ruler of the Faithful, must be like God—alone on his throne, and rule without the possibility of rivalry."

CHAPTER XV.

THE MONASTERY OF GRATCHANITZA, AND THE TOWN OF PRISHTINA.

WHEN, from the broken ground at the mouth of the Pass of Katchanik, one has fairly emerged on the plain of Kòssovo, it becomes possible to sit in the carriage, and even to proceed at a sort of jog-trot. This, however, is owing to the level, not to any superiority in the road, and the bridges are so rickety that one is recommended to take the precaution of getting out to traverse them on foot.

As for the scenery at this part of the way, there is nothing to be lost by passing it in a canopied coach. At every step the wood becomes more sparse, and the grass more mingled with sandy-looking soil, nor is this compensated by increasing signs of culture or human habitation. We passed some poor khans, and near, not through, a village said to be Albanian, its wretched huts surrounded and almost hidden by a hedge of interlaced roots and thorns. One of the khans is called by the Turks the New or Yeni Khan, but it proved as dilapidated as the oldest, and seems to retain its title only because there are none newer. It stands on the bank of the little river Neredimka, which we crossed immediately on leaving it. At mid-day we halted at the khan of Sasli, on ground that in winter forms the bog of Sasli, whence rises the river Sitnitza. On the brink of the stream there rested a drove of cattle; and as the hour was about milking time, we were given delicious milk with our coffee. Afterwards we crossed the Sitnitza, and next passed the khan of Rupofzé, to be remarked by travellers as a half-way house, distant five hours from Katchanik, five from Príshtina. A little farther on, the side track leading to Gratchanitza diverges from the Príshtina road.

We may mention that, some distance to the left of that road, and on the right bank of the Sitnitza, is to be found a village, containing some thirty Christian houses and a church. Hilferding remarks that its name, Liplan, is mentioned by Byzantine writers as early as the eleventh century, and in old times it was sufficiently important to be the seat of a metropolitan. To the right of the road between Sasli and Rupofzé lies the Bulgarian village of Babush. Till lately this village was remarkable as wholly belonging to a single family, whose members were exempt from taxation because their ancestors rendered service as scouts to the army of Sultan Amurath. It is said that their privilege has ceased since the issuing of the Tanzimat.

Late in the afternoon we drew near to the spurs of those hills which bound Kóssovo on the east, and here, in a low and sheltered spot, we came upon the monastery and village of Gratchanitza. Previously we had passed a lately erected chapel, of which the extreme smallness and entire lack of ornament show that hereabouts the Christians are still afraid to offend the Mussulmans by display. In telling contrast to this poor little modern church rises the old church of the monastery, the noble *zadushbina* (work for the soul) of a Serbian king. Seen from afar, it appears a cluster of arches and cupolas, culminating in one large dome. On nearer approach, one perceives that the smaller domes are four in number, and that among the curiously interlaced arches the higher are pointed, and the lower round. The principal merit of the structure is its general effect; and this, for Byzantine architecture, is so unusually graceful as to remind one of some churches in North Italy.

Evidence of Italian influence might doubtless be traced also in the frescoes of the interior, but injustice is done to these, as to everything else within the church, by the numerous subdivisions necessary to accommodate the inner to the outer form. Whether in the sanctuary, the nave, or the porch, one is always in a dark compartment, too narrow for its height. It would almost seem as if this blemish in Gratchanitza had served for a warning to the architect who built the church of the patriarchate at Ipek, for there outward beauty has evidently been sacrificed to giving the congregation a large well-lighted nave.

Among the frescoes at Gratchanitza are portraits of the founder, King Milutin, and of his queen, Simonida, daughter of the Emperor Andronicus II. Paleologus Milutin was the father of the king who built the church of Détchani, and the grandfather of Czar Dūshan; he reigned from 1275—1321, and it is said that he erected no less than forty-eight buildings for religious or benevolent purposes. The privileges decreed to the monastery of Gratchanitza are engraved on the wall of the church, and the monks call this inscription their archive.

The figures of saints which form the subject of several frescoes have suffered from the Turks, who fired pistols at them, and were also at the trouble to poke out their eyes. This latter injury evinced so much of the malice of deliberate insult, that it riled the Serbians more than wholesale destructions which might be supposed to have taken place in the confusion and heat of assault. Besides, the desecrated forms remain on the church wall, so that their injury can never be forgotten; and their marred faces meeting the upturned eyes of the worshippers, seem ever to cry out for retribution. In the Principality of Serbia, where some ruined churches have been rebuilt, these blinded pictures are left unrestored. An old bishop said to us, "We still need them—they are the archives of centuries of oppression; and our people must not lose sight of them so long as the oppressor still keeps foot on Serbian land." For the frescoes themselves this feeling is most fortunate, as it has saved them from the doom of whitewash; and it is only to be wished that some similar protection could be extended to the exterior sculptures and walls. While the modern phase of taste in Serbia is represented by the new cathedral of Belgrade, such monuments of the mediæval monarchy as survived the Turkish deluge, have more to dread from the zeal of the restorer, than aught that befell them from the ravages of the foe.

Among the frescoes at Gratchanitza, one alone has been preserved by the height of the dome, or, as the monks say, by a mysterious terror which seized on the destroyers, and saved the church itself. This rescued fresco is the Head of Christ, which in Eastern churches is usually depicted of colossal size, and looking down in the act of benediction. The conception of the face here drawn is as superior to the stiffness of the Byzantine, as to the weakness of modern schools. The artist who painted it would be a contemporary of Cimabue, and Luccio of Sienna; and, like theirs, his genius was strong enough to infuse power and grandeur even into the then conventional forms. Indeed, the Christ of Gratchanitza is of so stern a type, that one could almost believe the painter to have had a foreboding of the dark days in store for the church. Those awful eyes look down from under brows whereof the frown might well strike terror into desecrators engaged in their unhallowed sport.

There are a few Roman remains at Gratchanitza, consisting of stones with inscriptions and two stone aræ, the latter preserved within the church. Hahn conjectures that these were brought from the station Vicianum, on the great military road between Lissus on the Adriatic and Nissus, a few days' journey from the Danube. Outside the church we saw the lid of a large stone coffin, marked with the cross.

From our experience of Serbian monasteries, we had hoped to find at Gratchanitza both comfort and satisfaction, but nothing could present a stronger contrast to the state of convents in the principality than the condition of the convent here. We came, indeed, at an unlucky moment, for the prior had just been carried off captive, —a fate which by all accounts he richly merited; but which served as excuse for every passing Mussulman to bully the monks, and extort what he pleased. Under such circumstances, the presence of our zaptiés was a terrible infliction, and it was revolting to behold their insolence, together with the cringing alacrity with which the monks made haste to satisfy them. After a while, the sub-prior got our dragoman into a quiet corner, and told him how matters stood. Of course we at once sent to assure him that we would take away the zaptiés next day, and pay for all that we consumed.

The story related by the sub-prior, as to the misdeeds and imprisonment of his superior, was bad enough, and we afterwards heard it confirmed with additions which were not improvements. The captured Hegumon was a man much too young for his post, and who would seem to have attained it by bribery; he was imperious and passionate, and made enemies in the village. On the occasion of a wedding-feast, when raki had got into the heads assembled, the abbot of Gratchanitza received a blow, and returned it with interest, felling his assailant. The man came down on some hard substance and was seriously hurt; his family demanded reparation, and also indemnification for the loss of his work during the time the wound would take to heal; altogether 2,000 piastres, about £20. This the Hegumon thought extravagant, and declared that it would be enough for him to pay the doctor, meanwhile lodging and supporting the patient; but the relations insisted, and the fine was paid. The man got better, and went out to work as before, but after a time he caught cold, the half-healed wound inflamed, and he died. The family having been paid for the wound, and recognising the death as an accident over which the Hegumon had no control, made no further demand; but the neighbouring Turkish authorities thought to improve the occasion and extort money from the monastery. They therefore interfered, and demanded a second fine; the Hegumon could not or would not pay it, so they seized what money they could find, and carried him off to Prizren. He was condemned to prison for seven years, and if any one could have relied on the sentence being carried out, the whole country would have rejoiced to be quit of him. Unluckily it was well known that he would only be kept till the authorities were sure that he had paid them all the money he possessed, and then he would be sent back to Gratchanitza on the condition of raising more.

The wretchedness of the monks at Gratchanitza extends to what they call their school. Perhaps, considering that they live in an out-of-the-way part of Turkey, are but four in number, and have the services of the church to attend, it is rather creditable that they have a school at all, and should they acquire a good superior, the germ may develop into real usefulness. At present, however, their school is certainly far behind all others in the country, and that in more ways than one. In an unfurnished cell we found five miserable children with torn books under their arms. The books were the smallest Belgrade chitankas, and the scholars read out of them both old Slavonic and Serbian, but so glibly that we could not but suspect they were repeating by rote. We therefore opened the books at another place, and then they could scarcely read a word. Their teacher, a kindly-looking monk, apologized more candidly than many others of his calling, by taking the blame on his own ignorance; "however," said he, "I only teach them the first rudiments, and afterwards they will go to the good new school at Príshtina. As their poor little chitankas were torn, we gave them some, together with two New Testaments to the monks. Next day another monk came to us at Príshtina, and asked if we would give a Testament to him also, as he belonged to Gratchanitza, but happened during our visit to be from home.

Before leaving the schoolroom we ventured a very earnest remonstrance as to the mode in which the pupils had greeted us. At our entrance they had literally fallen down at our feet, and that with a sort of grovelling action which, if not revolting, would have been ludicrous. We asked how in the world they came to suppose we should wish to be thus received? Their teacher answered, "The Turks taught it us: their dignitaries require us Christians to prostrate ourselves before them." "But we are not Turks, and for Christians to enact or to permit such self-degradation is not only a shame but a sin. Have not some of you been in Free Serbia and seen how the school-children behave there?" "No, none of them." But at these words they exchanged glances, and began to cheer up a little. They invited us to come into the church, and presently brought thither a man from the village who *had* been in Free Serbia. This man wore a turban, was of uncouth aspect, and otherwise looked like the other rayahs; but he was far more outspoken than the monks. We desired him to say if the Serbian school-children prostrated themselves as these did. "Of course not," cried he, "but then in Serbia *everything* is different. There they have good roads, good judges, peace and prosperity; here there is nothing but disorder and zulum" (*Turk.*, violence and oppression).*

Prostrations like those of the school-children at Gratchanitza frequently greeted us during this journey, and we cannot think that any civilized traveller would see them with less distress than ourselves. But one's own feeling at thus witnessing the degradation of fellow-creatures and fellow-Christians gives but a faint idea of what is felt by the Serbs of the principality, to whom these rayahs stand in the relation of brethren of race, nay, often are near of kin. Monks, merchants, and emigrants of all sorts, constantly pass from the Turk-ruled districts to Free Serbia, and not even the accounts which they give of their position awake such indignation as the involuntary evidence of it afforded by their cringing demeanour, until they learn the manners of a new land. One instance among many may stand here. A young man working in Belgrade had committed some offence, and was sentenced to a term of imprisonment with labour. His old father, a Christian in Bulgaria, taking it for granted that the imprisonment would endure until he could be bought off, came to Belgrade, and found that the culprit, having served his time, was about to be

---

* For greater distinctness we shall use the term "Free Serbia" when speaking of the Danubian Principality, as distinguished from districts inhabited by Serbians, but ruled by Mahommedans. In the country, however, the name Serbia, without any prefix, is always understood to denote the free districts, the rest being called Old Serbia, &c.

set at liberty, and that there was no occasion for bribing any one. In his joy the father craved an interview of Prince Michael, in order to thank him for *pardoning* his son. This did not exactly please the prince, who is doing all in his power to break his own people of the habit of referring to him to comment on or change the sentence of the law; he feels that such a practice as this testifies to a state of society where the caprice of the despot takes the place of justice. However, as the old man came from far, and would not be satisfied without seeing him, he agreed to receive him, and walked into a room of his palace where the Bulgarian had been told to wait. The moment the man saw the prince, he fell down and grovelled at his feet, again and again with outstretched hand touching the floor and then his own brow. In vain he was entreated to rise, in vain assured that his degraded attitude inflicted on the prince the keenest pain; poor rayah! that was an idea which his mind could not readily take in. The scene was described to us by the prince himself,—the very recollection caused him to writhe: he added, "Je me suis dit, Voilà donc comment il faut se présenter devant un pasha."

As we were making our arrangements for departure from Gratchanitza, the new zaptiés who had come to meet us from Príshtina sent to say, that if we wished to continue the carriage they could compel the driver to go on with us,—we need not pay anything more. Of course we did not take advantage of this unjust proposition, but having sent the poor man home, as previously agreed, proceeded on our own journey on horseback.

The ride from Gratchanitza to Príshtina is not reckoned more than an hour and a half. The town stands in the undulating ground where surrounding hills mingle with the plain. It is dirty and small, but makes a fair show in the distance, owing to the minarets of eleven mosques, said to have been erected by Turkish women whose husbands fell at the battle of Kóssovo. A picturesque feature is the little eminence to the right, which at the time of our visit was dotted with white and green military tents. There is generally a cavalry regiment stationed on the field during summer; and in camp, as in city, the Turk shows his taste by relieving the glare of white with green.

The kaïmakam of Skopia had despatched a letter recommending us to the mudir of Príshtina; and this letter had an excellent effect, for besides sending to meet us at the monastery, he had provided us with capital quarters in the town. The house selected was that of the bishop, which, though not quite answering to the European idea of an episcopal palace (it boasted only four rooms, three small and one large), was nevertheless an agreeable residence. The prelate himself, a Fanariote, was naturally away at Constantinople, and the community deplored not his absence; neither did we, since in consequence we came in for his large, cool, pleasant room, with its row of windows shaded by the projecting roof. From these windows most pleasant is the view: the house, standing on a slope, looks down on the clustered town, and beyond it far over the plain to a shadowy frontier of distant hills.

Immediately on our arrival, the mudir of Príshtina sent to offer a visit, and then appeared, not as usual in the form of an obese and greasy-uniformed Osmanli, but as a gaunt Albanian in a green robe lined with fur. He was a fine-looking old man, with silver hair, glittering black eyes, a pale complexion, and with a look of blood unattainable to dignitaries who have earned promotion as a favourite pipe-lighter or café-gee. In a few minutes the companion of the mudir informed us that his superior came indeed of a noble race; and, as we displayed lively interest in the subject, the mudir himself took up the discourse, and told us the name of his family, adding that they were all Ghegga by race, and that in their country no one spoke a word of Turkish. Thus encouraged we proceeded to question him about other families of Northern Albania, and especially if he agreed with Consul Hahn's informant that the greatest houses were those of Ismael Pasha and Mahmut Begola. He said they were great, but that the last sprout of one of them had taken service under the Sultan, adding contemptuously, "He is a humpbacked little fellow," and imitating the humpback.

Referring to our journey, the mudir told us that he especially rejoiced to welcome us, inasmuch as at one time he had served under English command, and was well content with his treatment and pay. During the Crimean war he had accompanied an English consul through the districts of Ipek and Détchani in order to gain recruits. "The monastery of Détchani of course we knew—as it is the greatest in the world."

When the mudir was gone, the Serbian kodgia bashi came to ask us to visit the Christian school. After what we had seen at Gratchanitza our expectation was at the lowest ebb, and hence we were the more gratified with a very pleasing surprise. The schoolroom was large, airy, clean, properly fitted up, and embellished with texts from the Slavonic Bible written scrollwise on door and walls. These scrolls are the work of the schoolmaster, a Serb from Mitrovic, on the Austrian border of the Save; and he has imparted so much of his accomplishment to his pupils that they not only write well, but also draw. Two wonderful pictures representing the Madonna and St. George were given us to take away as keepsakes. The bright and vigorous-looking children that filled the school then proceeded to show us that they could read and cipher with ease; but they proved unusually backward in geography—which surprised us, inasmuch as a set of good maps appeared on the wall. In a while, however, we perceived that they were fastened so high that no one could look at them without getting a crick in the neck. The schoolmaster, being of the tidy persuasion, affirmed that this was necessary in order to keep them from being dirtied by the children's fingers.

The books at Príshtina were from Belgrade, but as they seemed only to have chitankas adapted for the youngest children, we asked if they had not some histories of Serbia. The master looked furtively around, and then said that he had some, but dared not to use them openly. "Why not?" "Because the officers of the Turkish regiments frequently come and loll about in our school, and the cavalry officers are often Hungarians or Cossacks or Poles, and can read the Slāvic books." "But these brief, dry histories contain nothing revolutionary, and surely the officers who are your fellow-Christians would not wish to calumniate you." "The rest would not, but the Poles are more Turkish than the Turks themselves. One day a Polish officer looked over the shoulder of one of the children, and called out, 'Halloa, master! what do I see here? These books are different from those used in Bulgaria; they come from the principality, and here is something about the history of Serbia. If I catch you at this again, I shall report you to the authorities.' I trembled from head to foot, and knew not what I should say or do; but luckily there was also present a Cossack, a deserter from the Russian service, a good man who had always befriended us; he got the Pole out of the room, and said to him in displeasure that they were not sent to Prìshtina to meddle with the Serb school. Since then all reading of our country's history has been in private." It need not be pointed out what ill service this Polish officer was doing the Sultan, in thus angering the Christians by suppressing the open school study of Serbian history, on a spot where its most exciting details are known to every man, woman, and child through the medium of national song. Unfortunately such malevolent tale-telling is not singular, and we have since heard how in one of the largest Slavonic towns in Turkey, the school histories of Serbia were seized. Of course the pasha had not read them himself, but some one told him of their existence, and that they contained passages tending to throw contempt on the Turkish government; fanatical Mahommedans raised a cry, and the Greek bishop proved a ready agent in the seizure. It is worthy of remark, that one of the more intelligent local Mussulmans, himself Slavonic and possessed of the suspected histories, objected to this measure on the ground that contempt for the Turkish government was far more likely to be engendered by such a step, than by anything contained in Serbian school-books. Having, like this Mussulman, read the book in question, we can unhesitatingly endorse his opinion.

Respecting the schoolmaster's assertion that Poles in the Ottoman army are more alienated from their oppressed fellow-Christians than the Mahommedans themselves, we must confess to have heard it often repeated, and with the bitterest emphasis. No doubt, at one time, these exiles were too apt to hate the Slavonic Christians in Turkey, inasmuch as they regarded them as clients of Russia. Subsequently, however, they showed more discrimination, and on the occasion of the bombardment of Belgrade, Poles as well as Hungarians offered their services to the Government of Serbia.

The school of Príshtina contains a second large room, which would just do for a class of girls; but as usual there is the lack of a female teacher, and the customs of this part of the country would oppose boys and girls being taught in one room. There is also another obstacle. Even the boys on their way to and fro are insulted by the Arnaout *gamins*,—what would be the fate of girls? This objection was urged by the kodgia bashi, and thereupon the schoolmaster said to him :—" Do you know what I have been told? The new mudir has informed the medjliss that it is the Sultan's pleasure that the children of his subjects should go to school, not excepting the children of Arnaouts. Now if the young Albanians were shut up at their tasks, ours could get through the street in peace." The kodgia bashi gave us a look, as if to see how much we believed, and then said shortly, "When the Arnaouts become quiet and go to school like other people, it will certainly be an excellent thing."

The said kodgia bashi was not particularly liberal-minded in respect to female education. He observed to us, that in their community many of the boys were yet untaught, and it would not be well that the women should know how to read and write before the men. Thereupon we showed him some handsomely-bound books, and told him that the contents were histories and records of travel written by women. He examined the works narrowly, and called upon the schoolmaster, who knew Latin letters, to decipher the title, adding, "Are you quite sure that it is neither a letter nor a song?" "Quite sure," answered we; and the schoolmaster confirmed our statement. Then said the kodgia bashi, "If women will write such books as these, we must see what ours can do."

After he was gone, the schoolmaster told us that the inhabitants of Príshtina have generally the gift of improvising poetry, and that to the national songs which they constantly recite, they add others composed on divers occurrences of their own life. Of course this gift is turned to account in courtship, and hence a notion exists that if women could write they would be for ever inditing love-letters. Such ideas naturally prevail in a country long subjected to Mahommedan influence, but the old songs tell us of Serbian ladies who "wrote like men."

Yet, with all his prejudices, the kodgia bashi is at Príshtina an apostle of progress. It is owing to him that the new school was built, and by him the schoolmaster was found and brought. In default of the absent bishop it is he who leads the little community of Serbs; moreover, although one of their poorest members, he is chosen to represent them in the medjliss, because he does them credit by his demeanour, and dares to speak out before the Turk. Of course he has been in Free Serbia. You see it at once; for, like the people over the border, he holds up his head and steps out like a man. The question is, Why did he return? This question we frequently put respecting persons who had similarly come back to their native town, although the state of things in it was one under which they groaned. The answer was as follows: In such cases all the family possesses— a bit of land, or a little shop—is in Turkey, and the Turks throw every impediment in the way of disposal of property for the purpose of emigration. Then, while some members of the family are willing to go, others cannot bear to leave their birthplace or the friends of their youth, and, rather than forsake their families, able-bodied men remain. Again, unless they go to Serbia before their mode of life is formed, they can seldom keep pace even with the workmen of the principality, and their habits are irregular and slothful; they cannot save enough to bring over their families, and rather than abandon these they go back to Turkey. But instead of themselves they send their children; the young son of the kodgia bashi was then on the eve of his journey.

CHAPTER XVI.

STARA SERBIA.

"Where the sword is, there is the true faith."—*Albanian Proverb*.
"It is under the torture that the hero is shown."—*Serbian Proverb*.

AND now finding ourselves at Príshtina, in the very heart of Old Serbia, it may be as well to inquire what extent of country is included under the name, what is its history, population, and condition. And here let us give notice, that if once we attempt an explanation which relates to various and conflicting elements of race, language, religion, and political interest, we are likely to spin out a long chapter. Readers who have no fancy to go in for it, need not do so in order to understand the allusions throughout our future narrative, if they will but consent to look at the subjoined map, and charge their memories with its explanation.

Even in the days of the czardom, it would appear that Serbia Proper was distinguished from the "Serb lands." The latter appellation included all the countries peopled by the Serbian race—Zeta, Bosnia, Herzegovina, &c.; but Serbia, in its strictest sense, denoted the tracts now comprehended in the Principality, together with those that intervene between the south of the Principality and Macedonia. Old maps of Turkey in Europe, which were drawn while all Serbia was subject to the Turks, give the whole of this country under its proper name; but now that the portion nearest the Danube has thrown off Mahommedan government, while the portion nearest Macedonia remains enslaved, map-makers have restricted the name of Serbia to the free districts, while the rest of the country is called by its Christian inhabitants Old or Stara Serbia.

This name is in use not only among the Slāvs in Turkey, but also with those throughout Austria and Russia, yet it is ignored equally by the Turkish authorities and by European Consuls in Turkey. The latter, with the exception of an Austrian at Prizren, are indeed stationed at too great a distance to know much of the local Christians; whereas they are aware that the Turks call the country Arnaoutluk, and that it is partly inhabited by Mahommedan Albanians. In the district itself both names may be heard. If you notice any instance of ruin or lawlessness, Turks and Serbians alike reply, "What do you expect in Arnaoutluk?" If you halt in wonder and admiration at the sight of an ancient church, and exclaim, "Who would have thought to find such a building hereabouts?" the priest who acts your cicerone draws near and whispers, "*We* call this country Stara Serbia."

The limits of Old Serbia have then no political definition, nor any definition except that which is assigned them by their Christian inhabitants. This, again, depends on historical associations, so that it is not easy to determine boundaries.

Yet, by way of giving some idea of the region, we will indicate a few of its geographical features, and begin with the frontiers as assigned by local tradition. On the *north*, *i.e.* where Old Serbia meets the southern frontier of the Principality, stands the town of Novi Bazaar; whence westward runs a chain of hills (Rogoshna Plánina), terminating in that mountain knot which culminates in the Montenegrīne Berdas. At the *south-*

STARA SERBIA.

western extremity of Old Serbia lies Prizren, the former "Czarigrad," and behind it the Scardus range, now called Shaar Plánina. As on the *west* a line from north to south is marked by the mountains of Herzegovina, Northern Albania, and Montenegro, so on the *east* a line from south to north may be drawn from the castle of Marco Kralïevich at Prilip to Skopia, and thence, following the range of the Bulgarian Cerna Gora, to Nish. Nish stands a little outside the boundary of the free districts, but it owns a monument erected by the Turks with the skulls of Serbians who fell in defence of freedom; and this monument, as Lamartine observed, marks the true frontier of Serbia.

Mountains.

At the point where Old Serbia meets with Montenegro, we find the highest mountains in Turkey in Europe, and their most elevated summits, Kom and Dormitor, rise from 8,000 to 9,000 feet. Liubatern, 6,000 feet, we have already noticed as marking the western end of the Shaar Plánina, at the corner where the Pass of Katchanik debouches on the plain of Kóssovo.

Plains, Rivers, Towns, &c.

The heart of Old Serbia, both historically and geographically, is formed by the sister plains of Metóchia and Kóssovo. On or near Kóssovo are situated the towns of Príshtina, Novo Berdo, Gilan, Vuchitern, the monastery of Gratchanitza, and the site of the famous old church of Samodresha. The castle of Svétchani, once a residence of the kings of Serbia, occupies an eminence at the northern entrance of the plain.

The field of Metóchia lies west of Kóssovo, and is

separated by the low chain of the Golesh hills. On this plain, as at once the centre of the Serb lands and a fertile spot in a defensible position, the Nemanides fixed their capital, and afterwards Stephen Dúshan transferred thither the seat of the Patriarch. The Czarigrad Prizren lay but a few hours distant from the ecclesiastical city Ipek, and between the two stood the famous church of Détchani, of which the king who built it felt so proud, that he took his name from it, and has gone down to posterity as Urosh Détchanski. Throughout national poetry Kóssovo is celebrated as the battle-field, Metóchia as the garden, of Serbia.

It would appear that the districts included in Stara Serbia, together with the southern part of the modern Principality, were in old times peopled by the richest and most civilised portion of the nation. Most of the higher nobles, whose family names are perpetuated in the Book of Serbian aristocracy,* appear to have held their residence in this part of the realm; while the beautiful churches still remaining either as ruins or partially preserved, show that a taste for the arts early penetrated regions which now are all but a desert.

The native sovereigns of Serbia were evidently liberal in their expenditure on works of piety or public usefulness. They took their surnames from the places where they had founded some holy house, and the impression left by their munificence on the mind of the people is to this day traceable in popular songs. We cite as a specimen the following curious ballad, whereof the scene is the convent of Gratchanitza, while the occasion is a Sabor held after the death of "Czar Némania."

"Behold," says the minstrel, "the Christian gentlemen of Serbia hold parliament in the fair church of

---

* Said to be preserved in a monastery of Mount Athos. A copy was shown us by M. Ljudevit Gaj, in Agram.

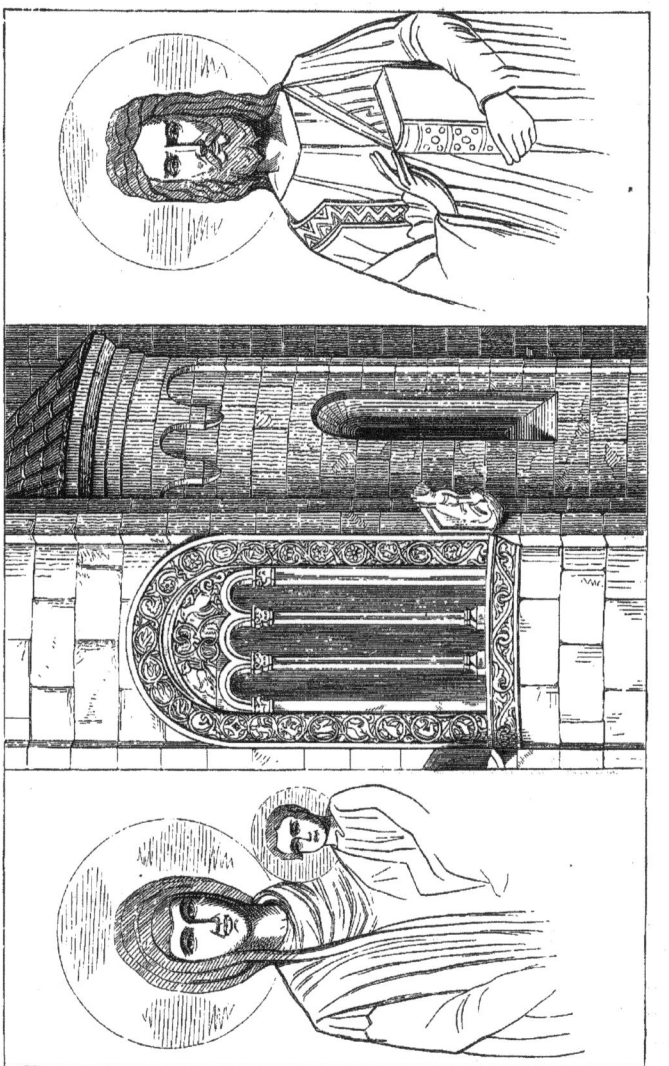

SPECIMEN OF SERBIAN ARCHITECTURE.

Gratchanitza, and they are saying one to another, Great God! what a miracle is this! The seven towers which Czar Némania heaped full of gold and silver now stand empty. Is it possible that the Czar should have wasted all this wealth on weapons, and battle-axes, and trappings for the war-horses?"

Then the Czar's son, Sava Némanjic, rises, and thus addresses the assembly:—" Ye Christian gentlemen, speak not foolishly, nor sin against my father's soul. My father did not waste his wealth on weapon or mace or trappings for the war-horse. My father worthily employed his wealth on many and noble 'works for the soul.' On the holy mountain of Athos he built the church of Hilindar, and for that he emptied two towers of gold. By the stream Bistritza he raised High Détchani, above Novi Bazaar the columns of St. George, in Stari Vla the white Laura of Studenitza; these cost him another tower." (Here follows a long list of names containing many churches really built by the descendants of Némania, but in this poem attributed to himself.) Then Sava adds:—

"What remained of my father's wealth he spent in making well-paved roads, in building bridges over the rivers, he divided it among the sick and blind, thus winning a place in Paradise for his soul. Truly several towers of treasure were emptied by the Czar my father, but on this manner was his wealth employed."

From Stara Serbia in the time of the Nemanides, we pass to it in our day. Previous to 1389, it was the most flourishing and favoured portion of European Serbia; at present, excepting the neighbouring mountains of Albania, it is the poorest and worst-ruled part of Turkey in Europe. The turning-point in its history is to be found in the victory of the Turks on Kóssovo, but the transformation of a fruitful land into a wilderness was a gradual process, and came about as follows:—

According to the terms made between the Sultan and the Serbians who first submitted to him, the church and the mosque were to stand side by side, and men were to worship in either as they might incline. But these conditions met with no better observance in Serbia than in Bulgaria. The moderation, the tolerance of the Turk, lasted only till he got a firm grip on the country, and then he appropriated to his own use whatever he did not destroy. Of the children that were not slain, the girls were dragged off to harems, the boys to the janissaries, while their elders could only save themselves by "ransoming their heads" (the original signification of the haratch). Such churches as escaped being destroyed or taken for mosques, owed it either to their smallness or to their occupying sites not convenient for Moslem worship, or finally because to save them the Christians were willing to pay large sums of money. In this manner Gratchanitza and Détchani still continue a source of income to the Mussulman.

Nevertheless, except the Ottoman colonies sent soon after the battle of Kóssovo to Skopia, Prizren, and Novo Berdo, the Mahommedanisation of Stara Serbia went on but slowly, so long as the population of the country were Serbs. But in the latter half of the seventeeth century, events occurred which nearly emptied the country of its original inhabitants.

The Turks having carried their depredations into the dominions of the Emperor of Germany,—having installed themselves in Hungary and besieged Vienna,—the House of Hapsburg took up the war against them in earnest, and the Serbian Christians south of the Danube were called on to lend their aid. At Adrianople the Patriarch of Serbia met George Brankovic, last scion of her last princes, and anointed him ruler; then both the secular and the spiritual chief undertook to raise the people to arms. We have in another chapter noticed the result of this effort. Austria, having used George Brankovic as a tool, held him captive for life at Eger; her generals having penetrated to the Kóssovo Poljé, mismanaged matters and had to retreat. Thereupon the greater part of the inland Serbian population, finding themselves given over to the Turks, and judging further contest in their own country hopeless, resolved to accept the Emperor's offer and emigrate to his dominions.

In the year 1690, 37,000 families passed from their fatherland under the leadership of the then reigning patriarch, Arsenius Tsrnoïevic; they were the remnant of wealth and valour in central Serbia, and preferred expatriation to unconditional submission. In their new settlements north of the Danube and Save they formed the greater part of that famous military frontier, which long served to protect Austria alike from the plunder of Oriental armies and from the contamination of Oriental disease.* The Emperor of Germany promised that their service in his dominions should be but temporary; that he would conquer their land back for them, and that meanwhile, if they would but help to defend his, they should continue to be governed by their own authorities, civil and religious.

But the old land has not been reconquered, and the

* In the rising of 1875 and 1876 the military frontier, which formerly served as the defence of Christian Europe against the Turks, has served as the bulwark of Islam against Christendom. Although it has been found practically impossible to restrain the sympathies of a kindred population, or to reckon upon the fidelity of every official, yet the northern frontier has been strictly guarded against the passing over of men with any sort of arms in their hands into Bosnia. Turkish barbarities have been committed within sight of Austrian soil, and attacks from Mussulmans on the lives and properties of Austrian subjects have been made with impunity, owing to the resolute determination of Austria-Hungary to keep peace with Turkey at any price.

new land was by no means freely accorded to its gallant defenders. The succession of the patriarchs was rendered dependent on the caprice of the cabinet of Vienna; the office of the Voivode was mulcted of real power; nay, some of the new settlers were so tormented in order to induce them to change their religion, that they left Austria for Russia.

At this moment, the Serbians under national government are not more enthusiastic patriots than those whose families have dwelt for 200 years on foreign ground; nay, young men among the Austrian Serbians take service in the principality rather than in the empire. Since the War of Liberation hundreds of families have passed over to Free Serbia, and should the Turks ever evacuate the more southerly districts, the bulk of the north Danubian colonists declare that they will return whence they came.

Significant of this unbroken adherence to their old fatherland, is the arrangement whereby the Austrian Serbs have consecrated a portion of their new territory *in memoriam*. The spot chosen is the so-called Frusca Gora, a hilly peninsula between the Danube and Save; there the newly arrived emigrants built churches named after those they had left behind them; thither they transferred their few treasures, and the bones of their last czar.

We visited the convent where Lázar lies. His body was carried from the field of Kóssovo first to Gratchanitza and thence to Ravanitza,—a church now included in the principality; finally to New Ravanitza, erected in the Frusca Gora. The day of the battle of Kóssovo is celebrated as the czar's anniversary; on it thousands of people make pilgrimages to his shrine, crowding around the open coffin wherein he lies, robed with the garments in which he fought and fell. A large picture of the battle is preserved in the same convent: it serves as a text for poems on the Turkish conquest, and for traditional descriptions of home.

Having now seen how Old Serbia lost her Christian and quasi-civilised inhabitants, we will examine how it came to be tenanted by barbarians and Islam.

The place of the fugitives who quitted the plains, both at the first emigration and afterwards, was filled up from the neighbouring hills by a descent of Skipetars, or Albanians, or, as the Turks call them, Arnaouts.

From the beginning of Serbian history there must have been districts where the Slavonic and Albanian elements existed side by side.* How far north the Albanians dwelt previous to their last ingress it is hard to determine; but it is certain that the Slavonians shared Albanian territory as far as Durazzo and Elbassan; also that, even before Némania's time, the little Serbian kingdom of Zeta united northern Skipetars and southern Slāvs. Afterwards, the laws of the empire speak of Albanians, both orthodox and catholic, as fellow-subjects with the Serb. Finally, after the breaking-up, first of the czardom, and then of Zeta itself, we find the Albanians under separate princes; but these princes— for instance, Scanderbeg himself—are relatives and allies of the Serbs.

Most of the northern Albanians dwelling near the Adriatic became adherents of the Latin Church. On the Mahommedan conquest it was the interest of the Ottoman to sow division between the Christian races. The

---

* M. Hahn is inclined to consider the Albanians as the aboriginal inhabitants, who vacated the fertile part of the country during the Serbian occupation for centuries. However this may be, both they themselves and the Slavonic inhabitants speak of their immigration as recent; in some places they have come down from the hills within the last fifty years, and constantly talk of returning thither.

Roman Catholics being in the minority were those to whom the most indulgences could be safely granted, and the mountaineers of Albania, unlike those of Montenegro, grew weary of acting breakwater to the flood of Turkish power. They therefore agreed to become subjects of the Sultan, on condition of a separate licence to maintain their religion and perpetuate their wild mode of life; these terms are still acted on by such tribes as dwell in the hills, and cannot well be reached by a Turkish army.

But when Albanians came down to live on the Serbian plains, they soon found that no better faith would be kept with them than with other Christians, and their fickle character and lack of definite purpose furnished poor stuff for patient endurance. Part of one tribe, called the Clementiner, did indeed emigrate with the Serbians; but those who remained in Turkey gradually yielded to the policy of the Porte, *i.e.* they became separated in interest from their brother-Christians, and purchased, at the price of apostacy, permission to hector over the rest of the population.

In Old Serbia the remnant of Roman Catholic Albanians is but small, although from time to time it is recruited by fresh arrivals from the hills. The newcomers usually follow the example of their predecessors, and after a while become Mahommedans. Even when they continue in the Latin faith, they compound for an exemption from haratch by lending the Sultan military service, and helping to keep down their fellow-Christians. Indeed, wherever the authorities are Mussulman and Mahommedan law is observed in courts of justice, it requires no small exertion on the part of the Roman Catholic priests, with occasional encouragement from foreign powers, to prevent all the so-called Latins in Old Serbia from going over to Islam. If once a few families in a village become Mahommedans, they never cease bullying the rest until they have made them follow their example, for apparently nothing annoys a renegade like the presence of constancy greater than his own. Waverers attempt to bridge over the passage between the two creeds by adopting Mahommedan names, and thus passing for Mussulmans abroad, while they remain Christians at home. We shall have occasion to speak of these Romanists hereafter—their principal parishes lie at Gilan, Ipek, Diakova, and Prizren.

As for the general characteristics and customs of the Northern Albanians, there exists a full and particular treatise on the subject, written by one who knows them and whom they know well. We refer to the book of M. Hecquard, late Consul of France at Scutari in Albania. At present it suffices to remark that the Arnaouts in Old Serbia belong to the division Ghegga, and, like all Gheggas, entertain a strong aversion for the southern Albanians, or Tosks. The Tosks are certainly very different from them, many being to a certain extent Hellenized, and exhibiting both in physique and character some affinity with the graceful, intelligent, and fickle Greeks. The Gheggas, on the other hand, are a sturdy and hardy type, and those settled in Slavonic districts have a strong tinge of Slavonic blood; indeed, some of their families are of Slāvic descent, for if a Serb forsakes his religion he at once loses the name of Serbian, and is henceforth termed "Arnaout."

The Albanian in Old Serbia is taller and more stalwart than the Albanian of Epirus; he is cleaner in his person, and his substantial and splendid dress displays more analogy with the Montenegrīne costume than with the Tosk fustanella and dangling sleeves. But a cross with the Serbian has not contributed to render the Ghegga character more amiable. If more stately than the Tosk, he is also more stubborn, and the Arnaouts now installed in the old city of the Patriarch, fully justify the merchant of Skopia's description, as the most lawless Mussulmans in Turkey. Their antagonism to the authority of the Porte is, however, quite as marked as their arrogance to the Christians. "Fear God little," say the Arnaouts of Ipek, "and as for the Sultan, do not know that he lives." They plunder the rayah, and are glad of the excuse of their creed for plundering, but they care about religion very little any way, and they and the Serbs are certainly not separated by hatred of race, as both are from the Osmanli. The Serbs look down on the Albanians for their inconstancy, lawlessness, and ignorance, but they admire their fighting qualities, and they declare that many Albanians joined the War of Liberation, and have since amalgamated with the Danubian Serbs.

We now come to the remnant of Serbian families who yet remain in the old country, and whom the emigration of their countrymen and the apostacy of the Arnaouts have left in the smallest minority formed by Christians in any part of Turkey in Europe.

In dialect, dress, and physique, the Old Serbians are identical with those on the southern frontier of the principality, and, like them, are as hardy a race as one could wish to see. Even among Mussulman neighbours their warlike qualities secure esteem; but they are slow to rouse, and this has often placed them at a disadvantage, both with Turks and Albanians, in cases where sudden and unscrupulous action wins the day. It is, however, in time of peace that appears the radical distinction between the Serbian and any of the Mahommedan peoples of Turkey. His idea of order and right is not Oriental, but European. In the principality, where he has his own way, popular government is found compatible with quiet and contentment; and his is the only country hereabouts where brigandage and official corruption are kept down.

In Arnaoutluk, and contrasted with the Arnaout, we have heard the Serbians called "good workers," but it is a comparison of laziness, for they certainly do not share the Bulgarian's disposition for agricultural labour. This lack of industry, together with a *dourness* which makes it difficult for them to yield in trials or to get on with others, constitute their most obvious faults. Fortitude, independent spirit, self-respect, and self-restraint, in fact a certain nobleness of character, cannot make up for such practical defects; nevertheless, in the Serbian, such qualities have a special value, inasmuch as they are precisely those which the other Christians of Turkey lack.

The government of the principality discourages the Old Serbians from emigrating to seek a home with their brethren, because they would thus abandon the old country entirely to Mahommedans. Of course, however, the existence in their neighbourhood of a free state governed by Serbians helps to give them self-confidence; and besides this, in Old Serbia, unlike Bosnia or Bulgaria, every proud memory is for the Christian.

The Asiatic Turk who conquered at Kóssovo has left few and sparse settlements in the country; the Albanian Mahommedan represents a doubly conquered race. He is a European who has lost not only liberty but religion, whose past is barbarian, his present apostacy, and his future either a sneaking return to his former faith, or slavery to a despotic government administered by foreign officials. The Christians, on the contrary, meeting at their festivals under the walls of the grand old churches, claim as their own all traditions of ancient empire, and of such civilisation as distinguished Old Serbia so long as it was a part of Christian Europe. And if the past be theirs, they have only to look forward to be sure that the future is theirs also; that sooner or later they must become a part of Christian Europe once more. Their kindred of race—often their own near relatives—are living as European Christians in Serbia and Austria; hence they know what is meant by freedom, and there is no confusion, no uncertainty in their prospects for their children, who are educated in the conviction that they at least will be free. But all this ideal life (which, as it has been truly observed, one can only get at by coming among a people with some knowledge of its language and history) is not inconsistent with an occasionally despairing view of things at present, and an occasional temptation to throw up everything and be gone.

The condition of the country is indeed bad enough to reduce to despair all its inhabitants, excepting of course those evil men who thrive on it. The Porte, having exerted energies sufficient to extinguish national liberty in Albania, and to drive great numbers of Albanians to apostatise, has never carried its pains to the point of bringing its new adherents into the attitude of orderly citizens. Whenever authority is exerted over them, it is in order to obtain recruits, or to impose Turkish officials in lieu of the old hereditary governors—not to enforce a just treatment of the Christians. The mode wherein the administration is conducted gives so good an idea of the state of society, that we will describe it in a few words.

In the towns of Stara Serbia the governor is a Turkish official; sometimes an Osmanli who does not know the language of the country, sometimes an Albanian who has served in the regular army. This official supports his authority by aid of a few zaptiés and cavasses in his own service, and these useful persons derive their pay chiefly from what they can rob from the people. The mudir, kaïmakam, or pasha, buys his post to begin with, and is then left to enjoy it so short a time that his chief aim is to reimburse himself as quickly as possible. Every one knows this, so Mussulmans and Christians alike ply him with bribes. But, besides enriching himself, he has to raise the Sultan's taxes. If the Mussulmans will not pay their share he must doubly fleece the Christians; for the Mussulmans are not to be trifled with, as, should he offend them, they may bribe some higher authority to remove him from his post. At Príshtina this was constantly the case; the mudir we found there was the second in a year, and before we left the district he was already deposed.

Supposing, however, that a governor will not be intimidated, and having friends among the higher powers, cannot be got rid of by fair means, force must be resorted to. At Ipek the kaïmakam being resolved to raise taxes from Mussulmans, not only obtained regular troops to support his designs, but seemed inclined to circumvent the local Mahommedans by conciliating the rayahs. Thereupon the Arnaouts waylaid him, and shot him from behind a bush. This instance came under our own observation, inasmuch as while at Príshtina, we took it into our heads to inquire if we could make a detour by the monastery of Détchani. The mudir told us that he could not send us thither, the road being beset with Albanians who had lately murdered the governor of Ipek, and who would not even respect the Sultan's firman. If we were resolved to go, we must make a round by Prizren, and ask the pasha for a guard of Nizam.

Next in authority to the Turkish governor comes the town-council, or medjliss. The members of the medjliss are (with the exception of one Christian) Mussulmans, and in Old Serbia the post is filled by the most influential chiefs among the Arnaouts. In former days, when the governor was a native, he usually had a strong party in his council, for many of its members were his kin; hence the Christians had only to bribe him in order to secure a certain amount of protection. Nowadays, the governor must still be bribed, but being a stranger he has not the same power to shelter his protégés, so all the medjliss must be bribed too, and in this respect the Christians themselves told us that their present state is worse than the first. The only chance is to play the foreign governor and the local Mussulmans against each other; but it is a dangerous game, as whenever the two sets of plunderers find it their interest to make peace, they make it at the rayahs' cost.

The Christians could do far more to help themselves if they were worthily represented in the medjliss, but this is rarely the case. In Old Serbia, as throughout Turkey in Europe, the Mussulmans congregate in the towns, and in order to keep out of their way, the Christians dwell in the country and villages. Hence the town community of every Christian district is comparatively small, and furnishes the Turkish Government with a pretext for restricting Christian representation in the medjliss to a single member, or, if there are both Roman Catholic and Oriental Christians, to two members. Even this is a late concession, and certain Turkish governors, who would be glad to use the Christians against the local Mussulmans, have themselves described to us the treatment which deprives the rayah member of the medjliss of all power. In the first place, he is one against many; secondly, he is used as a servant to hand pipes and coffee to the Mussulmans;

thirdly, he is sent out of the room whenever anything of importance is to be discussed. In consequence, few Christians, except such as are willing to expose themselves to ill-treatment, will consent to sit in the medjliss. Sometimes a poor wretch is put in and paid for it; sometimes a creature of the bishop's or the governor's is got in by intrigue, and then becomes the scourge of his own community. In Old Serbia the courage of the Christians shows itself by better men offering for the post; and those who have been for a while in Free Serbia bring to their office a resolute demeanour and a definiteness of purpose which enable them now and then to hold their own.

Of the Christian community the principal representative is properly the bishop; hence nothing could more effectually take the heart out of the Slāvs in Turkey than the transfer of this important office to Greeks, who do not care a rush for Slavonic interests. In most parts of Old Serbia the idea we found associated with a bishop was that of a person who carried off what few paras the Turks had left. When at home he would occasionally exert himself to prevent Christian children being carried off and made Mahommedans, but he was too often absent to be available even for this purpose. Of course, in this case, as in that of Turkish governors and Christian representatives in the medjliss, there are honourable exceptions to the general rule.

Under existing circumstances, the actual head of a Christian community is its primate or chief elder, usually known by the Turkish appellation, kodgia bashi. This personage is supposed to be elected by the Christians themselves. He has little political power; but his social influence is great for good or evil, as he helps to apportion the taxes, and acts as judge in civil cases. In the latter function he is aided by the chief men, called

Kmets, a title general among Slavonic tribes, and which may be traced back in the ancient annals of Bohemia, even to the days of Queen Libussa. The room wherein we lodged at Príshtina was used in the bishop's absence for the meeting of these kmets, who considered civil cases in the community itself; criminal cases are referred to the mudir's court, where, as we shall presently instance, Christian evidence is not received.

Having thus sketched the present condition of Old Serbia, we may conclude by quoting thereon the opinion of its inhabitants. This is,—that however in other parts of the empire improvement may be compatible with Turkish government, here that government is the very root of ill. The evils that desolate Old Serbia have their source in the antagonism of races and creeds: the first aim of a good government must be to appease these rivalries: the maintenance of Turkish rule depends on fomenting them. Hated alike by Albanian and Serb, the Asiatic conqueror, since the day he entered the country, has skilfully worn out the energies of his enemies by turning them against each other; should he ever allow them to make up their differences, their first act in concert would be to drive him from the land. That this will be the end of the matter is, in fact, the expectation of all parties; for the Arnaouts are only held to their present creed by interest; and the attempts lately made by the Porte to introduce the conscription and foreign officials have so disgusted them, that they have begun to ask themselves if they might not make a better bargain elsewhere. Their present profession of Mahommedanism is not an insurmountable obstacle: "they were all Christians once, and to gain anything they would be Christians again." During the last war with Montenegro it was very generally expected that a Serbian army would cross the border and co-operate with its kindred in the hills. On this occasion the Albanians in Old Serbia held assemblies and reasoned thus:—"We have long been fighting the Montenegrines, and know that they are good heroes; nevertheless we can hold our own against them, for they have not Frankish arms. But it is said that the Serbians on the Danube have cannon, and officers trained in Frankish schools. If they join the Montenegrines there will be another battle on Kóssovo; we shall be beaten, and then we must make terms. Let us seek persons who have been in Free Serbia, and ask what taxes are there paid." They were told that the Serbian government requires two ducats from every householder. "Two ducats? We will give three, if in return they will promise not to take us for nizam." Answer: "The Serbians do not care to have nizam, their soldiers are militia, who wear the national dress, and do not go on foreign service." "Good, good," cried the Arnaouts; "why, we should be better off under the Prince than we now are under the Sultan. Let but the Serbs march over the border, and we will negotiate with them through the Abbot of Détchani."

But a Serbian army could only cross the border in event of a Christian rising throughout Turkey—a rising which, even if successful, must entail massacre and pillage. No wonder, then, that some persons would desire to avert such extremities by diplomatic arrangement. According to them, we must find an agent for bringing this part of Turkey under civilisation, without necessarily detaching it from the Ottoman empire; such an agent is to be found in the native Christian government of Free Serbia. That government manages to keep order; and were the southern frontier of the principality extended so as to include Old Serbia, we should soon see brigandage put down, and all clans and classes equal before law. The present population is sparse, idle, and disorganized; but once let life and property become secure on the fertile plains of Metóchia and Kóssovo, and their inhabitants would be recruited from beyond the Danube by industrious and well-ordered colonists, able to retrieve their fathers' exile, and give back to Europe the Old Serbian land.

CHAPTER XVII.

FROM PRÍSHTINA TO VUCHITERN.

AT Príshtina we dismissed the kiradgees who had accompanied us from Monastir. Their grass-fed horses were becoming knocked up, and we spent so many days in resting, that it was bootless expense to pay for them when not in use. Scarcely had we parted, when the poor fellows met with a grievous mischance. As usual, to save paying for their horses in the khan, they drove them out to pasture. At nightfall, in a lonely place, they were accosted by some Arnaouts, who, pretending to be zaptiés, found fault with them for letting their horses graze in such and such spots, asked their names, and otherwise bothered them. When at last the kiradgees contrived to satisfy these tormentors and drove their horses together, they found that three were missing. At once they suspected that the *soi-disant* police were but members of a party of horse-stealers, and that they had engaged them with questions merely that the rest of the crew might have an opportunity of making off with the beasts. But it was now dark, no search could be made; and next morning at daybreak a diligent quest succeeded in recovering, not the horses, but the horses' tails—cut off, and left on the ground. On this discovery, the kiradgees considered it certain that their beasts had not merely strayed, and they repaired to the town to see if anything could be done towards reclaiming them from the thieves. To swear to the horses having been in their own possession overnight, they called in the evidence of our cavass, "*because his oath, as that of a Mussulman, would be received, and theirs would not.*" This he, a Mussulman, explained to us, when requesting leave to go with them.

So soon as the mudir heard what had happened, he determined to give the passing Frankish travellers a proof of his zeal; therefore he sent out into the bazaar, and captured the first two stranger Albanians on whom his zaptiés could lay their hands; then he let us know that the thieves were caught, and that he would send them, loaded with chains, to Prizren. Through our dragoman we questioned the kiradgees, if they thought the imprisoned Albanians were really the thieves. They answered that it was most unlikely, as the men who stole their horses would not be found next morning dawdling about the bazaar; they had doubtless made off, and the horses were with them. Besides, the poor kiradgees remarked, that what *they* wanted the mudir to catch was, not the thieves, but the stolen animals, and to this end no steps had yet been taken. We thought of a law of old Czar Dūshan, which ruled that if the magistrates and nobles of a district did not keep that district free from robbers, or, when a theft had occurred, could not find the robbers and force them to make restitution of stolen goods, they, the nobles and the magistrates, should indemnify the plundered voyager. It seemed that some law of this kind was still needed to quicken the execution of justice in Stara Serbia.

However, we asked the kiradgees whether, since they believed the captured Albanians not to be those who had stolen their horses, they would not say so, and have them released. But this no one would hear of: "*All* Arnaouts were thieves! If those now imprisoned had not stolen the horses in question, they had stolen others, or were about to steal them. The mudir himself had pronounced them *mauvais sujets*, their teskérés were not in proper order, and their testimony concerning themselves agreed not together. Let them stay in prison by all means; doubtless the mudir would let them out as soon as we were gone."

As the horses were not ours, nor any longer in our service, we did not see that we could intermeddle further, and we really dreaded to do so for fear of causing other persons to be thrown into jail. Evidently *justice* was beyond the mudir's functions, and all representations on our part would be considered simply as cries for vengeance. In this part of the world, if a privileged person demands justice, somebody is sure to be punished, and that promptly—whether he be the culprit or not is a matter of comparative indifference.

The road between Príshtina and Vuchitern lies over the actual battle-field of Kóssovo, and crosses the river Lab, which flowed between the hostile camps. To the right are passed the ruins of the old church of Samodresha— identified with many Sabors (parliaments), and with one account of the last sacrament partaken of by the Serbian army. The spot where Sultan Amurath was assassinated is covered by a small mosque, and all the neighbourhood between it and Príshtina is associated with legends of Milosh. By the Turks themselves a house is shown containing the tombs of the Vizier, and his companions slain by Milosh in his death-struggle. They also point out a mound on the top of which they say he planted himself, and killed all who attempted to approach. "All the graves around it are graves of Turks whom Milosh slew." But the most interesting monument has perished; three large stones placed at equal distance, and each marking the spot attained by Milosh in the three bounds that almost carried him to his horse's side. The third stone marked where he was cut down. Some years ago, when the mosque of Murad was rebuilt, these stones were removed and used as materials. Considering, however, how long they had been suffered to remain, it would not appear that the Turks intended, when removing them, to insult the Serbians; any more than the British peasant intends to insult the memory of the Druids when he breaks up their stone circles to build his cottage walls.

The hospitable sheikh from Bokhara, who entertained the winter travellers Zach and Hahn with tea, is still guardian of Amurath's tomb; but at the time of our visit he was absent at Prizren, and his black *locum tenens* was not communicative. He demurred at first about letting us enter, but whether as women or as ghiaours we knew not. However, the Usbashi gave a positive order, in the name of whom we also knew not; and the result was that not only were we admitted, but nothing was said about taking off shoes. There is little to be seen. The so-called tomb is a shabby likeness of some of those in Constantinople, *i.e.*, simply a room containing a large coffin. The body is not there, having been carried to Broussa, but over the coffin hangs a scarf, and at the head of it is fixed a sultan's turban. Once the actual vestments worn by Amurath when he received the blow were kept here; but the attendant assured us that the "old soiled ones had been thrown away, and that those we saw were bran new and sent from Stamboul." The turban is on the pattern of those worn by the lay figures in the hall of the Janissaries, a pyramid of linen coils monstrous to behold, and as unlike as possible to that most stately and simple of headgears, the turban, as it is still worn in Bosnia. At the top stands a little red fez, stiff and crimped as if with irons; this again is totally unlike the fez with its long flowing tassel as sported by the Albanians and Greeks.

It is said that the sword of Milosh Obilic used also to be kept here, but this we did not see, and the guards said it had been taken away. Having left the mosque, we remounted and rode onward for about half an hour, when the zaptié stopped to point out what the Turks call the site of Murad's tent; he showed us also a heap of stones where some Beg or other had fallen. Apparently the latter was of late origin, and referred to another battle on Kóssovo. Then we crossed the Lab, but not having with us any Christian from the neighbourhood, we could identify no spot connected with the Serbian battle array except the hills of Golesh (Slav. *gol*, naked), where Vūk Brankovic is said to have been stationed, and which have been cursed with barrenness for his sake.

But if the remembrance of their army's station is faded from all but uncertain local tradition, Serbian minstrels have not forgotten the order and manner of their heroes' fall—old Iūg Bogdan early in the day; eight of the brothers Iugovic side by side; the brave Ban Strahinia "where blood flowed knee-deep;" last the Standard-bearer Bosko is seen "chasing the enemy in flocks as a hawk chases pigeons, and driving them before him into the Sitnitza;" and where "the broken spears are strewn thickest and the bravest warriors lie slain," there is the spot where fell the Czar. Thus in the ever-darkening twilight we passed over that fatal field where once on the warm quiet Sabbath morning came forth the ministering "maiden of Kóssovo," with water to wash the blood of the wounded, with wine to freshen the lips of the faint, while still she sought her gay bridegroom of yesterday among the mangled corpses of to-day.*

---

* See one of the most touching Serbian ballads, "The Maiden of Kóssovo."

CHAPTER XVIII.

VUCHITERN.

WE had lingered so long on the way that it was dark when we reached Vuchitern, and then our dragoman, who had ridden on before, met us with a face of dismay, saying, "They have nothing for supper." However, it seemed that quarters had been bespoken, and we presently found ourselves in the house of the Serb pope, and in a room which, though it lacked window-panes and even shutters, was provided with a substantial goat's hair carpet. While we were improvising curtains the popadia entered, and by the time the luggage was brought up, we had made friends, and she whisperingly informed us that "a fowl was in the pot." Why then had they not said so at once? For this very sufficient reason. The pope and the kodgia bashi were standing without when the dragoman rode up and accosted them abruptly—behind him they saw Turkish horsemen. "You know," said the popadia, "we had not enough for all, and if those Turks had heard of supper in our house, they would never have gone to the khan."

The peasants from Príshtina went no farther than Vuchitern, and we sent back the postman with his obstreperous steeds, so that the operation of getting horses had to be performed all over again. We knew this would prevent us from starting in good time, and as our hosts appeared the sort of people likely to give information about the country, we agreed to spend next day where we were. This resolve we communicated to the mudir's son, who was in attendance the evening we arrived, and next morning at an early hour the mudir himself came to visit us. Our room was not yet arranged for the reception of company, so we agreed to receive him on the chardak,—a sort of covered balcony in form like a small room, which forms the outer saloon of most houses hereabouts, and where guests may be received without entering the house. However, when we came forth, we found him not reclining on the cushions of the chardak, but seated at the head of the stairs on a chair. The Arnaout or Bosnian Mussulman rarely affects foreign fashions, so we saw at once that this must be an Osmanli desirous to be thought cognizant of European manners. An Osmanli he was, and dressed in European costume, with an enormous pink waistcoat, which set off his *embonpoint* to the full. But an Osmanli shows much better when he is surrounded by menacing Arnaouts than when he is fattening on Bulgarian and Fanariote bribes; in the post of danger he is forced out of his sloth, his courage is called into play, his will too puts forth its real strength, while its imperiousness is restrained. Moreover, we found the mudir at Vuchitern both obliging and intelligent, and willing to tell what he knew about the place, though being himself a foreigner he had to call in assistance before replying to any question. Especially he was anxious to let us know that he had not always lived among barbarians. No—he had been mudir in the Roumelian provinces, and his son spoke Greek well. Encouraged by his amiability, and appealing to his civilised sentiments, we asked if we might visit the Mahommedan girls' school. The countenance of the mudir fell, and all present looked one upon another. This was not the first time we had made the request, but it was the first time we had asked point-blank ourselves. Our former messages had always met with some excuse : the schoolmaster was ill, the children had a holiday, or, as at Príshtina, it was Friday, and the school was not held. Yet we kept hearing of Arnaout girls' schools, and in the same breath that their women lived in gross ignorance. How were these accounts to be reconciled? Evidently we must see the schools.

The mudir of Vuchitern having no time to frame an excuse, waited only a minute to take breath, and then replied, that the request we had made was such as might be expected from civilised and enlightened travellers; further, he was well aware that it would be cheerfully complied with in Constantinople. But we were now in Arnaoutluk, and he regretted to say that the Mussulmans were fanatical and rude. However, he would take steps to secure that we should see what we desired ; the girls' school was next door to his harem, and if we would condescend to visit his khanum (lady), she and his son would escort us to the school. The visit was fixed for the afternoon, and all preliminaries were nearly settled, when we called to mind the slovenly déshabillé of the women at Katchanik, and therefore remarked to the mudir that we had heard much of the beauty and splendour of Albanian costume, and that we had long wished to judge of it for ourselves. He took the hint, and promised that in his harem we should see the best-dressed women in the town. At the same time, the cloud on his face gave way to a good-natured smile, as if this last trait had served to assure him that whatever we might ask or attempt, we had no motive deeper than feminine curiosity.

When the time for our visit came, the popadia offered to accompany us, and for that purpose arrayed herself in black serge; her tight-fitting garment reaching to the ankles, and scarcely differing from a long pelisse. We were heartily glad of her company, for such was her quickness of comprehension, that she contrived not only to understand our broken language, but also to interpret it to others. At the gate of the harem we found a sort of lodge, where we had to leave our cavass and dragoman, and where we were met by the Greek-speaking son, a dreadful little fellow in shabby uniform. He conducted us through a court to the chardak, on which carpets and cushions lay prepared. At the foot of the stair we were received by his mother. The khanum was a fat old Turkish woman, frightfully like an overfed bird of prey; her dress showed the same Frankish taste as her husband's pink silk waistcoat, for it was of brown European muslin, but its thin trousers and scanty bodice could hardly be said to become a corpulent and withered form. None the less, she was not emancipated from the fear of exciting dangerous admiration. While we sat sipping coffee, it happened that a zaptié having some message for her son, poked his head out of the lodge. Far off as he was, a hue and cry was raised, and the old dame ducked under the side of the chardak with all the haste that might have beseemed a fair one of eighteen. This incident recalled to us certain reflections that had occurred frequently in the female compartment of the steamers on the Bosphorus; namely, that if Turkish women value their prestige as beauties, they must oppose every attempt to draw them into public view; and for the following reasons. Most Oriental women have dark eyes, bright enough to look bewitching through the slit of the yashmak, and all can paint well enough to produce a complexion which seems roses and lilies when half seen through muslin folds. But alas for their charms should the veil be torn away, and the wearers be called on to show their faces honestly beside those of European women—the whole face, in broad daylight, exposed to sunshine, wind, and rain! Of course in the wealthy harem, where a high price is paid for beauty, and the faded rose is discarded or passed on, one sees exquisite forms arrayed with taste and splendour. But many of the officials in the European provinces cannot afford polygamy, nor to buy Circassian slaves; or as sometimes happens, they have inherited the favourite of some higher official—hence in this class, as a rule, the women are unpleasing to behold. Indeed it is hard to see how they could be otherwise. They destroy their teeth by smoking and eating bonbons, even when they do not blacken them on purpose. They dock their hair, they cultivate fatness, they bedaub their finger and toe nails with a coating that looks like red mud. Then, unless they have what is much admired, a broad, flat, featureless countenance, they exhibit the Turkish long nose, retreating brow, cutaway chin, and sallow complexion. Absence of intellectual occupations, and exclusion from cultivated society, deprive plain faces of a redeeming expression of intelligence, while even fine features bear the stamp of sloth, triviality, and too often of unbridled passion.

While we were at Constantinople, some persons who should have known better spread the report that a fête given by Fuad Pasha would be signalised by the emancipation of Turkish ladies—to wit, by their appearance outside the harem and dressed in Parisian toilettes. Of course, when the fête took place, there was nothing of the kind. Supposing, however, the report had proved true, is it not a question how far the moral elevation of the Turkish ladies would have been advanced by their mingling in Pera society, or by exchanging the dress of their country and climate for the foreign artifices of Parisian mode? Till the Mahommedan woman can receive an education calculated to arm her with self-restraint and self-respect, those would indeed assume a grave responsibility who should turn her loose on Oriental society, or suddenly divest her of her present guardians, the veil and the sacred walls of the harem. One might say more than this, and assume that until the women of Christian communities situated in Levantine cities shall make a more creditable use of their liberty, Mussulmans can hardly be expected to believe that the Eastern female possesses powers of self-guidance sufficient to justify a husband's confidence.

Such were our reflections while the khanum put numberless questions to the popadia: they were interrupted by her son taking leave, and then the door into the house opened, and a troop of ladies crowded in. In a few moments all were squatted on the chardak, staring at us, and we at them. Many of them were old and withered, and wore a heterogeneous costume; others were gaily coifed with seed-pearls and coins, but enveloped in a black serge pelisse like that of the popadia, and unlike any other dress that we saw in Turkey. These younger dames were painted to such a degree that at first we really thought they wore masks, and as their mask-like faces represent the ideal of beauty in this part of the world, we may state that this consists of cherry lips and cheeks, a very fair complexion, and jet-black eyebrows, strongly drawn. Among them all stood one unpainted fresh-looking girl—a bride—and, as we understood, the bride of the mudir's son; she it was who produced the fine clothes. Her trousseau was brought forth, bit by bit, and all wrapped in pretty handkerchiefs, for it is a *coquetterie de toilette* that the handkerchief should be handsome enough to correspond with the garment it enfolds. After a little coaxing she went in and dressed, reappearing in a suit of rose-coloured under-robes, with the over-robe of dark green velvet; a charming ensemble of which the idea seemed to be taken from a rosebud half folded in its leaves.

The details of the costume were as follows:—First, a garment of white silk gauze, the lower part of which disappears in voluminous trousers of rose-coloured silk, while over the upper part is worn a waistcoat of ruby-coloured velvet, showing the shirt in front and at the sleeves. Waistcoat and trousers are connected by a girdle, which, to match the dress, should be of the richest material; maybe the bride had a silver one at home, but that which she here wore was a piece of stuff. Over these garments, and open down the front, hangs a robe of silk, also rose-coloured, but lighter in shade than the trousers and vest; this robe has long sleeves. Lastly, comes the green velvet paletot, falling backwards and without any sleeves. Consisting, as this dress did, of so great a variety of parts, no portion of it was hidden by the rest, no item appeared *de trop*. As for the work on the robes, it was all in gold and exquisitely embroidered; yet when with pride they told us its enormous price, this did not exceed what is paid every day in Paris or London for perishable garnitures composed only of artificial flowers, ribbons, or tulle. The young girl's headgear consisted of a fillet of coins and seed-pearls, with a natural rose stuck behind the ear.

The dress being duly complimented, handmaidens brought forth bundles of handkerchiefs worked by the ladies present. They were of muslin or something like it, and embroidered in coloured worsted with a slight admixture of gold thread, but displayed little taste in hue or design. We supposed these handkerchiefs were worked at school. "No, at school the ladies did not work." "What! did they only read and write?" "No, all those present had been to school, but none of them could write or read." "Then what is it that you do learn there?" "To say our prayers, Turkish prayers."* "Can you understand these prayers?" "No." "Do any of you speak Turkish?" "No, no." Here the khanum interfered, highly amused at what she considered an enforced confession of inferiority. "*I* speak Turkish," quoth she, and then bursting out laughing, and spreading her hands over the assembly, she added, "but these women are every one of them Arnaouts."

Becoming wearied of this society, we at length proposed to adjourn to the school, when the khanum answered carelessly that there was no object in doing so; the school was empty, and the pupils were here. Former pupils, perhaps, but there were no little girls present; however we were about to yield the point when the good lady turned to the popadia, and with a wink at us and a scornful laugh said something about *ghiaour*. At the sound of the word *ghiaour* there flashed on our minds a recollection of the manifold excuses by which hitherto we had been dissuaded from seeing Mahommedan schools; we felt we were excluded as unbelievers, and that the cause of our exclusion was fanatical contempt. At once we determined to see the school. With a changed voice and frigid manner we turned to the popadia and said, "The mudir promised us to see the school, so be it full or empty we go there now." With these words we rose to our feet. What a hubbub in the chardak; the khanum exchanged her malicious triumph for a look of real alarm, and with deprecatory gestures hurried into the house. The Arnaout women scattered before us, as followed by the popadia we descended the stairs, walked to the lodge, and summoned our attendants. With them

* By *Turkish*, the Albanian and Bosniac mean Mahommedan.

came the mudir's son. "We are going to the school," said we, and therewith walked to the next door in the wall; it stood open and we passed in. Before us lay a sort of garden, and in the garden were a number of little girls who, half-frightened and half-curious, ran before us and showed the way. *En route* we came to an aperture in the wall between the school garden and that of the harem. It was stuffed with heads, among which we recognised those of the khanum and her visitors. Scarcely had we passed when the whole party, frantic with curiosity, clambered through the gap, and appeared in our train.

At the further end of the garden stood a house, with one door on the ground floor and another in the upper storey, the latter reached by an outside stair. At the top of the stairs we beheld a tall figure completely enveloped in mantle and veil, but at the sight of us she vanished instantly, and her place was taken by two unveiled women, who hurried down the stairs to meet us. And now the popadia, who evidently enjoyed the discomfiture of her fanatical neighbours, took the command, and laying hands on the little girls nearest her, began to push them in at the lower door. The other women called out to her that many of those children did not belong to the school. "Never mind," cried she, "scholars or no, let them get in and fill the room." In a few minutes we were invited to enter. To be sure, there was the school, *i.e.*, a little low den, with earthen unsmoothed floor, and a few broken benches. Of the scholars of course we could not judge, as many of those present were unaccustomed to attend, but in the front row sat some elder girls holding in their hands books dirty and torn, and written in Oriental characters. These girls were reciting or rather humming while they swayed their bodies to and fro. "You see," observed the popadia, "it is as they told you, what they learn here is to say the Turkish prayers." At that moment a voice sounded behind us, and one of the women of the house appeared. Her demeanour was nervous, and she asked very humbly what we were pleased to desire. "Here was the school, here were the scholars, as for the teacher (hodgia) she hoped we would not call on her to appear, she was a very reverend person." "She is sick," screeched a voice from the upper storey, "she cannot come: why don't you say she is sick?" "Ah, yes," said the former speaker, "that is it, she is sick, and very old too. Will you then be pleased to excuse her?" This we did gladly, and had they not betrayed themselves we never should have known that the hodgia did not choose to see us, any more than why they kept us from the school. It was only because we were excluded as ghiaours—a character shared by all the non-Mussulman inhabitants of Turkey—that we felt bound to carry the point. What right have they to shut Christians out of their schools, while Mussulmans walk into Christian schools without so much as asking leave?

The son of the mudir waited to escort us home. He seemed much agitated, and several times repeated, "O, this is not Constantinople, this is Arnaoutluk, Arnaoutluk!" But the grievances of Arnaoutluk were not at an end, our cavass had his story to tell. The horses sent in the morning for us to choose from were all miserable, and we had charged him to inquire for better. On our way to the harem we had encountered a drove, all strong and well-looking. He had been to inquire about these, and had found that the mudir dare not serve the firman on them because they belonged to Mussulmans. This story and the discussion thereon took us to the end of the bazaar, and then the popadia begged us to come with her and visit the Serbian kodgia bashi. On taking leave of the mudir's son we charged him with the following message:—All due thanks and compliments to his father, whose good intentions we fully recognised; but we were much surprised to find how little his Mussulman subjects cared either for the Sultan or for him. In spite of his order, the hodgia had refused to show us the school, and at this we were not so much angry as hurt, for we had intended only to show a friendly civility such as we were in the habit of paying to Christian schools. The Christians invited such visits, and took them as compliments, hence we perceived that hereabouts the Christians were the most enlightened and dutiful part of the community. Moreover, we were indignant to find that no good horses could be obtained for our journey, inasmuch as the Mussulmans would not obey the Sultan's firman, and give their horses for fair payment. The whole burden fell upon the Christians, who, being the poorer, could least bear it. Were the Mussulmans not also subjects of the Sultan? Had not the firman equal claims on them? As we finished these words we became aware that the end of the bazaar was filling with Arnaouts; and the thick gossamer veils which we wore as protection against sun and dust, could not altogether screen us from the flashes of angry eyes.

The mudir's son saw the eyes too: he was terribly frightened, flung his arm caressingly over the dragoman's shoulder, and speaking in a low voice assured him all would be well, his father would see to all. He then almost ran homewards, leaving for our protection a stout zaptié, who strode before us out of the bazaar; our cavass brought up the rear.

But a troop of urchins followed in our wake, and before we reached the kodgia bashi's dwelling we had ample grounds to credit the complaints made of the aggresive habits of these Mussulman gamins. Lurking in a body behind to watch favourable opportunities, they detach parties to run in front. These parties station themselves on each side of the way, and then first from one quarter and then another the victims are assailed by a pelt of small stones. In vain the zaptié swore and threatened, till at last, being struck himself, he furiously drew his hangiar and dispersed the tormentors with a sudden charge. Our cavass, a southern Albanian, was excessively incensed, and again and again assured us that in his part of the country the Mussulmans were not half so bad.

No wonder that the kodgia bashi's door was barred, and that cries from without afforded no inducement to undo it. At length the popadia caught sight of one of the family passing by, and asked him to use his voice in our behalf. When we had entered, and the door was closed behind us, what a change, and what a pleasant change! Instead of the parrot screams and excited gesticulations of the Arnaout females, or the khanum's medley of compliments, disputes, and insults, we were met by the sedate and hospitable greeting of a Serbian "house-father," and coffee was served by a gentle slender woman, modestly attired, and with unpainted face. Then came a half-hour's conversation, into which one could enter with earnestness and cheerfulness while resting in the well-cushioned "chardak," and looking down on the large and quiet garden.

Another interesting conversation was held that evening in the house of our host the priest. Pope Dantcha is a person well known throughout Old Serbia, and looked up to as he deserves. Without being previously aware of his reputation, we were much struck by his intelligence, his facility in communicating what he knew, and his courageous and upright bearing. In the presence of the mudir he showed none of that timid obsequiousness too common among the Christians in Turkey, while behind the mudir's back he abstained from reviling him, and did full justice to his difficult position. "There," said he, "the mudir sits—one man with half a dozen zaptiés—what can he effect? There are here but 200 Christian houses, and from 400 to 500 Mussulman, so the Arnaouts have it all their own way. They rob the Christians whenever and of whatever they please; sometimes walking into a shop, calling for what they want, and carrying it off on promise of payment, sometimes seizing it without further ado. Worse than this, their thoroughly savage, ignorant, and lawless way of living keeps the whole community in a state of barbarism, and as the Christians receive no support against them, no enlightenment nor hope from Constantinople, they naturally look for everything to Serbia;—to the Serbia of the past for inspiring memories, to the Principality for encouragement, counsel, and instruction."

The town of Vuchitern must needs have been once more important than it is at present, for it formed the seat of a bishop, and its old castle, whereof the ruins are used for the mudir's konak, was the residence of the hero Voina, brother-in-law of Czar Dūshan. One of the most fanciful of Serbian legends relates the feats of Voina's youngest son, and how he saved his imperial uncle "from the false friendship of the Latins." The old church of Vuchitern was destroyed, but a new one has been built. Not only is it of the plainest exterior, but lest it should overtop the houses of the Arnaouts it is sunk some feet in the ground. A similar church, but still further underground and almost dark, is to be seen at Nish, a town on the high road between Constantinople and Belgrade; but at Nish the Christians, having of late years got leave to build another church, have shown the joy of their hearts by beginning it on so large a scale that it towers over every building in the town. At Vuchitern there is a Serb school containing about sixteen children. We saw it, and though small it was clean and orderly, with an intelligent-looking lad for a teacher. A girls' school they have not, for the same reason as at Príshtina, but with a little encouragement they would be likely to start one, for the wife of Pope Dantcha would do her utmost, and is as energetic and clever as himself.

She said with pride, " I come from Ipek, and at Ipek there is a girls' school." We exclaimed, " But are not the Arnaouts of that district the most lawless in Turkey?" " So they are, but, on the other hand, the Christians of Ipek are the 'greatest-hearted' in Old Serbia. They have amongst them the church of the Patriarchate which is so stately and venerable; they have amongst them 'Katerina'—a woman whose equal is not to be found in the land. It was she who founded the female school." The pope added with pride, " My wife is her relative;" and feeling this a great recommendation, we asked many more questions about the school at Ipek. They said that it was provided with books, but not with maps, so we gave a set to be taken by the popadia on her next pilgrimage to her native town. Expecting soon to be in Free Serbia, we also left nearly all our remaining books to supply Pope Dantcha's school.

By way of rewarding us for these evidences of sympathy, the pope sat down on the carpet and gave us a sort of *catalogue raisonné* of all the churches, monasteries, and schools in the neighbourhood of Vuchitern. Most of them we shall presently have occasion to describe or allude to. All or almost all of the churches are old, some royal chapels and some formerly belonging to large convents. Many exist now only as ruins, but the people make pilgrimages to them regularly, and it is on or near their sites that new churches will rise. Unfortunately, while enumerating the ruins, the pope did not specially insist on the church of the old castle of Svétchani, and thus we passed it over on our way.

The glowing and affectionate praises bestowed by the popadia on the old city of the Patriarchate, and her husband's description of the church of Détchani, again roused our desire to go to Ipek; and we resolved to ask whether the route between it and Vuchitern was as dangerous as that from Príshtina. It was agreed, to try the effect of the firman, to send the servants early next morning with it and our request to the mudir. In order to give instructions to the dragoman we opened the door, and stood for a moment on the head of the stairs. He came, but with him Pope Dantcha in great apprehension, solemnly conjuring us not to appear outside with a light. "For fear of fire?" "No;" but the Arnaouts had been rather excited in the bazaar; some of them would now be lolling about on their way home, and talking angrily of our visit to the school. In that case our light might serve to "direct their mark!" In a room without shutters, this was no pleasant idea to sleep upon, so we put it out of our heads, assuring ourselves that the pope's apprehension led him to exaggerate. But we afterwards received the same warning from Mussulmans; and found that to take a suspicious stranger for a target is one of the recognised freaks of the Arnaout.

Next morning all was bustle, and by the time we had dressed and breakfasted the servants returned from the mudir. The firman had been read in full medjliss; to show proper dutifulness, the principal councillors declared that if we would go to Ipek, they would raise 100 Arnaouts and take us there. On the other hand, the mudir sent us his earnest advice by no means to make the attempt. According to the most recent tidings, the kaïmakam of Ipek had been murdered by the local Mussulmans while in the act of raising the Sultan's revenue, the whole district was in confusion, and who would receive us he could not say. As for himself, his zaptiés were few, and necessary for his support at Vuchitern; he could not give us enough for protection, and we should be at the mercy of an Arnaout guard. With less than 100 men the Arnaouts would not go, as they had feuds all over the country, and certainly would not return without a fight.

To such representations there was of course but one reply. "We grieved to find the Sultan's dominions in such a state, but as his officers were responsible for our safety we could not act against their advice." The fact was, that we might have got over the murdered kaïmakam and the general confusion, but we could not have answered it to ourselves to make a two days' journey through Christian villages, and to have halted at the monasteries described by Pope Dantcha, with a retinue of 100 fiends.

Scarcely was this matter decided when the mudir himself appeared. He enforced the arguments used by the dragoman, and further took occasion to express his regret at the discourtesy of the Arnaout hodgia. Now, he assured us, she was convinced of error, and he would be much obliged to us to give her an opportunity of proving penitence. Would we go to the school once more? The khanum was coming to return our visit, and would conduct us thither herself.

But we had had enough of the khanum; and hastened to deprecate her coming on the ground that we were engaged in packing and had not a room wherein to ask her to sit down. As for the school, for sake of precedent we thought it better to act on the mudir's invitation, but we intimated that, as we could not come forth expressly to pay it a second visit, we would take it on our way out of town. This we did, and experienced a reception so strongly contrasting with that of yesterday, that we could scarcely suppress a smile. At the first tap at the garden door, it was opened by a man in a turban who bade us welcome, and even carried his courtesy so far as to draw water from an adjacent well and offer it all round. He then led us into the school, which was this time filled with scholars, all duly rocking to and fro, and humming the prayers they did not understand. Even the recalcitrant hodgia was present, but with ill grace enough. Wrapped in yashmak and mantle as if for a walk through the crowded bazaar, she crouched against the wall in front of the first row; her back turned to us in the peculiar attitude adopted by Mahommedan women when desirous not to be seen. At our entrance she gave no sign, but about a moment later, espying one of the children raise its head to look at us, she dealt it a slap—such a vicious slap, its very sound spake of spite and rage.

Scarcely were we remounted, when, followed by his zaptiés, the mudir walked forward to bid farewell. He asked us formally if we were satisfied, and carried his pink waistcoat with additional dignity in the consciousness of having made himself obeyed. We did our utmost in the way of acknowledgment, feeling sincere admiration for his firmness, bearding the very Arnaouts whose brethren had just attacked his compeer, the luckless kaïmakam of Ipek. Poor old mudir! his post was not enviable, and probably offered but little emolument to reconcile him to its danger: apparently he had not even the luxury of a horse, or else, as a Turk, he would scarcely have presented himself to mounted strangers on foot. At the moment he turned to go, there appeared to escort us two of the principal members of the medjliss, so splendidly accoutred that we involuntarily thought of old Voina and his son. One of them bestrode a magnificent white horse, and the pistols in his belt were richly worked and gilded. These grandees rode speechless on either side of us, and as soon as we were out of town they turned back with a silent salute.

CHAPTER XIX.

FROM ARNAOUTLUK INTO BOSNIA.

FROM Vuchitern it takes but four hours to reach the northern boundary of Kóssovo, formed by the convergence of mountain ranges through which flows the river Ibar. The gate of the plain is the Castle of Svétchani, which rises from the banks of the stream, and, as seen from a distance, appears to fill up the angle between closing chains of hills. The eminence on which the castle stands is now richly clothed with wood; its sides, steep and tapered like a pyramid, look as if (like those of the hill of Castle Vissoko in Bosnia) they owed something of their form to art. In truth, the first dawn of history in these regions shows Svétchani as a fortified point, and it was probably a castle of the East Roman Empire before the immigration of the Serbs. In the beginning of the eleventh century all the surrounding country owned the sway of Samuel of Bulgaria, and when he was overthrown by the Byzantine Emperor Basil II., Svétchani was probably one of the numerous fortresses which sent its keys to the conqueror.*

The last Byzantine governor of Svétchani was ejected by Stephan Némania; and it was under the Serbian dynasty that this castle earned its tragical renown.

---

* In one district alone thirty-five are mentioned.—Hilferding's "History of Serbs and Bulgarians." See also Finlay's "Byzantine Empire," p. 450.

First a royal residence, it became a royal prison, and there King Urosh III., called Detchanski, was detained, and mysteriously died. Stephan Dūshan, the son of Urosh, who had superseded his father in the government, has been accused of giving the order for his death; but a cloud rests upon the whole transaction, and the Serbs are naturally anxious to exonerate their great czar. It is alleged that the sainted Detchanski, in his old age, fell under the power of the clergy, whereas his son, the strong-willed Dūshan, never was a favourite of theirs, —and the monks have had the telling of the tale. The most probable opinion is that cited by Mr. Finlay, viz., that nobles who had rebelled against the father murdered him to prevent a reconciliation between him and his son.

This tragedy in the Nemanjic family has furnished a topic to the modern Serbian poet, M. Iovan Subotic. His poem, called "Krāl Detchanski," tells its story simply and picturesquely in the easy language and metre of the popular songs;—language and metre so suited to each other that it almost seems as if good Serbian naturally utters itself in rhythmical flow. In this story the mischief-maker is Dūshan's stepmother, who, moreover, causes the death of his young bride, the daughter of a Zetan noble. The brothers Merliávchevic and other evil counsellors goad on the prince to take up arms, and then hastily murder the king, knowing that should he and Dūshan meet, their mutual affection would cause them to make peace. The scene of the king's death is laid at Neredimlïé, a country palace in the neighbourhood of Prizren; but history places it at Svétchani, a stronghold where it would be likely for the old monarch to retire with his treasures and wait for an opportunity of coming to terms with his son. Perhaps M. Subotic may have taken one idea in his narrative from the charter of the Detchansky Monastery, wherein Urosh himself, with touching words, refers to the misunderstanding caused by his Greek stepmother between him and his father, King Milutin. Naturally enough, the Serbians lay on these foreign consorts the blame of all quarrels in the Nemanjic family; for whatever may have been the faults of that dynasty, its members were certainly benevolent to the people, and left among them a memory of strong personal love. Not so the later and lesser rulers. Irene, the consort of one of the despots, has left a name proverbial in hatred, and her husband is allowed to bear his full share of blame.

At the foot of the hill of Svétchani lies the little town of Mitrovic, and at a short distance outside the town a khan marks the boundary between Bosnia and Arnaoutluk. Near the khan stands a great stone, and here it is customary for Mussulmans passing from one district to the other to slay a sheep, by way of thank-offering for the safety of the journey thus far.

The boundary represented by the stone of Mitrovic does not apply to the Christian population, which on both sides is alike Serb, calls its country Old Serbia, and insists that Bosnia does not properly begin till much farther to the north-west. But for the Mahommedans on either side Mitrovic the sacrificial stone marks a real frontier; the Mussulmans in Arnaoutluk being Albanian immigrants, while the Mussulmans in Bosnia are the renegade descendants of a native Slavonic aristocracy. In Bosnia the Mahommedan has not only more *prestige* than in Arnaoutluk, but his tenure of the land is far older; for the greater part of the Bosnian nobility became Mussulmans towards the end of the fifteenth century, whereas the Christian emigration from Old Serbia did not occur till the end of the seventeenth

MUSSULMAN BEYS AND CHRISTIAN PRIEST.

century, and the Arnaout renegades did not become masters of the soil till then. The relative position of Christian and Mussulman is also different in Arnaoutluk from what it is in Bosnia. In Old Serbia, where such noble families as did not perish in war gradually amalgamated with the people, they inspired the mass with their historic recollections, their proud obstinacy, and warlike spirit. Thus, although at a later period the Arnaouts obtained supremacy by adoption of the conqueror's creed, the Serbian still continues to feel himself their superior; and the renegade's slight attachment to his new faith causes him to be hated less as a Mahommedan than as a barbarian and a brigand. In Bosnia things went very differently. There the Christian population consists of that part of the nation which already before the Mahommedan conquest occupied the lowest room; while the Mahommedan represents the class which from time immemorial has been man-at-arms and lord of the soil. Hence in Bosnia antagonism fixes itself far more specifically on *creed* than in Arnaoutluk —difference of creed, not difference of race, being the barrier between the Bosnian Christian and Mahommedan: remove this, and they are one people.

It is curious to remark that the Croatians, and even the Serbs of the Principality, who are no longer oppressed by Mussulman landowners, look on the Mahommedan Bosniacs with great philosophy and even complacency as brethren of race, and the remnant of an old Slavonic nobility. They take a certain pride in observing that the Bosniac used to be the "Lion that guarded Stamboul;" that some of the greatest Turkish viziers were Bosniacs; nay, they glory in the Bosnian gentleman's superiority in stature and manly bearing as compared with the Osmanli official. It would not be hard for the Bosnian Mussulman to obtain good terms in a political arrangement with any South Slavonic community which is already free; but woe betide the haughty and oppressive landlord should he be left to the mercies of a successful rising of his own rayahs.

For ourselves, having travelled throughout the greater part of Bosnia, we have not to complain of the Mussulmans, who generally infused into such civilities as they rendered us a frankness and courtesy which savoured of the old noble. On the present occasion, although the orders to receive us with due observance had been the same to Mitrovic as to Vuchitern, at Mitrovic we met with a reception which showed how different was the disposition to interpret them.

The first thing we saw on approaching the Bosnian frontier was a troop of horsemen, richly dressed and armed; and soon we discerned that these included not only the mudir, but also the cadi and the whole medjliss. They were magnificent-looking fellows, and their welcome was full of hospitality. When to their salutation in Arabic we answered by a salutation in Slavonic, the ice was at once broken, and they talked away with real cordiality. They insisted that, if we would not pass the night at Mitrovic, we should at least halt there, and take some refreshment; and for this purpose conducted us, not to a Christian's humble dwelling, but to the best Mussulman house in the place, and there sat in state with us and drank coffee. The room in which we were entertained was very handsome, and bore every trace of belonging to old landowners, being filled with old arms and china and other family valuables. We conversed some time pleasantly, and among other questions asked our entertainers whether they had served in the last Montenegrīne war. As usual, the answer was, "No; the Albanians did, but not the Bosniacs." "Had the Sultan gained anything by the war?" "He had got back a *little* bit of Vassoïevitch." "Had he not got Cetinje?" "Certainly not."

No one made himself more agreeable than the cadi, a personage who in other places seldom came near us at all. He was a tall, fair man, with European features, and gave one an idea of the knights his forefathers, when they first put on the turban. He valued himself on his Arabic learning, but had a thorough abhorrence of Turkish and a strong love for his own language. As we were tolerably well up in the conventional phrases exchanged in Serbian meetings he imagined that we knew more of his language than we really did, and exclaimed: "It is a great pleasure to me to hear you speak Bosnian; *I* am a Bosniac (*Ja sam Bosniak*)." When we departed he and all the rest accompanied us, and before mounting our horses the mudir presented us with a bunch of roses.

But these Mussulman civilities cost us dear, and placed us for once in the position of those travellers who in passing through Turkey in Europe held converse only with Mahommedans. The same feeling which induced the Bosniacs of Mitrovic to deem it an honour to entertain us themselves, caused them to exclude the rayah from joining in the intercourse. We passed some Christians, standing near the road to have a look at us, and stopped to ask them about the castle on the hill, but they said they were strangers, and evidently did not choose to speak. In Mitrovic no rayahs appeared, and thus we heard nothing about their school, nor about the old castle, for the Mahommedans were of course oblivious of all local curiosities, and especially of Christian ruins. We afterwards heard that the Castle of Svétchani contains the remains of a church and several tombs, that it commands a magnificent view over the plain and the mountain ranges, and that the ascent is by no means so long and arduous as it appears from below. But all this was learned too late; our quarters for the night had been fixed for Banska, so we went on thither, and passed Svétchani by. This mistake caused us so much chagrin that we would do our best to secure other travellers against it by counselling them to divide their journey thus:—from Príshtina to Vuchitern in the morning, from Vuchitern to Mitrovic same afternoon; spend the night at Mitrovic. Next day go up to the castle and spend the night at Banska. If an extra day can be passed on the way, let it be at Mitrovic, not at Vuchitern.

When issuing from the street of Mitrovic we finally passed out of the plain of Kóssovo into that range of forest-mountain which divides it from the valley of Karanovac and the basin of Novi Bazaar. This so-called Zélena Plánina, with its long-drawn furrows, forms the natural bulwark of Danubian Serbia; Sultan Bajazet, though victor on the plain of Kóssovo, durst not attempt to cross the hills, and attack the Czarina in the town of Krushevac. Therefore he at once offered her favourable terms, and by his fair words opened the door he could not storm.

For some distance the road runs along the right bank of the Ibar and winds round the base of the castle hill, affording a striking view of the ruin. The change in scenery is attended by an equally sudden change in climate : one passes from hot and brilliant sunshine into the chill shadow of the hills.

At a turn of the winding road the way was stopped by a group of armed horsemen drawn up behind a tremendous figure, who was clothed from head to foot in crimson and mounted on a huge black steed. This red trooper proved to be the Bosnian chaoush of the little station of Banska, who had duly come out to meet us.

As he rode home before us, we rejoiced in having so fine a piece of colouring to relieve the grey rocks and drooping green boughs.

Near Banska the green became sparse, and the rocks began to assume a volcanic form and hue; the place is, as its name indiates, the site of a bath or mineral spring.* It is also a defensible point of the pass, and in Serbian times was held by that brave Banovic Strahinia who was killed on Kóssovo, and whose adventures and generosity form the subject of a stirring poem. While the inhabitants of all the neighbouring villages are Christians, those of Banska are exclusively Slavonic Mussulmans: may be the descendants of her ancient garrison, if, like some others, it apostatised to avoid laying down arms. The bath establishment at Banska is small, and as it was evening we did not go in; but we made the tour of the old citadel, now in the last stage of ruin. The high-walled enceinte contains nothing except the kula of a few zaptiés, who have also a watchman's post on the wall, uninhabited houses, and a deserted mosque; twenty years ago, they said, the houses were inhabited and the mosque used for worship. But traces remain of an earlier stage. From the ruined wall project the heads and forepaws of two stone lions, the rest of their bodies having been built up with the gate or pillars to which they belonged. The mosque too is in the form of an Eastern church, and the lower part of its apse displays some rows of beautiful masonry, marble of red and gray ranged in alternate layers and polished, like that which we afterwards saw at Détchani. Both church and castle appear to have been stately

* It seems however, doubtful whether it takes its name, like so many other places, from Banja, a bath, as it certainly possesses mineral springs, or, as is sometimes alleged, from its having been the residence of the Ban celebrated in Serbian song. A district ruled over by a Ban is called Banovina.

structures when in Serbian hands; indeed King Milutin, their founder, took from them his surname of Banski.

Here, on the subject of ruins in Bosnia, we may remark that the description which Mr. Paton gives of that country, from what he heard of it on the borders, though probably applicable at the time he heard it, is not so now. Omar Pasha, when putting down the last revolt, did much to reduce the Begs, who no longer occupy feudal strongholds, but live more or less meanly in towns, going into the country only to collect their rents; even when in the country they inhabit white houses, neither old nor of castellated exterior, though probably capable of being defended. Castles of the size and age of that of Marko Kralïevitch, at Prilip, may be seen near some of the towns or guarding the most important mountain passes; but they are either, like Marko's, totally ruined, or still nominally defended by a few rusty cannon and local guards under the name of Imperial fortresses. In fact, anything of a feudal residence on a large scale in Bosnia is so dilapidated as to give less idea of having been lately inhabited than the castles on the Danube and the Rhine. Such relics of architecture as the older castles exhibit, such legends of warlike owners as lend them a romantic interest, mostly refer to ante-Turkish times.

Our night's lodging had been prepared in the house of the chaoush himself; and though the room was small, it was interesting from its primitive ornaments in carving, old pottery, and arms. The officer himself received us with great hospitality, and presented to us with his own hand a large round cake (Slāv, *kolatch*), which he evidently thought a great dainty. We longed to bestow it on the poor Christian drivers, who must have spent an uncomfortable night. There are no fields near Banska, and it was hard to get forage for the horses; moreover, as the small khan would not hold them, they had to remain in the court of the chaoush's house.

But one good result accrued from their discomfort—they were ready to start at break of day. This is very necessary when the journey is from Banska to Novi Bazaar, for, although nominally only nine hours, it is nine hours of such mountain travelling as may be indefinitely prolonged. Not but that there is a road, *soi-disant tel*, made by the Turkish government, and, like others, answering its end so far as to serve for the transport of cannon, but extremely rough withal, and uncompromisingly steep both up and down hill. In every part it is wide enough for two bullocks to pass abreast, and we met several patient couples dragging the elementary cart of the country laden with the stems of trees. Altogether, we cannot quite endorse the opinion of the Polish officer who pronounced this road passable for a carriage containing ladies, *because* it is passable for wood and guns; but we are none the less obliged to him for his verdict, without which, in our then state of health, we should not have dared to attempt this route at all.

A day's riding in the Zélena Plánina (green forest-mountain), such as we came in for here and elsewhere, left us each time the richer by a memory of delight. It brings a fresh breeze over one for ever after, only to think of those forest hills, green as they are and windy as the summer downs in England, and yet with almost Grecian sunlight pouring on their brows. Greece herself has lost her forests, and so has beautiful Dalmatia, which the Venetians robbed of fertility when they bared her hills and left them to dry and bleach in the glare. It is well that the Serbian ranges did not share this fate, for they present comparatively little picturesqueness of form wherewith to atone for bleakness, and their inland scenery lacks the thousand charms inalienable from countries washed by a southern sea.

In the hills between Kóssovo and Novi Bazaar the grand monotony of greenness is only broken here and there by the grey walls of a far-off ruin. Svétchani is seen again and again as you round each new ascent; and farther on, the lone castle of Yelic appears on its eagle crag.

There would seem to be Roman remains in this neighbourhood; at a roadside fountain where the horses drank we descried on the trough a Latin inscription, and found that it was an ancient sarcophagus. After much questioning, which (no Christian being present) was difficult and unsatisfactory in the extreme, all we could elicit was, that this sarcophagus came from a village called Séochanitza. Séochanitza is said to lie two hours from the Kadiaschi Khan near the fountain where we saw the sarcophagus, six hours from Novi Bazaar, and four hours from the Serbian frontier; moreover many other stones covered with writing have been found there and walled into the little village khan. By all accounts the place is very small, and not abounding in konaks or food for horses, so we dared not turn out off the road to explore it.

Our chaoush, who had provoked us greatly by his "know-nothingness" about the Roman remains, was more communicative on the subject of the population here and on the Serbian border. He denied that there were any Albanians to be found in the neighbourhood, and said that from Banska to Novi Bazaar all the villages were Christian, or, as he called them, "Serb." On the other side of the border, as we doubtless knew, the Serbians had set up a state of their own. Last year they and the Sultan quarrelled; and he, the chaoush, and many other persons, had expected to see a Serbian army re-appear on the field of Kóssovo. The men on the Serbian border were fine fellows, and so were those on the Bosnian side; in fact "borderers always are the finest people of any country, as they are kept in fighting practice." We told him that one reason why the Serbs had not crossed the border was, that last year they had not good arms, but that now they had received a supply and had drilled 200,000 men. He answered, "We all know that quite well. They have also plenty of cannon; and, as I heard, not less than 300,000 men." "And how many fighting men do you think there are in Bosnia?" He answered, "They say 50,000; but they could never bring that number into the field."* Being a Bosniac, he spoke on this subject quite dispassionately, having probably made up his mind that, whatever the chances of a second battle of Kóssovo, he, like his forefathers, would make his terms with the victor.

With the chaoush and his fellow-borderers we must confess to have shared the anticipation of seeing the Serbs reappear on Kóssovo, when, the road attaining its highest bend, we turned back to take our last view of the field. We left our horses and walked to a little eminence where, resting under the trees, we could look over the winding of the mountain ranges, and past the spiral summit of Svétchani down on the far-off golden plain.

How many and divers travellers must have halted on this spot and been moved by this view! Here the contingent from Rascia and Bosnia, on their way to join the

---

* The immense disproportion between this number and that in the principality of Serbia, which has not a much larger population, is accounted for by remembering that in Bosnia the Christians, who form over two-thirds of the population, are not counted as fighting men.

camp of Czar Lāzar, must have seen the spot that was to behold their fall. Here the Mussulmans of Bosnia—all renegades and traitors as they be—when marching to vindicate against the Sultan their claim to govern their own provinces, broke out into the gloomy chant—"We march, brethren, to the plains of Kóssovo, where our forefathers lost their renown and their faith; there it may chance that we also may lose our renown and our faith—or that we shall maintain them, and return as victors to Bosnia." Here, day by day, the passing rayah prays, "that God will hasten the hour when a Christian army shall cross these mountains, to deliver Old Serbia, and redeem what their fathers lost on the old battle-plain of Kóssovo."

CHAPTER XX.

NOVI BAZAAR.

THE middle of this day we spent under the trees, near a dirty khan without any separate room. After leaving it we commenced the descent towards Novi Bazaar, passing by a short cut through a wood, of which the paths were spoilt by late rain, and so slippery that our horses could scarcely keep their feet. Emerging thence on the main road, we found ourselves at a beautiful point of view; we looked down on Novi Bazaar, lying in a basin of hills, traversed by the road that passes from Constantinople to Serajevo, and overtopped by a steep eminence on which rose the dome of a church.

At the foot of the last descent we met a zaptié, who instantly galloped off to give notice of our approach, and soon after we saw coming to meet us a train of horsemen, so numerous as to reduce that of Mitrovic to comparative insignificance. At their head rode three personages, all so portentous and dignified that for some time we could not discover which of them was the greatest. The most solemn wore plain clothes and a fez, and appeared to be so precious that, in case he should fall off his horse, a man walked at its side all ready to catch him; the handsomest and most brilliant wore a splendid Turkish uniform; while the fattest—and in Turkey this is often a criterion of high position—had what looked like a French uniform with voluminous scarlet trousers. In due time we learned that the civil governor of Novi Bazaar was gone on business to Seraïevo, and that the man in plain clothes was his *locum tenens*. The handsome soldier was military kaïmakam; the fat officer, a cavalry bimbashi; in their tail followed the medjliss of Novi Bazaar. Though heading the native Mussulmans in the ceremony of hospitable reception, the three superiors were Asiatics, and could speak nothing but Turkish, which our dragoman imperfectly understood. Hence the procession moved on in silence, the Turkish dignitaries acting as our outriders, the Bosniacs bringing up the rear. In this order we entered Novi Bazaar, and rode very slowly and very solemnly through the long charshia (market-place), round the foot of a hill covered with the houses of Mussulmans, and on and on, till between the holes, the stones, and the weary-footedness of our sorry steeds, we began to get into despair. At this juncture an incident took place which among any west-European crowd would have been saluted with roars of mirth. Down the central gutter of the sloping street flowed a brisk stream, swollen by recent rain; our poor horses were thirsty, one of them suddenly got his head down, stopped stock still, and drank. It was hopeless to get him to move till he had his fill; officious blows dealt by the cavass from behind only served to make him kick; so there we stuck fast, while the unconscious dignitaries rode out of sight, and the wondering Bosniacs pressed one upon another. On each side the shopkeepers sat cross-legged on their boards and stared at us—stared, yet did not smile. But from the lattice windows above peered down a galaxy of female eyes, and it was from these hidden spectators that the only expression of amusement at our ludicrous position escaped: almost on a level with our ears bubbled out the irrepressible giggle of a girl.

On rejoining the vanguard we found that it was leading us, not up the hill to the large houses of the Mussulmans, but down a narrow street to the marshy land near the river, *i.e.*, to the Christian quarter. Here we stopped before the dwelling of the Greek bishop, who, like his *confrère* of Príshtina, was spending his time more pleasantly at Constantinople. In his absence, the house was kept by his servant's family, and they had received orders to prepare the best room for our use. Bad's the best; small and unfurnished, it is like a slice off a passage, and has no glass in any of the four windows. Worst of all, these apertures look towards the street, whereby we are exposed to the observation not only of passers-by but also of the dwellers on the opposite side; the latter, stationed at their windows, stare at our doings as from the boxes of a theatre.

In places where we stayed more than one night it was customary for the Turkish authorities to appoint a zaptié to remain in our house, in order that we might send him to say if we required anything and have his protection if we walked abroad. For all these purposes one man was sufficient, and one could be managed without much inconvenience by the Christians with whom we lodged; give him good food and drink and a comfortable corner, and he would sit all day in a state of kef, or discuss horses and arms with our cavass, when the latter had time to attend to him. But in order to do us especial honour the authorities of Novi Bazaar left us, not one zaptié, but three, and these three proved an attraction to their comrades, who came constantly out and in. They were a terrible nuisance—those imperious, rapacious men turned loose in a rayah's dwelling; no part of the lower house was free from their presence, the women had to hide from them, and the young father of the family was ordered about as their slave.

We soon perceived that something was amiss by the repressed cringing air of the man, and sent our dragoman to say that we only wanted one zaptié and would only give bakshish to one. However, the other two would not stir, so all we could do was to ask the master of the house into our room, and try to reassure him with kind words. But the sound of our voices caused him to shake like a leaf, and to the most indifferent question he would only give a whispered reply.

The dragoman then told us that the zaptiés were sitting in a room just below our own; the man was in agonies lest they should hear us talking with him. Immediately we too whispered, assured the poor fellow that the obnoxious guards remained in his house contrary to our express desire, and that our inquiries proceeded from the sympathy we felt for the Serbian Christians, who through all our journey had treated us with hospitality and kindness. We then told the dragoman to ask him a few questions as to the state of the Christian community in Novi Bazaar, and meanwhile we talked to each other in a raised voice, for the benefit of the guards below. How curious a picture was the group in that little room! At one end, in the candlelight, we sat talking cheerfully on each side of our little table covered with English books and work; at the other end, where the shadow fell darkest, crouched the dragoman and the rayah, the former with his keen swarthy face bent down to catch the whispers of his companion—that companion a young man with the fresh colour and rounded contour of an European, but quaking, almost convulsed, with fear.

The whispers became quicker and more eager; our question as to the state of the Christians had acted like the sudden withdrawal of the dam from a stream, the pent-up waters overflowed, the rayah was pouring forth his tale. "The Christian community of Novi Bazaar is at the mercy of the Mussulmans; they enter houses both by day and night, take what they choose, and behave as they will. Raise an arm or speak a word, and you bring on yourself death or the loss of a limb. Make a representation to the authorities, and you are ruined by the revenge of those of whom you have dared to complain."

We asked if within the last few years things had become better or worse.

"In so far they are better, that the officials now sent from Constantinople are jealous of the Beys and the Beys of them, and the two opposing cliques act as some sort of check on each other. The Christians are less persecuted in their dress and other trifles, and they may enter their own quarter of the town on horseback, though it would still not be safe to ride past a Mussulman in the road or the bazaar. On the other hand, since last year great repression has been exercised, for fear of the Christians rising to join the Serbians over the border. We have been obliged to do forced labour in raising defences, and to contribute both in food and money to the maintenance of troops; and such troops! Do you know that last summer Bashi-bazouks were sent to Novi Bazaar? But no insult, no injury is so hard to bear, as that of Mussulmans carrying off Christian girls. Lately a maiden of the rayah community was servant in a Mussulman family. Suddenly her parents were informed that she had become a Mahommedan; she was not suffered to return to them nor see them, but was secretly sent off to Saraïevo. She escaped, came back to her family, and they ventured to give her shelter, but the Mussulmans tracked her home and their vengeance fell upon the whole Christian community. Out of its 110 houses at least 100 were, in their estimate, connected with the escape of the poor girl; all felt the weight of their wrath, and several were completely ruined."

This calamity was of recent occurrence, so it appeared uppermost in the narrator's mind; but when questioned as to whether he could say that a similar outrage had ever actually occurred in his own family, he answered straightforward that it had happened to his wife. Being a handsome young girl, the Mussulmans got hold of her, and she only escaped because the bishop was at home and took up the matter himself. As soon as she was released, the bishop married her to her present husband; when he left the town he put them in his house as one mode of providing for her safety.

Thus ran our landlord's tale, but he was not the only sufferer whose story came to our ears at Novi Bazaar. On the morning of our departure an old man knocked at our door, pushed into the hand of the dragoman a paper, and then turned and ran away. It contained some sentences in very crabbed Serbian written characters, which we could not decipher by ourselves, and knowing it was out of our power to redress the injuries of the writer, we deemed it wiser not to expose him to a risk of betrayal by showing it to any one in Turkey. We took it to Belgrade, where we were helped to read it, and found the meaning to be as follows:—" Gracious ladies, in God's name I welcome your visit to our town. Have pity, and save my unhappy daughter, whom the Mussulmans have carried away."

It has been said that the Christians in Turkey invalidate their complaints of Mahommedan oppression by the very fearlessness with which they complain, also that travellers detailing the grievances of these Christians have seldom had their stories first hand. We leave candid readers to judge whether either the one or the other of these explanations can be applied to the cases just detailed.*

At Novi Bazaar we passed three days, and one afternoon went to see the Serbian school. The zaptiés were left at home, our cicerone being the master of the house. Indeed he had volunteered to be our guide, and since last night appeared another man. He walked at our side stoutly, and spoke—although still in an undertone—cheerfully; neither did he show us any more of that servile homage which indicates terror mingled with hate. Such other Christians as were now presented to us, also opened out with friendly confidence, and one after another at convenient opportunities would whisper, "So you have been in Serbia?"—meaning the principality. The word "Serbia" is the Open Sesame of hearts between Prizren and Novi Bazaar.

Approaching the school our ears were saluted by a not inharmonious burst of children's voices singing "Welcome"; but when we reached the door we saw that the poor little choristers looked very miserable and ill. The atmosphere of the school was certainly not bracing—an exception to the rule hereabouts, where you find in every room open windows and draughts *ad libitum*. At the further end of this school we perceived a row of holy pictures with lighted lamps hanging before them, and we were told that the room was also used for a church. Hence the sickly after-smell of incense (worse even than that of tobacco) mingled with the unhealthy closeness of the air. We did not venture to remain more than a few minutes, and were glad to be invited to a stone seat outside, where we looked over the books, which were all from Belgrade. Meanwhile the schoolmaster released

---

* Consular reports testify that, so far is the offence here alluded to from being punished, that the man who carries off a Christian girl, and can make her become a Mahommedan, is rewarded by exemption from the conscription.

the poor children, who had been called together out of hours for us to see.

The bench assigned to us was an old tombstone, and others similar stood against the wall; but neither the priests nor the kodgia bashi could tell us anything about them. They cared rather to show us the town, of which this spot commands a view. Lovely it looks, in the narrow wooded valley, with its clustering white houses bedded in rank green; but evidently it lies in an airless caldron, and its inhabitants say that it is cursed with bad water and ague-breeding swamps. Smallpox had raged throughout the winter, and now the summer fever was in full force. Six persons of the richest families in the town had died of it lately within a few days. We now knew why that morning we awoke with the heavy feeling we hoped to have left behind at Skopia.

"To whom belong the houses on the hill?" "All to Mussulmans." "How many may there be?" The rayahs looked at each other, and hesitated, as if talking treason, then said in a low voice, "About 800, *we* believe. But the Turks themselves say 1,200 or even 1,400." "How many Christian houses?" "That is soon told; 110." "So few?" "Say rather, so many. God knows why any of us live here; better for us we should dwell in the woods and never see a town. Look at our quarter, in the lowest ground close to the river; the garden of the house where you are staying is all but a marsh." We turned our eyes to a high breezy terrace immediately above the town, and asked, "Why do you not build there? the Mussulmans have not taken that." The rayahs exclaimed, "We build there! the Begs dare not build there themselves. It is vakouf." "Vakouf" means that it belongs to a mosque, and thus at Novi Bazaar, as at Volo, on one pretext or another, the Turk has tabooed the most healthy site in the town.

NOVI BAZAAR.

We afterwards took a walk in this vakouf land, and thence perceived—rising on the top of the hill immediately above us—that beautiful light dome of a church which we had already admired from a distance on our approach to Novi Bazaar.

We were now told that this was the celebrated Giurgevi Stūpovi, or Monument of St. George,* built in the latter half of the twelfth century by the first Némania as a thank-offering. The church is supposed to cover the mouth of the cavern where that prince was confined by his elder brothers: St. George was the good friend who delivered him from their thrall. Two Serb priests had joined our party, and one of them, an outspoken intelligent person, offered to show us the church; our host persuaded some of his friends to lend us horses, and we set out forthwith.

The hill, which, from its steepness and commanding situation, appears from a distance of considerable height, may be ascended from the town in less than half an hour. The church stands on a point of rock; a little below it one arrives at a rough plateau, where from time immemorial it has been customary for pilgrims to leave their horses and approach the shrine on foot. This spot is marked by a large stone cross, strangely like some of the Celtic crosses, and also by three of the beacons erected last year by the Turks all along the frontier range of hills. The sight of the cross called forth the priest's enthusiasm at the humility of the Némanjic sovereigns, who dismounted thus far from the church door; the sight of the beacons elicited a cry of reprobation on the profaners of Némania's shrine. "Oh!" he exclaimed, "those Bashi-bazouks! God knows how they treated us here!"

* Stūpa, in Serbian, means literally "pillar" or "column;" but is also used in the sense of monumental erections that may consist of more than a mere column.

The shell of the church is still so far intact that until one is quite close it preserves a stately effect. First we reached a small building open on two sides and vaulted within; the pope supposed it to have been an outer chapel or a porch, but Hilferding describes it as the base of a campanile. Its walls are covered with frescoes, of which the colours are still in part fresh and the inscriptions legible; on one side is a picture of the Last Supper, and of SS. Cosmo, Damian, Pantaleon, &c.; on the other, portraits of the Némanjic family, in long gem-bordered garments and with glories round their heads. The priest declared this porch to be of later date than the church, and his opinion is confirmed in so far as that the royal personages there represented belong to a generation later than the first Némania.* In the church you see himself, represented as founder, holding the model of the building; there too is his son and coadjutor, St. Sava, depicted with a long fair beard; also his patron, St. George, with the dragon. The relics of another Némanjic used to lie in a side chapel, but were stolen thence some time ago; we saw the broken tomb, but did not distinctly gather who the occupant had been nor whither the body was gone. Hilferding calls him King Dragutin, and heard that his bones had been "lifted" by the family Znobic of Novi Bazaar, who thereby brought a curse on themselves and their posterity.

From the outer building it is some paces to the west door of the church, and on the way the priest pointed out a shattered column of red stone, which had formed

---

* We had unfortunately left pencils and notebooks behind us, so could not write down the names on the spot. Hilferding enumerates among the frescoes the following names:—1. Saint Simeon, Némania, lord of all the Serbian lands, 1159—1195. 2. Stephen Pervovencani, Simeon Monach, 1195—1228. 3. Stephan Kral Ourosh, Simeon Monach, 1240—1272. 4. Yelena Velika Kralitza, daughter of Emperor Baldwin, who then lived in Constantinople, and wife of Ourosh. 5. Stephen Ourosh, called Dragutin, 1272—1275. 6. Katherina Kralitza, daughter of Stephan V., King of Hungary, wife of Dragutin.

MANASSIA

INTERIOR OF SERBIAN CHURCH.

part of the doorway. He said, "This was thrown down quite lately by Turkish soldiers from Prizren."

The church of Giurgevi Stūpovi is one of the oldest specimens of Serbian architecture, it is also one of the most simple; the numerous little domes of other churches are wanting, and thereby the large dome in the centre gains infinitely in effect, its full swell reminding one of those island churches of Venice which look like bubbles blown from the sea. But while the outer shell is nearly entire, within the building is completely gutted, its pillagers having helped to exhibit its fair proportions by carrying off those doors and screens wherewith most Serbian churches are encumbered. In the principality, we know only Manassia where the interior proportions receive justice, and that because funds are still wanting to raise the picture-screen (iconostasis) to the wished-for height. The interior of Giurgevi Stūpovi must have been covered with frescoes, but it is only on that part of the walls which cannot well be reached, either from above or below, that any traces of painting remain. To obliterate the figure of Christ, the destroyers have broken up the plaster of the dome, while all the lower part of the frescoes has been picked off by mischievous hands. The paintings still extant are attainable only by throwing stones; and while we were in the act of looking at these a pebble rattled in through the door, and left its mark on the painted wall. Turning round, we perceived our zaptié, whom we had left with the horses, and who, striding in at the shattered entrance, rudely asked the priest, "What was here?" Our wrath was only increased by the civil and deprecatory tone in which answer was returned, and we peremptorily interfered, demanding of the intruder how he dared follow us, and ordering him back to his charge. Our cavass, who at first was in ecstasies of wonder and delight over the beautiful colours, on the entrance of his co-religionist, the zaptié, thought fit to adopt a nonchalant and scornful mien; finding the latter contemptuously expelled, he changed again, and exclaimed, "Really the Turks here surprise me; they are extremely mischievous, and destroy beautiful things." Then, with an after-thought highly creditable to his former employers, he added, "But you see, at Novi Bazaar there are *no consuls.*" From this date to the end of our journey, whenever he was struck with a case of Christian suffering, we used to hear him promising the people that the Queen of England would send a consul to their town. The behaviour of his co-religionists in these parts was not, however, without effect on our Albanian attendant, and we had to watch constantly to prevent him from making all sorts of unjust requirements in our name. On the way to Novi Bazaar he thought he recognised the lost horses of the kiradgees, and forthwith dispatched zaptiés to bring the drove and its drivers before the kaïmakam, when, by his own admission, he found that the horses were not the same. After this he made an attempt, unknown to us, to obtain for our journey the good horses lent to us to visit the church. So far as we could learn the price and quantity of what we used, we were most anxious to pay for it, but from time to time it came to light that the zaptié sent on beforehand ordered seven chickens where we ordered and paid for one, &c. Indeed, one of the great discouragements to travelling in these parts is that, with the best intentions, one cannot avoid being constantly oppressive to the inhabitants.

On the floor of the church we observed a piece of marble beautifully carved with old Slavonic letters. Outside the south door we discovered a fresco, with its colours as fresh as on the day when limned, but half smothered in a heap of rubbish; better that the whole had remained concealed, for doubtless it has only become visible to be destroyed.

On the north side of the church, and as it were hidden behind it, is a small plot, used as a Christian burying-ground. Before the south door there is a larger space, where the pilgrims assemble on St. George's Day, and where we found numbers of faded oak-boughs, which they bring along with them for shade. Here the pope showed us a small hole in the rock, hollowed as a reservoir for rain. The women of the district have a superstition that water from this sacred hole is a cure for fever, and the plants near it are decorated with scarlet threads, sacrifices drawn from holiday aprons in testimony of supposed cures. It is to be hoped that the inhabitants of this feverish district will not lose their faith in the rain water at the top of this rock until they have learnt how much fever patients may be benefited by a change from valley to hill air; especially during such short cheerful journeys as their holiday pilgrimage to the church of St. George.

From the rock of Giurgevi Stūpovi there is a fine view towards a range of hills, of which the names were written down for us by the priest. We give them here for the benefit of future travellers, who may thus be enabled to judge of the excursions best worth making from Novi Bazaar. Towards the north and east are the mountains Sokolovitza and Kopaonik; from the latter of which there is an extensive view of the lands between Macedonia and the Danube. Among the hills to the south lies Yelic, with its old castle just visible. South-west are the hills where the river Rashka has its source; among them lie the monastery of Sapotchani, and the so-called castle of Relja. North-west is seen a picturesque gorge in the hills, called the Ludsha Clissura; and further north rises a summit, conspicuous for its rich covering of grass and wood; it is called the Czerveni Verh (or Red Height).

The plain which stretches towards the Serbian frontier is called Dezevo Poljé; and one can see Dezevo, now a village inhabited by Mussulmans, but formerly a town "where the family of Némanjic loved to dwell." The road which leads thence in the direction of the hill Sokolovitza is called to this day the "Tsarska Ulitza," or the "street of the Czar;" and it is said that hereabouts lay the *divor* or country house of Czar Dūshan. The village Sudsko, also inhabited by Mussulmans, lies about a quarter of an hour from the "street of the Czar;" it marks where in old times the Serbian rulers used to hold their court of justice (Slāv, *sud*).

A heap of stones on the bank of the Rashka is called by the country people the house of Relia, and belonged to that hero in the winged helmet who appears in every gallery of Serbian worthies. Winged Relia is sung as the bond-brother of Marco, and one of the paladins of Lāzar; like Milosh Obilic, he was of unknown parentage, and was rejected by a haughty damsel as a foundling picked up in the streets of Novi Bazaar. There is a certain popular song which seems to have been composed in order to contrast the merciful rule of the native sovereigns with the tyranny of foreign lords, and in it Relia is intrusted with the punishment of the Czarine's own brothers, because they kept back the pay of the Czar's workmen. But in this song, which is very old, Relia lives, not at Novi, or New Bazaar, but at Stari, or Old Bazaar, the ruins of which were afterwards pointed out to us. This Old Bazaar would appear to have been no other than the capital of the so-called "kingdom of Rascia," one of the zupanias most frequently spoken of in Serbian annals, and by some supposed to have included the greater part of the country now known as Old Serbia.

Rascia is mentioned as a Serbian government by Byzantine historians as early as the ninth century; and in 1143 its bishop, Leontius, was one of the few prelates in Serbia belonging to the Orthodox Church. The father of Némania was zupan of Rascia before he succeeded his cousin Bodin, king of Zeta; afterwards he does not seem to have changed his title; and according to some reports, he continued to reside in Rascia. In the government of that district he was succeeded by his son Némania, though not till after a struggle with those relatives who are traditionally said to have imprisoned him in the cave. The prisoner, released by miraculous intervention, and abhorring the heresies of his rival brethren, was admitted by Bishop Leontius into the Orthodox communion in a little church near Novi Bazaar, still called by the country people the "Holy Metropolitan Cathedral of Rashka." Afterwards arriving at supreme power, he erected as a monument of his deliverance the large and beautiful church of St. George. Some writers say that the old capital of Rascia was destroyed in war: the legend says that it was overthrown by an earthquake. In either case, the new zupan would have to build a new town, which, lying like the old on the frontier between Serbia and Bulgaria, and succeeding to its position as a rendezvous of merchants, would, like it, be distinguished by some such name as the Turks have translated by *bazaar*.*

When the seat of Serbian government became fixed at

---

* In early Serbian history it is mentioned that an exchange of prisoners between Serbians and Bulgarians took place at this town of Rascia, as being then the frontier between Serbia and Bulgaria.

The Serbian name for that part of a town where the citizens live is *varosh*, in contradistinction to the *grad*, or citadel. *Terg* is the immediate market-place, whence *tergovac*, a merchant.

Prizren, Rascia gradually lost the position of a separate state, and its name is now associated only with the river Rashka, with the little metropolitan church of St. Peter and St. Paul, and with those emigrants who passed in the seventeenth century from this neighbourhood into Hungary, where to this day the appellation Rashki denotes Serbians of the Eastern Church.

According to the plan of journey made out at Monastir, Novi Bazaar was our last stage on the Mussulman side of the border; but the ride over Kóssovo and the Zélena Plánina had so far restored our health, and the descriptions of Ipek and Détchani had so strongly excited our interest, that we could not bear to leave all this unexplored country behind us and cross into the principality, where we knew every step of the road to Belgrade. Rather we bethought ourselves of a long-cherished scheme, viz., so turn back at Novi Bazaar, cross the hills to Ipek, and then pass viâ Prizren to Scutari in Albania.

Novi Bazaar is a principal station on the road between Constantinople and Seraïevo, and it was evident that the authorities were not ill-off for troops; no doubt they could spare us such an escort as was required. On the other hand, if we could not get to Ipek at least we might go a two days' tour further westward to Senitza, and cross thence to Serbia, in which case we should visit Uzitza, a part of the country we had not already seen. Of this change of plan it was necessary to apprise our friends at Belgrade, lest, should we not appear at the date when they expected us, they might express anxieties, which the Austrian papers would take up and cook into some absurd report or other.

At our request the kaïmakam of Novi Bazaar sent to the Serb capitan at Rashka to ask if some one would come over and speak with us. Forthwith, two Serbians

SERBIAN PEASANTS AND CITIZENS OF A COUNTRY TOWN.

rode across the border; not military men, for that might have excited suspicion, but quiet "house-fathers," members of the national guard.

These good people brought us pleasant tidings. They said we were expected, and orders given for our welcome. They told us that we should lodge in a good house at Rashka, and that if we would fix a day for crossing, the frontier capitan and his followers would meet us and bring us over with rejoicing. From Rashka onwards there is a good road, but the country is mountainous, and they added, that if we wished for a carriage they must send for it to Karanovac. The men looked peaceful and good-tempered, clean, calm, and comfortable, like the members of a well-ordered community, unlike either terrifiers or terrified; it really cost an effort to turn from them and their hospitable offers, and plunge again into a country where every one's hand is against his neighbour. However, as Serbians, they could not but highly commend our idea of a pilgrimage to Ipek and Détchani, and they promised that, lest after all we should be obliged to give up our plan and cross to the principality by Senitza, the capitan of adjacent Uzitza should be duly prepared to receive us.

Having sent news of movements to Belgrade, the next thing was to communicate with the Turks. The three dignitaries had duly sent to ask at what hour they should call, and we had appointed the afternoon, adding, that as there was not in the house a room large enough to accommodate them we would receive their visit in the garden. This garden was decidedly swampy, nevertheless cushions and carpets were carried into it; punctual to the hour, the Turks arrived with a numerous suite, and were conducted to the spot prepared; then we were apprised; but when we came down and found so many grave personages enthroned in the long grass, and surrounded by their attendants stooping under the boughs of the low fruit trees, we could scarcely suppress a smile. The dignitaries smiled too, and observed that like ourselves, they were strangers to Bosnia, and considered its climate and accommodation as things to be rather endured than enjoyed. On this we became quite grave, and assured them we prayed God that on the first convenient opportunity they all might be transferred to Asia. "Please God," responded they fervently, thus probably expressing the sentiment of every unlucky Turk quartered in the Slavonic provinces, and certainly that of their still more unlucky harems. The wife of a high-placed official once said to us, "Such Osmanlis as are sent to these parts are sent by their evil fate. This is Bosnia: every one knows what that means, and that it does not mean *our* land." We most heartily agreed with her.

After the usual round of compliments and coffee, we began to tell our visitors of the difficulty we had met with about going to Ipek, and how two governors had refused to send us there. The military kaïmakam observed superciliously, "that those little mudirs probably had no zaptiés to spare, but that *he* could provide us with an escort with which we might go whither we pleased." The civil officer further remarked that no doubt the mudirs were themselves Arnaouts, and did not wish us to penetrate into their country, but that, bearing with us the Sultan's firman, we should be properly received everywhere. As to the road from Novi Bazaar to Ipek, it certainly passed over the mountains, but the inhabitants were Bosniacs, and *konacs* could be secured. He also recommended us to go by Roshaï, a station on the frontier between Bosnia and Arnaoutluk, for there we should find a new mudir, a talented and liberal-minded person, who would receive us with every distinction. At this juncture some of the attendants interfered, and began telling a long story, when it appeared that, although living only two days' journey from Ipek, the governors of Novi Bazaar had not yet heard of the attack on the Ipek kaïmakam. At this news they rather abated their zeal, and the civil officer remarked that the mudirs who had warned us not to venture, might possibly, from their proximity to Ipek, be acquainted with sufficient reasons for their advice. However the military kaïmakam repeated "that with a Bosniac guard nothing was to be feared; those wretched Arnaouts were altogether barbarous, but Bosniacs could be depended on." At this point the matter was deferred for further reflection.

Wishing to know something about the state of the Montenegrīne frontier, which is here but twelve hours distant, we asked if they could send us to Berda.*

The Turks replied that they could send us to the border, but that on the other side they could answer for nothing: even our firman would be of no use to us there. It was evident that whatever might be pretended in Constantinople, these officers of the Porte were well aware that Montenegro had not been compelled to acknowledge the authority of the Sultan. We replied that we knew Montenegro perfectly, and that therein everything was quiet and well-ordered; our anxiety for safety referred solely to this side the frontier, and if they could guarantee that, well and good. However, we

---

* B'rda, or rocky mountains, is the name given par excellence to the north-eastern portion of Montenegro; Cerna Gora, or black-wooded mountain, being properly applied only to the part nearer the Adriatic. Both alike were included in the government of Zeta, of which the present principality of Montenegro claims to be the representative; but during the greatest distress of the Christians the champions of independence could only maintain themselves in a very small district, and it is under their present reigning family that they have re-asserted bit by bit their old territory, as one tribe after another dared to join them and openly to disclaim allegiance to the Sultan.

would think over our plans and let them know. Soon after they were gone our cavass came to us with a message from a Bosnian Mussulman. He had just come from the neighbourhood of Ipek, and could answer for it that at Roshaï we should find Bosniacs willing and proud to take us into the Arnaout country. Whatever information we wanted he could give us, and would tell us to whom to apply for help. "On no account," he said, "be persuaded not to go to Ipek; all the alarm about danger is a pretence of those beggarly Arnaouts." This was the only communication we had with native Mussulmans at Novi Bazaar. We should much have liked to find out some connections of our friends made in Bosnia the previous year, but we dreaded to remain longer in so unhealthy a spot. Then, too, we had no personal introductions, and under the circumstances it would have been difficult to adjust amicable relations with the Beys, considering our intercourse with their adversaries on either side—with the Turkish authorities and the Christian Serbs.

However, from the message now received it was evident that the Bosniacs thought there was no reason we should not go to Détchani; so we forthwith sent to the kaïmakam, saying that we had quite made up our minds to go to Ipek, unless he could formally declare it to be unsafe. He replied that he would take steps to make it safe, and that we had only to fix the day.

CHAPTER XXI.

THE BOSNIAN BORDERS.

"Little heart! do not get angry with me;
For if I were to get angry with thee
All Bosnia and Herzegovina
Could not make peace between us again."
Bosnian Love Song.

NECESSARY preliminaries having been adjusted, on the fourth morning after our arrival at Novi Bazaar we turned our horses' heads, not, as hitherto, towards Belgrade and the Danube, but towards Scodra and the Adriatic.

The first stage was to be Tutin, a Mahommedan village in the mountains; thither we sent our luggage on peasants' horses, and ourselves were lucky enough to follow on decent animals furnished by the menzil. The two popes came to escort us, as before leaving Novi Bazaar by the western end we were to ride a quarter of an hour to the east, and visit that little church of St. Peter and St. Paul, called by the country folks the cathedral of Rashka. Just as we were starting the kaïmakam was announced— come in person to accompany us out of town. What was to be done? We would not for the world miss seeing the place where Némania was baptized; so there was nothing for it but go thither, kaïmakam and all. Having slowly proceeded to the church, we entered it in company with the popes, but were well satisfied to remark that the official and his Turks remained outside.

The church is very small, with windows like gun-holes. It was built at least as early as the eleventh century, but was restored in 1728; owing probably to its unostentatious exterior and its situation without the town, the Christians have been allowed to retain it in use. A small side chapel contains the tomb of a Serbian patriarch; we were shown also part of a patriarch's staff inlaid with mother-of-pearl, an old candelabrum, in form like a griffin, and a curious little tryptich in gold. Lastly, the popes brought forth a Serbian copy of the Gospels, sent from Ipek, and began to explain the signification of some handwriting on the first page; but they moved and spoke nervously and hurriedly, ever with one eye on the door. And with good reason. While we were thus engaged the sound of tramping caused us to raise our heads, and behold the church fast filling with the figures of the kaïmakam and his train. Possibly they were only tired of waiting outside; more probably they suspected and hoped that some treasures were being brought from their hiding-place; but whatever the motive the entry was made with rude carelessness of all feelings except their own. Without speaking to the priests or waiting for guidance, the Turkish official walked straight through the church and through the principal door of the iconastasis into the sanctuary, where even Christian laymen may not enter without special invitation. Our first sight of him was when the tassel of his fez was already disappearing behind the screen, so all we could do was to get him out again as fast as possible by instantly quitting the church ourselves.

We had mounted our horses when the dragoman called our attention to the Turk, who had followed us and was striving to make a speech. He evidently saw that something was wrong, and therefore told us that he had been impressing on the priests the necessity of always keeping this church smart and clean, that it might remain a show to strangers. We replied that we hoped he would extend his solicitude to the beautiful church on the top of the hill; and in order that it might be preserved for admiration, that he would desire the Mussulmans to cease pulling it to pieces. To this the Turk answered, with some peevishness, that the church on the hill had been ruined ages ago, and turning to the pope he demanded what we meant. But the pope stood his ground, and declared that part of the building had been destroyed quite lately by the rude soldiery from Prizren; he also took occasion to inform the governor that near the very church where we stood the Christians had lately begun to build a little house for a priest, but that the Mussulmans had pulled it down. The governor was evidently not prepared for this statement of grievances before strangers, and he looked all the more cross when he saw that the priest's outspokenness pleased us well.

The procession now resumed its march, and the kaïmakam, with admirable patience, escorted us to the other end of the town. At parting, we offered him very sincere thanks for having secured our journey to Ipek; and contrasting the mode of our exit from Novi Bazaar with that of our countryman Mr. Paton, we felt that the introduction of a rival element, in the shape of officials from Constantinople, had here acted as a much needed curb on the fanaticism of the native Mussulmans.

Scarcely had we parted from the Turks when down came a pelt of rain; no one seemed to know where the next house stood, and for some time we galloped pell-mell along the road. Meanwhile the priests underwent a sudden metamorphosis; each drew from behind his saddle a wide red mantle, and flung it over, not only himself, but the greater part of his horse. Thus accoutred they looked so exceedingly like the heroes whose portraits adorn the walls of Serbian taverns, that we had only to strain our fancy a little to see old Relia tilting along on his own ground.

The first attempt at shelter was under a tumble-down shed, literally so called, for part of it tumbled on ourselves; while we were there the zaptiés discovered a Mussulman's cabin, and prepared it for our reception in the following manner. They caused the proprietors to make a good fire and then turned them out of doors, the father of the family improvising a harem by barring his women up in the maize shed. When we arrived nothing was to be seen save a hen hatching in the corner of the inner room, and on the floor a wooden trough of the favourite plant basilica. Before departing we got them to call the master of the house, in hopes that a bakshish might console him for his trouble.

The rest of this day's journey proved unexpectedly interesting, partly because the chaoush of the Bosniac guard turned out a great talker and knew something of the local traditions. Our way first pursued the left bank of the Rashka to a point where it is joined by another mountain stream. The angle between the rivers is occupied by a huge rock, and on the opposite side of the Rashka lies a small plain covered with low ruined walls. "Here," said the zaptié, "stood Stari Bazaar, which was a great town before Novi Bazaar was built. There are the stones of some of the houses, and in that great rock lived the king's daughter, called Morava. One day an earthquake destroyed the city, and shut the king's daughter up in her cell."

This, then, is the traditional site of the ancient town of Rashka, to which we have alluded in the preceding chapter.

Some distance up the glen to the right are the ruins of the famous church of Sapotcháni. We had much wished to see it, but were told this was impossible, as there were no konaks within several hours. Let not other travellers be thus deterred. Sapotcháni cannot be more than three hours distant from Novi Bazaar. It might be visited thence in one day, but if taken on the way to Ipek there is a house belonging to a certain Murad Bey, where one would probably find as good quarters as at Tutin.

Our way now left the course of the Rashka, for that of a smaller stream to the left; after a while we crossed this also, and struck over a wooded hill. Here all around is forest-mountain, its wild stillness broken only by the gurgle of unseen brooks, or by the fitful sobs of the breeze when rain is in the air. But though no human habitation is to be seen, the region is not really uninhabited; through these glens the Albanians have pushed from the borders of Montenegro to their north-western limit, namely, Senitza, a small town on the Serbian frontier. The Bosniac guards called our attention to one hill in particular, and said that in its glens lay ten villages which had never obeyed the Sultan nor paid tribute till some ten years ago. Then Reschid Pasha was sent to quiet the country. There was a great war in the glen, and the villagers lost many of their men, some being killed and some sent prisoners to Stamboul. We asked, "Do the villagers pay tribute now?"

"Not very punctually," he answered; "but they cannot rob their neighbours and go on as they used to do."

"Were the robbers Bosniacs or Albanians?"

"Mixed. The real boundary between Bosnia and Arnaoutluk is Roshaï, but you will find Albanians mixed with Bosniacs on this line as far as Senitza."

"Are there any Christians hereabouts?"

"Yes; but few, very few."

Finding the chaoush so communicative, we questioned him about the country through which we rode. Passing a beautiful ravine on the left one heard the sound of a descending torrent; thereupon he declared that not far off, in a spot called Ostravitza, was to be found an intermittent spring; he further told us that the hills we had passed were called Yelak and Ruya, and that we should next cross a high ridge named Kanima—all before we reached Tutin.

A new theme was then started by the menzilgee, who suddenly burst into a wild song, whooping exultingly such words as these: "I am a Bosniac, I carry shining arms."

We asked the chaoush, "What kind of military service do you Bosniacs prefer, the Nizam or the Bashibazouks, *i.e.*, regular or irregular?"

He answered, impetuously, "Not the Nizam; we will have nothing to do with Nizam; but the Bashi-bazouks are fine fellows, and have always good horses and fine clothes."

"Has the Sultan yet raised Nizam in Bosnia?"

"No, nor can he; the Bosniacs will not give him Nizam."

"How is that?" we asked; "the Arnaouts furnish Nizam."

"So they may, but the Bosniacs—no."

"And which, then, do you consider the best heroes—Albanians or Bosniacs?"

"Listen," he said. "The Albanians are heroes with guns, whereas with guns the Bosniacs are worth nothing; but the Bosniacs are heroes on horseback—hu!—such as there are not in the whole world."

The distant view of the Vassoïevic Mountains here suggested a change of subject, and we asked whether he or any of his people, had been fighting there last year. He said, "No, but the Albanians were."

"And what sort of heroes are the Vassoïevic?"

"Good—very good: heroes, and like the Albanians, with guns."

"Are they as good as the Arnaouts?"

As a Mussulman he would not allow this, and said the Arnaouts were better. Wanting to hear what he would say, we asked if it were true that Vassoïevic used not to belong to Montenegro, and if it was only during the last thirty years that even the Berdas had become free.

"Yes," he answered, "they do not belong to the old Montenegro, but now they are all free together."

We asked if they heard anything about the Danubian Serbians arming lately.

"Oh, yes," he cried, "but we don't care about them. It is true they have good cannon, but they are not heroes."

"Were they not good heroes in Kara George's time?"

"Yes, that they were; but now we know that they cannot be, for this reason, they have not fought these thirty years."

The sun was setting as we emerged from the thick woods of oak and beech. Before us lay the little mountain plain of Tutin, traversed by a stream, on the banks of which rise wooden houses with peaked roofs. At the entrance of the meadow, two well-mounted Bosniacs with their attendants were drawn up to await us. The elder was a fine old man in turban and robes; the other, middle-aged, wore over his linen tunic a crimson jacket lined with fur. The former led the way in silence; the latter said, "Dobro doshlé," and rode into the village at our side. At the door of the largest house the cavalcade stopped, the crimson jacket alighted, and seizing the nearest of his guests, literally *sous le bras*, half carried her up-stairs. All was dark, the steps broken, and the general impression that one would land in a granary. With pleasant surprise we found ourselves in a comfortable room, thoroughly carpeted, and containing a fireplace as well as a stove. The windows were very small, but the wooden walls were literally perforated with loopholes, whence to fire on a besieging foe; some of these were large, some small, and most covered with thick white paper, so as to exclude the air.

That evening we amused ourselves with recalling what we had heard about a personage whose forest realm we were now traversing, *i.e.*, the *vila*. Of her presence in the surrounding mountains the chaoush had spoken without a shade of doubt. He affirmed that she was frequently seen both by Mussulmans and Christians, provided they were natives of the country; but he did not think she vouchsafed to appear to strangers, whether Franks or Osmanli. "And what is she like, when seen?" asked we. He answered, "She does not always appear in the same way. Sometimes she looks like a fair maiden riding on a good horse." Such, indeed, is the usual description, with the further details that her dress is white, her bright hair flowing, and her steed swift as the wind. When not riding, she is represented with white wings. Albanians talk of her as well as Serbians, yet she would seem to be of Slăvic origin, for she is found in most Slavonic countries, and even in that half of Germany of which Latham says that " if it did but know, or would but own, it is Slavonia in disguise." Famed as are the vila's horses (a vila steed being proverbial as a good one), she has been seen mounted on other animals; for instance, on a stag, with a snake for bridle. But this is told of an eccentric old vila, who used to make travellers pay for troubling her woods and waters, and got her quietus from Marko Kralievitch.

The supernatural maiden on horseback reminds one of the Scandinavian *valkyr*, who rides wind and storm, and from whose horse's mane the drops fall as dew into the valleys, producing fertility and freshness. But the valkyr, though more than human, is human still; though termed the Maid of Odin, the Fair One of Valhalla, the Chooser of the Slain, she may also be the daughter of an earthly chief, the bride of an earthly hero.* In fact, the valkyr is the conception of a race whose christianized descendants carried the idealization of woman both into religion and daily practice, and as such she is the legitimate precursor of the high-bred, high-spirited, yet gentle "ladye" of chivalry. But the Serbian has no such female ideal. His free, powerful vila is one thing; his submissive, affectionate wife another; the former has no link with humanity save that of *posestrima*, or bond-sister, whereby certain heroes engage her, in order to secure aid in the hour of need.†

But if the vila has not the idealized humanity of the valkyr, as little has she the demoniacal taint of the northern race of elves and gnomes. We hear of no "tithe paid to hell," no uneasy forecasting of future condemnation, no terror of holy signs, no deceitful pomp and private wretchedness. Indeed the Serbians have not the same intimate acquaintance with demons as the Germans. The devil in person is not a hero, either of popular legends or religious epics; he is distinguished by a simple and awful name, "the Foe," while human enemies are merely called "not-friends," or, in Turkey, by a Turkish word—*dushman*.

---

* See "The Story of Svava and Helgi" in the Edda.

† That some vilas have domestic ties among their own people may be inferred as allusion is occasionally made to their children, though not to their fathers and mothers, brothers, lovers, or husbands.

Perhaps, although with important differences, the vila has most in common with the nymph of classic heathendom. We hear of her sleeping at mid-day in the deep shade of fir trees, while her feet are washed by the wavelets of a forest tarn. Near her the swans build their nests, and so do the *utvas*, or gold-winged ducks. In her realm the wild deer let themselves be tamed and bridled, and the lamb grazes confidently by the wolf's side. She has too her cloud-castle built on the hill-top, with its gates, one of scarlet, one of gold, one of pearl. In some cases she is even the "cloud-compeller,"—storm and thunder come at her call.

Now-a-days the most frequent appearance of the vila is as a spectator of human concerns. In that capacity the nymph most celebrated is she who dwells on the mountain Lovchen.

The peak of this hill overlooks Montenegro, and a poetic chronicle of events in that country usually begins by announcing that they were witnessed, heard of, lamented over, or predicted by the Lovchen vila. We happen to have seen two little modern poems, the one written by a poor Montenegrīne, the other by the present prince. The prince's poem describes the battle of Grahovo; that of his subject, the death of Prince Danilo; but in both the first lines introduce the vila, and throughout you are supposed to hear with her ears.

One might go on for ever instancing the actions attributed to the vila by the more ancient popular songs. We will merely give that which at this moment we can remember as her most purely benevolent deed.

The eyes of a poor lad have been put out with the connivance of his own mother, and he is left alone weeping among the hills. The vila washes his wounds in the brook, and then, "having prayed to God," she proceeds to make him new eyes. The ballad recording this is too long to stand here; it is called "Iovan and the Elder of the Deevi" (giants). We could fancy its scene among the weird caves of that deev-haunted region we afterwards traversed between Montenegro and Old Serbia.*

On the other hand, the most purely malevolent action we can remember of the vila consists in watching the hasty temper of one of two brothers; setting those brothers, who really loved each other, fighting, and when one is killed mocking the survivor with false hopes only to goad him to despair. The heroes of this legend are Slavonic Mussulmans, and it originates in a region bordering on Montenegro; hence the remarks of our Bosnian chaoush naturally introduce it here. We will give it under the name of

HASTY WRATH;

OR, THE VILA AS MISCHIEF-MAKER.

There were two brothers, Muyo and Ali, who lived together in wondrous love.

So lovingly did they live together that they changed horses with each other, that they changed with each other their shining arms.

One day they arose, and went together to the dark mountain-lake to chase the utva with golden wings. Muyo loosed his grey falcon. Ali sent forth his well-trained hawk. They caught the utva on the lake.

---

* There is much to be said about this word *deev*, or *div*, and its forms in different languages from Sanskrit downwards. In Serbian it is given to mythic giants to denote, not their size, but their supernatural character. *Divno*, adj., in Serbian expresses "wondrous," and when used for "wondrously good" or beautiful, the words "good" and "beautiful" are understood. The Albanian giant is also called *dev, def*; (see Hahn's "Journey from Belgrade to Salonica," p. 39;) he and the Serbian have several localities and exploits in common.

Muyo cried out, "The falcon struck it;" but Ali said, "Nay, it was the hawk,"—and his words vexed Muyo to the soul. And now they sat down under the trees, under green fir trees, drinking cool wine: over the wine sleep surprised them.

All this was seen by three white vilas, and the eldest of them said to the rest, "Behold two marvellous good heroes. A hundred sequins would I give to the vila that could set them quarrelling."

Then flew off the youngest vila—off she flew on her white wings, and alighted at Muyo's head. Burning tears she wept over him, wept till they fell on his face and scorched him. Up sprang Muyo, startled to fury; but when he looked, behold a damsel! Loud called he to his brother, "Rise, Ali, let us get home!" The young Turk bounds from the earth to his feet (but still half asleep and the wine dazing him; he sees, not one, but *two* damsels). "Ho, Muyo!" cries he; "may evil befall you! Two maidens for thee, and for me not one!" Again Ali's words stung Muyo, vexed him to the very soul. From his girdle he snatched the hangiar, and struck his brother through the heart.

Ali falls on the green grass. Muyo seizes his white steed, and throws the fair damsel behind him; off they go to his home in the hills. Ali's black steed neighs after them. Then wounded Ali calls to his brother, "Ho, Muyo, brother and murderer! Turn thee again, and take my little black horse, that it be not left uncared for on the hill. Else, better pluck out thine own eyes than meet such praise as thy comrades will give thee." Muyo returns, takes the black horse, and sets the fair damsel on its back; off again they go among the hills.

But lo! in the middle of the road there meets them a raven without its right wing. "Alas! poor raven!"

cries Muyo, "how wilt thou fare without thy right wing?"

With a loud croak the bird answers him, "I shall fare without my right wing, as a brother without his brother: as *thou*, Muyo, without Ali."

Then doth the Turk begin to say to himself, "Ill done, oh Muyo! was to-day's exploit. If the very birds upbraid thee, how much more thy kinsmen and comrades!" Thereupon out speaks the vila: "Turn thee again, oh Muyo! Once I knew something of leechcraft; maybe I could heal thy brother's wound."

Back they ride towards the dark lake; back they ride till now they have reached it. Then Muyo looks behind him; he beholds the black steed—the vila is gone.

Muyo falls on Ali's body, but already Ali has breathed out his soul. When the young Turk, Muyo, sees this, from his belt he snatches the hangiar, and plunges it into his own breast.*

---

* Parentheses mark where we have interpolated a line telling how Ali came to see two maidens when there was but one. Such an explanation we ourselves required, and think it likely others may need it also; but in the written version of the legend it is omitted, perhaps because the audience to whom it is usually recited know well enough that after drinking wine a man sometimes sees double.

CHAPTER XXII.

THE BOSNIAN BORDERS—(*continued*).

FROM TUTIN TO ROSHAÏ.

NEXT morning we started for Roshaï, but before departing we asked to speak with our host. He looked very sulky, and took our expression of thanks without any return of Oriental compliment. We asked whether the *pushki* (gun) holes with which the chamber was studded were still necessary for defence. He said, "No; but ten years ago they were constantly in use. In those days the Arnaouts plundered the country, and haunted the village to that degree that we and our rayah dare not stir beyond doors." "Who put an end to this state of things?" "Reschid Pasha—he who made an expedition into the mountains and erected so many kulas." "Was that the same pasha who fought with the ten villages that would not pay tribute?" At the mention of these villages the brow of the aga became still darker and his utterance slower; he knew nothing about *ten* villages; something like that to which we alluded had been spoken about in his hearing, but it only concerned *one* village, not ten." "Did he know the name of the village?" "No, he did not; it had no name." We then asked him some questions as to the road we were about to travel and the names of rivers and mountains. He told us that in winter the roads between Tutin and Novi Bazaar were filled up with snow, but the snow froze so hard that communications could be carried on without difficulty. Further, he said that the whole substance of the village consisted in cattle, the mountains being unfit for cultivation, but, as we saw, well-watered and abounding in pasture. "How many houses are there in Tutin?" He took up the string of beads which he was twirling in his fingers, and counted thus: "There is my house, and my uncle's, and Abraham Aga's—that makes three"—and so on—"in all seven." "And to whom does the village belong?" He again became sulky, and answered that he did not know what we meant, but that this village and all the district stood under the kaïmakam of Novi Bazaar. This struck us as a strange reply, for besides that the Bosniacs do not in general like to be reminded of the central authorities, in what country would a proprietor be likely to describe his estate as standing under the governor of the nearest town? Suspecting something amiss, we only added that we should much like to know his name, as that of a person who had entertained us hospitably. Without seeming aware that he thus replied to our former question, he answered readily, "I belong to the family Hamsa Agitch, and so do the other proprietors of this village, who are all my brothers and cousins—we and our rayah are the only people here." On coming outside the gate to mount our horses, we saw the representatives of "our rayah," in the shape of three or four supremely ugly women, clad in shirts and aprons and adorned with silver coins. They looked at us in a friendly and confiding manner, and smilingly stood forth to let us examine their weird head-gear and necklaces. It appears that they had inquired of our dragoman if we were really Mahommedans, as the aga had told them, and when they heard we were Christians they rejoiced greatly, for "was it not a fine thing to see

Christian women received with honours and lodged in the aga's house?" But if the rayah were glad to see us, so was not the old uncle in the turban. This morning he looked grimmer than ever, and again escorted us without uttering a word. We could not but marvel at this demeanour, as opposed to all we had formerly seen of Bosnian Mussulmans. But in due time the phenomenon was explained. The possession of a firman, the journey to Ipek at this crisis, perhaps also some expressions in the letter of the kaïmakam of Novi Bazaar, had given rise to the impression that we were emissaries from Constantinople. This was made known to us by our dragoman the moment we had taken leave of our host. Like us, he had been struck by the exceeding reserve and suspicion shown by all at Tutin. But during the evening one person after another had come to ask him if we were really the persons sent by the Sultan to investigate matters at Ipek. "This," he added, "was the reason they would tell you nothing more about the contumacious villages, indeed they were very vexed you should have heard of them at all." We asked the dragoman if the aga really thought we were Mahommedans? He answered, "Who knows? The kaïmakam probably did not tell to the contrary, for otherwise they might have objected to lodging you. At any rate they did not wish their rayah to think that they had been forced to receive ghiaours." We were by no means satisfied with this story. The sullenness of these Bosniacs was no good omen of the temper in which we should find the Arnaouts, who had an attack on the Sultan's representative on their consciences. If we were taken for emissaries at Tutin, how much more at Ipek! We had not forgotten that the Arnaout, when uncertain of the good intentions of strangers, is apt to quiet his mind by taking a shot at them, and under such circumstances we could not but fear lest the mudir of Roshaï should forbid our going farther. To be turned back a third time would have been too bad. All we could do was to bid our servants din in the ears of future inquirers that we were from England, not from Stamboul; and that we were not Mahommedans but Christians, on a pilgrimage to Détchani.

What a day's ride between Ipek and Roshaï! Here is again Zélena Plánina in all its shades—from fir to hazel; in all its forms, from the park-like valley to the grim ravine. Then ever and anon some break in the dark woods, opening like a break in rain-clouds, shows sunlit vistas of the eagle's realm, — of Montenegrine summits streaked with snow. It is in such scenes that one identifies the epithets wherewith the Slāvic language characterizes, and even seems in sound to describe, the varieties of highland landscape. There is the *shumá*, or great forest; the *plánina*, or mountain-chain; the *berda*, or knot of rocky mountains; the *cerna gora*, or black-wooded hills; and lastly, the *verh*, or individual height, whose huge grey shape, rising out of the blue-green, looks like the giant shepherd of the forest-mountain, his head enveloped in a misty *strooka*.*

A peak wherewith we made acquaintance to-day for the first time is Haïla, immediately above Roshaï. Rising as it does to the height of nearly 7,000 feet, its limestone crags retain even in the end of July a partial covering of snow, and it forms a magnificent feature in the landscape as seen at intervals from this forest ride. Presently our path emerged on a lovely little valley, its lawns strewn with fresh-mown hay and sloping to a rapid stream. At its farther end appear two twin

---

* *Strooka*, the plaid of the Montenegrine highlander; in tempestuous weather he wraps it about his head; in colour it is usually grey, black, or brown.

hillocks covered with the dark wood, while darker still —*cerna gora* in its gloomiest form—rises behind them the hill of Soko. Having traversed the valley we crossed the stream, and began climbing the fir-clad ascent.

Some years ago this region was so infested by robbers that none could pass it except in a large company; and the "thousand shining-armed wedding guests" celebrated in Serbian poetry would scarce have been too strong an escort for a bridal party between Tutin and Roshaï. Whether in self-congratulation on their present safety or from old habit, our zaptiés began to fire off their pistols and to whoop and shout with giant voices; the cavass, who, being badly mounted, had fallen back, came rushing up on foot, sword in hand, expecting to find us in a fray with haïduks. The dragoman was also behind, but did not rejoin us till long afterwards; he then told us that, like the cavass, he had dismounted, and, believing us attacked, had turned "as green as death." Here, however, the story broke off, and we were at liberty to suppose that the end of his exertions was to creep into a bush.

A long ascent brings you to the top of the pass—unluckily, not to the top of the hill, from whence the view must be magnificent. We saw the summit rising on the left, its apex a large rocky fragment, whereon a shepherd was keeping watch. We would fain have climbed this eyrie, but the wind blew chill and the horses were heated; the zaptié would scarcely let us halt even for a moment, whereas, we could have sat for hours to feast our eyes on the vale of bowery wood we were leaving behind. But a greater feast awaited them on the other side, when we began the descent towards Roshaï. This frontier hamlet, built of the rough wood of its own forest, lies at the foot of a deep glen, and "in the water and out of the water" of the Ibar, which here, near its source, is a powerful mountain burn. Right in front rises the peak of Haïla, now golden with the sunset on its snows, while on each side the woods open, showing pastures scattered over with herds, and glades dotted with heaps of green hay. Near the head of the glen a few roofs peep up from a Bosnian Mussulman village. There are Christian villages among the hills, but none in sight from any point of our way.

Within half an hour of Roshaï the mudir met us with all his following in full array. He bestrode a great black steed, and managed it in the Turkish style, *i.e.*, causing it to rear and bounce as if in conflict with a swarm of wasps. This looks very fine, till the poor brute becomes covered with foam, and one perceives that, being all the while perfectly quiet, it has been heated and wearied by the rider for show.

The whole population of Roshaï turned out to see us, and a truly picturesque community they appeared: many wore turbans, and all wore white and red garments that well set off their stalwart forms.

The dwelling prepared for us belonged to a Mussulman. We were not a little surprised at its size, cleanliness, and the proportion of glass to paper in the window frames; above all, there was a regular fireplace, such as one still sees in mediæval houses in England, with a peaked stone canopy for chimney-piece. The young mudir ushered us into the room and then seated himself á la Franca, threw off his fez, and ran his fingers throught abundant hair, which showed small sign of the Mussulman tonsure. He then began to talk at a great rate in Slavonic, and called to his counsels, *not* the master of the house, a dignified Bosniac, but the Christian kodgia bashi and pope, both of whom he introduced to us in a perfectly conventional style. In return, those representatives of the rayah treated the mudir with ease; nor could we discern in their behaviour anything of the usual traces of fear. The text of their discussion was the letter of the kaïmakam of Novi Bazaar, which had not been sent forward to the mudir as we expected, but reached him first by the zaptié who accompanied us. Hereupon it appeared that the mudir had not the slightest knowledge of such a place as Détchani, although the far-famed monastery lies but thirteen hours from Roshaï. Neither did he at first see any difficulty in our going to Ipek; but on this subject a second thought struck him, and he suddenly exclaimed, "By-the-bye, the last thing we heard from Ipek was, that the mudir and all the medjliss had been called to Prizren to answer for murdering their kaïmakam. It is a question who may now be there in authority, or in a temper to obey the Sultan's firman." Here was a difficulty. The Bosnian master of the house came forward, and said that he and his friends would take us to Ipek, maugre all the Arnaouts in the hills. But the mudir dismissed this idea rather impatiently, deciding that as we wished to go not only to Ipek but beyond it, it was peremptorily necessary to know how matters stood. Hereupon we suggested that he should send a messenger with a letter, enclosing the order of the kaïmakam, and we would await the answer at Roshaï.

This proposal found favour with all parties, and we ourselves were not sorry to have a day's rest. But now a fresh solicitude arose. Where was our luggage? We had not passed it on the way, and hence expected to have found it awaiting us, but no; and after the mudir was gone some time passed without its appearance. At length unpleasing ideas suggested themselves; either the drivers must have mistaken the road, or else some accident having happened, they had quietly resolved to wait where they were, counting that we should send to look after them. At last the mudir did despatch some zaptiés, but not till it was already dark and we had made up our minds to an uncomfortable night. However, about nine o'clock the wished-for tramp of horses was heard, and the drivers being called to account, explained that there had been no accident, nor had they lost their way, but they had taken a different road from ours, and in the middle of the day had indulged in a long rest. Roshaï was the limit of their district, so next day they and the Novi Bazaar zaptiés went home. So did the menzilgee, though we had engaged the menzil horses to Ipek; he insisted on returning with the guards, because, should he return alone, he was certain that the Arnaouts would shoot him and make off with his beasts.

Of the two days we spent at Roshaï waiting for an answer from Ipek, the first was unpleasantly taken up in getting over the effects of a chill caught the evening before. When it became known to our host that we were taking remedies for fever he begged us to prescribe for his eldest son, who had been suffering from it for a year, and a lad of fifteen was brought before us, terribly green-faced and glassy-eyed. We gave him some of the simple medicine we had found most useful, and thereupon the father applied for himself. Though a stout, well-built man, he had, like all the inhabitants we saw at Roshaï, an unhealthy, livid hue. After nightfall there came a message from the harem, hoping that "if we came back this way" we would prescribe for a woman who suffered much from her head. We were really glad not to be asked to see her this time, being afraid of doing mischief; nor did we ever attain the happy confidence wherewith so many amateurs can prescribe in total ignorance of a patient's constitution. With such scruples it is painful to be asked for medical aid, in a country where to refuse it would be considered irreligious as well as unkind.

There is not much to be seen at Roshaï, except the picturesque Ibar Glen and slight remains of an old castle. The pope told us that at some distance there lie the foundations of an ancient church, and that hither on great feast days the Christians gather, and hold divine service among its grass-grown stones. Making inquiries as to the road to Senitza, we heard of two ruined castles on the way. The convent of Biélopolyé lies also in that direction, and the pope said that its monks keep a school.

The kodgia bashi and the pope were loud in praise of the new mudir, and gave the following story of his appointment. Last year, during the Montenegrīne war, numbers of Christians were arrested on suspicion, and it was believed that the Mussulmans hatched a plot to kill, imprison, and exile every energetic and intelligent rayah; in fact, a plot similar to that which, in the beginning of this century, gave rise to the war of liberation in Serbia. Then came the bombardment of Belgrade, to which the Serbs replied by an unexpected show of teeth and claws, and the spirit of the rayah hereabouts was roused by the hope of a kindred army crossing the frontier. The Turkish government, having its hands full with Montenegro, dared not drive the Slavonic Christians to desperation, and orders were sent to let them alone. At the same time the late mudir of Roshaï was displaced and succeeded by the present. Now the former mudir was a fanatic Turk, and in all things went hand in hand with the native Mussulmans, but the present governor had come with instructions to conciliate the Christians, and was a man whose temper and antecedents disposed him to carry his orders out. For this very reason he was odious to the Mahommedans, and the Christians expected to see him murdered by these Bosniacs, as the kaïmakam of Ipek had been by the Arnaouts. The first part of this story we had heard before, for we had ourselves met with exiles from this part of the country at Travnik in Bosnia, and we now delivered their messages to their families, who thus first learned what had become of them. The second part of the tale, namely, the efforts of lately-appointed governors to win over the Serbian population, was also corroborated by several instances of our experience. Everywhere, however, with a like result, *i.e.*, while it fails to diminish the legitimate longing of the rayahs for a Christian administration, it has the effect of rousing the native Mahommedans to ominous discontent. The agent of this policy, now at Roshaï, may be taken as a superior specimen of his class. He also represents another remarkable though not numerous type, namely, the young generation of Bosnian aristocrats when transmuted into Turkish officials; thus furnishing an illustration of what bureaucracy, centralisation, and Stamboul life make of the tough old Slavonic Bey.

The day after our arrival the mudir came again to see us, and this time chose to talk Turkish, falling into Slavonic when necessary to make his meaning clear; probably he did not wish the people of the house to understand him, for he had much to say, nor did the deficiencies of our dragoman in Turkish discourage him from a conversation of some hours. This may be partly accounted for by the circumstance that he was talking of himself and his ancestors. Like Bosniacs in general, he had "ancestors," and no sooner knew that we had been in the Herzegovina, and seen Mostar, Blagaï, Stolac, than he poured forth their history and his own. He came of the house of Rizvan Beg, a relative of the famous Ali Pasha of the Herzegovina. The family seat was Stolac, and had been so ever since the Turkish conquest, but the rank and power of the family dated earlier; they had been great people in the days when Herzegovina was called the Duchy of St. Sava, and they came to Stolac when the last duke was driven from Blagaï by the Turks. One branch of the family renegaded to save its lands, the other followed the duke into exile, and became nobles of the free city Ragusa; but between both branches friendly intercourse continued, and the family of Rizvan Begovic always remained on good terms with the Latins. At last came the grand revolt of the Bosnian Mussulmans against the Porte; one after another the great families found their ruin, and the turn came to that of Rizvan Begovic. Advantage was taken of its old connections to accuse it of treasonable negotiations with the Latins, and a firman of the Sultan empowered Omar Pasha to deprive its members of their lands and bring them captive to Stamboul.

At the end of this story the mudir drew a long breath, and then asked—

"At Stolac did you see a factory built by an European merchant?"

"We did."

"Well, the merchant who built that factory agreed to set it up at his own expense, on condition that for a certain number of years he should hold it free of rent. During the war the factory could not work, the merchant lost money, and he called on my family to indemnify him. But at that time all our rents were paid in to the Sultan, and we lived on a yearly allowance from the treasury; therefore it was settled that the

Sultan should indemnify the merchant, and stop the amount out of our revenue. Thus ever since we have been shut out of our estates; but they say that by next year all will have been repaid, and that we shall get our lands again. Meanwhile my father lives in Constantinople, and there I was born and educated. My mother was a Circassian: it was from my father I learned the Bosnian tongue. I spoke it when I was a child, but I never had occasion to speak it since, till I came here two months ago."

We told the mudir that much of his story was already known to us, and that we had met other families of Bosnia and the Herzegovina in the same position as his own.

"Yes," he said, "in Bosnia and the Herzegovina there is scarcely one whole family spared. Do you know any of these?"—and he named one after another the great Bosnian houses.

"Yes, we know some of them, and also some of those that went over to Ragusa and have fallen under Austria; and a Herzegovinian family we know that would not submit either to the Turks or to the Latins, and are now princes of Montenegro."

"Ah!" he exclaimed with a start, "ah, indeed! Well, my family was once almost as great as princes, and when Montenegrines came to Stamboul, they always visited my father. Pray tell me what sort of place is Montenegro."

Thinking of the adjacent Arnaoutluk, we answered, "It is a place where robbery has been put down, and where even a woman may walk in safety by day or night, carrying any property she pleases."

He interrupted impatiently, "I don't mean that kind of thing: is it a comfortable place to live in? I have heard that it is all mountains. What sort of house has the prince?"

We answered, that the prince had a good house, but that the most of the country was mountainous, and that to preserve their freedom the people were constantly at war.

"Yes, yes," he said, "that is just as it was described to me; but now tell me, have you been at Bucharest?"

"No."

"Well, that is a delightful place; it would surprise you to see such a European-looking city in this out-of-the-way part of the world. Now that is the sort of place I should like to live in. The truth is, I have become used to large cities, and if to-morrow the Sultan were to give me back all our estates, and say, 'Now you may go back to the Herzegovina,' I would beg him to keep them. I could not go."

These last words he said with a tone and air absurdly like *blasé* young gentlemen elsewhere, and apparently like them he believed that his utterances bore the impress of great mental superiority. As, however, we gave no sign of admiration he changed the subject, and began thus:

"I have been in England. One of my relatives is attached to the embassy, and I was sent to him on business. What a great city London is! but when I was there it was almost as dark as night."

We asked him if the climate had not disagreed with him.

"No, indeed; the climate of England is not bad, but it is a climate wherein it is necessary to drink a little spirits."

We asked him if he had ever seen English people in this part of the world before.

"Not here," he answered, "but once, while I was mudir in Caramania, an English gentleman came to dig for antiquities. He had a huge train of servants and

BOSNIAN RAYAH PAYING TRIBUTE.

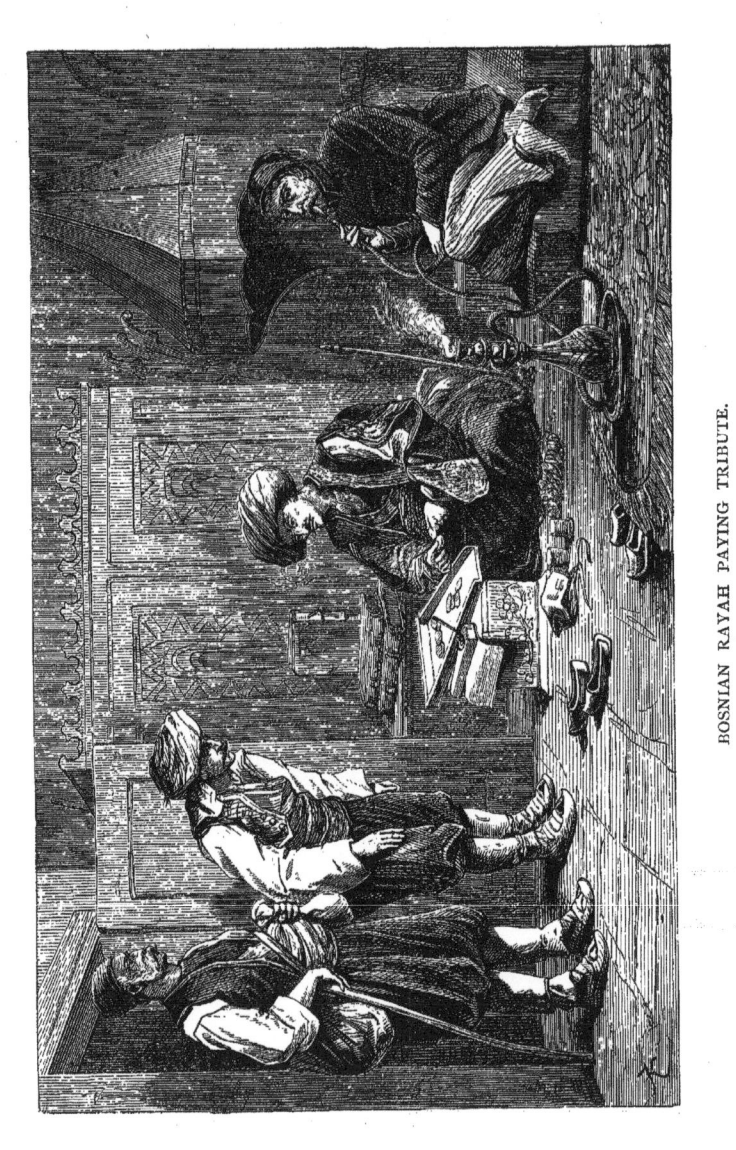

baggage, and like you he carried a firman. I went out to meet him as I did to meet you, on my best horse, with all my people, but the English gentleman coming thus suddenly on a great company of armed men took us for robbers and turned to flee: with difficulty he was persuaded to return. Ah!" added the mudir, presently, "Asia Minor is a much nicer place than this. There, if I wanted any number of horses I had only to send out a zaptié, and the people brought them at once; here, if I require horses, I may send a dozen zaptiés and not get them after all. The people here are headstrong to a degree; they do not even care to earn money. If horses are wanted for travellers, the travellers pay for them at a fixed rate; if they are wanted for government service the owners receive in exchange a receipt, and when the tax-gatherer goes round he remits the equivalent. Yet rather than thus gain money the people of this district will let a horse stay idle at home."

In qualification of this statement we were aware, first, that the government pay is too low to defray the expenses of horse and man; secondly, that the receipt is not always honoured by the tax-gatherer, while the horses are starved, overdriven, and not unfrequently taken away altogether. However we only remarked that so far as the Christians were concerned they felt it a hardship to be called on for horses when the demand was not equally served on Mussulmans.

"That," said the young governor, "is the fault of the mudirs: they are afraid of the Mussulmans and do not force them to do their duty. But I am not afraid; they may kill me if they will; but I have the Sultan's authority for it, and I will make them obey. Why should there be any difference between men of one faith and another? For my part what do I care who is Christian and who Islam?"

We remarked that with such sentiments it was a pity he did not live in the Herzegovina, for there the Mussulmans in their fanaticism were always goading the Christians to revolt. He answered, "It would do no good; nothing can make these Mussulmans act otherwise."

"But your ancestors used to make themselves listened to, why should not you?"

"True," he said, "you are right. If I were restored to the Herzegovina, it might be an excellent thing for the people: but you see, it would not be at all pleasant for myself." Presently he added, "To show you what a set of people I have to deal with, I must tell you that the Christian pope finds a better friend in me than among his own flock. His dues are small enough, but the rayah would not pay him unless I forced them. What do you think of that?"

We thought that, whatever it proved for the mudir, it told very badly for the priest.

The conversation finally turned on Serbia. Of the new roads and schools the mudir had heard, and he much wished to visit the country. He said, "I have heard that Serbia has kept up the old ways, and has not, like Bucharest, become *European*. But they say there is justice for the poor in Serbia, and that rich and poor are equal before law." Then he added, "I did not mean that Bucharest is a *good* place, only that it is a place where a man can enjoy life. They say there are good schools in Serbia. I was at school in Constantinople; my brother went to a school where he learned French and Greek, and I should have liked to have learned Greek, for it is the most beautiful of all languages; but in the Mahommedan school there is nothing taught but Turkish."

"Is nothing taught but Turkish in the Mahommedan schools in the Herzegovina?"

"Nothing," he replied; "but the Christians are taught Serbian, and we will send our children to the Christian schools rather than they forget their fathers' tongue."

The morning before we left Roshaï, the mudir, who was evidently a great dandy, sent to ask if we could spare him a pair of gloves. At first we feared that none of ours would be large enough, but as he was a little fellow, with the hand and foot of his Oriental mother, we decided to try a pair of ample German gloves we had bought for riding—the only specimens to be got at Salonica. Of course we supposed they were to be kept for his next visit to Novi Bazaar; so, conceive our amusement when, at the door of our house, we found him on his prancing charger, and with the great black *handschuhs* carefully buttoned.

Early on the morning of Monday a message came from Ipek to this effect: "The pasha of Nish holds court in Prizren, and thither all holders of authority at Ipek have been summoned to answer for the attack on their kaïmakam; meanwhile, in the room of the kaïmakam a new mudir has been appointed at Ipek, and he will be glad to receive you with honour, in obedience to the Sultan's firman." Hereupon we made ready to depart, the master of the house at Roshaï hospitably inviting us to return. "Only," added he, "this thing I pray you: when you think to come here write not to the mudir, but to me; and if you want horses apply not to him, but to us residents. This time, if you had asked me, I would have procured you capital horses from my friends; but you have applied to him—see what miserable beasts he has got!"

END OF VOL. I.

TRAVELS IN

THE SLAVONIC PROVINCES OF
TURKEY-IN-EUROPE

TRAVELS IN

THE SLAVONIC PROVINCES
OF TURKEY-IN-EUROPE

BY G. MUIR MACKENZIE AND A. P. IRBY

WITH A PREFACE BY
THE RIGHT HON. W. E. GLADSTONE, M.P.

IN TWO VOLUMES.—II.

FIFTH EDITION

LONDON
DALDY, ISBISTER & CO.
56, LUDGATE HILL

LONDON
PRINTED BY VIRTUE AND CO., LIMITED
CITY ROAD

CONTENTS OF VOL. II.

CHAPTER XXIII.
THE BOSNIAN BORDERS—ROSHAÏ TO IPEK 1

CHAPTER XXIV.
THE NATIONAL CHURCH OF SERBIA 14

CHAPTER XXV.
THE PATRIARCHATE OF IPEK 34

CHAPTER XXVI.
FROM IPEK TO DÉTCHANI 60

CHAPTER XXVII.
MONASTERY AND CHURCH OF VISSOKO DÉTCHANI 67

CHAPTER XXVIII.
HERMITAGES IN THE GLEN OF DÉTCHANI 79

CHAPTER XXIX.
DIAKOVO TO PRIZREN 93

CHAPTER XXX.
PRIZREN, THE OLD SERBIAN CZARIGRAD 100

CONTENTS.

CHAPTER XXXI.
	PAGE
MODERN PRIZREN AND ITS INHABITANTS	115

CHAPTER XXXII.
A HIGH ROAD IN NORTHERN ALBANIA—PRIZREN TO SCODRA . . 130

CHAPTER XXXIII.
SCUTARI IN ALBANIA, SCODRA, OR SKADAR 164

CHAPTER XXXIV.
SERBIA ON THE ADRIATIC 193

CHAPTER XXXV.
CHRISTMAS IN MONTENEGRO 213

CHAPTER XXXVI.
THE STORY OF SERBIA.—PART I. 280

CHAPTER XXXVII.
THE STORY OF SERBIA.—PART II. 302

APPENDIX.

A.—VENICE ON THE ADRIATIC, AND VENETA ON THE BALTIC . 328
B.—DESCRIPTION OF THE SERBIAN VILLAGE COMMUNITY AS EXISTING IN FREE SERBIA 329
C.—ALBANIAN DISTRICTS AROUND DÉTCHANI 332
D.—TABLE OF DATES OF LEADING EVENTS IN SERBIAN HISTORY . 339
E.—TABLE OF DATES OF LEADING EVENTS IN HISTORY OF THE SERBS IN MONTENEGRO, SINCE THE BREAKING-UP OF THE CZARDOM 341
GLOSSARY 342

LIST OF ILLUSTRATIONS.

VOL. II.

BOCCHE DI CATTARO, OPENING ON THE ADRIATIC	*Frontispiece*
CHURCH FESTIVAL IN FREE SERBIA	facing p. 14
CASTLE OF PRIZREN	100
ALBANIANS IN MOUNTAINS ABOVE SCODRA	160
ZABLIAK: CASTLE OF IVAN TSERNOÏEVIC, LAST PRINCE OF ZETA AND FIRST OF MONTENEGRO	182
MONTENEGRINS BRINGING TURKISH CANNON TO CETINJE AFTER THE BATTLE OF GRAHOVO	208
UNDER THE TREE AT CETINJE	243
PORTAL OF WHITE MARBLE CHURCH OF STUDENITZA, BUILT BY NÉMANIA	289
MUSSULMANS AND RAYAHS	316

CHAPTER XXIII.

THE BOSNIAN BORDERS.

ROSHAÏ TO IPEK.

"Then fled they through the country, and through the world, until they came to the forest-mountain of the Deevi, and there found they a cool cave."—*Serbian Legend.*

IN the bright sunshine of a July morning we started for Ipek, and, crossing the Ibar, climbed the side of the opposite hill. By orders of the kaïmakam of Novi Bazaar we had an escort of twenty men, apparently the whole available force of Roshaï, for some of those on foot were boys, others feeble and grey-headed. The mudir pointed out to us one remarkably fine-looking fellow, wearing the Montenegrīne strooka on his shoulder. "See," said he, "that is a rayah." We expressed great satisfaction to find a Christian carrying arms. "Ah," said the mudir with a sigh, "if you could only have seen *our* rayahs in the Herzegovina, how beautifully they were armed, how faithfully they fought for us!" It is said that Ali of Stolac held out longer than any of the other chiefs, because he armed his Christian vassals, and trusted for his defence to them.

After a while, the mudir and leading Bosniacs of Roshaï turned homewards, leaving us under the leadership of a broad-shouldered, sallow-faced uzbashi. We were much disappointed to find that the greater part of our escort did not go back at the same time, for the clanging and trampling of so many men and horses throughout a journey of nine or ten hours was an infliction for which we had not bargained. But, instead of diminishing, our party was doomed to an accession. Within an hour's distance of Roshaï, we met a troop of Arnaouts, sent over from Ipek to fetch us. Their leader we afterwards heard described as the greatest villain in Arnaoutluk,—probably on that account he was made answerable for our safety. His red figure starting up in the green wilds might have done duty for that of Zamiel in the "Freischütz." Tall, weedy, and of a livid complexion, he had lank black hair, and black eyes hidden by the lids. He was quite young, but cruelty and pitiless greed had effaced every trace of youthful geniality; the nose was sharp, the under-lip protruding, the voice shrill. Among the Slavonic race, both Mussulman and Christian, we saw many a man famed for ferocity, but never one without some trace of human heart, some turn of countenance that suggested he might be kind to children, gentle in his own family, and,—when his suspicions were not roused,—hospitable. But in this Arnaout and other of his species, the smile is more hideous than the frown, the laugh more cruel than the threat, the whole instinct seems prey. Among beasts the Bosniac would answer to the bear—the Arnaout to the wolf or the hyena. So much for the man, but his dress was admirable: we were now entering the region of Ghegga costumes, and one description may do for a specimen. Our guide rode a milk-white horse, which was splendidly accoutred. His tunic was of scarlet cloth, bordered with gold, and reached to the knee; round the waist it was girded with a shawl, hiding a leathern belt, whence issued the usual complement of silver-mounted arms. His sleeves hung so long behind, that when riding he had to draw them through his girdle, but in front they flew open, displaying to the shoulder a wide under-sleeve of silk gauze, white and gleaming in its richness, and bordered with a fine-wrought fringe. On his head he wore a scarlet fez, with a dark-blue tassel of enormous size; in addition to this a yellow silk handkerchief, which ought to have been wrapped around it as a turban, but in deference to new fashion was fastened under the fez, tying up the neck and jaws. This last addition to the toilette proved an unlucky one, for it gave the wearer, with his drawn and sallow features, the air of a corpse dressed out in its best clothes.

The first part of our way climbed a green hill; Haïla in full view before us, behind the forest-glen of the Ibar. After a while we came to a spring of water, surrounded by a grove of trees; the uzbashi told us that at this spot the Mahommedan women from both sides of the mountain meet on the first day of summer, to drink the water and deck themselves with flowers. After this the path ran along the mountain side, and became so narrow and slippery that the guards could not keep to it, but dispersed on all sides, cutting their way through the fragrant pasture. Picturesque fellow-travellers, this troop of thirty men—the only living creatures to be seen in the solitude; their garments, white and crimson, brushing the high grass, their arms flashing in the sunlight and ringing through the silence of the hills.

When we halted for the walkers to rest, the uzbashi pointed out the Christian, and said, "This is Iova, our Serb, who was with us in the war."

We asked, "Did he take part in any battle?"

"Nay," cried the uzbashi, "how could he? He is a Christian; would he fight against the Montenegrines? But he comes from Podgoritza, where the Serbs are all good heroes, so he is glad to be allowed to bear arms, and we are glad to have him. He is one of our best men; and when the war broke out, and we had to go to the border, we paid him to take care of our children and our houses: that he was ready to do, but no one expected him to fight against the Montenegrines. Why, don't you know they are all Serbs together?"

"Yes," we answered, "we have heard that before; and also that they and the Bosniacs are one people. It is true, is it not? for you all speak the same language.; and if true, one must hope that some of these days you will cease biting and devouring each other."

The Serb looked up suddenly, and the uzbashi said to him, "Eh, Iova, do you hear that? We and the Serbs are not to fight each other any more, because we are one people, and speak one tongue." Then turning to us, he added, "What you say is true; before these countries were taken by Sultan Murad, they all belonged to the Serbs. You will find many castles which were built to keep down the country when it was first conquered; there is at Roshaï a little ruined one, which was put up at that time."

We remounted and rode on, the uzbashi seeming deep in thought. At last he said, "The Sultan is a good master, and under him I have a good place, and many piastres a year; the Prince of Montenegro is so poor that he cannot feed his people, much less pay them. But there is something which I have heard, and I shall be obliged if you can tell me if I heard aright. It is said that the Serbians near the Danube are not poor like the Montenegrines; now, will you tell me frankly, is the Prince of Serbia rich?"

We answered, "Certainly Prince Michael is a wealthy man; and instead of draining the country for his pleasures, he often makes the people presents, builds bridges, and gives food to the poor."

"Does he, indeed?" said the uzbashi thoughtfully. "Well, in that case it is a pity the Serbs are not better heroes."

"What is your reason for thinking they are not heroes?"

Like the chaoush from Novi Bazaar, he answered conclusively, "they have not fought for thirty years. Now, no one can deny that the Black Mountaineers are good heroes; and if the Prince of Montenegro had as many piastres as the Prince of Serbia, we should see *great changes.*"

Suiting the action to the words, he suddenly swung his arm forward with a gesture expressive of a "clean sweep."

At the next halting place the uzbashi broached a new subject. Last year he had taken part in the attack on Vassoïevic, and showed us a patch in the front of his jacket where a bullet had gone in, and another patch behind where it had gone out, after merely grazing his side; he had also taken part in firing a church, which seemed to have been the chief exploit of the campaign.

"When we burnt their church," said he, "you should have seen the Christians' despair. After that they did not attempt to keep the plain; they left their villages, and drove their cattle into the hills."

By his own account the narrator had been a mighty man of valour, but the Christians at Roshaï had desired our dragoman to warn us against believing in the uzbashi's statements. They said he had mingled little in the war, and spent most of his time on the sick list. Waiting for a favourable opportunity, we asked him if, in addition to other obstacles, the Turkish army had not to contend with sickness.

"That it had," he cried; "many of our best men

were carried off, and many others spent most of their time laid up with fever. I myself was among the number."

Not trusting too far to the account of the uzbashi, but uniting the testimonies of friend and foe, we made out the story of Vassoïevic, and here give it as a specimen of neighbourly relations in this part of the world. The district inhabited by the children of Vasso —Christian tribes of Serbian extraction—lies about twelve hours distant from the southern frontier of Free Serbia, and on the extreme east of the Montenegrīne borders. The tribe is said to be descended from three brothers, whose colonisation of the country is related in a curious legend;* some of their villages are situated in the mountains, some in an arable plain. In old time the whole formed part of Zeta; but after 1489, when these regions fell into anarchy, several clans nominally acknowledged the Sultan, while all lived in a state of barbarism and isolation. At length the family of Nïegūsh, in Montenegro, succeeded in reasserting a central authority, and gradually brought all the tribes of the mountain to follow their standard, and take laws from Cetigne. The hill villages of Vassoïevic went with the rest of the Berdas, or hill districts, but the villages in the plain found more difficulty in gaining their independence. The Mussulman community of Plava and Gūssinié claimed the right of gathering tribute from Vassoïevic, and therein took occasion for many excesses; but at length the Vassoïevic raised their war-cry—"He who is born of a Serbian mother let him come out and fight for freedom"—drove away the Mussulman, and declared that their own elders should carry their tribute to the pasha of Scodra. They then continued in a state of chronic squabble with their neighbours, till, in the year 1859,

* See Hecquard's "La Haute Albainie," "Détchanski Pervenatz," &c.

the Turkish government was obliged to recognise Montenegro as a separate state, and the commissioners of the five great powers came to define its boundary. The task was not perhaps an easy one, but, according to all accounts, it lay in the power of these commissioners to put an end to much of the lawlessness and brigandage which desolate those lands, by drawing their boundary line so as to divide the Christian mountaineers of the Oriental Church from the Albanian Roman Catholics and Mussulman Bosniacs. There is not in the whole district an acre of land about which it is worth the Sultan's while to bicker; while it is evidently for the Sultan's interest that the Prince of Montenegro be responsible for maintaining order among the Serbian mountaineers. Unfortunately, the commissioners went upon a different theory. Insufficiently impressed with the necessity of avoiding future quarrels, they exaggerated the importance of representing in puppet-show the jealousies of certain European powers. From the testimony of most parties concerned, and from their censures of each other, it appears that the commissioners gave up visiting some of the wildest parts of the country, and drew a portion of the boundary merely from maps and reports. Then—some of them deeming it a point of honour to stickle for every inch of soil on behalf of Turkey—they drew another portion of the boundary so as to divide the lands of tribes and of villages. Thus the Sultan became obliged to defend territory wherein he cannot pretend to keep order; while for the next Montenegrine contest was prepared a band of landless desperadoes for whose depredations the Prince cannot be brought to book, inasmuch as they are no subjects of his. All this would be of less moment if its effect had not been to reduce some thousands of brave men to the life of haïduks, and to give up whole districts to rapine and brawl.

As for Vassoïevic, in particular, the frontier line cut its territory in two, and left all the arable ground away from the mountaineers. Thereupon the whole clan transferred their dwellings to the Montenegrine side, and crossed over day by day to cultivate and reap their land. Of course an arrangement so inconvenient to all parties proved the cause of constant quarrelling; and the upshot was, that when in the spring of 1862 war broke out between Turkey and Montenegro, the small cultivatable territory of Vassoïevic was reduced to desolation. The Sultan, to whom the possession of the region in dispute is utterly valueless, had to spend borrowed money and sacrifice the population of an ill-peopled country by way of "maintaining his frontier at Vassoïevic." Nay, long after the war was at an end, at the time we were at Roshaï, he was still obliged to guard the said frontier—a detachment of regular troops living, as was then described to us by the Turks themselves, in tents among the ruins of burnt villages.

To return to our day's march. From the hillside we passed to a sort of mountain meadow, where some Arnaout women were cutting hay. The uzbashi pointed them out to us, remarking, like the zaptié in the pass of Katchanik, that they had never worn the yashmak, and were fiercer and better shots than the men. From this meadow the path descended into a deep glen, at the foot of which the Alagina Rïeka flows at a right angle into the Bistritza, and the mountain track leading from Roshaï meets the paved bridle-road between Vassoïevic and Ipek.

On the side of this glen we made our mid-day halt, had a fire lit, and drank coffee. The Arnaout from Ipek politely offered us to share a greasy meal-cake which he had brought with him. Its appearance was not tempting, and we afterwards felt all the more glad we had not touched it, when we learned that he had passed the night in a Christian village, and had forced the inhabitants to provide food, on the ground that we should want refreshment by the way.

While the rest were preparing for a fresh start we climbed the bank above them, in hope of obtaining a view of the pass which we were about to traverse. Like many others in the neighbourhood, it is a long glen, running out of the level country of Old Serbia, into that tremendous hill-knot which links the mountain chains of Turkey with the southernmost ends of the Dinaric and Carnic Alps.

The rocks of this ravine are higher, and its whole scenery is sterner, than anything we had met with east of Montenegro. Nevertheless it is really beautiful, for it is one of those passes of which the windings, how mazy and intricate soever, can be taken in by the eye at a given point of view. Our point was the top of the bank beneath which the two rivers meet; as seen from thence the nearer hills do not hide those behind them, the bases of bare cliffs are mantled by a foreground of wooded slopes, while the whole landscape is so grouped that its highest mountain range forms its background, and, as it were, its frame.

And now descending the steep and crossing the stream, we began to tread the right bank of the little river Bistritza. The Arnaouts told us that if, instead of following it down to Ipek, we had followed it up to its source, we should have arrived at a place called Maria Chesma, or the Fountain of Mary, and that there we should have found a wonder-working water, an Arnaout village, and a mosque. We asked many questions about this Maria Chesma, but could make out very little by the answers. Its name seemed to denote a spring dedicated to the Virgin Mary, yet the Christians cared nothing about it, and Mussulmans told us of it. We beg that the first travellers who visit it will not fail to let us know what they find.

The paved bridle-path we now traversed was declared to have been lately made to get at the Montenegrine frontier, but although it may have been lately repaired, traces of ancient fortification show it to have been used in early times: the superior of a convent assured us that it had been made by the Romans (?). At present it is dangerous for riders, being narrow and without parapet, besides abounding in precipitous ascents and descents. In many places our cavalcade had to ride single file, which rendered the procession slow and tedious; at last even the reckless Arnaouts walked up and down most of the hills. As we advanced, the opposite side of the ravine became ever steeper and more grand, more of rock and less of wood; here and there a row of forked grey summits shot out of a bed of luxuriant green.

In one of the grimmest closes our Arnaout guide suddenly turned round, pointed with his skinny arms to the cliffs, and shrieked out in Serbian, but with a most un-Serbian sharpness of voice and accent, "Look there, and tell me if this is a place for cannon and nizam! What power has the Sultan's firman here, and who that lives here ever heard of the Tanzimat? These cliffs belong to us, and are inhabited by our men." We laughed quietly, and said the cliffs were quite beautiful, we had seen nothing on our journey that had pleased us better; moreover, if the whole country were his, we esteemed ourselves fortunate in having him for our guide. Perhaps, however, as the sun was setting, we had better not stand talking here.

The Bosniac drew him on, and they walked hand in hand together, while behind his back we could not help exchanging glances with each other, and wondering whether this ostentatious depreciation of the firman meant anything or nothing.

After some conversation with the Bosniac, the Arnaout turned round again and ordered the dragoman to inform us that he and his men had burned Cetigne in Montenegro. He saw we did not believe him, and yelled it out afresh. On this we lost patience, and asked him if he did not happen to know that we had been in Montenegro since the war, and had lodged in the Cetigne he professed to have destroyed. This caused great sensation, so the Arnaout qualified his assertion, saying he did not mean Cetigne but Rïeka, the citadel of Ivan Beg.

The Bosniac also chimed in and remarked:

"It is of no consequence. Look at our fine clothes, and recognise the comfortable position of the Sultan's men. No one denies that the Montenegrīnes fight well, but what do they fight for? They are hungry, ill-clothed, without a para: their prince cannot even supply them with powder and shot! Speak, Iova! you are a Serb: speak—is it not as I say?"

Iova seemed not to hear, and before they could repeat the question one of us answered, "If it be as you say, the Montenegrīnes are all the greater heroes."

This Iova heard at once, and repeated triumphantly, giving its full meaning in good Serbian. "She says, 'If they can fight you hungry, ill-clothed, and ill-provided with powder and shot, that proves them to be heroes indeed.'"

"Heroes indeed!" cried the Bosniac; "but what is the *use* of being such heroes? Fight without food, without pay! Allah!" and taking the Arnaout by one hand, with the other he clapped his well-filled belt, and the worthy brethren-in-arms strode down the hill, doubtless exchanging vows that *they* would never fight for the Sultan on such meagre terms.

Presently we came to a ruined khan, and there halted for awhile. Our guides bade us look at the rocks on the other side of the river, and remark the *pétchi*,* or caverns. These pétchi occur at intervals, and at a considerable height above the water; their openings are small and squared. After what we had seen at Stari Bazaar, nothing but their inaccessible situation precluded the idea that they had been made by tools, and farther on, the rocks on all sides exhibited traces of habitation. We were gaining the end of the pass. The cliffs draw closer, the road becomes a mere thread, mounting up and down like a ladder and crossing and re-crossing the stream; till, as it were the lock on a doorway, a tiny fortress hangs on the crag,—literally hangs, for it has not standing-room, and its builders have been reduced to connect and fortify a series of caves. Who the builders were is uncertain; the Arnaouts call it, in common with most other ruins which they found in the Serb countries, the Grad of Irene; the Serbs call it the Grad of Yelena—meaning, perhaps, the empress of Dūshan; perhaps a widowed czarina of Bulgaria, who came to these regions to die. Some hint that the weird little castle was there placed by the "Romans;" others name the scarcely less unknown Deevi, the giants of the Zélena Plánina. "Perhaps the Deevi built it to keep the Romans out of the mountains; perhaps the Romans built it to bar the Deevi out of the plains."

If we had had any notion that our road would lead us past such curious ruins, we should have made arrangements for examining all these "castles" and "caves." As it was, coming on them by surprise, towards evening, and in a dangerous path, we were obliged to content

---

* Possibly Ipek, of which the modern Serbian name is Pétch, is so called from the number of caves in its neighbourhood.

ourselves with noting their existence as a hint to future explorers.

The Grad defends the entrance of the pass, and when you have passed through it, the rocks close behind you like folding portals. In front the banks on each side decrease in steepness, and the road becomes more even. But we had not done with wonders. On the opposite shore of the river is seen the mouth of a large cave built in with a wall, and you are told that this forms a hermitage and chapel. Close by the road stand two rocks, which the Arnaouts call the Arab and the Maiden. "The maiden was pursued by a black man, and could only save herself by springing into the river; when God had mercy on her, and changed both her and the Arab into stone." Many legends in these countries commemorate the brutality of the Moors, including under that name all those dark-skinned myrmidons who followed the Turks in their plundering career.

We were so busy asking questions, hearing stories, and noting marvels, that we forgot to look—as during some hours of the day we had been wearily and anxiously looking—for the first sign of approaching our goal. Now, before we were aware, we found ourselves under the white walls of a monastery; and, our Arnaout guide clapping spurs to his horse, whooped out, "Behold the Patriarchate!"

Those who choose to follow his example, and gallop helter-skelter into the convent, will meet us there at the beginning of Chapter XXV. Others who care not to visit any historical shrine without knowing something of its history, will find in the next few pages a short account of the Church in Serbia, and of its founder, the metropolitan St. Sava.

CHAPTER XXIV.

THE NATIONAL CHURCH OF SERBIA.

WE have already noticed that statistics respecting the numbers of the Slavonic inhabitants of Turkey are difficult to obtain, and, when obtained, unworthy of reliance. The statistics of their creeds are more imperfect still. Returns exist, by way of officials, on which the taxes are apportioned; but this very circumstance involves "the numbering of the people" with that machinery of bribery and corruption by which every class attempts to escape its share of public burdens.

The Mahommedans who do not pay haratch, and who in one way or another shift most of the taxes off their shoulders, gratify their pride, at least in conversation with a stranger, by exaggerating their own numbers; the rayahs, on whom the weight of taxation devolves, fear to tell how numerous they really are. Then, if you attempt to question the rival creeds as to each other's numbers, the Mussulman often ignores the Christians altogether; while a Christian, interrogated respecting Mahommedans, will seem half afraid to give an opinion, finally answering, "They themselves say that they have 1,500 houses in this town, but" (lowering his voice) "we do not believe that they have more than 1,200."

However, making use of such imperfect statistics as exist, and taking together the 10,000,000 or 12,000,000 Southern Slāvs in Turkey and Austria, it has been com-

CHURCH FESTIVAL IN FREE SERBIA.

puted that some 780,000 are Mussulmans, over 2,600,000 Romanists, and that all the rest belong to the Slavonic branch of the Oriental Church.

The Slavonic Mussulman says his prayers in Arabic, which he neither speaks nor comprehends; part of the Catholics pray in Latin, a language not understood by the people; some Bulgarian congregations are still constrained to attend services in Greek; but the bulk of the South Slavonic Christians are distinguished alike in the Eastern and Western Church by using for their Scriptures and liturgy an ancient dialect of the Slavonic tongue. On this community of ecclesiastical language, Iugo-Slāvic patriots, both Catholic and Orthodox, build hopes of future union; and trust to see their nation, now divided under rival communions, one day united in a national Church. Of course, as to the finishing stroke, whereby union is to be achieved and declared, nothing can be settled as yet. The Catholics would advise recognition of the Pope's authority, on condition of autonomy, as already accorded to the United Greeks; the Orthodox would have church government by a synod, as already practised in Russia. But, postponing the final question, Catholics and Orthodox work to the same end: Croatians endeavour to substitute Slavonic for Latin throughout their parishes; Serbs and Bulgarians seek to expunge Greek and Russianisms from their liturgy. Rather than be græcised, Bulgarian congregations place themselves under the Roman pontiff; rather than be latinised, Croatian priests have entered the Oriental Church. Each party has for its badge, national unity; each comprises the liberals of its denomination, and sees its enemies in Phanariotes and Jesuits. Both go about their business noiselessly, and are solicitous rather to lay foundations deep and broad than to raise their structure above ground. Hence, distant spectators see nothing. But those on the spot may satisfy themselves that labour is going on, and steadily enlarging its sphere, forming part of that regenerating process of Slavonian life which may yet change for the better the face of south-eastern Europe.

There are three Iugo-Slāvic churches; the Serb and the Bulgarian, belonging to the Eastern Church; the Croatian, belonging to the Western Church.

At present we speak only of the Serbs. The Serbian division of the Eastern Church counts nearly three millions of members, and claims for their ecclesiastical medium a Serbized dialect of the ancient Slavonic. For the Church Slavonic has its different dialects, modifications introduced by Russian, Serbian, and Bulgarian monks, when copying the Scriptures for their respective peoples. According to the Serbs, their version of the old Slavonic is the most systematic, that of the Russians least; for the Serb writers made their alterations on a rule and within an early date, while the Russians continued modifying to the sixteenth century. In early times the South Slavonic nations were more civilised than the Russian, and their priests, invited to northern sees, exercised on ecclesiastical literature an influence whereof traces are yet extant. But the situation was reversed when the Russians had shaken off the Tartar, and the Iugo-Slāv fell under the Turk. For the last hundred years, most of the church books have been printed in Russia; and at the present hour—except in some remote districts of the Herzegovina, russianised Slavonic is generally in use among Bulgarians and Serbs. The change met with no objection so long as the South Slavonic MSS. and incunabula were all hidden or scattered, or while there were no Iugo-Slāvic philologists to decipher them; but of late years Serbian literati, averse to Panslavistic fusion, have exposed the difference between Serbian and Russian Slavonic, and demand a restoration of services on the national model.

It is said that the government of the Czar does not take kindly to this; while Iugo-Slāvic patriots urge forward the publication of Serbian MSS., Russia is correspondingly slow to give those in her possession to the light. Thus many Serbian MSS. await resurrection in northern libraries. Some found their way thither in the fourteenth century, when an abbot of Détchani became archbishop of Kieff; many within the last century, in change for modern church books. So long as the Academy of Belgrade lies within range of a Turkish fortress the Serbs cannot aspire to be the guardians of their own literary treasures; hence they are dependent on the publication of those preserved in Russia and Austria.*

Among the earliest works extant in Serbized Slavonic is a biography of Némania, written in the thirteenth century by his son Sava, first metropolitan of Serbia. Then come the biographies of kings and metropolitans, written by Archbishop Danilo.

These oldest known specimens of Serbian authorship are not considered the first literary effort in the tongue. Burning heretical books is recorded among the acts of Némania; and as, prior to his adoption of the Orthodox faith, all Serb people might be set down as heretics, it seems too likely that the flames of his zeal devoured the earliest national literature.

A store of documents, chronologically arranged, has lately been published in the "Monumenta Serbica." †
Among these are charters of monasteries dating from the twelfth century.

Further specimens of Serbized Slavonic are the books

---
* Soon after the publication of the first edition of these volumes the British troops were withdrawn from Belgrade.
† "Monumenta Serbica." Miklosich. Braumuller. Vienna. 1858.

called Serbliak, containing services for the national saints. Many of these saints were archbishops and kings, and the services written for their festivals were composed by the most exalted persons in the state. Thus, the service for St. Simeon Némania has for its author St. Sava; that of St. Sava is by the metropolitan, his successor; and the service for Czar Lāzar is referred to the nun Euphemia, a widow of royal rank.

Besides MSS., the Serb Church has its incunabula, and books printed between 1493 and 1635. One of the earliest typographies is that of Montenegro, and its types were not melted down into bullets before they had given forth some of the first works printed in Cyrillic characters.

Again, a Montenegrīne noble (Bozidar Vukovic, vlastelīne of Zeta), set up a printing press at his own expense in Venice, in acknowledgment of which service to civilisation he was created Baron of the Holy Roman Empire by the Emperor Charles V. A fine specimen of his typography is preserved in the library of Belgrade, — a miniæon, illuminated on parchment.. Therein it is stated that the printer has established his press at Venice, in the hope of transferring it to his own country whenever the barbarous Moslem shall be thence expelled.*

At present the Serbian Church in the principality and in Austria has theological schools at Belgrade, Carlovic, Carlstadt, Versec, and in Dalmatia. We do not here speak of normal schools and gymnasia, nor of the academy in Belgrade, where religious instruction is also given. In the Serb provinces under Turkish rule there

* These words were penned in 1519 by one noble of Zeta, while his companions, forsaking every luxury of comparative civilisation, undertook the defence of the Black Mountain. In 1862, when the few thousand warriors of Montenegro were combating the army of the Ottoman Empire, a new printing press was set up at Cetinge.

was not at the time of our visit one printing press, nor a single higher school.*

As for the architecture and works of art still remaining in the Serbian Church, we have already noticed how rich it once was in *zadushbiné*, or works for the soul, reared and endowed by pious sovereigns. Although roads, bridges, almshouses, and hostelries for travellers were included among the zadūshbiné, yet, according to the spirit of the times, most of them were monasteries. The greater number were destroyed by the Turks, and though several have been lately restored, it is not on the ancient scale of splendour, for the present bent of the people is contrary to monastic life. But in some cases where the monastery perished, or has been replaced by an ugly modern building, its beautiful mediæval church has outlived the days of ill, and remains to show the combination of Eastern and Western influences on the civilisation of ancient Serbia. The best church architecture and frescoes date from the end of the twelfth to the beginning of the fifteenth century, and yield fine specimens of Byzantine form quickened by Italian spirit. In Free Serbia the most beautiful churches are those of Studenitza, Ravanitza, and Manassia; in Old Serbia, there are the ruins of Sapochani and Giurgevi Stūpovi, and the well-preserved churches of Gratchanitza and Détchani. Of inferior excellence are some small chapels remaining in Prizren, and the church of the patriarchate at Ipek.

The members of the Serbian Church scattered in Turkey and in Austria are divided into four distinct ecclesiastical administrations.

I. The patriarchate of Carlovic in Austria, representative of the original patriarchate of Ipek.

II. The vladikate of Montenegro, acknowledging no

* There is now a printing press at Serajevo, capital of Bosnia.

direct superior, and sending its vladika, or metropolitan, for consecration either to Carlovi or Moscow.

III. The Church of the Principality of Serbia, governed by a synod, which elects its metropolitan and bishops. Like the state of which it forms part, this division of the Serbian Church, though virtually self-governing, is tributary; and pays an annual subsidy to the patriarch of Constantinople, answering to the tribute paid by the Principality to the Sultan.

IV. The fourth division of the Serbian Church comprises the Orthodox congregations in the Serbian provinces of Turkey; it is ruled in civil matters by Turkish officials, and in matters ecclesiastical by Greek prelates from the Phanar.

In old times these divers administrations did not exist, the whole Serbian Church being governed by a native metropolitan, whom Czar Dūshan, when assuming for himself the imperial title, raised to the rank of patriarch (1347). The ancient seat of the metropolitan was Zitcha, a monastery in Danubian Serbia; but the seat chosen for the patriarchate was Ipek, a town not far from the "imperial city" Prizren.

The battle of Kóssovo, which broke up the unity of the Serbian state, did not materially affect its church. The Sultan promised the same religious autonomy to the Serbian Christians as to the Bulgarians and Greeks; and so long as the Patriarch continued to reside at Ipek, his whole flock, however politically divided, acknowledged one ecclesiastical sway.

Although, as the Turks gradually gained footing in the country, they violated all their promises of toleration, seized Christian churches for mosques, and interdicted the open observance of Christian rites; yet it was not till 1646 that they actually laid hands on a Serbian Patriarch, carried him off to Broussa, and had him hanged.

It was after this outrage that the new Patriarch, Arsenius Tzernoïevic, led 37,000 families into Austria, that the vladika of Montenegro refused to acknowledge any superior dwelling under foreign control, and that the Porte, having first attempted to force creatures of its own into the Ipek chair, reduced all such Serbs as remained in its dominions, in common with the Bulgarians, under the Patriarch of Constantinople. We have already referred to the use made by the Phanariotes of this extended jurisdiction: it is one of the most deplorable incidents in the history of the Greek Church. Wisely applied, here was a means by which the resolute and strong-handed Serbian might have become content to find his spokesman in the eloquent and ingenious Greek; nobly used, here was a channel through which the learning and European relations of the Greek might help forward and civilise the Serb. That neither wisdom nor nobility dictated the acts of a Patriarch of Constantinople—trembling under the Ottoman's paw, removable at his pleasure, dependant for position on bribes to his slaves—this may be understood and excused. But that, of his own proper movement, the head of the Eastern Church should appoint to his Serb flocks Greek bishops unacquainted with the Slavonic language; that those bishops should hold Greek services in churches founded by Serbian kings; that despite should thus be thrown on all traditions of intercourse between Greeks and Serbs in the days of freedom, and the very tongue and name of Greek be rendered odious to his brethren in captivity—surely this was unlike the sagacity of the wiliest of peoples.

Throughout the Serb provinces still under Turkey—Bosnia, Herzegovina, and Stara Serbia—we found all the bishops Greeks. One only was present in his diocese, and he had but lately returned from Constantinople to squeeze from the wretched peasantry that revenue which his compeers were staying in Constantinople to spend. In default of payment, the Turkish authorities are invoked to extort the bishop's dues; and the minor clergy, fleeced by their superiors, are constrained to sell every rite of the Church. One peasant affirmed that the corpse of his brother had been left lying in his house until he could raise what the priest asked to bury it—two gold ducats paid in advance. The result of such a *régime* might have been foreseen. Throughout the Slavonic provinces the Greek bishop has become enrolled in the same category as the Turkish governors; and so soon as a million of Serbs secured to themselves autonomous administration, they placed their relation to the œcumenical Patriarch on the same footing as their vassalage to the Padishah.

Among the prelates of the Serbian Church who have become most historically famous, we may name Arsenius Tzernoïevic, who led the 37,000 families into Austria. By birth he was a scion of those vlastela of Zeta who ever defied Mahommedan rule; and had the Emperor of Germany made good the promises on which he invited the Serbians to settle in his dominions, Arsenius would have transmitted his power to a line of powerful princes of the Church.

As it was, after his death the title of Patriarch was forbidden to his successors until 1848, when the Austrians, needing the support of the Serbs, permitted the election of Joseph Rajacsics.

But the Austrian government will never allow so influential a post to be held by any save a creature of its own; and though both the Patriarch of Carlovic and the Patriarch of Constantinople claim the rank of head of the Serbian Church, yet in the eyes of the Serbs themselves that position is held by the virtually independent archbishop of Belgrade, who bears the title of "Metropolitan of all Serbia."

Other notable prelates were those ecclesiastical phenomena the independent vladikas of Montenegro, who between 1516—1851 united the functions of priest, prince, and military leader. Their most distinguished representatives belong to the family of Niégūsh. First, Daniel, who, having been for a time held treacherously prisoner by the Turks, raised his people to slay all such Mussulmans as had found their way into the mountain, with all such cowardly Christians as had adopted Mahommedanism, and thus, in the darkest days of the Turkish deluge, rallied the Serbs of the Black Mountain to freedom. Of his successors two are specially distinguished—St. Peter and Peter II. St. Peter defeated the Turks in pitched battles, gave his subjects written laws, and moreover taught them to cultivate potatoes. Peter II. established on the mountain a regular government with security of person and property; he also left his people a highly prized poetic treasure of epics, war-songs, and laments.

But not Arsenius Tzernoïevic—not even the Montenegrīne vladikas—enjoy the veneration of the Serbian people in the same degree as St. Sava, their first metropolitan, and the founder of their national hierarchy. It would be impossible to conclude a notice of the Church of Serbia without giving some account of this personage, even did not his biography throw light on the last days of that great ruler, his father, and present a curious picture of the manners of his country and age.

The secular name of Sava was Rastko, and he was the younger son of Grand Zupan Némania, of whom it is recorded not only that he was the first to unite all the Serbian lands under one ruler, but also that he was the first to establish in Serbia the one Orthodox creed.

It would appear that in the beginning the Christianity of the Serbs had come from Byzance, for when the Emperor Heraclius invited tribes from White Serbia to pass the Carpathians and the Danube, and to people his provinces desolated by the Avars, he invited them also to profess the religion of the Byzantine Empire. But, lying midway between Constantinople and Rome, the ecclesiastical allegiance of the Serbs was for several centuries divided and capricious; profiting by the confusion, a sect, styled heretical,* gained among them numbers and strength. At length the Oriental Church made a convert of Némania, who rendered it the ruling creed in Serbia, and caused himself to be regularly rebaptized by an Orthodox bishop.

No doubt the dignity conferred by this association on the little dark church of St. Peter and St. Paul is one reason why the title of "Metropolitan Cathedral of Rashka" has never been transferred from it to its beautiful neighbour the church of St. George.

We may be sure that the three sons of Zupan Némania, Stephan, Vūk, and Rastko, were educated in principles of the most intolerant Orthodoxy; fortunately they seem to have inherited much of their father's intelligence and strength of character, and never to have allowed their partiality for the Oriental Church to override their allegiance to their own nation.

* In the ill-fated land of Bosnia the history of this sect has been peculiarly disastrous. A premature and erratic Protestantism, after provoking the fury of Papal persecution, became itself lost in Mahommedanism. The last of the early Dissidents of Bosnia perished as martyrs or saved their lives by strengthening the ranks of Islam. But they had rendered service in handing on the glimmer of light they were unable to cherish, nor can northern Europe refuse to recognise some debt of gratitude to the early Slavonian Paterenes and Bogomiles. See the historical preface to Mr. Evans's "Through Bosnia" (Longmans), and the result of the investigations in which he is now occupied in Ragusa.

The youngest brother, Rastko, was endowed with a pious and gentle disposition and a love of contemplation or retirement; but he had not much opportunity of indulging these tastes, for he was early entrusted with the government of a province, and steps were taken to provide him with a wife. But the young prince was steadfastly minded to devote himself exclusively to God's service; and God blessed the pious desire, by turning his talents into a channel, wherein, contrary to all expectation, they were destined to become of the widest use.

One day, some caloyers from Mount Athos (known throughout Slavonic lands as the Svéta Gora, or Holy Mountain) came to collect alms at the Serbian court. One of them was an old man, a Russian, and with him Rastko made great friends, and took delight in hearing his stories of the still life of the monasteries. At length the young prince persuaded the monks to take him back with them to Mount Athos. There was no hope of gaining his parents' consent, for already they were making preparation to marry him; so when the caloyers were about to depart, Rastko asked his father's leave to go on a hunting expedition. He then seized an occasion to elude his companions, and at nightfall joined the monks, who were waiting for him.

The parents of Sava were sorely grieved when they found him missing, and none the less when at length they learned that he was gone with the caloyers to Mount Athos. Némania immediately dispatched messengers, desiring that his son should be restored, and they obtained a letter from the eparch of Salonica, requiring the monks to give him up.

But when the messengers appeared in the Holy Mountain, Sava persuaded them to tarry there a night; and next morning, when they came for him, he walked to meet them in his caloyer's frock, told them he had taken the vows, that he was no longer Rastko, but the monk Sava, and bade them take back to his parents, instead of himself, his worldly garments. To his father he sent a message, saying that he hoped yet to see him in Mount Athos.

And the time did come when the warlike zupan desired to end his days in the quiet of a monastery. Some say that it was in Rascia that he usually held his dvor, or court; at any rate, it was there that he had formerly been imprisoned by his relatives, and had been solemnly received into the Orthodox faith; and thither he gathered his last sābor, calling "all the chief men in the Serbian lands." "Before this assembly he stated his intention of abdicating; he reminded them of the anarchy and weakness in which he had found the divided provinces of Serbia, and how by uniting them he had formed a great nation; he exhorted his people to live in love, and preserve the union wherein their strength lay. His eldest son he appointed his successor; to his second he gave the government of Zeta together with the title of Grand Count, and desired him to obey his elder brother."

Then, in the church of St. Peter and St. Paul, he took his crown from off his head, and set it on the head of his successor, Stephan, and hailed him by the title of Grand Zupan. After this he gave a feast to the assembled nobles and took his leave of them all.

The profession of Némania, who now became the monk Simeon, and of his consort, who is said to have become the nun Anastasia,* took place some days later in the beautiful white marble church of Studenitza, still to be seen in Danubian Serbia. There he resided for two

* Her story is differently told by Byzantine historians: possibly there may be a confusion as to names.

years, at the end of which time, longing to be with his son Sava, he transferred his residence to the Holy Mountain. He was accompanied by his elder son as far as the Serbian frontier, but beyond it—even into the seclusion of the cloister—by many of the elder vlastela, his old companions in council and in war, who would not part from him on this side the grave.

The arrival of his father in the Holy Mountain marks an epoch in the life of Sava. From henceforth we find him no more a recluse, but taking lively interest in all that concerns his country, and actively using his influence in its behalf. Herein the Serbs resemble the Russians, that their national worthies earn canonisation by patriotism rather than by asceticism; by useful actions rather than by posthumous miracles.

The retired zupan first dwelt in the Greek monastery of Vatopædion, but wishing for a residence to himself he induced the Byzantine Emperor to cede to him the site of a ruined convent, called Hilindar, and began to build it anew. It is said that, while engaged in the work, an old man appeared to him, and suggested that he should make of Hilindar a Serbian convent, wherein Serbians, retiring to the Holy Mountain, might worship God in their native tongue and elect a hegumon of their own. Doubtless Némania was well aware that the Greek superior of Mount Athos would not be likely to tolerate this order of things; for he sent his son to Constantinople to obtain from the Emperor a charter for Hilindar, emancipating it from all control except that of the Emperor himself. It is especially recorded that Némania had brought part of his treasures with him from Serbia; and though he liberally distributed them to the monasteries of Mount Athos, he kept back enough to send Sava to Constantinople furnished with a golden key.

The mission was completely successful; the Emperor presented Hilindar with a sceptre, which, when the monks were assembled to elect a hegumon, was to be placed in the midst of them as a representation of the imperial presence and a sign that they had the imperial authority to ratify their choice.

Old Grand Zupan Némania, who, even as a monk thus exerted himself in behalf of his countrymen, died in the convent he had reared. No wonder that his nobles in parliament decided that his treasures had been well expended, even if, as the ballad hath it, "before he finished the monastery of Hilindar he had emptied two towers of gold."

This foundation of a self-governing Serbian monastery on Mount Athos proved the forecast of Sava's later and greater work, the foundation of a self-governing Serbian Church in the Orthodox Oriental communion.

The last injunction of St. Simeon Némania was that his bones should be carried to Serbia, and rest in his favourite laura of Studenitza. Sava carried out his parent's wishes, and chose for the transfer of the body an occasion when his brothers Stephan and Vūk, having been quarrelling over their inheritance, prayed him to come and make peace between them. Great multitudes followed their old ruler to his last resting-place; and according to his parting injunction, the union of his family and people was cemented over his grave. His relics are still to be seen at Studenitza, and were shown us there, together with the cross and robes of Sava himself.

The biographers of Sava are eloquent in their record of his good deeds, during the period which, at this time and afterwards, he spent in his own country. He made peace between the Serbs and the Hungarians, and again between the Serbs and the Bulgarians; he healed dissensions in his own family; he built the church and monastery of Zitcha in Danubian Serbia, which he intended for the seat of the metropolitan; he "completed his father's work of rooting out heresy"; he preached the Gospel to the poor.

We pass on to his great achievement—the foundation of the Independent National Church of Serbia. In the beginning of the thirteenth century two events contributed to give the Pope a sudden accession of influence in the lands east of the Adriatic—the taking of Constantinople by the Latins, and the marriage of the Serbian zupan Stephen to a relative of the Doge of Venice. Moreover, the zupan wished to assume the title of king, and considered it necessary that he should be recognised either by Eastern or by Western authority, by the Greek Emperor or by the Pope of Rome. The Pope was as ready to recognise Stephen of Serbia as two hundred years previously his predecessor had been to recognise Stephen of Hungary: of course, on the same conditions, viz., that the new-made kingdom should be subject to the Latin see. But Sava considered that it would be possible to secure for his brother the desired recognition without making a concession to any foreign ruler; he undertook the negotiation, and set out for Nicæa, whither the Greek Emperor and Patriarch had retired. The former readily agreed to acknowledge Stephen as king, and to the latter Sava addressed the following argument: "If," said he, "the Serbian Church is to resist the claims of the Pope, you must agree to acknowledge it as independent (*autocephalous*); for let it once be settled that we are to have a foreigner to rule over us, and it will be all one whether he reside at Constantinople or at Rome." The Greek prelates assembled at Nicæa had the sense to admit this argument, and in 1220 the Patriarch consecrated Sava independent archbishop of the National Church of Serbia. As such he was to appoint its bishops, and all future metropolitans were to be elected by their own clergy.

Sava then returned to Serbia, enthroned himself as metropolitan at Zitcha, called thither a great sābor, and on the ensuing Ascension Day crowned his brother Stephen king of all the "Serbian lands and the Pomorïé." A picture of this ceremony may be found in almost every monastery in Serbia, and it is said that in consequence of wisely conducted negotiations in Italy a Serbian bishop was entrusted to bring his sovereign's crown from Rome.

The Serbian lands were then divided into twelve bishoprics, comprising Danubian and ancient Serbia, Zeta, Herzegovina, part of Bosnia, and the Pomorïé. The names are preserved,* but we cannot say how far they correspond to any existing division of eparchates.

The last act of Sava is characteristic both of the times in which he lived and of his own love for his native land. His father, his brother, his nephews, and he himself, had built and endowed many churches; but these churches wanted what in those days was necessary in order to constitute them places of pilgrimage, and to give them repute among the people. According to the ideas of the times, they in great measure lacked the patronage of the saints until they should become the resting-place of *relics*. The affairs which required Sava's guidance being settled, he undertook his second pilgrimage to the East, everywhere gathering relics, ornaments, and holy pictures wherewith to endow the churches of his fatherland. He visited, "not Jerusalem only, but also Egypt, Libya, the Thebaid, Judea, Baby-

---

* The names are—1. Zahumlïé. 2. Ston (Stagno). 3. Dibr. 4. Budimlïé. 5. Rascia. 6. Studenitza. 7. Prizren. 8. Gratchanitza. 9. Toplitza. 10. Branitchevo. 11. Moravitza. 12. Beograd.

THE NATIONAL CHURCH OF SERBIA. 31

lon, Mount Sinai, &c., passing through countries in the hands of Mahommedans. His fame had gone before him; it is recorded that the patriarchs of Jerusalem, Alexandria, and Antioch, received him with exceeding honour, and that even the sultans showed him hospitality and favour to a degree that excited the astonishment of their own subjects." At the end of this journey, and having amassed a treasure of sacred objects, Sava returned to his own land.

He had left it, according to his biographer, starting from Dioclea, and thence, it would seem, passing through the Lake of Scodra by the river Boyana to the Adriatic Sea. He returned through Bulgaria; and on the road visited the Bulgarian Czar Asen, a prince who at that time enjoyed great power and reputation south of the Danube, and whose friendship Sava had conciliated for the royal house of Serbia, by obtaining the hand of his daughter for the young King Radoslav.*

At Tirnova, the then capital of Bulgaria, Sava spent his last Christmas. He spent there also the feast of the Blessing of the Waters, which is still celebrated throughout the Slavonic countries, without regard to the inclemency of a climate so different from the East, where the custom originated. On this occasion, as we have ourselves seen at Belgrade, an altar of ice blocks is erected on the ice, and down to the river's brink the sovereign, followed by his ministers of state and by multitudes of all classes, marches in procession, and bareheaded.

---

* The chronology and nomenclature of this period are very confused, and Serbian and Byzantine authors frequently disagree. Finlay records that Asen was assassinated in 1196, and succeeded first by his brother Peter, and then by a younger brother called Joanice (Slav. "Yanik," *i.e.*, Johnny). A Bulgarian biographer of Czar Asen calls this successor Ivan (John) Asen, and makes him the son of the elder Asen. This must have been the Czar Asen visited by Sava, as his coming occurred in 1336—7.

The function is performed by the native metropolitan in person, but on the occasion of Sava's visit, as a mark of high honour and distinction, the Bulgarian Patriarch requested the Serbian archbishop to officiate in his stead.

To bless the waters must be even colder work at hilly Tirnova than at Belgrade, and hence highly conducive to fever in the case of an aged traveller just returned from the East. No wonder that the next thing we hear is of Archbishop Sava being dangerously ill. Anxious to the last for his Serbian churches he caused his treasures to be brought before him, selected thence a present for the Bulgarian Patriarch, and hastily sent off the rest to Serbia under an escort of his own people.

St. Sava died at the beginning of the year 1237, and the 14th of January is celebrated as the anniversary of his death. He is acknowledged as a saint both in the Eastern and Western Church by the title of the First Serbian Metropolitan and Enlightener.

Soon after his death the body of Sava was transferred from Tirnova to Serbia, and deposited in the monastery of Mileshévo in the Herzegovina, for which the saint, while living, is said to have manifested a strong preference. The monastery, though lying in wild and secluded mountains, soon attained repute as a place of pilgrimage; and when that part of the country became a separate duchy it took for its name Ducatus S. Sabbæ, as being the resting-place of so great a saint. In 1595 the Turks made it their business to seek out this monastery and to destroy it; but not content that the destruction of the saint's body should be perpetrated in a corner, they troubled themselves to transport it to Belgrade, and there, on the Vratchar, in all publicity, they burnt it and scattered its ashes to the winds.

For some time the Serb people sought to mark the spot where this outrage occurred by setting a fence round it, but this fence the Turks threw down. The memory of Sava has been more worthily preserved. In every Serbian school his picture is honoured as that of the national "Enlightener" and his day celebrated with a special service. Within sight of the spot where his earthly remains were given to the flames has arisen the stately new Academy of Belgrade, which was opened by the Prince of Serbia on St. Sava's Day (14th January 1863).

CHAPTER XXV.

THE PATRIARCHATE[*] OF IPEK.

"Surely oppression maketh a wise man mad."—Ecclesiastes vii. 7.

WE now return to the point at which we broke off the recital of our adventures, *i.e.*, to the gate of the Patriarchate of Ipek. The foot soldiers filled the court, the Arnaouts clattered in on their prancing steeds, the monks, drawn up in line, with their superior at their head, received us with profound salaams; but it was in vain that we returned their salutation with all imaginable cordiality—evidently they were frightened to death.

Their first declaration was to the effect that nothing had been prepared for us, inasmuch as they believed we should lodge with the kodgia bashi, in Ipek. We reflected a moment, and then considering that our presence might not be more desired by the kodgia bashi than by the monks, we remarked that we were very tired, and would gladly see such rooms as they were in the habit of assigning to strangers.

On this they led us to a chamber surrounded on three sides by glassless windows; its whole furniture consisted of some faded cushions, while a threadbare carpet

---

[*] We call this monastery and church the "Patriarchate," following the example of the people of the country, who do not trouble themselves each time to repeat "Church" or "Monastery of the Patriarchate" (Patriarshia).

scarcely covered a plank floor between the planks of which the light shone.

This would not do, so we returned to our horses, and were in the act of remounting when our eyes fell on the opposite side of the court, on a building provided with glazed windows.

"Pray," said we, "allow us to look also at those rooms." With very ill grace the monks agreed, and sure enough behind the glass panes we found comfortable chambers, containing a large table and other comparatively substantial furniture. The prior explained that these were his own: had he known of our coming they would have been prepared for us, but in their present state he really feared lest we should find them "full of fleas."

In answer to this excuse we had the door shut, to the exclusion of our Mussulman attendants, and said to the prior, "We are Christians, and we do not desire to annoy you. If you wish it, we will depart at once; but we are excessively fatigued and would rather go no further to-day. If you allow us to remain, we will send away all the Arnaouts, and pay for whatever we consume."

The poor monks seemed a good deal comforted, and said we must excuse their apparent inhospitality. They had had a terrible day. Early in the morning a troop of Arnaouts had come to them, and devoured all the food they could find, and scarcely were they gone when our forerunners arrived. They would have no objection to lodge us, but they feared our presence would prove an excuse for that of every Arnaout in our train.

On this we at once summoned the uzbashi together with our Albanian guide, and desired both to take themselves off with their whole retinue. The uzbashi we paid off that he might return to Roshaï, but we desired the Arnaouts to proceed to Ipek and inform the mudir that we should remain where we were till afternoon next day, and that on no pretext whatever should zaptiés or Albanians enter the convent.

In due time the court was cleared, and as each successive Mussulman freed it from his presence the brow of the prior cleared also. When all were gone he hinted that on a third side of the court there was to be found a suit of guest chambers which, not having been lately inhabited, would prove cleaner than his rooms.

Thither we gladly removed, and commenced installing ourselves for the night. But while thus engaged the noise of trampling and prancing again broke on us, and we saw the court again filling with armed men. A monk rushed in to say that here was the son of the mudir: would he and his men remain all night? "No, no," we answered; "they shall be gone—every one of them. Pray tell them to go."

"Nay," he cried, "you must tell them so yourselves, and, I beseech you, be civil to the Bey, else he will be wroth."

The Bey now appeared and greeted us, but his aspect was not in his favour. His fat form was buttoned up in a snuff-coloured uniform, his face was purple, and his eyes red and heavy. He had moreover an odd, confused way with him for which we could not account, until afterwards we heard that he was a confirmed drunkard.

A civil spoken Albanian did most of the conversation, speaking Serbian, with which, like other Albanians in Ipek, he seemed perfectly familiar. He informed us that the mudir was much annoyed with our guide for having lodged us in the Patriarchate, since he had caused all proper preparation for receiving us to be made in the town. To this we replied by promising to lodge in Ipek the succeeding night, but we strictly prohibited any zaptié being meanwhile left to guard us. The Bey agreed, remarking that in the monastery we were safe enough, and now only asked if we desired that his father should come out to receive us with all his train. Under some circumstances we should have caught at the opportunity in order to see the Arnaouts in their best array; but we were now too anxious to avoid noise and fuss, so entreated that he would spare himself all parade.

Preliminaries being thus settled the Bey sat awhile, gravely blinking like an owl in the daylight, and then took his leave, whereupon the preparation of our quarters for the night recommenced. The windows had been originally devoid of panes, but after the Turks were gone, glazed frames were carried into the room. Neither frames nor windows were numbered, and before each was fitted it had to be tried in and disputed over three or four times. The march, with the clanging and whooping of a troop of irregulars in our ears, had lasted from ten to eleven hours, the negotiations with monks and Turks had proved alike lengthy and tiresome, and now came the bungling over the window-panes. At length we got to bed, but tired to that degree at which one wishes oneself and all things connected with one at the bottom of the sea. Our last orders to our dragoman were to the effect that *advienne que pourra*—a fire, a revolution, an earthquake—no one should presume to arouse us from our slumbers.

Next day—but not till 10 a.m.—we awoke refreshed, and full of glee and thankfulness to find ourselves safe and sound in the Patriarchate of Ipek. It was well, however, that we had taken measures to ensure our sleep from being disturbed, for no sooner were we ready to receive than we had to hold converse with three deputations.

The report of our intended pilgrimage to Détchani,

the unwonted spectacle of Christian women travelling alone in a Mussulman country, the firman, the kaïmakam's letter, and the peremptory dismissal of our guard the evening before—all these circumstances had impressed the population of Ipek with the idea that we must be persons of great importance. One theory was, that the British sovereign, being a woman, employs women on her private errands, and had sent us to ascertain the condition of the dominions of her queer ally the Turk.

Of course we only found out this hallucination bit by bit, but meanwhile we profited by its effects so far as to obtain versions of every story from each of the opposing parties concerned. Having noted down all we heard from the lips of the speakers, and compared all accounts together, we must give it as our testimony that it is simply impossible to arrive at certainty as to the details of any incident, but that all accounts agree as to the state of society. For instance, the stories told us by the Christians represented the native Mussulmans as oppressing, robbing, and insulting the rayah—"for a rayah to be prosperous is to mark him out for destruction; thus industry is deterred and the country ruined." Further, they declared that the native Mussulmans would not obey the Turkish authorities, and that the latter had not power to control them. Now, everywhere this general picture was confirmed by the Turkish authorities themselves, who thus excuse the disorderly state of the country, while the Arnaouts bore sufficient testimony to their own dispositions by attacking the Turkish kaïmakam.

Again, as to the Roman Catholic Albanians, the Serbs averred that they had hitherto injured rather than aided the Christian cause, because they were always ready to take part against other Christians in order to purchase concessions for themselves. The Roman Catholics unintentionally confirmed these accusations, by rather making boast of their line of policy.

Finally, as to themselves, the Serbs assured us that they desired progress and education, and pointed to the portion of their race which is already free as that whence improvement and help must come. All that we heard from others confirmed these statements, while we ourselves found among them not only careful preservation of every relic of ancient civilisation, but schools newly founded by themselves, while all their books and teachers do certainly come from Free Serbia.

One of the deputations which visited us in the Patriarchate was that of the Serbian elders of Ipek, who, reserved and stately, merely bade us welcome, and announced that all was prepared for us at the house of their kodgia bashi. In reply we told them that no assurances on their part were needed, seeing what hospitality we had always met with among their people, especially in Free Serbia. As usual, at the magic name every face brightened with a slow smile: they answered, that in hospitable intention Serbians are the same everywhere, but those in a free country have more in their power.

Less discreet visitors were the plausible and loquacious Roman Catholic Albanians, with whom we made our first acquaintance to-day. They wore the white fustanella, and were otherwise well dressed, cleanly, and smart; in person they were tall, well-made, sallow complexioned; their manners had little dignity, but much shrewdness, politeness, and *savoir faire*.

The chief speaker began with treating us to a dose of flattery, and then joined with the rest in a chorus of most dismal whining. For some time we were unable to discover what had happened. A great many questions

—each of which with furtive instinct they began by evading—at last elicited the following particulars:

"They were Roman Catholics, poor Christians. During four hundred years their forefathers had dwelt as faithful subjects under the Sultans; they had served in all the Sultan's wars; and in return the Turks had never asked haratch of them, nor confused them with the *schismatic* Christians under the comtemptuous name of 'ghiaour.' But this year, alas! alas! the Turks had begun to distrain them for haratch." Now, as we have before said, haratch, which was formerly a tax whereby the Infidel ransomed his head, has now received the name of a tax on those exempted from military service. Accordingly we asked if these poor Roman Catholics still served as formerly in the Sultan's wars? Why, not exactly. There had been a hitch last year. During the war with Montenegro, the prince of the Miridites and the Roman Catholic bishop had had a difference of opinion, and both had differed with various minor chiefs as to whether the Latin Christians should march against the Montenegrīnes or not. In consequence of this uncertainty, some Roman Catholic Albanians had served against the Montenegrīnes and some had stayed at home.

"And what course was pursued by the Albanians of Ipek?"

"Those in the town would not go forth, but those in the country went to war. The terrible thing is, that this year all alike are being called on for haratch."

"Well," said we, "by your own account your forefathers made a capital bargain with the Mahommedan, and you have had the benefit of it for 400 years. All we can remark on the subject is, that English people have little sympathy for those who shelter themselves at the expense of their brethren in affliction; and that our respect is rather for those with whom you say the Turks have never confused you, viz., with such Christians as pay haratch and endure the name of 'ghiaour,' but who do not serve against the Christian cause."

The Latins looked at each other, and seemed about to enter on a long story, but we bade them farewell. At the door they turned round to ask if we would visit their church at Ipek, and this we promised for the next day.

We have kept to the last an account of the deputation which waited on us first in point of time; when we awoke, its members were sitting outside our door, on pretext that they had come to bring us a trout fresh out of the Bistritza. This deputation consisted of three women, to whom our opening question was, "Do you know the schoolmistress, Katerina Simitch?" They were delighted, and announced that she stood among them.

As Katerina is one of the most remarkable persons we met in Turkey, and the bravest woman we know anywhere, we will herewith give her portrait and history. A woman advanced in middle age, above middle height, with a pale calm face and singularly refined expression. She has nothing saintish about her, still less anything wheedling and sly; but perfectly self-possessed and gentle, the authority of her presence makes itself felt. Her story is, that she was taught to read by a pope—whether her own husband or her sister's we could not quite make out. She became a widow, and her only child died. Then, in her own words, "Having no children to bring up of my own, I began to teach the children of others. At last the bishop came from Prizren" (we shall afterwards allude to this prelate). "It happened that he understood Serb, and he said to me, 'Would you not like to be a nun, and to give up the world, and dedicate yourself to God's work?' I answered, 'If I become a nun, can I go on teaching children?' He said, 'Assuredly you can; nay, you will teach them better.'

So nun I became, and what he said proved true. My religious character gave me authority; the people listened and sent their children, and other women joined themselves to me. After a time, the good Alexander Hilferding visited this place, and when he went home he induced a society of Christian people in Russia to send us yearly some assistance; also he sent us a provision of books."

We asked Katerina how she contrived to get her school-girls through the streets, since elsewhere this proved so great an obstacle. She answered, it was at first a great difficulty; it could only be overcome by making up one's mind to put up with anything rather than relinquish a good purpose, trusting that God would help at last. Of course the Arnaouts did all they could to oppose her, and twice they had broken into her school and carried off whatever they could find; luckily it was so poor that they had little inducement to rob it often.

The women then joined in asking us to come and visit the school, as this would encourage their community and deter the Arnaouts from meddling with them. They had come hither to make this request, because in the town of Ipek it would be more difficult to speak without being overheard. Certainly we could not form to ourselves an idea of the state of Ipek. The Arnaouts carry their ill behaviour to such a pitch that when the Christians bear out the dead for burial they throw stones at the corpse and cover it with dust and dirt.

At these words one of the women suddenly burst into tears, threw herself at our feet, and amid agonies of sobbing, told us what she had come to tell. "Her family was in trouble, brought on it by the calamity that had overtaken one of its members. The trouble began in the winter, when one night a woman of the Serb community was taken ill. The master of the household went out to call assistance, and an Arnaout who had a grudge against him shot him dead.

"In an evil hour the Christian community of Ipek, knowing the murderer, denounced him to the kaïmakam, and thereupon the Arnaouts seized on another Christian, and declared that he, not an Arnaout, was guilty of the deed. Christian evidence going for nothing against a Mussulman, of course the Serbian could not be cleared. The kaïmakam threw him into prison. Months passed: in prison he lay still—the working man of the family. Who is to provide for his wife and children? At length the Arnaouts shot at the kaïmakam himself; the whole medjliss of Ipek were called to Prizren to be judged by the pasha; thither the prisoners in the Ipek gaol had been also carried. The man falsely accused of murder was taken with the rest, but did not return; and lately his mother had gone to Prizren to try and see him." At this point in her story the poor woman's voice became lost in sobbing. We looked at Katerina, who moved her head in the Oriental sign of affirmation, and said, "Thus is it." She did not weep, her face was stern. The other woman now recovered herself, and said, "The ladies are going to Prizren, will they speak for this poor Serb?" We felt much distressed, and said to Katerina, "You must not let these poor people think that we have any influence with the Turkish authorities: they are bound to further our journey, and provide for our safety, but that is all. We are grieved to hear of your troubles, and this sad story we will mention to the first consul we meet, and relate it in our own land. More we cannot do." Katerina repeated this to the other woman, adding, "They are friends, they will not forget us, they will tell of our troubles in their own country." The other woman answered: "We do not know who you are, but ever since your coming was talked of the

Arnaouts have not dared to meddle with us—they are quite hushed, and sit so," and she crossed her hands over her breast. "Ay," quoth Katerina, "that is what they always do when a consul is coming; but they make up for it afterwards, insulting and tormenting us, and exclaiming, 'Do not fancy your turn has come yet.'" Our dinner was now brought in, so the women bade us adieu, trysting for the morrow at the Serbian school. After they had left us we looked out of the window and watched them on their path to the town. The two others cowered behind Katerina, who, humble but steadfast, firmly pursued her way.

It seems that our mode of receiving our visitors was such as to give the monks some confidence in our good intentions, for they sent to tell us that, before leaving, they hoped we would not fail to visit their church; "they had things to show quite as old and curious as those at Détchani." They added a request that we would come at once, before the Mussulmans returned to escort us to Ipek. Unluckily, just as we were walking through the court, who should meet us but our unwished-for Arnaout cavalier of yesterday. We begged he would walk up stairs and make himself comfortable, and then set our cavass to keep guard over him; but the apparition had been more than enough to throw back the prior and his suite into all their original terror, and hence we lost the sight of various treasures, while all special information was dried up at its source. They scarcely dared even to indulge us with the view of a saintly mummy, because it was bedizened with various rings; and when we asked after such ancient MSS. and jewels as had escaped spoliation, a monk more intelligent than the rest took upon him to save the prior's conscience an useless burden of *Néma* (there is nothing), by telling us frankly that with Mussulmans actually in the monastery they dared not draw treasures from their hiding-place. Nor could we blame their caution. The once considerable wealth of their church was first spoiled by two Greek monks, who, previous to the abolition of the Serbian patriarchate, were sent to seize its treasures and bring them to Constantinople for sale. Afterwards, several precious objects were transferred to Cetinje in Montenegro. If the monks whom we saw are of any use to their nation, it is chiefly as guardians of national relics; and criminal indeed would be their recklessness, if, to indulge a traveller's curiosity, they should risk the safety of some yet remaining cross or goblet, handed down from patriarchs and kings.

To return to our examination of the church. A wall passing through the court of the monastery parts off the sacred building, and to some extent hides it; only on entering the inner inclosure did we see anything to remind us that we stood within the venerable patriarchate of Ipek. The original church, built in the thirteenth century by Archbishop Arsenius, the successor of St. Sava, was afterwards almost destroyed by the Turks; the present building is a structure of the sixteenth and seventeenth centuries, when art in Serbia had sensibly declined from what it was in the days of freedom. Hence this church is far less beautiful, both as regards form and frescoes, than some others; on the other hand it is richer than any in relics and tombs.

The central edifice and its two large side chapels are surmounted each with a dome, seen from without, these three leaden cupolas in a row look heavy and tasteless enough. However, their windows throw an effective and, for the East, an unusual flood of light on the interior; in the two side chapels these windows have coloured glass—a rarity in Serbian churches.

Over the north door of the narthex there is an

inscription, referring to the restoration of the church. It records that the "trouble and heartfelt care of the very reverend and blessed Archbishop and Patriarch Macaria restored this sacred *prestol* (altar, throne) of all the Serbian lands, of the western sea-coast (Pomorïe) and of the northern (Danubian) countries, in the year 7070 (1562)."

The nave is, as we have said, well lighted and large, but low in proportion to its length. It is full of monuments, among which the handsomest are two white marble tombs, belonging respectively to Arsenius and to the Patriarch Ioanik. Of relics we were shown the body of Archbishop Nicodemus and the heads of the five so-called "nimbus martyrs," the latter brought hither from Tirnova by Archishop Arsenius, and probably forming part of the collection imported from the East by St. Sava. One of the most interesting objects in the church is the white marble throne of the Serbian patriarchs; it stands on the right side of the altar steps.

The north chapel contains the tombs of St. Sava the fourth and of the Patriarch St. Spiridion, but otherwise, nothing that caught our notice. In the south chapel we found a miraculous icon of the Madonna, adorned with a notable necklace of gold coins. Here too we saw Archbishop Nicodemus's mitre, carefully preserved under glass, and a patriarch's staff, said to be very old, and inscribed with letters partly Greek and partly mysterious—at least they proved so to the monks and ourselves. In this chapel the principal tomb is that of an archbishop called St. Danilo. The wall above it displays a fresco representing the saint, together with his patron, Daniel the prophet. This painting is pointed out as the original production of an inhabitant of the monastery.

Before leaving the church we inquired of the priests respecting the so-called Grad of Irene, and the rock cells we had seen in the way. They knew, or professed to know, little about either, directing us to the neighbourhood of Détchani for more interesting hermitages, and to the works of Hilferding for a description of them. We have not been able to find any such details in the Serbian translation of his book, and they had better have sent us to Katerina as the most fertile source of information on these subjects. As we left the south door we perceived the inner enclosure lined with people, especially children; but the gate into the outer court was open, and immediately beyond loomed the red coat of the Arnaout. Between him and the entrance our cavass had interposed himself, and neither of them dared to transgress our orders literally by passing the barrier; but the attitude of our young retainer, standing on tiptoe, with stretched neck and straining eyes, seemed more calculated to appease his own curiosity than to impose restraint on that of his countryman.

From the patriarchate to the town of Ipek is scarce a quarter of an hour's ride. Our way was thronged with sturdy little boys, whose beautifully clean though coarse garments consisted of a white tunic surmounted by a waistcoat; the latter, crossed over the chest, protects the vital organs while leaving the limbs free. These were Christian children, and displayed none of the aggressiveness of the young Arnaouts at Vuchitern; nevertheless, we had much ado to prevent our guards from driving them away. One fine little fellow broke from the zaptiés, and darting off as an outrunner was ready to receive us at the kodgia bashi's door. Then came the Serbkinias, for Katerina had made the most of the occasion, and drawn up her school on a green plot outside the town—pretty little girls, glowing with health and excitement, smooth-haired, and dressed in their holiday attire. The quaint grey figures of the nun and her assistants marshalled their white and crimson ranks.

From this pleasing picture our attention was recalled to avoid rickety bridges, splash through pools, and slip and splutter over huge-stoned pavements, with other dignified incidents common to entering a Turkish town; but especially to entering the town of Ipek, whose streets are literally made use of as watercourses.

We stopped before the door of a high-walled court, and were received by the kodgia bashi of the Serbs. Our course then led up a stair, through the chardak, and into an inner chamber looking on the garden and hidden from without by the high garden wall. Here evidence of household industry appeared in handsome carpets and cushions; here, too, we were greeted by the women of the family. One of these, the daughter-in-law of the house, was a bride, and in person and attire a thing of beauty. Her lithe form, above the middle height, was rounded like a classic statue; her features were delicate, and her skin so fair that we could not but suspect a tinge of art in the intense blackness of eyebrows and hair. Her dress consisted of that creamy silk gauze reared and spun for Turkish trousseaux; the wide sleeves hung open, and the full skirt was gathered in at each ankle. Over this she wore a long paletot without sleeves, of scarlet cloth bordered with gold. Her head and neck were encircled with gold coins and seed-pearls strung on scarlet, while behind fell a veil of the palest yellow gauze, contrasting charmingly with her raven braids. This dress as a whole was the most tasteful we saw in Turkey, being ample for modesty yet not surcharged. At Prizren we recognised its elements on the persons of two rich

Mahommedan dames, but then the transparent white gauze proved sadly inadequate to drape or disguise a world of fatness. Again at Scodra we found both tunic and robe, but over and above these a catalogue of jackets, not to speak of a wide-spreading apron, extending from the chest to the knee.

Except the bride none of the women were finely dressed, but even the elder ones were nice-looking, an exception to the rule in Turkey, where beauty is emphatically *du diable*. We remarked that nowhere in these countries had we seen women past the first bloom so slender and fresh, or so refined in complexion and expression, as the Serb matrons of Ipek; for this there may be the following reasons. Their Slāvic blood is untinged with southern sallowness, their Christian customs save them from the corpulence contracted in the slothful harem; while the necessity of wearing the yashmak, which Arnaout licence imposes even on the non-Mussulman women of Ipek, protects them from that sun-burning and weather-beating which darken beauty in Serbia and Montenegro.

Suddenly our hostess and her guests took to flight; the mudir and a bimbashi were come to call. The former, an Arnaout Bey of Prizren, proved an aristocratic-looking personage in an European suit of white; the latter was an Osmanli, panting in a tight Turkish uniform. The mudir had served under English command during the Crimean campaign, and both he and an old Bashi-bazouk who afterwards came to see us spoke warmly of their officers, and of their "regular pay." We asked him whether the English commander tolerated plundering of the villagers, as practised by the Bashi-bazouks in the Turkish service. "God forbid!" cried he; "the English commander put those who plundered in irons; by the way, this fate befell a respectable personage whom you lately met with as mudir of Prishtina." We expressed a hope that the good example of the speakers would work a change on their countrymen, and in reply they confirmed all we had heard of the incorrigibility of the Ipek gentry. Let a Turk fancy that you appeal to him personally as more enlightened than his brethren, and he will frequently tell you stories of their misdeeds, which you would not credit if reported only by the rayah.

A trifling incident connected with this visit seemed to us sufficiently significant. When we arrived, coffee was brought in by the beautiful daughter-in-law, and the cups were supported by zarfs of silver filigree, to which the mistress of the house directed our attention with some pride. When the Turks were present, coffee was again served, but by an old woman, and in a service of the commonest kind.

Next morning we received a message from the mudir inviting us to visit the Arnaout girls' school; we had also to see the church of the Latins and the two schools of the Serbs.

The first visit was to the Serb boys' school, which we found small and low, but well filled with children. They received us singing at the top of their voices, and accompanying themselves on pieces of metal which they struck into a jangling like that of small bells. The clamour was intolerable, and ended not until in agony we lifted up our eyes to the face of the master, who took the hint and called out "dosta" (enough). The school-books were, as usual, from Belgrade, but we found, as the popadia of Vuchitern had told us, that they lacked maps, and we could but regret having lost the pleasure of offering our supply. However, when it was explained that Pope Dantcha would bring them on his next pilgrimage to Ipek, with one voice all exclaimed that they were in trustworthy keeping.

Katerina's school proved still humbler than that of the boys, for the Arnaouts tolerate no display. Twenty-seven little girls could read Serbian and Old Slavonic, and write a little. Quoth Katerina, "That is all that we can teach them, for it is all we know ourselves, but those who can read have it in their power to learn more." She was glad to hear of a supply of books, for they had none but those first sent by the Russian traveller, Hilferding. From the school-room we were conducted to Katerina's own, and there introduced to the grown-up pupils and their mothers. They wore a grey mantle with sleeves, constituting a sort of monastic garb; for although, except Katerina herself, none had taken regular vows, yet all were self-dedicated to a single life spent in good works, teaching, and prayer. As we knew of a community in search of a Slavonic schoolmistress, we inquired on what terms one of these maidens would undertake the office. As a rule, the primary obstacle is the high salary required, before a woman educated in any civilised locality will bury herself in these wild districts. Secondly, there is the ambition to marry, which takes a young mistress from her profession so soon as she has saved her dowry, and sometimes cumbers her engagement with restrictions like the following:—"The schoolmistress shall live in the —— consulate, and never go out unchaperoned, else no man of this country will consent to marry her." Now all this sort of thing would be escaped in the case of Katerina's nuns, who do not seek husbands, and who teach from a desire to do God's work. Nevertheless the matter required some negotiation. No Ipek damsel even at the age of twenty-seven will go forth without her mother, and most mothers are home-tied; besides, as the unlettered parent cannot teach, her support is an extra charge for which every community may not be willing to pay. There stood in Katerina's room but one maiden whose mother was free to accompany her, and she did not content us, for she looked sickly, sleepy, and timid. On the other hand, our regards were fixed by Katerina's own assistant, a superb girl, by name Petra, alert, intelligent, resolute, and in whose doing and ordering we recognised the noiseless swiftness of thorough efficiency. Of Petra, Katerina at first said, that she could not possibly quit her family, but when we suggested that to start a school required both cleverness and courage, and that, once the school started, Petra could return to Ipek, leaving the work to proceed under another, the good dame entered into the idea, and agreed that it should be submitted to the kodgia bashi. He gave his consent, and fixed the required salary at 2,000 piastres (about £20). Of the loss of Petra's services to herself, of the dangers and difficulties of the journey, of the loneliness of the damsel in a strange place, Katerina spoke not a word. After long travelling in a land of harems, it is impossible to say how refreshing we felt it to converse with a woman whose mind had thus grasped the idea of self-devotion for the general good.

At Katerina's house we saw a Montenegrine woman who had come to Ipek through Podgoritza and the valley of the Moratcha. Not long ago, there had been also a nun from the Montenegrine convent of Ostrog; and the story of the latter was as follows:—Princess Darinka had tried to use her for teaching girls, but it seems she preferred working miracles, so the Prince told her that some day he hoped to have several nuns at Ostrog, but that meanwhile it was not good for a woman to be alone, so she had better go to Ipek. Thither she came, and remained till the Arnaouts heard of her, and began to ask if she were not the Prince's sister. On this the Serb community started her again on her journey, and she landed ultimately with the Bulgarian nuns at Samakoff. The peregrination of the Ostrog nun had served to spread the fame of the Prince and Princess of Cerna Gora, and when afterwards news of Danilo's murder reached Ipek, the mourning was great indeed. We had with us a photograph of Princess Darinka. Katerina gazed on it with an intensity of feeling scarcely conceivable in a stranger, and at length murmured, "Now I have seen her portrait, oh that I could speak with her face to face!"

At Ipek we were indebted to the Montenegrines for an illustration wherewith to combat a revolting custom practised by many of our kindly visitors. Like the children in the school at Gratchanitza, they absolutely fell down before us, kissing our hands and our skirts. We strove to make them understand that this was unworthy of Christians who were all brethren, but in vain; so we bethought ourselves of asking if such prostrations were customary with the Montenegrines. With one voice they exclaimed, "Né, né, Cernogorac digné glavu," (the Montenegrine lifts the head)—a description no less true than graphic of the lion-like carriage of the mountaineer.

Our next visit was to the Latin Church. We found it small and bran new. The roof ascended in a curious conical form, the altar was gaily decked, and a high screen from the altar steps to the door severed male and female worshippers. The books were from Rome, and contained prayers in two languages, Latin on one side and Albanian on the other; the latter printed in Roman letters with additional signs for special Albanian sounds. The priest wore a purple cope over his ordinary clothes, he spoke Italian, and seemed more intelligent than the monks in the patriarchate, but less so than the popes of Novi Bazaar and Vuchitern. He told us there were but 15 to 20 Latin houses in Ipek, and in the parish 100 to 200; no school. We asked him if the Turks treated the Latins better than they did the Serbs. He said they had done so until lately, inasmuch as the Latins furnished troops for their wars, but that now they were beginning to demand haratch. If the Latins paid haratch they would come to be called *kauri* (ghiaours) like the other Christians,—the name applying hereabouts to Christians less as unbelievers than as payers of tribute, or rather being considered by the Albanians simply as an expression of contempt. He, the priest, did not know how the people would bear *that*. This was said with a doleful whine, but somehow we could not see that it was a case for pity. Either the Latins were now refusing to keep to their bargain with the Sultan, and hence they had no right to complain if he did not keep to his bargain with them; or else, in order to secure themselves from persecution, they were prepared to aid in holding down their brother Christians, and in that case they had no right to sympathy from any one bearing the Christian name.

By this time the heat of the day was set in, and we returned to our quarters more than half dead. We found some monks from Détchani come to fetch us, and wanting us to start at once, as after dark the road was unsafe. But here we begged to be excused; far more than robbers we dreaded fever, and fever we were certain to incur by further exposure to the sun. The monks then agreed to go first, and await us on the border of their own territory, but on taking leave, they urgently entreated us not to bring any Turks to Détchani.

After dinner we had a long talk with Katerina, who is full of information about country and people; but when all was ready for departure, the kodgia bashi himself entered, and turned out his wife and all other women except the nun. He then sat down, and said to us solemnly, "I do not know your home nor your family. I know not if you are friends, and may be trusted, or whether I can speak before you with safety or not." We did not choose to give assurances, so answered nothing, and there was a pause. Then he exclaimed suddenly, "I will speak. We are suffering what no tongue can tell, what flesh and blood will endure no longer; our lives and property, our wives and children, are at the mercy of a pack of robbers. Our governors and medjliss, our judges and police, all are thieves, villains, and blood-guilty. If one among them would do better than the rest, if he try to do us ever so little justice, the rest fall on him and destroy him. You have heard what they did to that wretched kaïmakam."

"Was then the kaïmakam a good governor?"

"Good and not good. What shall I say? Not good as a governor should be, but too good for them. They resolved to make away with him: you heard the tale?"

"What sort of a man is the new mudir?"

"He has been here but a few days. I do not yet know him, and I will speak nothing for or against any one except from my own knowledge. But this I do know, either he must do like the rest or he cannot stay here."

"What sort of a man is he who escorted us over the mountain? We heard he was the son of a powerful Bey."

The kodgia bashi groaned.

"Do you want to know who *he* is? His father a Bey

indeed! He and his father are the scum of the earth, the lowest of the rabble, robbers of robbers, and rogues of rogues. Every para in their pouch, plunder; every rag on their backs, plunder:—plunder of the industrious and the poor. Did you mark his sleeves—those long white silken sleeves? He tore them from the women that wove them. Ladies, I am not a fanatic. I have been in Free Serbia. I have heard the talk of educated people. I know that a man is not bad *because* he is of this or that religion. I am content that the Mussulman should have his mosque, and the Jew his—(what do you call it, Katerina?) But a fellow like him you speak of is a bad man; he tramples, he spits on that which I hold sacred. Whose law is it that I must stand by defenceless and look on?"

We turned to Katerina and asked, "Did you not say that if the new mudir were supported by regular soldiers (nizam) he could keep the Arnaouts in bounds?"

She said to the kodgia bashi soothingly, "Have you not heard that the new mudir has brought some nizam with him?"

We went on. "Is it not expected that more consuls will be sent to Prizren?"

She again turned to him: "You know there is some talk of a Russian consul coming to Prizren."

The Serb elder raised his huge form from the divan, and spake deliberately and sternly: "Nizam are better than Bashi-bazouks—at first; but in a place like this I have ever seen them become like the rest. A consul who could stand up for the Christians would benefit us; but such consuls as I have known at Prizren are powerless, and do no good. I do not say that things cannot improve, but I say that unless they utterly change we Serbs of Ipek must do as our fathers did—we must *go!*" He opened the door, and left us.

The nun and we looked at each other. Then we took her hands and said: "Katerina, you will not let them go? After holding out so many hundred years, would they now leave the patriarchate to the mercy of the Arnaouts? Katerina, you will make them understand that better times must be at hand." She answered quietly, "Since last year's war we have been shut out from Serbia; times do not grow better, but worse."

* * * * * *

The greater number of the Orthodox Christian inhabitants of Old Serbia are now (1877) exiles in the Principality. The fate of Katerina we know not.

I give the following account of the present condition of Ipek or Petch from a correspondence in the *Glas Crnogorska*:—

CORRESPONDENCE IN THE "GLAS CRNOGORSKA."

"*From* Old Serbia, Petch, *Dec.* 25, 1876.

"When Serbia and Montenegro went to war with the Porte, the rest of the Serbian nation in the Nahia of Petch and in all Old Serbia who were unable to join the Serb armies under the standard of the Petrovic and Obrenovic suffered indescribable and terrible persecution. Even in the beginning of the war Turkish robber bands went about the Nahia of Petch killing our people and plundering at their will whatever belonged to Serbs. These robbers were sent and commissioned by the authorities of Petch, in order to slake their fanatic rage and revenge the great losses of the Turkish army and the injuries inflicted by the brave Montenegrin troops. We hear that peace has been made, but it is only to our ill and infinite harm. For instance, they have just killed the best man among us, with five others. The Proto was going into the church of the Patriarchate to perform the evening service, when the Turks lay in wait for him at the doors of the court, wounded him frightfully, and killed his companions. On this day our happy brethren throughout the Pravoslav world are celebrating in peace and joy the birth of the Saviour; but we are praising God that this morning we did not all fall victims to the bloodthirstiness of the Turks, and I thank God who has kept me alive to publish to the world the unheard-of oppressions which the Turks are now exercising upon us. This morning before daybreak we went to the sacred Patriarchate to hear the Divine service, but the Turks had filled the hill Kestenova, which rises immediately above the church, with their ruffians, and when the pious people were assembled in the churchyard these Mussulmans fired upon us across the hedge. A second and a third time they fired. Thus on the day of the birth of Christ the blood of innocent men, women, and children was shed about and around the church. The happiest day which our Church celebrates we have spent in the greatest grief and sorrow. Instead of hymns of joy have resounded funeral lamentations and wailings of women and children. We have buried to-day twenty-nine men, sixteen women, and eight little children, killed by Turkish guns. This is our 'peace on earth.' After this terrible slaughter and ill-keeping of Christmas, the Turks called our chief men and asked them, 'What do you mean by firing guns at Christmas?' They answered, 'It was not we who fired, but ruffians who fired on us, and they have killed many.' 'But we know,' said the kadi, 'it is your custom to make a noise at Christmas.' 'Effendi, we had not finished the service when you attacked us.' The mudir then shook his stick at the knez, saying, 'It was not I who killed you, ye sons of slaves.' The knez Marko, with his companions, left the court, but was summoned again at 8 P.M. The zaptiés were lying wait for him, and killed him. The next day it was proclaimed in the market-place that the church of the Patriarchate is closed, and the Serb school, and all the Serb shops. In short, the Turks have now inflicted the greatest sufferings ever before heard of. They have closed our church of the sacred Patriarchate, which has never been closed since Kóssovo. The prisons are full of our people. The Turkish judges imprisoned a Roman Catholic, and when the frater heard it he took his stick, went to the mudir, and said, 'I am not "the Vlaski Pope;" let out the man.' We are here despised of all, and whoever likes may avenge the Sultan's army upon us. The Nahia of Petch is left almost empty. All our best men are in prison. The rope hangs over the head of every one. We are lost; there is help from nowhere. From nowhere is there any one to save us from the claws of the bloodthirsty dragon which drinks up our blood like water, nor are there any to care."

"[Lay this at the door of Europe, brethren, who gave you up into the hands of the Turks in 1856, taking you away from the Russian protection, and placing you under her own 'guarantee,' which is nothing else than a 'privilege' to the Turks, that they may exterminate you. We, on our parts (that is, Montenegro), have done what we could; that we have done and will do, be God and history our witness!"—Note of the Editor of *Glas Crnogorska*.]

CHAPTER XXVI.

FROM IPEK TO DÉTCHANI.

A RED-TUNICKED Arnaout, with his Bashi-bazouks; an uzbashi of nizam, with six troopers carrying flags; mounted citizens, among whom we recognised the Latin elder and a Serb pope; these formed our escort out of Ipek. We drew up before the Mahommedan girls' school. A door in the garden wall was opened by its turbaned keeper, and as we entered it each of us was seized by a hodgia (teacher), more like a harpy. We were embraced, dragged, carried through the court into the house, and finally deposited on a low divan in the corner of a small close room stuffed with women. The harpies began tearing off our riding things and fanning us: the first was enormously fat and red-faced; the second we forget; but the third, haggard and vulture-beaked, was coifed with a pale-green veil. The noise they made was stunning; and among their outcries we distinguished, "Are you Mahommedans? are you Mahommedans?" At first, not feeling sure of consequences, we took no notice of this query; but, rendered desperate by their civilities, at last cried out, "No; we are Christians." These words acted like a spell. The three hodgias fell back, the crowd closed on them, even the voices underwent a lull; we, profiting by this result, contemplated the tenants of the school-room.

Except a few puzzled-looking children, all were grown up, and many past their prime, evidently an assembly of the Arnaout ladies of Ipek. Among the motley garments we recognised the black pelisse and mask-like face of a woman from Vuchitern. Presently we asked, in Serbian, if they would kindly show us their books. Thereupon the harpies-in-chief reappeared. "What did we want? Coffee was coming." Suddenly a voice sounded behind us, and we perceived outside the low window a woman holding a baby, who looked into the room over our shoulders. She spoke Serbian, and said, "You wish them to read, do you not?" Then, lifting up her voice, she shouted into the room, "They want you to teach—*teach*, I say." General hubbub, every one with a different outcry. "What do you want?" "Books," "Coffee," "Teach." At this juncture the fat hodgia leant over us, and, with hospitable intent to make our seat more comfortable, began clawing up the fusty cushions behind us, and clapping them. Stifled, we sprang to our feet, and as courteously as the crisis permitted, dived and waded through the squatting forms. At the door we met the coffee, but as it had been brewed since the discovery of our ghiaourism, we were not tempted to do more than put our lips to it. The turbaned keeper laughed good-naturedly at our suffering aspect, and hastened to undo the garden entrance. Once without, the red-coated Arnaout and the uzbashi, the nizam, the Serbs, and the Latins—all appeared saints and angels after the crew within the school.

The patriarchate of Ipek and the monastery of Víssoko Détchani are divided by a distance of three hours, and each lies at the point where a stream called Bistritza*

---

* The name Bistritza signifies clear, bright, glancing, and is a common denomination for little rivers in Slavonic countries. In this neighbourhood there are three Bistritzas, tributaries of the Drina.

flows from the mountain gorges into the plain. The town of Ipek occupies an angle between the hills Peklen and Kopaonik; the former heading the chain that runs to Mitrovic, and the latter that which joins the Albanian Koronitza. From this angle to the foot of the Shaar Plánina stretches the fertile plain of Metóchia, divided from that of Kóssovo by a furrow of low hills, marked at its south-west corner by Prizren, on the north-west by Ipek and Détchani.

Our way lay along the base of the Kopaonik, a wooded range shooting up into high fantastic crags, now peaked as an obelisk, now crenelated like the battlements of a castle. Beneath the grey cliff the mountain forest showed an emerald verdure these lands but seldom see; from the forest downwards stretched fields and pastures dotted with groves and fragrant with green hay. It was evening, and this landscape, beautiful with the varied and luxuriant beauty of the west, was bathed in the halo of an eastern sunset.

Nor did the picture lack due foreground; only instead of patient oxen and labourers wending home, we had the flags of cavalry and their prancing steeds, the gold and crimson tunic and long gun of the Arnaout. These warlike ensigns called up to our fancy a cavalcade which some five hundred years ago may have been seen wending its way along the road between Détchani and Ipek. We pictured to ourselves King Urosh returning at eventide from viewing the progress of that fair "Zadūshbina" whose name has come down to posterity interwoven with his own. The aspect of the royal saint is weary and mild, as of a much-tried man near death; verily he was a gentle and bounteous king, and his vague and venerated image is dear to his people yet. But in his train ride those broad-shouldered, eagle-eyed Vlastela whose type still lives in the Bay of Bosnia and in the free-descended

Montenegrine. Goodly must they have been, those nobles of Serbia, in stately manliness, in bearing and array, for all the pomp of oriential conquerors has not effaced them from the popular eye, and centuries of foreign rule have not reduced their people to borrow a term for "lordliness" from the conqueror's tongue.*

We have already alluded to the fact, that the plain of Metóchia, lying as it did in old time between the great monasteries of Ipek, Détchani, and Prizren, received its name as being mostly church-land ($\mu\epsilon\tau\acute{o}\chi\iota a$). Since the emigration of the Serb inhabitants, and the descent of the Arnaouts from the hills, the latter have called it from their old home "Dukadjin." These two names express the change that has come over this on e favoured region. Of all the haunts where the cowardly brigand firing from his ambush plunders the industrious and defenceless, none is now more notorious than the northern corner of Dukadjin; and here the central authority of the Porte cannot even keep up that show of order which elsewhere whitens the sepulchre of freedom. For it is not only the rayah, the peasant, the merchant, and the traveller whose life and property are in peril; the lieutenants of the Sultan, escorted by the Sultan's nizam, should they presume to raise taxes from Mussulmans, are shot down in open day. Not far from the road we were now traversing, according to one version of the story, the luckless kaïmakam met his fate. Passing from one village to another in his progress to raise the revenue, he was shot from behind a hedge, and, well

* *Gospodstvo*, lordliness, and, by implication, stateliness, is taken from the Serbian *gospod*, lord. The term *plemenit*, *i.e.*, noble in the sense of high-born, is from the Serbian *plémé*, family. We find these native words, with others denoting authority, high office, splendour, and every branch and attribute of administration, in parts of Serbia where every rich and powerful man is, or for centuries was, a Turk. They have lived in the popular songs.

knowing the character of his assailants, would not allow his soldiers to enter the bushes in pursuit. Though not killed, as was at first reported, he was severely wounded; to Ipek he dared not return, and to Prizren he had to be conveyed in a litter.

Such being the associations of our road, we were not surprised when, in crossing a tract of brushwood, the escort divided into three parts, some forming the vanguard, some the rear, while the rest scampered up and down among the bushes with intent to dislodge a lurking gun.

Rather more than half-way between Ipek and Détchani we found the second hegumon of the monastery waiting for us with his companions. Their first anxiety was to remind us of our promise to dismiss the Turks. We accordingly summoned the two leaders, thanked them for their escort, and desired them to return home. They simply refused: "it was too late; besides, their horses could not go back to Ipek without stopping somewhere to bait." But Hadgi Kyril said this was nonsense: if they could go on to Détchani they could go back to Ipek, the distance was nearly equal either way. He "hoped we would insist on it," and evidently became uneasy. The situation was embarrassing, when luckily we espied a minaret peeping out of the greenwood,—sure sign that some Mussulman hamlet was nigh at hand. Thereupon we called the uzbashi, trusting that as a regular soldier he might prove the more amenable, and told him that if he wanted to rest for the night and feed his horses, here was a village convenient for both purposes—no need for him to come a step further. He tried hard to reverse our decision, alleging that he and his soldiers would not hurt the convent, and that they had even their horses' food with them; nay, that should he quit us half-way, the mudir might be seriously displeased. "Is that all?" said we, and tearing a leaf from a pocket-book wrote on it a few words (in English, of course), and delivered it to him, saying, "Take this to the mudir, and he will be satisfied with your conduct; but if you persist in coming on to the convent, we will write him a letter to-morrow to say that you disobeyed our orders." In the interior of Turkey the most stubborn Mussulman is strangely moved by the sight of writing, especially of a woman writing, and this was not the first time the discovery had stood us in good stead. The document, administered with a bakshish, decided the uzbashi to obey, and even the red-coated Arnaout felt staggered. To him we had given no second order, not being certain how far it might be prudent to drive him against the grain. But he now rode up to the dragoman, and said that if he also received a "paper" and (*sous-entendu*) a bakshish, he also would go home.

Quiet, deeper than the stillness of evening, seemed to settle on all around us when these ministers of misrule were gone. Protection we lacked not, for soon the foot-guards of the monastery emerged from under a spreading tree; when once freed from the presence of the Arnaout, the monks, who had hitherto shrunk sulkily behind, rode at our side, and directed our attention to the objects of interest on the way. At length we caught our first view of the "fair" church of Víssoko Détchani. In the opening of a dark glen, at the foot of wooded hills, the clear-cut outline of those marble walls streamed through the twilight with pearly brightness. After a day spent among the savageries of Arnaoutluk, night brought with it the testimony that this was once a Christian land.

At the great gate of the monastery court stood Hadgi Seraphine, the portly abbot, and with him three priests carrying banners and clad in scarlet, crimson, and white. As we alighted, these priests turned about, and marched before us towards the church, the abbot beckoning to follow in procession. We passed into the shadow of the marble nave, and halted before the gate of the sanctuary. A short prayer was chanted by the priests, a silent prayer followed, and then the abbot welcomed us to Détchani.

CHAPTER XXVII.

MONASTERY AND CHURCH OF VÍSSOKO DÉTCHANI.

"Seeing 'works for the soul' worthy of czars, let men know that we reigned."
Serbian Song.
"Even the Turks say, when they see these churches: 'By these ruins one perceives that the Serbians also must have had their czars.'"—*Shafarik.*

THE monastery is built on the north side of the church, and to keep the Arnaouts out of those places where they could do most mischief, a second wall has been raised through the court, and joins the church at the west end. Within this inner enclosure are the guest chambers, with large windows opening on a front gallery, and with small loopholes looking on the river Bistritza. The chamber assigned to us was large and painted, and provided, besides the divan, with a table and chairs. It was built and furnished with money from Serbia; a tablet hid in the wall records the gift of Prince Milosh. Cool and shady as it is in the midst of summer, the traveller will at first pronounce this room delightful, but let him not rejoice too soon. The absence of glass in any of the windows, the draught that pierces through and through, the chill night air off stream and hill, are highly provocative of rheumatism and fever to the frame of a new-comer from the Ipek plain. We suffered so much that the sub-prior Hadgi Kyril, in whose chamber the windows are glazed, kindly gave it up to us; still illness did much to impede a full use of the ten days we spent in the convent.

To console us we were told the following story :—

"Some years ago a wealthy matron in the principality of Serbia, having tried many doctors and divers sorts of baths to restore her son from consumption and melancholy, resolved to take him on a pilgrimage to the royal shrine at Détchani. They contentedly remained in the convent for months, indeed throughout an entire winter." To be sure, the invalid died; but that was "God's will."

In the time of its founder the monastery of Détchani was a royal residence, but after the battle of Kóssovo the Turks sacked all except the church, and when the widow of the last Serbian czar came thither she found (in the words of the charter), "this lovely spot, the resting-place of the sainted King Urosh III., so laboured and cared for by its pious benefactor, now by God's permission given on account of our sins, burnt and destroyed of the evil tribe of Ishmael." Czaritza Militza raised the monastery from its ashes, and granted it a new charter and privileges. Since then, however, it was ravaged by "Tatar Khan," a mysterious barbarian who stands godfather to most destructions in this part of the world. It was probably in this last calamity that perished the campanile which used to surmount the great court gateway. A picture of the church and monastery, dated 1747, gives this belfry, and also on a neighbouring rising ground the little chapel of St. George, but all is caricatured and too much out of drawing to afford an idea of the building as it really stood. At any rate this is an instance, besides that of Giurgevi Stūpovi, of a separate campanile belonging to a Serbian church.

Of the old house of King Detchanski there still remain the kitchen, with its central fireplace, and the rooms, renovated from their foundations, where the royal saint, when on a visit to the monastery, entertained his numerous guests. The higher room is for the richer sort, the lower for the poor; the latter has a board long enough to accommodate one hundred persons, and at its upper end are preserved the small stone table and chair where "the good king sat and looked on." According to Serbian custom there is a day in every year kept in commemoration of the first baptism of the family, and called the "day of the Christian name." On this day the master of the house, be he peasant or czar, is required to wait on his guests, and one of the best modern Serbian poems celebrates King Detchanski thus entertaining rich and poor. An ancient ballad relates that the mighty Czar Dūshan once took it upon him to omit this pious duty so far as not to serve the wine with his own hand; thereupon his patron, the archangel Michael, who so long as the czar waited on his guests had been standing on his right shoulder and fanning him with his wing, struck the wing in his face, and flew out of the court in a rage. No one saw the angel go except an old man sitting in the yard, but he at once raised hue and cry; the revelry ceased, the feast was turned into a fast, and the fast lasted three days before the offended patron was appeased.

We were told that this "feast of the Christian name" is observed by all the South Slavonic peoples of the Eastern communion, but not by those of the same Church who are Greeks by race. Another designation for the festival is simply the "Sláva," or "glory," and it has been suggested that its celebration possibly dates from heathen times, when each Slavonic plémé, or clan, had its household god. On adoption of Christianity, the family would not be willing to forego supernatural protection; hence, on the day of its own baptism, it would bestow on its patron divinity a *Christian name*, exchanging him for some Christian saint who henceforth received equal honours, and was supposed to requite his votaries with equal care. Families having the same patron saint are held to be spiritually related, and at one time could not intermarry; an idea naturally arising from the circumstance that originally those enrolled under the same saint were really near of kin.

Among the curiosities of the convent of Détchani the country-people had prepared us to find the real drinking-cup of Marko Kralïevic, engraved with figures of himself and his spouse. When we asked for this, the monks brought forth a great vessel bearing a coat of arms, and graven with letters. The supporters of these arms are a man and a woman, both with fishes' tails. "How is this?" cried we; "you surely don't suppose that your great hero Marko was half a fish?" Reverent and incurious, the younger monk answered, "God knows, I cannot tell;" but Hadgi Kyril, with a sly twinkle in his eye, suggested that the cup might have belonged to some noble family in the neighbourhood, and that these were their heraldic bearings. He added, that there is at this moment a great house in Russia which traces its descent from Serbian emigrants, and still bears its Serbian arms.*

Of MSS. there is a store at Détchani kept in a chest in the narthex of the church; thence they were roughly pulled for our inspection, the monks declaring that constant visits from the Arnaouts deterred them from displaying their books in a library. Hadgi Kyril hunted long for a volume which, according to him, gives

* There are many families of Serb descent in Russia. Mr. Wesselitzky, a Russian subject, who has laboured so earnestly at Ragusa and elsewhere for the relief of the Herzegovinian fugitives, is the descendant of a Herzegovinian family which emigrated to Russia.

account of "fifty years during which the daughters of the Christians were dragged off to harems, and their boys to the Janissaries; when, moreover, no priest dared openly to celebrate the ordinances of religion, or even to show himself abroad, so that fathers baptized their own children." Many of the MSS. were written in rock hermitages in the glen behind the convent, and after these cells had long been deserted two volumes in metal binding were found, and brought to the church. In one of them, a translation from the Greek, the possessor has added a note on the title-page. We begged that it might be deciphered, and it proved to be a quaint lamentation on the destructions effected by "that filthy people" the Turks.

The best view of the church of Détchani is when, approaching from the east, you catch its first and characteristic effect of pearly brightness, finish, and grace. The walls are of three kinds of marble, white, grey, and red, ranged in alternate layers, and some slabs so highly polished that the country-people take them for crystal. The material of the building, like that of Studenitza in the principality, is a product of its neighbourhood, now lying unrecked of in its glen. If we would judge of the effect of Turkish rule on ecclesiastical architecture in Serbia, we need but contrast the marble and fine masonry of these ancient shrines with the rough stones and the whitewash wherewith, in modern times, church and mosque are alike bedaubed.

The outline of Détchani is cruciform, the church consisting of narthex, nave, sanctuary, and two small side-chapels; unlike many other Serbian churches, it is not cumbered with an extra porch.

A cross, said to be of massive silver, surmounts the single dome. The monks declare this cupola was to have been only one of twenty-four, and that the interior is vaulted to correspond with that number. But, as the end of the royal founder drew nigh, it became unlikely he could complete twenty-four domes; so St. Nicolas, appearing in a dream, desired him to finish up with one, and to dedicate the church to the One God in Trinity. On high festivals the dome of Détchani is illuminated, and can then be seen as far as Prizren—cheery light for the Christian in these plains, once Metóchia, now Dukadjin.

To describe Détchani in detail without the aid of drawings is vain (and the artist to whose kind assistance we owe our other illustrations has unfortunately never yet been able to visit this church); but to gather some notion of its most striking points we invite the reader to join us in one of our oft-repeated strolls round the walls. First we will station ourselves in the monastery garden opposite the east end.

Hence we see the sanctuary with its five round apses, the full wave of the centre receding in two smaller ones on either side. In the principal apse is a beautiful three-light window divided by slender columns, and surmounted by a projecting round arch. The pillars of this arch support two monsters, and their base rests on a crouching human form. Throughout the carving is rich, and its ornament often beautiful; for instance, there is a nest full of eaglets stretching out their heads for food, while the eagle shelters them with outspread wings. Below the arch is carved a human head, from whose mouth issues a vine; the tendrils winding right and left encircle the window and unite beneath it; in its foliage nestle all sorts of birds and creatures of fantastic form.

Let us now leave the garden and betake ourselves to the south door, which, together with the east and west doors, is in the narthex. On our way we find that some poor hand has scratched the polished wall with the words, *némam chleba*—*i.e.*, " I have not bread." We pass under the windows of the nave. Of these the two outer are single lights, but the two centre double lights, and divided by a column. Whereas both at the east and west ends the arch of the windows is round, it is pointed in the narrower windows on each side of the church.

The south door is the least handsome of the three, and the carving under its arch is comparatively rude; it represents the baptism of our Saviour. Here, however, we find an inscription recording the name of the architect:—

" Frater Veit (Frater Minorum), Protomaster of the royal city of Cattaro, built this holy church of the Pantokrator, for King Stephen Urosh III., and for his son, the illustrious, great, and glorious King Stephen. He built it in eight years, and completed it in the year 6843—(1335)."

From the south door we turn the corner to the west, where we find two windows on each side of the portal, and two in a line immediately above it. This door is the principal entrance, and is surmounted by a representation of Him to whom the church is dedicated, the Svederzitel (Παντοκράτωρ), seated on a throne, holding a book with seven seals. The whole window is surmounted with a projecting arch as by a canopy.

The first window over the entrance resembles the large one in the east end, save that one of its monsters has perished in defence of the holy place. " The Mussulmans thought to take Détchani for a mosque, and their hodgia bowed before the door in prayer; but down fell the monster and crushed the hodgia's head, thus giving the misbelievers a lesson which has lasted them till now."

Of the windows at the west end the lower has three lights, and the higher but two, the scale of proportions diminishing in breadth from the massive portal upwards. The effect thus attained, together with the luxuriance of ornament, renders this one of the most beautiful portions of the church.

As for the north side, its windows resemble those on the south; but the north door, instead of figures, bears a cross interwoven with lilies, and the inscription, "Jesus Christ, King of Glory." Here a pillar of the arch is broken, one of the comparatively few pieces of damage that the church has sustained.

All round the walls immediately under the roof runs a frieze of round arches, resting on human heads; all round the walls near the ground runs a stone bench for the repose of weary pilgrims. On this bench on a sunny afternoon you are sure to find seated the elder hegumon, by name Archimandrite Seraphine, waiting for vespers. Under his guidance we will enter the church.

The narthex is paved with red and white marble, and its vaulted roof rests on four marble columns, of which the capitals and pedestals are ornamented variously with birds, beasts, and flowers. The walls are covered with frescoes painted with sacred and historic subjects, and on the north side of the door, leading into the nave, are the figures of the founder and his son. Their inscriptions run thus :—

> Saint Urosh III., King of all Serbian lands and the Pomorié,
> Founder of this Holy Place.
> Stephen, through Christ-God, right-believing Greek Emperor, King of all Serbian lands and the Pomorié, Founder of this Holy Place.

Hence it appears that Stephen Dūshan contributed to his father's "Zadūshbina" of Détchani, and this idea is confirmed by the tenor of another half-obliterated inscription over the west door. Above the said inscription is a hole in the wall, also connected with the sainted king; for here it was that his relics lay concealed during the attack of Mussulmans under Tatar Khan.

In the narthex stand three tombs with inscriptions of the latter half of the fourteenth century. Near the entrance leading into the nave we noticed a round marble font, and beyond it, painted on the wall, the genealogy of the race of Némania.

The door into the nave has an elaborate round arch, supported on pillars of red and white marble in rows of six on each side. At the pillars' base crouches a great lion, its fore paws resting on a man's head. From their capitals spring small lions, that on the left being winged and holding a beast's head in its paw.

The nave has four columns like those in the narthex, and besides these, eight painted pillars, four of which stand between the choir and the sanctuary, four between the nave and choir. The transepts terminate each in a small chapel occupying the outer apses. A low wall of marble, partly enclosing the choir, is concealed on each side by the wooden stalls, and in front by the iconastasis, but none of these divisions are high enough to break the full expanse of the roof.

Entering from the narthex, your eye falls on two tombs covered with red velvet which stand side by side to your right. These are in memory of the royal founder, and of St. Yelena, his sister, and wife of Michael, the Bulgarian Czar.* One evening during vespers we saw a

* So we were told. The Detchanski King had a sister married to Michael, Czar of Bulgaria, whose name was Néda, and who may have become a nun under the name of Yelena. But the widowed Empress of Dūshan was certainly called Helena (*Serb.* Yelena), and is known to have become a nun after her son's death. She, however, was not loved by the people. They believe she was not loyal to her son, and regard her late sanctity as that of a penitent. Doubtless some old document would show which Yelena is here meant.

woman spread a cloth on the pavement by the side of the Czarine's coffin, and deposit thereon a shrivelled babe, covering its little head with the velvet. Throughout the service the infant lay mute and motionless; at the close its mother picked it up, believing it strengthened by virtue from St. Yelena. Considering the chill from the marble, we could only wonder that she did not find it dead.

Opposite the iconastasis are two stalls, one the bishop's, and the other the old marble seat of Serbian kings. The position of the ambo is not raised, but marked by a cross pattern on the floor.

The iconastasis is of wood carved and gilt, and exhibits a number of dusky icons. On the left side of the altar doors are the relics of the sainted king, the body lying in a painted and gilt coffin, clad in silken garments; the place where the face should be is surrounded with a metal glory. The feet are extended to view in costly shoes, and one black withered hand is covered with rings. The dress of the saint is enriched by a handsome waist-clasp, or *golphia*, and a bracelet set thick with pearls. In his coffin lie two small crosses; one, containing some hairs of Christ, was given to St. Sava by the patriarch Jeremy of Jerusalem; it was afterwards presented to this monastery by King Detchanski, who had it set in silver and gold in the form of a cruciform church with domes. This cross has a separate pedestal, on which are engraved the four evangelists, the saints of the Némania family—Simeon, Sava, and Milutin—and the Serbian arms.

Besides the principal apse, one of the side-apses is included in the sanctuary; the other is screened off, and forms (as we understood the monks) a repository for lumber. Within the sanctuary are a stone synthronus and a marble altar; also a few valuables, among which were shown several crosses and a so-called model of the church, well bejewelled, but clumsy and unlike. Two *ripidi* (flat round plates with tinkling bits attached) are kept here in store, and bear date 1750 ; on high days they are carried on long staves at each side of the cross. There is also a holy picture, a Virgin and Child by St. Luke himself, but from the canvas of which the figure of St. John has been cut out, all save one hand. The country-people call it the *Three*-handed Madonna, and look on it with a sort of puzzled awe.

To those who read this description of Détchani, it will doubtless occur, as it did to us, "How has a church so costly and so fair escaped destruction or appropriation by the Moslem?" Détchani, like Prizren, was beset by Tatar Khan (whose name the more learned of the monks are now trying to improve into "Tamerlane"). How comes it then that this Tatar Khan destroyed Dūshan's great church of St. Michael Archangel, and left the church of Détchani intact? Old Abbot Seraphine settled the point with an appropriate miracle, but Hadgi Kyril, seeing us still unsatisfied, allowed that Détchani had generally been more able than most monasteries to buy off the destroyer, for there was scarcely anything the Serbs would not give to preserve their favourite shrine. Besides, while the churches of Prizren, forming part of a fortified town, were approached by Mussulmans in the fury of assault, and used by the Christians as places of shelter, Détchani escaped most of these dangers by its situation in a secluded glen. Nevertheless the High Church of the Serbs was nearly lost to them but a few years ago. It was at the time of the Crimean war that a well-meaning French emissary, hearing of the poverty and perils of the monks, is said to have promised them a pension and the protection of his Government, if they would place their establishment under the Latin pontiff. Good Hadgi Seraphine was well known in the principalities as a persistent beggar; but to this proposition he answered : " It was not in his power to bargain about transferring the sanctuary of Détchani, inasmuch as it belonged not to him, not even the bishop or the patriarch, but to the whole congregation of the Orthodox Church."

CHAPTER XXVIII.

HERMITAGES IN THE GLEN OF DÉTCHANI.

WE have said that many of the MSS. at Détchani were written in the neighbouring hermitages. These hermitages are cells in the banks of the Bistritza, for the monastery stands at the mouth of a rocky glen, through which the river Bistritza has torn itself a way. On the south side of the stream the hills are wooded, but of the north bank the base only is clothed, and above rises the bare limestone crag. The hill nearest the convent is called Plïesh, and its elevated summit commands a wide view. On the top of a wooded height to the south remains the wall of an ancient fortress, and on one of the crags to the north are traces of fortification. From these eminences to the further end of the glen is a journey of four hours, which would bring one to the village of Belaï, now Albanian, but containing the ruins of a small Serbian convent and a cemetery with four hundred graves. Between this village and the monastery of Détchani the sides of the glen are perforated with hermitages, little chapels, and cells, half rock, half wall, some still retaining the paintings traced five hundred years ago. Two of these hermitages were inhabited, respectively, for some years by King Uresh and St. Yelena.

Now in an ancient charter of Détchani it is forbidden for *vlahi*—that is, shepherds—to intrude within its demesnes; but since the monks lost power to enforce this restriction, their hills have become a summer pasture for Albanian flocks, and their cells are not secure from Albanian visitors. Thus the hermitages have been abandoned as residences or studios; nay, the danger of straying about the hills deters the monks from even visiting them. Meanwhile the shepherd Arnaouts use some of the cells as sheds for their goats, climb into others to dig for treasure, burn the woodwork, throw down the walls, and pick off the frescoes bit by bit. Considering that these curious hermitages are certain to become objects of interest and protection so soon as they are known to European travellers, it is grievous to see them thus, as it were, perishing in sight of land.

During our stay we visited five rock-cells; Hadgi Kyril, a younger monk, our cavass, and the convent zaptié acting as escort. But to get at the cells is a puzzle, for many of them are inaccessible without the ladder or the plank which their whilom inhabitants used to extend to visitors. Persons not addicted to scrambling may be consoled to know that a good view can be had from the path on the north side of the Bistritza, about a quarter of an hour from the convent. Thence we see the hermitage of Svéti Kral, like a high narrow house with windows and a door, and the side-rock for its back wall. Lower down on the bare face of the cliff is the hermitage of St. Yelena, which, being deprived of its front, gives to view two arched clefts with a rose-bush between them. For nearer inspection we crossed the Bistritza, clambered up the steep bank on the other side, and passed by a spring of excellent water called Kralïeva Chesma. Arrived at the cell, the monk was about to lead us in, when with a cry of dismay he pointed to the traces of fire: "They have burned the staircase! all is destroyed!" Too true: Arnaouts seeking shelter in the entrance had lit a fire, using the stair for their chimney, and thus had burnt not only the means of ascent, but the very floor of the upper room. After lasting out five hundred years!

Perhaps a ladder would make it possible to get in from outside, and, entering by the windows, one might find a footing on the rock half of the cell; but, unprepared for the disaster, the monks had not even a rope with them. Imagine our feelings, when a moment later we found one of the perpetrators of the mischief nonchalantly looking on at our side—Arnaout, of course, a half-naked, stunted savage duly carrying his gun—by way of herding goats. The sight of a depredator so close to the church did more than all the lamentations of the monks to show us how the wild beast of the wood has broken into this goodly vineyard.

To gain St. Yelena's chapel is not easy, for the destruction of wood and wall has left scarce footing across the face of the cliff. The portly monks altogether declined venturing, but the convent carpenter, who had once been a refugee in the mountains, proved a zealous and clever guide. In the first cell there is nothing to be seen; and pushing through the rose-bush you get to a second, the sanctuary of the hermit's chapel. A slab cut in the rock represents the altar, and the icons are painted on a stucco coating. On one side, indeed, and on the lower row of the other, the little Arnaout children have picked off the saints; but the second and third row still remain tolerably distinct, and surprisingly fresh in colouring. First come the portraits of saints, with names inscribed under each still legible, and above this the picture of a scene that may be either baptism or martyrdom. The saint, stripped to the middle, stands in a cauldron, and is surrounded by divers figures; a mysterious personage, whose robe floats without touching the earth, appears about to bless, or it may be to rescue, the patient.

Intent on the paintings, we were barely in time to arrest our attendants on the brink of sacrilege. 1st. They were breaking off a bit of the frescoes for us to carry off as a remembrance. 2nd. In order to facilitate our exit, they were conspiring to cut down the rosebush. They were going to cut down St. Yelena's rose—a marvel in spring-time for its wealth of bloom, and over which such pilgrims as cannot climb up hither rejoice and wonder from the opposite bank. What if next May the pilgrims had found it gone!

A third hermitage lies at the foot of a neighbouring crag, and must be sought under the surface of a large stone. The refugee had not been there for years, so spent some time in hunting up the hole, and when he had done so it looked so small that cavass and monk alike disdained to enter. However, the carpenter begged so hard, that we declared our resolution to make the attempt. He crawled in, struck a light, and then we followed. We found ourselves in a little stone chamber, half choked with earth and sticks. This opened into an inner cell, free from rubbish, smoothly built, arched at the top, and wide enough on all sides for a man to span with outstretched arms. We could not descry a trace of painting or inscription. Returning to daylight, we found a narrow path winding from this cell upwards to the cliff till it ended in a square opening like that of a tomb. A grave the monk opined it to be; but the carpenter, who had been there twice, declared that it was a hermitage; whether there be writing on the wall he could not tell, inasmuch as he had never looked.

Higher up the hill is a large hermitage, wherein was found a sword we afterwards saw in the monastery. Though covered with rust it bends with ease, and traced in gold on the blade we found a minute cross and globe.

Next day we again started in quest of hermitages. After riding for about an hour along the left bank of the Bistritza, we stopped opposite a ravine, with a hermitage on one side, and a chapel on the other. The former, denuded of its front wall, looks like the mouth of a shallow cave; the latter is indicated by a doorway, with wooden posts let into the side of the cliff, and without any external approach whatever. Observing that the site of these cells lay nearer the top of the bank than the foot, we asked Hadgi Kyril why he had not led us to them from above. No words can paint the consternation of the monk at a question which betrayed our intention of visiting them. After protesting it was impossible, he finished up by pointing to his own portly frame, and groaning out, "*I*, at least, can never get up there." Leaving him below, we started on our climb up a crumbly bank of earth and stones. Here and there footing was found on the roots of the trees, and between these one held on by boughs. From the bank we passed to a ledge of rock, and now the threshold of the little church seemed near. Already we were triumphing at thought of the frescoes, nay, of the books said to lie within, when between us and the door appeared a space of rock from which all support for footsteps had been carefully smoothed. This was the gulf of separation over which the former inmate used at will to extend his drawbridge, and when he departed he took it away with him, and left his hermitage shut up for aye.

Digesting our disappointment as best we might, we now climbed to the top of the ravine, and descended to examine the opposite hermitage. This was one of the most famous in the mountain, and here were found the Gospels exhibited in the monastery. Enough remains of wall to show that it once had a front like that of Svéti Kral; but this is destroyed, and, instead, a barrier of sticks has converted it into a goat-shed. A few steps further on, happening to look up, we espied a square opening in the rock, and above it the face of the Madonna, rudely sketched in red. We now knew whence the spot takes its name, *i.e.*, "Chapel of the Mother of God" (Bogoróditza). The convent guard told us he remembered the cliff on each side covered with paintings; but this is hard to believe, for not a trace remains.

While we were still examining these cells, a voice sounded behind us, and we beheld an Albanian peering round a corner. Unlike those we had hitherto met, he was not defiant-looking and careless, but worn-out and scared, like a hunted animal in human form. The cavass accosted him in his own tongue, asking if he would show us any way to the opening above. At once he crept along the ledges like a cat, and sought, but without success, for footing whereby one might approach the cave. During this process he kept up a running conversation with the cavass, and when both were once more on level ground, the latter turned to us and said, laughing, "Really, this poor rayah is most hospitable and kindly. He says, that if you delight in ruins like these, you should come to his village, where there are far better ones; he offers you entertainment in his house, and will set before you all he has, namely, honey and kaimak." We inquired where the man lived, and who he was. "Oh," cried the cavass, "he is the most miserable rayah in the world. It seems that he and his family are the only Latins in a village that was once all Latin, and that the families which have become Mussulman bully their very life out of them. At last they have agreed to bear Mussulman names—

Hussein, Muyo, and such like; but he says he cannot bear to change altogether yet—he calls it 'to forsake Jesus Christ,' and it is in Christ's name that he bids you to his house. He thinks that if you see how things really stand, you will bid his tormentors desist, and save him and his kinsfolk from being driven to desert their creed. I tell him, I only wish *my* consul dwelt in this part of the world." We were not surprised at the cavass's advocacy, for an Albanian usually stands by an Albanian—as he would fight him—*i.e.*, without regard to creed.

Meanwhile, the poor man stood eagerly watching our faces. When the cavass finished speaking, he said in Slavonic, and in a low lamentable voice: "For Christ's sake! For the sweet name of Jesus." In these regions, by Serbs as by Albanians, the invocation "for Christ's sake," "in God's name," is an appeal none may disregard. If possible, assistance must be given, but at any rate sympathy; in the popular songs even dumb creatures and inanimate objects are represented as answering when thus adjured. We were greatly touched, but of course, before deciding on anything it was necessary to return to the horses and consult the monk. The Latin pointed out a mode of descent more easy than that by which we had mounted; and we set off at a pace which caused the cavass again and again to exclaim: "Allah! You run; you run. Truly the rayah is oppressed, and he is good and hospitable; but is this a place to run in? What would your friends say could they see you?"

After all, our haste was bootless. The Latin's village proved to be much too distant for us to visit it that evening, and the priest thought the temper of its Mussulman occupants so doubtful that he shuddered at the idea of our going there at all. "Besides," said

Mussulman broke the strength of the Christians in these parts, and that, this bargain once made, their mischievousness has had little to do with creed. Still, so long as they call themselves Christians, they maintain a link with civilising influences. Priests, educated in Italy, penetrate to some of the wildest districts, and though sometimes these priests are mere agents of political intrigue or superstition, often they show examples of courage, self-devotion, and charity, and generally they try to implant the rudiments of education. Moreover, the Roman Catholic Albanians being themselves under the protection of some Christian power, they are often drawn to the coast, nay, over the sea, and bring back ideas of order and progress to their wild home. But all these links are severed so soon as they adopt Mahommedanism, or rather, that "no creed but self-interest," which they, as well as more civilised renegades, find it convenient to call Mahommedanism. Then are they indeed cut off from Europe, and, however insubordinate they may prove to Turkish governors, they henceforth identify their interests with upholding that system of violence and corruption whereby Mussulman supremacy is upheld.

The case of the Latin in the Bistritza glen confirmed a statement that we frequently heard, *i.e.*, that the number of Mussulman Albanians must not be reckoned as commensurate with the number of Albanians who call themselves Mussulmans. Whole villages of *soi-disant* Mahommedans are concealed Christians. Some have confessed this since the publication of the Hatt-i-humayoun, others may be expected to do so on the first movement unfavourable to Mahommedan rule. Even in the case of the genuine Arnaouts the change of creed has been too recent to wipe out a superstitious veneration for Christian rites. When sick, they ask prayers he, "who are these Albanians that any one should know how to help them? Doubtless, the man's story is true, for there are cases like his all over the country; but what made him and his clan come to these parts, if they cannot bear bullying or hold to their faith. The village they inhabit belonged to the monastery; the ruins he talks of are churches, hermitages, and graves of monks. His people were Latins when they drove the monks away and destroyed the places; what could Mahommedans do worse? If they cannot do better, or bear persecution, let them get back whence they came."

We consulted the cavass as to what could be done, and at length it was agreed to give the poor man bakshish for trying to help us into the cave; also to commission him to bring next day a piece of wood to supply our lost tent-pole. To such material comfort the cavass added consolation after his own fashion, and made a long speech garnished with frequent mention of the Queen of England and of consuls. Being in Albanian, we could not tell what it might portend; but we saw the Latin's face flush and brighten, and we heard how he cried out to the priest, while he bounded along at our horses' side, "They have looked graciously on me, and listened to me, 'for Christ's sake.'"

When he was gone, we rode silently home, musing over his strange story, and the state of things it revealed. We could not but wonder at the tenacity of sentiment which held these two ignorant and half-wild Albanian families to a faith of which they knew almost nothing, when their adhesion to it involved daily and hourly persecution; we could not but think how different might be the state of these regions, if such tenacity had been as general among Albanians as among Serbs. It is true, as the priests often said, that the bargain which made the Latin Albanians allies of the from Christian priests, and on certain festivals they fill the church of Détchani, and attend service in honour of saints, whose resentment they still fear. The old prior hinted, with grim satisfaction, that their pains were vain; "the saints will take no account of their attendance, since they never pay the priest his due."

Of other festivals the Albanians show their observance in a different manner; they repair to a chapel in the neighbourhood where Christians assemble to take the sacrament, and there, having surrounded the doors, allow no one to pass out without paying toll. As for the way in which Arnaouts prey on the convent, this formed a constant theme of the monks' lamentation. According to the decree of its founder, Détchani was to be a "royal house," where any poor man might be sure of a piece of bread; fields and pastures were assigned from which to provide its hospitality. The order is now changed. To sustain the convent, Christian peasants give of their poverty; while the lazy Mussulman, having taken away most of the pastures and fields, yet demands at his pleasure food, lodging, provender for his horses, raki for his feasts, and, when all is supplied, regards it only as tribute for his forbearance in letting the convent stand. Travelling pachas and their locust suites frequently quarter themselves in the monastery for days; during the Montenegrine war, parties of nizam, bashi-bazouks, sick, wounded, all found quarters there in turn—all devoured, no one paid. We ourselves saw how of an evening any number of Arnaouts would stalk in and demand supper and a night's lodging, giving no better reason for their intrusion than that they were tired, and did not wish to walk to their homes that night. After supper there is often a brawl, and the zaptié, paid by the monks to protect them, has, ere this, been wounded in his attempt to keep order; while nothing but the consideration that they would thus lose their free hostelry deters these wild guests from burning the convent any day. Again, when the Albanians hold a feast, they scruple not to borrow the dishes, clothes, vessels of the monastery, wherewith to make a show; nay, at their weddings, they dress the bride in the gorgeous gold-heavy vestments which have descended to the monks from ancient times. Profanation apart, this is the least of grievances, for the Arnaouts keep strict watch upon each other, and every article thus borrowed is returned, in order that it may be forthcoming when next wanted.

To supply the constant demands of the Mussulmans, and yet keep up the church and monastery, the monks must eke out the produce of their few fields and the contributions of the Christian neighbourhood by begging journeys through Austria, Russia, Serbia. All in all, their life is hard, and one cannot be surprised to learn that every day it becomes more difficult to find monks for Détchani.

As for the state of the country during our visit to these parts, both Mussulmans and Christians told us that it was quite exceptional, the attack on the kaïmakam of Ipek having called the pasha of Nish and his nizam to make a progress through the country, during which progress the Arnaouts held their breath. Prior to the pasha's coming, and while the late outbreak was brewing, a ramble in the glen of Détchani would have been at the risk of our lives. Luckily, the Arnaouts connected the pasha's visit and ours together, and hence were careful that no one should do us harm. At the same time, they felt all the more certain that our coming had some political significance, and that we did not trouble ourselves to pry into such nooks and corners without an idea of appropriating them. On one occasion, on returning from a hermitage, we found the monk who had remained with the horses in a very disturbed state of spirits, and we could perceive an Arnaout skulking off with his gun. When once more near the convent, the monk explained that during our absence this visitor had been tormenting him with questions as to our doings and intentions. The monk pleaded ignorance, whereupon his questioner lost patience and exclaimed: "Oh, it is very well for you to pretend to know nothing; you are afraid we should find out that they have brought your monasteries many thousand ducats. But we know all about it, and were it not that the pasha and his nizam are just now upon us, we would just let see what *hangs up in Arnaout houses.*" At the latter words he significantly tapped his gun, adding, "How would your Kralitze like that?"

We asked, "Whom does he mean by Kralitze?"

The monk answered: "Whom but yourselves? Did any one ever see women who were not kralitze (queens) care about countries and peoples like you?"

Much amused as we were with this notion, we could not but fear lest the report of our bringing a gift to the convent might draw on the monks new demands; while our own small gifts were certain to be henceforward received with discontent. We afterwards heard that the Arnaouts were indignant we did not shower gold on all who approached us. "Why should we spare it, when, having the mint at our disposal, we could coin as much more as we pleased?"

But before leaving the convent we heard another *canard*, which threw that just related quite into the shade. This new story not only gave us names, but explained the reason of our coming in a fashion which certainly did credit to the imagination of the inventor, whether he intended his tale for circulation among credulous semi-savages, or had it told to us in hopes of eliciting an explanation, and a confession that our visit had some political end. Before repeating this story, however, we will indicate where some of its ideas came from. The year of our visit to Arnaoutluk was that of the Princess of Serbia's visit to London; the great Christian lady of these parts is the Princess of Montenegro; the Princess Dowager Darinka is known to take an interest in political arrangements. But most necessary is it to explain that the backing of Turkey by England throughout the late Montenegro campaign is commented on throughout the ballads about the war, and is accounted for by supposing that the Sultan has engaged the English Queen in a bond of "probratimstvo," whereby she is bound to assist him as the vila did Marko, even if she would rather not.

And now for the tale. One morning, the convent court filled with Arnaouts. Their elders told the prior that on no account would they depart "without seeing us, and speaking us fair while yet it was time." The prior assured them that we still slept, and also that it would be contrary to all custom for us to hold converse in so public a fashion. "Besides," said he, "what can you want to say to two non-official voyagers? Whom do you take them to be?" The elders drew near, and spoke in low terms. "Of course it is a secret, but if any one knows the truth you must; and we may as well ask you about what we hear. People say that, of these travellers, one is Princess Darinka of Montenegro, and another even the English Queen." "Indeed," cried the prior, "that would be a fine thing. And pray, how do they account for such personages coming on pilgrimage to our poor shrine?" "Your church is the greatest in the world," was the answer, "and known in all countries; nevertheless, the pilgrimage is, as we suppose, a mere pretext. The real reason of their coming you may guess as well as we. We all know that during the late war the Sultan had to borrow money, powder and shot, arms and engineers, everything he required, from England, and the Queen of England sent them, for is she not his bond sister? He promised to repay her, and now he finds he cannot; so they have settled between them that, instead of gold, he is to make over to her some of those bits of country about which he is always quarrelling with the Serbs. It is said that these parts are to go too, and as they are far from England and border on Montenegro, the Prince of Montenegro has obtained that he shall be allowed to try if he cannot keep them quiet; and he has sent Darinka to show the English Queen the land. Thus have they two come here together, secretly, to see our country, and to find out if all they heard about it be true."

CHAPTER XXIX.

DIAKOVO TO PRIZREN.

DURING the whole of our stay at Détchani we were beset by offers of escort for our onward journey. Now it was our old nizam acquaintances from Ipek, who managed after all to spend one night in the convent. Then came a deputation from the neighbouring town of Diakovo, saying that it was not for the Ipek people to send but for the Diakovo people to fetch us, and beseeching us to appoint a day when the whole community might come out and meet us. Finally the Austrian agent in Prizren despatched his cavass to see who we were, and even to propose himself as the attendant of our movements. All we dismissed, but not without an expenditure of bakshish, which, together with the present bestowed in recompense for our entertainment at the convent, left us merely funds sufficient for the continuance of our route. We entreated the good folks on this side and on that not to trouble themselves about our departure; we could fix nothing, except that if we went to Diakovo we meant to lodge with Katerina's brother-in-law, the Serbian pope, by name Stephan. As for escort, we would give notice in time. Then, one quiet afternoon, old Seraphine lent us the convent horses, and we rode over to Diakovo without further ado.

A monk joined the party, and for his benefit took one of the convent guards, a Serb, and member of that little band of refugees who have had to invoke the protection of the sanctuary for having avenged a wife's dishonour or a brother's death. It happened to be the day of Diakovo market, and we met numbers of returning Arnaouts, lawless and defiant-looking enough, many in rags and some barefoot, but all armed. In passing they looked at the priest askance; he laughed and said to us, "Those are my good friends, I know them well. To-night, were I to return alone, they would stop me and demand bakshish. Should I refuse, they would tap their guns and answer, 'Oh! a priest has always paras to spare.' But in Iova's company no one will meddle with me." Iova quietly observed, "Yes, they knew me long enough in the mountains." The priest explained, "He was in the mountains when tracking his brother's murderer."

The road from Détchani to Diakovo lies first through hay-fields and lanes, and hard by a village with its walls set full of loop-holes, and every house marked with gun-shot. At length one forsakes the mountain region for a treeless plain that continues to Prizren.

It was during our last halt in the greenwood that we were beset by some all but naked Gipsies, who, seeing strangers mounted and guarded, began begging in broken Turkish, then in Albanian, and as a last resource in Serbian. In reward for a Slavonic "God help you," we scattered some paras, just to show them that there are still *gospoda* (gentry) who love to hear the Christian's tongue.

Our desire to slip quietly into Diakovo succeeded so far that outside the town we were met only by six zaptiés; but within, the houses seemed to have emptied themselves on the streets, and nowhere else were we conscious of such staring.

We should have met with something worse than staring had we entered Diakovo three months earlier. At

DIAKOVO TO PRIZREN.

present the Arnaouts were in a subdued tone of mind, and still under the influence of a dressing administered during the late visit of the Pasha of Nish. The outbreak against the kaïmakam of Ipek had caused an " opening of books " all over the country, and even in Arnaoutluk sensation was caused by the discovery that since the last official visit to Diakovo 400 Arnaouts had killed each other in party squabbles, without reckoning rayahs murdered by Mussulmans, of whom probably no account was found. Accordingly a placard was stuck up in the bazaar, threatening with pains and penalties every one who should provoke another by word or deed. Nizam, too, were left with intent to keep the peace, and we were edified by the sight of regular soldiers standing sentry at their barrack gate.

Of those who came in for a cut of the pasha's whip were the Latins, who had been threatened with haratch with a seriousness which provoked them to declare that, rather than submit to it, they would do one of two things: return to their hills, or—become Mahommedans.

The Serbs, on the other hand, besides the satisfaction inseparable from the disgrace of their adversaries, had got soft words, and a promise of better times. But, alas! said they, of two things we have had so much that we care not to have more, " promises and patience."

In return for some of the pasha's promises one man took heart of grace, and told him that the Arnaouts had a proverb, " In time of flood the stream seems as if it would sweep all before it, but the flood subsides, and the stones and shingle remain." " The pasha," said he, " is the flood, and the Arnaouts are the shingle and stones." We afterwards heard that these misgivings had proved but too well founded. In a week or two the pasha left the district, and the Arnaouts resumed their former misrule.

It was late when we alighted at Pope Stephan's door, so we excused ourselves from giving audience to the mudir. The room in which we were located for the night was small and low, but hung round with various objects and different sorts of arms, while its shelves displayed cups, plates, and a few books. From the arrangements of the house it was evident that the pope was poor; and the popadia, Katerina's sister, had a sad and careworn aspect. This good woman told us that we should find the Christians at Diakovo far inferior to those of the city of the patriarchate, and this opinion was confirmed by the aspect of the women who came to see us next morning. They entered covered with the yashmak, like Mahommedans; the prostrations were worse than ever, nor could we make them understand our objections even by the Montenegrine simile. To give them an occasion for reflecting on the subject, we hunted up from among our books a little poem, and left it with the pope for their edification. The poet records his visit to the Black Mountain, and how he fell down before young Prince Nicolas, "but the gospodar raised him with a rebuke, and bade him remember that all free Serbs are brethren."

The women of Diakovo showed us some of the silk spun in their town, but it was yellow-looking and dear. They told us it was all raised by Mahommedans, the Christian women being too poor even to provide the mulberry leaves necessary for the silkworms. Then two small coins were brought, found, it was said, in a ruined church in the neighbouring mountainous district of Malesia. They were discovered by a girl who dreamed of a treasure hid in the place, and afterwards digging there, got out a pot of coins. Some were large, and she had sold them, others she had kept for her necklace and head-dress, those shown us were very small and thin. Lastly, they brought a diamond ring, containing a large central stone surrounded by smaller ones; they said it belonged to an Arnaout Bey, who wanted to dispose of it. With a little ready money one might buy up many curious ornaments hereabouts, besides what are more tempting, old richly ornamented arms. The Bey's ring did not much please us; but seeing the people look disappointed, we told them frankly that all money we had with us was necessary for travelling expenses, and that, had we any over, we should give it to them for their churches and schools. And sorely we wished for an extra handful of ducats when we came to see the school and church at Diakovo. Let no one think slightingly of Pope Stephan, as at first we did, and have had many a twinge of remorse in consequence. He lacks the prepossessing manner and the gift of eloquence characteristic of many of his compeers; he talks fast and fussily, gets his story into a bungle, is hard to be understood by a foreigner, and puts a dragoman out of patience. But the energy and devotion of Pope Stephan are worthy of any Christian pastor. When he came to his parish there was no church and no school; and what wonder, when there are in the town of Diakovo but fifteen or sixteen Serbian houses? But Pope Stephan had been in Free Serbia, and could not let his flock stay as he found it. He contrived to gather and to spare till he had money enough to build a walled enclosure, and safe within it a clean little church and school, also to lay in a stock of Belgrade school-books. Well might Katerina say, "The community at Diakovo is small, but it has a great will."

Unfortunately, having got thus far, Pope Stephan's achievements are brought to a stand-still. Who is to teach his school? Himself? Even were he capable, his duties as parish priest do not leave him the time, and where is he to find payment for a regular teacher? From Russia he had a present of about 1,000 piastres to start with. From Serbia he is promised 1,000 piastres (10*l*.) a-year; but the only teacher he could find went away declaring this salary too small, and now none will come for less than 1,200 piastres. The small congregation of Diakovo could not at the time of our visit guarantee even the additional 200; so there stood the school without a master. Throughout Turkey we met with no case more deserving of assistance, but unfortunately at the moment we were so much afraid of running short of money before getting to Scodra that we dared not give Pope Stephan more than the usual bakshish for our lodging and entertainment. Afterwards, the kindness of a British consul enabled us to send a small remittance to this and other schools in the neighbourhood.

The ride to Prizren, with a halt in the middle of the day, occupied from six to seven hours; luckily, the mudir had sent us really nice horses, one of them lent, at his request, by a Turkish official. In consequence of the pasha's late transit, the road was for the moment safe, but we were told that it was usually brigand-ridden, and in our passage over the dusty plain we scarcely met a living creature. About two hours from Diakovo we forded the river Drina, close to a high bridge of many arches, said to have been originally built by the Serbian king Milutin.

The khan wherein we halted was wretched, its only separate room serving for a hen-roost, and neither in nor near it did we see any signs of traffic. During the afternoon we rode round the foot of a little hill, bearing on its side a Mahommedan village with its mosque, in the vicinity of which are said to be vineyards that belonged to the Serbian kings. Every object has now its legend connecting it with the monarchs who held their residence in this neighbourhood; for our road is once more leaving the plain for the hills, and as it turns the summit of the first rising ground we come in sight of the town of PRIZREN, ancient capital of Serbia.

CHAPTER XXX.

PRIZREN, THE OLD SERBIAN CZARIGRAD.

SITUATED on the northern slope of the Shaar Plánina, the town now called Prizren in Albania contains only about four thousand houses * and is without political or commercial importance. To the left the river Drina passes on its way to the Adriatic; around lie the plains of Metóchia and Kóssovo; behind rise mountains rich in wood and ore; but the Drina is not at present navigable; the field, though fertile, is never cultivated; the hill-forest is so much cover for brigands. One asks for an explanation of this state of things, and one hears that the lord of the land is a Mahommedan, a foreigner, and far off; he cares not to develop the resources of a remote and hostile province; it is enough if he can hold it down; and for lack of better instruments, he uses the arm of the Arnaout to break the arm of the Serb.

But Prizren has seen better days. For some 200 years she was the Serbian czarigrad, *i.e.*, the residence of the sovereign, the seat of government, and the usual place of meeting for the sābor. During this period,

---

* The number given by the Austrian consul of the inhabitants of Prizren was as follows:—

    32,000 Mahommedans.
    12,000 Christians of the Orthodox Church.
    2,000 Roman Catholics.
    ―――
    46,000

CASTLE OF PRIZREN.

according to all record, she was a prosperous and progressing city. At the great fair of Prizren, Serbia and Bulgaria exchanged their produce for the merchandise of the west. Protected highways on the Roman track united her with the Danube and the Adriatic. Between her and Cattaro, Ragusa, and even Venice, there was constant intercourse, and the laws of Czar Dūshan attest the desire of the Serbian rulers to facilitate the passage of merchants through their lands.

Besides such advantages as were incident to the residence of the court, Prizren enjoyed the security belonging to her strong position in the heart of the Serbian lands; she remained undisturbed by wars on the frontier, and for several generations her walls never saw a foe. It is said that her neighbourhood used to contain 360 churches and monasteries, while the city itself was enriched with benevolent foundations of every sort, from the cathedral to the great hostelry for travellers attributed to Czar Lāzar.

But the central position of Prizren told both ways, first for her advantage and afterwards to her hurt; the fortunes of the czarigrad followed the fortunes of the czardom. When Némania transplanted Serbian royalty northward of Zeta, Prizren was chosen as the seat of empire; when the tide turned, and the rock-fortress of Zeta became the sole shelter of Serbian freedom, Prizren naturally lost her pride of place. Though not taken by the Turks till 1455, she ceased to be the residence of Serbian rulers from the day that they exchanged their frontier wars with European neighbours for a life or death struggle with the invading Mussulman.

Prior to the battle of Kóssovo the last Czar removed his seat to Krushevac, within the bounds of Danubian Serbia; after the battle of Kóssovo his successors retired to fortified cities on the Danube, until at length the advancing Moslem compelled them to take refuge on the northern bank of the stream.

It is only within the last half-century that the Serbs have again had a capital on their own soil, and that capital is not the ancient czarigrad, which has not as yet shared their freedom. But even were the frontier of Free Serbia so extended as to include Prizren, there is little likelihood that she would resume her former position; she might be honoured as a Serbian Moscow, but she can never become a Serbian Petersburg. For an *inland* capital the day is past; in order that Serbia may enjoy free intercourse with her neighbours and due influence over kindred populations, it is of the first necessity that the seat of her government should be a natural centre of civilisation and commerce. For the future, the chief city of Serbia must lie in the neighbourhood either of the sea or of one of the great European arteries, and this necessity is so deeply felt, that even in the tenacious imagination of the people "Prizren on the Shaar Mountains" is beginning to be supplanted by Belgrade on the junction of the rivers Danube and Save. Even in the proudest and most hopeful visions of the future this change of the national capital reconciles itself with a change in national feeling and policy; the old exclusive seat of Serbian czardom gives way to a metropolis for the South Slavonic race.

Four centuries of Turkish rule have stripped Prizren of architectural ornament, and debarred her from making any advance towards the well-built streets of a European city; but she still retains something of that majesty of attitude and general effect which has been observed to cling to royalty deposed. The traveller approaching from north, or east, or west, sees before him a great white city enthroned on the plánina, with its skirts sweeping the plain; he marks that here meet the highways from the Danube, the Adriatic, and the Ægean; he might still fancy himself coming up to the residence of the ruler of the surrounding lands.

From a picturesque mass of white and green there stands out imposingly a broad platform. Does it support the "Dvor" of the Némanides? No; a modern Turkish fortress, which like Turkish fortresses in general, is more formidable to the town than to outward foe. Behind this castle a spear-like rock shoots up, rearing on its summit the tatters of a tower; this tower, according to the testimony of the inhabitants, is all that remains of the stronghold of Czar Dūshan.

On entering the town each telling feature speaks of an Arnaout present and a Serbian past. The minaret of the principal mosque is a wooden pepper-box, but it has for base a broad stone tower; behind the tower rise the five cupolas of a church. The portico of another mosque rests on pillars torn from an adjacent monastery, and the stones still bear the sign of the cross. Then, if from the lower street you raise your eyes to the houses on the hill, which here seem to crowd one above another in perpendicular steepness, among them, too, stand out here and there the unmistakable arches and domes.

Before entering the town we were met by a number of dignified persons, among whose fezes we descried the consular cap of the Austrian agent.

That zealous official received us with great civility, and conducted us to what he called "the only good house in Prizren," no other than the palace of the Roman Catholic bishop. Its chambers stood empty, for the late possessor was dead and the new incumbent not yet installed. Of two good rooms with glazed windows, the one was a genuine parlour, with table, chairs, sofas, and even a bookcase; the other, a bedroom in the Turkish style, *i.e.*, surrounded with a divan, had sufficient space in the centre for the erection of our establishment. On the wall hung a picture of the Sultan, side by side with a picture of the Pope.

We remained three days at Prizren, and took our sight-seeing but lazily, the great heat keeping us in doors till within two hours of sunset. Our cicerone was a Serbian parish priest, who had acted as guide to the Russian Hilferding, and who was resolved that, willing or unwilling, we should leave nothing unseen that Hilferding saw. To this end he drove us ruthlessly from church to mosque, up hills, and through bazaars; for which we were truly thankful to him afterwards, but at the moment—not at all.

First, we must needs visit his own church, built by Némania, and dedicated to St. George. The entrance lies through a high walled court and a graveyard, wherein we observed small vessels of oil stationed beside most of the tombs. The old church is small and low, and in its dim recesses we could scarce mark details; if it have any special interest the priest did not point it out. A half built new church rises at its side. This is on a large scale, and at its entrance stands a headless row of white stone columns. Pope Kosta led us into the building, and several respectably dressed Serbs followed. In a corner shaded from observation they stood still and told their story. The unfinished church was not, as we fancied, checked in its growth by want of funds, but part of the ground comprehended in the plan had been appropriated by a Mussulman neighbour. We inquired how long the Turk had held the land? Fourteen years. And how long since the church was begun? Eight. Why, then, did you build on a scale exceeding the ground actually in your possession? They answered, "Because the land is ours, and we have documents to prove it. From ancient times it has belonged to our old church, and we have a right to use it for our new one." Possibly we did not understand the story: it seems more likely that a Prizren architect should have miscalculated the area required, than that Prizren rayahs would speculate on getting back ground that a Mussulman had held for fourteen years.

From St. George's Church we ascended the hill by a path so steep that our horses almost lost their footing, but at last we found ourselves enjoying a view of the whole city from the site of a little church. This building consists of two parts, side by side, the larger being a modern church added for the convenience of worshippers. The other and older part is very small, but gracefully vaulted, and its walls retain pictures of the Némanja family.

As the popes will neither tell nor show anything in the presence of a Mussulman, we had as usual left our zaptié at the door, but turning round from an inspection of the frescoes we found him spying and and prying behind us. We ordered him to be gone with the single Turkish word "Haïdé;" he, applying the injunction to anybody but himself, forthwith drove out two old women. Great was the surprise of all present when we reversed this order of things, expelling the Turk, and with apologies inviting the terrified crones to return. There could be no question that the Mussulman was an intruder, and that the old women, as members of the congregation, had a perfect right to crowd up the chapel, kiss the icons, and stare at the foreign visitors, hence our judgment was merest justice; yet we might not have had courage to execute it could we have foreseen the consequences. The delight, the triumph, the embraces of the reinstated old women knew no bounds; the crowd, no longer afraid of the zaptiés, pressed around us, kissing our hands, our feet, our clothes, with greetings and good wishes that swelled to a hubbub. Frightful was the homage of a poor dumb man, uttered in those unearthly sounds which were all that nature had left him. When we saw this unfortunate preparing to join the procession that escorted us down hill we hastily sent our servant to him with bakshish, and an entreaty that he would fatigue himself no further.

Pope Kosta now led us to one of the principal mosques, bade us observe the columns of its portico, the carving, and the cross-marked stones; all brought hither from the great Church of the Archangel Michael, built by Dūshan at the foot of his Grad. As by all accounts there was nothing to be seen within this mosque we contented ourselves with an outside view.

Then the pope started down a narrow road running alongside of a swift-flowing stream. The sun was setting, and the air from the water came so chill that we scarcely appreciated this excursion, especially as we encountered a lot of nizam—those "regular soldiers who are to civilise Turkey." At first, only seeing a cavalcade headed by a Christian priest, they prepared to push us, as they did others, into the water; we drew up, and left them no choice but to do the thing deliberately or get out of our way. Perceiving our European dress, the zaptié, and the cavass, they just avoided an actual shove; but in passing uttered a long low howl of hatred.

Having made a circuit, we re-entered through the skirts of the city, and stopped before what was once the cathedral. This edifice is said to have witnessed a solemn peace-making between the Greek and Serbian branches of the Oriental Church, when a quarrel which broke out during the reign of Dūshan, was made up under the gentle and pious Lāzar. At the Turkish conquest this cathedral was dismantled, and long suffered to stand in ruins; but lately the Mussulmans have made a mosque of it, and perched a minaret on the broad summit of the western tower. Seen from below, this tiny pointed superstructure looks like a peak-hatted dwarf stuck still while playing at leap-frog over a giant; its incongruous and insolent effect gives no bad idea of the attitude of modern Albanian Mahommedanism in Old Serbia.

The Austrian consul had told us we could not possibly enter this mosque, but Pope Kosta was enterprising, and we had the pasha's order for seeing everything; so the hodgia was called to open the door. He came not, but sent a message saying the key could nowhere be found. Meanwhile, a side door was open, so in we went up a stair into a gallery, apparently the ancient belfry, commanding a full view of the interior. The zaptié offered to take us up to the gallery of the minaret, "whence we should see all Prizren;" this offer, however, we thought it most prudent to decline, and descended the stair to go quietly away. But the door by which we had entered was locked, and as a screen barred us out from the interior of the mosque, there we were, and could neither get backward nor forward.

It was an embarrassing moment, but only a moment; our zaptié, making a ladder of the carved wood of the screen, swung himself over it, and thus gaining the inside of the mosque, hunted up the hodgia, who thereupon found the key. The zaptié then returned to us, accompanied by an Arab porter whom he compelled to follow him over the top of the screen. We were liberated, and, by way of reparation, invited to re-enter by the principal door.

The interior of the Prizren Cathedral was originally, like that of Gratchanitza, divided into several parts, hence it is peculiarly unfitted for a Mussulman place of worship. The imaum's pulpit and holy place do not occupy the apse, but are twisted aside to look towards Mecca, so that when facing them the worshippers cannot stand in the usual way across the building, but must form a line which stretches along the church from the east end to the west door. The frescoes on the walls and cupola are whitewashed or perhaps destroyed, for the workmen who repaired the dome boasted that they had "picked off Christ with his saints and thrown them down on the pavement." The deformation of this fine old minster is the more vexatious because it took place lately, and since the Christians in Turkey have been formally entitled to the use of churches. The Cathedral of Prizren stood in ruins for centuries, and now the hope began to dawn that it might be restored to Christian worship; it must have been a heavy day for the little Orthodox community when at this juncture they saw their church taken and deformed in order to adapt it for Mussulman use. Nor were the Mahommedans themselves satisfied, for so apparent is the original character of the building that many do not regard it as a real mosque, and some nizam passing through Prizren were greatly offended at being led to worship in what appeared to them to be a church. "Pray, what is that?" asked some of them, pointing to the western tower. "It is the place," answered a bystander, "whence bells used to ring." "They used to ring!" exclaimed the soldiers; "aye, and so they will again."

By the time we left the mosque the mood of its porter had undergone a change; he pointed to the door which so unwillingly he had opened to admit us, and coaxingly asked the ghiaour for bakshish.

Before going home, Pope Kosta insisted that we should once more ascend the hill to visit the residence of the bishop, and the adjacent church of St. Nicholas. Until lately this church was practically subterranean, from the surrounding accumulations of rubbish. Part of this is now cleared away, but you still descend some steps to the entrance, and the interior is dark and cold as a pit. The house of the Orthodox prelate is larger than that of the Roman Catholic, but, so far as we saw, not furnished à la Franca. The bishop himself was absent at Constantinople, spending the money he had squeezed from his flock on a bid for the Patriarchal Chair. We saw his sister, a doleful-looking woman; according to Pope Kosta both she and all the Orthodox community wept day and night for the absence of their pastor. But of this more hereafter.

Our second day's sight-seeing in Prizren took us to the ruins of Dūshan's Grad. The way thither leads under the walls of the Turkish fortress, whence there is a fine view of the town. You then thread the ravine of the Prizrenska Bistritza, till the path becomes too narrow for riding. You must proceed on foot, sending your horses round to await you below the Grad. All that remains of Dūshan's stronghold is now borne aloft on the point of a rock, whose base is encoiled by the swift mountain stream; to climb from below would be difficult and perilous, and even the approach from the neighbouring bank is slippery. Worst of all, unlike the ruins we had lately visited, there is here literally nothing to see. The fragment of a tower and some tatters of wall are all that remain of fortifications which used, it is said, to cover the hill. Possibly much of the ruin has been choked up with earth, and thus contributes to give the bank its present form, for it would be incredible that so steep a peak should ever have accommodated a building larger than a watch-tower. It struck us that this castle must have been merely a stronghold, and that the far-famed Dvor of the Czars had occupied the less inaccessible and broader position of the present Turkish fortress. Pope Kosta scouted this idea, declaring that thirty years ago nothing stood on the latter site; but we afterwards found other persons who shared our impression.

"Look," continued Pope Kosta, pointing to the swift mountain stream that coils round the base of the rock, "that is the Prizrenska Bistritza, and there are two other rivers of the same name; the Detchanska and the Ipekska Bistritza. All three fall into the Drina, and in all there is caught one particular kind of fish. This Bistritza comes down from the plánina, which you must cross on your way to Skadar." We could not help thinking that this must be the very plánina wherein Czar Dūshan held his famous hunting party with old Iūg Bogdan and the nine Iugovics, preparatory to asking their sister in marriage for his favourite page Lāzar; doubtless among the delicacies of the banquet which the page prepared for their return were some of the excellent trout of the river Bistritza.

In the church of the monastery below this Grad (or else in the great church of the town) assembled the great sābor wherein, on the extinction of the line of Némania, Lāzar Grebliánovic was elected to the throne. One popular legend has also chosen the Grad Dūshanovi for the scene of the great Czar's death, instead of Devoli, where it really occurred. This legend is curious from its description of the dying scene, and also because it attributes to Dūshan in his last moments that overbearing will which carried him through so much during his lifetime, but left to a semi-developed people, wrangling nobles, and a traitorous guardian, a task to which they were not equal when he was gone. Here it is, rudely translated from the fragment of a half-lost poem :—

In the pleasant city Prizren,
Stephen, Serbian Czar, falls sick,
Sorely sick, and like to die.
When the Czaritza perceives this
(She who wrote like any man)
Quick she takes the pen, inditing
Three, four letters, and forth sends them
To four quarters of the czardom,
To all provinces in order,
Duly calling all the lords.
"Hearken, ye our lords of Serbia!
Heavy sickness weighs Czar Stephen,
Weighs him down, so that he die.
Therefore haste to Prizren Castle,
That ye haply find him living,
That ye hear his last behest
And to whom he leaves the realm."

Swift the nobles catch her meaning;
Each one speeds him as he may;
And their ways all meet at Prizren,
In the castle, in the chamber
Of the mighty Serbian Stephen;
Haply find they him still living,
And they stand around the Czar.

Vukashine the King steps forward,
Lifts the Czar from silken pillows,
Wraps him in the silken covering,
On his face drops bitter tears.

Then looks up the great Czar Stephen,
Sees his nobles stand about him,
Rouses him, and speaketh thus:

"Thou, King Vukashine, dear cousin,
In thy trust I leave my czardom:
In thy keeping all my castles,
And my provinces and warriors,
All that in my realm was mine.
And to thy care leave I Urosh,
Yet an infant in the cradle.
Do thou rule for seven years,
Then give mine empire to my son."

But King Vukashine makes answer,
"Nay, Czar Stephen, nay, dear cousin,
Not for me to rule thine empire;
I am overdone with trouble
By my restless self-willed boy
Whom they call the King's Son Marko.
Where he will there goes he, asking
Leave of none; and where he resteth

> There he drinks; and everywhere
> Seeks he quarrel, rakes up strife."
>
> Speaks the great Czar Stephen—" Cousin!
> If *I* bridled my proud captains
> And all states throughout mine empire,
> Canst not *thou* thine own child bridle?
> So be it as I said; my czardom
> In trust to thee I leave; all my castles,
> All my warriors, all my states;
> In thy care I leave my Urosh;
> Rule for seven years, and then
> Yield mine empire to my son."
>
> Thus spake the Serbian Czar, great Stephen,
> And wrestled with his parting soul.
> As the word ended the soul fled." *

* * * * * *

The descent from the ruins of the castle on the rock to the ruins of the laura at its foot, is less of a path than a slide, or if there be a path our guide could not find it, and we each tumbled down as best we could. At the bottom used to stand the great monastery, from which the Turks carried away the columns for their mosque. At present scarce anything remains above ground, but Pope Kosta seemed to know what each part had been, and among others pointed out to us the place formerly occupied by the altar and sanctuary. In old times a bridge crossed the Bistritza below the convent; it is now gone, so we had to ride through the stream, and in order not to have to dismount frequently in passing along a narrow rocky path on the other side we continued to follow the course of the river, constantly crossing and recrossing as we found

---

* The Czar and Vukashīne really call each other *mili kroomé*, lit., dear *koom* —a name given to godfathers, brideleaders, and all sorts of voluntary connections, by which friends in Serbia usually create a relationship between them, held as sacred, or more sacred, than the ties of blood. As the word has no English equivalent, we substitute the word "cousin" as that frequently used in the Middle Ages among persons of royal rank who were not really related. Vukashīne is remembered among the people as the early friend and creature of Dūshan, whom he had raised to the second place in the empire, and on whose fidelity he therefore relied, but in whom, as the event showed, he was mistaken.

footing on either side. The sun had set, a weird flare lit up the rocks, along which a herd of goats happened to pass. The whole scene strongly resembled one of Salvator Rosa's landscapes. On the face of the cliff we observed a number of recesses similar to those at Détchani, and Pope Kosta confirmed our supposition that these also were hermitages, and formerly peopled from the laura.

Next day the good pope was very anxious that we should accompany him on a tour of the monasteries in the neighbourhood; of these he gave the following description, which we bequeath to the first traveller who has time and strength to profit by it. Whereas, according to the priests, there were in old times no less than 360 monasteries and churches in the neighbourhood of Prizren; at present there are but twenty-one. Of these, two, called Svéti Marko and Svéta Troitza, are inhabited and comparatively modern; the monastery of Korisha is ancient and deserted. On the slope of the Shaar Plánina, once stood a church in the style of Czerna Rïeka, with cells in the sides of the rock and remnants of paintings and inscriptions. The monastery belonging to this church is now deserted, having been pillaged by the Arnaouts and its village destroyed. Still more curious are the ruins of a church built by order of Czar Dūshan, in honour of a young caloyer whom he highly esteemed. This monk, when meditating in the mountains, was beset by the devil, but being aided by the Archangel Gabriel, he rid himself of the evil one by casting him over the brow of a precipice. In order that the church might be reared on the very scene of the exploit, arches were raised by the side of the rock and on them a chapel was built. The Mahommedans have destroyed it, but the arches are said to remain, together with a fragment of wall still painted with the figures of saints.

The Arnaouts, otherwise unable to get at these, have riddled them with shot.

Lastly, and historically most interesting, about a mile from the site of the old palace of Neredimlié, one may see the spot where young Czar Urosh was murdered, and the church of Our Lady where his body was laid.

MORNING ON THE ADRIATIC.

CHAPTER XXXI.

MODERN PRIZREN AND ITS INHABITANTS.

THE larger of our rooms in the bishop's palace was destined, as we were told, for receptions, and nowhere throughout our journey had we more need of such an apartment than at Prizren. Our visitors comprised Mussulmans, Roman Catholics, and Serbs. Among the first, came various deputies of the pasha, to pay compliments and receive orders, also the poor old mudir of Príshtina, already gone the way of Príshtinski mudirs. The Austrian agent and his wife we found both kind and civil to the utmost of their power; they were curious about old jewellery, and showed us some beautiful rings and antique gems bought up from impoverished Beys. Then there was the pro tem. master of the house, the Padre Vicario, an intelligent Italian of the Franciscan order, and various Albanian priests from the mountain parishes, who presented alike in dress and countenance a strange compromise between the Miridite and the monk. An incongruous pair, representing each variety, drew the yoke of the ménage, the one a young Italian friar, the other an Albanian schoolmaster. One of our visitors was an old man, who brought a bottle of excellent red wine, and told us it was from a vineyard planted in Stephen Dūshan's time. He was so shabbily dressed that we thought of paying for the wine, and thereupon found out that he was the richest merchant in the place. The most interesting members of the Orthodox community waited to be summoned, and then came the mistress of the girls' school, Pope Stephan, and Pope Kosta and his wife. Pope Kosta is a native of Vassoïevic, and besides being an energetic cicerone, is generally intelligent and not wanting in tact.

From the conversation and testimony of all these persons we extracted the following information respecting the present condition and inhabitants of the whilom Serbian czarigrad. In its streets are spoken Serbian, Albanian, Turkish; the presence of the latter language being accounted for as follows. On the first conquest of Prizren its size, strength, and importance caused some genuine Ottoman families to settle there, while others were left in charge of the town; now-a-days the sons of the richer Prizren Mussulmans often go for their education to Stamboul; and from both these causes Turkish, which is ignored in Ipek and Diakovo, forms one of the three languages of Prizren. That Serbian should still be considered the chief tongue, although the Christian inhabitants are in a minority, is due to the inalienably Serbian character and associations of the town; partly also, it is said, because some of the Mahommedans are of Serbian origin. The majority are Arnaouts.

Prizren is the seat of a pasha, but subordinate to a superior pashalic, lately that of Scodra, now of Nish. From the presence of regular troops and the admixture of Ottoman families the Arnaouts of Prizren comport themselves less unruly to the central government, less robber-like towards the Christians, than in Ipek and Diakovo. Still they are a bad lot, their chief families going to poverty and given up to vice and slothfulness. The most creditable members of the Moslem community would seem to be those craftsmen in steel who make the celebrated Prizren knives and scissors.

As to the chief town of the district, it is to Prizren that grave cases are referred for judgment; and throughout Stara Serbia we were constantly hearing of criminals sent thither "in chains." It was therefore with additional regret that we heard from a source friendly to the Turks of the injustice and corruption of the Prizren administration. The terrible accounts of the state of the prison made us think of those dungeons celebrated in the old songs of Serbia, into which heroes sometimes fell when engaged on distant campaigns. These are described as filled with "water up to the shoulders, bones up to the knee, and in the water, snakes and reptiles. In hope of ransom the captives are to be kept nine years, till the feet rot from their legs and the arms from their shoulders, till the serpents have sucked out their eyes; then turn them out into the street to beg their bread from the pity of the passers by." If the prison of Prizren be not full of water and snakes, it is by all accounts full of filth and vermin; and if the prisoners are not kept nine years for ransom, they are certainly detained without judgment until they can bribe the authorities; innocent and guilty, healthy and fever-struck, huddled together for an unlimited time; moreover they must be provisioned by their relations or they may expect to die of want. Not only for the sake of the Christian population between this and the Serbian frontier, but also to rouse and back the pasha in executing long-promised reforms, the presence of a sufficient number of energetic consuls is much desired at Prizren. At present, except the Austrian vice-consul, there is no European representative in the whole region of Old Serbia.

We saw a Bey of Prizren at home in the harem of the ex-mudir of Príshtina. Poor old man! he was scarcely recognisable; and in spite of conventionalities as to the "will of Allah," showed himself so put out by his deposition that we were glad to please him by agreeing to visit his dames. As an inducement he proffered the acquaintance of his sister, who had been married to a pasha, and in her widowhood occupies a house next door to his own. She was, as he informed us, a properly educated and polished lady, and had been much in Stamboul. As the Stamboul ladies we had seen in the provinces usually wore a gown of European cotton or muslin, we assured him that we were especially anxious to see the Albanian ladies of his harem and should be much gratified by their wearing their national costume. Accordingly, the wife and daughter of the mudir received us in all the glory of white gauze and velvet over-robes, the latter magnificently worked and heavy with gold. Here, however, the ladies' beauty began and ended; within the robes there appeared clumsy corpulence, above them painted faces and tawdry head-dress, and below, stockingless feet and toe-nails thickly bedaubed with henna. The Stamboul sister must have been very handsome; her features, though wasted, were still refined. In virtue of her alliance with a pasha, she played the grande dame of the harem; it was she who met us, led us in, and seated herself to entertain us, the fat wife and daughter brought the coffee, and afterwards stood fanning us. They made no attempt to join in the conversation, which flagged considerably, for we knew no Albanian and these dames but little Slāv. When we rose to depart the mudir and his ladies invited us to take a walk in the garden "to see the water." So the mudir led the way and Madame Pasha accompanied us, gathering up her scanty gown, and thereby exposing bare feet and ankles. We passed through some long grass and a few small trees to a door in the wall; the door was opened, and behold! a running stream,

After this walk in the pleasure ground we took our leave.

In this and other harems we were amused to see attendants and mistresses watching our behaviour in order to detect some of those signs which in the East so precisely indicate who is to be considered the chief guest. The idea that people can be of equal position and pay no attention to the minutiæ of etiquette, is in these countries almost inconceivable; nor could our hostess be made to understand that we chose our places on the divan with regard to light and draught. For long we knew nothing of their observances, and with involuntary humility often seated ourselves in the lowest room, our only care being that inculcated alike by European and Christian rules of courtesy, viz., not to seize on that place which we supposed to be the best. Afterwards we sometimes amused ourselves with puzzling our hosts, nicely dividing between us all the infinitesimal marks of distinction; when they remarked this they did the same, now and then bestowing any indivisible attention on her whom they might think the oldest.

And now for the Roman Catholics. The Albanians of this persuasion are patronised and assisted with money from France, Austria, and Italy, and have colleges and schoolmasters provided from Rome; the only consular agent in Prizren is the Roman Catholic agent of Austria sent for their special protection—hence we were a little surprised to hear from the Latins far more whining, begging, and lamentations than from the unbefriended Serbs. The fact is, that what with their Romanist allegiance drawing them off from the other native Christians, and what with their division into divers hostile tribes, precluding all settled aim and national consciousness; above all, from their habit of making Judas bargains with the Turks, and expecting everything to be done for them by foreign powers—these people are demoralised as they never need have been by mere servitude, however hard. The best hope for their regeneration is that the French influence, which is now predominant, is used to promote union among all the Christians in the country. After the Roman Catholic Albanians found that we were inclined to applaud unity they began to protest of their kindly feeling towards their Christian brethren; but when we first arrived, supposing that, as English, we should wish to believe the Christians of Turkey disunited among themselves, for the benefit of the Mahommedan, they sang a very different song. Not that among these Latin communities there are not some good specimens; a foreign education gives many of their priests more polish than can be boasted by the Serb popes. Moreover their ecclesiastical authorities stand up bravely in their defence, and exert themselves for their interests in a way the Greek prelates seldom or never do. The late Roman Catholic bishop of Prizren is said to have been respected by men of all faiths—a testimony confirmed even by the Russian Hilferding; it is due to his influence that the old cathedral was not utterly destroyed. It also speaks well for his taste that, even after the fine new episcopal residence was finished, he continued in his previous humble dwelling, and used the palace only for meetings. Doubtless he felt, what must strike every one at Prizren, that for the pastor to live in a style superior to all around him, while the community is poor and the church wretchedly small, is an anomaly discreditable to any creed.

On the day of our arrival the padre vicario was absent on a mission to Diakovo; on his return he told us its import and begged us to join his supplications and efforts. In the first place, he was troubled about some Roman Catholic congregations in the mountains. During the heat of persecution they had pretended to be Mahommedans; but when persecution decreased and military service became a burden, they declared their Christianity and agreed to pay haratch. No sooner, however, was the haratch paid than the Turks demanded military service also, ignored the return to Christianity, and required them to observe Mahommedan customs as before. Secondly, the padre vicario was troubled about some Roman Catholic congregations in the plain. They had come down from the hills comparatively lately and were colonists, *i.e.*, tenants, not possessors of the soil. They used to prefer fighting for the Sultan to paying him tribute, and in the Crimean war lost many men. But the injustice they suffered and the embezzlement of their pay had rendered them unwilling to render such service again; last year they would not march against Montenegro; hence the Turks were now demanding haratch. In both cases the padre complained against the Turks: "when they want haratch they treat our people as Christians; when they want soldiers they take them for Moslems." Those who know the Turks will not think this statement improbable; but those who also know the Roman Catholic Albanians may believe the Turks have some reason on their side when they assert that "these Latins are all Mussulmans to the tax-gatherer, and all Christians when called to war." The colonists of the plain about Diakovo, knowing that their brethren in the mountains were able to defy the demand for haratch, had declared their resolution to return whence they came. "And why not?" said we; "for whose benefit do they stay where they now are? With the Turks they cannot agree; with the Christians they do not join; for themselves they prefer labouring in a less fertile soil to parting with the fruit of their labour in taxes; and as for the land, so far as it is improved by any agriculture of theirs, they may as well scratch the earth in the mountain as in the plain." "Nay, nay," cried the padre; "you do not understand the question. If the Roman Catholics withdraw from these parts, *we pastors shall be left without flocks.*"

The padre vicario told us that in sickness Mussulmans often asked for the prayers of the priests, apparently by way of a spell; and that the other day a hodgia came to him, and besought him to breathe on him and give him his blessing as a means of curing some disease. The padre objected, representing that since the hodgia had no *faith* the blessing would do him no good. "Never mind," cried the hodgia, "only bless me; faith or no faith, it can do me no harm." The priest laughed heartily at the hodgia's stupidity; but it struck us as somewhat suspicious that he should have found fault only with lack of faith, instead of frankly stating that neither blessing nor breathing of his could avail to cure disease. It occurred to us from this anecdote that the Roman Catholic monks in Albania, like their Bosniac brethren, may profess to heal their congregations by means of all sorts of absurd practices, and possibly, like them, increase their slender incomes by writing talismans, of which the virtue is believed in by the ignorant Christians and no less by the ignorant Turks.

The Roman Catholic priests we saw at Prizren gave us a good many interesting details respecting the chief of the most powerful tribe of Latin Albanians, commonly called the Prince of the Miridites. The title itself is a mistake, being really Prink or Prenk (Peter), which is a common name in the chieftain's family. A former Prenk held the rank of a general of brigade in the Turkish army—a circumstance which sufficiently marks the distinction between his position and that of his Orthodox neighbour the independent prince of Montenegro. We were anxious to hear how far this distinction was answered to by a difference in their respective modes of living and in the condition of their subjects. Some persons have been prompt to assume that as regards the comfort, quiet, and civilisation of the highlanders of Montenegro, the only spoke in the wheel is the persistence of their prince not to recognise the nominal authority of the Sultan, thus compelling the Turks to treat them as foes. Like several other theories affecting the Montenegrines, this one should not be indulged without reference to the actual condition of the Latin Albanians who do acknowledge the Sultan's authority, and even render him military service. From all that can be learnt on the subject, it seems certain that these Albanians are in a more barbarous condition than the wildest of the Montenegrines and quite as impoverished and predatory; while they lack all signs of such modern improvement and organization as that by which the last rulers of Montenegro have succeeded in establishing security and order within their own domains. Descriptions of Orosh, the residence of the Miridite chief, show it to be without even those features of the tiny capital of Montenegro which indicate (to use the Prince of Serbia's expression referring to his own dominions) "that at least the people have the intention to become civilised." Such travellers as have made the acquaintance of the Princess and Princess Dowager of Montenegro may judge of the difference between Montenegrine and Miridite manners, when they learn that it is customary for the Prenk, not to marry a Christian woman, but to carry off a Mahommedan and baptize her on purpose. During M. Hecquard's visit to Orosh, the women's apartments in the chief's residence were tenanted by two widows, who had survived all their immediate male relatives, and having each killed a man in order that the number of dead might be equal on both sides, thereupon agreed to forgive the past and live under one roof for the rest of their days.

But to return to Prizren, where we have still to notice the Orthodox (Pravoslāv) community. The archbishop was absent, and of him we heard contradictory opinions. Some said that he was on the mother's side Bulgarian, and a friend to the Slavonic people and nation; that he celebrated the liturgy in Slāv, and protected deserving Serbians like Pope Kosta and Katerina of Ipek. Others said he was a Greek from Seres, where there is a large Bulgarian population; hence, knowing the Slavonic language, he was less distasteful to his flock, but nevertheless selfish and addicted to Phanariote intrigue. He was even accused of being hostile to education, and of preventing the establishment of a higher Serbian school. Pope Kosta, as the archbishop's secretary, came in for his share of blame. But whatever the archbishop may have done about a higher school, we can testify to the existence of two normal schools at Prizren. The boys' school we visited, and found it a creditable structure and provided with books from Belgrade. The girls' school was in embryo, partly because many families are too poor to spare their children from home, partly from lack of communal funds sufficient to dispense instruction gratis, but chiefly because there is no competent teacher. The Prizren schoolmistress is a humble, good woman, in despair at her own ignorance, and really anxious to do her best. But Pope Kosta remarked, "We want a woman like Katerina. Her religious character gives her authority, she goes from house to house, finds out the children, and takes them. Such a woman would fill our school."

One obstacle to prosperity in the Serbian community of Prizren is that its most vigorous members draft off to the principality. By their own account no less than 500 families had lately emigrated; and though the Austrian consul thought this number exaggerated, he allowed that as many, and more, would go but for the hindrance of the Turkish authorities. The associations of the old Czarigrad keep alive the spirit of freedom, and, unlike emigrants from more demoralised districts, the Prizrenites take kindly to European institutions, and having once walked with head erect will never again stoop to the yoke. They offer their families all aid to follow them, but not even a refusal will induce them to return. More than one mother, bemoaning to us a son's absence, imitated the gesture with which he forswore Mussulman dominion, shaking one side of the garment and spitting violently on the ground. The few energetic men who remain are kept at home by the fears of timid relatives, and Pope Kosta pointed to his wife as the hindrance to his not holding a good position on the other side of the border. No sooner did the obstructive party suspect the approach of the contested subject than she opened her batteries, crying, spreading out her hands, and conjuring him not to separate her from home and kin. The Serbian nation is obliged to such good matrons, for it certainly ought not to sever the last link between itself and the old lands; we have already noticed, that the government of the principality does not encourage emigration from Old Serbia.

At parting we gave Pope Kosta our last Serbian Testament, little anticipating how welcome the gift would prove. He received the book without appearance of pleasure, and took it home with him the evening before we left Prizren. But next morning he reappeared radiant and accompanied by his wife and another relative,

He said that he had begun reading to the women, and the language being such as they commonly use the words came home to them familiarly, as never in the Church Slavonic version. They had sat up till late, poring over the book, and now the pope was going forth into the villages to read it out to all the people.

We cannot take leave of the Serbs of Prizren without giving the following story. One morning our dragoman ushered in a lad, who earnestly begged leave to tell us somewhat. "The matter," said he, "is none of mine, but I was entrusted to bring it before you by a poor mother who had to leave Prizren before your arrival. In my childhood I myself was carried off by the Turks and barely escaped being made a Mussulman, and the tale I come to tell you is of a boy carried off in like manner. He is the son of a widow at Vuchitern; his family lived next door to rich Moslems, who, so long as the boy's father lived, showed themselves friendly neighbours. On the father's death the Mussulmans proposed that the boy should come to their house and do what little services he could, promising to treat him kindly and give him food. The mother, being very poor, agreed; but no sooner did the Turks get hold of the child, than they began to coax him to change his faith, and one day they dressed the little ragged fellow in a complete set of good clothes, and promised to give them to him if he would become a Mussulman. At last the boy consented, and then forthwith he was spirited off to Prizren, and given in charge to the pasha's zaptiés. So soon as the relatives could discover what had become of him they followed hither, and objected that so young a child could not legally change his faith. The bishop was absent, but his secretary, Pope Kosta, pleaded the cause. He asked: 'What says the law? May a child declare a change of religion before he has attained years of discretion, or may he not? Bring the book, we will abide by what is written.' The law was read out. 'No change of faith is legal below a certain age.' Then asked the pope, 'Has the child attained that age?' No one could pretend that it was more than eight years old. Hence the case seemed beyond dispute, when the pasha neutralised the whole value of the decision by appointing that till the child be of age it shall remain in charge of his zaptiés. In vain the kinsfolk urged that by law the boy ought to be returned to them, or at least should spend the interval under the protection of the Orthodox bishop. The pasha kept to his judgment, and to give it a colour of justice, turned to the little fellow and asked whether he demanded to be removed from his present associates. As might be expected the child whimpered out 'No,' and thereupon the pasha dismissed the case. Henceforth the zaptiés kept strictest watch over their prize. His poor mother came from Vuchitern, but after spending all her money had to return without seeing him." In parting she laid a solemn charge on the lad who told us the tale not to lose sight of her boy. Further, knowing of our expected arrival, she besought him to lay the matter before us. "I have done my best," said he, "to fulfil her trust. It is hard to get speech of the boy, for the zaptiés keep him aloof from the Christians, but when I do he cries for his mother and would be glad to return to her; at other times I see him among the Mussulmans merry and happy enough."

We could not but remark that the narrator of this story in no way sought to garnish the tale, or to invest the child's fate with exaggerated horror. He merely contended, that on the part of the Turks to carry off the boy was a breach of trust, and to detain him a breach of law. We asked the name of the child; this his advocate dared not reveal; that of the mother, or of the friends—not a word. This reluctance is usual in cases where the rayah is not certain of being protected; what amazed us was, that the witness readily gave his own name and allowed us to write it down. But the day we left Prizren a woman sprang into our chamber, trembling and crying, and bringing us as bakshish a pair of red socks embroidered with flowers. She was the mother of the boy who had told us "that story;" if it became known the Turks would kill him, and we had "written down his name." Restoring the bakshish, we opened our note-book, showed the poor mother the name of her son, and effaced it before her eyes.

But we were not left without authority that might be quoted in support of the tale. The narrator had referred us to Pope Kosta, and the pope gave full details with permission to use his name; he promised further to give his evidence in writing should the matter be investigated.

"And now," said we, "what can we do? To *you* it is not necessary to state we do not possess the power attributed to us by these poor people, but at Scodra there are European consuls: will it be of any use to tell your story to them?"

He answered, "Yes. A consul could help us."

"Then we will tell the Russian consul."

"The Russian!" cried Pope Kosta: "his interference would only give the pasha an excuse for setting down the whole matter as political intrigue. You must tell the French consul."

"But the stolen child is a Serb—not a Latin."

"No matter," insisted the pope, "for the French it is enough that he is a Christian; besides, theirs is the only consul who can make the Turks mind him." *

---

* M. Hecquard, a man who would have left his mark anywhere, was at that time French consul at Scutari.

"And what can the French consul do in this matter?"

"He will investigate the case, and make sure what he is about, and then he will write a line to the pasha, saying, 'Such a child is illegally detained by your zaptiés, let him be given up at the orthodox bishop's house.' Any consul could make this reclamation, for the child's detention is illegal; but unless the pasha is aware that the demand will be followed up, he will answer that he knows of no such child, or that the child remains of its own free will, or that it may depart when it pleases—and the zaptiés would keep it as before."

CHAPTER XXXII.

A HIGH ROAD IN NORTHERN ALBANIA.

FROM PRIZREN TO THE TOWN VARIOUSLY CALLED SCUTARI IN ALBANIA, SKADAR, AND SCODRA.

IF questioned as to the most disagreeable part of our journeys through Turkey in Europe, we should give the palm to that spent in traversing scorching plains, either on horseback or in a Scythian waggon which conveyed us from Rodosto to Adrianople. But perhaps the most dangerous journey was that between Prizren and Scodra, through the region called Old Dukadjin.

The Abbot of Détchani advised us not to attempt it, but rather diverge over Dibra, and get to Scodra by way of Ochrida, Elbassan, and Croja. This route has no greater objections as to roughness than the direct one; it traverses magnificent scenery, and by it one might visit several remote convents, and find out if any ruin remains of the old palace of Neredimlïe.

But to do all this would take many more days than to go straight from Prizren to Scodra; we were becoming rather short of strength, and our stock of silver was waxing low, and could not be replenished on this side Scutari. Besides, we had often heard of the road through Old Dukadjin as traversing the wildest country in Turkey in Europe, and this wild country we wanted to see.

The road from Prizren to Scodra is a high road, and a post road; it is the route of commerce between Prizren with the district behind her and the coast of the Adriatic. Unfortunately in Turkey all this hinders not that it be a rough bridle-track through tangled forests and stony hills, narrow and slippery, crossing precipices and crossed by streams. Private houses there are few or none to be found; the khans are but stables, and, being known as the rendezvous of travellers, have become also the rendezvous of robbers, of whom, report says, the khangees are chief.

The Albanians of the district belong to the tribes of Haluia and Puka, and are about half Mussulmans and half Latins. The Latins generally go to war under the chief of the Miridites; like the Miridites they pay no tribute, and furnish men to the Sultan's wars at the rate of one per house. The Mussulmans enjoy a terrible character among their neighbours; and though they tolerate kulas for zaptiés at intervals along the road, yet they seem little amenable to any police power. It is certainly unfortunate that the only route between Prizren and the coast should pass for days through such wild country, and one cannot but wish that it were possible to discover and clear an old road which in the time of the Némanias used to unite Metóchia and Zeta. The country people say that by it one could get from Ipek to Scodra in sixteen hours, whereas the distance between Prizren and Scodra is now called four days. Under the existing régime, however, the district of Malesia, through which ran Némania's road, is as unsettled as that of Dukadjin; its greater proximity to the Montenegrine frontier is probably another reason why the old route has been disused since Prizren passed into Mussulman hands.

Such is the habit one contracts in the East of crediting but half what one hears, that we scarcely believed in the perils before us until we had made experience of their reality. However, in justice to our acquaintance, we must say that they did not let us start without warning. First, the good prior of Détchani told us, that if he had to get to the coast of the Adriatic, he would rather make his way through Bulgaria and Macedonia to Thessalonica, and there take ship and come round, than he would again risk his person on the few days' journey between Prizren and Scodra. Next, the wife of the Austrian Vice-Consul, who like the prior was of portly size, dwelt on her dangers while passing over so narrow a track, and on the fatigue of incessantly dismounting in order to cross the worst places on foot. In case we might neglect this precaution, she told us of a hapless priest who quite lately had been killed by a fall from the narrow road in the bed of the stream below. We were also told, both at Prizren and at Scodra, of a young Italian merchant who caught fever on the way, and from lack of proper food and rest died in a wretched khan, just as he had reached the journey's end.

The day before we started, two people called on us and offered to obtain letters from certain persons in Prizren to certain khangees on the road. They said: "These khans are the regular resort of robbers, and the people cannot be dealt with by any pasha. But if one comes to them with letters from their friends, the innkeepers will send men of their own from station to station, and under such escort no one will meddle with you."

Hardly were these comforters gone than the pasha himself sent us the following message:—"I give you for your guide one zaptié, a well-known and trustworthy person, who will do for you all that can be done. I have told him that if you are stopped by the Albanians he must say you carry the Sultan's firman, and we hope that after hearing this, the people will let you go on.

More I cannot do, nor is there any use in sending you with a greater number of guards, for those through whose land you are about to pass are not amenable to any regular authority."

But more scaring to our minds than all the rumours of haiduks, was the certainty that the inns wherein we were about to lodge were unprovided with separate chambers. We could not make up our minds to rough it as the poor Austrian consuless had done, and sleep night after night in full travelling costume on a shakedown in the stable; cavass and zaptié, with cocked pistols, being interposed between us and the rest of the wayfarers. This obstacle would have fairly turned us back, but for our hitherto useless tent, which now came into play, and was pronounced small enough to find room inside the walls of a khan.

Of course it was not to be expected that on a road leading through such lawless communities, the pasha's fiat would be sufficient to provide us with horses from point to point. We must once more look out for kiradgees, and this proved the greatest trouble of all. According to a whisper we afterwards heard among our visitors, Christian kiradgees were to be obtained at a regular price of 50 piastres per horse; but it happened that the kijaja of the pasha had a favourite, for whom he wished to get a job. Hence he informed us that Christian kiradgees were not to be had, but that he could recommend a Mussulman, the most trustworthy kiradgee in the world; one to whose escort were confided all the Government goods and official harems that passed to and fro on that road; one, moreover, that had been honoured by the patronage of the Austrian consul when he came last spring. The model kiradgee came to make his bargain, and demanded for each horse 120 piastres; we, thinking this price exorbitant, sent a note to the Austrian consul, which was answered to the effect that he and his wife had paid but 80 piastres per horse. The matter was then referred to the pasha, and in consequence the man reappeared before us in a more subdued frame of mind. However, the kijaja recommended us, in order to secure him,—the very pink and prince of kiradgees, —to compound for 90 piastres; and this the rather as, with any other, the pasha could not really be answerable for our safety, and in order to go with us the kiradgee was surrendering the conveyance of a cargo paid at 100 piastres per horse.

To save bother we consented to this compromise, but bother was not thus to be saved. To make up the deducted price, our carrier bethought him of adding to the convoy an extra horse. His excuse for this was that he could not bring back his full complement of return loads from Scutari without his full complement of packsaddles; and, therefore, as we chose to use saddles of our own, he must have an extra horse to carry the packsaddles belonging to our steeds. As the pack-saddles were going wholly for his convenience, and a similar charge had never been made on us before, this demand was deemed unjust. It ended in our agreeing to pay half price for the extra horse—whereupon the kiradgee added various articles to its burden which he must otherwise have transported at his own expense.

Nor was he yet finished with. He demanded to be paid beforehand at least half the hire. But on this head we would hold no parley, for we knew quite well that, being a Mussulman, a favourite of the kijaja, and thus protected against all fear of punishment, our only hold on him was the hope of his fee. Pay him half of that beforehand, and we had no security that he might not take offence at something, and turn back half-way. The event proved that we were right; but, nevertheless, this point was not easily got over. The pasha's kijaja came himself to speak with us, ostensibly about something else, but soon contriving to insinuate that in his opinion we really ought to make the kiradgee some advance, inasmuch as (to his certain knowledge) the carrier had debts, and might be prevented by his creditors from leaving town. We answered that if the kiradgee could not go with us we should not break our hearts about it, having already found him indocile and troublesome; on the other hand, if he had creditors, it was clear that he had also friends, and that from these he might crave an advance to pay his debts more appropriately than from ourselves. This hint struck the kijaja like a shot; not one word more did he say about the kiradgee's debts, but immediately advised him to go with us without further ado.

Next morning, having risen early, and looking into the yard to see our baggage start before us, we perceived that the carrier had after all contrived to smuggle in an extra horse by loading the baggage on five horses instead of four. This would not do; before entering on so adventurous a journey, it was necessary before all things that our servitors should understand that our will was to be done—not theirs.

We counter-ordered all preparations for departure, and sitting down with almost Turkish phlegm, let the early hours pass in waiting till the pasha should take his seat in the konak. Then we ordered our dragoman to go before him with bitter complaints that a carrier so wily and stubborn should have been recommended by his kijaja. Indeed we absolutely refused to have anything to do with such a person, unless before departure some pledge were given that he should play no more tricks, stick to the agreement, and engage not to demand one para of his payment until we were safely delivered into the hands of a consul at Scodra. After much delay a respectable surety was found, a certain sum deposited with the pasha as security for good behaviour, and then the kiradgee, thoroughly tamed for the time being, reloaded the horses and set out; we ourselves followed in the cool of the afternoon.

The first night was to be spent at a khan near the Drina, between four and five hours from Prizren. After leaving the town, the road continues level, but stony, and without any features of beauty or interest. It was already dark when we reached our quarters, and we rejoiced to find that the kiradgee—efficient when he chose, and now anxious to conciliate us—had caused our tent to be pitched in the khan. We would rather have had it placed outside, but all persons consulted on the subject declared that the night air in these regions is too chill to be braved without danger, especially on the margin of a river; also that the Albanian fancy to take lights for a target would make it dangerous to sleep in a chamber without solid walls. So we were obliged to remain within the khan, which was merely a stable, surrounded with mangers for the horses, and having for fireplace a large stone. Of course, we had much to suffer from heat and stable odours, and our little bell-tent proved too small for convenience. However, of this we could not complain, since, if larger, it could not have been got into the khan; under the circumstances, indeed, we felt thankful to have a separate apartment capable of containing beds, bath, and tea-table. We had brought with us chickens ready roasted, and milk had been procured, so there was nothing to find fault with in the way of supper; nor was our sleep disturbed by sound or motion on the part of the other tenants of this rough hostelry.

But the repose of the night was amply made up by

the fatigues that came with morning. Never had it seemed to us that the carriers took such an endless time to load; if we ceased urging them for a moment, they dropped their arms and sat down. Our servants, who usually presided at this part of the business, appeared to have some cause of pre-occupation. At last the dragoman came to tell us that the khangee was demanding an altogether exorbitant price; on the ground that to accommodate us he had refused other passers-by to rest in his khan the night before. Thus beset, we resolved to adopt the course which we saw was followed by the Arnaouts themselves. Get all ready, mount your horse, and ride clear out of the khan; then take out of your pocket that which you know to be the khangee's due, put it into his hand, and be off. On this occasion we sent the luggage first, and then started ourselves with the zaptié, giving our servants orders to pay the host and follow; but they followed not, so after a time we had to come to a halt and await them. First the cavass pelted up in a towering passion, followed at a distance by his more deliberate companion, and both were not only angry, but frightened. The former exclaimed, "Never was I among such fellows as these Arnaout khangees: why, they think nothing of threatening to shoot one. Not that I should mind their *threatening*, if I could be sure that they would not do it." At this juncture, who should spring out from behind some bushes but the kiradgee. He laughed loudly, and addressed the dragoman: "Ha, ha! so you have had a *barufa*. I saw you were going to have one, and took myself off, inasmuch as you had not asked me to help you. If you had asked me, I could have managed for you, for I know the price of everything, and that wretched khangee never would have dared to charge me what he charged you. Why, you gave twice too much for everything. Last night you had only some milk, and two chickens to take on with you to-day. With a few piastres I could have paid for all; but how can *you* understand the people of these parts!" He then proceeded to give a sketch of the character of his countrymen, mingling open reprobation with half-concealed pride, as a mother sometimes does when telling of the unmanageableness of her naughty boy. Quoth he: "The people hereabouts cannot be brought to order by any one who does not belong to themselves. To a stranger they will not listen, let him be who he may. Your zaptié cannot help you here, nor could he though he were a consul. What do you think happened, when I was conveying the Austrian consul and his wife? An Albanian to whom I owed money caught his horse by the bridle, and forbade us to proceed till I had paid my dues. The consul called out, 'Let go instantly! I am the agent of the Emperor of Austria, and this horse is in my service.' But the Albanian took no heed of him: what did he know of the Emperor of Austria? nor would he leave go until I begged and entreated, and prevailed on him to let me complete my engagement, in order that I might obtain money wherewith to pay my debt. Such are the manners of this people, and thus must one deal with them. Angry words are of no use here; for amongst the Arnaouts the life of a man is of no more value than the life of a chicken."

Our course for the rest of the day lay along the banks of the Drina, and beholding its bed very shallow and full of rocks, we could not but doubt the possibility about which the Prizren consul had talked to us, of navigating the river by steamer. For the country north of Prizren need is felt of a navigable outlet to the Adriatic; and at the very time of our visit the same Consul Hahn who had formerly explored the route between Belgrade and Salonica in the interests of a railway, was preparing an expedition, with the view to ascertain if the Drina stream could be used for small steamers, and thus open up the fine woods of Stara Serbia and Northern Albania. We afterwards heard that, on careful investigation, he was obliged to relinquish the idea.

Before arriving at our mid-day halt we had to cross a bend of the river; the bridge was so rickety and steep that the kiradgee compelled the whole party to dismount, and pass it on foot. On the further side we found a zaptié's kula; and while the horses were being led over the bridge, we sat ourselves down in a rude out-door saloon, with pillars of unbarked wood and a roof of leafy boughs. Dirty, disorderly, and ruin-stricken as are Albanian habitations indoors,—for repose and recreation in the open air, for a good site, good water, and a good view, leave the Oriental to choose. If there be a failure more costly, uncomfortable, and pretentious than another, it is the regulation summerhouse of Europe, and that notably in grand gardens, where no expense is spared. But in the East you need only provide yourself with a carpet, and let your guard spread it for you,—he will hit exactly the one spot where, when the rest of the landscape is uninteresting, there is something you could watch for hours; where, when the air is sultry, you catch a delicious breeze; and when the sun is scorching, some thick stem or bough interposes itself as shade. There sit down—for the present just where we happen to be,—outside this zaptié's kula in Albania, and look at the delicious view. Can anything be more picturesque than that snakelike bridge, with its little arches of irregular height? Through those arches, the swift stream wheels round the foot of the bank; and directly opposite us, apparently within a stone's throw, rises a huge mountain, so wrapped in the haze of noon that it seems, not a mass of rock and earth, but all purple shadow and silvery sheen.

Mid-day was spent in the khan of "Brod." This name is the Slavonic for "ford," and is often found applied to inns and towns in the neighbourhood of bridges or ferries.

From the foot of the mountain Gallitch to the khan of Brod stretches a pretty valley, abounding in green pastures, and here and there cultivated. While we rested the shepherds brought in their flocks, and our dragoman was able to obtain a supply of milk. The inn of Brod had a *soi-disant* separate room, and on account of this we were advised to select it for our first night's halt. But the boasted room proved merely a compartment used by the khangee for storehouse and kitchen, and separated from the stable by boards so roughly knocked together that it was easy to see between them.

At Brod we were to enter the district particularly infested by thieves, hence our zaptié desired that two men from the nearest kula should go on with us as guides.

Soon the path re-enters the river gorge, and arrives at a second bridge less infirm than the former; on the approach to this bridge we came in for a perilous but absurd adventure. The cavass, who was riding behind, suddenly pushed his horse past ours, and overtook the guard walking in front, pulled him round, and called upon him instantly to "look at that fellow and fire." The guard did not fire, but he stood for a minute with his gun pointed at some object on the opposite side of the stream. "What is the matter?" said we. The cavass answered in great excitement, "Do you not see?

Crouching behind a stone is a man taking aim at us,—now he sees the guard taking aim at him, he has dropped his gun." "Nonsense," interrupted the guard, in his turn lowering his weapon, "the man meant no harm, he was trying to shoot fish in the river." "Whatever he was trying to shoot, it was at us that he pointed the gun," answered the cavass, sulkily.

On the other side of the river there stood the ruins of a large khan, of which part evidently served for a kula. In front four or five Albanians were drawn up behind our chief kiradgee, who now looked quite warlike with a gun on his shoulder.

He ran forward to meet us, and said, "Look, look what I have done! I have waited to see you safely over the river, and these brave fellows are drawn out to protect you. I was sure that man would try to shoot some of you, even as he tried to shoot some of us. While we were passing, he called out to frighten the men—'Ho, there! I am going to kill you;' so as the baggage horses had to go slowly across the bridge I stood with my gun pointed at him, shouting that if he fired I would shoot him stone dead."

We replied that it was sheer nonsense to suppose that a man would sit under a stone all day on the chance of shooting a passenger or two on so unfrequented a road. The people answered, "He is a shepherd, and while he is sitting with his sheep he amuses himself trying how far off he can hit, wounding or frightening the passers-by. However, he does not want to rob you, it is purely *per spasso*." The idea of such fun was so original that we could not help laughing, without well knowing how much to believe.

On this very spot where life was so cheaply held, the zaptiés had a little foundling boy who lived with them in their kula. They said his father came to grief on the journey, and that they brought up the child as theirs, while passengers would now and then contribute bakshish towards his keep. He looked very hardy and happy, and evidently was a great pet with his rough hosts.

The khan where all this happened is called the Vezir Khan; it is now in ruins, but used to be known as one of the largest on the road; and M. Hecquard mentions it as marking the boundary between the pashaliks of Prizren and Scodra.

The rest of that day's ride took us along the wooded banks of the river, under cool shade, and looking down on the stream, which here flowed strong and clear. All along the way the guards and kiradgee scoured the wood paths shouting lustily,—as they said, to apprize and frighten away lurking guns; their cries served to attract some few country people, who brought water-melons and green apples to sell. We passed several very small khans, and when it became dark were obliged to stop at one of them. Its roof was too low to admit the tent in other than a squatting attitude; we spent the night under difficulties, and could not but envy our attendants the fresh air of their bivouac outside. In front of the khan there was a sort of open shed, so the kiradgee spared us the company of his horses; only one horse was permitted to remain in the stable, and that at our own request. It belonged to an old Turk, on his way from the Eastern provinces to Scodra to visit his son, who, as he said, had been taken from him to serve in the Sultan's nizam. The old fellow had made friends with our cavass, and joined our convoy for protection, and this the rather because at Prizren, where horses are cheap, he had invested in a nice little nag, with intent to pay his travelling expenses by selling it, for twice or three times what he paid for it, to some cavalry officer at Skadar. The horse arrived this evening hot, and the old man was leading it into the stable, when our zaptié authoritatively ordered him out, and said his beast must take its chance with the rest.

Luckily we were at hand; knowing the value of the horse, and seeing the despairing look of the old man, we reversed the harsh decree. We had given no previous order that horses should be turned out of the khan, so the exclusion of the old man was an entirely gratuitous injustice on the part of the zaptié. This was one of the many instances we saw of the Turks' imperious want of consideration even for each other.

This small khan was so ill provided with food that had we not brought chickens and milk from Brod we must have gone supperless to bed. Indeed, excepting the khangee, the only living thing we saw on the premises was a scorpion, and that we found the next morning crawling on the canvas of the tent. The dragoman told us that in these countries the remedy used for a scorpion's bite is an application composed of the bodies of scorpions scalded to death, and kept in a bottle of sweet oil. At Scodra we saw a bottle containing this nostrum, which is kept in most native houses ready-made: one of the consuls attested its powers, and said that it is in general use.

Next day an hour and a half's riding brought us to a very tolerable hostelry, rejoicing in a new and clean stable, and numerous fowls running about the yard. No one had told us of it previously, so doubtless it was of recent date, and ere this may be dilapidated like its fellows. A short distance before reaching it we espied the only vestige of an old castle that occurred between Prizren and Scodra. It was quite a ruin, and stood high above the river on the bank opposite to that whereon we rode. And at this point we parted company for a while with the river Drina, fording the broad and shallow stream, nor saw it again till we debouched together from the mountains on the plain of Scodra.

We rode, or rather scrambled, up the bank on the opposite side, whence our view was no longer restricted to the Drina glen, and an opening in the forest suddenly revealed a magnificent vista of limestone crags towering in the distance. Strangely their name sounded—Cerna Gora, the Black Mountain, Montenegro; as seen from the dark forests of Albania, they appear rather as the Biéla Gora, or White Mountains. Especially is this true, if we take the word *white* in its figurative Slavonic sense, and contrast the forest of the aimless savage, with those hills, however barren, which are the abode of tribes at once disciplined and free.

The large khan of Sachat, at which we arrived about mid-day, enjoys a grand upland position, commanding views over ravines and passes on every side, and looking down on every winding of the little river below. This advantageous situation has secured for it the patronage of numerous haïduks, and, together with its neighbour khan of Vlet, it enjoys the reputation of being a very head-quarters for rogues. It is also a station of zaptiés, and the khangee, who is generally reputed to be the confederate or captain of thieves, here gives orders as head of the police. The instance was not a solitary one, and altogether the relation of Turkish police to Arnaout bandits, and of zaptiés' kulas to Arnaout khans, remained to us a mystery culminating in the mixed character assumed by the khangees.

One of the talismanic bits of paper that were to ensure us protection bore the name of the khangee of Sachat. To him accordingly we delivered it; but he gave it a very doubtful reception, at first announcing that he knew nothing of the writer. Finally, however, he muttered something about having heard that we were coming, and being prepared to give us an escort; at the same time comforting us so far as to declare that, *for the present*, there was no robber-band quartered between his khan and that of Vlet. "Pray," interposed we, " do not let that circumstance deter you from giving us a guide;" so, to humour us, as he graciously termed it, he at last desired a half-clad ragamuffin to head our cavalcade. While the guide was preparing for the journey, we eat our luncheon in a compartment of the stable, which (one degree less exclusive than the compartment at Brod) was fenced in with a ridge of boards that only reached half-way between the floor and the roof. The meal in this cell has remained impressed on our memories, because, when replacing our utensils, we omitted to pack up one silver spoon, and left it behind us when we went away. Thus, by our own carelessness, it was lost; but the companion spoon, together with two silver forks, returned in safety to England— having voyaged up and down Turkey in daily use, and certainly not owing their preservation to any secretiveness of ours. Our knives, as we have already said, could not thus brave publicity, for in Albania a good dinner knife can be put to more uses than one.

The Albanian who was to act as guide from the khan of Sachat to that of Vlet, fitted himself out for the journey with a pair of tight and very short linen pantaloons, a shirt thrown open at neck and sleeves, and a gun. In this light marching order, with stooped shoulders and round back, he stuck himself on a small rough pony, which bore him unfalteringly up and down tracks of headlong steepness, narrow as the Mussulman's bridge to Paradise.

The road now began to be bad, even in the Albanian sense of the word. The hill-side was slashed with ravines, of the character attributed in Scotland to the finger-marks left by the "Devil's grandmother," when scratching her way up from the bottom of precipices, down which she had been thrown by her graceless nurseling. Wherever the path rounds a groove thus scooped by the old dame's finger, it becomes so narrow that a single false step would send horse and rider to the depths below. The ground is, moreover, of a crumbling description, so that rolling stones are always choking the track, and threaten at every moment to efface it altogether. The Albanians ride through thick and thin, and testimony to their recklessness is found in carcasses of horses and stories of neck-broken travellers; indeed, the perilous passages occur so often, that towards the end of a long day, even a Frankish traveller becomes inured to them, and sick of constantly hopping on and off, so that courage and sloth alike incline one to stick to the saddle. Our servants, who heaped rugs and bedding under them till they sat uplifted as on a throne, were naturally loth to descend from an eminence which it took both time and ingenuity to regain. On the other hand, the zaptiés, and all other persons who have good horses, take a care of their property which they would not take of themselves, and on approaching a steep or crumbling bit of road, regularly dismount and lead the horse.

If the way to Vlet Khan was dangerous, fortunately it was short. We found the tent already prepared, and hoped to get early to bed. But here a difficulty occurred about provisions. Having procured nothing at our last night's lodging, we did not as usual come provided, and had to wait till our supper could be bargained for. The people said that milk had already been sent for; but the flocks were far off on mountain pasture, and if the messenger ever went, he certainly did not return. A number of fowls were running about the doors; but at first the khangee refused to sell them, and finally professed himself unable to have them caught. A good hour was wasted in fruitless attempts at catching chickens; now chasing them, then casting stones at them, while of course between each effort the hunters sat down to rest and smoke. At last, having finished all our part of the evening preparations, we awoke to the fact that supper was no nearer, and desperately desired a couple of fowls to be *shot*.

This fell in with the humour of the natives; forthwith, a gun was discharged right into the khan, causing the tethered horses to plunge frantically, and sending the startled poultry in a screaming flutter about our heads. One chicken sank wounded to the ground, and thereupon the executioner walked up with a demand for bakshish.

Thus, after all, it was late when we retired to rest. Weary and unrefreshed, we slept ill, and next morning there were symptoms of fever.

Now, since our misadventure at Gornishevo, all bugbears seemed to us as nothing compared with fever, which renders one low-spirited and restless, and lays one up in a dirty khan. Nothing avails to avert these kind of attacks like timely rest. Therefore, although the khan of Vlet lay in the very centre of the most notorious country on our road, though nothing could be more ill-advised than to expose our baggage and purses to the tender mercies of its owners one hour longer than was necessary, yet, to escape fever, we determined to risk all else, and to remain where we were and to rest one whole day. In this resolve we were strengthened by the circumstance that we must have started without a supply of food, and could not tell what we should find on the way; also, that this khan stands in a healthy open spot among hills and running streams, while, for aught we knew, our next quarters might lie low on the borders of some swamp.

The announcement that we meant to stay all day produced great dissatisfaction and hubbub. The khangee did not wish to take the trouble of getting us provisions, our servants did not like the trouble of urging him, the zaptié disapproved of our lingering in a dangerous spot; worst of all, the headstrong kiradgee, being paid at so much per horse, not at so much per day, was anxious to hurry to the journey's end. "Well," said we to ourselves, "it is very plain that we shall not get our will done here with a good grace, so if we must insist, let it be for something worth insisting on." One of us came forth, and without appearing to notice their displeasure, gave directions for a boy to go to the flocks and bring back a good supply of milk, sufficient for tea and for *café au lait;* also a kid, for we were tired of chickens. A fire was to be lighted outside the khan, and coffee, toast, and roast meat were to be prepared. It was added, that those who brought provisions from a distance should be adequately paid, and that when we remained an extra day on the road, the food of the horses should be added to the payment for their hire, and paid for when we got to Skadar. Having given these directions, we both remained shut up in the tent. Without, there was an interval of silence, then whispers, then mutterings, and at last a chorus of voices vociferating Albanian in their angriest key. After a while we interrupted it by calling to our dragoman, and desiring him to tell the others to be quiet. He answered in a querulous voice: "I will tell them so; but first I must tell one thing to you. The kiradgee declares that he did not bring money with him sufficient to pay the horses' food for more than a night or two; that if you stay here, you must immediately give him ninety piastres, or else he will go away with his horses, and leave us all where we are." As this conciliatory speech came to an end, the audience, who evidently knew its import, confirmed it by a burst of wrathful sounds. The kiradgee talked loud and in a determined and threatening tone, while neither cavass nor zaptié attempted to quiet him, evidently cowed by his bullying, and thinking he had the best of it on his own ground. Perhaps we were as frightened as they, but, luckily, we had two sets of fears which counterbalanced each other. To be left in the midst of this wilderness, three days from Prizren, three from Skadar, ill, and insufficiently guarded, was certainly a perilous position; but equally perilous, so it seemed to us, would it be to unpack our boxes in this robber's den, get out money, and pay it on threat. Once let these people see gold, and that we were to be frightened into parting with it, and between exorbitant payments and ever-recurring bakshish, they would soon fleece us of every para. Having so fleeced us, the kiradgee would scarcely choose to face the pasha and consuls at Scutari, and might leave us *plantées là*, after all.

Each possibility weighing equally with the other, the scale was turned by that propensity to resist which naturally arises when an attempt is made to bully one. After a short consultation, we said deliberately from within the tent, "Dragoman, you must inform the kiradgee, that by demanding money on the road he is breaking the agreement made before the pasha of Prizren, therefore we will have nothing more to do with him. Let him begone." Then, after a moment's pause: "We shall stay here till we are rested, and despatch the zaptié to Scodra with a letter to the *French* consul; he will send for us, and will also telegraph to Prizren, to let the pasha know how the kiradgee has behaved."

It was a mercy that our expedient was not put to the test; for, as it happened, although we did not know it, the French consul to whom we had letters was not then at Scutari, nor was any one there who could or would have acted promptly or imperiously enough to help us. But with these barbarians, our experience proved what instinct had suggested; viz., that a firm front scares them, as it does a turkey-cock. The tone of the dragoman, when translating our last words, already sounded reassurance, and the tone of the kiradgee when answering them was quite ludicrous in its contrast to that in which we last heard him. Obsequiously, hesitatingly, he framed his excuse. "He did not wish to leave us; he had no thought of breaking his engagement—only, when we got to Scutari would we pay the *ninety* piastres, *i.e.* ten piastres for each horse's food."

"That is already promised."

"Oh, then he begged a thousand pardons, it was all a mistake! He had understood that we objected to pay more than *eighty* piastres!" The dragoman repeating all this, added significantly, "Adesso é contento."

We replied, "Well, for this time we will be content also; but in case those around you never before served travellers who are English, or travellers who carry a firman—bid all lay to heart, that a firman entitles those who bear it to respect from every subject of the Sultan; and that what English people say, they mean."

This last message the dragoman repeated in a sententious and haughty tone, which caused us to shake with stifled laughter, especially when we heard the emphasis which marked the comfortable word firman. Amid abject professions from the kiradgee, and exclamations of "God forbid!" from the rest of the men, the khan emptied and the great door was closed.

A HIGH ROAD IN NORTHERN ALBANIA.

That day we rested on a hard-fought field. The milk was brought, the kid was brought, and never in Turkey did we live better, or pass hours more undisturbed than during our halt in the khan of Vlet.

At this date we find in a note-book a list of Albanian words in daily use. Our cavass told us that he found the pronunciation of the Ghegga population so far different from the Tosk, that every sound was more guttural or more harsh. The term for " good," which he pronounced " meer," was by the Gheggas pronounced " murr," and so on.

The next day's journey was a long one; the Mussulmans themselves advising us not to venture into any of the smaller khans within their territory, inasmuch as the baggage would hardly escape. Push on, said they, for the khan of Kirvet—that stands on the Latin territory—there the Albanians are Christians, and none will steal from you or make you afraid. We had indeed enough of Mussulman khangees; for though our present host sent two of his men to see us safely out of his district, he not only made a difficulty about selling us necessary food, but finally demanded a huge price for our entertainment. " Do you think," cried he, " that I would have cleaned the floor of my stable and poured water to lay the dust, even for my own father—how much less for a party of Ghiaours?" When this speech was made we were already outside the khan, but he resolutely shut the doors of the court on our servants, till the kiradgee interfered, admonishing him to abate his terms, and to let the payment stand as part of a debt which the innkeeper owed to him (the kiradgee). The morning before, the carrier had declared himself in need of funds to pay his bill at this very khan. To effect their escape, the servants agreed to pay what the kiradgee required, and he then liberated them, remarking that he would get the money repaid to him at Scodra, or have our lives.

Having delivered himself of this threat, our eccentric guide resumed all his hilarity, and proceeded to fulfil an oft-repeated promise of showing us where "the pope broke his neck." The road seemed singularly propitious for such an incident, and it was an agreeable surprise to find that we were exempted from going over it; the bed of a stream, being dry at this season, left us room to pass round the foot of the rocks. Overhead we saw the path, without a vestige of parapet, running along the face of the crumbling cliff. The narrow and dangerous portion of it continued throughout a long way, and for this reason the priest, an old man and weary, was unwilling to pass over it on foot. The kiradgee said that, as in duty bound, he had warned and urged him to dismount. At last the priest himself took fright, and attempted to get off in the narrowest part of all. Of course this was the worst thing he could have done, and whether the bank gave way under him, or his descending weight pulled the horse off his balance, beast and rider fell sheer over the precipice to the very bottom. When his companions got down to him he was still breathing; but he could not be moved, and there he died.

When, from listening to this dolorous story, we turned our attention to what was going on around, we saw that the pass had peopled itself with Albanians of every age and size, from old men to quite young boys, all in ragged and dirty white garments, and all carrying long guns. As they seemed to go the same way as ourselves, and to resolve their movements into an order of march, we conjectured that they meant no ill. Presently the zaptié, taking occasion to fall behind, informed us that as the glens hereabouts swarm with haïduks, or rather, as every inhabitant is a haïduk, he had by the pasha's order called on a number of men to augment our escort. "And who are they?" we asked, "are they zaptiés?" He answered, "They are the very individuals who, if they were not guarding, would be robbing you."

We passed several hamlets hidden in the green wood, whence issued a crowd of ragged begging children, swarming out of the bushes, the rocks, the water—wherever they happened to be disporting themselves—to pursue us with uplifted hands and cries. If their company was unpleasant we had ourselves to thank for it, having imprudently bestowed on the first we met the extravagant alms of a whole piastre.

At last the ravine came to an end, and we had to begin climbing anew. Our road passed the door of a khan, and we wished to stop a little to rest; but this the zaptié forbade, and hurried us on. We soon knew why. At this khan all the ragamuffins composing our escort came to a halt, and were relieved by another party. Apparently they expected us to halt too, and when we did not they overtook us, marching in somewhat threatening array, and calling on the zaptié in tones of remonstrance. To our surprise he did not as usual refer to us for orders, nor even desire the dragoman to translate; he held parley on his own account, and in a determined and authoritative tone. We took the hint, and did not interfere.

Soon the colloquy assumed no friendly aspect; we saw the faces of the Albanians darken, they rattled their belt-arms, shifted their guns about menacingly, scowled at us, and finally began talking among themselves. Suddenly the zaptié broke on their consultation, and pointed to us with outstretched arm. We heard the word "firman" uttered in a voice of thunder. "Yok, yok," (no, no), cried the Albanians, with deprecatory gestures; the guns were replaced on every shoulder and the company turned to go. Presently one of them came back, approached our guard coaxingly and whispered to him; the zaptié relaxed his frown and replied in gracious tones. Then the whole party walked off, and we proceeded in peace. We observed, however, that no one escorted us except the two men from the khan of Vlet.

When fairly out of sight and hearing of our late companions, the zaptié halted and explained what had passed. "Rogues, villains, robbers," began he—"such are these men, every one of them. I called on them to guárd you from haïduks, and they proved haïduks themselves. They followed us to ask for bakshish. I know what bakshish means. Whatever they crave you must give, it is robbery under a fairer name. So at once I refused. I said you were travelling with the Sultan's firman, and all of us, from the pasha downwards, were bound to serve you without bakshish. You saw how they took my answer; they began to rattle their guns, so I thought it best to cut matters short. I pointed to you, and cried out, 'Here they are with the Sultan's firman on their persons, shoot them if you dare; if not, let us pass." On that you heard them cry, 'Yok, yok.' The rogues! I am up to their bullying ways."

We asked what the last Albanian had returned to crave of him? "Only this, that as we had not given bakshish to them I would promise to give it to no one else. Our only excuse for not giving them bakshish must be that we gave it to none. This I promised gladly, as you may believe."

"But because you have promised to give no bakshish, the second edition of our escort has not chosen to come on with us?"

"Never mind; now we can do without them."

"But," cried the dragoman, "we must promise something to the two men from the khan of Vlet, else they likewise will turn back, and we shall be left alone." Here we also interposed, saying, that the men had walked a long way, and in common justice must have reward.

But the zaptié was not to be moved. His word was pledged, and of all hazards the greatest would be to let the Albanians find out it had not been kept. If we gave to one we must to all, so on this day's march nothing was to be given. We had to acquiesce, for he was responsible for our safety.

The Vlet men walked on before us yet awhile; then they interchanged words, and when we came to a comfortable seat under a spreading tree, they sat them down and allowed us to pass by. The zaptié said, "It cannot be helped; the next guard-house is not far off—we must press on, and get there before meeting any one." But the road was not favourable for pressing on, being drawn threadlike athwart the side of precipices; the zaptié no longer dismounted, even at the most ticklish places, and we followed him without a word. To make things better, our cavass chose this situation for getting into a dispute with the kiradgee. The Tosk used an Albanian word which the Ghegga supposed to convey an insult; the Ghegga forbade it to be uttered in his presence; the Tosk declared that in his country it had no offensive meaning, and repeated it over and over again. Fortunately the whole length of our single file cavalcade was interposed between the disputants; the kiradgee being in front, the zaptié stopped so as to keep us all back until he had got on well ahead, and then sternly enforced on the cavass the necessity of maintaining a conciliatory demeanour.

Having doubled this stormy point, we came on another, which perhaps involved the greatest risk of all.

The way led across a gravel bank sliding down into a deep ravine; the loose stones and dust had effaced the path so that it scarcely showed the prints of human footsteps, while, as if to warn quadrupeds from attempting it, just beneath lay a horse's skeleton. Yet across this slide the zaptié rode, and we following him, scarce saw where we were going until too far on to halt.

Without a word, without daring to look back, and dreading every moment to hear the crash of a fall behind, those in front passed on in succession. Slowly, slowly—one, two, three, four, five—each horse footed its way over the slide.

The zaptié only paused to see that we were all on the right side of this "bad step," and then rode hastily on, till in about a quarter of an hour we found ourselves at the wished-for guard-house. Then, for the first time, he spoke, saying:—"I knew very well that was not a place for you to ride over, but to dismount would have made a noise, and to lead the horse would have taken time, and there was no saying who might hear and who might come."

This was the climax of our troubles. After it we got on without accident worse than a hail shower, and that deferred its descent until we were within short distance of a khan.

The clearing off of this storm showed the wooded hill scenery in all its wild luxuriant grandeur, and we enjoyed many a view such as can only be seen in primæval forest-land. From the woods we at length emerged on an open highland, and over this made our way to the night's quarters, which we did not reach till dark.

Every rug and wrap in the bundles was dragged out to cover us in the khan of Kirvet, for its situation is one of those bleak uplands which know not summer, and are colder than the hill-top. Here, however, we went to sleep with the comfortable consciousness of safety, and next morning the zaptié, the kiradgee, and all who knew the country, congratulated us on having entered the Christian land, for now no danger was to be feared. We here tell only what was told to us by guides themselves Mahommedans, and therefore not partial witnesses. We ourselves remarked that the Latin khangee used no threats, that in the kulas guards were ready to march, and relieved each other without solicitation or demur; also from time to time a person better dressed than the rest would respectfully greet us in Italian. Yet every one to his taste! to us this last stage of the journey between Prizren and Scutari, although the least perilous, was the most wearisome. Danger awakes a corresponding excitement; but oh! the patience that is called for in order to sit a tired horse stumbling over ground where every footstep falls on a stone.

If we had not known the Adriatic country, we really should have wondered where we were getting to, when we found the soil, the grass, the mosses, all vanishing from a skeleton of rock. The pudding-loving Austrians, who are condemned to garrison inhospitable Dalmatia, have some ground for their hypothesis that the stalwart race of men that line this coast, having nothing else to live on, live on the fine air. But the coast of the Adriatic is "fayrie land," according to the Scotch idea of "fayrie"—that is to say, it is at once wretched and fascinating; such is the witchery of its beauty, that you cannot help falling in love with it, let physical discomforts torment you as they may. While we marked the soil dwindle from beneath our horses' feet, giving place to sharp bare points of white bleached rock—as we exchanged the fir, the beech, the hazel, for silver-lined olives and wild figs—as the atmosphere became sun-dried and rarefied, and the lights and colours grew clearer and more clear, we felt the old magic telling on us, and fairly cheered the first glimpse of that blue and silvery sea, the Signe Moré * of Serbian song.

When we descended from the hill-top into the stifling valley our way-weariness made itself felt, and we were almost desperate with fatigue before reaching the khan of Dugagne. At this point we endeavoured to gain information as to our distance from Scutari. One nonchalant Albanian said we were three hours' off, another four, another six, till we felt we could not rely on a word. We did not choose to risk arriving late at night, considering the chances that nothing might be prepared for us, and that our letters sent from Prizren by private hand might not yet have reached the consuls of Skadar. Fortunate that we thus judged—the said letters arrived after we had been at Skadar a week.

The khan at Dugagne has a separate room, and its landlord appeared far more obliging and acquiescent than any we had found on the way. But it was still so early, that hearing of another khan about two hours farther on, we resolved to make that our night's quarters, and sent on our baggage and tent.

The extra time we occupied in visiting an Albanian homestead. At Prizren we had heard from the priests that a large household dwelt near Dugagne, which might be taken as a good specimen of its kind. One of this family happened to be loitering about the khan, and in answer to our inquiries he at once welcomed us to visit his abode. The family mansion stood in a field, and at the foot of a hill. It consisted of two parts, the so-called

* Pronounce Signe, Dugagne, Trebigne, and all similar names, as they would be pronounced in a French song, accent on the second syllable, and the final *e* slightly sounded. The Latin-Croatian alphabet expresses this sound by the combination *nje*.

house, devoted to the kitchen, women, and children, and the kula, a fortress which was solidly built, and provided with loopholes through which to shoot on a besieging foe. The whole presented a very unromantic, uncastle-like appearance, and in comfort was decidedly on the lowest par. The reception room was in the kula. Thither we were led upstairs through several small apartments, empty and uncarpeted, to a balcony, where the only two men of the family who happened to be at home reclined and smoked. One of them was the head of the house, a stubborn, sulky-looking fellow; the other proved more intelligent, and spoke Slavonic. He told us that he had been among the Montenegrīnes, and witnessed so warmly to their good treatment of the last batch of Albanian prisoners, that we almost suspected he must have been amongst the number. He energetically declared that the Miridites did not bear arms against Montenegro in the last war, and that they never would do so in future. He and his family spoke favourably of the late chief, Bib Doda, and very sulkily of his treatment by the Porte. They said he was a brave warrior, and hinted the Porte had put him out of the way because he expressed the feelings of his countrymen in not taking part against their brother-Christians. How far this supposition is correct, of course we are not in a position to decide; but we may here mention, that while Bib Doda was at Constantinople, a Montenegrīne voivode asked if the British ambassador could be persuaded to interest himself in securing that he got back to Albania safe and sound. We remarked that, the Miridite being a Latin, a Protestant representative would probably not feel justified in interfering in his concerns with the Porte. "My God!" exclaimed the mountaineer, "are we never to cease hearing of Latins, Protestants, and Orthodox, and never to begin hearing of *Christians* helping each other as bond-brothers. Even we Serbs, whom you call barbarous, are beginning to get over such divisions, and will the civilised English allow themselves to think of them." The speaker was no Montenegrine educated in Paris, but an elderly man of the old school.

In the balcony lay a gusla, and at our request the young Miridite began to play on it, and that much faster, and in a more lively style than we had hitherto heard. With affected bashfulness he refused to sing, which we much regretted, for, to judge from wild fragments sung by the kiradgee, there must be some not unpleasing Albanian airs. In laying down the gusla, he asked us if we had heard it played in Montenegro, remarking that in that country women were allowed to try their skill. "And are they not so with you?" asked we. He repeated our question to the master of the house, who exclaimed brusquely, suiting the action to the words, "If we catch them at it we hew off their hands." His companion seemed rather ashamed of such barbarity, and tried to atone for it by telling us that they allow their women the use of the gun, and that they are capital shots. "Ay," rejoined his surly brother, "better shots than many a man."

We asked what were the occupations of the women when not engaged in shooting, and were told that they nurse the babies, cook, and spin. Then, observing that we were curious about them, the brothers carried their politeness so far as to ask if we would come downstairs and see the "house." This proved to be a separate building, or rather shed, used for every purpose of domestic economy except sleeping, for which the inhabitants adjourn to the more secure kula. Three or four women seemed busy cooking, and though not old, were withered and red-nosed, with figures that looked utterly shapeless in bundled-up bodies and kilted petticoats.

ALBANIANS IN MOUNTAINS ABOVE SCODRA.

We could not but regard that jealousy as most unreasonable which debarred them from singing to the gusla for fear of their too great fascinating powers.

Dugagno is a pretty spot, and well watered, we rode from it over a wilderness of stones to a dry feverish site, where our ill-luck destined us to pass the night. Yet this spot, though barren, and lacking even a well, was not devoid of interest. The high grey rocks rear themselves above it in fantastic shapes, and not far off the river Drina forces its way through a causeway of crags, and broadens out into the Skadar plain. Near the khan there is a little church, apparently old, but lately restored. The French consul at Scutari was named as the person who had caused it to be rendered fit for Divine worship; perhaps he also caused the new Latin cross to be inscribed over the doorway, and thus may have appropriated to Roman Catholic use an old temple of the Orthodox rite. The rest of the building is in what we had learned to call the Serbian style; and what now stands for a whole church seemed to us as if originally it had formed part of a larger edifice. While supper was preparing we spent some time in examining this church and wondering what might be the epoch of its foundation. Nothing we had yet seen warranted us in attributing it to Albanians; but the Venetians may have built it, or more probably the Serbians, for the ground we now tread belonged to the old Serbian principality of Zeta.*

The khan, which is intended for the convenience of travellers crossing the Drina, was, at the time of our visit, a new one, and contained two tiny rooms on the higher story; however, our tent being ready, we remained below. Perhaps we should have done better to

---

* M. Hecquard mentions several such churches, known to have been founded under the Serbian rulers. He also notes that throughout the Miridite country the people communicate in both kinds and have Greek crosses on their churches. In Orosh there is such a cross, very old.

use the upper chambers, however small; certainly we could not have been worse off than where we were, for the heat was stifling, and in proportion to the heat the unsavoury exhalations, the stinging and creeping things. Having borne it all till past midnight, in hopes that then the air must be cool, we could bear it no longer; we called our servants, broke up the encampment, and were on the road to Scodra, so soon as there was a glimmer of light to show the way.

To our great joy and refreshment we found that the first thing to be done was to ford the Drina. In the delicate light of early morning it would be impossible to imagine a lovelier scene. A broad expanse of shallow water, thronged with figures of men and horses, lies like a silver-paved court in front of those half-open rock-gates through which the river pours into the plain. The rocks, whose colour by daylight is a hard and colourless grey, are now dipped in the halo of dawn—a pale rose-leaf tint slowly brightening into crimson and orange, until it glows like flame on cliff and shore, and mirrors itself in the glassy stream. Deep in shadow, on the further brink of the river, there lies one of those bowery glens that redeem the aridity of Adriatic landscape—a group of small white houses, half buried in the olive wood, nestle in a crevice of the crag.

Through the cool plashing water our horses slowly waded to the opposite bank, and now we found ourselves on the road to Scutari market, in company with numbers of country people driving asses laden with poultry and fruit. The track became something like a road partly bordered with hedgerows, and the dust, which lay thick on every leaf, caused us to congratulate ourselves on the early departure which had given us the start of sun and wind. Yet even as it was, when we quite emerged from the shade of the rocks, a sharp burning stroke, falling on the back of the neck, warned us to hasten to shelter.

The sun's rays, before they fell on us, lighted up certain pale, vague masses, lying beyond us on the plain, and we saw that these were our goal. Yet a long hour elapsed before we found ourselves entering the "city on the Bojana"—beneath the rock of the ill-starred "white castle of Skadar."

CHAPTER XXXIII.

SCUTARI IN ALBANIA, SCODRA, OR SKADAR.

WITH SOME NOTES ON THE PRINCIPALITY OF ZETA, OF WHICH IT WAS SOMETIME THE CHIEF TOWN.

SCUTARI IN ALBANIA, as diplomatists call it, was named by the Turks Iskendrié, probably from associations with the Albanian hero Scanderbeg. The Serbians call it Skadar, and have some right to call it what they please, seeing that they built its fortress and held the district about 700 years. Perhaps, however, the oldest name is that of Scodra, still in use among the Albanians, and which is to be found in the account given by Livy of a Roman expedition into these lands.

But what's in the name of a city in the Ottoman empire, so long as, call it what you will, it answers to the same lamentable description—natural advantages unimproved, trade hampered, streets ill-built, and inhabitants ignorant and misruled.

Such a Turkish city is Scodra; but nature has marked it out for a flourishing emporium between the sea-coast and the interior.

To the north lies the one great lake in the South-Slavonic lands, "Skāderski jezero," as it is called in Serbian song; its northern, western, and part of its eastern shores are inhabited by Serbians; the southern and south-eastern by Skipetārs. Between Scodra and the Adriatic, uniting the lake with the sea, runs a large stream, the Bojana, considered by the inhabitants as the continuation of a stream flowing from Montenegro, of which the current is perceptible in its course through the lake. This river, which in its two parts forms the link between the country north and south of the lake of Scodra, is called Zenta, or Zeta, and has given its name to this whole district, at least since the days of Justinian.

Another river flows through the plain of Scodra into the Adriatic at Alessio—the Drina, formed by the confluence of two branches: the Black Drin from the lake of Ochrida, and the White Drin, our fellow traveller from the plain of Metochia.

To complete these natural advantages by rendering the city available as a place of defence, a ridge of low hills, rising near the southern outlet of the lake, culminates in a fine rock, which has been fortified since the earliest times.

Thrice, say the old chroniclers, have the inhabitants of Scodra built a city on this site. First they occupied a part of the plain on each side of a small river, the Chiri, and on this town being destroyed by an incursion of barbarians they took refuge on the Castle rock, and built a new city round the fortress in the form of a cone. This, which was probably the town occupied by the Serb rulers from the seventh century to 1401, passed from them to the Venetians, the Hungarians, and back to the Venetians, till, in 1477, it was taken by the Turks and ruined, after which the present position was fixed on about a mile further east.

From the time of the Turkish conquest to the first half of the present century, the government of Scodra was held by native families, especially by the great house Bouchatti, which traced its descent to a renegade branch of the Serbian princes of Zeta. Lately, in Albania as in Bosnia, Turkish officials have taken the rule out of the hands of the local Mussulmans, and have thereby greatly diminished their affection for the Sultan's sway. During the Montenegrine war of 1862, Scutari in Albania became known to newspaper readers as the head-quarters of Omar Pasha. At the time of our visit, the inhabitants of the town and district still complained of the presence and burden of a number of troops.

Having given these few historical particulars, we must go back to our own entry into the town, and tell of matters concerning it in the order in which they came under our observation.

Although from a distance Scutari makes a fair show, it is so stragglingly built that on nearer approach it seems less a town than an aggregation of villages, or rather of 4500 detached houses, gardens, and courtyards.

One of the first objects that attracted our attention was a large Roman Catholic church in process of erection.

Until the French consul, M. Hecquard, set this work on foot, the Latins worshipped in the open air; moreover, they had no school, and in his book he calls on France and Rome to give them one, if only to prevent their entire dependence on instruction provided by Austria. The Serbian (Orthodox Slāv) community, although far less numerous than the Latins, have contrived to build a little church for themselves, and pay for a school out of their communal fund.

While still nearly a mile from the part of Scodra called the town, we passed through the bazaar, where the shops were already open.

A good living is here made by tailors, who display on their stalls the grandly embroidered jackets worn both by men and women. Those with long dangling sleeves cost from £7 to £10. Unfortunately it is now becoming the fashion to wear gloomy and undecided colours, and patterns supposed to be French; with some difficulty, and only by taking a velvet vest already worn, did we procure a specimen of the true Albanian crimson embroidered in a grotesque and original style. Women returning from early shopping met us in large cloaks of scarlet cloth embroidered with gold; as we never saw a garment of the species near enough to judge of all its peculiar characteristics, we can only say that, except that they are longer and wider, they reminded us of those worn in Salonica.

At last, having for some time wandered about, and more than once stopped at the wrong door, we arrived at the British consulate.

The British consul then at Scutari was the late Sir Francis Gilbert, who at the time of our visit was in a weak state of health, aggravated by a disastrous accident, to which we shall presently allude. This, however, did not deter him from showing us every courteous kindness, and assisting us so far as we required throughout the short time of our stay. The letter of introduction sent from Prizren did not indeed reach him till long after we were in Scutari ourselves, but he had already been prepared to see us by a notice from Monastir, and a packet of letters from home was awaiting us in his care.

It was at the consulate that we paid the kiradgee, in case of his repeating extravagant demands. But that worthy, so bold on his own ground, no sooner saw us under adequate protection than he became meek as a lamb; and when every para of the stipulated sum was paid to him, even to the khan bill extorted at Vlet, his joy knew no end and he bounded like a kid. Our dragoman thought fit to improve the occasion, and said to him, "We know quite well that the payment you made us promise at Vlet is more than you are entitled to, but having been promised, it is paid." The kiradgee answered with an exclamation of high glee, "I now see that with English travellers it is an unnecessary precaution to demand payment in advance."

A still more satisfactory parting took place with the zaptié, who had proved far the best specimen of his class we ever knew. He was a tall, large, elderly man, dressed in dark colours, without a single ornament or a single rag—which sobriety and solidity of clothing made it scarcely possible to credit that he was by birth an Albanian, though mellowed by long absence from home. After being paid he asked permission to say good-bye to ourselves, and then expressed very gravely and heartily his satisfaction at seeing us safely housed after the dangers of that "desperate road." We thanked him as the person to whose wisdom and courage we mainly owed our safety; then casting about in our minds what we could add to his bakshish by way of a special compliment, we bethought ourselves of writing a testimonial in German for the Austrian consul to read to the pasha. This opportunity served not only to praise the zaptié, but to warn against making over other travellers to the kijaja's pet kiradgee.

Trusting to what we had heard of the comparative civilisation of Scodra, we did not send our bujourdi before us to the pasha, or apply to the authorities for quarters. We hoped to be able to find some sort of hotel or lodging and to hire for ourselves; nor were we disappointed. The rooms found for us by the consul's cavass, although by no means elegant or convenient, had about them more of Dalmatia than of Turkey. They were kept by a woman from Ragusa, and, though not up to the style even of Ragusan *locande*, yet they boasted a few European luxuries, such as beds, tables, washing-stands, and chairs. Theoretically we preferred the Turkish kind of room, with its range of windows, open fire-place, gaily clad divans, and ample space; nevertheless, when coming in tired, we rejoiced unfeignedly not to be called on to furnish a bed-chamber for ourselves.

We had a good deal of little business to get through at Scodra. From thence it was necessary to send back the careful and well-trained young cavass lent us by the consul at Monastir, and we had to look out for some one to fill his place. Then too we had to find a merchant who could and would cash bills on Trieste; and lastly we resolved to bring away some specimens of the work and costumes for which this district is renowned. The perquisitions requisite to compass these objects helped us to make the acquaintance of divers specimens of the population; yet we found that Scodra, like all semi-europeanized towns in Turkey, is a less favourable position for knowing the natives than the unsophisticated districts in the interior.

No doubt if 'you want to see Albanians, whether Mahommedans or Latins, this is the place for it; nowhere else will you behold so grand a show of flouncing fustanellas, such long-tasselled fezes, such grandly embroidered jackets, or such a chevaux de frise of arms sticking out of every belt. The swaggering bullying manner of the skipetār is here shown off to the full; the pasha supplied us with horses and zaptiés, and when we rode abroad the zaptiés would make a show of fierceness in driving even an old woman out of the road. When recruits were wanted for the Montenegrine war these fine fellows suddenly vanished from the bazaar, and had to be sought under the divans of their harems. Many when brought to close quarters ran away or suffered themselves to be taken prisoners, whilst some simply refused to fight at all, turning their pistols on their

Turkish commander when ordered to disembark on Montenegrïne ground. To this behaviour witness was borne by the Italian and British consuls, while a Turkish officer told the English engineer of the steamer that he would be sorry to command a thousand of the men of Scodra opposed to one hundred Montenegrïnes. Of course in reckoning anecdotes like these, allowance is to be made for the fact that the Albanians loathe the Osmanli, and that the objection they showed to fight the Montenegrïnes in the Sultan's quarrel by no means applied in former times to fighting them in quarrels of their own. Moreover, on this occasion the Montenegrïnes lost no opportunity of announcing that they wished to be friends with all Christian tribes, and many Skipetār clans, whose bravery cannot be doubted, were exceedingly slow to move in behalf of the Turks.

Distinct alike from the mountain warriors and from the showy flaneurs in the bazaar, is the class of Scutarine silk merchants, who are mostly Latins, and seem to be an industrious and thriving set of men. With one of these we made acquaintance in the person of him who cashed our bill, and who afterwards invited us to visit his wife. The firm consisted of three brothers, whose wives jointly inhabited one handsome dwelling. Our acquaintance was the second brother, and he remained at home to receive us, while his wife served us with sweetmeats; nevertheless it was the spouse of the elder brother who did the honours as lady of the house.

The dress of these dames was exceedingly rich, but as tastelessly composed and as awkwardly put on, as if they had belonged to the middle class in Germany. They wore voluminous trousers of purple gauze, but instead of allowing them to fall over the feet—which is the graceful fashion of the interior districts—they caught them up above the ankle in a bulge. The head gear was formed of ornaments and a red handkerchief. A red waistcoat was worn over a red striped dress, and a hideous adjunct to the toilette was formed by an apron, or rather a shawl folded square, pinned across the whole front of the person with a certain appearance of prudery. A little girl belonging to one of the ladies was brought in; on examination it proved that she wore three jackets, one over the other, all richly embroidered and each more or less hid by its supernumerary companions. After we had partaken of coffee and sweetmeats, the latter consisting in delicious bon-bons and dried Nice fruits, we were shown some choice bits of white silk gauze. Scodra is famed for this manufacture, and some very fine pieces had been brought to these ladies in order that they might each choose a dress for their approaching visit to Milan. The brother merchants were about to emigrate at least for several years, and instead of letting their wives buy clothes in Italy they resolved to provide them with a trousseau beforehand. The piece of silk we most admired was in the original style of the country, *i.e.*, crêpé in furrows like curly hair. But the favourite of the three ladies was that which most resembled French gaze de soie, and one such had been chosen for their best gowns.

The next object of exhibition was of a very different character, viz., the little girl's new book of devotion, which she had yet to learn to read. It was Albanian on one side and Italian on the other, and the open page contained a commentary on the Ave Maria. The father of the household then held forth a little on the education of women in Scutari, which he represented as nil— "perhaps no bad thing, since, should they become more intelligent, they might become less passive members of society, and no longer consent to be handed over to husbands they had never seen." We hinted that such a custom involved a degree of passiveness on the husband's part at least as astonishing as that on the bride's; whereupon he laughed, and said that, after all, the practice answered very well; he believed there were as few unhappy marriages in Scodra as elsewhere; adding, with a kindly look at the dames, "We three brothers, at least, have no reason to complain, and we married our wives without having seen them previously."

The recent cession of the Ionian Islands furnished matter for a little political discussion. The merchant wondered if "England intended to carry out her public professions on this subject to their logical consequences, and acquaint the Sultan that she could no longer *assist him* in keeping down peoples that would infinitely prefer to govern themselves." We in return asked whether, if the Albanians were to be emancipated from Osmanli rule, they would prefer to unite with Greece as a whole, or to be divided, the Tosks joining Greece, and the Northern Albanians joining the Slāvs. He answered cautiously, "Those are right who believe that the Albanians hereabouts have far more sympathy for the Slāv than for the Greek." We afterwards heard another Latin of Scodra excuse the lukewarmness of the citizens during the war, by saying, "The truth is, most of them expected the Christian powers to help the Prince of Montenegro, and would not have been sorry to see him enter Scodra."

There would seem to be no place in Turkey where the Christians are less oppressed than in Scodra, because of the neighbourhood of their powerful kinsfolk, the Albanian Miridites and the Montenegrīnes. Still the townsfolk are sufficiently outnumbered and hectored over by the Mahommedan element to dread coming forward in witness of injuries committed by Mussulmans against themselves, even after begging for consular interference; and wherever this reluctance exists it may be taken as a sign that they do not feel certain either that a sentence in their favour will be carried out, or that in the end they will not be made to suffer for having called in Frankish aid against the Turks.* In such cases nothing can give the Christian courage except the personal character of the consul who undertakes his case; the weak know by instinct the sort of man who will really stand up on their behalf. Hitherto in Scutari the only agent who inspired this confidence was the French consul, who cared less for a punctilious observance of the rules of etiquette, or even of legality, than he did for throwing such weight into the scale of the Christian as shall enable him to balance the Turk. No doubt his ways and means were sometimes not very scrupulous. Neither in Turkey nor elsewhere, is a roll in the dust, with a sound beating, the legal penalty for jostling one's neighbour in the street. Yet by all accounts M. Hecquard did much for society in Scodra when, some ten years ago, for the first time since the Turkish conquest, a Mussulman Bey was rolled in the dust and soundly beaten by his cavasses, for having pushed out of the road a Christian member of the French consulate. After many years' labour, the same agent made the characteristic announcement—" I am now glad to see that, occasionally, a Christian is insolent to a Mussulman."

The achievement of another French consul is now

* How vain it is to expect that oppressed people will complain openly, or stand to their assertions, when exposed to the vengeance of those against whom their evidence would go, is found in English workhouses as much as in Turkish cities. Unfortunately this has not always been taken account of by persons entrusted to watch that abuses do not occur. It is curious to observe how it was recognised by the old Serbian law, which, when decreeing that the peasant might call his lord into court, took care to decree also that the judge should exact bail from the lord, sufficient to ensure his not taking future vengeance on the peasant.

fairly enrolled among the hero-legends of Scodra. We heard it related at least twenty times in Skadar itself, in Prizren, and in Montenegro. We repeat it as told by the people, without vouching for accuracy of detail. At the time of the Montenegrīne war a certain priest, called Dom Gaspar (Latin priests in Albania are called Dom, even as Scotch schoolmasters used to be called Dominie), dared boldly to preach that it was a sin and a shame for the Roman Catholic Albanians to fight in the interest of Mussulmans against their free Christian brethren the Montenegrīnes. By all accounts this man's sermons addressed themselves to motives far higher and more generous than any that had for ages prompted the deeds of these poor selfish barbarians, and to the credit of the people, he had immense success, while the best possible comment on his lectures was afforded by the studious kindness bestowed by the Prince of Montenegro on the 600 Albanian prisoners who fell into his hands at the beginning of the war. But the Turks by no means approved such doctrines, and after various manœuvres and strenuous bribery got Dom Gaspar into their power, and prepared to send him to Constantinople for trial. Austria is the so-styled protectress of the Roman Catholic Christians in Albania, and according to consular etiquette it was to be supposed that if Austria did not give her consul orders to interfere on Dom Gaspar's behalf, nothing would be done. But the French consul interfered on his own responsibility, and declared that the Porte had no right to meddle with Dom Gaspar's teaching, and that in no case should he be transferred to a Turkish prison from his present scene of usefulness. As a rule there is nothing a consul will say to which a pasha will not seem to agree, but there is nothing a consul can demand which a pasha will not contrive to evade. Having put off the French consul with a series of compliments and speeches, Omar Pasha, then commanding at Scutari, waited for the Mahommedan feast, Bairam, when the Mussulmans filled the streets and were in a state of excited fanaticism, and then quietly ordered Dom Gaspar to be conducted from the town to the sea-coast. Already the priest and his guard were in the street, when the French consul was apprised by his vigilant scouts, and instantly—without waiting to consult with other consuls or remonstrate with the pasha—accompanied only by his two cavasses, he dashed off to the rescue. From the very midst of the guards, surrounded as they were with a Mahommedan crowd, he bore off Dom Gaspar, and brought him safely to the French consulate. Once there, the pasha accepted the logic of facts and attempted nothing more; the Albanians accepted it also, and henceforward Dom Gaspar's teachings were placed on a pinnacle. Poor Bib Doda, as we have seen, was not thus fortunate; but lured off to Constantinople, was tried, acquitted, and never returned.

At the time of our visit to Scodra the prestige of the French agents was not shared by the representative of Her Britannic Majesty; instead of shielding others from injustice, this poor man could not even obtain justice for himself. Shortly before our visit Sir F. Gilbert went to try sea baths at Durazzo, and the following account of what happened there is taken from his own lips. The consul had two cavasses, both Christian Albanians, and while he rested after his bath they obtained permission to walk in the bazaar. Dulcigno being a nest of fanaticisim and of general unmannerliness, they were not long without being insulted as "ghiaours," and so far punished the insult as to push a boy, who was making faces at them, out of their way. The Mussulmans did not attack them then and there, for two stout men, fully armed, would have sold their lives dear; but, rushing to the mudir, they demanded vengeance. The mudir told them he would speak to the consul next day, but meanwhile could do nothing; whereupon the townsmen left him, vowing revenge. The mudir neither warned the consul nor took any steps to maintain order. That night, while all in the consulate were asleep, a body of men came to the gate and craved admittance. The cavasses hastened to the door to ask their business, and forthwith the townspeople fired a volley into the court, and ran away. The consul, suddenly awakened by the noise, hastened to the gate, and found one of his cavasses wounded mortally and weltering in blood. The shock told terribly on the sick man, who scarcely had an hour's sleep for weeks afterwards. At the end of a few months we heard that he had left Scodra and returned to England to die.

Some English travellers happened to visit Scodra at this time, and when the news of the outrage arrived the pasha rushed out of their presence, exclaiming, "The whole set shall be hanged! I'll see them hanged myself!" He showed true Turkish savoir dire, for this indignant outcry was duly chronicled by his auditors; but a month later, when we came to Scodra no one was hanged, and no hanging was intended. In vain the consul demanded justice; it was answered that some of the culprits having got away to the mountains it would be unjust to put the rest to death till all were caught; and nobody took the pains to catch them.

An Italian ship appeared off Dulcigno and was supposed to be an English ship; at once the mudir took steps to secure some of the guilty, but the mistake was discovered before they had been punished; when at length an English ship appeared off Antivari, and the captain came to Scutari, he was obliged to go away without getting more than protestations. Whether eventually any of the assassins were executed we have not heard; but at the time of our visit the case, as generally recognised by the consuls and by the Christian townsmen, was simply that the Turkish authorities did not choose to make an example of Mussulmans for putting to death a ghiaour; the precedent was not one that they desired, and it was perfectly well known that the English government would not quarrel about it. To be sure Albania is not exactly the place wherein to allow the dwellings of European representatives to be fired into with impunity; and the Italian consul said on this subject, "My country is at present a second-rate power, yet I should be very sorry to eat the amount of dirt swallowed by English consuls in Turkey. At least nous autres are not ordered to support, against the native Christians and in opposition to other consular agents, those very Mussulman authorities whose acts we condemn."

And now, speaking of the Italian consul, we may give an idea of some of the difficulties that beset the life of a consul's wife in Turkey, by repeating the story of his charming little *consulessa* as to her arrival in Scodra. Possessed of private means, and provided with all that could make their new abode comfortable, the newly-wedded pair landed at Antivari, and there found the roads in such a state from floods and snows that they had to push on to Scodra on good horses, leaving the baggage to follow when it could. On their arrival they found that the vice-consul had only succeeded in hiring for them a single room; in it they must needs remain for many days, their discomforts being aggravated by the necessity of receiving and paying visits of etiquette. Not till long after did they obtain their luggage, and longer still was it ere they could make a bargain for a house. Then they got it from the owner because it was half ruined. They had to spend large sums before it became habitable; and after all he would only let it for two years, so they were liable to have it soon taken from them. This habit of letting houses in order to get them repaired, and then resuming them, is common in Turkey, and tells heavily on the incomes of such consuls as must provide accommodation for wife and family.

We did not make out a visit to any Mahommedan lady in Scodra—partly we were too tired and the weather too hot to make much exertion, partly we had often enough visited the harems of Turkish officials, and cared not to repeat the process. To the Mussulman Albanian families we had not brought introductions such as those that opened to us the Bosnian harems. If we may believe what we were told, the Scodra Beys are not exempt from the law of decay at work on all of their creed and kind. They are growing poor, the presence of the Turkish officials deprives them of real authority, while the garrison takes off them the responsibility of defending their city; besides, they cannot tax or plunder their Christian townsmen as they did in the good old times. Bouchat, a sort of suburb, built during the Venetian occupation, used to contain handsome country houses belonging to the Mussulmans of Scodra; at present it shows only dilapidated remains; the quarter called Tabachi—formerly the town residence of many Beys, who were at constant war with the rest of the Scutarines—is now little more than a ruin. Involuntarily the Turkish government is doing the native Christians a great service by weakening and impoverishing the local Mussulmans. They will hardly be capable of reasserting their old supremacy even should the Porte be obliged to draw her troops from the Montenegrine frontier to more pressing work elsewhere.

One thing in Scodra Mussulmans and Christians have in common, and that is the legend about the building of its castle. Differing in minor details, both agree that the walls could not be raised until a woman was built up in the foundations; both agree also that the woman when immured was suckling her infant, and that to this day a moisture on the outer wall represents her milk, and is resorted to as a place of pilgrimage by mothers who lack nourishment for their babes. The terrible story connected with its foundation has invested the Castle of Scodra with a reputation of bad luck; possess it who may —and it has had many masters—it brings no good to any of them. Among other evils, it is found to be more fever-ridden than the town, although standing on higher ground; the Turkish commandant has lately been obliged to give up living in it as a bad job.

Rosapha, the name of the castle of Scutari, is sometimes said by the Albanians to be derived from those of its founders, Rosa and his sister Fa; history as well as tradition imputes its erection to Serbian rulers, and one tradition calls these the three brothers Merliávchevic, of whom the eldest, Vukashīne, was king of Zeta, under Czar Dūshan. M. Hecquard, in his description of the fortress, says, that it has scarcely been altered from the original plan, except that the Venetians replaced its square towers with bastions, and that the Turks have let much of it go to ruin. It used to contain several subterranean passages, of which one led to the Bojana; the entrance of this passage was lately found, but no one had the courage to venture into it, so it was covered up again, and the trace lost. Two entrances admit to the castle, one of which is a small postern; the other, on the eastern side, has a portal engraved with the lion of St. Mark, and is reached by a broad but ill-paved road winding up the steep ascent.

By this road we approached the fortress from the bazaar at the foot of the hill.

In the interior of the citadel we found the usual tumble-down houses which serve in Turkey for barracks and magazines, a mosque, which was once a Latin church, and the konak, recently evacuated by the governor. Among the cannon we were shown a gun said to have been taken from the Montenegrines. "The taking of Montenegrine cannon" was one of the jokes current at Constantinople during the course of the war, for after every skirmish with the mountaineers certain journals duly registered "cannon" as taken, varying the number as fancy dictated. An order was published more than once that some of these trophies should be forwarded to the capital; but they came not; and it was whispered that the poor Montenegrines had not as many cannon in the field during the whole war as the journals took from them in a single battle; that the seizures, when not purely imaginary, consisted in the Turks retaking such pieces of their own as the mountaineers had captured in some late skirmish, and were not able to use or carry away. Austria shutting up the ports of the Adriatic against the passage of material of war, the Montenegrines had scarcely any good guns, or even rifles, except what they took from the enemy. The proverb, "Our arsenals and our studs are in Turkey," is no empty boast: the Prince's guard was armed with rifles taken at the battle of Grahovo; and the French used to say that the best way to send a supply of ammunition to Montenegro was to supply some to a Turkish army on the frontier.

To return to the castle. Its position commands at once the course of the Bojana, and the roads that lead between the sea-coast and the interior. H. Hecquard considers that to render it impregnable it would suffice to fortify the hill called Torobos and the mountain Casina, by both of which it is commanded, and which ere this have been turned to account by besiegers. Of such points we of course were no judges; but we long lingered to enjoy the lovely view, which varies at every turn of the castle wall.

On one side there is the town, built on the slopes of little hills and stretching far into the plain; its white houses and bright minarets shining through a bower of trees. From another side your eye can follow the course of the Bojana and its tributary, the Chiri, which flow past Scutari towards the sea-coast, between banks at first covered with houses and gardens, then with green pasture land. But the loveliest view is that of the lake, its surface smooth and bright as a silver shield, overlooked by mountains, some barren, and some wooded— closed at a distance by its rocky islands, and losing itself in a sheeny haze, through which loom the huge forms of the Montenegrine hills.

According to the legend of the country, the waters of the Lake of Scutari cover a number of submerged towns and villages; on calm days it is said that the roofs of houses may be seen through its clear waves.

On the northern shores of this lake lie some spots famous in the early annals of Zeta. The neighbourhood of Podgoritza (hill foot) contains the site of ancient Dioclea, within the territory of Montenegro, and as already mentioned the capital of the first Serbian kings. The district of Podgoritza has still a Christian and Serbian population, and in all parts of Turkey we heard of its stalwart and handsome men. This fame it has enjoyed from early times, and shared with certain Herzegovinian districts bordering on Montenegro. The Montenegrine marches have given birth to most of the leading Serbian families, among others, those of Nemanyic, Tsernoïevic, and

Petrovic of Nïegŭsh. Indeed, some persons allege that the families of Milosh and of Kara George, before distinguishing themselves in Danubian Serbia, emigrated from the borders of Montenegro.

Another celebrated site is Zabliak, last capital of a Zetan prince before driven to bay on the neighbouring Black Mountain.

We twice traversed the Lake of Skadar, once on the Turkish steamer and once in a Montenegrīne barge, which last took us from Rïeka to visit the prince's sister in her house at Tsernitza. On neither occasion did we make out a halt at Podgoritza, but the Montenegrīnes rowed us as close as possible under the foot of the castle hill of Zabliak, telling us all the time how Ivan Tsernoïevic once lived there in his "white castle," and how, rather than become a Mahommedan and hold his land in vassalage of the Sultan, he and his warriors betook themselves to the hills. Near the Montenegrīne village Rïeka, Ivan had a tower called Obod, and somewhere thereabouts he lies buried, or rather sleeping, in a cave, while the vilas watch him. He and Marko Kralïevitch may be expected to awake about the same time.

This Ivan Tsernoïevic, or Ivan Beg, as the Turks called him, was one of those princes of Zeta under whom it maintained independence for about 100 years after the battle of Kóssovo. From the time that the rulers of Serbia took to residing in the inland districts Zeta was frequently the appanage of the second person in the realm. Stephen Némania assigned it to his second son. Stephen Dūshan is said to have held it during the lifetime of his father, and certainly Kral Vukashīne held it during the lifetime of Czar Dūshan. The Merliávchevic family was succeeded by that of Balsha, said to be of Albanian origin, and allied by marriage to the then

ZABLIAK.—CASTLE OF IVAN TSERNOÏÉVIC, LAST PRINCE OF ZETA AND FIRST OF MONTENEGRO.

reigning family in Serbia. Ivan Tsernoïevic, a Serbian of Podgoritza, and a relative to the Balshas, was chosen by the people to succeed them. He was nearly allied to the Albanian prince, George Castriote, better known by his Turkish name Scanderbeg, and shared in most of the victories in which this valiant warrior repulsed the Turks. During these vicissitudes the old capital Dioclea was exchanged for Scodra, Scodra for Zabliak, and at length Zabliak for Cetinje. In Cetinje a chief is to be found at the present day styling himself Prince of the Black Mountain of Zeta.*

All this is matter of history; but it is difficult to say how far there may be historical foundation for the famous legend about Ivan Tsernoïevic wooing a Venetian for his son. This story is the text of a poem, the longest and, some think, the finest effort of Serbian ballad poetry. Its subject, however, is not a pleasing one, nor are its personages the noble characters that come before us in ballads of the era of Czar Lāzar.

From the castle of Scodra, looking north and south, one can see great part of the region that furnishes the scenes of this tale; here, therefore, may be a good place for telling it.

It came to pass, that Ivan Tsernoïevic bethought himself of asking in marriage for his son Maxim the daughter of the Doge of Venice; and he visited Venice in order to arrange the match. While bidding the Doge adieu he made the unguarded boast, that he would

* The late Prince of Montenegro addressed the following circular to the cabinets of the Great Powers of Europe after the Treaty of Paris, 1856: "Dans les conférences de Paris, en présence des plénipotentiaires de toutes les Puissances, Aali Pasha a avancé que la Porte considère le Monténégro comme une de ses provinces. Cette assertion est insoutenable. Les Monténégrins auraient bien plutôt droit de prétendre à la moitié de l'Albanie et à toute l'Herzégovine, puisque mes prédécesseurs, Princes indépendants du Monténégro, Ducs de Zeta (Zenta), ont possédé autrefois ces territoires, tandis que les Turcs n'ont jamais possédé le Monténégro.'

bring across the sea a thousand wedding guests, the Doge might meet him with another thousand, and the bridegroom would bear off the palm of manly beauty from them all. On returning home great was the horror of Ivan to find that during his absence the beautiful Maxim had been afflicted with the smallpox. His limbs remained strong, his figure stately, his eyes clear-sighted, but his face was black and yellow, and scarred, and seamed—in short, says the bard, instead of the handsomest, he had become the ugliest of men. For nine long years Ivan made no further mention of his son's match; at the end of that time the Doge roused him with a letter, upbraiding him for delay. Thereupon Ivan, hoping to make up for Maxim's ugliness by the brilliance of his following and to overawe the bride's relations by the presence of a numerous host, called together all his kinsfolk and their followers to accompany him over the sea. From Antivari and Dulcigno come the lowlanders, from Berda and the Black Mountain the highlanders, from Podgoritza the kinsmen of the Prince, —all gather on the plain of Zabliak. Ivan exults over their number and brilliance, but his nephew, the leader or capetan of the mountaineers, reproaches him for thus drawing off on a distant expedition the flower and the strength of the country, who are wanted to defend it against the advancing Turk. But Ivan will go ; and as he rides over the plain to the sea, and beholds on one side of him the black face of Maxim and on the other the blooming countenance of his cousin Milosh Obrenbegovic of Antivari, an idea strikes him : he may yet redeem his boast ! Milosh shall personate the bridegroom, carry off the palm of beauty at Venice, bring the bride safe to Zabliak, and then resign her to Maxim, receiving for his reward the wedding gifts.

Milosh consents, Maxim dares not object. At

Venice it is acknowledged that Ivan's pledge is amply redeemed; magnificent presents are given with the bride; the sea is crossed in safety, and the capetan of Montenegro, who acts "bride-leader," is riding at the lady's side on the way homeward, when Maxim gallops on to bring the news to his mother. Then Milosh spurring up to the bride, playfully touches her; she looks up, sees his wondrous beauty, and, taking him for her bridegroom, in a transport of delight throws back her veil and holds out her hands. On this, father-in-law Ivan is obliged to explain the deception. Bitterly does the damsel reproach him—not, however, for the cause one might suppose. To her credit it must be said, that she cares not whether her real bridegroom's countenance be blooming or no. He has still, says she, the sight of his eyes, and his heart has not changed with his face. Why, then, should she disregard him? Unfortunately, however, although careless about beauty, the daughter of the merchant city is not indifferent to the loss of the bridal gifts. On this head she utters bitters words and threats, recalls Maxim, and appeals to him to avenge her rights on Milosh. Maxim, already envious and now stung to rage, suddenly strikes his cousin dead. The kinsmen of the slain fall on those of the slayer, a bloody fight covers the plain with dead. The capetan of the Black Mountain dies, seeing his foreboding of disaster come true. As for Maxim, hating the Venetian as the cause of his wicked action, and feeling himself henceforth an outcast among his kinsfolk, he sends her back to her father, and himself leaves the country and goes over to the Turks. So does his cousin, John Obrenbegovic, brother of the murdered Milosh, but from widely different motives. As his relatives bid him adieu, he says to them that he must follow on the track of Maxim, and watch for his attempting to stir up the Sultan against his fatherland. "Maxim is of bad blood," says John, "and will seek to do you a mischief; but if you have to do with him he shall have to do with me. Fear not, my children, so long as you know that I am in Stamboul."

The poem ends by telling how, when the Sultan had taken these countries, he gave to the Obrenbegovic the pashalik of New Dukadjin, in the fertile plain about Ipek, and to Maxim the pashalik of Scodra. The Scodra family, called Bouchatlia, or Bouchatti, from their residence at Bouchat, reigned till 1831, when their representative, Mustapha Pasha, was obliged to leave his country and accept a government in Asia Minor. Strange to say, at one time a member of the house all but returned to Christianity in order to obtain from Austria a promise of the sovereignty of Albania. The Bouchatti pashas were the bitterest enemies of Montenegro. One of the greatest victories the mountaineers ever gained was over Kara Mahmud, whose skull is or was preserved at Cetinje.

The fortunes of the Christian successor of Ivan Tsernoïevic we shall relate when we follow him to Montenegro. Meanwhile we have to do with that part of Zeta which fell under Mussulman government. It is curious to remark how, in this Serbo-Albanian region, the fiercest Mussulman Arnaout families proudly insist on their Serbian lineage, while their most honourable traditions—the traditions woven round the great name of Scanderbeg—celebrate a heroic resistance to the Turk and alliance and kinship with the Serb. Long as the northern Skipetārs and the Montenegrines have worried each other in border forays, long as differences of creed have served them as excuse for violence and pillage, often as the foe has used and may still use their mutual jealousy to turn their swords against each other —nevertheless they yet share, and know that they share, their ancient history and their grudge against the Osmanli. Common memories and common grievances furnish a tolerably broad basis whereon to found an alliance for common interests: should such an alliance ever be realised, those will not be wrong who have observed that the name of Zeta united Serbian and Albanian once, and may again.

We still stood looking on the Lake of Skadar, thinking over the traditions interwoven with its name, its neighbouring plains and cities, and its mountain shores, when we were suddenly reminded of the tale connected with Rosapha by the zaptié telling us he had been making inquiries as to the part of the wall where the woman was immured. When we left the castle the locality was duly pointed out to us, but we could not get to the spot famed as the source of a milky spring. Perhaps our readers have had enough of legends; at any rate, we will not attempt to tell the legend that ought to stand here in our own words, seeing how well it is told by Sir John Bowring in his translations of Serbian poetry. From that source, for those who care to read it, we quote the story of "The Building of Skadra."

The Building of Skadra.

[The quantity of the proper names throughout this poem seems to be regulated by the translator to suit his measure, and differs from that given in the original and in Talvi's German translation. The name Skadar is also given Skadra, its form in the genitive, instead of Skadar the nominative form.]

BROTHERS three combined to build a fortress,
Brothers three, the brothers Mrljavchevich.
Kral Vukashin was the eldest brother;
And the second was Uglesha-Voivode;
And the third, the youngest brother, Goiko.

Full three years they laboured at the fortress,
Skadra's fortress on Bojana's river;

Full three years three hundred workmen labour'd,
Vain th' attempt to fix the wall's foundation,
Vainer still to elevate the fortress:
Whatsoe'er at eve had raised the workmen
Did the Vila raze ere dawn of morning.

When the fourth year had begun its labours,
Lo! the Vila from the forest mountain
Call'd, "Thou King Vukashin! vain thine efforts!
Vain thine efforts—all thy treasures wasting!
Never, never wilt thou build the fortress
If thou find not two same titled beings,
If thou find not Stojan and Stojana: *
And these two—these two young twins so loving,
They must be immured in the foundation.
Thus alone will the foundations serve thee:
Thus alone can ye erect your fortress."

When Vukashin heard the Vila's language
Soon he called to Dessimir, his servant:
"Listen, Dessimir, my trusty servant!
Thou hast been my trusty servant ever;
Thou shalt be my son from this day onward.
Fasten thou my coursers to my chariot;
Load it with six lasts of golden treasures;
Travel through the whole wide world, and bring me,
Bring me back those two same-titled beings:
Bring me back that pair of twins so loving:
Bring me hither Stojan and Stojana.
Steal them, if with gold thou canst not buy them,
Bring them here to Scadra on Bojana:
We'll inter them in the wall's foundation:
So the wall's foundation will be strengthen'd;
So we shall build up our Scadra's fortress."

Dessimir obey'd his master's mandate;
Fasten'd, straight, the horses to the chariot;
Fill'd it with six lasts of golden treasures;
Through the whole wide world the trusty servant
Wander'd—asking for the same-named beings—
For the twins—for Stojan and Stojana.
Full three years he sought them—sought them vainly:
Nowhere could he find these same-named beings—
Nowhere found he Stojan and Stojana.
Then he hasten'd homewards to his master;
Gave the king his horses and his chariot;
Gave him his six lasts of golden treasures:

* These are both Serbian names, and the point of the ballad must be seen in their affinity to the verb *stojiti*, to stand.

"Here, my sov'reign, are thy steeds and chariot:
Here thou hast thy lasts of golden treasures.
Nowhere could I find those same-named beings:
Nowhere found I Stojan and Stojana."

When Vukashin had dismissed his servant
Straight he call'd his builder, Master Rado.
Rado called on his three hundred workmen,
And they built up Scadra on Bojana;
But, at even did the Vila raze it.
Vainly did they raise the wall's foundation;
Vainly seek to build up Scadra's fortress.
And the Vila, from the mountain-forest,
Cried, "Vukashin, listen! listen to me!
Thou dost spill thy wealth and waste thy labour;
Vainly seek'st to fix the wall's foundations;
Vainly seek'st to elevate the fortress.
Listen now to me! Ye are three brothers:
Each a faithful wife at home possesses.
Her who comes to-morrow to Bojana,
Her who brings the rations to the workmen—
Her immure within the wall's foundations.
So shall the foundations fix them firmly:
So shalt thou erect Bojana's fortress."

When the king Vukashin heard the Vila
Both his brothers speedily he summon'd:
"Hear my words, now hear my words, my brothers!
From the forest-hill the Vila told me
That we should no longer waste our treasures
In the vain attempt to raise the fortress
On a shifting, insecure foundation.
Said the Vila of the forest-mountain,
'Each of you a faithful wife possesses;
Each a faithful bride that keeps your dwellings:
Her who to the fortress comes to-morrow,
Her who brings their rations to the workmen—
Her immure within the wall's foundations.
So will the foundations bear the fortress;
So Bojana's fortress be erected.'
Now then, brothers! in God's holy presence
Let each swear to keep the awful secret;
Leave to chance whose fate 'twill be to-morrow
First to wend her way to Scadra's river."
And each brother swore, in God's high presence,
From his wife to keep the awful secret.

When the night had on the earth descended
Each one hastened to his own white dwelling;
Each one shared the sweet repast of evening;
Each one sought his bed of quiet slumber.

Lo! there happen'd then a wondrous marvel!
First, Vukashin on his oath he trampled,
Whisp'ring to his wife the awful secret:
"Shelter thee, my faithful wife! be shelter'd!
Go not thou to-morrow to Bojana.
Bring not to the workmen food to-morrow.
Else, my fair! thy early life 'twill cost thee,
And beneath the walls they will immure thee!"

On his oath too did Uglesha trample.
And he gave his wife this early warning:
"Be not thou betray'd, sweet love, to danger!
Go not thou to-morrow to Bojana.
Carry not their rations to the workmen.
Else in earliest youth thy friend might lose thee:
Thou might'st be immured in the foundation!"

Faithful to his oath, young Goiko whisper'd
Not a breath to warn his lovely consort.

When the morning dawn'd upon the morrow
All the brothers roused them at the day-break,
And each sped, as wont, to the Bojana.

Now, behold! two young and noble women;
They, half-sisters—they, the eldest sisters—
One is bringing up her snow-bleach'd linen,
Yet once more in summer sun to bleach it.
See! she comes on to the bleaching meadows;
There she stops—she comes not one step farther.
Lo! the second, with a red-clay pitcher;
Lo! she comes—she fills it at the streamlet;
There she talks with other women—lingers—
Yes! she lingers—comes not one step farther.

Goiko's youthful wife at home is tarrying,
For she has an infant in the cradle
Not a full moon old, the little nursling;
But the moment of repast approaches,
And her aged mother then bestirs her;
Fain would call the serving-maid, and bid her
Take the noon-tide meal to the Bojana.
"Nay, not so!" said the young wife of Goiko;
"Stay, sit down in peace, I pray thee, mother!
Rock the little infant in his cradle:
I myself will bear the food to Scadra.
In the sight of God it were a scandal,
An affront and shame among all people,
If of three, no one were found to bear it."

So she staid at home, the aged mother,
And she rock'd the nursling in the cradle.

Then arose the youthful wife of Goiko,
Call'd around her all the serving-maidens,
Gave them the repast and bade them forward.
When they reach'd Bojana's flowing river
They were seen by Mrljavchevich Goiko,
On his youthful wife, heart-rent, he threw him;
Flung his strong right arm around her body;
Kiss'd a thousand times her snowy forehead.
Burning tears stream'd swiftly from his eyelids,
As he spoke, in melancholy language:

"O my wife, my own! my full heart's sorrow!
Didst thou never dream that thou must perish?
Why hast thou our little one abandoned?
Who will bathe our little one, thou absent?
Who will bare the breast to feed the nursling?"
More, and more, and more, he fain would utter;
But the king allowed it not. Vukashin
By her white hand seizes her, and summons
Master Rado—he the master-builder;
And he summons his three hundred workmen.

But the young-espoused one smiles, and deems it
All a laughing jest—no fear o'ercame her.

Gathering round her, the three hundred workmen
Pile the stones and pile the beams about her.
They have now immured her to the girdle.

Higher rose the walls and beams, and higher;
Then the wretch first saw the fate prepared her,
And she shriek'd aloud in her despairing,
In her woe implored her husband's brothers:

"Can ye think of God? Have ye no pity?
Can ye thus immure me, young and healthful?"
But in vain, in vain were her entreaties;
And her brothers left her thus imploring.

Shame and fear succeeded then to censure,
And she piteously invoked her husband:
"Can it be, can it be, my lord and husband,
That so young, thou, reckless, would'st immure me?
Let us go and seek my aged mother—
Let us go—my mother she is wealthy;
She will buy a slave—a man or woman,
To be buried in the wall's foundations."

When the mother-wife, the wife and mother,
Found her earnest plaints and prayers neglected,

She address'd herself to Neimar * Rado:
"In God's name, my brother, Neimar Rado,
Leave a window for this snowy bosom,
Let this snowy bosom heave it freely;
When my voiceless Jovo shall come near her,
When he comes, Oh let him drain my bosom!"
Rado bade the workmen all obey her:
"Leave a window for that snowy bosom,
Let that snowy bosom heave it freely;
When her voiceless Jovo shall come near her,
When he comes, he'll drink from out her bosom."

Once again she cried to Neimar Rado:
"Neimar Rado! in God's name, my brother!
Leave for these mine eyes a little window,
That these eyes may see her own white dwelling
When my Jovo shall be brought towards me,
When my Jovo shall be carried homeward."
Rado bade the workmen all obey her:
"Leave for those bright eyes a little window
That her eyes may see her own white dwelling
When they bring her infant Jovo to her,
When they take the infant Jovo homeward."

So they built the heavy wall about her
And then brought the infant in his cradle,
Which a long, long while his mother suckled.
Then her voice grew feeble—then was silent.
Still the stream flowed forth and nursed the infant:
Full a year he hung upon her bosom;
Still the stream flow'd forth—and still it floweth.
Women, when the life-stream dries within them,
Thither come—the place retains its virtue—
Thither come to still their crying infants.

* Neimar—master.

CHAPTER XXXIV.

SERBIA ON THE ADRIATIC.

FROM Scutari in Albania to the Adriatic, the direct route lies by Antivari, or Anti-Bari, a town situated opposite Bari, on the coast of Italy, and itself called in Slavonic—Bar. In 1863 we visited Antivari, and in very appropriate company; for the Austrian steamer which took us from Cattaro to Corfu conveyed also the Montenegrine commissioners, then on their way to Constantinople. Part of their business was to negotiate for the cession of a port to Montenegro, and to represent the inconvenience of existing arrangements, especially with regard to Antivari; but neither of them had yet seen Antivari, therefore it was proposed that, while the steamer took in her cargo, they should escort us on our expedition to the town.

A walk of about three miles brought us to the city on its present picturesque site, a rock backed by a ridge of jagged hills; beneath stretches a slope covered with olive-trees, subsiding into the flat land near the bay. The town looks miserably desolate—Scodra is quite thronged and thriving in comparison, but we beheld remnants of that Italian style of architecture common to the cities on the eastern shore of the Adriatic; and in the narrow streets we saw high houses, whose dilapidated walls still bear the arms of Venetian nobility.

The story of Antivari is this. Probably a Roman colony, certainly a flourishing emporium under the Byzantine emperors, it continued prosperous throughout Serbian and Venetian rule, and for a short time enjoyed the position of a "free burgh." In those days the city is said to have spread itself along the shores of the bay; and its citizens, whose Slavonic race was blended with an infusion of the Latin element, showed as great a capacity for commerce as their Slāvo-Italian neighbours in Ragusa and Dalmatia. Constant attacks of pirates at length induced them to retire from the immediate neighbourhood of the sea, and to secure for their town the stronger position it now occupies. Here, in 1571, they stood the siege that delivered them to the Turk; an event fatal to the prosperity, almost to the existence, of the town. The garrison of Antivari consented to capitulate on honourable terms, but no sooner was the Turk master of the place than he gave it up to massacre and pillage. Similar acts of treachery are to be found constantly recorded in the history of places and persons in this part of the world, and to this day nothing is found more difficult than to arrange interviews between pashas and native chiefs, even when the discussion of a matter is obviously for the advantage of both parties. Those who have engaged in attempts of the kind bear ample evidence to the suspicion of Turkish treachery, implanted by long experience, not only among Christians, but common alike to Albanians and Serbs.

Antivari numbered about 250 houses, huddled around a ruinous keep. The population is said to consist of some 50 Turkish families in the fortress, and in the city, or *varosh*, of about 2,500 Mussulmans, 800 Latin Christians, and 600 of the so-called Orthodox.

The Slavonic name *varosh* is given to that part of the

town not included in the fortress, and Slavonic patronymics (for instance, Mediminovic, the surname of a "noble Frankish family" in the days of the Turkish conquest) would indicate that here, as in the northern coast cities, Latin as well as Orthodox Christians were not of Albanian, but Slavonic lineage. The country population between Antivari and Dalmatia is entirely Slavonic, and mainly consists of a gallant clan called Pastrovic, who long held out against the Turks, and by descent, religion, and sympathies are identical with the Montenegrines. Austria has possessed herself of that part of their territory that lies near the coast at Budua, and Turkey has laid hold on that between Spizza and Antivari; so that their destinies are no longer in their own hands. They are an industrious, intelligent, and trading people, and should their district ever come to be included in an extension of the Montenegrine frontier, the incorporation would do much to give a commercial direction to the energies of their mountain kin.

The Slavonic tongue, wherein one of the commissioners asked his way to Bar, soon brought a countryman eager to act as guide. In a low voice he began relating the vexations practised on the Christians during the war, and after many piteous stories ended with remarking, "The Turks were always saying to us, 'You know full well that nothing would please you better than to have the Montenegrines here in our stead.' So indeed it was,—long, long we expected every day to see them cross the hills." To all such communications the Montenegrine commissioner, restrained by prudence from avowing his real sentiments, answered with half-articulated growls, which grew less and less repressible when he reached the town and beheld the traces of whilom Christian rule. At last he fairly broke out, "How different would this poor city look in a year's time, if they gave it to our Prince for his winter residence!"

Seeing us inclined to smile at the idea, he added, "That is rather a picturesque way of putting it, but the fact is, if we had a harbour on this coast, we could probably hold out inducements to Christian merchants which would cause them to prefer it as a settlement to any port of Turkish Albania. However, we are not insisting on Antivari; we should be now content even with Spizza, the dent in the shore which you see over there." Following the direction of his pointed finger, we looked at the coveted bay, which indeed seemed little desirable among all the harbours in its neighbourhood.

This was not our only sight of Spizza, for it so happened that our first journey in the South Slavonic countries took us down the eastern coast of the Adriatic, and we afterwards repeated the voyage. Each time we were struck by the number and excellence of the harbours on this the Slāvic shore, contrasting with the comparative lack of them on the opposite coast of Italy. It is truly deplorable that the inland countries should be cut off from their natural outlet. The harbours and cities of Dalmatia have been transferred from Venice to Austria. Bosnia and Herzegovina still belong to Turkey.

For the small free state of Montenegro the true harbour is without doubt Cattaro, whose winding gulf, popularly called the "Bocche," washes the foot of the Montenegrīne hills; while its shores are inhabited by a people of Serb lineage, who so warmly sympathize with their mountain neighbours that, during the late war, they formed companies to march to their assistance, and could only be dispersed by Austrian interference. In

1814 Cattaro was actually made over to the Montenegrīnes, and that by the English, in return for their assistance in dislodging its French garrison. But Russia quickly forced them to resign it, and then transferred it to Austria. To reclaim it from that power is more than they dared hope; so what they asked in 1862-3 was the little Bay of Spizza, which is really, as the commissioner called it, a mere dent in the shore between the Austrian frontier and Antivari. Nominally it belongs to Turkey, but it is of no use to any one; while it is overlooked by the mountain territory, and goods there imported could be carried up without let or hindrance to Montenegro. Nevertheless, Spizza was withheld; and instead, the treaty at the end of the last war stipulated that all articles not used in warfare might be imported free by Montenegrīnes at Antivari.

Antivari is the port of the Turkish garrison town, Scodra; it is separated from Cetinje by considerable mountain ranges, and (unless the frontier of the principality be rectified) between the harbour and the nearest point of Montenegro some time must be spent in traversing Turkish ground. Furthermore, the free importation at Antivari was limited to articles not used in the manufacture of arms and gunpowder, and this limitation served as excuse for prying into every cargo, and keeping a watch over all that goes on. We found the green tents of Turkish soldiers pitched down to the water's edge.

We have described Antivari as a point to which negotiation has been directed, although it was not the point where, on this journey, we reached the Adriatic. From Scodra we went to Montenegro, and descended to the sea at Cattaro.

This was our third visit to the mountain, and we had been much pressed to return, so we were received as old friends. The Montenegrine agent at Scodra wrote to say that we were coming, and to mention our wish if possible to secure a separate dwelling, where we might remain as long as we pleased, and do what we liked, without trespassing on hospitality. When all was ready, the pasha sent us in his steamer across the lake as far as the fortress of Lessendria; and thither the Prince sent to meet us a barge commanded by one of his capetanos, who dazzled all eyes with his brilliant array. The capetano escorted us by water to the little lake port of Rïeka, where we visited the churchyard in which the Turks had recently wreaked on the dead the vengeance which, in the campaign of 1862-3, they were unable to satisfy on the living. The Montenegrines had not yet had time to remove the traces of the outrage. Tombstones were broken, heaps of earth and bones from the torn-up graves were lying tossed about. We were told how the Turks had been assisted in this campaign by the knowledge of the country gained by an English consul during his travels in Montenegro.

One of the songs current after the war of 1862 was a sort of parody on the "Anglo-Turkish alliance." The Turkish Sultan is represented as writing to his dear Bond-sister, the English Queen:—"Dear sister," says he, "I am in great difficulties. I have got into a war with a terrible people called the Montenegrines, and I have no means to fight them. No money to pay my troops; no engineers to fortify my castles; no good cannon, no powder, no shot." And so on with a long lamentation. To this the Queen is made to answer:— "Dear Bond-brother Turkish Sultan,—Fear nothing. I will make you able to fight, nay, to gain a victory over the Montenegrines. Of money I will send you plenty; my engineers shall look at your castles; my arsenals at Corfu shall furnish you with all you require. And as your officers cannot draw maps, and have never been in Montenegro, I will send you a consul called Churchill, who can draw; and who, having been once in Montenegro as a friend, has provided himself with sketches enough," &c., &c. The Sultan is now represented as going to war with a good courage, and succeeding in repulsing his redoutable enemies, who are, after all, only the poor black mountaineers, themselves without money or ammunition or cannon. The song concludes with asking the hearers if they are not astonished that a great and free Christian nation should have been anxious to strengthen the Sultan against a few free Christian highlanders who were taking the rayahs' part.

The English engineer of the Scutari steamer told us it was reported at Scodra that, on the taking of Rïeka, shots were observed to proceed from a house on a little eminence, and several persons passing near it were struck down. Suspecting an ambush, a cannon was sent for, and meanwhile a party of Albanians made a vigorous assault. No one opposed their entry, and behind the riddled walls they found a Montenegrīne woman with two muskets, and her little boy who loaded for her as fast as she fired. We saw one lad of twelve years old, at that time deprived of arms because a student at the Cetinje school, but who during the war had been called out, and shouldered his musket at his father's side. Corpses of children under fourteen were frequently reported as found among the slain, and cited with exultation by Stamboul journalists as a proof that the highlanders were becoming scant of men. With respect to this child, our remarks were answered by "What is he there for, if he cannot be of use when needed? He is young, but he is a Montenegrīne."

The women of the Black Mountain, known as its principal agriculturists and traders, are also not backward to take their part in a campaign. "Pity she is not a boy, she would be a second Mirko," was a remark often made in admiration of the Prince's sister, who, whenever her father would suffer it, followed him to the scene of war.

The women used to repair to the camp to supply their husbands with raki and food, and then returned home to tend their children, weave clothes, and till the ground. But on certain days the women did not return; for if there was a fight they remained to look on, stationing themselves on some commanding rock-point, and thence encouraging the warriors with their cries: "On, on, ye Serbian heroes! For the Holy Cross, for Serbian freedom!" (Za chastni krst i slobodu Srbsku.) Should the heroes give way, they cry, "Shame, shame! Do ye call yourselves men? Give us your guns; we will redeem the fight." The Serbian word for shame is *srámota*, and terribly grates the harsh *sr* over the tongue of the Montenegrīne.

The finest story of a "fair warrior" in Montenegro was told us by one of her fellow-combatants, who seemed truly proud of his countrywoman. Her husband was a standard-bearer. He fell in battle, and was succeeded in office by the eldest of his grown-up sons. That son fell, and was followed by a second, and he in his turn by a third. The woman's fourth and last son was still a child, so she shouldered the banner herself, saying, "I will bear it till my son be grown."

It would be unfair to notice these traits of highland heroism without alluding to the barbarous customs imputed to the mountaineers in their treatment of enemies. Certain newspaper correspondents gave a terrible but somewhat confused account of the ferocity with which the war of 1862-3 was carried on on both sides, and declared that the Turks did not bring in a single prisoner.

Without palliating the general cruelty of the Turks, we may mention that in this instance the fault may not have been wholly theirs, inasmuch as the Montenegrines mention this very circumstance not with deprecation, but with pride. It is a point of honour on the mountain rather to die than be taken captive, and friend will cut off the head of friend rather than let him fall into the hands of the foe.

This desperate resolution used to be partly inspired by the prospect of tortures which not long ago were undoubtedly practised by the Mussulmans on their prisoners, but it is also an object to prevent the heads of the slain from being afterwards shown as trophies. This custom was common on both sides, and many persons assured us that the Mussulmans indulged in it still. Till lately the Montenegrines on their side certainly regarded it as necessary to authenticate their exploits by bringing home the heads of those they slew; the late Prince Danilo went strongly in the face of popular opinion when he banished garlands of skulls from the towers at Cetinje, and at the entrance of the valley of Tzernitza. The present prince is still more strenuous in his prohibition of barbarous shows, and we can witness that, having heard of certain heads clandestinely exhibited in an out-of-the-way part of his dominions, he forthwith repaired to the spot, whereupon the forbidden trophies disappeared. But two days earlier we saw them, three in a row, dangling on an apple-tree; and on our expression of horror were told that it was simply absurd to associate an idea of cruelty with cutting off a man's head *after he was dead*. Besides, "the case was a peculiar one." Two lads, aged sixteen and eighteen, had been sent to Constantinople to make their fortunes under the care of an uncle and in a peaceful career. On the breaking out of the war they returned, and, without even seeing their family, hastened straight to the seat of war, slew three Turks with their own hand, and brought home the skulls to their mother. "Would you not," said the narrator, "encourage schoolboys by giving them prizes to show at home, and are not these far more glorious prizes, of which any mother may be proud?"

But if the Montenegrines are yielding slowly and unwillingly in the matter of cutting off the heads of dead foes, they appear to have been brought to relinquish a practice which they could not deny to be cruel, namely, cutting off the nose of a living foe. The determined severity of their rulers really seems to have put down this barbarism in Montenegro itself; every foreign agent to whom we referred was of opinion that no noseless patients had been seen or authenticated at Scodra. On the other hand, it appears that such were seen at Ragusa and on board steamers for Corfu, and there are grounds for believing what the mountaineers assert, viz., that those mutilated suffered at the hands of the Herzegovinian insurgents, whose barbarities the Prince of Montenegro cannot control, and who, being Turkish rayahs, behave as such.

The cruelties and oppressions whereby the Mahommedans roused the rayahs in Herzegovina are beyond all dispute; indeed, some European agents on the spot, while doing their utmost in the Turkish interest, were driven to accuse certain pashas, who, making money by the war, intentionally increased the people's exasperation and despair.

One very cruel punishment is said to have been inflicted in the presence of Omar Pasha before he left Herzegovina; but as the person who related the incident to us did not witness it, although he said he had heard of it from eye-witnesses, we would not allude to it but for the remarkable case of the criminal on whom it is said to have been executed. It is curious to find an old classical story reacted in the nineteenth century, and in Herzegovina.

An elder, highly venerated among the Christian communes of the insurgent district, fell into the hands of the Turks. Omar Pasha, to whom his acquaintance with the Serbian language has always given great power in arguing with and pacifying these people, ordered this prisoner to be brought before him, and condescended to enter into discourse. He set before the rayah elder the promise of redress and better days held out to those who should lay down their arms; he insisted also upon the utter hopelessness of the Herzegovinians prolonging a successful resistance, and the direful consequences of being subdued by force. Finally, he offered to the elder himself reward and favour if he would exert his influence to quiet the people; if he would go with a Turkish escort to the neighbourhood of some spot where they lay in hiding, hold a parley with them, and induce them to submit. The man agreed, and was accordingly conducted to the border of some wood or stream, and there lifting up his voice in the shrill call of these mountaineers, soon collected various of his former neighbours; among them leaders of the insurgent villages, all anxious to hear what terms such a staunch old Turk-hater had agreed to propound. "Then," said he, "my children, I am, as you see, the pasha's prisoner, and cannot help or lead you further. But this I can do, I warn you not to trust the pasha's promises. He speaks fair, but so he spoke last time, and we all know how he deceived us and the Bosniacs after the last insurrection; thus will he deceive us again. Better die with arms in your hands than lie down to be trodden like worms."

One knows how the Carthaginians treated a prisoner

when he disconcerted their overtures of peace in a similar fashion, and one may well believe that Omar Pasha would make an example of the man who had deceived him, and defeated his well-meant scheme. Nevertheless, we will not here repeat what was told us as the punishment of the Herzegovinian Regulus, for one cannot hear of such extraordinary atrocity without being inclined to pronounce it incredible, at least in the case of a man who, like Omar Pasha, was educated as a civilised being. Unfortunately, it is impossible to give the benefit of doubt to other instances of outrage, especially those perpetrated on Herzegovinian women, and of these outrages the perpetrators held high rank in the service of the Porte.

A Montenegrīne "hero without fear and without reproach" is Peter Vūkotic, the father of the young Princess, of whom even his enemies bear this witness, "If Peter said it, it is true." Peter was in his youth considered a model of beauty, and as such, it is said, sat for the fancy likeness of a favourite Serbian hero, in which character his portrait has been preserved; now, toil and privation have worn his features, but they still present a noble type of countenance, wherein an expression of gentleness and guilelessness softens an eagle eye and wide commanding brow. His speech is remarkable, not only for the eloquence wherewith he sways assemblies, but for a distinct song-like utterance, which at once shows you why Serbian is called the Slavonic Italian. Peter Vūkotic is the hero of the following episode of a mountain campaign.

There is a part of Montenegro where the valleys, on either side held by the Turks, run up into the hills, and almost cut the mountain territory in two; at each end stands a Turkish fortress, the northern called Niksitch, the southern Spuz.* This is the weak point of Montenegro; and those who followed the newspaper accounts of the war will remember that here Dervish Pasha again and again attempted to march through with the army of the Herzegovina, and effect a junction with the troops of Omar Pasha on the Albanian side. But the district of the Herzegovina bordering on Montenegro was insurgent against the Turks, and in that district lies the long, narrow, winding pass of Duga, through which, according to ordinary calculation, a Turkish army must march before entering the mountain itself. To dispute this pass, started, early in the spring of 1862, a chosen band of Montenegrines, under command of Peter Vūkotic. They remained at their post till the snows were melted and the summer heats began, and throughout that time underwent the extremities of hunger and thirst. At that time of year the hills around them brought forth nothing fit for food; the people of the plains would willingly have sold them food, but the country was swept bare by the Turk. Peter and his band lived on such supplies as they could wrench from Turkish foraging parties; when the heats came on in that dry land, they more than once were reduced to such moisture as they could lick off grass and leaves. Thus went by month after month; then came to Peter a Herzegovinian in hot haste, crying, "The Turks are passing you; some one has shown them another way; they are on the road to Kita, and will be in Montenegro before yourselves." Peter and his men set off, tearing across the hills to get to Kita before the Turks. Herein they were successful; the advance guard of Dervish Pasha, halting after a forced march, was sud-

* See Sir G. Wilkinson on Montenegro. We cannot too much recommend the account given by this traveller to all who would have some idea of the country, history, and disposition of the Montenegrines.

denly fallen on by the mountaineers. The troops, surprised and totally ignorant as to the number of their assailants, were panic-stricken, and lost many men before they could retreat.

This was the first battle of Kita, and in it Peter came off victorious. But his band was reduced and weary, and now that the Turks had found a road other than the pass of Duga, he knew well that their second attempt would be deferred only till they had recruited their numbers and strength.

In due time they marched again to the entrance of Montenegro, and again found the Montenegrines waiting for them. But this time the highlanders were too weak to attack, and even to resist seemed all but hopeless. The Prince met them from Ostrog, and did his best to cheer the worn-out and hungry men, but he brought few followers, and, believing it impossible that they would be able to maintain their position, they insisted that the Gospodar should place his life out of danger. Then, putting the slender funds of the expedition in a bag, they hung it round the neck of a man, and hid him behind a rock, with orders, so soon as the battle went against them, to get off with the money and tidings to Cetinje. Thus they waited all the morning, to mid-day, to afternoon, and then they saw the Turks move. But the Turks do not come forward; they go backward. "Yes, they are turning about and taking themselves off by the way they came." It was afterwards known that Dervish Pasha was disappointed of a guide who was to show him the way to Spuz, and uncertain of the road and of the force before him, he had not dared to involve himself in the hills.

At last, however, a traitor bribed by Omar Pasha met the army of the Herzegovina at the entrance to Montenegro, and led it through to Spuz. By one of those faults

of generalship which it is said went far to neutralise the
effect of individual prowess, the Montenegrines rarely in
this campaign concentrated their force on any one point,
and hence, though it is considered they never had a better
opportunity than this of crushing the army of Dervish
Pasha while entangled in the hills, no force was sent
against him large enough to do more than harass his
march. Thus, after all Peter's pains, the Turks made
their way through Montenegro, the Berda were cut off
from Cetinje, and the Ottoman army of the Herzegovina
effected its junction with the army at Scutari.

The great disadvantage of the Montenegrines throughout the war lay in their old-fashioned muskets and their lack of ammunition. We were told by a voivode that in several skirmishes he and his comrades had no more than ammunition for five charges; when they had fired it all off, they sprang from behind their earthworks and met the enemy in a hand-to-hand combat with the hangiar. During one of these unequal fights the firing was audible at Cetinje, where the Prince happened to be. One of his companions described to us how, lying with an ear on the ground, they heard the Turkish cannon answered by the Montenegrine musketry, "as it were, the roar of thunder answered by the patter of hail."

Of course the loss of life was great, but nothing like what was reported. From 2,000 to 3,000 men were the utmost we could hear from any one in Montenegro, the force in the field having been about 15,000. The report of 2,000 *widows* in Montenegro, which was generally credited and confirmed, might be taken to imply a far larger number of slain; but then, it is said, the men marry so young that very few died without leaving a widow. The great drain on the force of the mountain at the time when the war ended was in men *hors de combat* from wounds and fever, and the prostration brought on by hunger, thirst, and heat. Of these many even desperately wounded recovered to a degree almost incredible, owing, according to themselves, to the skill of Montenegrine surgery,—according to the Prince's indignant French doctor, solely to mountain air. The number of fighting men in Montenegro has since been, to a certain extent, made up from the Turk-ruled districts; rayahs who had been insurgents applied for admission to the principality, and received in some cases the lands of the slain.

We once met boatfuls of these new immigrants, shouting and singing on their way to a gathering, and were told it was the first time they had openly mustered as free men.

But terrible was the devastation in certain families; for, as the Serbian proverb has it, "The mother of a brave son is the first to become childless." One day we passed a white-haired man, wearily hoeing at a little plot of ground. The Prince's cousin, who was escorting us, pointed him out, saying, "This time last year that man had eight stout sons; all fell in the war, and now he is left to toil in his old age."

No doubt, the hope of obtaining, by some chance of war, at once a port on the Adriatic and acres of arable land in the Herzegovina, did much towards deciding the Montenegrine government to espouse the cause of those Christians in its immediate neighbourhood who, in 1861-2, rose against the Turk. But the Turks and the Herzegovinian Christians have been at war, off and on, ever since the first Turk showed himself in Herzegovina; the insurgents have asked aid of their mountain neighbours, and have received aid again and again. As things at present stand, the poorer among the mountaineers behold in an expedition into the low

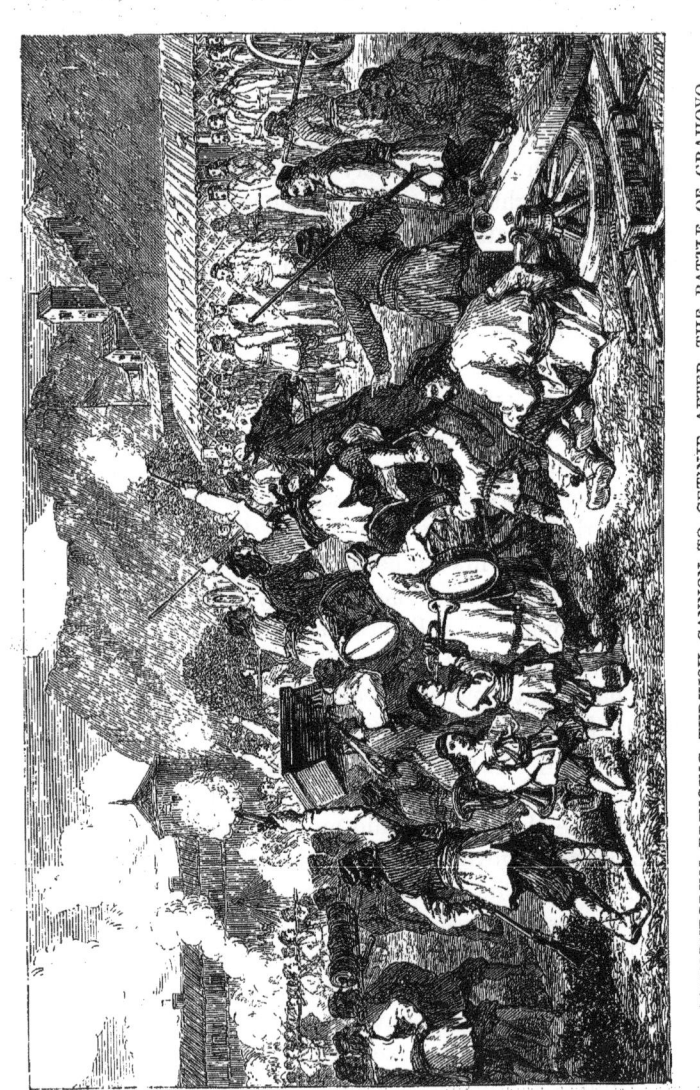

MONTENEGRINS BRINGING TURKISH CANNON TO CETINJE AFTER THE BATTLE OF GRAHOVO.

STARA (OLD) SERBIA

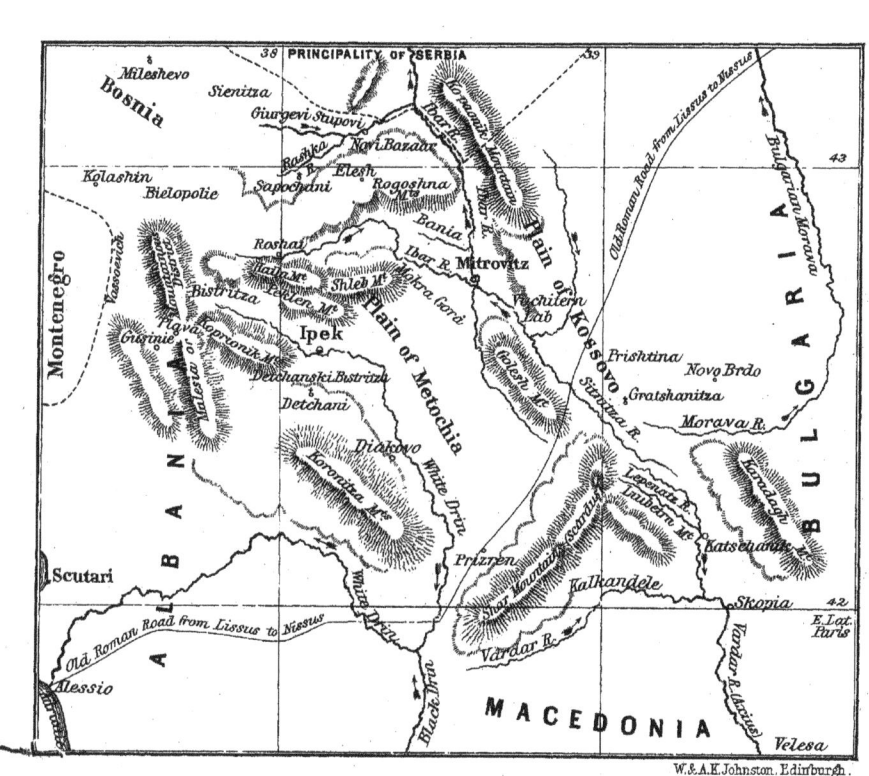

STARA (OLD) SERBIA.—A district between Macedonia and the south of the Serbian Principality. In consular reports it is included in Northern Albania, and the Mussulmans call it Arnaoutluk.

POPULATION.—Numbers very uncertain—some say about half-a-million.

RACES.—Serbian. Gheggha-Albanian. The Osmanlee is represented by a few troops and governors of towns and some families in Prizren. The Greek only by the Bishops.

LANGUAGES.—Serbian and Albanian. Turkish spoken only by officials, and as one of three languages in Prizren. Greek only by Bishops and their Secretaries.

RELIGIONS.—Serbians, Christians of the Oriental communion. Albanians, mostly Mahometans, some Roman Catholic.

country the only means of retrieving a bad harvest; the chief men view in war with Turkey the only honourable career open to them. The original *raison d'être* of Montenegro was as the retreat of a number of Serbians who did not choose to bow to Mussulman yoke; if Turkey ceases to attack them, the primary occupation of defenders of the Black Mountain is gone. But there still remains cause enough for war, either in order to liberate the adjacent rayahs, or to obtain for Montenegro such a territory as can be occupied by human beings in a higher state of civilisation than that of the goatherd or guerrilla.

One can hardly blame the Montenegrines if they will not purchase a return to plains and cities at the price of becoming Turkish rayahs, or even by exchanging their present independence for the Austrian taxes and conscription. But should it ever be possible for them to inhabit the adjacent sea-coast or Herzegovina without a surrender of independence, the greater part of them would certainly return to the districts whither their fathers came, and there is no reason to suppose that they would not grow into enterprising and successful traders, like their kinsmen and neighbours the Bocchese. They have already shown their willingness to resume a peaceful existence by emigrating in numbers to Danubian Serbia so soon as it was relieved from Mussulman administration. Montenegrines who go for work to Constantinople—they are reputed good gardeners and vine-dressers—always return to spend their earnings at home; but those who go to Danubian Serbia remain there, and though for some time restless and fitful, in a generation settle down into yeomen and militiamen like their neighbours. We saw many of the descendants of the first comers. The most noted among them all was the venerated Garashanin, prime minister of Danubian Serbia, who retained, under the forms of civilised life, the towering stature, commanding presence, and energetic will of the Black Mountaineer.

The limits within which the Montenegrīnes could maintain liberty were once very much more restricted than at present; indeed, every ruler of the family now reigning has left the principality larger than he found it. This precedent, and the daily-felt impossibility of civilised existence within its present bounds, may give some idea how little the Montenegrīnes can be expected to resist any temptation to extend their territory such as may be offered them by the promise of help from without, or by the prospect of seeing the Porte's forces drawn off to meet foes elsewhere. Turkey, on her side, is proverbially slow to understand that there can be wisdom in concession, or dignity in doing promptly with a good grace what must be eventually done.

The remarks we had occasion to make on the lowland of the Vassoïevic country apply equally to all the region known as the insurgent districts of the Herzegovina. These districts border on Montenegro, and would long ago have shared its freedom, but that their ground is less defensible. As it is, ever since the Turk first laid claim to them, they have been the scene of constant petty but bloody insurrections, which can only cease when they shall be subjected to some government at once capable of keeping them in order, and interested in improving their condition.

If a Montenegrīne frontier is to be recognised at all, it certainly ought to include these tribes. They are Christians, and will not tolerate among them the presence of Mahommedans; in war they follow the standard of the Black Mountain; in peace their disputes are referred to the tribunal of Cetinje. Yet, if oppressed rayahs in the low country call on them for help; if on their own account they make a raid on the adjacent champaign, or if it suits their mountain neighbours to incite them to disturbance; in short, do what they may, the Prince of Montenegro cannot be called to account, for the offenders are not recognised as his subjects. Meanwhile, the Turkish authorities in Herzegovina do not even pretend to control the clans on the frontier, nor to protect peaceful people from their depredations; so that were those clans regularly included in Montenegro, the Sultan would not thereby lose a single subject, nor would the fighting force of the Prince be swelled by the accession of one man whose service he does not already command. On the other hand, by making the Prince responsible for the behaviour of these borderers, several districts of the Herzegovina would cease to be a battle-ground for Turkish troops and rayah guerrillas, who now plunder them in turn. Montenegro has again and again demanded a rectification of her border, again and again has satisfaction been promised, and it has been well remarked by Lord Strangford that she has a "natural though limited line of probable annexation on her north-western frontier, in the Christian districts of the Herzegovina towards Niksich and Trebinje."* In the interest

* What use the Turks are making of this territory in the meantime may be judged from the report of an eye-witness, who saw what he describes in the autumn of 1865:—"We pulled up our horses at the edge of a precipitous slope, and looked down upon the beautiful plain of Niksich, in the Herzegovina, clothed in perennial green and interlaced by two or three small streams of water. To the north this plain is backed by a range of mountains—the true geographical frontier of Montenegro, but at present in the occupation of the Turks. This range was formerly wooded, and even yet remains of noble forests in some parts blacken the slope of the limestone mountains. When we looked at it, however, the whole range was almost concealed by dense clouds of smoke. For eighteen months these mountains have been burning, and the magnificent oaks and beeches which furnished the country around with the choicest timber are now almost wholly destroyed. This has been done by orders from Constantinople, in order to form a sterile frontier, but its effect will be to destroy the plain which lies at the foot of the mountains, and to reduce it to the condition of the arid plains of Albania on the other frontier of Montenegro. But it will do

of all parties it is to be wished that this natural annexation should be effected as soon as possible.

more than even this: it will dry up the tributaries of the Zeta which flow through Montenegro, and render barren much of the scanty territory possessed by these people." . . . . It is also remarked, "Within the last three or four years, a circle of forty-eight small fortresses has been built close to the frontier of Montenegro."—See "A Ride through Montenegro," by Rev. William Denton, *Good Words*, September 1, 1866.

CHAPTER XXXV.

CHRISTMAS IN MONTENEGRO.*

"The eagle builds her nest on the mountain, because freedom is not in the plains."—*Slavonic Poem.*

SUMMER is the season when Cetinje sees most visitors, and such descriptions as we happen to know of describe it at the sunny time of year. It happened to us to pay our first visit in winter, when the little Alpine plain wears a very different face; when, too, occurs the ceremony of the Badniak, peculiar to the Christmas feast. A picture of Montenegro at Christmas-time is, therefore, what we offer, although to do so we must go back a year and a half.

Towards the end of December, 1861, during that fortnight which intervenes between the Latin Christmas and the Greek, we found ourselves on board an Austrian Lloyd steamer, entering the Bocche di Cattaro. As we approached the head of the gulf, the rock-walls on each side drew closer, and we could discern the town of Cattaro crouched under the shadow of its citadel. From the Austrian fortress upwards a white path winds over the face of the cliff; your eye can follow it to the mountain's brow, where it vanishes between two crags; it has reached the gates of the fortress of Montenegro.

"Look there," cried the old captain of the steamer; "that is the ladder you must climb to-morrow, if you

* Published in "Vacation Tourists," 1862.

mean to go to Cetinje." An individual in a soiled white uniform, who had been put on board at Castel Nuovo, here observed, "It is very dangerous to go to Montenegro." "You have been there?" said we inquiringly. "No, indeed, we may not." "They may not," explained the captain; "for, since last year, when Prince Danilo was shot in Cattaro, the Montenegrines do not choose to see Austrians at Cetinje."

The steamer stopped at a short distance from the shore, and boats came to take off the passengers. There was a numerous second class pressing out, and we expected to be met by the Prince of Montenegro's agent, so we remained seated on the deck, trying to identify the localities about us with those scenes to which the captain had alluded when he spoke of Prince Danilo being shot in Cattaro.

Immediately in front, the gulf runs into the land, forming a point so narrow that it may be rounded in a few minutes' walk. A short way down the left shore lies the village Perzanjo, on our right the Marine Platz of Cattaro, with an incipient public garden, and a free space where the band plays. It was at Perzanjo that the late Prince and Princess of Montenegro resided, during that visit which terminated so fatally. The health of the Princess required sea baths, and her husband insisted on accompanying her, contrary to the advice of many of his counsellors, who did not consider his life safe on Austrian ground. At first, all went well; deputations from the various parts of the Bocche waited on Danilo, and among the inhabitants of Cattaro, including the chief Austrian officials and their families, the Prince and Princess soon became objects of affection and respect. On fine summer evenings, when the band played on the Marine Platz, Princess Darinka liked to come and hear it: and it was at the close of one of these entertainments that the murder took place. The scene was described to us by eye-witnesses. It was already twilight, and Danilo was in the act of handing his wife into the boat, when a pistol, fired from behind, shot him in the back, and he fell. The confusion that ensued was terrible. The attendants of the Prince, deeming themselves betrayed by the Austrians, fired upon the crowd; the crowd, expecting to be massacred by the highlanders, fled in the wildest terror. Strange to say, no one was hurt; even the assassin escaped to a distance, where he was arrested by the Austrian sentinels. At length, a guard of soldiers formed round the body of Danilo, and the Princess herself assisting to support him, he was carried into Cattaro to the house of his agent. There, next day at the same hour, he died.*

The assassin was executed in Cattaro; but not till on the way to execution did he confess the crime: it is said that he declared himself to have been instigated by Austria. Certain it is that this version of the story was believed by many of the Montenegrines, although there are a hundred other versions based on grounds of private quarrel. The assassin belonged to a faction, banished from Montenegro for opposing Danilo's reforms: the chiefs of that party reside at Zara, the Austrian capital of Dalmatia, and subsist on pensions from the Austrian government. It is true the murdered Prince had lived on good terms with Austria; and, in 1848, he offered to support the Croats, rising in defence of the monarchy; but, in 1859, Montenegro was the ally of France; and in case of a national movement among the Southern Slāvs, talents, policy, and position marked Danilo as its leader.

Signor B——, under whose roof Danilo died, was the person who came on board to meet us. He brought the

* August, 1860.

welcome tidings that tolerable quarters were in readiness, and conducted us through the narrow lanes and small dark squares of Cattaro to a house that had seen better days. Its present owners, an elderly widow and her daughter, let us our lodging as a sort of favour. Signor B—— advised us, by all means, to take advantage of the present mild and lovely weather, since in the middle of winter we must not count on its continuance. There had not as yet been snow to speak of, so the road to Cetinje would present few difficulties; he was afraid we should get miserable horses, but he would make our bargain, and secure good attendants. He then left us to get our passports viséd for Montenegro.

Our next care was to inquire about a courier, whom we had been prepared to find at Cattaro. This was no other than a Montenegrīne, adopted in childhood and educated by an Austrian officer, who intended to have made him his heir—now, by his patron's sudden death, left destitute. Great was our disappointment to learn that this accomplished person had just gone to seek his fortune in Constantinople: we did not like undertaking the next day's journey without some one who could speak Italian, and on whom we might rely to order our cavalcade. Count N—— went to find us another escort, and returned followed by a tall Montenegrīne. "I bring you," said Signor N——, "a friend of mine, who is going home to spend Christmas with his family, and agrees to start two days earlier than he intended, in order to be of use to you. He is a merchant, and speaks Italian; he has made more than one voyage to Trieste, and has an idea of what civilised travellers require." The Montenegrīne added that "if, after we had visited Cetinje, we chose to go on to Rïeka, and would so far honour his humble home, he cordially invited us for the

Christmas feast." Hereupon followed some arrangements for the journey, and then our intended escort begged to ask whether the large book before us was not a "travelling book," and if it gave an account of Cerna Gora. It happened to be a translation of Sir Gardner Wilkinson's valuable work on Dalmatia and Montenegro, and we made haste to show him the portrait of the last Vladika. But when the mountaineer found that the account of his country was written in a language he could not read, a cloud came over his face, and he remarked that, had he not neglected his opportunities, he might have understood German. As on this occasion we only spent one night at Cattaro, we did not then make the acquaintance of a family who afterwards treated us with hospitable kindness—the family of the Austrian commandant. This officer had been some years at his post, and expressed liberal opinions towards two bodies not generally favourites with Austrian *employés*—the Slāvs of the Greek Church and the Montenegrīnes. To our question whether he did not find the latter unruly neighbours, he replied that on no one occasion had they given him trouble. In the town they never disagreed with the citizens, and in the country, where bickerings did take place, he thought the fault lay quite as often with the Bocchese as with the mountaineers. "I should never think," he continued, "of describing the Montenegrīnes as robber tribes; those raids on the Turkish frontiers are no more than border forays, such as, according to your own history, went on between the English and Scotch. A great deal is said about their cutting off the heads of their enemies; but who are their enemies? The Turks and Albanians, whose warfare comprehends barbarities rather greater than the cutting off of heads. Besides, fighting against enormous odds, as the Montenegrīnes usually do, how could they let their prisoners go? and how bestow their food and time on nursing wounded Turks? To kill them at once is much less cruel than to leave them perishing on the field, and the Montenegrīne beheads his own companion rather than let him fall into the hands of the enemy. Then they are accused of making raids in time of peace; at least, the Mahommedan borderers have no right to complain of this, for they have always done it themselves, not only on the Montenegrīnes, but even on us, in the military frontier." The commandant also affirmed, what we had previously been assured of, that since the time of the last Vladika, perfect security of person and property exists within the Montenegrīne boundary, while even in their wildest days these highlanders never molested a woman.

On the subject of the Slāvs of the Greek Church in Austria we had a question to ask: Had they kept open shops on the Latin Christmas Day? Till lately, in the Austrian empire, all sects must needs honour the Roman festival; but henceforth no religious community is obliged to keep any feast but its own. In the Bocche more than half the population are members of the Greek Church, but the Latins, long supreme, had not quite made up their minds to see their Christmas disregarded. It was said, "the government would take it as an insult." However, the Greeks made use of their privilege, and kept open shops on the holiday of their rivals. When the commandant spoke to us about this, he added, "Many people were scandalised, but what could we expect? We Romanists have never thought of shutting our shops on the Greek Christmas. The other day I was placed in a difficult position. The Greeks required our soldiers to figure in their ecclesiastical processions, as they figure in those of the Latin Church. Now I have orders to let the soldiers march in the Latin processions, and I have no orders with regard to the Greek. I answered that I would write for instructions."

Next morning our party assembled soon after sunrise; that is to say, a little past eight. We had three horses, of which one was for the luggage, small weak animals, the three men who led them far better able to carry us than they; but the men carried nothing save their arms, two pistols and a hangiar stuck in the girdle. Two boys from the Bocche followed with extra baggage. Besides these, our regular attendants, we had as escort Giorgio the merchant, and the Cetinje postman. The latter was a splendid fellow, some six feet four in height, and with as honest and kindly a face as one could wish to see. His weapons were beautifully ornamented with silver, and on his bonnet he wore the badge which constitutes in itself the uniform of the Montenegrīne guard. This postman had orders to keep by us on the way, and then to announce our approach, and deliver our letters of introduction at Cetinje.

Our starting-point was the so-called bazaar, an open space flanked by a single row of stone sheds; it lies immediately at the foot of the rock, and outside the gate of the town. Hither, thrice in the week, the mountaineers bring their produce and hold their market; for, except the Prince and the senators, the Montenegrīnes are not allowed to enter Cattaro armed, and rather than go in unarmed, they mostly prefer not to go in at all. But for the Montenegrīne bazaar the citizens of Cattaro must often hunger. Their coast-strip between rocks and sea gives them little but wine and oil; the mutton, the poultry, the scoranze (dried fish from the Lake of Scutari), the eggs, the milk that store their market, come from Montenegro. Besides these products, the southern valleys of the Black Mountain yield corn, wine, silk, tobacco, and a wood called sumac, valued for its yellow dye. These the mountaineer wants to exchange for manufactured goods, weapons, and ammunition. But here he feels the inconvenience of a political arrangement which gives the natural port of his country into Austria's keeping. The duties levied in the Austrian custom-house are found excessive even by Austrians residing in Cattaro; and worse than these is an embargo laid on the sale of arms, whenever it suits Austria to leave Montenegro defenceless. At the moment of which we are speaking, there was peace between the Austrian government and that of Montenegro, and yet, with Omar Pasha on the Montenegrine frontier, Austria forbade that arms and ammunition should be sold at Cattaro to Montenegrines. Since then an arrangement has been entered into more favourable to the mountaineers, but the real grievance remains untouched, so long as trade with Montenegro depends on Austrian policy and good pleasure.

The bazaar used to be the place where strangers went to see the rich and warlike costumes of the mountaineers; but for long after the death of Danilo his people wore mourning—the men carried their arms reversed, and turned the golden embroidery on their vests inside.

On the morning after Danilo's assassination, 8,000 Montenegrines gathered in the open space before the bazaar, swearing that if their gospodar were not given up to them, they would burn Cattaro. The Prince was dying; but the Princess sent a message: "Children, as soon as your gospodar * can be moved without pain we will bring him up to Cetinje; meanwhile his bidding

---

* *Gospodar*, "lord," title given by the Montenegrines to their secular sovereign. *Vladika* was the title of their ecclesiastical sovereigns or metropolitans, of whom the last, Peter II., died in 1851. His nephew, Danilo, separated the ecclesiastical from the secular dignity, and, as the head of an independent principality, definitively declared Montenegro exempt from all claims of foreign suzerainty, whether Turkish or Russian.

to every one of you is, Go home." "And like children," said an eye-witness, "they went home; with downcast heads and in silence, that terrible gathering melted away."

The Prince could not be moved without pain, nor were they able to bring him up to Cetinje alive. It was here, at the foot of the rock, that his body was delivered to his own people. By order of the Emperor, Danilo was to receive the funeral of an Austrian marshal; the cannons sounded, the troops were drawn out, Austrian soldiers bore him through the streets of Cattaro. To the beginning of the ascent Princess Darinka followed the bier on foot; up the mountain she followed it on horseback. To picture that funeral procession one must have mounted the Ladder of Cattaro.

The path climbs a rock 4,000 feet high, by an endless series of zigzags. As far as the Montenegrīne frontier it is kept by Austria; but even on this, the best part of the road, in rainy weather it serves for a torrent's course, and is covered with large and pointed stones. Its windings exhaust the patience of the mountaineers, who most of them bound straight down the hill; while to escape its roughness, those who, driving mules or cattle, are obliged to follow the track, walk along the smooth flags which bind it, on the verge of the precipice. Our horses also preferred easy footing. Whenever for a moment we ceased pulling at their heads, we found ourselves in a perpendicular line above the harbour and roofs of Cattaro. Riding up the hill, this made us rather giddy; but when it came to walking down, we were ourselves glad to step along the edge-stones, without giving a thought to the housetops.

Although it was not market-day, the Ladder of Cattaro swarmed with Montenegrīnes, as the ladder of a bee-hive with bees. Such as were going the same way as ourselves would for a time join our party, and walk by our horses. Among the women we remarked one very tall, with fine features and brilliant eyes. Most were middle-sized, thick-set, and with weather-beaten complexions. However weighty their burdens, they walked under them with an elastic tread, talking, laughing, and often knitting the while. However rough their work, not one had a coarse or brazen expression. Indeed, the countenance of the Montenegrine woman is generally pleasing, being intelligent as well as cheerful and modest. These women still wore mourning; a long coat of coarse white cloth over the white chemise and petticoat, a black apron, and black serge veil hanging behind like that of a nun; their crimson embroideries were laid aside, so were ornaments, except in a few instances the ponderous belt, comprising three rows of large cornelians massively set in silver or brass.

The men were also dressed in white. Their coat is no longer than the knee, open in front, and girt round the waist with a sash, and with the leathern belt which supports their weapons. Each carried also a long gun swinging behind. They had dark blue trousers, short and full, rather like knickerbockers, white gaiters, and the shoes called *opanke*, made of ox-hide, and said to be the best for rock-walking. The lofty stature of these highlanders, their athletic proportions and warlike air, did not strike us more than the square brow and intelligent eye. They wear moustache, but not beard; the mouth and chin are firmly moulded; the teeth fine; the nose short, but high; hair brown; large eyes, brown or blue, or oftener a dark grey—we seldom saw either hair or eyes black; the complexion is of a sunburnt red, rather than the dusky yellow of the Italian and Greek. They are larger men than the Tosk Albanians, even than the Gheggas, and they lack that unpleasing expression of cunning which strikes one in the Scodra people.

Men and women walked and talked together, the conversation proceeding in a most lively style; in their intercourse we could not but remark, as did the German Kohl, the absence of embarrassment, rudeness, or coquetry. A less pleasing characteristic is the loudness of their voices. To speak continuously, so as to be heard for miles off, is a highly valued accomplishment.

As we approached the entrance to Montenegro the way became rougher—there is no object in making it too easy—and the path was slippery with the unsunned frost of the morning. We had been obliged to dismount, when down came a drove of cattle, solemnly marching in the midst of the road, leaving us to choose between the cliff and the precipice. The mountaineers were eager to help; the women almost lifting us on to the ledges of rock, where we were out of harm's way. When again en route, they appeared disappointed unless we constantly halted and admired the landscape.

At every stage of the ascent the view becomes more striking. First, you look right down on Cattaro, into the squares of the city, upon the decks of the ships. Gradually, bend after bend of the winding fiord becomes visible, as like a silver way it threads the passes of the rocks. At last, the rocks themselves no longer shut out the sea, and when you gain the topmost step of the Ladder, the Adriatic lies before you unrolled to the horizon. At this point we turned our backs on the world, and passed into the Black Mountain. Giorgio, the travelled merchant, exclaimed, with a half-stifled sigh, "Ecco il Montenero!" and another member of the party, who scarcely knew Italian enough to make himself intelligible, pointed to the crags speckled with snow, and called out, "Now, signore, you are in Montenegro; now you are in a free country; here you may go where you like, and do what you like by day or night; here no one will do you harm."

That this was a free country was its recommendation to its first settlers, who, forsaking the more fertile but enslaved Herzegovina, where they had dwelt under the hill Nïegūsh, became the defenders of this rock-walled fortress, and called their new home after their old one. Of this band of freemen come the reigning family of Montenegro; his own patronymic suffices to remind a prince of the house of Petrovic de Nïegūsh that the land of his ancestor still serves the oppressor, and has a claim on his aid to set it free.

The district of Nïegūsh comprehends two or three villages dotted over a small, broken plain. We here found the "half-way house," an inn affording at one end a counter where raki is sold, and at the other a room without windows or chimney, wherein passengers who wish for a fire may light it in the middle of the floor. Since our first visit, there has been added a more civilised apartment containing a bed. Giorgio managed the raki-drinking part of the company, and we sat by the fire, and ate the luncheon we had brought from Cattaro.

Recollecting that at Nïegūsh a former traveller was assailed by dogs, we asked what had become of the garrison. "Oh!" answered our guide, "there used to be dogs in every village, but since the Vladika and the late Prince brought things into order, we have no need of dogs, and many a house has not even one."

The road between Nïegūsh and Cetinje is merely a pathway, crossing one after another ridges the slopes of which are clothed with low wood. Here the ground was covered with snow, waxing deeper as we proceeded. We heard that much had fallen during the night, and testified our regret at the circumstance. But our escort was of a different mind. "How I do like the snow," quoth Giorgio; "see, this is good black soil, and here every spot that is not rock is cultivated; during the winter it is the snow that keeps it warm."

We came on a troop of small hill-cattle, and their herd, a lad, armed like the rest. Afterwards we met people bringing home wood. The women carried bundles of branches, and the men dragged the heavier stems after them, sticking the hatchet into the log, and fastening a cord to the hatchet. Hereabouts we were accosted by a beggar. We asked Giorgio what became of those who were too old and sick to work. "What becomes of them?" cried he; "why, if in the family there are a few who cannot work, there are always plenty of strong ones who can." These words reminded us that the old Slavonic family organisation continues in Montenegro in full force; thereby each family supports its own poor; widows are not left without protection, and as some one said to us, "there are no orphans." Nevertheless, after the late war it was melancholy to note the increase of begging; we could scarcely walk a step without being pursued by little children praying for alms.

That the road from Nïegūsh looks grand in a snow-storm, we had occasion to know when we next traversed it; in ordinary circumstances its only fine point is a view. This shows you Montenegro, as it were a rocky sea, whose waves, thrown up "mountains high," culminate in one great chain. In the midst lies a sheet of snow—a fairy ring fenced about on all sides with jutting crags. This is the alpine plain of Cetinje, the last fortress of the Serb empire, and for long the only spot where Serbians could be at once Christian and free.

The village, palace, and convent of Cetinje, situated

behind a promontory of rock, are not visible until one is close upon them. From Cattaro the journey is counted six hours; we took seven, but our horses were miserable, one so rickety that its hapless rider was reduced to walk the last miles in the snow. Very tired, we arrived at the locanda of Cetinje, which, in the days of Sir Gardner Wilkinson and Kohl, seems to have been a creditable inn. Unluckily, "since the Prince's death," so few strangers had visited it, that the landlord meant to go away, and had not of late repaired his window-panes. The upper chamber to which we were conducted was, however, better furnished than in many Dalmatian inns; and that the floor and tables had lately undergone a washing was evident from the fact that they were not yet dry.

We were not long left to make observations. So soon as the Prince received the letters we had entrusted to the postman, he sent his French doctor to offer us better quarters. "His Highness regrets," said the doctor, "that he cannot accommodate you *chez lui*, but he has taken his whole family to live with him, and one wing of the palace is under repair. He has ordered a lodging to be prepared for you in the house of his cousin Kertso Petrovic, Vice-President of the Senate." We soon found ourselves in a warm comfortable room, and heard with satisfaction that there was settled at Cetinje a Bocchese woman who spoke Italian, and had been trained as a servant in Cattaro. She acted housemaid to the doctor's family, and would be happy to wait upon us.

That evening we dined at the palace, "*en bourgeois*," as the invitation ran, and "to save us the trouble of ordering supper." To ensure our getting supper was the real meaning of the last part of the message; and we learned to thank the Prince's consideration on discovering that the strict Greek fast before Christmas had begun, and that it would have been difficult for us to procure animal food. Equal kindness provisioned us throughout our sojourn, and from the next day forward our meals were sent from the palace kitchen. The French doctor congratulated us. "In virtue of my office," said he, "my wife and daughter and I are expected to take our meals in the Prince's house, but in bad weather it is no joke plodding through the snow. As for the fare at the locanda, I can tell you, from the experience of a friend of mine, that had you been dependent on that, *vous auriez mangé des choses impossibles.*"

Sometimes a little house, or part of one, stands empty during the temporary absence of some functionary, and after our first visit we always made our coming conditional on being able to find some place of this sort where we could be what the Germans call *ungenirt*. We brought servants able to cook, and with a little difficulty procured all necessary food.

The doctor at Cetinje is no longer M. Tedeschi, who took many photographic views, and wrote an interesting little account of Montenegro. At the time of our visit his successor had only filled his post eight months; being a married man, he could not be accommodated in the palace, and as he made no attempt to learn the language, he was much cut off from intercourse with the people. On the other hand, the light of his science was scarcely appreciated by the Montenegrines. "He may be a good man," said one of them, "but it seems to us that the Prince pays a great deal of money for a doctor to give medicine to his people, and his people do not like medicine." Then said another, "a foreign doctor may know something about physic, but do you think a Montenegrine would let him meddle with broken bones? In the world there are no such surgeons as our own—if you had seen the wounds they healed after the battle of Grahovo!"

This is not altogether a vain boast; many travellers allude to the surgical skill of the Southern Slāvs. It has been even said they can *trepan*, and are in the habit of trepanning as a cure for neuralgia and for—madness (?).

Since Sir Gardner Wilkinson visited the vladika, the interior of the palace of Cetinje has undergone transformation; its transformer was the first lady who has ruled society in Cetinje since the Venetian consort of Prince George Tsernoïevic (1516). Out of the bachelor quarters of a warrior bishop, Princess Darinka succeeded in forming a comfortable, almost an elegant, residence; and coming on such among the rocks of Montenegro we, as British travellers, were reminded of a first-rate shooting-lodge in the Highlands of Scotland. This analogy was carried out by the dinner, which, though well cooked and served in the European style, was plain, and owed its chief delicacy to a splendid trout from the Lake of Scutari. As in our Highlands, too, master and servants alike wore the Highland dress.

In the drawing-room of the palace at Cetinje hang two large portraits of the Emperor and Empress of the French, presented by themselves; also smaller ones of the Emperor and Empress of Austria, and of Danilo and the Princess Darinka. The most interesting picture is that of the Vladika Peter II., a man of European education, and the author of many remarkable poems, some of which were published in Vienna, some in his own monastery. He acutely felt his isolation among an uncivilised community, and used to describe himself as the hermit of Cetinje.

The customs of the Greek fast prevented our meeting on this occasion several members of the palace circle. Neither the mother nor the sister of the Prince was present; and as soon as dinner was announced, the Prince's wife took the arm of her father-in-law, and both withdrew.

At that time the Princess was only fifteen, but already talked of as a beauty. She wore the mourning dress with little difference from that of the other women, except that under the white coat appeared a black silk skirt, that the cloth of the coat was exquisitely fine, and in front was adorned with gold. We afterwards had many occasions of improving our acquaintance with the young Princess. Her name is Milïena, and she is daughter of the Voivode Peter Vūkotic. When we last saw her, she was much grown and strikingly handsome; she has something of her father's charm of voice and manner, and the Serbian language sounds very musical in her mouth. Unluckily for visitors, at that time she had acquired no other tongue, for her former home, Chévo, lies far from the sea-coast, and there she was brought up; this circumstance, together with her extreme youth at the time of her marriage, acted unfavourably on the chances of foreign intercourse penetrating to the ladies of Cetinje. The Princess Darinka, widow of the last Prince, descends from a Serbian family of the Bocche, but received a careful education at Trieste. With her infant daughter Olga, she has been much at Paris and St. Petersburg since her husband died.

Grand Voivode Mirko Petrovic[*] is the elder brother of the late Prince, as well as father of the present. A chief esteemed in council and in war, he has twice stood aside in the succession to power, and been content to give place to a younger because he did not receive a European education. Mirko is the hero of Grahovo; and with respect to his sagacity, we were told that had Danilo listened to its suggestions he would not have perished as he did. "Mirko," said a Montenegrīne to us, "is a simple highlander; he cannot speak any foreign tongue, he can read and write nothing but a little

---

[*] Mirko died of cholera in 1865.

Serb, but not in Paris, not in Vienna will you find a man with more head." (Here the speaker tapped his own.) "With the good Mirko is good, but his eye knows the wicked, and the wicked know that they cannot deceive Mirko, therefore do they hate and fear him." That is to say, Mirko has many enemies, and when we add that he is close-fisted in money matters, it may be guessed what colour for evil stories his character lends to Austrian journalists. We had heard that he wished to close Montenegro against civilisation and foreign intercourse; nay more, that corn sent from Odessa for distribution among the poor had been sold and its price pocketed by Mirko. The more impatient spirits among the Austrian Slāvs who wished Montenegro at once to back the insurrection in the Herzegovina were also foes to Mirko, and at one time accused him of taking a bribe from Omar Pasha to abandon the hapless Christians. Most of these imputations have met with refutation, and in due time the corn which Mirko was represented to have sold was found never to have left the magazine.

Some idea of Mirko's political ideas may be formed from an anecdote. When it was rumoured that Montenegro was about openly to head the rising of the Christians in Turkey, a young officer in the service of the Prince of Serbia gave up his commission at home, and came to offer his services to the cause. Prince Nicolas happened to be out riding, so the volunteer was brought to Mirko, and the person who told us the story was present at his introduction. The Grand Voivode was walking up and down before the palace, smoking his long pipe; he received the officer graciously, and asked him his object in visiting Montenegro. The young soldier stated it, and all around smiled approval. Mirko answered, and his voice made the hearers tremble. "Are there not many thousand Turks still in Serbia? Turn them out, and then come and help us with the Turks in the Herzegovina."

When Princess Milïena and her father-in-law had quitted us, the only member of the family left was the Prince himself, who, as host, remained, and did the honours of the dinner-table. Prince Nicolas was then only twenty years of age, but already one of the largest men in his dominions; though unusually dark, he has the fine stature, fine head, and frank smile of the Montenegrïne. In case of Danilo leaving no son, his nephew had been designated as his successor, and was the first of his dynasty sent for education, not to St. Petersburg, but to Paris. He speaks French fluently, understands German, Italian, and Russian, and is a fair poet in his own tongue.

In consideration of our ignorance of the Serb language, no one spoke at dinner who could not speak in French. The conversation thus lost much in interest. But in no company in Montenegro could one topic pass untouched, the topic of Danilo's loss. The young Prince spoke thereon with much feeling. "If you had seen the country before my uncle died," said he, "you would not know it again. In former times, only because you are strangers, the population of Nïegūsh would have come out to meet you, and offered you fruits, and sung songs, and fired pistols; now, though it is Christmas time, you will not hear a shot fired or a song sung. I do not believe you will even see a fine garment. It is more than a year since the whole population went into mourning, but there are still no signs of its being laid aside." At another part of the conversation, the French doctor related that on board the steamer in which he came to Cetinje there were several Montenegrïnes, who appeared quite delighted to return to their Black Mountain. He added, "your highness would scarcely believe it." "I not believe it?" exclaimed the Prince. "Have I not felt the same myself? Why, when I left Montenegro to go to Paris, I climbed on the highest part of the deck to catch the last sight of the mountains; and when I came back, I climbed up again to catch the first glimpse of them. *Allez!* I at least know what *that* is."

How far young Prince Nicolas may be expected ever to fill the place of Danilo is an anxious question in Montenegro, and an important one for the Christians of Turkey. It is satisfactory to know that Danilo himself, as successor to Peter II., and even Peter II., as successor to Peter I., were each, at the commencement of their respective reigns, the object of a similar discussion.

In the winter of 1861,* the greatest embarrassment of Prince Nicolas was his position towards the insurgents in the Herzegovina. As Slāv against Turk, as European against Oriental, as Christian against Mussulman—the free Serb of Montenegro thought himself bound to support his brethren in arms against the oppressor. Moreover, the Prince of Montenegro, as representative of the Princes of Zèta, regards the Herzegovina as a part of his dominions, only kept separate from the rest by force. In 1861, the Christian Slāvs, insurgent against Turkey, urged these pleas and begged for assistance; their petition was backed by that faction among the Western Slāvs whom we have described as the impatient spirits; both parties spoke as if the support of Montenegro were alone needed to make the Herzegovina free. For Prince Nicolas, on his first accession to power, to refuse that support, imperilled his popularity at home and his influence in the Slavonic world. On the other hand, France and Russia bade

---

* As in 1875-6. For the most recent information on this subject, see Mr. Stillman's excellent book, "Herzegovina and the Uprising." Longmans, 1877.

him wait. For a rising of the Slāvs to be successful, it must be general. Bosnia and Serbia were not ready. For the interference of Montenegro in behalf of the Christians not to be worse than useless, it must be certain that Austria would not take this as an excuse for her own interference on behalf of Turkey. . . . . While we were at Cetinje the government of Montenegro was reported neutral; in the Herzegovina, Luka Vukalovic and his desperate band held out against Omar Pasha, and not a day passed but volunteers went from Montenegro to join the "Forlorn Hope."

How ready both prince and people were to welcome an excuse for quitting this passive attitude, may be guessed from the following story. During the autumn, a report reached Cetinje that Omar Pasha had attacked the Montenegrīne frontier. That morning the Prince's secretary was awakened by the sudden entrance of the young gospodar, crying out, "Hurrah! The Turk has attacked the frontier, now we *must* fight." When the secretary went out, he found the great flag waving over the palace—no flag had waved there since Danilo's death. All day the Prince and the people were busy together with preparations for war; and in the evening, the Prince sat under the great tree on the plain, the people stood round him, and he read them national war-songs out of the book of the vladika's poems. Some hundred men started at once; as they set out the Prince said to them, "This day our war with the Turks begins; our national mourning is at an end." And now comes a dispatch from Omar Pasha. The infringement of the mountain territory is a mistake; he trusts that the good understanding with Montenegro will continue. It was as if some great calamity had befallen the nation. The warriors who had departed with songs, returned carrying their arms reversed; the national mourning continued as before.

We now, and afterwards, saw some of the leading men in Montenegro. As compared with the behaviour of Turk and rayah, it is scarcely necessary to say that the difference between them and their poorer countrymen was nothing that indicated mastery on the one side or servility on the other. Every Montenegrine is equal before law; every one has a right to wear arms and to give his voice in the Assembly of the people. Except in the family of the sovereign, there is no such thing as hereditary office; and, except the sovereign himself, every one, even Mirko, is called simply by his Christian name. Superiority in the social scale can only be obtained in three ways—by the industry which makes a family rich; by the sagacity or courage which procures for the individual election to the post of senator, voivode, judge; and, thirdly, by a European education; which last is, as we have seen, a *sine quâ non* in a candidate for the throne.

It is easy to know if a Montenegrine is rich, for he carries a good part of his wealth on his person, in the form of splendidly mounted arms. Also, under the white tunic, he wears a crimson waistcoat, embroidered with gold, and over the tunic a crimson jacket without sleeves, handsomely worked, and adorned with massive buttons. Some have, besides, a sort of breastplate, or collar of silver; and in cold weather surcoats with fur and fur caps. It is a rich dress, and, from its contrasts of white and crimson, beautiful; but, as compared with that of the Scottish Highlander, is perhaps lacking in drapery. Even the strooka, a sort of plaid, is stiff and narrow, and in fine weather is not wrapped about the figure, but left to trail in a straight line from one shoulder to the ground.

At the time we were in Montenegro an air of troubled thought and sadness might be observed in most of the leading men. To sit with arms crossed, while their brethren in the Herzegovina called for aid, was a hard trial for the old chiefs who had beaten the Turks again and again, and, relying on the experience of the battle of Grahovo, could not believe that there is any real superiority in regular to irregular troops. Then, too, Danilo's loss fell heaviest on those who stood nearest to him. Many a one, we were told, had never looked up since. It was enough to see the cloud of gloom that settled on the face of our landlord, Kertso, when he showed us a likeness of Danilo. With a sigh, almost a groan, he pressed the portrait to his lips, and spoke not a word.

Kertso was a Montenegrīne of the old school; simple, kindly, even child-like in all circumstances but the heat of battle, and absolutely unconscious that any idea of horror can be associated with cutting off the head of a Turk. At the time we first saw him Kertso had lately acquired a yataghan, mounted in silver and coral; he was very fond and rather vain of it. One day he bade the Prince's secretary tell us that he hoped we did not mind his coming into our presence armed: "there was no need to be afraid of him, though he had, with his own hand, killed fifteen Turks." Then, drawing his beautiful yataghan, he passed his finger slowly along its edge, and observed that it had already cut off two Turkish heads.

There are always several young Montenegrīnes at college in St. Petersburg and Paris, and when their education is finished they travel. We just missed the son of a senator, who had been giving the Prince an account of his voyage. No place had made such an impression on him as London. "Ah!" said an elder man, alluding to him, "when we get a seaport, learning will come to us in our own country; now we must send away our children if they are to see foreigners and know what goes on in the world, and few among us are rich enough to give them such an education as that."

The morrow of our arrival in Cerna Gora, and often subsequently during our stay, we walked on the mountain plain, and climbed its sides to various points of view. The best of the latter we did not indeed reach, the snow lying too deep on the hill; but we recommend no visitor to leave Cetinje without having seen it from the Rïeka road, and from the rock above the convent. The former commands the greater part of the valley, and the hamlets that stud its grey circlet of crag. Hence, too, appears, in most picturesque grouping, the village of Cetinje, with palace and convent, lying at the foot of a rocky promontory, and surmounted by a round tower.

Tower, convent, palace, and village, all are modern, forming the third encampment where two have been burnt by their own inhabitants at the approach of the foe. It is in the rock-wreathed plain itself that you behold the capital of Montenegro. There, while the surrounding lands have been groaning under Moslem yoke, the last free Serbs have met in their national parliament, a Christian bishop has held his see. Twice, indeed, during the history of Montenegro have the Turkish armies penetrated to Cetinje—the second time by means of a treacherous stratagem.* No sooner, however, was the main force withdrawn, than the mountaineers came forth from their rocks, massacred every Turk that remained, and set up their independent state

---

* Thirty-seven Montenegrine chiefs being invited to the Turkish camp to settle conditions of peace, were treacherously put to death, and this was the signal for the Turkish army to cross the Montenegrine frontier.

as before. Of course there is no knowing what trials may yet be in store for the little country, or how far it may be able to surmount them; but at present for the Sublime Porte to call Montenegro an integral part of its dominions is of a piece with the belief of the common Osmanli, that all the kings of Frangistan are vassals of their Sultan, that the Queen of Great Britain and the Emperor of France hold their crowns of his goodwill.*

The tower on the rock appears never to have been finished, and can never have been inhabited, for it has no door. On its walls used to hang a garland of Turkish heads, trophies which so shocked Sir Gardner Wilkinson, that he urged the then reigning vladika to have them removed. This the vladika was himself forward to do, and his moral influence effected thus much, that, although in battle the Montenegrīnes still decapitated their enemies, the heads, instead of being exposed, were rolled into a pit of water. The vladika excused the barbarism of his people by pointing out that they had barbarians to deal with; and, in fact, when Sir Gardner Wilkinson reached Mostar, he found that the Turks not only stuck on the castle the heads of their slain foes, but tortured their captives and impaled them alive.

Between the tower and the convent rears itself a stone house, three stories high, and no broader than a single room. This was the dwelling of the vladikas before the present residence was built. Certainly archi-

---

* There is said to be in the archive of Cetinje a document signed by the Sultan reigning in 1799, which recognises in so many words "that the Montenegrīnes were never subject to our court." There is also another document, copy of an answer sent to an attempt at dictation on the part of Russia; therein the highlanders declare, "Le peuple du Monténégro et de la Berda n'était jamais sujet à la Russie. Nous ne reconnaissons la protection de la Russie qu'autant qu'elle résulte de l'égalité de la religion. Nous n'avons jamais subi une assujétion, ni par traité ni en échange de priviléges, et il n'y a point d'État qui soit notre protecteur."

tecture does not flourish at Cetinje. The only edifice of interest is the convent, and that boasts little save a row of double arches. The original foundation stood on the plain, and is said to have been a larger, finer building. The present monastery preserves in its wall a tablet taken from the ruins, and sculptured with the two-headed eagle of Serbia. In the old church were kept jewels and church valuables belonging to the princes and primates of Zeta. But when the Turks approached Cetinje, the old convent was blown up by its own monks, and its treasures have never reappeared. A store of valuable objects and of trophies are now kept in the palace. Among the latter may be seen English medals taken at the battle of Grahovo from Turks, who, having earned them before Sebastopol, lost them before Cerna Gora.

The convent of Cetinje contains the principal church and school of Montenegro; it is also the residence of an archimandrite, who shortly afterwards received consecration as vladika. We were shown into the apartments of the rev. father—very comfortable rooms, furnished in the European style. The archimandrite himself had the long hair and flowing robes of an Eastern monk; but the parish priests or popes of Montenegro wear the national dress, and carry arms, which they only lay aside while reading service. They are generally "good heroes," the first at a gathering, the leaders of their flocks in war.

In the apartments of the archimandrite we met the then "Minister" of Montenegro, a Dalmatian educated in Trieste; also the Bohemian secretary of the Prince, a "Bosniak" come to Cetinje on a mission from the Christians in Turkey; and a little Siberian engineer, engaged on a strategical map of Montenegro.

As to the school of Cetinje: our visit happened in

the Christmas holidays, when regular lessons were not going on; but one afternoon, hearing from without the voices of children singing hymns, we entered, and found scholars but no teacher. It appeared that the boys of the first class were met to sing and read together. Their song was rough-voiced, as that in a Scotch kirk; the books they had just laid down were church books; we were told that the Cyrillic translation of the Bible can be mastered with ease by a Montenegrine child. Reading, writing, arithmetic, history, geography, are taught at Cetinje; but the master not being present, there was no one to put the class through its manœuvres. The boys showed their copy-books, in which the writing was very fair; of course in the Cyrillic character. Like the rest of the race, the Slāvs of Montenegro show much eagerness for historical knowledge, and quickness in picking up foreign languages. At present the poetic gift is common among them, and a poem on the death of the last Prince was produced by the Cetinje scholars. Schools were established by Danilo in many a village; but since his death the unsettled state of the surrounding country has gone much against their progress. In case of a Turkish inroad, the people know that their villages will be burnt, and everything like civilisation put an end to; and in the meantime, we heard of schoolmasters forsaking their desks for the more congenial post of volunteers in the Herzegovina. No subject appears to be more earnestly taken up by the present Prince than that of education.

The church in the monastery of Cetinje is in form and adornment an ordinary Greek chapel, but it contains the tomb of Danilo and the mummy of St. Peter. The secretary told us that for eight weeks after the late Prince's death the chapel was filled day and night with people lamenting over his grave. "And not women alone," added he, "but huge sunburnt warriors, weeping like very children."

Homage of another kind is rendered to the body of St. Peter, which lies displayed in priestly robes, with nothing but the face covered. St. Peter was in his lifetime Vladika Peter I.; now he is the patron saint of Montenegro, and has an intelligible title to his post, which is more than can be said of his neighbour, St. Blasius of Ragusa. In the cathedral of the "Slāvic Athens," we were shown the skull of its protector, magnificently set in jewels; we asked by what benefit to the city St. Blasius had entitled himself to a higher place in her homage than those great Dalmatians, St. Hilary and St. Jerome. "When the Venetians bombarded our city," was the answer, "the image of St. Blasius caught the balls in its hands; and once he saved Ragusa from being taken, by revealing the enemy's project in a vision to a priest." Ask a Montenegrīne what St. Peter did for Montenegro, and he tells you: "There are still with us men who lived under St. Peter's rule, heard his words, and saw his life. For fifty years he governed us, and fought and negotiated for us, and walked before us in pureness and uprightness from day to day. He gave us good laws, and put an end to the disorderly state of the country; he enlarged our frontier, and drove away our enemies; even on his deathbed he spoke words to our elders which have kept peace among us since he is gone. While he yet lived we swore by his name; we felt his smile a blessing and his anger a curse; we do so still."

St. Peter was the fourth ruler of the line of Nīegūsh. Danilo, its founder, was the deliverer of Montenegro in the worst danger it ever ran from the Turks, and it was in consideration of his services that the office of

Vladika was made hereditary in his family. The fifth was the last Vladika—the national poet of Cerna Gora; the sixth was Danilo, who resuscitated the princely dignity, and obtained a recognised frontier for Montenegro.

Perhaps, however, the greatest benefit Danilo rendered to the Serbian cause was, when for himself and his descendants he disclaimed every right that could endanger the unity of the nation. From Prague to Bosnia are repeated the noble words which he addressed to Milosh: "Prince, go forward, and I also will go forward. Whenever our ways meet, trust me for being the first to hail you as Czar of the Serbs."

From the convent at Cetinje a few steps bring you to the palace—a long one-storied building in the centre of an open court, flanked by four towers. Close by is soon to be erected a hall for the Senate, which now assembles in a room of the palace. A portion of the plain is pointed out as the place where the Parliament, or General National Assembly of Montenegro, meets in the open air.

From the gates of the palace-court starts that line of street which, crossed at its further end by another line, forms the little village of Cetinje. "You think there are but few stone houses in Cetinje," said a Montenegrine to us; "you would think there are a great many if you had seen Cetinje twenty years ago, when there were only two."

Most of the houses at Cetinje have an upper storey, and in many of the private dwellings this is well furnished, and even carpeted, the rarest luxury being a stove. There are also several small locandas, and in summer a stranger accustomed to rough it would easily find tolerable quarters; in winter this is more difficult, the absence of fire rendering most locandas intolerable.

At this season the kitchen is the only warm part of the house. There, on a slight elevation at one end of the floor, you will find not only fire but company, and, if you understand the language, more instruction and entertainment than anywhere else. It is round the kitchen fire that those songs are sung and stories told wherein the Serbs of Montenegro hold intercourse with their brethren in Danubian Serbia, Herzegovina, and even Bosnia and Dalmatia. Centuries of separation have not loosed this tie, and Kara George, the liberator of Serbia in our own day, is not less a national hero of the whole Southern Slavonic race than Milosh Obilic in the fourteenth century.

As for the resources of Cetinje, food—that is to say, fish, dried mutton, bread, and cheese—can be obtained in the locandas; and, in the way of apparel, we bought a good woollen strooka from the household where it was made. For a trifle any girl will undertake the six hours' walk to Cattaro, and bring you back whatever its dear and ill-supplied shops afford. Still, the little daughter of the French doctor was not far wrong in describing Cetinje as "une ville où les ressources sont rares, et l'on ne trouve qu'un bon air." The air is indeed "bon"— even with snow on the ground it never felt chilly—the sunshine was bright, the atmosphere clear.

To us the great grievance in Cetinje was the street. There the snow lay, and to use the expression, "got leave to lie," drift, freeze, crack, or melt under the eyes of all those great fellows, who at this season have nothing to do. For their negligence two excuses were alleged. First, that at any moment the wind might change, and clear the valley in a few hours. Secondly, that the inhabitants of Cetinje do not themselves fear the snow, and that in winter they are not accustomed to visitors. But what excuse is admissible when one is

UNDER THE TREE AT CETINJE.

hobbling and plunging from hole to hole where giant footsteps have trod before?

Every day, as we went out walking, we could see the crowd gathered round Mirko, where, sitting at the door of a house, he judged the people and gave ear to their petitions. This is his office as President of the Senate. To the Senate are referred cases which the judge of each separate village has failed to settle satisfactorily; and from the Senate a last appeal lies to the gospodar. Therefore, while causes are pleaded before Mirko, the Prince is often present, and, as it was described to us, "walks up and down, listening to what goes on, and frequently explaining the decisions to the people."

Another office was discharged by Mirko. There had been drought in Montenegro—cattle died, and the harvest suffered; to keep the poor alive, the government had to buy Indian corn, and of this Mirko was the distributor. To swell his store, supplies were sent from Russia and France—from Russia, as by race and creed the natural ally of the Montenegrines—from France, in order to save them from being wholly dependent on Russia. The Montenegrines are duly grateful, but still they feel that he is badly off who depends for daily bread on charity; and rather than live on the subsidies of foreign powers, they ask if it were not better to return to the old highland fashion, and gain winter provision by a so-called *tchéta* on the low country. These *tchétas* are plundering excursions on the Turkish territory, and the perpetrators being, as suggested by M. Broniewski, unacquainted with the high-sounding epithets of contribution, requisition, forced loans, &c., call pillage by its own name, and excuse it by such arguments as the following:—By force the Turk took that country from us, by force he keeps it from us; have we not the right in our turn to take its produce by force from him?

The late Vladika and Danilo, being resolved to elevate Montenegro into the community of civilised states, ordered *tchétas* to be given up. What then? Comes a bad harvest in the Mountain, how are the inhabitants to live? The answer is, that while the sovereigns of Montenegro were teaching their people to keep within the border, they looked to an arrangement with the great powers whereby Montenegro should receive a territory within which civilised beings could live. They had in view, first, that Turkey should be obliged to acquiesce in a definition of the Montenegrine frontier; and, secondly, an extension of that frontier to the coast at Antivari; or, at least, as far as Spizza.

In 1859, after Mirko's victory at Grahovo, and when the Herzegovina only waited the signal to join him, the Porte did find itself obliged to recognise Montenegro as a separate state, and agree to the delineation of a Montenegrine boundary. The great powers sent their emissaries to draw the line; it was drawn, and on every side fell short of the sea. This was a terrible disappointment for the Montenegrines; they impute it partly to the influence of Austria, whose own frontier lies close to Spizza, and whose jealous policy it has hitherto been to exclude independent southern Slāvs from the Adriatic.

Sir Gardner Wilkinson complains that most travellers who ascend to Montenegro from the Bocche go no further than Cetinje, and then come back, saying, that in the Ladder of Cattaro they have found the secret of Montenegrine independence. He advises those who desire to learn the real secret of Montenegrine freedom to prolong their expedition to the Turkish frontier at Niksich and at Spuz. There, on each side, valleys run into the mountain, and the Montenegrine territory is only twelve miles broad. Yet there the highlanders dwell fearlessly, without rampart or defence of any kind save their individual valour.

Nothing would have pleased us better than to obey the injunction of the great traveller, but our visit falling in the depth of winter, the roads to Niksich and Spuz were blockaded by snow. We did our best in making out Rïeka, which lies not far from the Turkish border, in a valley opening to the Lake of Scutari. Rïeka was the home of our good friend Giorgio; but he had kindly halted at Cetinje while we did, and although we had declined his invitation for the Christmas feast, we accepted of his escort with thankfulness. Another welcome companion was the Bosniak, on an embassy from the convent party to buy their Christmas dessert at the Rïeka Bazaar. We have already alluded to the graver mission which brought this gentleman to Cetinje. Besides his experience of Montenegro, he had much to tell us about the Slāv populations in Austria and Turkey.

Our "equipage" on this expedition was worse than ever. One of us obtained a reddish-coloured pony and a leathern saddle; but the other had to put up with a lame mule, and a seat formed by wooden bars; an end of rope, fastened to one side of the bit, served for bridle.

Our road led, first, across the plain, in a direction opposite to that by which we had reached Cetinje; soon it began to climb the rocks, and brought us, on their further side, to the point called Gránitza, or the boundary. Thence the view is beautiful and singular. Cetinje lies in the Katunska, or Alpine canton, Rïeka in the River canton. Between the two, you stand as on a rampart, and look, on the one hand, into the court of the citadel; on the other, down the castle rock to the valley and the enemies' country. Eastward, the Albanian mountains stretch chain after chain of snow-covered summits; at their base, two streams fall into the Lake of Scutari, one is commonly known as the River (Slāv, Rïeka), the other is named Moratcha; in the distance the lake spreads its waters, blue and sunlit, as far as the eye can reach.

We were shown the site on the shores of the lake where rises the Castle of Zabliak, whence the last Prince of Zeta removed his residence to Cetinje. In 1485, Ivan Tsernoïevic, finding he could no longer defend the level country against the Turk, called around him his best heroes, and took of them an oath on the New Testament to abide true to their faith and nation, and rather die than accept terms of the infidel. Whoever broke this oath should be invested with a woman's apron, and hooted from the ranks of men. Then the Prince of Zeta turned his back on his "white castle" and fertile lands, and led his devoted band into the mountains. On the rock-girt plain of Cetinje he planted the eagle-banner of Serbia, and erected a Christian church: thither he transferred the throne of the Princes of Zeta and the see of the metropolitans.

Soon after this the plains of Zeta became the province of a Turkish pasha; and the highlands of Zeta acquired their distinctive name of "Black Mountain;" in Serbian, Cerna Gora; in the Venetian dialect, Montenegro.

Ivan was succeeded by his son, George, who fought valiantly against the Turks; but, having no children, and wishing to end his days in peace, eventually abdicated, and withdrew to Venice. But first, in the Assembly of the Nation, he solemnly made over his power to the metropolitan; and from the date of his departure, 1516, till 1852, Montenegro was ruled by a Vladika, or bishop. Under its Vladikas, the Black Mountain weathered the severest storms of its history; and the fidelity of the Montenegrīnes to the Christian religion, at a time when so many other tribes "fell off," may, at least in part, have been owing to the character of their government. A Christian priest would surely be the last to sanction partnership with the Mahommedan; and the uncompromising policy of the Montenegrīne Vladikas has come down to us in the declaration of their last representative. He was a youth of twenty, and but lately come to the throne. Mehemet Redschid Pasha invited him to make submission to the Sultan, promising to reward him with the Berat. Peter II. answered: "So long as Montenegro is independent, no Berat is needed to constitute me its ruler: should the independence of Montenegro be surrendered, the Berat were but a mockery."

We have already told that, since 1697, the office of Vladika has been hereditary in the Petrovic family; also, that, in 1852, Danilo Petrovic separated the secular from the ecclesiastic dignity, and revived the original title of prince. Had Danilo lived another year he hoped to have retraced the steps of the first prince, and transferred his residence from Cetinje to the shores of the Lake of Scutari, or at least to the neighbourhood of Rïeka.

At the Granitza we began to descend, winding down the side of a long hill; the path was rough, and at first coated with ice, which grew less and less frequent as we proceeded.

In those gorges of the Black Mountain which open on the east and south, the climate is that of Central Italy—as spring to winter, compared with the climate of Cetinje. The valleys yield in abundance fruits, tobacco, vines, and mulberry-trees; the wine produced is red, and considered to be more wholesome than any in Dalmatia; and the Montenegrīne cocoons of silk are of a superior quality. But in the more mountainous regions culture is very laborious, and on the way to Rïeka we remarked patches no larger than flower-beds dotted about in the very clefts of the rock.

The Bosniak remarked them too, and exclaimed, "Every inch of soil turned to account; verily, it is a thrifty people."

"It is not then true," we asked, "that good land on the plain of Cetinje lies neglected?"

He answered, "Whoever told you so knows nothing of Montenegro. What the men leave undone is done by the women; it is astonishing, with their constant warfare and their few resources, what these poor people get out of their ground. Where the plain of Cetinje is not worked, it is either necessary as pasture for the cattle, or the soil is not deep enough for cultivation."

We then inquired if he thought that the industry of the Montenegrīnes in eking out a subsistence from their barren mountains might be taken as a sign that they were naturally diligent and persevering, and would prove these qualities if tried on a wider stage. We had been told that in the Mountain territory lay coal only waiting to be worked till they had a seaport of their own. Was it likely that the highlanders would accommodate themselves to continuous labour like that of working coal? Would they know how to make a civilised use of a seaport, supposing they had one?

"That," said he, "need never be a question. When Montenegro has a port on the Adriatic, as a free port under a Serbian government, it will attract to it the Serb merchants who now trade in Trieste and elsewhere. If the coal is worth anything, there would soon be a company to undertake it. You must observe, that in the present state of matters not Montenegro alone, all the Serb countries are cut off from the sea; a port given to one would be a benefit to all."

We here quoted the remark of a Dalmatian, given by Mr. Paton in his "Highlands and Islands of the Adriatic" : "Dalmatia without Bosnia is a face without a head."

"To be sure it is," answered the Bosniak, "and Bosnia without Dalmatia is a head without a face. Bosnia has the produce, Dalmatia has the ports; to part them, as for ages they have been parted, is to bar the natural development of both."

"Did not Austria at one time hope to add Bosnia and Herzegovina to her empire?"

"Indeed she did, but in the meantime, instead of annexing, she has been losing provinces. Of course one cannot tell what may yet come about. What we would wish to see is, not Bosnia and the Herzegovina added to Dalmatia, but Dalmatia added to Bosnia and the Herzegovina. All three countries are peopled by the same race, and should ever a Christian and a Serb government be firmly established in the inland regions, there can be little doubt but that the coast will make out her junction with them."

"But surely," we said, "though the population in Dalmatia and Bosnia are of one race with those in Serbia, the Herzegovina, and Montenegro, they are divided from them as to religion. We have heard that in Bosnia the descendants of those who, 400 years ago, renegaded from Christianity, hate the Christians more and are more hateful to them than the original Turks."

"The story of the Mussulman Bosniaks is this:— When, at the time of the Turkish conquest, the nobles of Bosnia found that rank and riches were continued to those who apostatised, rather than forfeit their wealth they changed their religion. The poor, who had less to lose, remained faithful; it was a case of the camel and the needle's eye. Further, I can tell you as a fact, that 400 years of apostacy have not obliterated among the Bosnian Mussulmans a sort of superstitious trust in the efficacy of their fathers' faith. In case of desperate illness they call in a Christian priest, and they will cause Christian prayers to be said over their parents' graves. There lingers among them even a tradition that their fathers' race will resume empire, and *lettres de noblesse* and title-deeds of estates received from Serb and Christian monarchs have been handed down in renegade families from an idea that they will be of advantage to the possessors when the Christian kingdom is restored."

"But are not the Dalmatian and other Christian Slāvs Romanists, and as such divided from the Slāvs of the Greek Church?"

"They are, and at one time their sectarian jealousies drove many a brave man into the ranks of the Mahommedan. But nowadays influences are at work whose tendency is to absorb such differences as separate Christians into Latin and Greek. You may have remarked that the Bohemians, who are Catholics, do not therefore wish the less kindly to us, and among the lower classes, even in Dalmatia, religious prejudices do not prevent the Romanist from singing songs about national heroes who are Greek. I am pretty sure that the national sympathy will prove too strong for the sectarian antipathy, at least where, as in the case of Bosnia and Dalmatia, the material interests of the populations demand their union."

After a while he resumed: "I call myself a Bosniak because my forefathers were Bosniaks; but they left the Turkish provinces and settled within the Austrian frontier. My little property is in Slavonia. I was one of those employed by the late Ban Jelachic to bring out plans for improving agriculture."

"Perhaps then you can tell us if the Slāvs on the

military frontier are inclined to assist their brethren against Turkey."

He replied, " Were they not, I should not be here ; " and then, at our request, proceeded further to explain the state of matters. We repeat the substance of what he said, if only to show how the Southern Slāvs in Austria echo the sentiments of those in Turkey. " To have a clear idea you must begin at the beginning. The military frontier was originally organised to defend Christendom against the Turks. Such a barrier was then needed, and the Slāv populations, of which it was chiefly composed, lent themselves gladly to any system which had for its aim to keep out the Mahommedan. It was on the lands of the Slāv, as those lying nearest to Asia, that the Mahommedan swarm principally settled; and, if we except Constantinople and the Greek provinces, it may almost be said that while the Mahommedan remains in Europe he remains on Slavonic ground. The Russian has already driven out the Tartar, the Serbian must drive out the Turk; and till the Turk is gone, Northern and Southern Slāv are alike bound never to lay down arms. Well, nowadays, the Turkish power is broken, in so far that it can no longer molest the portion of Christendom comprehended in the Austrian empire. At this point Austria bids us halt. She does not abolish the military frontier, although she has been much pressed to do so; and although it is not needed for defence, she insists on retaining it; but she uses its soldiers on foreign service, and refuses to let the Slāvs who form it come to the aid of their southren brethren now finishing the common work."

" Perhaps," we suggested, " she thinks it a bad example for the subjects of different governments to meddle in each other's quarrels."

" She had no such scruples in 1848-49, when, during

her own quarrel with the Magyars, our kinsmen from the Turkish provinces crossed the frontier to join us in fighting for her. But now that the Turkish Slāvs are striving for their freedom and nationality, now that it is our turn to help, we may not even give house-room to their stores, shelter to their women and children. Because I was discovered giving shelter to such fugitives and house-room to such stores, the ammunition and provisions on my premises were seized, and I myself was to be made prisoner. Instead of that I crossed the frontier to Bosnia, and then came here to try what could be done for my people in another way."

"But if," said we, "the Serbs have an enemy in Austria, they have powerful friends in France and Russia."

"Powerful friends who, when their service is rendered, may take care to repay themselves at our expense, while, in the meantime, all open patronage from Russia draws on us the hostility of Austria and England."

At this we laughed and said, "Come, do not try to persuade us you would not be glad of such help to start with as Napoleon gave the Italians."

"Of course we should be glad of it, but what we want far more than foreign intervention is *non-intervention* applied to our cause as it was to the Italian. We might do without open aid from France or Russia, if we were certain that Austria would not co-operate with Turkey, and that England would not secure the Porte money wherewith to maintain the war."

"And when you have gained the day, are we still to practice non-intervention while you effect a junction with your northern brethern, and inaugurate the empire of Panslavism?"

He laughed. "You English people are too clever by

half. You can look so far forward as to imagine the union of the whole Slavonic race under one government, but you do not recognise that at this moment the southern division of that race is struggling to assert an independent nationality. You can discern champions against Panslavism in the Austrian and Turk; you do not see that in order to render Panslavism impossible, you have only to balance Sláv against Sláv."

We thought this argument sounded very like those in Count Krasinski's treatise on Panslavism; and certainly we had heard almost the same words from the lips of Slávs of various nationalities in Dalmatia, and Vienna, and Prague.

As we descended the rock-gorge to Rïeka, a wailing cry broke on our ears; it ended in a sustained drone. "Hark!" quoth Giorgio, "that is the lament. Women who have lost a relative in the Herzegovina, will gather to the bazaar to-morrow to mourn him, sing his exploits, and how he fell." Again the wail rang through the hills; it startled us painfully, and the tone of the last long note was heartrending. Giorgio said, "When we are at Rïeka, I will show you one of these laments written in a book." The book proved to be that of the Vladika's poems, and we found therein a lamentation full of wild and touching poetry. It is the bewailment of a sister over her brother.

"My falcon, my eagle!" she calls the departed, using the Montenegrīne epithet for a hero, "whither hast thou flown from me? Didst thou not know the treacherous Turks? didst thou not know that they would deceive thee? Oh! my deep wound, my wound without cure! Alas! for my lost world, my world dearer than the sun! Thou pride of brothers! Had thy place been at the side of the emperor, thou wouldst have become his chief minister. If thy place had been at the side of the king, he would have made thee his general. Oh! my brother, where is thy beautiful head? Could I but kiss it! could I but comb its long hair! But the enemy will desecrate thy beloved head; he will deck with it the walls of Travnik!" The singer frequently speaks of herself as a "poor cuckoo" (kukavitza); for, according to Serb legend, the voice of the cuckoo is that of a sister calling on her lost brother, and who will not be comforted, because he answers not.

But for the general mourning for Danilo, we should, at the bazaar, have heard something better than laments—ballads celebrating the feats of national heroes, chanted by minstrels who are heroes themselves. Travellers, more fortunate than us, describe these Montenegrīne singers as realising the bards in Homer's Odyssey.

From Cetinje to Rïeka is a three hours' journey; but we had been late in setting out, and now arrived when it was too dark for a good view of the valley. We could just see that the houses of the village were surrounded by a verandah, and in a different style to those of Cetinje; and we also caught the outline of Danilo's stone bridge, which spans the river below the town.

Above Rïeka stands a small fort; its story is curious. George Tsernoïevic here erected his printing-press, where church books were printed as early as 1494. Specimens of these still exist, and are among the oldest printed works in Cyrillic character. Eventually, the printing establishment was turned into a fort; and the types, melted into bullets, were shot off against the Turks.

At Rïeka we had been promised quarters better than at Cetinje; great, therefore, was our chagrin to find the one lodging with a stove already full. It was, we understood, a house belonging to the Prince, and we afterwards occupied it when Rïeka had been burnt, and when it was almost the only dwelling roofed in. The guest-chamber of the inn was fireless, and had broken windows; against each of its walls stood a bed large enough for the accommodation of half a dozen giants; one corner displayed a cupboard with glass doors, of which every pane was cracked; a gaily painted chest occupied the other. Between the windows hung a daub, representing the Emperor and Empress of the French, with their son. Even here we only obtained a resting-place by the courtesy of persons who resigned their prior claim; and we certainly never should have got meat for supper had not our companions insisted on our behalf. We felt a little out of countenance when the landlady, bringing in our fowl, made the remark: "It was plain we did not belong to their religion, or we never should have asked meat during the Christmas fast." No one else touched even milk or cheese.

But though we did eat meat during the Christmas fast, every one gave themselves the utmost trouble to make us comfortable; as for Giorgio, no sooner had he seen his wife and child, than he returned to the inn, and there remained till he had taken all necessary care for our well-being.

That night the wind changed; and the bright mild weather that had favoured us since we left Cattaro gave way to a snow-storm. This, at the moment of the Christmas fair, was a real calamity; hundreds of people were prevented from attending; others suffered much on the journey. The show of stalls was proportionately small; and of all the good things in requisition for the convent feast, nothing was to be found but walnuts strung together in long necklaces.

The bazaar was held in an open court surrounded by houses, of which the lower storey served for a shop; the upper, ascended by an outer stair, for dwellings. To see about some specimens of costume, we paid a visit to the court tailor, whose achievements we had especially admired in the dress of the Prince and the crimson and gold jacket of the Bosniak. It appeared, however, that he sold nothing ready made, and could make nothing to order within three or four months. We therefore left with him three dolls to be dressed, one as a Montenegrine, one as a woman in her holiday garb, the other in the mourning costume worn while we were in Cerna Gora. We also bought a cap, on the subject of which we still feel puzzled.

Sir G. Wilkinson says that the Montenegrine head-dress is a fez, surrounded by a turban : we never saw a Montenegrine in either. Instead, they wore a round crimson bonnet, without tassel, worked in a corner of the crown with gold, and trimmed round the rim with a black silk band. These Montenegrine bonnets became fashionable in Corfu, as smoking-caps, and some of them were to be seen in the London Exhibition among the things sent from the Ionian Islands. We were repeatedly assured that they were the characteristic Montenegrine head-gear, and were told, further, that the broad red field on the crown represents fatal Kóssovo, while the golden corner is free Montenegro ; the black band is worn as mourning for those of the Serbian lands which are still occupied by the Turk.

Presently Giorgio invited us to see his dwelling, and led the way to a tidy upper chamber. "Had my room contained a stove," said he, "I should have offered it to you for last night." We could not help asking why he, who evidently knew the comfort of a fireplace, did not put up one for himself. "We Montenegrines," he answered, "do not require warm houses. In winter evenings it is enough for us to sit together in the kitchen. We are healthy and strong: even our infants* do not need to be swaddled or coddled; we just wrap them in a cloth, and if it is cold weather, we set them near the fire." Coffee was brought to us by Giorgio's wife, a pretty young woman, on whom the mourning costume looked quite tasteful—we were shown some of her holiday garb, jackets in form like the Greek, crimson and purple velvet, embroidered in gold.

As we left the house we caught sight of Giorgio's little boy; he was not quite well that day, but seemed to us a fine chubby little fellow. After all the father had been telling us about hardiness, his only son appeared warmly clad.

We then returned to the inn, and for some time sat round the kitchen fire. The changing society was sufficiently amusing. Now entered a voivode grandly attired, now quite a poor man in vile raiment, but the richest appeared not to think he had a superior right to a seat, nor did the poorest give up his place, or seem abashed at the neighbourhood of finer clothes than his own. As regards ourselves, we were never in any place where the presence of strangers was so quietly taken, no one noticed us except so far as to make room for us by the fire. On the other hand, if we chose to commence a conversation, it was sure to be continued with liveliness and courtesy.

And now the question began to be mooted, should we or should we not return to Cetinje that day? The snow was falling thick; crossing the hill would not be pleasant, but then if frost set in to-morrow, the road

---

* "Le défaut de soins médicaux fait que peu d'enfants faibles arrivent à l'adolescence, de manière que ceux qui y parviennent sont tous forts et bien constitués. L'absence de travaux d'esprit, la vie en plein air, leurs rudes labeurs par le grand soleil et le froid, l'influence de l'hérédité, la sobriété et la tempérance sensuelle viennent encore ajouter à ces causes de vigueur."—*Notice médicale sur le Monténégro*, par M. Tedeschi.

would become impassable for horses, and here we were at Rïeka, in a fireless room with broken windows. At present many people were leaving the bazaar for Cetinje: if we started at once, we should have company, and, if need be, assistance by the way.

We started. Giorgio brought his great capote for an extra wrap, and engaged two stout fellows to take his place with us. He said he would have himself seen us safe back to Cattaro, but for the Christmas feast and the illness of his child. We bade him good-bye with great regret; he had left his business in order to accompany us, and had undertaken all the trouble of the journey, yet he made no charge for his services, and seemed quite taken aback when, at parting, we gave him something for his little boy.

We have since learnt that the day we crossed the hill from Rïeka was the worst of all that winter. Now that it is well over, we are glad to know what the Black Mountain looks like in bad weather. The snow fell in thick flakes, all around was snow; the Montenegrines in their white garments, and heads enveloped in their *strookas*, hurried past us, filling the air with their shrill voices. As evening drew on, the scene became unearthly, like the ghost of the scene of yesterday. Winding up the mountains the path was very steep, and as our beasts grew tired they frequently came to a dead halt. The luckless mule was lamer than ever, and more than once fell down on its nose. So long, however, as it did not roll over on its side, the best chance was to stick to it, seeing that one could not have hoped to walk, where the mountaineers themselves were scarcely able to keep their feet. How we looked forward to the top of the hill! It proved the commencement of worse troubles. Descending to Cetinje the snow lay thick, and a tremendous wind had sprung up; not a north wind, that would have finished us, but a wind that melted the snow, so that every step was a plunge. Here the mule did better than the pony; its sagacity in choosing sure footing was marvellous, and, at any rate, we were well off in comparison to the walkers. The women, who had hitherto been trudging along, talking, laughing, and encouraging each other, now tumbled down repeatedly, and under their burdens it was not so easy to rise. At length one of these hardy, patient creatures began to cry; she was not as strong-looking as the rest. We saw her again next day all right, and brave and merry as ever.

How we looked forward to the house of Kertso! But here, once more, we were doomed to disappointment. The men who had escorted us from Rïeka knocked; our hostess herself opened, spoke to the guides, then turned and shut us out. We supposed she was gone for a light, and, in fact, soon the door reopened. This time it was Kertso himself; he also spoke to the guides—we distinguished the word "locanda"—then again the door clapped to, and we were shut out again. What to do did not at first appear; the Bosniak, having seen us to the entrance of Kertso's house, had departed to his own, and with the guides we could not speak. They were dragging our beasts to the comfortless locanda, when from the farther line of street a light streamed over the snow, and a loud cheery voice hailed us. Again our poor beasts were pulled along; and arrived at the light, we this time found an open house, and hosts who bade us welcome. A young woman assisted us to dismount and an old woman led us into a large kitchen, where she made us sit by the fire.

We found ourselves in a regular Montenegrīne house, and unable to make a soul understand us; but our hosts were of the kindest—they took off our cloaks, spoke coaxingly to us, and pitied us as if we were children. And now a known tongue sounded behind us, and the Bosniak entered. He apologized for having taken for granted that when we got to Kertso's door we were all right; and added, "This also is a little locanda, and upstairs there is a chamber with a stove; the person who rents it is at present in Cattaro, and you must take possession of it till you can get a better. I have ordered the stove to be lighted, but till the room becomes warm, I am afraid you must remain here." So there we sat round the fire, and the old woman brought us coffee. But soon the kitchen began to fill with water, which at first content with coming in at the door, ere long poured through a hole in the wall— wider and wider grew the pools, closer and closer the circle by the hearth—at length a hissing sound announced that the logs would soon cease to blaze. The women lifted what they could out of harm's way, but viewed the mishap calmly, as if accustomed to it; meanwhile the landlord was telling a long story to the Bosniak. "Ha!" cried the latter, "water has burst into the house of Kertso, and the rooms are flooded. I know that last summer the roof wanted repairs, which it did not get; no doubt it has broken in. Well for you that you were not there." At last the room upstairs was reputed habitable, and retiring thither we inquired into the state of our carpet-bag—thanks to the gallant bearing of the maiden who carried it over the mountain, some part of its contents were dry. The old woman came to us, and when she had otherwise helped us as much as she could, seated herself before the fire, and held up various of our articles to dry. Of her consolatory talk we could only understand a word or two, but the motherly tone was intelligible enough.

And now it was the stove's turn to exhibit alarming

peculiarities; it soon let us know that unless carefully attended to, it might be expected to set the house on fire. Meanwhile, without, the storm increased in fury, the wind was tremendous, there was thunder and lightning; we were told that the inmates thought it likely their roof would follow the example of Kertso's Altogether the chances were that we should be disturbed that night, so we lay down without undressing. Tired as we were, we slept at once, only awakened at intervals by crashes and flashes.

At dawn the tumult ceased, and when we arose and asked after our neighbours, we heard that the floor of the kitchen was once more dry land, and that such inhabitants of Cetinje as had been storm-stayed at Rïeka, came now trooping across the hill unscathed. Of course, no one had expected us the preceding evening, but so soon as our return and its attendant circumstances were known, the prince sent to tell us that arrangements had been made for our occupying the upper story of a house whose usual tenant was in the Herzegovina. The abode was in charge of the Bocchese housemaid and her husband, an Austrian deserter, who made himself generally useful. Extra furniture was sent from the palace, and the princess's maid, a purpose-like Bohemian, came to see that we were all right. Before evening we were installed in two (water-tight) rooms, with a spring arm-chair, a sofa, and a stove that had a good idea of its functions.

And now began the most enjoyable part of our stay in Montenegro. Frost had set in, and the road to Cattaro was impassable for horses, so there we were with time to rest and to pick up information. We did not want for society, nor, after the first day, for exercise, and the little girl of the French doctor showed us some capital walks about Cetinje.

The doctor himself came to see us the morning after our ride from Rïeka, and having ascertained that we were none the worse, poured forth the recital of his own grievances. "Je vous dirai, mesdames," he began, "that you must have excellent constitutions not to have suffered from the effects of that storm. For myself, I confess that life in Montenegro does not suit me; for the last three weeks I have had a cold; I am lodged with my wife and child in a single room. When it is bad weather, we cannot go to dinner at the palace. Yesterday evening, for example, it was impossible to cross the road. During last night, from the violence of the tempest, the house rocked to its foundations." We could not resist answering, that his experience of life in Montenegro doubtless increased his admiration for the Montenegrīnes, who during centuries had borne what he bore, and worse, rather than submit to the Turk. "Pardon," interrupted he; "that is a sentiment to which I do not aspire. Often I ask myself, Qu'est-ce que c'est que la liberté monténégrine? Cannot any one be independent who chooses to dwell on the top of a rock? I avow, that rather than cultivate such liberty, I would a thousand times be subject to the Turk." With considerable irritation the Bosniak answered him —"Do you suppose you would better your condition by exchanging it for subjection to the Turk? Try life in the Herzegovina, and see if you find it pleasanter than life in Montenegro. The Montenegrīne bears privations; the Christian subjects of the Turk must be content to bear cruelties, insults, shame. You see yourself that at the end of four centuries it is he that can endure his position no longer; that with hands folded, the subject of the Turk begs for help of the Montenegrīne." The doctor hastily changed the subject. "If you knew," he said to us afterwards, "how monotonous is the conversation of these Slāvs! It is the fashion, chez nous, to find them clever and witty; to me they seem to have but one idea—to think and talk of nothing but their eternal nationality and freedom."

When the prince's secretary and the Bosniak visited us, the text of discourse was usually some published account of Montenegro. They would point out wherein its statements seemed to them inaccurate, and what changes had taken place since it was written. Many were the anecdotes related; the life and work of Danilo became better known to us; the information about country and people would fill a book; it is difficult to select what may find space in a few pages.

One day we said to the secretary—"Do you know what a travelled and accomplished Englishman told us, 'That at this hour, in Montenegro, there is no code but revenge'?" "Indeed!" answered he; "then to-morrow I had better bring our code to show you." He brought it, and translated for us some of the articles from the Serb. There is a published translation in Italian, and a French translation may be found in M. Delarue's Memoir.

The code* now in force in Montenegro is that of Danilo. It comprises ninety-five articles, and has for its basis the ordinances of St. Peter. A third, and somewhat less primitive code, rendered necessary by the more civilised state of the people, is now in process of compilation. Even by St. Peter's law—the first *written* law in Cerna Gora—private feuds and the vendetta are abolished, but at that time there were no regular officers of justice, and it was necessary to hold out rewards to private persons who would punish an offender caught in the act. Nowadays the corps of so-called "perianiks" undertake the duty of police, and each company in its

* 1861.

own village brings criminals before the judge, and sees to the execution of sentences. Capital offenders are shot, and for smaller transgressions there are fines and a state prison at Cetinje. But the prison is often empty, and has rarely more than two or three tenants; indeed, in a poor country like Montenegro precautions are taken not to let captivity become a resource for the improvident or the lazy. The victuals of the prisoners are paid for by themselves, and an article of the code provides that criminals sentenced to prison shall be employed in mending the roads, or on other works of public utility.

The ordinance abolishing vendetta runs thus— "Whereas, in Montenegro and the Berda there exists a custom of vendetta, by which vengeance falls not only on the murderer or guilty individual, but also on his innocent relatives, these vendetta are rigorously prohibited. No one shall dare to molest the brother or other guiltless relatives of the criminal, and he who kills an innocent person shall himself be put to death. The murderer alone, who shall be sought for and brought to justice, shall atone for the murder with his head."

Articles 24, 25, 26, are directed against *tchétas* and all infringement of the enemy's country in time of truce. "In order to preserve with neighbouring countries the tranquillity needful to our reciprocal interests and the welfare of the State, theft, brigandage, and depredations of what kind soever, are prohibited in time of peace. . . . In time of peace or of truce (*bessa*) with the parts of Turkey bordering on our country, brigandage, theft, and all depredations are forbidden, and should they occur, the booty shall be returned to those from whom it has been taken, and the guilty parties shall be punished. In case of transgression on the territory of a neighbouring country, the culprit shall receive the same punishment as if his offence had been committed against a brother Montenegrīne."

Other sentences are primitive enough; one has come down unaltered from the days of the first prince. The man who does not take arms when his country is attacked shall be deprived of his weapons, and never may he again wear them. He can never hold any place of honour in his country's service, and he shall be condemned to wear a woman's apron, that every one may be informed that he has not the heart of a man.

Several articles are directed against insults—not only insulting actions, such as a kick, or a blow with the pipe, for which it is lawful to retaliate by killing the offender on the spot, but also against insulting words. We were told that such abusive epithets as are commonly bandied about among the lower ranks of other countries, would be held to sully the mouth and the honour of the poorest Montenegrīne. It is enacted that, "The Montenegrīne who insults a judge, voivode, or elder, shall pay a fine of twenty talari, and a fine of twenty talari shall be paid by any judge, voivode, or elder who insults a common Montenegrīne."

A thief for his first offence is fined, for his third offence is shot. During the year 1859, they said, there were fifteen thefts committed in Montenegro; in the course of 1861, there were only two crimes, and one of these was a theft to the amount of a few pence.

We will next quote one or two articles of the code of Montenegro, which may help to answer the doctor's question—"Qu'est-ce que c'est que la liberté monténégrine?"

"Article 1. All Montenegrīnes are equal before law.

"Article 2. (French translation.) En vertu de la liberté héréditaire jusqu'ici conservée, l'honneur, la probité, la vie, et la liberté demeurent assurés à tout Monténégrin, et personne ne peut toucher à ces choses sacrées qu'en vertu d'un jugement."

On the question of religious toleration, it is written:

"Article 90. Although in our State there is no nationality but the Slāvic-Serbian, and no religion but the Orthodox Eastern Church, nevertheless the professor of any other religion may live among us freely, and enjoy the same privileges as a brother Montenegrīne."

On the right of asylum:

"According to the will and testament of St. Peter, who was our sovereign, every fugitive setting foot in our free State shall there be safe, and no one shall dare to molest him, so long as he behaves peaceably. He shall enjoy the same rights as a native Montenegrīne, and if he does evil, he shall be chastised according to this code."

We asked the secretary if any person not members of the Eastern Church resided in Montenegro. He answered —"I myself am a Roman Catholic; the servants who occupy this house are Roman Catholics. There are at this moment a few Mahommedan fugitives residing within our territory, and the prince has given them permission to erect a place of worship whenever they choose. For fear they should not have full confidence in his sanction he has offered them money to assist the building, and not even Mirko has a word to say against it."

As for St. Peter's ordinance respecting the right of asylum, it was elicited by the following incident:—An Austrian soldier escaped hither in order to avoid a flogging. The Austrians demanded that he should be given up. St. Peter, who knew that the man's offence had been slight, and that his superior officer was cruel, refused, except on condition that his punishment should be remitted. The Austrians promised this—they gave the promise in writing; still St. Peter would not turn out the fugitive, but only showed him the written promise, and left him to take his own way. The fugitive gave himself up, and no sooner did the Austrians see him in their power than they had him flogged to death.

Dreadful was the wrath of St. Peter; he beheld in this incident a stain on the honour of Montenegro, and in his will he laid a curse on every Montenegrīne who, on any plea or consideration whatever, should give up a fugitive to his persecutors.

We were anxious to learn what sort of position the law of Montenegro assigns to women.

According to Danilo's code, the Montenegrīne woman has, in every respect, the same legal rights as a man, and especial provision is made to secure her a full share in the division of property. When a father's possessions are parted among his children, daughters inherit as well as sons, and an only daughter can succeed to the whole property of both her parents. When a woman marries, she receives a dowry which passes to her husband's family, but in return, should she be left a widow, she is entitled to her husband's share in the common stock, and, should she marry again, the family of her first husband must continue her a certain pension. In cases of domestic quarrel, where the man refuses to dwell with his wife, they are at liberty to separate, but not to break the marriage. Neither of them may wed any one else, and the maintenance of the wife must be provided for by the husband. Further, care is taken by law that no woman be married against her inclination. When, as is usual, persons have been affianced in childhood, the priest is forbidden to marry them without having ascertained that the bride is a willing party; and if a girl should dislike the spouse chosen for her by her parents, and choose one for herself, the family is not allowed to interfere. "Such couples," so runs the sentence, "are united by love."

"A woman who murders her husband shall be put to death like any other murderer, only no weapon may be employed in her execution, for it is shameful to use arms against one who cannot take arms in defence." By what agency a woman shall be executed is not provided by the code of Danilo, but, according to ancient usage, in cases of gross crime she is stoned, her father casting the first stone. With this fearful doom was visited every transgression of social purity, and though Danilo's code sanctions capital punishment only in the case of a married woman, by popular custom there is no exception. Nor, according to Montenegrine standard, is crime less degrading to the stronger than to the weaker culprit; the male offender equally forfeits his life, the honour of his family receives as deep a stain; while her father undertakes the punishment of the girl, the man is shot by his own relatives. Thus have they "put the evil away from among them;" the Montenegrine spurns social impurity as unworthy of his manhood, and even when dealing with their Mahommedan enemies, even in their wildest tchétas, with these "barbarians" a woman is safe.

It has been remarked that the social virtue of the Montenegrine is not less admirable in itself than as an evidence of what the precepts of Christianity can do for the moral life of a people even when its material life has been reduced to the verge of barbarism.

That the Montenegrine considers it as below him to offer violence to the defenceless, sufficed for the protection of women and their property even before the establishment of law and police. Through any part of the country they might walk unguarded and carry what they would without fear of molestation, and it was even sufficient for the security of any person, be he stranger or fugitive, that a woman should take him under her charge. It is not, however, to be denied, that in a country where war is the business of life, the very fact of being defenceless is considered the mark of an inferior being. The vast, the immeasurable superiority of one who can take care of himself and others, over one who requires to be taken care of, needs no demonstration, it is taken for granted; and so long in Montenegro as war shall continue to be the business of life, this feeling cannot change. In the meantime there is no feeling of dislike or suspicion against a woman who rises above the general position of inferiority. "Why should they not do as we do if they have the spirit?" These words we heard from the lips of a Montenegrīne. A woman who has ever taken part in the defence of her country is highly prized, and made the subject of national poems; a former traveller records having seen a Montenegrin girl who by some exploit acquired the right to wear arms; and we were ourselves witnesses of the honour in which Montenegrīnes hold the sister of Prince Nicolas, because she begged her father to allow her to accompany him to the seat of war.

Some conventional usages, more or less characteristic of a great part of the whole Southern Slavonic race, appear in the behaviour of the Montenegrīne woman. Her salutation to her husband and her husband's guest is the same as that generally offered to the gospodar; she kisses the hand and the hem of the tunic. A more curious custom is that which regards it as indelicate for a young married woman to address her husband before company; from a like feeling, the husband avoids mention of his wife; and if he cannot help speaking of her, premises her name with a sort of apology.

Of a different character is the use of the invocation,

"My brother, or my sister, in God." To claim the assistance of the most absolute stranger, it is only necessary to address by this term. "Are we not all His offspring?" is the original idea; and in Serbian poetry, the sun, the moon, the bird, the tree, every creature of the One Father, is called on to aid the sufferer as "a brother or sister in God." From her greater weakness, it is the woman who most frequently makes appeals of this nature; and the vengeance of Heaven would instantly overtake him who should either refuse aid thus invoked, or abuse his office of protector.

Another custom, still in force in Montenegro, is that of swearing "brotherhood." Two individuals bind themselves by solemn oaths to mutual aid, attachment, fidelity: their tie is stronger and more sacred than that of blood. The idea of such a relationship is not Montenegrine; it is human, world-old; we have world-famous instances of it in Achilles and Patroclus, in David and Jonathan. What would seem to be characteristic of the Southern Slavonic "friendship bond" is that women, as well as men, are accustomed to engage in it. Two women may, and do, thus bind themselves, and solemnly receive the Church's blessing on their contract; or, a woman pledges herself as a "bond-sister" to a man; and it is said that there never was an instance of the association degenerating from its fraternal character.

As for the material existence of the Montenegrine woman, one need scarcely say that it has its full share of the toil and hardship of life on the mountain. War and agriculture are the employments of man; on woman devolves often, besides a good deal of field labour, the work of the household, the manufacture of clothing, and the carriage of produce to market. By the latter arrangement a great part of the commerce of Montenegro passes through the hands of women; but strangers riding up 'to Cetinje from Cattaro, and meeting the highlanders on their way to the Bazaar, are not favourably impressed by the sight of heavy burdens on female shoulders.

Laborious as are the occupations of woman in Montenegro, they are not such as to impair her health, or debase her social character. Would that the same could be said of the life of women in more civilised countries! On this head we have the testimony of one who ought to be a good judge—a physician, and a Frenchman. The Montenegrīne women, he says, work more than the men. "On les voit portant des fardeaux énormes, cheminer lestement aux bords des précipices; souvent comme si elles ne sentaient pas le poids qui les charge, elles tiennent à la main leurs fuseaux ou leurs chaussettes, et, tout en filant ou en tricotant, elles causent ensemble. Mais ces travaux n'humilient pas la femme; elle est inviolable, elle ne conçoit point l'amour sans le mariage ou sans le meurtre du séducteur. Si les rudes labeurs lui enlèvent vite certains charmes, ils lui procurent aussi des dédommagements : une santé toujours florissante, une grande vigueur et l'innocence des mœurs ; bienfaits dont sont privées beaucoup de filles de nos grandes villes, dont la vie sédentaire et souvent oisive les livre à tous les écarts de leur imagination et à tous les égarements des passions qui flétrissent la beauté avant l'heure." *

And now the long Christmas fast was drawing to a close; the Christmas feast was to begin. It was high time, for, by reason of abstinence, every face had grown thin and yellow; but joy had fled from the coming holiday; it was, like the last, to be celebrated in mourning —without songs, without shooting, without any of its

* M. Tedeschi, " Notice médicale sur le Monténégro."

festive characteristics, saving only the quasi-religious ceremony of the "badniak."

A few days after our arrival at Cetinje, the prince, with his "following," had gone into the mountains to cut down the yule log; on Christmas-eve it was to be brought home. He now sent us a message to the effect that he would have asked us to witness the ceremony in his house, were it not contrary to the custom of the country that on this occasion foreigners should be present in the household circle. A like pretext served for the banishment of the French doctor. Considering that the Christmas party at the palace was to be a family gathering, and that very few of the prince's relatives speak any language but Serb, we did not find anything mysterious in a custom which excluded foreigners from their meeting. We were, however, afterwards told that this time the exclusion was really owing to that suspicious dislike to intimacy with foreigners entertained by Mirko since his brother's murder—the English from their patronage of the Turks being for the moment almost as odious as the Austrians, in whose land Danilo died.

But it would have been vexatious on this account to miss witnessing the badniak, and with no small satisfaction we heard of the following arrangement:—It happened that the proprietors of the locanda in which we passed the night of the storm belonged to a family not long resident in Cetinje, who had but lately set up for themselves. For the young couple and their mother to keep Christmas alone seemed dolorous enough, and already old Yovana had been crying over it; therefore it was agreed that the bringing home of the log should be duly held in Andrea's kitchen, and that we and some others, who, like our hosts, were passing the Christmas away from our own fire-side, should be present at the ceremony. "You will excuse me," said the tall young landlord, "if I am awkward and cannot make fine speeches, for this is the first time I have acted house-father." "Ah," quoth another of the party, "you should see the log brought home in some of our large houses. We have here a family numbering seventy guns, besides old men, women, and children."

About half-past six o'clock on Christmas-eve (January 5th, New Style), Andrea came for us, and with his assistance, united to that of the Bocchese maid, we steered clear of the snow-drifts and pool of water that lay between his door and our own. Arrived in the locanda we found the kitchen swept clean and the kitchen fire in a cheery blaze. Around the hearth was a row of seats, and at one end of this circle places were assigned to us. By degrees our "scratch" party gathered, and then the ceremony began. First entered old Yovana. Nothing could exceed the gravity of her aspect; she carried a lighted taper, and took her station in front of the fire. Then came the house-father, bringing in the badniak—three logs, or rather trees, their stems protruding from under his arms, their branches trailing behind him along the floor. At the entrance of the badniak all rose, and the men, taking off their caps, greeted it in words like these:—"Welcome, O log! God save thee!" The badniak was then placed on the fire, and the house-father sprinkled it with raki, uttering the while benedictions on all friends, and wishes for the coming year. Glasses of raki were then handed round, and each guest drank to his host. When it came to the turn of the Bosniak, he, being accustomed to the ceremony, made a speech of some length, wishing Andrea a house of his own and a son. The Montenegrīne answered, "May God give our prince a long arm and a sharp sword from the field of Kóssovo."

This has been a Serb toast for nearly five hundred years.

In a rich family we should now have sat down to table; but Andrea's house boasted no table, and supper was represented by two plates of cakes brought in by the mistress, and set on the floor before the fire. These cakes were made of apple, and really delicious; unluckily, we have forgotten what they are called, but in Montenegro they take the place of shortbread and bun in Scotland. Before the cakes were presented to the company, a portion of them was thrown upon the logs, the housefather making an invocation. Herewith the ceremonies ended. All sat round the fire and chatted, old Yovana especially distinguishing herself. The prince's secretary translated to us the conversation. Meanwhile the young house-father, released from his difficult duties, slipped into a seat behind the blaze, and began confidential discourse with the Bosniak. Their talk was of the next campaign, and Andrea proposed that they should be brothers and fight side by side. The mutual obligation of such brothers is this: should one of them be slightly wounded, it is his friend who carries him out of the battle; should one of them be desperately wounded, and no chance remain of saving him from the enemy, it is his friend who strikes off his head.

Properly speaking, the evening of the badniak should conclude with a grand letting off of firearms, wherein families of seventy guns come out to great advantage. Because of the national mourning, not a shot was heard in Cetinje, and our little party separated in quiet, our friends promising to call for us next day on their way to the ten o'clock mass.

On Christmas morning before dawn we were awakened by the ringing of bells, and, for the first time since our arrival, beheld the sun rise on Cetinje. After that day we never missed the sight, so beautiful was the effect of the grey rocks and snowy field, tinged first with a pallid blue and then with a glowing blush. But while we enjoyed this scene of our Christmas morn, we little thought of what we were losing. Contrary to expectation the prince and his family attended mass, not at ten, but at six A.M.; and as the sun rose on the plain the young "gospodar," in kalpak and plume, issued from the door of the convent chapel and received the Christmas greeting of his people. Hundreds of the white-clad mountain warriors—those old unconquerable champions of Christendom—gathered round their chief with the salutation, "Truly, this day Christ is born!"

Our ill luck was shared by those who had taught us to rely on mass taking place at the usual hour, and at first no one could account for the change. Afterwards it was explained as a kindly device on the part of the archimandrite to hasten the hour of breakfast for the exhausted people. Some of our friends were roused from their slumbers by a summons to keep their feast with the prince. Said one of these, "I do not feel as if it were Christmas-day, for I have had no mass." Others, whose duty bound them to be at least as alert as their sovereign, received no bidding to the palace, and lost both mass and breakfast.

We were honoured with various calls, every visitor dressed in his best, and some wearing the highland dress who were not born to it. On this occasion we were able to assure ourselves that, with the Montenegriïnes at least, it is not "fine feathers that make the fine bird;" the white close-fitting coat and gaiter form an unmerciful costume for any but the athletic mountaineer. Later in the day we offered our good wishes at the palace, and after dinner received congratulatory visitors of a poorer class, till we had exchanged greetings with every one we had seen in Cetinje, including the palace servants and the two women from the locanda. Each brought us something—an orange, an apple, a pomegranate—gifts too small to be offered except in Cetinje; but there, owing to the absolute dearth of luxuries, more acceptable than can readily be conceived. (Some time afterwards a hamper of oranges and lemons came as a present to one of the convent party; and "gallantries," consisting of one orange and lemon, were forthwith sent round to his principal acquaintance.) These compliments of the season we returned as well as we could, and made the discovery that maraschino is the refreshment conventionally offered to Christmas callers. Last of all the visitors appeared our young host of the preceding evening. His errand was to thank us for a Christmas gift made to his wife, and to renew his apologies for having awkwardly acted the part of house-father. "Besides all that," said he, "you must forgive the poverty of the feast. I know well that many a one would have spent sixty or seventy guldens to have entertained you properly, but at present, as you may be aware, we in Montenegro are poor."

The disappointment on Christmas morn was in some sort made up to us by another opportunity of seeing the gospodar, surrounded by his senators, voivodes, and heroes of many fights. Every day, about three P.M., this goodly company used to take its station in front of the palace-court, and there to practise shooting at the target. One afternoon we were invited to look on.

We found together some hundred warriors—picked men they would be anywhere—the poorer, with white garments; the wealthy, in picturesque and richly-coloured attire. Distinctive uniform they had none, saving the badge of the Serbian eagle; many wore splendidly mounted weapons, not a few Turkish spoil.

Contemplating this assemblage, and contrasting it with similar assemblies in other lands, we could not but recognise the words of the old Serb ballad to be as true to-day as in the time of Ivan Tsernoïevic: "The Latins are rich, they have gold and silver, and the skill of workmen; but the Serbs have the proud and princely bearing, and the glad, fearless eye of heroes."

Among his "following" the gospodar was distinguished by his lofty stature and tunic of green and gold. Eagerly watching the marksmen stands his sister—a dame of resolute mien, with loaded pistols at her girdle—and from a window in one of the court-towers looks forth the sweet face of little Princess Milïena.

The gun used by the shooters was long and slender, its stock inlaid with mother-of-pearl; the target was set at first a short way off, afterwards much farther; but the difference between foreign and English measurements prevented us from ascertaining the distance in yards. As for the skill of the Montenegrine marksmen, we, of course, could be no judges; such opinions as we have heard or read are in its favour. The shooters stood in a throng; we could perceive no sort of military formality in their practice; a good deal of talking went on, but no cheering, or any demonstration, which might have told us what we afterwards learnt, that they were shooting for a prize. The winner was the patriarch of a large family, and reputed the most honest man in Montenegro; as such, chosen for the state-treasurer.

The gospodar advanced to greet us, and then returned to take his turn with the rest. His shot seemed invariably to hit the target; and we were told that, like his two predecessors, he is one of the best marksmen in the realm. Presently the Grand Voivode, Mirko, came up, and held a conversation through the medium of the secretary. As Mirko, not to mention being the hero of

Grahovo, is himself a bard, a singer of valorous exploits, we appealed to him to point out some of the most distinguished warriors present. Casting his eye round the circle, he indicated a Montenegrīne poorly dressed, shorter of stature than the rest, of especially simple and unpretending aspect. "That man," said Mirko, "has with his own hand killed twenty-five Turks; his cousin has killed thirty-five—but he is in the Herzegovina." The secretary added: "In a hand-to-hand combat the mountaineers reckon ten Turks for each Montenegrīne; the cousins noted by Mirko are therefore really something more than common, for they are still young, and can between them answer for sixty Turks. In this computation foes merely shot down do not count—to gain credit for having slain a Turk, a Montenegrīne must have struck off his head." After this conversation it must be supposed that Mirko ceased to suspect us, for he sent his aide-de-camp to tell us that if the house we were in pleased us, and we wished to retain it for future visits, it was his property, and he would be happy to sell or let it to us.

Perhaps it is as well to add, that while the Montenegrīne regards the slaughter of Turks under existing relations as pleasing in the sight of Heaven and of all good men, he does not, like a Mahommedan or a Crusader, practise war with the infidel as a short cut to Paradise. He requires no such stimulus: the Turk is to him the trampler of his religion, the oppressor of his nation, the robber of his country, the abuser of women — he fights not to proselytise and conquer, but to defend or avenge.

The sun was setting and we turned to leave the shooters, when a cavalcade was seen crossing the plain. The French and Russian consuls from Ragusa, whom the storm had prevented from coming earlier, brought the young gospodar of Montenegro a Christmas greeting and their good wishes for the coming year.

Before that year began, we had bade farewell to Cerna Gora; and having run some risk in a snow-storm between Cetinje and Nïegūsh, found ourselves once more at the gates of the rock-citadel, looking down on the olive-woods and white villages of the Bocche. A Montenegrīne who had been charged to escort us pointed beyond the barrier mountains to the blue waters of the Adriatic; he stretched out his arm to the sea and called out "England."

To the dweller on the Black Mountain the sea is England, and the day that opens his country to the sea opens it to intercourse with England—to English sympathy, to English commerce. The subsidies of foreign powers will never stand him in stead of a seaport of his own, nor can the patronage of military empires give him his place among civilised nations, until he receives the right hand of fellowship from the great commercial people of the West. Also, it is a fixed idea with the Montenegrīne, that if England really knew that what he wants is access to the ocean—to that great world-highway on which the ships of England are the carriers—she would be the first to admit and to advocate his claim. We cannot close this record of a Christmas spent in the Black Mountain of Zeta without delivering the message intrusted to us by an old highlandman, "Tell your great English Queen that we Montenegrīnes can live no longer without a bit of sea."

* * * * *

CHAPTER XXXVI.

THE STORY OF SERBIA.*

PART I.—HER GROWTH AND HER GLORY.

"The occupancy of the Servians Proper is, as we expect, Servia. But many countries are more or less Servian. Bosnia, Turkish Croatia, and Herzegovina are Servian. Dalmatia is, in its essentials of blood and language, Servian. Carinthia, Carniola, and Croatia, the language of which is sometimes called Vend, and sometimes Illyrian, are Servian. Montenegro is Servian. The Uskoks and Morlakians are closely akin to the Servians."—LATHAM's *Ethnology*.

"La Serbie, débris d'un état jadis puissant, contient le germe d'un royaume futur."—UBICINI: *Les Serbes de Turquie*.

THE story of Serbia consists of four parts—growth, glory, fall, and rising again. Here we may recognise in her fortunes something in common with those of Russia and of Spain; nations that, like her, were once bowed low before the blast of Mussulman conquest, and when that blast had spent its strength, gradually but steadily raised their heads.

The four epochs of Serbian history have each its representative man. The first of these is Stephen Némania,

---

* We call the following sketch the "story" rather than the history of Serbia, partly because it is impossible to crowd anything deserving the name of history into a few pages, but chiefly because what we would try to bring before our readers is the popular "story" of Serbia, with its salient phases and characters, as it is known to every child and sung on every hearth. It has often been remarked that Serbians, even to the poorest and least lettered, are well versed in their history, and feel and speak about kings and heroes who lived centuries ago as if they were personages of the present day. A similar disposition among the Russians in the form of connecting religion with their national history is commented on by the author of "Lectures on the Eastern Church." In Serbia the popular view of history has an immense influence on the people, and it is necessary to be up with them on this point, if one would understand them at all.

who, in the middle of the twelfth century, welded several detached and vassal governments into an independent monarchy. The second is Czar Stephen Dūshan, who, in the middle of the fourteenth century, raised the monarchy into an empire, and aimed to defend the whole peninsula against the attacks of Turkish Mussulmans, by uniting its peoples in one strong realm. The third epoch is marked by the fall of Czar Lāzar, who, in 1389, lost the decisive battle of Kóssovo; after which Serbia became tributary to the Turks. The fourth epoch dates from the opening of the present century, and is identified with the name of Milosh Obrenovic. An insurrection of Serbian rayahs had ended in disaster, and its heroic leader, Kara George, worn out and disheartened, fled into Austria. Then Milosh took up the lost game, tore from under the Turk a fragment of Serbian land on the south bank of the Danube, and made that fragment the germ of a European state.

But to begin at the beginning: who the Serbians are, and whence they come. Shafarik is of opinion that the name Serb denotes "nation, gens," and that it must have been one of the earliest by which Slavonic tribes were known amongst themselves. Slovieni, or those who speak, is another generic designation; marking those who spoke one language as distinguished from the Niemtzi or *dumb* foreigners.

A list of native sources on Serbian history prior to 1830 is given in Shafarik's "Geschichte des Serbischen Schriftthums," and the Dictionary of Danichitch explains ancient terms and names. We may mention that we were particularly requested to conform to the practice of French and German authors, and write Ser*b*ia instead of Ser*v*ia, the Greek form of the name. Many authors are of opinion that the modern word Slave, as used among European nations, takes its origin from the number of Slavonic captives of war taken and sold by the Franks and Saxons, at a time when a great part of what is now Germany had to be reconquered from the Slavs. But some persons have gone further, and would connect the name Servian with the Latin *servus*, a mistake which the Serbians are by no means anxious to encourage by the substitution of *v* for *b* in the pronunciation of their name.

It seems that the Slavonic tribes which first filled the countries between Trieste and Thessalonica called themselves Slovieni, or Slaviani. Of their descendants remain to the present day the Slavonic Bulgarians, and the Slovenes inhabiting Carinthia, Carniola, and part of Styria. Both these peoples regard themselves as older tenants of the south Danubian regions than the Croato-Serbs, whose settlement intervenes between them; and their dialects, though now differing from each other, show more resemblance to the most ancient written form of Slavonic speech than is presented by the Serbian tongue.*

The immigration of the Serbo-Croats is said to have happened on this wise. In the beginning of the seventh century, the northern provinces of the East Roman Empire were overrun by the Avars, a Tartar horde which, true to its origin, not only conquered but depopulated and destroyed. To root out this swarm and repeople the land, the Emperor Heraclius invited into his dominions certain Slavonic tribes who, having left their original seats, were hovering on the north bank of the Danube.

The land whence these tribes came lay beyond the Carpathian mountains, and extended thence far into Russia. Its general name, Serbia, would seem merely to have denoted a country peopled by Slavonic tribes, but it was specially known as *White* Serbia, to distinguish it from Black Serbia, a district labouring under foreign yoke. The western and mountainous portion

---

* Shafarik, " Slavische Alterthümer," vol. i. p. 180. At the time when Cyril and Methodios began their translation of the Scriptures, Shafarik believes that the language of the Slavonic peoples in Thrace, Macedonia, and Mœsia, was still called Slovene; even as that of the Slavonic inhabitants of Carinthia and Carniola is to this day. Supposing (as it is generally supposed), that the name Bulgaria is of Tartar origin, it may be said that in Bulgaria as in Russia, a Slavonic nation has absorbed the foreign race which gave it its first dynasty, while that dynasty has given its name to the land.

was called Chrobatia (from *chrb*, hill, height), and moreover "red and white," or the beautiful and free. The Chrobatians were the first to move, and to them the invitation of the Emperor is said to have been directed; some of their Serbian kinsmen followed them, some remain in their ancient seats unto this day. On arriving south of the Danube the Croato-Serb immigrants called their new colonies after their old homes.*

The tribes which settled nearest the Bulgarians gave the name of Serbia to their land, of which the south-eastern boundary extended from the river Timok to the Adriatic at Antivari. The Croats, who had the first choice, established themselves on the north and west. Hence came it that on their adoption of Christianity, the Serbs fell under the jurisdiction of Byzance, the Croats under that of Rome; an accident fraught with dissension and disaster after the separation of the Western from the Eastern Church.

The Croats upheld a separate monarchy till the beginning of the twelfth century, when they placed the crown on the head of a prince who was already King of Hungary. It is now worn by the Emperor of Austria; but in all his dealings with the so-called triune-kingdom of Dalmatia, Slavonia, and Croatia, he is bound to use the title not of kaiser, but of king. Throughout the middle ages, alliance with powerful neighbours saved Croatia from the Turks; with whom, however, she has been constantly at war almost to the present day. A still more savage enemy was repulsed by her in that

---

* In Croatia we were shown a ruined castle on the site where "used to stand the three castles belonging to Czech, Lech, and Russ or Moch, who colonized Bohemia, Poland, and Muscovy, or Russia." This legend, which reverses the direction of the stream of emigration, is very confused, and may, in its present form, be an attempt to connect a local legend with the old famous one about the three brothers who, in Bohemia and Poland, are said to have come from the Carpathian Chrobatia.

horde of Mongols which, during the thirteenth century, overran the whole of Hungary; but was totally defeated and brought to a stand by the Croats on the field of Graves (Sláv. Grobnik), near Fiume (1241).

The present capital of Croatia, Agram, forms the focus of such South Slavonic patriotism and literature as are to be found in the Latin Church. When we visited it, the Croats were trying to get back that self-government for which they stipulated when their crown was placed on the head of a Hapsburg. In moments of embarrassment the emperor has hitherto made concessions, only to be retracted or neutralised so soon as he finds himself relieved. Hence, perhaps, in the long run less practical result is to be looked for from the political negotiations of the Croats, whether carried on at Vienna or at Pesth, than from their determination to reinstate Slavonic instead of Latin services throughout their churches, and from their recognition of national kinship with Serbia by adopting her literary dialect as their own.

We have thus far digressed on the subject of the Croatians, lest it might be wondered what had become of them; we now go back to their brother-immigrants, the Serbs. The fact principally to be remarked of this people for the first five centuries after their settlement south of the Danube, is that communal organisation which, having survived all after superstructure, remains among them at the present day.[*]

According to some records, that special district of White Serbia from which the colonists came was called Boiki, or the land of the warlike; and it certainly would appear that the men of the first immigration were warriors, and, unlike the Slavonic settlers of Bulgaria,

---

[*] Mr. Maine, who finds traces of this kind of organisation among at least all races of the Indo-European stock, remarks on its continuance to the present day in various stages of development among the Hindoos, the Russians, and the Slavonians in Turkey and Austria.—MAINE's *Ancient Law*.

crossed the Danube as an organized community, commanded by princes. Afterwards they acknowledged sometimes the Byzantine emperor, sometimes the Bulgarian czar, but they were never governed except by their own chiefs.

The earliest form of Serbian government is that of the zupa or zupania, which was common to all Slavonic populations in the same part of the world.* To this day in Croatia, zupan denotes a municipal officer of high rank; while, in Hungary (where the constitution has a Slāvic substratum), this name may be traced through various forms from the title of a county sheriff to that of the palatine. The original meaning of zupa is a "sunny land," and herein we at once recognise those sunlit valley plains, surrounded by amphitheatres of hills, which form the most frequent geographical configuration in the countries peopled by Serbs. At the time of the first immigration many of the mountainous regions were, as they still are, tenanted by Albanians, or by half Latinised aborigines called by the Slāvs, Vlachi, or shepherds.† Even those Serbians who settled among hills long maintained an independent clannish life. But the "sunny lands" became the seats of villages; the villagers, combining for government and defence, chose one judge and leader for their whole zupa; and from this magistrate's title of zupan, his government in time became known as a zupania. In each zupa there was a fortress, or "grad," which, together with the office of governor, soon became the inheritance of a family. Among the zupans one was distinguished by the prefix

* Joopaan—pronounce z as j in the French word *jour*.

† Because these shepherds spoke a Latin dialect, all peoples speaking Latin dialects, whether Roumans or Italians, came to be called by the Serbians, Vlachi; while the name "Latins" was applied, without regard to race, to all nations belonging to the Romish Church. Strangely enough, the Serbians themselves, in Herzegovina and elsewhere, were afterwards called Vlachi by the Mahommedans, who applied the name to all Christians of the Eastern Church.

of "grand" (*veliki*); but he appears to have stood to the rest rather in the position of *primus inter pares*, than as the wielder of any central powers. Some writers call the earliest residence of a Serbian grand zupan, the town of Destinika, or Desnitza, and place its situation between the rivers Bosna and Drina.

Long did the Serbian zupanias carry on their uncentralised democratic régime; each obscure commune exercising free choice in the regulation of its obscure concerns—unheeding, and unheeded by, the world. This sort of passive socialism seems natural to many nations of Slavonic race. It is only with effort that they rouse themselves into caring what goes on beyond their commune; or cease disputing amongst themselves about trifles, in order to speak with authority out of doors. When they do at last wake up, it is generally because forced to rid themselves of foreign domination; or because they are headed by one of those great men born to be the champions and arbiters of mankind. Especially at a time when brute force ruled the world—as it did in the middle ages—a Slavonic state could only become powerful by thus concentrating its strength in the hands of an individual able to lead.

Thus, the epoch of Serbian growth began when, from among the zupans, there arose a race capable of uniting and heading the rest in an hereditary monarchy. This race took birth on the mountain shores of the Adriatic sea, in a district which still nurses the hardiest specimens of the Southern Slāvs, and where independence, early asserted, is upheld unto this day.

Not far from the eastern coast of the Adriatic lies the only large lake within the heritage of Serbian tribes; behind this lake a knot of mountains rises to between eight and nine thousand feet. From the mountains to the lake, from the lake to the sea, run navigable rivers over fertile plains; one of these rivers, the Zenta, or Zeta, early gave its name to the country around.

Near the northern shore of the lake the Romans founded a city, called Dioclea, said to be the birthplace of the Emperor Diocletian. Afterwards, that city, like many others in the same part of the world, set up as a small republic, and was taken possession of by the Serbs, who made it the capital of Zupania. Latin civilisation told on its new citizens, and the annals of ancient Zeta were recorded by the "chronicler of Dioclea."

The Serbians of Zeta could not persevere in the passive existence of their inland kindred, for their position brought them into constant friction with divers neighbours; at Ochrida with the subjects of the Bulgarian czardom; at Antivari with those of the Byzantine empire; afterwards with the peoples of the West. Their lake, and the rich plains beyond, invited visitors, and together with the vicinity of the sea, engendered the spirit of commerce. In its train came the spirit of acquisition: the Zetans extended their rule inland, in one direction to Trebinje, and in another to Elbassan and Croya, while along the coast they stretched their arms to Durazzo. To maintain this position it was necessary to preserve the compact order of a warlike front, which was further needed in order to exact respect from their neighbours in the hills—those plundering Albanians who, so long as they feared the Serb, remained his fellow-subjects and very good friends. Hence was it that at Zeta a Serbian zupania brought forth captains by sea and by land, and that a Serbian zupan developed into a king.*

One of the early Zetan kings we have already mentioned, namely, the St. Vladimir who wedded the daughter of Bulgarian Samuel, and whose tomb lies at

---

* The title Rex is indifferently given to most of them, even prior to Michael, who, Shafarik says, actually received a crown from Rome, 1078.

Elbassan.* Another, called Bodin, appears at the siege of Durazzo, assisting the Normans against the Eastern Empire. At home, this king extended the power of Zeta, and forced Bosnia and Rascia to take zupans of his choice. His cousin and successor is called by Byzantine historians Bachin, and is noticed by them on account of the single combat wherein he engaged their emperor Manuel Comnenus. Serbian writers call him variously, but all know him as the father of their great Némania.

By this time most of the Serb lands had zupans belonging to the Zetan family, and when Bachin died he left territories to all his sons, to his youngest son Némania the territory of Rascia. After the father's death, certain brothers and cousins disputed Némania's inheritance; he succeeded in vanquishing these opponents, made Zeta and Bosnia recognise his supremacy, and was acknowledged grand zupan of the Serbs (1162).

In his hands the title brought with it almost monarchical authority at home, and the power to extend it abroad. Némania took from Byzantine governors all such fortified towns as they still held in territories peopled by Serbs; and in this manner possessed himself of Nish, Skopia, and Prizren. The last-named city, lying on the northern slope of the Scardus Mountains, offered a convenient position whence to rule territories situated between Bulgaria, the Danube, and the Adriatic. Thus in due time Prizren became the Serbian Czarigrad, or city of the ruler.†

At length Némania no longer chose to remain even nominally subordinate to the Byzantine emperor, and

---

* Hilferding's "History of Serbians and Bulgarians," chap. iii. part 2.
† The name "czar," while especially used to express "emperor," is given to all supreme rulers; thus, although a Serbian sovereign was not regularly entitled emperor till the middle of the fourteenth century, all the Némanides are popularly called czar. At the present day, while the Emperor of Russia is known as the Czar Russki, the Turkish Sultan is the Czar Turski, and so on,

PORTAL OF WHITE MARBLE CHURCH OF STUDENITZA, BUILT BY NEMANIA.

aimed to secure for himself a crown, and for Serbia a European position. To this end he met the Western Kaiser, Frederick Barbarossa, on his way to the Holy War, and offered to do him homage for Nish and certain other cities, on condition of being recognised as King of the Serbs. But Frederick could not then engage in negotiations that might involve a quarrel with the Greek Emperor, and passed on to his crusade and grave. Némania died a grand zupan, with no status except that he owed to the election of his own people. But his son Stephen, called the "first crowned king," obtained a recognition of his title, both from the Pope and from the Greek Emperor of Nicæa.

Hereafter we shall have occasion to refer to the founder of the Némanyitch dynasty, as to him who established the Eastern Church in Serbia; at present we know him only as the uniter of the zupanias into a monarchical state. His death occurred in 1195, and from that date till 1367 the rulers of Serbia were all Némanides; a list of them and of their queens is subjoined at the end of this volume. Of most of them we will say nothing now, but give our attention to the change that came over the Serbian nation during its existence as a mediæval kingdom.

Serbia was more accessible to foreign intercourse throughout this period of her history than at any other, before or since. Her kings, intermarrying with the daughters of Byzantium, France, and Venice, brought the influence of the most civilised nations in Europe to bear upon their peoples; and such churches, frescoes,

our own sovereign however being named, as the Turks name her, merely *kralitza*. This title is the feminine of *kral*, or king, a name applied to the kinglets before Némania, or to rulers subject to an emperor; it was, like many other Slavic words, borrowed by the Turks, and by them bestowed on all Christian rulers, until most of these formally insisted on being addressed as the equals of the Ottoman sovereign. *Czarivati* means, in Serbian, to rule as an emperor.

and MSS. as have escaped destruction, witness to the progress then made in the fine arts. There was moreover a native channel through which Western influence filtered into the wilds of Serbia; namely, the free cities on the eastern shore of the Adriatic, which, Slavonic by lineage, occupied the site of Roman colonies, and combined the civilisation of Italy with allegiance to a Serbian king. Of this number we might cite several small republics, which maintained their status almost to our own day; but among the most noted cities were Antivari, Cattaro, and Ragusa, whose merchants were once to be found in every Serbian mart, while the names of their artists still remain, graven on Serbian church portals or handed down in song. Various laws were introduced, with especial reference to Latin commercial travellers, and special regulations were made for their benefit. For example, for a certain toll paid to the king he engaged to protect them from highwaymen, or, should they be robbed, to make good their loss; the local authorities were obliged to convoy them from point to point, and in case they came into court with a native, half the jury were to consist of their own people. It was even considered a work of religious merit to smooth the path of travellers by making "good roads, building good bridges, and providing good quarters." The memory of the great hostelry of Prizren has been preserved, together with that of her yearly fair.

But the Serbian kingdom had also direct relations with the great Slavonic-named Latin city, Venice;* and perhaps no foreign influence is so clearly to be traced among Serbian remains as hers. The coinage, for which material came from mines at Novo Berdo and Rudnik, was probably struck at Venice, and certainly from Venetian models. Specimens of it are to be now found in the

* See Appendix A.

museum of Belgrade, which exhibits a collection dating from 1195 to 1457.

Some of these coins bear a Latin inscription, all of them bear an inscription in Slavonic; and this circumstance illustrates a principle which seems to have regulated the intercourse of Serbia with foreigners. Foreign fashions might modify her own, but might not oust them; the stranger was welcome to her as a merchant or a craftsman, but did not become her lawgiver, or ruler, or priest. As for the Serbian language—though its next neighbours were Latin and Greek—it held its own as the medium both of legislation and religious teaching. The Holy Scriptures and the Civil Code were written in a serbianised dialect of ancient Slavonic; so were the chronicles, poetry, and inscriptions; while the native tongue was used for social intercourse among all classes, courtly as well as rural, clerical as well as lay. Even a person unacquainted with the history might gather from these facts, 1st, that the native language must have been early cultivated; 2ndly, that the chief offices in the state cannot have been entrusted to foreigners, nor even to a caste which had so far outgrown the common people as to affect a foreign form of civilisation. In the thirteenth and fourteenth centuries the possession of a dynasty and aristocracy of genuine native growth distinguishes Serbia from many contemporary states; the use of her own language characterizes her as compared with Croatia, Hungary, and Poland, where the cultivation of the native tongue was all but smothered by a Latin overgrowth.

The "Book of Serbian Nobility" exhibits Slavonic names, and as aristocracy was not introduced by conquest one is inclined to ask how it came to arise among the patriarchal and democratic Serbs. We were told by one of the few remaining representatives of a genuine

South Slavonic noblesse, that the Serbian aristocracy drew its titles originally, not from territorial possession but from office, and hence derived its name of *vlastela*, literally, holders of *vlast*, authority; the greater office-bearers being termed *velika vlastela*, and the smaller *vlastelitchitchi*.* Among the great vlastela appear various titles, more or less hereditary; first zupans, then kneses and bans, with their governments, called after them knesovina, banovina, &c. A rank of military origin was that of voivode, leader in war, a name which has found its way through German into English under the meaningless cacophony of "waywode." Under the monarchy, the voivodes appear as companions in arms of the sovereign; and the office was bestowed on a talented general, whatever might be his descent or social rank. Afterwards it denoted the possession of a duchy; but to this day in Montenegro the voivode bears his original position, which is hereditary only in so far as warlike talent is often hereditary in the best blood of the land.

The "lords of Serbia," whether with or without office, had a voice in the administration, and we find them, under the name of *góspoda*, attending the sábor or parliament. The assembling of a sábor is identified with the principal historical acts of the Serbian kings, such as ascending or abdicating the throne, assuming a new title, creating an office, or publishing a decree. Thus, for instance, we hear of the abdication of Némania at the sábor of Rascia, and the coronation of his son at that of Zicha. Stephen Dūshan took the title of emperor under the auspices of the sábor of Skopia, and on its authority was issued the code of laws that bears his name. The Serbian Patriarch was appointed at the sábor of Seres; and on the extinction of the line of Némania a new ruler was

---

* Some interesting articles on Serbian titles, official dignities, and first and second orders of nobility, are to be found in the Dictionary of Danichic.

elected at the sābor of Prizren. Besides these historical parliaments, popular songs speak of the assembled *serbski góspoda* exercising control over most monarchical acts; and one meeting, to which we shall further allude, is mentioned as demanding and receiving, after the death of Némania, an account of the manner in which his treasures had been employed.

Besides the góspoda, or great lords, we find frequently Serbian sābors, the little lords, or gospodichic, and the promulgation of new decrees receives their sanction, as well as that of the higher nobles, the metropolitan, and the sovereign. Under the mediæval monarchy the first and second orders of nobility probably stood to one another somewhat as the untitled nobles of Hungary stood to the titled or magnates. But in earlier days, the Serbian gospodichic may have had much in common with the Bohemian vladyka, or head of a family, who as such attended the national assembly, and had as good a right to give his voice as the richer and more powerful lords. On certain great occasions, the Serbian sovereign is said to have called together " all men of note throughout his lands." The skoopshina of the modern principality of Serbia gives no idea of the ancient sābor, inasmuch as its members are elected. But in Montenegro, where Serbian tribes fell back on primitive forms, the old name is still in use, together with the assembly in its most rudimentary stage. A portion of the plain of Cetinje is known as "the meeting-place of the s'bor." And the s'bor is attended, not by elected delegates or representatives, but by heads of families and persons of influence; while in times of danger it is considered as much the right and duty of a free man to attend the assembly as to carry arms.*

* The *mali s'bor*, or little parliament, used to gather together principal persons and heads of districts, in contradistinction to the great s'bor or general

Under the kings of the house of Némania, Serbia increased in warlike strength, and in old documents and inscriptions her monarchy is described as extending over all "Serbian lands and the Primorïé," or sea-coast. For a moment it aspired to do more—to sway and absorb divers nations, assimilate a foreign civilisation, and take the lead in south-eastern Europe. But this was not the idea of Serbia; her people never rose to the height of it; it lived and died with one man.

The name of this man was Stephen Dūshan, and he was surnamed Silni. Stephen, or "the crowned," is a designation common to most kings of Serbia, and seems to have been assumed on coronation; Dūshan is a Serbian name, derived from *dusha*, "soul"; *silni* means "mighty." If there exist an authentic portrait of Dūshan it may be one of those taken from life, and still preserved on the walls of some old church enriched by his gifts. That which we saw represents him as a very Saul in height and strength of frame; chestnut-haired, and fair-complexioned. His large, full, grey eye is expressive at once of speculation and command—faculties perhaps more common in Serbians of the fourteenth century than they are now in the descendants of a race long shut out alike from intellectual cultivation and from government on a large scale. Both form and head, standing out as they do in a row of pinched and elongated saints depicted in the Byzantine style of art, give to the beholder a singular impression of power both in body and spirit— such power as earned the name of Dūshan Silni.*

assembly. Its debates, which were sufficiently tumultuous, could only be quieted by the metropolitan ordering the church bell to be tolled; now most of its functions are more regularly performed by the so-called senate or council of the prince, wherein, however, there is still loud talking enough.

* Dūshan is said to have had a younger brother called Dūshitza, or "little soul." We are told that similarly resembling names among members of a family are sometimes a *jeu d'esprit* of the god-parents, who in Serbia decide the child's name. In the ballad called "The Building of Scadar" this custom is alluded to.

The idea of Stephen Dūshan was this: "While the Serbian nation grows the Greek Empire is dwindling away; and while numerous candidates squabble for the imperial name the Ottoman draws daily nearer to Europe. Why should not Dūshan anticipate the Turk, take Constantinople, wear the crown of empire, and wield the united strength of Slavon and Greek? Thus he might turn the tide of Moslem conquest, and pour the vigour of his young northern peoples into the exhausted frame of a long-civilised realm." It was a grand dream, and had it come true perhaps this portion of the old Roman Empire would, like the West, have seen a revival of national energy and classic culture, and the south-eastern peninsula might have become a second Italy. To defeat Dūshan's scheme a Greek Emperor called in the host of the Ottoman, and we have the result in Turkey in Europe.

Part of Dūshan's youth was spent at Constantinople, and there, doubtless, he imbibed ideas that regulated his future policy; indeed one account makes a Greek Empress suggest that he should marry her daughter and assume the purple. After he was king of Serbia, John Cantacuzene, candidate for the imperial crown, came to his court and besought aid; which Dūshan willingly granted, on condition that every city taken from the enemy should declare as it pleased for the Greek or for him. Many towns and districts of the empire, having Slavonic populations, preferred the rule of the Serb.

Another peculiarity connected with the names of noted personages has given occasion to not a little confusion; that is to say, a king or queen will have *three* names: one bestowed on birth, which is of Slavonic origin, and with a signification, such as Militza, which means "darling," Dūshan,' &c. Added to this there is the name bestowed at baptism, usually that of a saint. Then, if in old age the royal personage assumes the monastic habit, he or she adopts another name, by which after death they are themselves known as saints. When in addition we have *sur noms*, and names assumed on coronation, the difficulties of identification are multiplied without end.

Cantacuzene became jealous, and having triumphed over his original rivals, quarrelled with his old protector, and sought a new one in the Turk. It is said that prior to this quarrel the allies had exchanged the oath of brotherhood; hence, even after their rupture, the Serbian would not personally meet his "bond-brother" in battle, and none of his paladins would have dared to hurt so much as a hair of his head. But the time had come for Dūshan to act in his own name, and he now assumed the title of "Emperor of all Serbs and Greeks."

A mighty army was gathered to give effect to his claims; but before starting on his decisive campaign he called his notables together, and made such arrangements as should preserve order in his absence and ensure the welfare of the Serbian realm. His idea was, to come among the Greeks, not as a foreign conqueror, but as a powerful candidate for the crown of the Eastern Empire; even as kings of France and Spain offered themselves as candidates for the Western imperial throne. Henceforth, therefore, his residence was to be Constantinople, and his task the combat with the Turk; Serbia could no longer be his sole care, and his intention was to prepare her for this change in her destinies. To this end it would appear that the sābor of Skopia was called upon to digest and sanction what is called "Czar Dūshan's Code." The form of this code, and the illusions wherewith it abounds, testify that it contains neither the only nor the earliest laws of Serbia, but merely those revised or promulgated in one particular parliament. We have already alluded to some of the older laws therein mentioned or improved. To the institutions of Serbia as a separate kingdom Dūshan added imperial ordinances; he added also imperial offices; most of these offices and ordinances, being of foreign origin, may be detected by their Greek names.

At this time, not only Macedonia but Thessaly received governors from the Serbian ruler; his dominion extended from the Ægean to the Ionian Sea—from the walls of Arta to those of Thessalonica. Over these extensive dominions Dūshan appointed under himself as Czar, divers responsible deputies, entitled, according to their rank, king or kral, despot, cæsar, sevastocrator. All were intended as imperial officials to act as a check on the unruly or separatist tendencies of local lords.

For this reason the new dignities appear to have been mostly committed to the hands of individuals personally devoted to the Czar. For instance, Vukashīne, to whom we have alluded in the story of Marko, became one of the krals, his next brother a despot, and the youngest a voivode. Popular tradition calls them the three brothers Merliávchevic, and says that they were men of naught, but companions of Dūshan's youth and owing everything to his favour. Then too the sturdy old Bogdan, despot of the southern territories, was induced to give his only daughter to a favourite page of Dūshan's, and that page was made Count of Sirmium, a northern frontier-land between the Danube and the Save. So much has been said about the subordinate position assigned to women in Serbia, that we may here mention that one province was committed to the rule of the Empress—that the Czar even associated her in the imperial government, and caused the coinage to bear her image with his own.

These arrangements completed, Czar Dūshan placed himself at the head of his troops, his standards displaying the double eagle of empire. His march was directed towards Constantinople, but it reached no farther than the village of Devoli,* for there fever attacked him and he died, aged about fifty years (1355).

Around the couch of the dying sovereign the great office-bearers eyed each other, muttering, "Who shall rule the empire now?" Who indeed? Dūshan could bequeath his realm, he could not bequeath his power to rule; and recognising this, he mourned as a

ARMS OF CZAR DŪSHAN.†

great man must who knows his work unfinished yet feels that he must die. His last sorrowing thought for his land has found expression in a pathetic legend, which is preserved among the Serbian people as part

---

* The situation of Devoli is uncertain. Some suppose it to have been a village in Thrace, twelve leagues from Constantinople; others a village near Ochrida.

† Herein are to be seen the arms of Danubian Serbia and of Zeta, where Serbians have at this day native rulers, together with the arms of those South Slavonic countries at present ruled by Austria or Turkey. This engraving is taken from an old Serbian "Book of Nobility."

of the history of their mighty-souled Czar. We give it in the simple traditionary words: "When Stephen Dūshan felt the hand of death upon him he bade them carry him to the top of a hill, from whence he could look, on the one hand towards Constantinople and on the other towards the Serbian lands; and behold, when he had looked this way and that, bitter tears gathered in the eyes of the Czar. Then said his secretary, the King's Son Marko, 'Wherefore weepest thou, O Czar?' The Czar answered him, 'Therefor weep I, not because I am about to leave the countries where I have made good roads, and builded good bridges, and appointed good governors; but because I must leave them without taking the City of Empire, and I see the gate standing open by which the enemy of the land will enter in.' Then the secretary Marko made haste and wrote down the words of the Czar, that they might be remembered by his son, the boy Urosh; that they might be remembered by the Serbian nation; that they might be remembered by all peoples among the Slāvs."

CHAPTER XXXVII.

THE STORY OF SERBIA—(*continued*).

PART II.—HER FALL AND RISING AGAIN.*

"We came this morning from the plain of Kóssovo. There we saw two mighty armies, that fought together yesterday. Both of the Czars lie dead, and of the Turks the remnant is but small; but of the Serbians there remains not one that is not wounded and covered with blood."—*Serbian ballad.*

"La Serbie est le point de mire, le kiblé, comme disent les Arabes, de ces populations qui, en proie à des malaises divers, aspirent à échapper à leurs dominateurs actuels. C'est chez elle que se réfugient, comme dans un lieu d'asile, les raias opprimés de la Vieille Serbie et de la Bosnie, les révoltés de l'Herzegovine, les Albanais persécutés, les Bulgares nécessiteux. Les Serbes d'Autriche, ballottés sans cesse entre Vienne et Pesth, se tournent vers Belgrade, et regardent le Prince Michael comme le chef et le protecteur naturel de leur race."—*Revue des Deux Mondes, mai* 15, 1864.

PERHAPS the instructors of youth in modern Serbia are justified in blaming as they do an enterprise the success of which hung on the life of one man, and in deeming that the overstrain of the reign of Dūshan resulted in a reaction after he was gone. Others, however, are of opinion that all the South Slavonic peoples have shown themselves unenterprising to a fault, forgetting that he who "aims the sky, shoots higher far than

---

* A study of the history of this period will, we believe, justify the assumption on which we proceed throughout the story of Serbia's fall, viz., that although Serbia shared religious communion and geographical position with part of the Greek Empire, yet otherwise she had far more in common with her neighbours on the West, together with whom Byzantine writers of course class her as "barbarian." We remark this because, in noticing the causes that had to do with the fall of Serbia, we in no way pretend to enter into those that led to the fall of the Eastern Empire. As little do we presume to give an opinion on the causes that led to the great success of the Turks during their day of conquering

he that aims a tree," and that to carry the war into the enemy's country is often the best way of defending your own. Certain it is, that while Dūshan met the Turks on the shores of the Ægean, his own kingdom was untrodden by hostile armies; the unambitious Czar who succeeded him waited for the Turks within his frontier, and one lost battle laid Serbia at their feet.

But to continue our narrative. The only son left by Dūshan was still a lad and of feeble character; till he should come of age the regency was committed to his father's protégé, the kral Vukashīne. So long as the young Czar submitted to dictation this guardian was content to let him live; but he grew up, and married, and his wife and mother bade fair to secure the chief influence over him. The regent could not make up his mind to resign the government, and therefore took an opportunity to murder his charge while out hunting. The deed was for the time concealed, and the common people were led to believe that Urosh had disappeared on some distant pilgrimage, a pretence to which his piety gave ground. Vukashīne wielded the supreme

power. It is generally admitted that they united great courage and statecraft to a belief that they were commissioned to ensure the triumph of the Mahommedan religion with the sword, and to a disregard of all considerations that could fetter them in the way to conquest. The murder of a Sultan's male relatives to escape the dangers of a war of succession; the exaction of tribute children in order to form out of them a wholly devoted military corps; the massacre of captives on a tremendous scale—have been cited as instances of the latter kind. They had generally, also, the tact to grant very easy conditions to a defeated enemy so long as he retained any strength, trusting to their hold once fixed on a country for the power to exact afterwards what they pleased. Like their descendants in the present day, they had a real genius for "promising." This is, however, one reason why nations that have once been subject to them, and afterwards become free, will never trust them politically, or even allow them to reside in their country. As respects the immediate influence of the Turks on the fall of Serbia, it is enough that they were an advancing military power, from whatever cause, far more formidable than any wherewith she had hitherto had to do, or than any her Christian neighbours could have brought against her at the time. Dissensions between Greek and Latin Christians afterwards did much to prevent the fall of Serbia from being retrieved.

authority, but the despots, bans, and other great vlastela ruled each his province in virtual independence. During this interregnum the high prestige still clinging to the very name of Némanyitch may be recognised in the fact that the dead Urosh continued to be invoked as Czar; and that while Vukashīne struck coins bearing his own image and superscription, the other governors used one impressed with the figure of the son of Dūshan surrounded with the halo of a saint.

Meanwhile the Turks, conceding to Constantinople the melancholy privilege of being devoured last, were daily gaining firmer footing in Europe, and at length extended their ravages to Serbian ground. Vukashīne drove back the invaders, and in the heydey of triumph followed them to the neighbourhood of Adrianople. There he halted and held a carouse; the Turks rallied, made a night attack, surprised and routed the Serbs. Vukashīne, accompanied only by his standard-bearer, escaped from the field alive; already he had reached a place of safety, when, as he stopped to drink at a fountain, there fell out of his vest the insignia of the golden double eagle which he had taken from the breast of Urosh. Up to that moment the death of the young Czar had ever been left doubtful, and none dared name the suspected murderer. But at this sight the standard-bearer accused his master. In the horror of the moment Vukashīne found neither words nor arms to defend himself, and the indignant Serb slew him on the spot. Then, taking up the eagle as a proof that both Urosh and Vukashīne were slain, the standard-bearer carried it to Lāzar, knez of Sirmium, the youngest and noblest of Dūshan's favourites, who forthwith published the direful news. Thereupon the notables of Serbia, being convinced that the male line of Némania was indeed extinct, and feeling the necessity of union under a vigorous head, assembled in a great sābor at Prizren, and elected Lāzar Grebliánovic to be czar.

But for this sābor, and the election wherein it resulted, it might be supposed that the Turkish conquest of Serbia was sufficiently accounted for by her intestine divisions; but, in fact, for some years before her fall, she was united and energetically ruled under a legally elected head. No doubt there were malcontent nobles or disappointed pretenders to the throne, who entered into treaties with the enemy. But such was the case in every country in Europe, and the English seldom entered France, or the French Italy, without the complicity of some disloyal lord; yet this amount of division did not bring on the Western nations the wholesale destruction that overtook Serbia.

Of course it was still more disgraceful for a Christian noble to ally himself against his native sovereign with the general enemies of their religion, than to seek the aid of a neighbouring Christian king; and one would be glad to suppose that Western Christians would not have done what Eastern Christians did in helping to bring the infidel into Christendom. Unfortunately, Byzantine annals tell how Mussulman armies numbered many a Frankish knight and Varangian adventurer, whom revenge or greed had driven to its ranks; and at a far later date the Protestant nobles of Hungary and Transylvania openly preferred an Ottoman Sultan to a Catholic Kaiser. Further, one must allow that if the burden of Mussulman empire has fallen chiefly on the Christians of the East, the jealousies of Western nations permitted its consolidation, and at this very day they guarantee its maintenance.

These facts should be borne in mind, inasmuch as among us Westerns, there is the same sort of disposition to judge harshly of those nations on whom fell the weight of the Turk, as there was among the Jews to judge harshly of those men on whom fell the tower of Siloam. It is pleasant to conclude that, because we escaped destruction, we must have been better than those who were destroyed; instead of recognising that, at the time of the Mahommedan flood-tide, the chief difference between us and them lay in the advantage of our geographical position. A valley in the interior of the country may escape, while a plain on the coast is submerged; even if the flood spread inland, much of its force is spent on the way. In like manner, when a Mussulman army advanced into Central or Western Europe, it lost the power of covering a defeat, or of following up a victory, which was easy for it when nearer home. The parts of Europe lying nearest Asia and Africa served as a breakwater for the inner lands; to use the expression of their inhabitants — no Mussulman spear struck our shield without first passing through their breast.*

As respects Serbia in particular. In spite of all imperfections and weaknesses, she had shown herself, up to the time of the Turkish onslaught, able to hold her own, and to keep pace with the age. Had she continued to have to do only with her European neighbours, she

---

* "It may be worth while here to notice another of those fallacious clamours with which national annals often falsify the pages of history. Western Europe long kept up such an incessant boasting concerning the defeat of Abderahman, one of the lieutenants of the Caliph Hescham, who led a division of the Saracen armies on a plundering expedition into France, that this insignificant affair has been considered the first great check given to the power of the Caliphs. Charles Martel, who led the Frank troops, had been raised to the rank of a Christian hero. Anna Comnena would have been warranted in citing this vain-glorious boast as a proof of her assertion that the Franks were the greatest babblers on the face of the earth. The force of the Saracen empire—a force far superior to any that ever appeared even in Spain—was first broken by Leo the Iconoclast, and the choicest veterans of the Mussulmans were slain under the walls of Constantinople. . . . The idle tale that a governor of Spain would lead an army of 300,000 men into a depopulated region like France in the time of Charles Martel requires no refutation."—FINLAY, *On the Characteristic Features of Byzantine History*, p. 27.

would, according to all appearance, have remained a free
state, gradually working out her civilisation, and her
junction with surrounding kindred peoples. It was the
misfortune of Serbia, that while still in the unsettled
and uncentralized condition common to most European
states in the middle ages, she should be exposed to a
tremendous shock from without; a shock which she
came in for on account of her position right in the line
of the Mussulman wave. Herein, at the time, she
shared the fate of the greater part of Hungary. At
different periods both Spain and Russia underwent a
similar calamity. Countries in less exposed stations
escaped; but if, during their early history, they had
been called on to stem the full current of so violent a
destructive force, the degree to which they suffered
from less formidable invasions, leaves them little right
to suppose but that for a time they might have succumbed. Some of these nations were indeed attacked,
and impute their salvation to the triumphant result of
some great battle or siege. But no such isolated victory
could shake the hold of the invader when once fixed on
the nearer lands. On them the attack was renewed
year by year; year by year harvests were burnt, and
thousands of prisoners carried away. Even when the
Turk could not complete his conquests, he forced the
assaulted nations to relinquish every object in life
except that of a struggle for freedom; during which
struggle their resources were exhausted and their infant
civilisation destroyed. Supposing gallantry equal on
both sides,—and no one has yet accused Hungarians or
Serbians of lacking warlike valour,—how hard is the
case when a people of settled domicile, requiring peace
for the development of industry, is obliged to wear itself
out in a trial of brute force with such troops as the
janissaries—warrior-slaves cut off from country and

home, who consider their one business in this world, their title to happiness in the next, to be a life spent in the prosecution of "Holy War."

Perhaps we shall judge most fairly of such inner sins as weakened Serbia for her encounter with the Ottoman, and also be certain not to palliate them, if we realise that in these respects she was neither much better nor much worse than contemporary and neighbouring states, with whose history we are more familiar. Religious intolerance, petty jealousies, and divisions about everything and nothing; these were the weaknesses of mediæval Christendom, look where we will.

But look where we will, we shall also find—among the throng of passion and intrigue—here and there a character of pure gold, worthy the best age this world ever saw. Such characters exhibit the noblest type of mediæval Christianity, for they unite hardihood and strength of will with lofty-mindedness and deep religious feeling—with purity, humility, and abnegation of self.

If we may trust the portrait handed down by the traditions of his people, such a Christian champion was the last Serbian czar. History shows him to us as an energetic ruler and valiant warrior; but it is the people who have remembered that "the churches he built were not paid for by tears of the poor," and that he was one of those who, to use the popular expression, "knew that God would be served with clean hands." *

Lāzar Greblianovic, knez of Sirmium, although

---

* In their exemplary domestic lives, the last czar, and his son the first despot, are favourably distinguished from some of the Némanides, whose quarrels with their relatives and foreign wives have lost nothing by transmission through Greek gossip. The Serbians, as a nation, can hardly, however, have been demoralised in this sense; they preserved their simple manners, and to this day the family tie is held far more sacred among them and the Bulgarians than among any other races in their neighbourhood.

duly crowned and acknowledged czar, forbore to assume the style of the great Dūshan, and modestly contented himself with the title bestowed on him by his master while living. Thus he is usually known by the name of Knez Lāzar; *knez* meaning prince or count.

One of his chief cares was to arrange old feuds, secular and ecclesiastic, with the Greek Empire; then, while he unsparingly drove forth such vassals as disputed his election, he made friends with those bans and kneses who in Bosnia, Albania, and Zeta, had been tempted by Vukashīne's misrule to establish princedoms for themselves. Through his wise and beautiful czarine, Militza, he was connected with the line of Némania, and thus obtained the respect and alliance of the oldest ruling houses in Serbia; but the highest grades in the state, together with his personal friendship, were freely accorded to every Serbian distinguished by talent and bravery. The traditional heroes, Relia and Milosh, were of origin so obscure, that report called one of them the foundling of a gipsy, and the other the suckling of a mare.

Entering on his functions at a time when the nation was smarting under a defeat by the Turks, Lāzar had to purchase an interval of peace by treaty, wherein, according to the spirit of the times, he promised the payment of a certain sum annually, together with assistance to the Sultan in wars with Mussulmans in Asia. It is allowed that even for this unloved enterprise he selected a band of his bravest and best-armed cavaliers; but when the contingent returned, its voivode strongly represented to Lāzar the ignominy of such service, and the superiority of his troops to the Turks, both in weapons and in discipline. His words moved the czar, who also reflected that the continued payment of tribute would not shield him for a moment after the Sultan should find it convenient to attack, and that it was better to choose his own time for fighting than to await the leisure of the Turk. The Albanians were eager to strike. The Bosnians and the already weakened Bulgarians promised to stand by the Serbs. Hungary engaged to send help, which did not come in time. Next year Lāzar Greblīánovic refused to continue the payment of tribute, and called together the confederate Christian forces on the great upland plain of Kóssovo, which lies a few days' journey to the north-west of Macedonian Edessa.

When the Ottoman Sultan Amurath, or, as the Serbians called him, Turski Czar Murad, heard of Serbia's determination to resist, he was already at Adrianople, and forthwith recalled from Asia Minor his two sons, Jacub and Bajazet, together with the troops under their command. He then marched on Serbia, passing mostly through the territories of small Christian potentates, already his vassals; they, overawed by his formidable presence, duteously showed him the way, and provided him with food. At Karatova he was met by the herald of Czar Lāzar, who brought him his master's challenge.

Two ideas seem at this time to have possessed the more patriotic and spirited among the Serbs. First, that every day's delay would enable the Ottoman to attack them with greater advantage; that indeed he was only waiting to attack until he had finished with other enemies, or saw them involved in some domestic quarrel. The other idea was, that duty called on the czar of Serbia to risk his all in striking a bold blow for Christendom; such a blow as, if successful, would palpably weaken the Turks and deliver all surrounding countries from the danger that hung over them. This last is the popular view of the motives that induced Czar Lāzar to challenge the Sultan, or, as some ballads say, to accept the Sultan's challenge; and it is because he was thus ready to die for the Cross, that he is popularly honoured as a martyr and a saint.

We have in an earlier chapter given the details of the combat that ensued on the plain of Kóssovo; its name is scarcely known in England, yet few battles have been more decisive, or in their consequences more disastrous to civilisation. The defeat of the Serbian army broke the barrier between the Turks and the Danube, and opened to the janissary the road to Belgrade, Buda, and Vienna.

The field of Kóssovo was watered with the blood of both czars—Amurath the Ottoman, and Lāzar the Serb. The throne of each passed to his son. But the successor of Amurath was the terrible Bajazet, already known as Ilderim, or the Lightning, and he stood at the head of a victorious army; whereas the son of Lāzar appears to have been yet a lad, for the first overtures of peace were chiefly addressed by the Sultan to the widowed czarine. Stephen Lāzarevic found himself for the moment without a force sufficient to take the field; but the victory of Kóssovo had cost Bajazet dear, and he could not then proceed on a career of conquest. Therefore he treated amicably with the vanquished, asking only tribute and an auxiliary force as formerly contributed, together with a daughter of the late czar to wife.*

This last condition, together with the family intercourse to which it gave rise, made all the difference to the Serbs. The young prince Stephen, overcome by the

---

* Another Serbian princess was afterwards married to a Sultan, and they were not the only Christian princesses thus allied; hence it is curious to remark that some of the earlier and greater Sultans were the sons and husbands of illustrious Christian ladies, whereas the Sultans of our day are the husbands and sons of slaves.

Bajazet is said to have been extremely fond of his beautiful Serbian sultana, and proud of her birth; when reproaching Tamerlane with scornful treatment of himself and his consort, he remarked with indignation that she was the daughter of the Serbian king.

friendly professions of the triumphant Bajazet, from that hour identified his interests with those of his brother-in-law, and became the fast friend of the Turkish Sultan, supporting him in person against Mahommedan foes in Asia, and the armies of the Latins in Europe. Nay, on the defeat and capture of Bajazet by Tamerlane, when an opportunity was given for all nations subject to the Turks to break the leash, the Prince of Serbia saved one of the Sultan's sons, and supported his claims.

The notion of Stephen Lazarevic seems to have been, that the last generation of Serbians had erred in their estimate of the Ottoman; that when not attacked he would not molest, that if a fearful foe, he could be a trusty friend. Perhaps it was natural that the successor of the hapless Lāzar should adopt a policy the reverse of his own; and undoubtedly Stephen acted with the most loyal intentions. He was, for the times, a singularly pure character, as well as a gentle ruler and a valiant soldier. Yet his friendship for Bajazet and the sons of Bajazet cost Serbia her last chance of freedom; while the employment of his troops in retrieving Turkish battles separated the cause of Serbia from that of Christendom, alienated the sympathy of her neighbours, and forfeited her claim to their aid.

Of course, when the Ottoman had recovered his strength, and Serbia had worn out hers, he robbed her bit by bit of her land, and trampled her royalty in the dust. Why not, forsooth? Had not God sent this blind friendship of the Ghiaours, in common with all their other mistakes and blindnesses, in order to serve the true believer's turn? Serbians are not the only Ghiaours who have shown themselves thus gullible; and the Turk is still as fair-spoken as of yore. Mr. Palgrave notices the inherent and masterly dissimulation of the Osmanli character; how at the present day he baits the English hook with commerce, the Austrian with policy, the French with bombast—for the Serbian he baited it with those brotherly ties which a Slavonic people holds most sacred.*

It were tedious to go into the details of Serbia's decline and destitution between 1389, the date of the battle of Kóssovo, and 1804, the date of the rising under Kara George. This much may be said, that although the empire fell nearly 500 years ago, the spirit of the people has never said "die." After the battle of Kóssovo, the Serb rulers were called despots or princes, and paid tribute to the Sultan; while the western districts maintained for another hundred years a show of independence under the name of the kingdom of Bosnia. Mussulman conquest was rendered easy by dissensions and jealousies between the Christians of the Western and of the Eastern Church. Both Serbs and Bosnians have often preferred to trust the promised toleration of the Mahommedan, rather than face the uncompromising spirit of the proselytism of the Latin. The Turks, though long ostensibly friends, having once gained entrance to the country, deprived

* Palgrave's "Central and Eastern Arabia," vol. i. p. 300. "A Turk in action (at least such has been my experience) has rarely either head or heart save for his own individual rapacity and sensuality; the same Turk in theory is a Metternich in statesmanship and a Wilberforce in benevolence. . . . . But while the diplomatic Turks are fully aware of their own extraordinary talent for imposture, they have a yet shrewder insight into the weakness of those with whom they deal, and know where and when to employ flattery or interest, to lavish promises and fair speeches, to bait the English hook with commerce, the Austrian with policy, and the French with bombast, all swallowed as readily down the hundredth time as the first, so appropriately is it administered, so well is the recipient disposed."

On one occasion Stephen refused to join a league against the Turks because he had promised Bajazet always to stand by his sons. Of his relations with the Sultan, Ranke says, "As the translation of Dukas, which is rather free, expresses it: 'Volse che Stephano sotto il suo imperio esercitasse la militia, ed in qualunque loco fosse l'imperatore, se trovasse la sua persona.'" During the battle of Nikopolis, Hammer relates, "Already they (the French and Bavarian troops) had beaten back the janissaries; already they were about to overthrow the spahis, when the despot of Serbia, who fought as Bajazet's ally, rushed to his aid with five thousand valiant followers, and decided the victory in his favour.'

the native rulers of one province after another, and finally forced them to cross the Danube. The last scion of Serbian princes was by name George Brankovic. Having been induced to call his people to arms in aid of an Austrian invasion of Turkey, he was then seized by order of the German emperor, and kept a prisoner till his death, 1711. But before this, many of the inhabitants of the inland provinces, finding the contest in their own country hopeless, crossed the Danube, fought the Turk in the armies of the Emperor of Germany, and formed the celebrated military frontier. Others found refuge in the highlands of Zeta, which, under the name of Montenegro, has sheltered a free Serbian community to this day.

Meanwhile it is of some consequence to trace the social change that came over the nation in its passage from the middle ages to the beginning of the present century. During this phase, almost everything that had been superinduced on the old Slavonic commune was swept away by the besom of Turkish conquest; the modern Serbian, where free, and not living immediately in the neighbourhood of towns, comes before us at nearly the same patriarchal stage as his fathers prior to the time of Némania. The so-called feudal nobility vanished, and it may well be asked what became of them. As for the higher *vlastela*, the battle of Kóssovo, with other ensuing and equally bloody struggles, made terrible havoc in their ranks; and when the Turks got possession of the land, some of its original lords became Mussulmans rather than become rayahs. Others joined the princes of Zeta, and their descendants still do battle on the Black Mountains; others emigrated to Christian countries, and amalgamated with the nobles of Hungary, Dalmatia, and Venice. But wherever they went, these Serbian magnates lost all such badges as may have hitherto distinguished them among the Serbian people. This is not the case nowadays with nobles of France, Italy, and Poland, when forced to leave their country on account of political troubles. They do not lay aside their titles, for they are the titles of a whole family, and identified with family domains; but if, as some maintain, the Serbian titles were still merely official, then, where the offices ceased, the titles would naturally cease with them. And this was really the case; such emigrants as occupied a high position in the countries whither they had betaken them, took foreign rank; thus in Croatia and Dalmatia we find old Serbian families decorated with German titles.

But while such was the fate of the higher nobility, the lesser nobles and yeomanry of Serbia became thoroughly welded with the people, and leavened the lump with their independent spirit and their warlike mode of life. Not that this happened alike in all portions of the Serb lands; and we have already had occasion to allude to the distinction between those populations where Turkish conquest cut off the people from the gentry, and those where it welded them into one mass. This difference was illustrated to us by describing the Christians in some parts as milk that has been skimmed, and in others as milk stirred up with its cream. To the latter sort belong the people in the Danubian districts, and in the so-called Old Serbia which we have visited; in these parts the foreign yoke has never been able to crush the spirit of the freeman.

It is also to be remarked that the Turkish conquest, although it obliterated from among the Serbs their titled families, did not root out the elements of leading families, for it left beneath the surface many a house whom the people were accustomed to follow, and who could transmit the habit to lead.

As instances of this we may mention that there are

districts well known in Danubian Serbia, where, until a duly elected and organized native government took the law into its own hands, the people regularly grouped round some one family from generation to generation, in peace and in war. The same custom prevailed in Herzegovina. An emigrant, now vice-president of the Serbian senate, told us that his family had been obliged to leave home because of a quarrel with the local Mussulmans. This quarrel it had headed as leader of the surrounding villages; an office which by tacit election had devolved on the same family for at least two hundred years.

Respecting the lowest classes of the population, it has been assumed that for them at least the Turkish conquest must have been a benefit, by sweeping away the tenures of a feudal nobility. It would seem, however, that the change in this respect was more apparent than real. The Sultan doled out the revenues of conquered lands to his spahis, on condition of military service. The rayah had no property in the soil, but had to pay for the right of cultivating it, by yielding part of its fruits to the landholder, and working for him at divers kinds of service on certain days of the week and certain weeks of the year. Supposing this to have been no worse than was required of him by his Christian lord, yet points may be discerned which place their mutual relations in a somewhat harder light. To give one instance: according to the law of the Mahommedan conqueror, the oath of the rayah was not received in a court of justice against a Mussulman, and in the districts to which we refer this practice is still in full force. Between the landholder and the peasant under the old Serbian law no such distinction existed. One class of peasants was free, but the laws mention another class, who are called *meropch* or *neropch*, a non-Serbian word of which the meaning is obscure. Some persons

MUSSULMANS AND RAYAHS.

suppose it originally indicated such cultivators of the soil as the Serbian immigrants may have found in the country after it had been harried by the Avars; and whoever the merops were, in due time they appear to have been absorbed, for nowadays one finds among the Serbians no class considered lower than the rest. But while the merops were still merops, *i.e.* avowedly not free, it is especially provided by Serbian law that any of them could call his lord into court, or that, if any person had injured him, whether "noble or prelate, the czar, or the czarine," he could obtain justice against that person; while the judge was bound to exact bail sufficient to ensure that in all future time the powerful defendant should not take vengeance on his poor prosecutor.*

Of course it is impossible to say whether the aristocracy of Serbia might have become more and more separated from the people, more and more a burden on their labour, even as Christian aristocracies certainly did become in France, Poland, Wallachia, and elsewhere. Had it become so, perhaps the evil for the lower classes might have been worse than the evils entailed by Mahommedan conquest. But there is not sufficient evidence to show that at the time of the Turkish invasion the Serbian aristocracy had actually attained this stage; on the other hand, it is self-evident that the conquest took the land out of the hands of an upper class which shared with the people community of race and creed, and put it into the hands of an upper class separated from the people either by creed or by race, and in many instances by both,—a class which based its tenure on right of conquest, or on adoption of the conqueror's faith. Under such circumstances it would hardly be reasonable to assume that the

---

* See Shafarik, "Geschichte des Serbischen Schriftthums," p. 53; also the Dictionary of Danichic, &c.

oppression of the lower classes must have decreased, even if the Serbian peasant had not given us a hint of his own opinion on the subject. The word he uses to denote oppression is a Turkish word, and he chooses for his hero Marko Kralïevic, a native noble, who is frequently represented as defending him from the Turk.

The very bitterness wherewith Christians in Turkey declaim against the evils brought on them by Mahommedan conquest, together with the readiness with which they refer all their shortcomings to that sole cause, prompts many of their hearers to ask, "Does one not take Turkish destructiveness rather too much for granted? Has it really injured these countries as much as is assumed?" This question suggested itself the rather to ourselves because we were familiar with the laments of various nations in the Austrian empire, who, although members of a Christian state, seem to think that no peoples on earth have to complain of greater injuries than they.

Without attempting fully to answer the question, we will herewith state a few facts that came before us on the subject.

The Turkish conquest robbed Serbia of advantages that she naturally derived from geographical position; it shut out from her the stream of commerce that would have passed through her between Western Europe and Constantinople, and it cut her off from her natural harbours on the Adriatic. At the same time it converted her into a battle-ground whereon the armies of the Ottoman met those of Hungary and Germany, and by which she was desolated by each in turn. The isolation which is at present so striking a feature in the position of Serbia,—an isolation which among ourselves is constantly testified by persons "who never heard of her,"— was the natural result of these circumstances incidental to the Turkish conquest. Moreover, Serbia was shut out from the thought as well as from the commerce of Europe. Art could not take root on her war-ploughed soil: we read of her first printing-presses moved from place to place, till they had to seek shelter in Venice. We find her history and her literature reduced to unwritten national songs.

A glance at the districts still ruled by Turkey,—at Bosnia, Herzegovina, and Old Serbia,—shows us at the present day (1867) ruins and poverty, lack of communications, lack of cultivation, life and property far from secure, and all classes hating the Government and each other. The Christian, too, still labours under palpable disadvantages on account of his creed. But let us look back to the times before Mahommedan prestige declined and the Turk was obliged to admit the interference of European agents. In those days Christian worship was held underground; the Christian had to dismount in presence of the Turk; his women dared not go abroad without the Mussulman disguise (still a matter of necessity in some towns); nor durst the rayah display in dress or dwelling any ensign but that of meanness and poverty. Worst of all, the flower of the Christian youth was exacted as "tribute" to swell the ranks of the enemies of their kindred and their faith.

At the beginning of the last century, we find Serbia thus described by an impartial eye-witness:—"We crossed the deserts of Servia," writes Lady Mary Wortley Montagu, "almost quite overgrown with wood, through a country naturally fertile. The inhabitants are industrious; but the oppression of the peasants is so great, they are forced to abandon their houses and neglect their tillage; all they have being a prey to the janissaries, whenever they please to seize upon it. We had a guard of 500 of them, and I was almost in tears, every day, to see their insolences in the poor villages through which we passed. After seven days' travelling through thick woods, we came to Nissa .... in a very good air, and so fruitful a soil, that the great plenty is hardly credible. The happiness of this plenty is scarcely perceived by the oppressed people. .... The desert woods of Servia are the common refuge of thieves, who rob fifty in a company, so that we had need of all our guards to secure us; and the villages are so poor, that only force could extort from them the necessary provisions. Indeed, the janissaries had no mercy on their poverty, killing all the poultry and sheep they could find, without asking to whom they belonged. .... When the pashas travel it is yet worse." At the beginning of the present century, Serbia is described by other writers as in an equally pitiable condition.

At length the Ottoman Empire began to enter on that change which has been variously described and defined; but which, both in its origin and in the mind of the sovereign and in its effects on his subjects, may be partly characterized as a change from the anarchy of mediæval feudalism to the centralized government of a modern despotism. The career of Mahommedan conquest was at an end, the hereditary pashas spent their time in plundering provinces and making war on one another. An energetic sultan arose, who resolved to save the empire from falling to pieces, by bringing it under his own control. The attempt involved him in war with the more turbulent among his Mahommedan subjects; at the same time he had to repel assaults from Russia. Two outlying Christian populations, the southern Greeks and the Danubian Serbians, used the opportunity to make good their deliverance from Mahommedan rule.*

* * * * * *

* See Ranke's "History of Serbia and the Serbian Revolution." This work,

THE STORY OF SERBIA.

In Milosh Obrenovic, first prince of modern Serbia, we must not expect to find the wide schemes of the first Némania, the comprehensive policy of Stephen Dūshan, or the Christian chivalry of Czar Lāzar; for Milosh was the representative of a people that had served the Turk nigh four hundred years. Uncivilised—nay, unprincipled, whimsical, greedy, and revengeful, he exhibited on his own person the brand of the barbarian yoke. Yet he was a patriot rough-hewn, and when he deemed the cause hopeless, could propose to his little band of freemen that, rather than submit, they should slay their women and children, take to the woods, and spend their lives in avenging the country on its oppressors.

We have already said that the Turkish conquest of Serbia was not only gradual, but partial; the submission of the people was more partial still, since, besides those who held out in Zeta, numbers transferred themselves to Croatia and Sirmium, and repulsed the invader under foreign standards. Nevertheless, from the middle of the fifteenth to the beginning of the nineteenth century, no portion of the old czardom reasserted its existence under the Serbian name, or was recognised by Europe. It is because Milosh regained this position, at least for a small portion of his native land, that we take him for the representative of "Serbia Rediviva," rather than that redoubtable hero, his ill-fated precursor—Kara George.

George the Black, whose head and countenance bear so strange a resemblance to those of the great Napoleon, was indeed a war-chief of the first order; his successes, considering the smallness of his means and the lack of sympathy from Europe—which, unlike Greece, Serbia

which has been translated by Mrs. Alexander Kerr, gives a graphic account of the events that led to these risings, and of the changes effected by Sultan Mahmoud. It should be read by all who wish to form an idea what the rule was from which the Serbians freed themselves.

had to brook—have been considered among the most wonderful ever obtained in irregular campaigns. In 1804 he took the lead in an insurrection against the unbearable tyranny of plundering governors, whom the Sultan could neither remove nor control, and who had formed a plan for massacring every leading man among the Serbs. For ten years Kara George upheld the unequal contest; but at length he succumbed, and in a moment of weariness and despair abandoned the land and fled to Russia. Perhaps Serbia never lay lower at the feet of her enemy than at the moment when her interests came into the care of Milosh Obrenovic.*

In his early years Milosh was at once a "leader of heroes" and a swine-herd. Indeed throughout Serbia, while under the Turks, these two offices frequently met

* When the other leaders exiled themselves, Milosh refused to follow, saying: "What will my life profit me in Austria? while in the meantime the enemy will sell into slavery my wife and child, and my aged mother. No! whatever may be the fate of my countrymen, shall be mine also." (Ranke, p. 188.) We heard much of Milosh from his personal associates. The scenes of his early life and rising were described to us in his native village, and many of them by the son of his standard-bearer. As for Kara George, subsequently he returned, but unexpectedly, and at a moment when to have risen would have been certain destruction. The Turks heard of it, so did Milosh, and while uncertain what to do, he received a message from the Pasha of Belgrade, demanding the head of Kara George or his own. There are many versions of the story; we heard it from one who was present at the consultation that followed. What was to be done? At last one loud voice exclaimed, "Gospodar, we must do with Kara George as with the lamb on Easter-day." (In other words, he must be the sacrifice of the people.) On this, Milosh at last resolved to send a messenger to Kara George, representing the necessity of recrossing to Austria to wait for a favourable moment. If he would not listen to reason, his blood must be upon his own head. What with trial and long waiting, Kara George had become distraught, and imperiously summoned Milosh to his presence; so there was nothing for it "but the first time he fell asleep to knock him quietly on the head." "His skull, stuffed with straw and presented to allay the suspicions of the Pasha, served his country at that moment, as his brains had done in days gone by." The adherents or special admirers of the heroic Kara George can hear no excuse for Milosh on this head. That which the friends of Milosh allege is, that in the first place it was certainly a question between Kara George's life and his own; and secondly, that it was, to all appearance, a question between the destruction of Kara George and that of Serbia. One version of the story says, that Milosh yielded so far to these considerations as to anticipate the Pasha's hearing from others of Kara George's return, by informing him of it himself.

in the same person. The youth who watched over herds of half-wild swine, ranging in the mountain-forest, was thus withdrawn from the eye of the Turkish landlord; he had opportunity to harden himself, to learn the use of arms, and to hold unseen consultation with his fellows. On the death of an elder brother, Milosh succeeded to his position as head of a commune; when Kara George was gone, he enjoyed sufficient consideration among the people for the Turks to choose him as their deputy in the collection of tribute. It was while thus brought daily into communication with these astute barbarians that Milosh learned how to oppose them. That is to say, not only with courage equal to their courage, but with craft equal to their craft, dissimulation equal to their dissimulation, unscrupulousness and tenacity equal to theirs.

Ranke, in his admirable story of the Revolution, and Mr. Paton in his description of the principality, have given graphic sketches of the process of freeing and organizing Danubian Serbia. They have described also the first reign of Milosh, ending as it did in his expulsion by the people he had saved. The truth is, that those very qualities which made Milosh a match for cruel and guileful pashas, caused him afterwards to rule somewhat in the pasha style; and although the Christian was no longer oppressed as a Christian, nor the Serbian insulted as a Serb, yet no one was safe from oppression and insult should he incur the anger of the prince. Nor could such faults be cured by remonstrance. Milosh had no idea of government, except in the Oriental mode; thus the rising generation of Serbian statesmen—who had been educated since the French Revolution in European universities,—beheld no course open to them but to expel their wayward knez. Unluckily, they could not effect this object without asking assistance of the enemies of the nation. Thus the good end was soiled by unworthy means, and the liberal constitution imposed on Milosh's successor was clogged with conditions that left him powerless in the hands of a senate which the Porte might terrorise or bribe.

But the Turks never expected resistance on the part of one so young and apparently so gentle as the youth of eighteen whom Milosh had left behind. Herein, however, they were disappointed. The young Prince Michael, while willing to act up to the Constitution, showed himself stubborn against dictation; and, rather than accept councillors imposed on him, he resigned his office and left the land.

The Serbians now gave an instance of their attachment to the families of those who have served them. Although the country abounded in able and ambitious men, the people chose for their new prince the son of the liberator Kara George, a lad of whom, except that he was the son of Kara George, no one knew anything good, or, indeed, anything at all. He proved a docile vassal of the Sultan, and an acquiescent neighbour of Austria; and his quietness stood the Serbians in good stead during the interval necessary for organizing society, and making the first step in progressive civilisation. Thus much done, the spirit of the nation rebelled at seeing what it called the "Austrian consul acting Prince of Serbia," while the Turks still garrisoning the fortresses treated the citizens *de haut en bas*. It was observed, too, that the young generation was growing up less hardy, less able to defend the country than their forefathers; that Serbia was sinking from her place as "voivoda" of the Southern Slāvs. At the time of the Crimean war, when the Bulgarians hoped for an improvement in their position, they offered their crown, not to any member of the reigning family of Serbia, but to Michael Obrenovic, an exile at Vienna. The example was ominous, and the Serbians began to cry, " Let us bring back our Milosh, with him will return our glory."

At length the deposition of Karageorgevic was effected in a legal manner by the voice of the national assembly, and the Obrenovics were invited to return. No one opposed the choice of the people; yet many urged that it would be most prudent to recall, not the father, but the son. However, the revolution had been effected by the armed yeomen from the country districts; the idea of giving a son precedence over his parent was abhorrent to their patriarchal notions; besides, it was their aged Liberator whom they knew, and whom they loved. One of the most influential men in Serbia told us that he made a speech on this question; and was answered with one thundering shout, " Give us back our OLD Milosh."

So Milosh was brought back, and old he was indeed; but the tenacity of his nature showed itself in his oft-repeated saying, that "he *would not die* except as Prince of Serbia." During his exile his son had travelled throughout the greater part of Europe, and become a thorough European; but it was not to be expected that he himself should greatly change. It is true that on the day of his return—when, after an absence of nineteen years, the people clung round him and wept for joy—he published a general amnesty to those who had formerly taken part in driving him away. Nevertheless, so long as he lived it was an anxious time for all who knew that he had aught against them. Most of these prudently withdrew beyond his reach; waiting, in obedience to the outspoken will of the nation, till the government of Serbia should drop from the grasp of the grand old barbarian to that of his better-instructed son.

This took place in 1860, when Prince Michael Obrenovic succeeded his father, and inaugurated a change of system by the declaration that "henceforth the law should be supreme in Serbia." His reign witnessed the departure of the Turks from all the fortresses, with the exception of Mali Zwornik, on the Drina. His untimely death by the hands of assassins, May 29th, 1868, greatly checked the internal progress and development of the little state. Milan, his successor, the grandson of a younger brother of the old Prince Milosh, was at that time fourteen years old.

The Principality of Serbia is in extent about one-fifth smaller than Scotland. Her population, according to an official return given in the *Almanach de Gotha*, 1875, numbered, before the war, 1,338,505. Belgrade, the modern capital, stands at the junction of two navigable rivers, the Danube and Save, and forms a natural terminus for railways that would unite the North Sea with the Ægean, the Euxine with the Adriatic; in commerce, as in war, it is the key of the East, and has been pointed out by the great British free-trader, Mr. Cobden, as one of the future free ports of Europe. The history of war between Austria, Hungary, and the Ottoman tells how often Belgrade has changed masters, becoming by turns the rampart of Western civilisation and the prison-gate of Turkish barbarism. But neither the powerful empire of Germany nor the gallant kingdom of Hungary could permanently retain it for Christendom; at length it was won by peasants in a rising which they commenced with no arms but their staves, and ended with weapons taken from the enemy.

The frontier of the modern principality is not the boundary of the "Serbian" lands. With Montenegro, *i.e.* Serbia on the Adriatic, Danubian Serbia shares the melancholy honour of remaining the sole representative of a czardom which once spread from the Danube to the sea; with Montenegro she also shares the responsibility of providing a nucleus of self-defence and self-government for many of her neighbours. She now lies exhausted by her brave and generous but rash response to the cries for help which reached her in 1876 from the Serbs of Bosnia and the Herzegovina.*

* I have no space here for the full evidence which has been pouring in on all sides to disprove the assertion that these heavings of deep and irresistible forces were produced by Russian intrigue and outside agitation. Nor would aught but the presumption of ignorance dare to suggest a plan for the construction of order out of the present chaos. But let the charge of cowardice so wantonly made against Serbian soldiers be answered in the words of a Serbian senator. "A nation of less than a million and a half has defied and attacked the Ottoman Empire, and held its highly disciplined battalions in check for four months, during which time that empire removed its troops to Europe from Africa and Asia. Our troops were a badly armed, badly disciplined mass of peasants and shopkeepers, officered only lately by foreigners. And yet the Turks have got no farther than Alexinatz." Dr. Sandwith writes in the midst of the war: "Brave the Serbians certainly are, and full of fighting qualities. The other day a convoy of wounded volunteers came to the Hospital of Uziza; the oldest was seventy-two, the youngest sixteen. Self-mutilation has been charged against the Serbians largely. Doubtless, there has been about as much of this as might have been expected in an army of married men of business, many of whom were ruined by their absence from home; but when men are defending breastworks the head and hands are those parts which are most exposed, and it is hardly fair to make every hand wound a case of self-mutilation, or even half of them."

APPENDIX

A.

VENICE, Venezia, Venedig, Veneta, on the Adriatic. Vineta, Saxon name for a Slavonic city on the Baltic, at the mouth of the Oder, destroyed by the Danes in the eleventh century. In both cases the name is held to mean " city of the Vends "—Vend, or Vind, being the German designation for the Slāv. The citizens of Vineta on the Baltic were undoubtedly Slavonic, and a Vendic population still so called inhabits territories marching with those of Venice on the Adriatic. The Slāvs, however, never called themselves Vends or Vinds; nor was it they who called Vineta or Venice " the city of the Vends." The Slavonic name for Venice is Mletci, " city of the shoals." We may mention that an idea exists that the first Latin settlers on the site of Venice found it already visited, if not inhabited, by the Slavonic tribes in the neighbourhood; and a Croatian literatus, following up this idea, thought he found traces of Slavonic origin, especially in the larger island, whose quay is termed Riva dei Schiavoni. He found that the inhabitants of that island held themselves as somehow or other traditionally distinguished from those of the other islands, that they wore caps of a different colour, and held a yearly fight with the other islanders, of which the origin was forgotten. He also affirmed that during a dispute he heard a sailor of the larger island call out, " What have I to do with you others? Son' Schiavon';" and on inquiry found that he and his fellows were accustomed to call themselves Schiavoni, but did not know what it meant; though evidently in their mouths it did not mean *schiavo* in the sense of a bond-servant. It is historically certain that Venice had extensive relations with the Serbian peoples; that while she ruled Dalmatia her sailors mostly came from the eastern shore of the Adriatic; and that such of her noble names as end in " igo " are Italianised from

Slavonic names ending in "ic." Few persons who have seen the handsome, athletic, and dignified Dalmatians can mistake the type as it sometimes appears in the old Venetian pictures. But it is on the eastern shore of the Adriatic that one finds a real specimen of latinised Slavonic, viz., the beautiful city of Ragusa, which was never subject to Venice, and developed a fine Slavonic literature; where, nevertheless, the Italian language is naturalised and there is a considerable infusion of Italian blood. It is curious to remark, as a sign of the times, that formerly in Ragusa many Slãvic names were Italianised, whereas at present families of real Italian origin are taking to write their names Slãvicè.

B.

DESCRIPTION OF THE SERBIAN VILLAGE COMMUNITY AS EXISTING IN FREE SERBIA.

From an Article in the "Oestr. Revue," VIII., 1865, entitled "Das Serbische Bauernhaus," by F. KANITZ.

"THE constitution is patriarchal, limited by the rights of the individuals of the family. The head of the family, the *stareshina*, is elected by the free choice of its members, the *zadrooga*. The most competent is usually elected. Should he prove unequal to the position a fresh choice can be made. He represents the whole household before the political authorities, settles disputes, and conducts the work of the "house," in which the whole family takes part. The men and women labour in the fields and the woods, the children herd the cattle, and go in turn to school.

"Willing obedience is yielded to the regulations of the stareshina. He divides all income and expense of the house among the members, and cares for them as for himself. The agricultural profits, obtained chiefly from orchards and vineyards, from the breeding of cattle and specially of swine, the sale of the skins of beasts, of wood for fire and for building, constitute the principal common sources of income. For sales, for more important purchases, and for the taxation of the common property, the consent of the majority of the members is necessary.

"The stareshina is the guardian of the younger orphan children. He is bound, in conjunction with their mother (according to § 519 of the Serb municipal law), to bring them up in such a manner "that they shall become good and honest men, and useful to their country.'

"The widow herself, even if childless, is entitled to her deceased husband's share in the house communion, but is bound to promote to the utmost its interests. Should she remarry, she, like the daughters of the house communion, receives from the joint-stock a suitable portion.

"The law in § 528 fixes the right of inheritance in the zadrooga as follows:—

"'Relationship in the house communion gives right of inheritance before even a higher degree of relationship out of the communion. The rights of an adopted member precede in respect of inheritance even those of blood relations without the house communion, if this adoption took place with the open consent of the communion. Children under age who accompany their mother when she leaves the communion preserve their own rights, though out of the communion. Also in cases of capture, or other similar misfortune and danger, in the country's service, the right of relationship will be held valid out of the house communion.'

"The interests of the separate members of the zadrooga are most intimately connected with those of the whole. By so much more that the individual by his labour contributes to the prosperity of the zadrooga, so much the larger is his claim on the joint-stock in case of his exit from the association—so much the richer the inheritance he can leave to his children. The individual industry of the members of the association, far from being hindered by the house communion, is encouraged and developed.

"These features of the Serbian zadrooga form and characterize the outward appearance and inner arrangements of the Serb peasant's home.

"In the most prominent position stands the house of the stareshina, distinguished by its size and better style as the seat of the head of the family, and forming the central point around which the small houses of the married members are severally grouped. Those little offset houses are usually only arranged for temporary requirements. They contain the sleeping apartments of the married members of the family, and whatever separate earnings they may acquire. The general stores of fruit, cattle, utensils, &c., are preserved in the barns and chambers common to the whole house. They are called *vajate* (pl.), are either four-sided or round, are made of woven osier or reed, and are raised, like the wigwams of the Indians, on posts, in order to secure the contents from the domestic animals allowed the run of the yard.

APPENDIX.

"The common house economy is conducted alternately by one of the married women. She then bears the name of *redusha* (from *red*, order, *i.e.*, she to whom the order comes); with the help of the youngest female members she provides the meals of the whole family, and arranges how the remaining women of the house shall be available for field labour and other service. As among all the South Slavonic races, the Serbian wife shares in almost all the labours of the men. She is never idle, always occupied. On her return from hard labour in the fields she spins, weaves, bleaches, or dyes the stuff for the linen or clothes of the house. Greater prosperity or the fulfilment of motherly cares makes little difference in this. The Serbian wife is laborious, in a far higher degree than the comfort-loving man. In Serbia neither men nor children are ever seen in tattered linen, and this is the best criterion of the love of order and work of the Serb women.

"Evening finds the family by the household hearth, by the bright-burning fire in the house of the stareshina. The men cut and repair the agricultural tools and house vessels. The elder rest from their labours, smoke, and discuss what is to be done next day or the events of the village and the country. The women group themselves, quietly working, in a circle near them; the merry little ones play at the feet of their parents, or beg the grandfather to relate to them about Czar Troyan or Marko Kralïevitch. Then the stareshina, or one of the other men, takes the one-stringed gusla from the wall. To its singular monotonous accompaniment are sung legends, heroic songs, and such as in burning words relate the need of the fatherland and its wars of liberation. Thus the house of the stareshina becomes the social gathering point of the whole family. At his hearth is kindled the love of individuals for the old traditions of the family and people, and the inspiring enthusiasm of all for the freedom and prosperity of their native land."

* * * * * *

A passage in the old Bohemian poem, "The Judgment of Queen Libussa," gives the following poetic account of the main features of the Slavonic family law :—

> "Every father in his household ruleth;
> Man must till and clothes be made by women.
> If the household's head be gone, the children
> Rule together jointly his possessions,
> Choosing from the household a vladyka
> For the common weal to seek the assembly
> With the kmets, the lechs, and the vladykas."*

---

* From the Translation, by Rev. A. H. Wratislaw, of "The Queen's Court Manuscript."

C.

ALBANIAN DISTRICTS AROUND DÉTCHANI.

THE following extracts are translated from an account of the Monastery of Détchani, the Patriarshia of Ipek, and parts of the surrounding country, written by a Serbian priest, whilom monk of Détchani, now prior of a Serbian monastery in the Frusca Gora: *Détchanski Pervenatz (the Firstling of Détchani),* by GIDEON JOSEPH IURITITCH, Ieromonach of Détchani. Neusatz, 1852.

Describing the route from the monastery, along the Bistritza, to the small towns of Plava and Gusinïé, and thence to Podgoritza on the Lake of Scutari, the author gives this account of a visit to the Albanian tribe of the Clementi (p. 77):—

"From Gusinïé polié on the west are reached the mountain villages of the Clementi, and beyond these, on the river Tsievna, lies the town of Podgoritza. In these Clementi districts are about ten villages. The inhabitants are Christians of the Western Church; among them are some few of the Mahommedan religion, or, more truly speaking, of none at all, for they neither cross themselves nor bow, and whatsoever seems to them right that they do; all are merely haïduks (robbers).

"In a village of the Clementi, Seltzi by name, I was compelled on one occasion to pass the night. I arrived before a stone house. It was raining a little. My fellow traveller, Zachariah, a monk of Détchani, asked in Albanian, 'May we pass the night here?' They answered, 'You may. Whence are you?' We replied, 'From Détchani.' At that name, 'Welcome!' and we were led up into the house, under which, on the ground-floor, was the stable. The paterfamilias, Mirat Kolya, seated us by the fire, then took from us our arms and hung them up by his, according to the custom there. The younger ones made up the fire; and while we were resting and drying ourselves some women came to take off our shoes. Ignorant of their usage, and thinking of no etiquette, I presented my left foot first, whereon my attendant seized me by the right foot, stretched it out, and set to work to take off the shoe. The host, seeing me smile at her rough pull, said, 'With us it is customary to take off the shoe from the right foot before the left.' I replied, through my companion, here also my interpreter, 'You are right, for the right side is more noble than the left.' While we were taking off our clothes and talking they strewed in front of the fire some hay, and some of their 'spreading;' they laid over this our own carpets, which we carried on our backs, and invited us to sit down thereon. Then they gave us coffee. Having some raki in our chutera (wooden bottle), we drank and offered to them. This done once in a row, we drink another cup of coffee. In the course of conversation the host announces that he belongs to the Roman Catholic Church, and says that he has been at Détchani. I ask him, 'How do you pray to God? and where do you celebrate your religion?' He replies, 'We have here in the village a church and a frater; to-morrow, when you leave us, you will pass by the church.' I ask him further, 'Where does your priest come from?' 'He is sent hither from Rome.' This sounded strange to me. I asked, 'How do you converse when he does not understand your tongue?' 'This frater, who comes to us, learns by degrees to speak Albanian; when he first arrives, he understands all that we say, but cannot answer well. In time he learns better; for whoever comes to us lives here six or seven years; after that he goes to Rome, and receives a good living as a recompense for all his troubles here.' 'And do you give him anything for serving you?' 'Every married man of us gives the priest twenty okas of hay, a fleece of wool, a lump of cheese; for a baptism we give him stockings and a towel; for a wedding we give paras, for a funeral we give paras; besides this one gives him a sheep, another a lamb for his food; what remains over he sells.' 'And whom has he with him?' 'One servant.' 'And do you send your children to learn of him?' 'We do not.' 'And why do you not? Perhaps your children could learn of him, and could become priests.' At this saying of mine the father and all the household fell into a loud laughter, saying, 'What good would that do us? *we* will not turn fraters. They send us out of Rome priests who celebrate our religion.' 'Perhaps you have somewhere near a bishop, who sends you priests; they could not send you priests so far from Rome.' 'We have a bishop in Scodra,' said the father; 'he sends here, they come to him from Rome—so they tell us—and our priest goes to Scodra four times a year to talk with the bishop.' 'And do spahis come to your village?' 'They come when it is time to take the tenth.' 'And do they oppress you?' 'No, there are enough of us; we do not permit it; our frater would fall out with the spahis forthwith if they demanded more than their due.' 'Once our spahi,' continued the father, 'here in the village struck a youth with his chibouque; we all sprang up, and would have killed the spahi, but the priest ran and separated us. On this our priest goes to Scodra and tells the bishop, and the bishop tells the pasha; from that time the spahi has not come to our village, but has sent his son to collect what is his.' Here came the supper. We all sat round the sofra (a low round table), except the women and children, who supped after us. After this we lay ourselves to sleep, and on the morrow we arise early and prepare for the journey. The father gives us coffee, and invites us to eat something; we will not, so he provides a little bread for our wallet. We thank him for his hospitality, and proceed along the river Tsievna, which passes through the village, and below the town of Podgoritza flows into the lake, which, from the supplies of many rivers, there forms a large piece of water.

"The father accompanied us out to the other side of the village. Near the river we find a small church, and by it a neat little house. I wished to see their priest, but at that time he was in Scodra. Above the village is a very high rock, which looks exactly as if it would fall over on the houses. Our host remarked, ' On a certain day every year we carry up an offering on this rock.' I exclaimed eagerly, ' What offering?' ' Once a year we celebrate a certain day on which all slay a sheep, a lamb, or a goat on this rock, and dance all day long on the hill.' 'And why do you do this?' 'That the rock may not fall over on the village.' I, smiling at him, answer, ' It will not fall; do not fear. Have you done this for long?' ' It has come down to us from our forefathers, and on no account would we spoil the custom, for on that rock have our forefathers always slain an offering.' ' Perhaps when your fathers were ignorant of the true God they slew on that rock an offering to the false god— the idol.' He replied, ' So says our frater; but now from long custom we go up the hill on a certain day, and afterwards have a merrymaking in the village.' 'And does the priest come to your merrymaking?' 'He comes and sits among us the whole day, sees our children play; in the evening we all go away together, come first to the church, sprinkle ourselves with holy water, and disperse, each to his own house.' Observing the church had been newly whitewashed, I ask, 'When did you build the church?' He replies, ' Lately; we burnt lime, and carried stone, and the bishop paid the workmen for the church and for the school.' Thus conversing, we reached the other side of the village, and then our host turned homewards.

"Journeying onward, I say to my companion, the said priest Zachariah, ' How I vexed myself last night to know where we should sleep, lest some danger should befall us. Now I am glad that we have passed the night in that village, for we have made experience of some of the customs of that people, and also of the practice of the Romish Church there. Thou seest, my Zachariah, what a control the Church of Rome has over her flock in these wild, almost forgotten regions, if not wholly to educate the people (for that for the present is impossible), at least by every possible means to maintain the true religion, to shelter it from every danger, and even to stretch out a helping hand; while our bishops* would skin the nation bare, and always say, 'You do not know what we have to give on your account in Constantinople.' Quoth Zachariah, 'I would never ask help from the bishop, and all which is his I would gladly give, but he further demands that we should lend to him, and this loan is for ever; if one does not give to him, then, with the help of the Turks, he imposes a fine, divides the money with the Turks, imprisons the monks and priests, and thus, in the place of archiepiscopal instruction, brings the people torment. Thou knowest how our Prizren bishop, Ignatius, seized some priests and drove them bound to Prizren; and when we of Détchani complain he gives 25,000 piastres to the kaïmakam of Prizren, only to come to the monastery and carry off our hegumon Antim, bound, to Prizren, in order to terrify the people, that he might the more easily extort money from them. I cannot think what is come to these Greek bishops,' continued Zachariah, 'that they so hate our nation, for indeed the people give them whatever they demand. If we had not had friends among the Turks and the Arnaouts our hegumon Antim would certainly have been taken prisoner and our monastery destroyed. Thanks be to the kaïmakam, he accepted 25,000 piastres from the bishop and then left the monastery as he found it, the only injury being that the monastery had been obliged to entertain him with his troop of 100 horsemen; and thanks be to God, He called the bishop to the patriarchate, or this malice of the vladika would have brought us no good. See what a difference between the bishops of the Eastern and the bishops of the Western Church in the Turkish empire! When it is also remembered that we in our parts have no good instructors nor schools where the children could to some extent receive education, neither is any teacher willing to come to our parts—for in the first place, our poor people would not be able to maintain them, and still worse, without protection they could not be sure of their lives—how can the education of our native people be deemed possible?' To these remarks of Zachariah I added further that 'the clergy of the Church of Rome enjoy a great protection from the Austrian consulate in Scodra, and that Austria (as a relative in Scodra told me) protects the bishops of Scodra and Prizren, and sends them remittances, that they may be able to maintain themselves according to their dignity in these

* Greeks from Constantinople, placed over Slavonic flocks.

wretched districts. When they are thus protected themselves, of course they are able to protect their own people.' Here we arrived at the town of Podgoritza, on the river Tsievna, in which, among five or six hundred Turkish, there are also Serb houses. On the north-east of Podgoritza lies the stony district of Kutchi, in which live two or three thousand families, all Serb."

Describing the Mussulman-Albanian districts in the neighbourhood of Détchani, he proceeds (p. 86) :—

"To the south of Détchani is the mountain district of Malesia. Here is a scattered population of some three thousand Mussulman-Albanians. They are inveterate haïduks and acknowledge no authority. They belong to the nahia of Diakovo in the Prizren pashalik. This district is shut out by high mountains and wooded hills. It is entered on one side only, coming from Diakovo. It borders on the nahia of Scodra. Through Malesia, in the time of the Némanias, there was a road to Scodra made by the Némanias. By this road, the people say, you may reach Scodra from Ipek and Diakovo in sixteen hours; but the road by which one goes now from these towns to Scodra requires four days and is a very dangerous road. Malesia is a hilly district, but cultivated; in it everything grows; there are also pretty hay pastures, as in the other cultivated lands in that part. In Malesia are more haïduks than anywhere else; almost all the inhabitants are robbers by profession. They, with the Arnaouts of the nahias of Diakovo, Petch, Novi Bazaar, and Vuchitern, commit violence openly rather than in secret, and greatly torment the Serbian people. In these days their ill-doing has reached the highest pitch.

"These Arnaouts are divided into tribes :—

"One is called Gasha; among the people here it is said that this tribe used to acknowledge for its patron saints St. John and St. Peter, and to keep *slava* on their days.

"Another is called Shala; they used to celebrate (*slavali su*) St. George.

"The third, Hotti, are Clementi; they celebrated the Sts. Vrachi (the holy physicians Cosmas and Damianus). Many of them are Roman Catholics.

"The fourth, Krinicha, celebrated St. Arandjel (the archangel Michael).

"The fifth, Berishai, celebrated St. Nicolas.

"Members of the same tribe do not intermarry. Often they quarrel among themselves, and two or three, or sometimes more, fall on the spot. When two tribes disagree, then indeed madly do they kill

Lightning Source UK Ltd.
Milton Keynes UK
UKHW01f0623180718
325892UK00005B/586/P